JUVENILE DELINQUENCY:
A Reader

JUVENILE DELINQUENCY

A Reader

Edited by

James E. Teele
BOSTON UNIVERSITY

F. E. PEACOCK PUBLISHERS, INC. • ITASCA • ILLINOIS

Preface

THE LITERATURE BEARING on the study of delinquency has grown prodigiously in the past few years, a fact which suggested the need for organization of and selection from this literature. The present reader has been designed for use in undergraduate classes on delinquency. Since it was prepared for use as a basic text, an attempt was made to include theoretical and research selections bearing on most of the major controversies and problems which engage specialists in this field. Naturally, it was possible to select only a small fraction of the many fine scholarly articles and to include excerpts from only a few of the books written by social scientists in the field.

While most of the material presented in this book is reprinted from previously published works—primarily reprints, in entirety, of articles from the professional journals in social science—one of the articles was prepared especially for inclusion in this volume. Many fine relevant contributions from scholarly journals in other fields were not considered for this book because of space limitations.

Whether or not the numbers of delinquents and delinquent acts are increasing—and there is disagreement on this issue—there is agreement that juvenile delinquency is *a*, perhaps *the*, major youth problem. The measurement of unrecorded as well as of recorded delinquency, the extent to which changes occur over time, the degree to which these changes are due to definitions and to the behavior of agents of prevention and control, the causes of delinquency, and the treatment of delinquents are some of the problems and issues dealt with in this reader on delinquency.

An attempt to present material bearing on more than one "side" of an issue has been earnestly made. Also, because of the recently increased attention now being focused on the role of labelling in delinquency, a special effort was made in this area and a variety of articles bearing on this issue appear in the first two sections of the book.

Acknowledgment is gratefully made to the many authors and publishers who have given me permission to reprint their works. I am also grateful to the many authors whose works were read but not included since these works enhanced my knowledge in this field. My thanks go, too, to Edgar F. Borgatta and Edward Rothstein for their suggestions on the preparation of this reader. Finally, I also wish to thank Ann Teele for her helpful comments on the editor's introductions and Jean Brady for her valuable secretarial assistance.

JAMES E. TEELE

Boston, Massachusetts
September, 1970

Contents

CHAPTER I

On Measures and Statistics of Delinquency

EDITOR'S INTRODUCTION

T HE DESIGNATION of a child as delinquent is likely to mean anything from the loose employment of a value-judgment in the description of the child to the official judgment of a court about his behavior. A look at the literature on delinquency indicates that a great many different approaches have been applied to the task of defining delinquency. A typical approach to the definition of delinquency has been through the application of the professional's discipline. Thus, the sociologist would be likely to define delinquency as "deviance from legal norms" while the psychiatrist or social worker might define delinquency as an inherent property of individuals who are "maladjusted" or "antisocial." Moreover, within each discipline, substantial differences in definitions exist among members of that particular discipline. Some sociologists, for example, might employ a strictly legal definition of delinquency while others might rely on a behavioral definition.

Another approach to the definition of delinquency is apparent through analysis of the relevant sociological research: this is the reliance on operational definitions. These operational definitions differ from one another depending upon whether the authors focus upon one or more of the following criteria: the *number* of delinquent acts committed by a youth, the *frequency* with which delinquent acts are committed over a time period, the *seriousness* of the act, the *motivations* of the actor, the *judgment* of the behavior by legal agents, and so on.[1] Because of the variety of definitions employed by social scientists and others in the study of delinquency, the measures used to quantify juvenile behavior and the statistics used to report the extent of delinquency vary a great deal between studies and raise questions about the reliability of measures used and the adequacy of substantive conclusions.

The articles in Chapter I were selected so as to give the student an introduction to some of the problems of definition and measurement. Sol Rubin, in "The Legal Character of Juvenile Delinquency," explores the problem of defining delinquency in connection with the standards of conduct for children. Rubin also takes up the issue of the effects of the delinquency tag or label—a matter which will be considered again in Chapter II. Following Rubin's article is a reprint by James Short and Ivan Nye, "Extent of Unrecorded Juvenile Delinquency: Tentative Conclusions." Following their assumption that

only a portion of delinquent behavior is followed by arrest and conviction [and] further, that conviction and commitment to a "training school" is much more likely to follow delinquent behavior if the adolescent is from the "wrong side of the tracks,"

Short and Nye used self-report instruments in documenting their hunches. This article is followed by one by Ball, Ross and Simpson who present a new procedure for estimating the prevalence of delinquency in a given population (i.e., the percent of youth in a population appearing in court before age 18).

The next paper, by William Arnold, returns the student to the use of self-reports in measuring type and extent of delinquent behavior among high school students.[2] Arnold's paper is a forecast of things to come for he suggests that self-report data could be used in connection with the technique introduced by Ball, Ross and Simpson to estimate the proportion of (all) antisocial behavior which is officially known.

Because contact with legal authorities is so often used as the defining criterion of delinquency, the next paper (following Arnold's) deals explicitly with the role of the police in the "delinquency process." This paper, by Piliavin and Briar, reports the results of the authors' observational study of police officers' contacts with juveniles. These authors show some of the results of officers' wide discretionary power in disposing

---

[1]For a fuller treatment of the problem of operationally defining delinquency see Travis Hirschi and Hanan Selvin, *Delinquency Research: An Appraisal of Analytic Methods* (New York: The Free Press, 1967).

[2]For a full treatment of all major aspects of the problem of measuring delinquency see T. Sellin and M. Wolfgang, *The Measurement of Delinquency* (New York: John Wiley & Sons, Inc., 1964).

of these contacts. The authors relate their research to the issue of labelling suggesting that police judgments are often very harmful to juveniles.

Another important agency in the handling of juvenile behavior is the court. Erickson and Empey employed official records and interviews with four purposively-drawn subsamples in an attempt to assess the nature of decision-making by court authorities. Their study includes data on undetected and unacted upon (by courts) violations as well as correlations between court appearances and reported number of violations for different categories of offenses. The authors also present comparisons among non-delinquents, one-time offenders, repeat offenders on probation, and incarcerated offenders on extent of self-reported violations.

The last paper in Chapter I is the one by Stanton Wheeler, "Criminal Statistics: A Reformulation of the Problem." This article is included because it represents a kind of synthesis and summary by Wheeler of many of the major weaknesses of delinquency definitions, measures, and statistics which were discussed by authors of the preceding six papers. Wheeler, however, takes a fresh view of these problems and recommends that students of crime and delinquency analyze all of the actions and inactions by those who are involved in the process of defining, reporting and preventing crime and delinquency. As such, his paper is appropriately viewed not only as the final piece in this section on measurement and statistics but also as an introduction to the more sustained consideration of labelling theory which is taken up in Chapter II.[3] Fittingly, and consistent with the foregoing papers, Wheeler discusses the question of how students of crime and delinquency can improve the value of both the numerator and the denominator of crime and delinquency formulations.

---

[3]Since nearly all the articles printed in this volume contain numerous additional references for those who wish to explore special subjects in delinquency, this volume is also appropriate for use as a basic text in graduate courses.

1.

Sol Rubin

THE LEGAL CHARACTER OF JUVENILE DELINQUENCY

The underlying purposes of the juvenile court movement are twofold—one, to remove child offenders from the ordinary criminal courts to courts specially adapted for dealing with children on a social treatment rather than a penal basis; and two, to have this specialized court render protection and treatment to other children needing them. The law is at the service of these admirable purposes.

With regard to the first purpose, it is considered that, for children in any event, the ordinary procedure obtaining in a criminal court is objectionable as being based on the personal responsibility of the offender. Contention between defendants and the state has produced an intricate, highly formalized procedure, the specific purpose of which is to determine the responsibility of the individual defendant for his act.

But in the development of juvenile courts there has been established a new type of proceeding for a group of offenders formerly dealt with in the criminal courts. For juveniles a procedure has been established in all states, although not applicable to all juveniles, which is informal, which does not limit itself to a particular act as does the criminal court, and whose function of social treatment of the offender is very widely asserted, becoming indeed the guiding principle of the court.

With regard to the second purpose of the juvenile court—to render special assistance to children needing protection—we may note that juvenile courts generally include in their jurisdiction children who are dependent and neglected, as well as children who are delinquent. It may have other jurisdiction as well. For these children the court renders judicial decree or order according to the needs of the child.

The creation of juvenile courts has been recognized everywhere as a first-rank development in the treatment of children. It is true, however, that the courts have had varying degrees of success. They have not reached their full expectations, for reasons which are well known and not denied. Two decades ago in *The Annals* they were summarized in an attack on the court entitled "The Juvenile Court at the Bar," by J. Prentice Murphy, then executive secretary of the Children's Bureau in Philadelphia. In brief, the inadequacies of the court were and are generally considered to be related primarily to personnel standards—the caliber of the judge, the training and education of the probation staff, and their sufficiency in numbers.

It is agreed that the philosophy of the court is sound. However, the fact that the juvenile courts have been upheld as a constitutional device and as an important development in socialized justice does not obviate the need of examining them with a critical eye unrelated to constitutional requirements but focused rather on the social effectiveness of the court and its legal provisions.

WHAT IS JUVENILE DELINQUENCY?

First of all, *juvenile delinquency is what the law says it is.* It is a legal and sociological concept, not psychological. When psychologists and psychiatrists use the term, they use it in the legal sense, or more loosely as a sociological concept.[1]

As indicated, a chief purpose of the juvenile

Source: Sol Rubin, "The Legal Character of Juvenile Delinquency," *The Annals of the American Academy of Political and Social Science*, 261 (January, 1949): 1–8. Reprinted with the permission of the American Academy of Political and Social Science and the author.

[1] Fritz Schmidl comments, "We hear psychiatrists make a distinction between 'neurotic' and 'delinquent' behavior. [But] we have searched in vain for a definition of the term 'delinquent' in the psychiatric literature." "The Rorschach Test in Juvenile Delinquency Research," *American Journal of Orthopsychiatry,* January, 1947.

court is to take child offenders out of the criminal court and protect them from criminal procedure and its effects. We therefore find in the juvenile-court acts that every definition of delinquency includes violations of laws and ordinances by children. The definition of delinquency does not, however, stop there, but *starts* there. The list of other acts or conditions which may bring a child within the jurisdiction of the juvenile courts as a delinquent is painstakingly long. The following is a list of abbreviated definitions of acts or conditions included under the heading of delinquency in the juvenile court laws of the United States:

Violates any law or ordinance
Immoral or indecent conduct
Immoral conduct around school
Engages in illegal occupation
(Knowingly) associates with vicious or immoral persons
Grows up in idleness or crime
(Knowingly) enters, visits house of ill repute
Patronizes, visits policy shop or gaming place
Patronizes saloon or dram house where intoxicating liquor is sold
Patronizes public poolroom or bucket shops
Wanders in streets at night, not on lawful business (curfew)
(Habitually) wanders about railroad yards or tracks
Jumps train or enters car or engine without authority
Habitually truant from school
Incorrigible
(Habitually) uses vile, obscene, or vulgar language (in public place)
Absents self from home without consent
Loiters, sleeps in alleys
Refuses to obey parent, guardian
Uses intoxicating liquors
Is found in place for permitting which adult may be punished
Deports self so as to injure self or others
Smokes cigarettes (around public place)
In occupation or situation dangerous to self or others
Begs or receives alms (or in street for purpose of)

Of course not every state, nor any state, has all these items in its definition of delinquency. However, the laws average eight or nine items in addition to violations of law. *No* juvenile court law confines its definition of delinquency to violations of laws and ordinances.

Nor are these jurisdictional possibilities neglected. The . . . national statistics of juvenile delinquency, the United States Children's Bureau juvenile courts statistics for 1944 and 1945,

inform us that "ungovernable" was the reason for reference to 380 juvenile courts in 9,853 cases, and running away in 9,688 cases—18 per cent of the total delinquency cases. Some of these possibly could have been represented as some violation of law. But undoubtedly many of these cases represented no violation of a penal law. Twenty per cent of the cases were referred for "acts of carelessness or mischief." Very likely many of these were not violations of penal law. Some would be torts rather than crimes if committed by adults.

As we have already said, the juvenile court laws go far beyond the purpose of taking child offenders out of the criminal courts. The juvenile courts have a proper function beyond delinquency jurisdiction. This question is present, however: Does inclusion in the delinquency definition of children who are not offenders but may be in need of protection complicate the concepts of the juvenile court? Does it confuse them?

There is no serious question that the juvenile court in its handling of child offenders is better —less harmful—than the criminal court. When the court goes beyond violators of the penal code, and takes in children who are not subject to the jurisdiction of a criminal court, the test becomes more exacting. It must then be established that the juvenile court, by initiating treatment of a group of children designated as delinquents who could not be criminals under the penal laws of the state, is making a positive contribution to the well-being of the community. Does the juvenile court by means of this widely inclusive delinquency definition lessen delinquency, or does it contribute to the solution of other problems of children and the community?

We must face the question of quality in the administration and practice of juvenile courts. It being recognized that probation staffs are inadequate in many courts, and that judges are inadequate in many courts, is it wise to augment the definition of delinquency as broadly as is done? Where the staff is not adequate, such augmentation may not only fail to help children who do not violate laws, but may impede the proper handling of children who are offenders against the penal law.

Furthermore the extravagant expansion of the definition of delinquency may have a retrograde effect on jurisdiction over child offenders. At present the jurisdiction of some juvenile courts is severely limited as to child offenders. Although the age jurisdiction goes as high as 18 in a majority of the states, in a substantial number of states it stops at 16. In a number of states the juvenile court is not given exclusive jurisdiction, and many child offenders are tried in the criminal courts. In some states certain offenses are *exclusively* the province of the *criminal court*.

The result is that although the juvenile courts everywhere go beyond the concept of a court only for child offenders, in many states they have not been given complete jurisdiction to fulfill their function of taking child offenders out of the criminal courts, and in some states the court has lost jurisdiction originally given to it.

It is perhaps in keeping with the present state of development of juvenile courts that jurisdiction be made most complete over child offenders before shaping delinquency definitions that include standards of conduct which go far beyond the prohibitions of the penal code.

STANDARDS OF CONDUCT FOR CHILDREN

Aside from the argument that as a matter of proper development of the juvenile court the delinquency definition ought not to be greatly expanded until well-nigh all child offenders have been taken out of the criminal courts, the problem of how comprehensive the definition of delinquency ought to be requires a socio-psychological examination. Do these parts of the delinquency definitions establish standards of conduct for children which are preferred rather than required? If there is justification for including in the delinquency definitions behavior which would *not* be criminal under the penal code, the justification would be most cogent as to behavior which is clearly predelinquent and likely to lead to delinquent or criminal behavior. If the behavior is dangerous to the community, or is intolerable behavior, delinquency is indicated. If, however, the *child*, and *not* the

community, is in danger, the child needs protection, but delinquency is not indicated.

It is relevant to look to the penal codes not as standards of child behavior, but as guides to what the community considers dangerous and intolerable. A child who associates with immoral persons is doing nothing which in an adult would be considered criminal. Of course such a child requires community attention; but we are talking here of *delinquency* definitions. A child who absents himself from home without consent is doing nothing which in an adult would be deemed criminal.

Children and adolescents coming within the age jurisdiction of the juvenile courts are in process of continuous growth, experimentation, and development. Stringent rules of conduct are not realistic. Yet the adult is not so closely bound by the penal code as the child is by the delinquency definitions.

Perhaps we do not like children to smoke or drink. But there is no proof that children who smoke or drink are likely to become criminal offenders. Indeed, smoking and drinking are now important adult graces. Using vile or obscene language is not nice. Nor is it nor should it be criminal or delinquent. Highly questionable in a delinquency definition are such provisions as patronizing poolrooms or bucket shops. If these places are sufficiently awful, they should be wiped out.

An "ungovernable" child may require attention. Is categorizing such a child as "delinquent" the kind of attention required? Perhaps the parents need help. Perhaps the child would be "governable" if community facilities were available for greater assistance to parents and child.

BREADTH OF DELINQUENCY DEFINITIONS

It is clear from a reading of the various items that go into delinquency definitions that standards of conduct are applied to children which are not applied to adults, at least so far as the penal laws are concerned. Since we are greatly concerned with the wide incidence of delinquency, since the very finding of delinquency is popularly, sometimes officially, considered to be only a lesser evil than a conviction for crime, since, furthermore, the consequences of an adjudication of delinquency are sometimes evil,[2] the broad delinquency definitions should be carefully examined to give these adverse factors full weight. It is a matter to which far less attention has been given than the problem deserves.

The Standard Juvenile Court Act, published by the National Probation and Parole Association and most recently endorsed as a model for all the states at the National Conference on Juvenile Delinquency held in 1946, avoids most of these delinquency classes. The Standard Act includes in its provisions corresponding to the usual delinquency definition only two items in addition to violation of law or ordinance. These items are: a child "who deserts his home or who is habitually disobedient or is beyond the control of his parent or other custodian; who, being required by law to attend school, willfully violates rules thereof or absents himself therefrom."

It is universally recognized that truancy is a mere symptom of more basic maladjustment. Modern school authorities wish to rely as little as possible on juvenile court proceedings in handling truancy. The Standard Act does not categorize truancy as delinquency, since it does not use the categories. Most juvenile courts do categorize truancy as delinquency.

With regard to the only other item contained in the Standard Act and usually found in the delinquency definition, I should like to see the psychologists and sociologists engage in a discussion of it. A child "who deserts his home or who is habitually disobedient or beyond the control of his parent . . ."—to what extent is this a family problem only, involving no inherent socially destructive element other than family disharmony? Should this be included in the delinquency definition? Would "neglect" be a sounder category? The Standard Act does not categorize disobedience as either delinquency or neglect. In many juvenile court laws such behavior is included in the definition of delinquency. This seems to have been accepted more or less routinely, without sufficient consideration.

With the present broad definitions of delinquency, a vast population of children, particularly children in slum areas, could be adjudicated delinquent. It would be hard to justify such a concept, just as it is hard to explain away the experience in California where a judge closed a juvenile institution because he was disgusted with the absence of sound treatment. The children had been neglected and abused in the institution. Most were simply sent home by the judge; some were placed in foster homes. The police predicted a crime wave; it never came. Six months later, out of 140 children taken out of the institution, only 10 were in trouble again.

AVOIDING THE DELINQUENCY TAG

We have referred to the delinquency categories in the Standard Juvenile Court Act. The Standard Act, however, does not define delinquency, but merely describes situations and classifications of children over which the court has jurisdiction. Thus in the Standard Act a disobedient child is not called a delinquent. About half a dozen juvenile court acts similarly avoid the delinquency tag.

What is the purpose of avoiding the delinquency tag? It is to support the underlying philosophy that in a juvenile court a child is being protected and helped and not being categorized as antisocial. Avoiding the delinquency tag thus implements the common legislative declaration of policy that a juvenile court proceeding is noncriminal. It requires, in turn, administrative and community implementation. However, it is clearly an advantage, although the same result should obtain where the delinquency tag *is* used, since the effect of an adjudication of delinquency is likewise noncriminal. It is also true that the distinction between delinquency and neglect is not always clear; the concepts cannot always be separated.

Does avoiding the delinquency tag have any other advantage? None is apparent.

An incidental advantage in the *use* of the categories is facility in statistical reporting (although more is required than mere existence

---

[2]Our training schools for delinquents have been called junior prisons and schools of crime; delinquency is sometimes a quasi-criminal finding in effect.

of the categories before statistics of delinquency can attain reliability). There are more important advantages in the use of the categories.

Where the categories of children within the jurisdiction of the juvenile court are separated into delinquent, dependent, and neglected, it is frequently provided that only the delinquent children may be committed to the training school or other institution for delinquent children. Where the delinquency tag is not used, a danger exists in the legal possibility that *any* child within the jurisdiction of the court, including dependent and neglected children, may be committed to the institution for delinquents. Possibly there are rare cases where a child not adjudicated delinquent would benefit from commitment to the training school. The question of training school commitments is apart from this discussion. It would seem, however, that the lost opportunity of placing in the training school children who are not delinquent is more than compensated for by lessening the danger of improper commitments of this kind.

There is also the danger, where the categories are not used, that the thinking of a court may become too vague for the proper protection of the child. A court without categories may engage in deciding that a child before it might benefit from the court facilities, without concerning itself with a clear legal test of jurisdiction and proof. With the categories, the court has to decide that the child is either dependent, neglected, or delinquent, and not merely that the court finds the child to be within its very generally described jurisdictional sections. If the distinction between delinquency and neglect is not always clear, the difficulty is not overcome by avoiding the terms. Avoiding the use of the terms "delinquency" and "neglect" does not avoid the use of categories, but merely avoids naming them.

AGE FLOOR FOR DELINQUENCY

Again, bearing in mind the inadequacies of many courts and juvenile institutions and the need for the most careful selection in institutional commitments, means of controlling commitments should be welcomed. Where the delinquency tag is used, it is possible to place an age floor on delinquency, therefore on children committable to the training schools.

The common law rule and the most common statutory rule is that a child under seven is conclusively presumed to be incapable of committing crime. A child between seven and fourteen is presumed incapable of committing crime. In a criminal proceeding the state must prove affirmatively that such a child has sufficient capacity to entertain a criminal intent (*doli capax*). In a juvenile court, these presumptions against responsibility of children do not exist. Some writers have accepted without discussion the proposition that in some way the rule carries over to the juvenile court. However, the presumptions are not in fact retained in the juvenile court laws as to delinquency. In several of the states the penal law provides that a child under a particular age—twelve years, or ten—may not be convicted of *crime*. In these states, however, a child under the specified age *may* be found delinquent for an act prohibited by the penal law. Children under seven years of age are adjudicated delinquents.

Is not the reason of the rule exempting children from criminal responsibilities applicable to delinquency? Accordingly, in some juvenile court acts the provision appears that a child under a stated age cannot be a delinquent, therefore cannot be committed as a delinquent. In Mississippi and Texas, for example, a child under ten cannot be adjudicated a delinquent. New York has an age floor of seven. By far most juvenile court laws have no floor; the definition applies to "children under 18" or whatever the upper age limit may be.

Retaining the delinquency tag permits a definition of delinquency to be applicable to a specifically limited age group, thus keeping the younger children out of the training schools. The same effect might be obtained in the noncategorized laws by providing that any one of the defined situations shall apply to children of a particular age. This is not done. It would require a corresponding particularity in the disposition section. Or it might be done by suitable provisions in the statute governing the institutions.

EUROPEAN AGE LIMITS

To a European juvenile court representative, the suggestion that an age floor be fixed in the delinquency definition would appear as a laggard proposition. It would be a matter of approaching what has long been established in a number of countries. Reviewing the delinquency jurisdiction of juvenile courts in Europe, M. Grünhut writes:

At present, the lower limit is 8 in England (though the law presumes that a child under 14 is *doli incapax* unless the prosecution rebuts the presumption by proving that the child understood the criminal nature of his act); 13 in France and Poland; 14 in Austria, Czechoslovakia, Germany, Norway; 15 in Denmark and Sweden. In Sweden the police have suggested a raising of the age limit to 16. The higher age limit is 17 in England and Poland and 18 in Austria, Czechoslovakia and Germany. Belgium, which followed the French *Code Pénal* in that it substituted the requirement of *discernement* for a statutory lower age limit, has the higher age limit of 16, and Holland likewise of 18. . . .[3]

For those cases of children whose delinquency consists of a criminal act as defined in the penal code, the term "criminal responsibility" is frankly used in the European juvenile court laws, as distinguished from the jurisdiction of the juvenile court over neglected and wayward children.

Can the delinquency age floor be safely lifted? Grünhut says:

To a certain extent, such age limits depend on ethnological factors which vary in different countries. Another factor is even more important. The more a thorough social and educational service by a Court, a Youth Welfare Authority, or the co-operation of both, has been developed and is working satisfactorily with regard to the treatment of wayward children, the more can the lower age limit of a Juvenile Court for offenders be raised. The Scandinavian countries with their well-established Child Welfare Councils have the highest lower age limit for juvenile offenders eligible for trial.

[3] In an article entitled "The Juvenile Court: Its Competence and Constitution," in *Lawless Youth, A Challenge to the New Europe*, a Policy for the Juvenile Courts prepared by the International Committee of the Howard League for Penal Reform, 1942–1945, by Margery Fry, M. Grünhut, Hermann Mannheim, Wanda Grabinska, and D. C. Reckham (London: George Allen and Unwin, Ltd., 1947).

In a court with excellent personnel, facilities (including institutions), and practices, these factors supporting the use of the delinquency tag would have little relevancy. The court's discretion would be sufficient protection. This is perhaps applicable to model legislation also. In many courts, however, at the present state of their development, the categories, including delinquency, may still serve an important, desirable function.

A CHOICE OF JUVENILE COURT CONCEPTS

Juvenile courts, like other social institutions, are in a continuous state of change. Some of our juvenile courts do not go far beyond the function of taking child offenders out of the criminal courts, and by having a comprehensive and exclusive jurisdiction they fulfill this function. Other juvenile courts perform this function rather poorly, leaving a wide jurisdiction over child offenders in the criminal courts. Many juvenile courts operate under laws which are concerned with standards of conduct on the part of children, standards which are not established as related to crime prevention.

Despite the 50 years' growth of the juvenile courts, they are still beset with difficulties on all sides. It might be the part of wisdom for the juvenile courts to go slow, to achieve important although limited purposes before embarking upon projects of doubtful urgency. If the juvenile court is to go beyond the problems of child offenders, if the juvenile court law is to set up special standards of conduct for children, it ought to do so cautiously and slowly, on the basis of generally accepted concepts on which child behavior experts are agreed. It may be that that is the course of speediest and most successful development for juvenile courts in the future.

If some of the foregoing concepts are controversial, the discussion is warranted. It will be beneficial if it is entered into by others, with tight hold of the single precept—what is best for the child. Jealousy of jurisdiction, or devotion to precedent for its own sake, ought to have no place in the development of the best means for protecting children. Not controversial, however, is the proposition that the delinquency definition is relatively unimportant when compared with the need for adequate court personnel and services, as well as other welfare and institutional services for children. It is the inade-quacy of these services that often results in a court referral or institutionalization rather than a welfare service solution. Where social services are inadequate, it helps neither child nor court to increase the scope of the delinquency definition.

2.

JAMES F. SHORT, JR. AND F. IVAN NYE

EXTENT OF UNRECORDED JUVENILE DELINQUENCY: TENTATIVE CONCLUSIONS

The frequency and nature of delinquent behavior committed by adolescents never arrested or committed to institutions has been regarded by criminologists as an important but unknown dimension of delinquent behavior. The informed layman also is aware that only a portion of delinquent behavior is followed by arrest and conviction; further, that conviction and committal to a "training school" is much more likely to follow delinquent behavior if the adolescent is from the "wrong side of the tracks." The picture of delinquent behavior obtained from official records only, and particularly the punitive action of the courts, is known to be incomplete and seriously biased.

That concern with unrecorded delinquency is high is indicated by the great interest shown in the pioneer studies of Robison,[1] Schwartz,[2] Por-terfield,[3] and the Cambridge-Somerville Youth Study,[4] in texts and in recent papers by the writers.[5] Cohen has called for an extension of such studies,[6] and a number of other investigators are pursuing research projects dealing with unrecorded delinquency.[7]

The methodology of the investigations which form the basis for this paper have been described elsewhere and will not be repeated here.[8] The

SOURCE: James F. Short, Jr. and F. Ivan Nye, "Extent of Unrecorded Juvenile Delinquency: Tentative Conclusions," *Journal of Criminal Law, Criminology and Police Science* 49, no. 4. (December, 1958): 296-302. Reprinted by Special Permission of the *Journal of Criminal Law, Criminology and Police Science* (Northwestern University School of Law), Copyright © 1958. From two larger studies of adolescent delinquency and adjustment supported in part by grants from the Social Science Research Council and the College Committee on Research of the State College of Washington.

[1]Sophia Robison, *Can Delinquency Be Measured* (New York: Columbia University Press, 1936).

[2]Edward E. Schwartz, "A Community Experiment in the Measurement of Juvenile Delinquency," *National Probation Association Yearbook, 1945* (Washington, D.C.: Government Printing Office, 1947).

[3]Austin L. Porterfield, *Youth in Trouble* (Fort Worth, Tex.: Leo Potishman Foundation, 1946) chap. 2.

[4]Fred J. Murphy, Mary M. Shirley, and Helen L. Witner, "The Incidence of Hidden Delinquency," *American Journal of Orthopsychiatry* 16 (October, 1946): 686–96.

[5]Albert K. Cohen, *Delinquent Boys: The Culture of the Gang* (New York: The Free Press, 1955), pp. 37–41; For the authors' statement as to the importance of such data, see James F. Short, Jr. and F. Ivan Nye, "Reported Behavior as a Criterion of Deviant Behavior," *Social Problems*, Winter, 1957–1958.

[6]Albert K. Cohen, Sociological Research in Juvenile Delinquency (Paper read before American Orthopsychiatric Association, March, 1956).

[7]The authors are aware of studies under way in Chicago, Kansas City, Indiana, Tennessee, Columbus, Ohio, New York City, and in the State of Washington.

[8]F. Ivan Nye and James F. Short, Jr., "Scaling Delinquent Behavior," *American Sociological Review*, 22 (June, 1957); F. Ivan Nye, *Family Relationships and Delinquent Behavior* (New York:

present paper deals with (1) types and frequency of delinquent behavior as indicated by 23 specific delinquent acts ranging from driving without a license to grand larceny and drug use, and by the use of delinquency scales derived from these items; (2) comparison of delinquent behavior in western and mid-western high school students; and (3) comparison of unrecorded delinquency with official records of delinquency.

The data were gathered by anonymous questionnaire in the classroom under the supervision of the writers. A 75 percent sample was taken from the three western high schools (cities of 10,000 to 30,000 population) and a 100 percent sample in three smaller mid-western communities. Approximately 99 percent of the questionnaires were usable.[9] In addition to being considered generally suitable for present research purposes, these particular communities possessed the positive advantage that active and informed lay people were ready to sponsor the project and interpret it to the community.

The measures of delinquent behavior used in this paper are based upon a list of behavior items commonly referred to in the laws relating to delinquent and criminal behavior. Delinquency has been defined in descriptive terms rather than in terms of legalistic categories. For example, we refer to stealing things of a certain value, rather than to descriptions of property offenses, e.g., robbery, burglary, larceny, etc.

HIGH SCHOOL POPULATIONS

Because they seem likely to be more representative of the general population than are college or training school populations, we have concentrated our research on high school populations. Table 1–1 presents the percentage of boys in our two high school samples, western and mid-

John Wiley & Sons, Inc., 1958), chap. 1; James F. Short, Jr., "The Study of Juvenile Delinquency by Reported Behavior: An Experiment in Method and Preliminary Findings" (Paper read at the annual meetings of the American Sociological Society, Washington, D.C., 1955 [dittoed]).

[9]Questionnaires were administered by one or both writers, assisted by other staff members or graduate students of the Department of Sociology of the State College of Washington. For further methodological details, see references cited in n. 8.

western, and in the western training school group, who report committing each of 21 delinquency items, and the percentage who admit committing these offenses more than once or twice. Table 1–2 presents these data for the high school and training school girls.

From these tables it is apparent that the types of delinquent behavior studied are extensive and variable in the populations studies. We have compared students in the western and mid-western samples in order to secure an estimate of the stability of responses in two non-institutionalized populations. Populations in these two regional samples differ in such respects as city size and population mobility. The mid-western sample is comprised of three small communities: a suburb of a large city, a rural town, and a consolidated rural school district. The western sample comprises three small contiguous cities. The population of the mid-western communities has been fairly stable since 1940, in contrast to the rapid population growth experienced by the western cities. These samples are alike in important respects, however. Ethnic composition is similar, both populations being overwhelmingly native caucasian, and age and sex are controlled. Perhaps of greater importance, both populations are non-institutionalized.

Few statistically significant differences between our two non-institutionalized groups are found in Tables 1–1 and 1–2.[10] This may be

[10]Samples from both finite and hypothetical universes are treated. The western state samples represent 25 percent regular-interval samples of the high school population. Mid-western and training school samples represent 100 percent samples of the individuals in those selected grades in the mid-western high schools and 100 percent samples of the training schools.

Nine of 21 possible comparisons of the percentage of western and mid-western boys who admit committing these offenses are significant at least at the .05 level. Eight of these nine offenses are committed by a higher percentage of mid-western boys. When percentage of boys admitting commission of these offenses more than once or twice is compared, only six significant differences (at .05 level) are found, five of these being higher for the mid-western boys. When mid-western and western girls are compared as to commission of these offenses, five significant differences are found, all being committed by a higher percentage of mid-western girls. Only one significant difference between these groups of non-institutionalized girls is found when percentages admitting commission of the 21 offenses more than once or twice are compared.

TABLE 1–1.

REPORTED DELINQUENT BEHAVIOR AMONG BOYS IN THREE SAMPLES

Type of Offense	Percent Admitting Commission of Offense			Percent Admitting Commission of Offense More than Once or Twice		
	M.W.	West	Tr.S.	M.W.	West	Tr.S.
Driven a car without a driver's license or permit	81.1	75.3	91.1	61.2	49.0	73.4
Skipped school	54.4	53.0	95.3	24.4	23.8	85.9
Had fist fight with one person	86.7	80.7	95.3	32.6	31.9	75.0
"Run away" from home	12.9	13.0	68.1	2.8	2.4	37.7
School probation or expulsion	15.3	11.3	67.8	2.1	2.9	31.3
Defied parents' authority	22.2	33.1	52.4	1.4	6.3	23.6
Driven too fast or recklessly	49.7	46.0	76.3	22.7	19.1	51.6
Taken little things (worth less than $2) that did not belong to you	62.7	60.6	91.8	18.5	12.9	65.1
Taken things of medium value ($2–$50)	17.1	15.8	91.0	3.8	3.8	61.4
Taken things of large value ($50)	3.5	5.0	90.8	1.1	2.1	47.7
Used force (strong-arm methods) to get money from another person	6.3	—	67.7	2.4	—	35.5
Taken part in "gang fights"	24.3	22.5	67.4	6.7	5.2	47.4
Taken a car for a ride without the owner's knowledge ..	11.2	14.8	75.2	4.5	4.0	53.4
Bought or drank beer, wine, or liquor (include drinking at home)	67.7	57.2	89.7	35.8	29.5	79.4
Bought or drank beer, wine, or liquor (outside your home)	43.0	—	87.0	21.1	—	75.0
Drank beer, wine, or liquor in your own home	57.0	—	62.8	24.1	—	31.9
Deliberate property damage	60.7	44.8	84.3	17.5	8.2	49.7
Used or sold narcotic drugs	1.4	2.2	23.1	0.7	1.6	12.6
Had sex relations with another person of the same sex (not masturbation)	12.0	8.8	10.9	3.9	2.9	3.1
Had sex relations with a person of the opposite sex	38.8	40.4	87.5	20.3	19.9	73.4
Gone hunting or fishing without a license (or violated other game laws)	74.0	62.7	66.7	39.6	23.5	44.8
Taken things you didn't want	15.7	22.5	56.8	1.4	3.1	26.8
"Beat up" on kids who hadn't done anything to you	15.7	13.9	48.7	3.1	2.8	26.2
Hurt someone to see them squirm	22.7	15.8	33.4	2.8	3.2	17.5

taken as an indication of stability and reliability of the responses obtained from the two samples. Comparison of 16 and 17 year old high school boys on a seven-item delinquency scale, based upon these same data, indicates agreement between the two groups of boys in 90.7 percent of the scale responses.[11] We note that such differences as are found in Tables 1–1 and 1–2 indicate that delinquent behavior is somewhat more widespread in the smaller, older, more structured mid-western sample than in the larger, newer, growing western communities.

The most common offenses reported "more than once or twice" by high school boys and girls in Tables 1–1 and 1–2 are traffic offenses,

truancy, and drinking. Boys also report considerable fighting, stealing (of small things), heterosexual relations, and game violations.

Comparisons of western institutionalized and non-institutionalized boys and girls on the delinquency items in Tables 1–1 and 1–2 indicate that significantly higher proportions of the "official" delinquents commit virtually all of the offenses, and commit them more often, than do the high school students.[12] Exceptions to this pattern are found only in the case of homosexual relations among the boys, driving a car without a license among girls, and game violations among both boys and girls. In spite of the statistical

[11]These data are described and graphically presented in Nye and Short, op. cit.

[12]This conclusion is based upon statistical comparison of figures presented in Tables 1–1 and 1–2, for our institutionalized and non-institutionalized western state boys and girls.

TABLE 1–2.

REPORTED DELINQUENT BEHAVIOR AMONG GIRLS IN THREE SAMPLES

Type of Offense	Percent Admitting Commission of Offense			Percent Admitting Commission of Offense More than Once or Twice		
	M.W.	West.	Tr.S.	M.W.	West.	Tr.S.
Driven a car without a driver's license or permit	60.1	58.2	68.3	33.6	29.9	54.4
Skipped school	40.3	41.0	94.0	10.1	12.2	66.3
Had fist fight with one person	32.7	28.2	72.3	7.4	5.7	44.6
"Run away" from home	9.8	11.3	85.5	1.0	1.0	51.8
School probation or expulsion	2.7	3.7	63.4	0.3	0.2	29.3
Defied parents' authority	33.0	30.6	68.3	3.7	5.0	39.0
Driven too fast or recklessly	20.9	16.3	47.5	5.7	5.4	35.0
Taken little things (worth less than $2) that did not belong to you	36.0	30.0	77.8	5.7	3.5	48.1
Taken things of medium value ($2–$50)	3.4	3.9	58.0	1.0	0.6	29.6
Taken things of large value ($50)	2.0	1.3	30.4	1.7	0.9	10.1
Used force (strong-arm methods) to get money from another person	1.3	—	36.7	0.3	—	21.5
Taken part in "gang fights"	9.7	6.5	59.0	1.7	1.1	27.7
Taken a car for a ride without the owner's knowledge ..	5.4	4.5	36.6	1.0	0.6	20.7
Bought or drank beer, wine, or liquor (include drinking at home)	62.7	44.5	90.2	23.1	17.6	80.5
Bought or drank beer, wine, or liquor (outside your home)	28.7	—	83.9	10.8	—	75.3
Drank beer, wine, or liquor in your own home	54.2	—	71.1	16.4	—	42.2
Deliberate property damage	21.7	13.6	65.4	5.7	1.6	32.1
Used or sold narcotic drugs	1.3	0.5	36.9	0.3	0.3	23.8
Had sex relations with another person of the same sex (not masturbation)	5.4	3.6	25.0	1.7	0.5	12.5
Had sex relations with a person of the opposite sex	12.5	14.1	95.1	4.1	4.8	81.5
Gone hunting or fishing without a license (or violated other game laws)	20.6	20.3	27.5	5.7	3.9	21.3
Taken things you didn't want	6.4	3.6	43.0	0.7	0.6	13.9
"Beat up" on kids who hadn't done anything to you	5.7	3.1	37.8	1.0	0.9	18.3
Hurt someone to see them squirm	10.4	9.3	35.4	1.0	1.1	20.7

significance of these comparisons, however, it is apparent that there is a good deal of "overlapping" between institutionalized and non-institutionalized boys and girls in the frequency of commission of our delinquency items.

In order to specify more precisely the amount of such overlapping, indexes of delinquent behavior in the form of Guttman-type scales have been constructed. Scales for 16 and 17 year old boys, consisting of seven and eleven delinquency items, have been described elsewhere.[13] These

scales proved to be nearly equal in their ability to differentiate between institutionalized and non-institutionalized boys. On the seven-item scale, a cutting point is found which maximizes the difference in delinquency involvement between the two groups of boys at 71 percent (see Table 1–3). At this cutting point, 86 percent of the non-institutionalized boys had been ac-

[13]Nye and Short, op. cit. The seven-item scale included the following delinquency items: driving a car without a license or permit, taking little things (worth less than $2) that did not belong to you, buying or drinking beer, wine, or liquor (include drinking at home), skipping school without a legitimate excuse, purposely damaging or destroying public or private property, sex relations with a

person of the opposite sex, and defying parents' authority to their faces. Offenses added for the eleven-item scale were: taking things of medium value, taking things of large value, running away from home, and narcotics violations. These data were rescored following the Israel "Gamma" technique in order to remove "idiosyncratic" elements, prior to scaling. For the procedure, and an exposition of its rationale, see M. W. Riley, J. W. Riley and Jackson Toby, *Scale Analysis* (New Brunswick, N.J.: Rutgers University Press, 1954), chap. 18.

TABLE 1-3.

DELINQUENT BEHAVIOR SCORES OF HIGH SCHOOL
AND TRAINING SCHOOL BOYS AGED
16 AND 17[*]

		High School		Training School	
Scale Type	Delinquent Behavior Score	Frequency	Cumulative Percent	Frequency	Cumulative Percent
1	00	0	0	0	0
2	01	128	22	0	0
3	02	40	29	0	0
4	03	60	40	0	0
5	04	105	58	3	2
6	05	28	63	2	4
7	06	26	68	3	6
8	07	25	72	2	8
9	08	80	86	7	14
10	09	31	92	24	32
11	10	27	96	8	39
12	11	6	97	11	48
13	12	6	98	15	60
14	13	5	99	16	72
15	14	3	100	34	100
		570		125	

[*]No scores were obtained for one training school and eight high school boys.

TABLE 1-4.

DELINQUENT BEHAVIOR SCORES OF HIGH SCHOOL
AND TRAINING SCHOOL GIRLS AGED
16 AND 17[*]

		High School		Training School	
Scale Type	Delinquent Behavior Score	Frequency	Cumulative Percent	Frequency	Cumulative Percent
1	00	135	26	1	2
2	01	72	40	0	2
3	02	21	44	1	4
4	03	74	59	1	6
5	04	61	71	0	6
6	05	52	81	0	6
7	06	15	84	1	8
8	07	11	86	1	10
9	08	22	90	0	10
10	09	10	92	1	12
11	10	23	97	6	25
12	11	9	99	4	33
13	12	2	99	7	48
14	13	5	100	25	100
		512		48	

[*]No scores were obtained for two training school and one high school girls.

counted for, as compared with only 14 percent of the training school boys. This difference on the eleven-item scale was maximized at 67 percent.[14] The amount of overlapping between institutionalized and non-institutionalized boys is here specified more closely than has been done in previous research. We have cited only the maximum differences between the two groups. Thus, if we were to study "delinquent" and "non-delinquent" boys by comparing our institutionalized and non-institutionalized groups, on the basis of the seven-item scale we would in fact be studying a group of delinquent boys, 14 percent of whom are less delinquent than are 14 percent of the "non-delinquent" boys. Comparisons can, of course, be obtained at any point along the scale.

A nine-item scale for the 16 and 17 year old western high school and training school girls differentiates somewhat more clearly between the two groups.[15] On this scale a maximum difference of 80 percent is found at scale type 09 (See Table 1–4). At this point on the scale 90.4 percent of the high school girls and only 10.4 percent of the training school girls are accounted for. That is, only about 10 percent of the high school girls are more delinquent than is indicated by scale type 08, while nearly 90 percent of the training school girls fall into this more delinquent category.

SEX DIFFERENCES

Comparison of boys and girls within the high

[14]It is interesting to compare these findings with results of the delinquency scale of the California Psychological Inventory, as obtained by Gough. Comparing a broad cross section of delinquents (as indicated by their being institutionalized or classed as "high school disciplinary problems") and non-delinquents on this scale, he found a cutting point above which 70 **percent** of his male delinquents fell, as compared to 20 percent of his male non-delinquents. See Harrison Gough, "Systematic Validation of a Test for Delinquency," (Paper delivered at the annual meeting of the American Psychological Association, 1954 [mimeographed]).

[15]The girls' scale consisted of the offenses included in the eleven-item boys' scale, with the exception of taking things of large value and narcotics violations.

school sample indicates a higher proportion of boys committing nearly all offenses. With few exceptions such differences are statistically significant (at .01 level). This finding is similar to that revealed by official data, though the 5 to 1 ratio of boys to girls reported by the Children's Bureau[16] is not found in many cases, suggesting a bias in under-reporting female delinquency on the part of official data. Offenses for which significant differences between the sexes are not found are generally those offenses for which girls are most often apprehended, e.g. running away from home, defying parents' authority (incorrigibility), and drinking. The fact that significantly higher proportions of boys in both samples report engaging in heterosexual relations and the fact that girls are most often referred to court for such activities presumably reflects society's greater concern for the unsupervised activities of girls.

Fewer statistically significant differences are found between training school boys and girls than was the case in our samples of high school students. Significantly greater percentages of the boys report committing 11 of the 24 offenses studied, and 13 of these offenses "more than once or twice." For nine of these offenses the recorded differences are not significant. Four of the offenses are reported by larger percentages of training school girls. These include running away from home, defying parents' authority, narcotics violations, and homosexual relations. A higher percentage of girls also report heterosexual relations, though this difference is not statistically significant. With the exception of narcotics violations, these are offenses for which girls are most often apprehended. The offenses reported by the highest percentage of training school boys, with the exception of fighting, which is a part of "growing up," are also those for which boys are most often apprehended, viz., stealing and traffic offenses.

ARREST RATES

Arrest rates for the high school and training school samples described above are not available. Data from the first phase of our research program, comparing college and training school students, indicates that non-institutionalized (college) students experience arrest in a far smaller proportion of offenses which they report committing than do training school students.[17] This is especially true of girls, for college girls report arrests for only traffic offenses. These arrest data bear a close relationship to officially available data. For both training school boys and girls arrest rates are highest for offenses against the person exclusive of sex offenses. Arrest rates for property offenses are more than twice as high among boys as among girls in the training school populations, while the reverse is true of sex offenses among these groups. Arrests among college men are reported in only a small percentage of property offenses (.3 percent as compared to 13.7 percent for training school boys), behavior problem offenses (2.3 percent compared to 15.1 percent for training school boys), and "casual" offenses (1.9 percent compared to 5.2 percent).

SOCIO-ECONOMIC DISTRIBUTION

Finally, the socio-economic characteristics associated with delinquent behavior among our high school and training school populations have been studied.[18] For this purpose analysis of delinquent behavior by individual behavior items and by scale type was made, holding constant sex categories and two age groups in the western and mid-western states. Similar analysis was made for adolescents 16 and older in the "training schools" of the western state. Few significant differences were found between socio-economic strata. Such differences as were found indicated greater delinquent involvement within

[16]U. S. Department of Health, Education, and Welfare, Social Security Administration, Children's Bureau, *Juvenile Court Statistics, 1955,* Children's Bureau Statistical Series, No. 37.

[17]James F. Short, Jr., "A Report on the Incidence of Criminal Behavior, Arrests, and Convictions in Selected Groups," Proceedings of the Pacific Sociological Society, 1954, published as vol. 22, no. 2 of *Research Studies of the State College of Washington* (June, 1954), 110-18, see Table 3, p. 117. [Not reprinted in this volume.]

[18]F. Ivan Nye, James F. Short, Jr., and V. J. Olson, "Socio-Economic Status and Delinquent Behavior," *American Journal of Sociology,* vol. 63 (January, 1958).

the highest socio-economic category as often as in the lowest.

CONCLUSIONS

While recognizing the limitations of our definition of delinquent behavior, in terms of the behavior categories studied, and the limitations of the sample employed, it appears that the following tentative conclusions regarding the extent of juvenile delinquency in the non-institutionalized population are warranted:

1. Delinquent conduct in the non-institutionalized population is extensive and variable;

2. Delinquent conduct as we have measured it is similar in extent and nature among non-institutionalized high school students in widely separated sections of the country;

3. Delinquent conduct *reported* by institutionalized and non-institutionalized students is similar to delinquency and crime as treated officially in the following respects:

(1) sex ratio—non-institutionalized boys admit committing virtually all delinquencies more frequently than do non-institutionalized girls, "once or twice" and "more than once or twice"; fewer differences exist, and these differences are smaller, between institutionalized boys and girls;

(2) the offenses for which boys are most often arrested are generally those which they most often admit committing, e.g., property offenses, traffic violations, truancy, destruction of property, drinking; a few offenses are reported by large proportions of boys which are not often recorded in official statistics, e.g., game violations and fist fights;

(3) the offenses for which girls are most often arrested are, with the exception of sex offenses among high school girls, generally the offenses which girls most often admit committing, e.g., sex offenses, incorrigibility, running away; a few offenses are reported by high proportions of girls which do not find their way into official statistics;

(4) significantly greater proportions of training school boys and girls admit committing virtually all delinquencies, and admit committing them more frequently, than do high school boys and girls;

(5) when training school students are compared with high school students on a composite scale of delinquency activities there is considerable overlapping between groups of both boys and girls, but training school students as a group rank significantly higher, in terms of seriousness of involvement in delinquent behavior, than do high school students;

(6) differences on the delinquency scales, and in the commission of individual delinquencies, are greater between high school and training school girls than between high school and training school boys;

(7) variation in the proportion of reported delinquencies which result in arrest are similar to variations in the "cleared by arrest" figures collected by the Federal Bureau of Investigation.

4. Delinquent conduct reported by non-institutionalized students differs from official data in the following ways:

(1) arrests—comparison of college and training school students indicates that training school students are arrested in higher proportions of all classes of delinquencies which they admit committing than college students;

(2) socio-economic status—delinquency within the non-institutionalized populations studied is distributed more evenly throughout the socio-economic structure of society than are official cases, which are found disproportionately in the lower socio-economic strata.

Further research of this nature may be expected to provide additional clues as to the extent and nature of delinquent behavior in various segments of the population. By such means the structural correlates of delinquency, together with other important etiological considerations, may be better understood. Reported delinquent behavior as a method warrants and requires further investigation.[19] The present status of research by reported behavior is regarded as still in a pioneer stage. It provides an alternative to the use of institutionalized populations and court records, with new opportunities for research in delinquent behavior and comprehension of it.

---

[19]For a discussion of advantages, as well as methodological problems of this approach, see Short and Nye, op. cit.

3.

JOHN C. BALL, ALAN ROSS AND ALICE SIMPSON

INCIDENCE AND ESTIMATED PREVALENCE OF RECORDED DELINQUENCY IN A METROPOLITAN AREA

Accurate delineation of the incidence and prevalence of juvenile delinquency is an indispensable prerequisite to analysis of adolescent behavior;[1] it is important, if not imperative, to know whether 2 per cent, 20 per cent or 40 per cent of American adolescents appear in court before adulthood.[2]

SOURCE: John C. Ball, Alan Ross, and Alice Simpson, "Incidence and Estimated Prevalence of Recorded Delinquency in a Metropolitan Area," *American Sociological Review*, 29, no. 1 (February, 1964): 90–93. Reprinted by Permission of the authors and the American Sociological Association.

[1] Paul W. Tappan, *Juvenile Delinquency* (New York: McGraw-Hill Book Company, 1949), chap. 2; Thorsten Sellin, "The Significance of Records of Crime," *The Law Quarterly Review* 67 (1951): 489–504; Ronald H. Beattie, "Problems of Criminal Statistics in the United States," *Journal of Criminal Law, Criminology, and Police Science* 46 (July–August, 1955): 178–86; I. Richard Perlman, "Delinquency Prevention: The Size of the Problem," *Annals of the American Academy of Political and Social Science*, 322 (March, 1959); 1–9.

[2] Various delinquency rates have been reported. In one study of 12 year old boys, the rates of *police or court contact* varied from 8 to 23 per cent. Walter C. Reckless, Simon Dinitz and Barbara Kay, "The Self Component in Potential Delinquency and Potential Non-Delinquency," *American Sociological Review* 22 (October, 1957): 567. Perlman estimates that 20 per cent of all boys in the United States will appear in *court* before age 18; loc. cit., p. 3. Starke R. Hathaway, Elis D. Monachesi and Lawrence A. Young found that 34 per cent of a statewide sample of Minnesota boys had *police or court contact* before age 17.5 "Delinquency Rates and Personality," *Journal of Criminal Law, Criminology, and Police Science* 50 (February, 1960): 435. Monahan reported that 22 per cent of Philadelphia boys would appear in *court* before age 18. Thomas P. Monahan, "On the Incidence of Delinquency," *Social Forces* 39 (October, 1960): 66–72. In a Nashville study of white boys *still in school*, 8 per cent were known to the court as delinquent. Albert J. Reiss, Jr. and Albert Lewis Rhodes, "The Distribution of Juvenile Delinquency in the Social Class Structure," *American Sociological Review* 26 (October, 1961): 720–32. In a high delinquency area of Philadelphia, 59 per cent of the boys had acquired *delinquency records* by age 18. Leonard Savitz, "Delinquency and Migra-

tion," in *The Sociology of Crime and Delinquency*, eds. Marvin E. Wolfgang, Leonard Savitz, and Norman Johnston (New York: John Wiley & Sons, Inc., 1962), p. 205. In a Kentucky study of ninth grade students, 11 per cent of the boys were *known to police or court officials* as delinquents. John C. Ball, *Social Deviancy and Adolescent Personality* (Lexington: University of Kentucky Press, 1962), p. 32.

[3] For a recent consideration of this issue see James F. Short, Jr., Ray A. Tennyson, and Kenneth I. Howard, "Behavior Dimensions of Gang Delinquency," *American Sociological Review* 28 (June, 1963): 413.

[4] Paul W. Tappan, *Crime, Justice and Correction* (New York: McGraw-Hill Book Company, 1960), p. 53.

The relation of recorded delinquency to undetected antisocial acts is an important but as yet unresolved question.[3] Whatever the relation between the commission of acts and officially recorded delinquency, however, the fact of official cognizance and confrontation remains as a social datum. We are inclined to agree with Tappan that juvenile court statistics are the most adequate data generally available throughout the United States.[4]

Our purpose in this study was to depict the extent of juvenile delinquency in Fayette County, Kentucky (which is coterminous with the Lexington Standard Metropolitan Statistical Area of 131,906 population). Computation of incidence figures did not pose any unforeseen statistical problems, but the prevalence rates involved application of conditional probability notions. The outcome of our study is a new procedure for estimating the prevalence of delinquency in a given population.

THE INCIDENCE OF JUVENILE DELINQUENCY

The age and sex distribution of juveniles who appeared before the Fayette County Juvenile

Court in 1960 is shown in Table 1–5. Of the total population of the county in 1960, 25,656 were from 6 through 17 years of age. During this year 363 different juveniles appeared in court. For boys, this incidence was 2.3 per cent of the juvenile population; for girls, it was 0.5 per cent.

Of the 363 juveniles, 113 or 31 per cent were Negroes. This figure is somewhat higher than the percentage of nonwhites in the general population aged 5–19 in 1960—14.9 per cent, reflecting the higher delinquency rates found among metropolitan youth of lower socio-economic status.

Among the charges or offenses that resulted in appearance before the juvenile court, property offenses, particularly larceny and burglary, were predominant. Because the traffic court handles common vehicular violations by juveniles, our incidence rates include only serious or unusual traffic offenses.

For boys, the incidence of delinquency doubles from age 11 to 12 and then more than triples from 12 to 17. In the latter age group, 7 per cent of the total male population were delinquent by virtue of court appearance in 1960.

THE PREVALENCE OF JUVENILE DELINQUENCY

In 1960, 236 of the 363 delinquents appeared in juvenile court for the first time. The age and sex distribution of these offenders is presented in Table 1–6. To determine the prevalence of delinquency in the Lexington SMSA, delinquency risk rates were computed for these first offenders. Under our definition of prevalence—one or more juvenile court appearances before age 18—second and subsequent offenses were excluded. Thus, the probability that a child or youth would appear in court before age 18 was the probability that he appeared for the first time at age 6, *plus* the probability that he appeared for the first time at age 7, and so on through the risk of first delinquency at age 17. Thus, the prevalence figure of 20.7 per cent for boys is a summation of the annual risks from age 6 through 17. The mathematics involved in this procedure are straightforward and based on simple probability concepts.[5]

---

[5]H. C. Fryer, *Elements of Statistics* (New York: John Wiley & Sons, Inc., 1954), chap. 3.

TABLE 1-5.

INCIDENCE: AGE AND SEX OF 363 DELINQUENTS WHO APPEARED IN JUVENILE COURT IN 1960

Age	Delinquent Boys (N = 301)			Delinquent Girls (N = 62)		
	Number of Delinquents	Total Population of SMSA, 1960*	Incidence of Delinquency (Per Cent)	Number of Delinquents	Total Population of SMSA, 1960*	Incidence of Delinquency (Per Cent)
6	2	1306	0.2%	—	1291	—
7	3	1279	0.2	—	1317	—
8	7	1238	0.6	1	1222	0.1%
9	3	1204	0.2	1	1094	0.1
10	9	1166	0.8	2	1137	0.2
11	11	1126	1.0	—	1157	—
12	23	1116	2.1	6	1166	0.5
13	39	1181	3.3	10	1167	0.9
14	50	804	6.2	10	780	1.3
15	48	805	6.0	17[a]	767	2.2
16	50	845	5.9	8	814	1.0
17	56	798	7.0	7	876	0.8
Total	301	12,868	2.3	62	12,788	0.5

*Enumeration district 57, in tract 28, was subtracted from the SMSA totals; this district is a juvenile reformatory.
[a]Includes one girl of unknown age who was assigned to the modal age group.

TABLE 1-6.

PREVALENCE: AGE AND SEX OF 236 FIRST OFFENDERS WHO APPEARED IN
JUVENILE COURT IN 1960

Age	Delinquent Boys ($N = 189$)			Delinquent Girls ($N = 47$)		
	Number of First Offenders	Total Population in SMSA*	Prevalence of Delinquency (Per Cent)	Number of First Offenders	Total Population in SMSA*	Prevalence of Delinquency (Per Cent)
6	2	1306	0.15%	—	1291	—
7	3	1279	0.23	—	1317	—
8	5	1238	0.40	1	1222	0.08%
9	3	1204	0.25	1	1094	0.09
10	6	1166	0.51	2	1137	0.18
11	5	1126	0.44	—	1157	—
12	13	1116	1.16	5	1166	0.43
13	30	1181	2.54	9	1167	0.77
14	36	804	4.48	8	780	1.03
15	32	805	3.98	12[a]	767	1.56
16	28	845	3.31	5	814	0.61
17	26	798	3.26	4	876	0.46
Total	189	12,868	20.71	47	12,788	5.21

*Enumeration district 57, in tract 28, was subtracted from the SMSA totals; this district is a juvenile reformatory.

[a]Includes one girl of unknown age who was assigned to the modal age group.

CALCULATION OF THE PREVALENCE ESTIMATE

Several assumptions were employed in estimating prevalence. The first pertains to population mobility. We assume that the first offenses committed outside the county by county adolescents are comparable to those committed within the county by outside adolescents. This assumption can be empirically assessed as incidence data from surrounding jurisdictions are obtained. For example, a given city might have a high incidence rate by virtue of a congregation of adolescents from surrounding areas for recreational purposes, or conversely, a low incidence might merely reflect the absence of facilities associated with adolescent interests. In the present case, lacking accurate incidence data for the contiguous counties and considering that 95.6 per cent of the 363 juveniles who appeared in court were residents of the metropolitan area, we decided to assume for purposes of calculation that the in- and out-movements of delinquents were comparable.

We assume, secondly, that the probability of first court appearance is stable over time for each age-sex group, e.g., the probability for 12 year old males is the same in 1955 and 1960. Let

p_i = probability of (first) incident during i-th year of age, $i = a, a+1, \ldots, t$.

P = probability of at least one incident during the years $a, a+1, \ldots, t$.

P is the prevalence to be estimated, for $a = 6$, $t = 17$.

Defining the two mutually exclusive classes, (1) persons who have never experienced an incident and (2) persons who have experienced one or more incidents, allows us to construct a simple probability relationship for P.

$$P = p_6 + (1-p_6)p_7 + (1-p_6)(1-p_7)p_8 + \ldots + \ldots (1-p_{17})p_{18}$$

Thus, prevalence is the chance of first court appearance at age 6 plus the chance of first appearance at age 7 *given* that no incident occurred at age 6, and so on.

Following a cohort from age 6 through the 17th year provides all the information required for P. Let N_6 = number of persons entering the cohort at age 6 and let n_1 = number who appeared in court for first time at age i ($i = 6, \ldots, 17$). In this case $P = (1/N_6) \Sigma n_i$.

The age-specific rates p_i are

$$p_6 = \frac{n_6}{N_6},$$

$$p_7 = \frac{n_7}{(1-p_6)N_6} = \frac{n_7}{N_7},$$

$$p_8 = \frac{n_8}{(1-p_6)(1-p_7)N_6} = \frac{n_8}{N_8}, \text{ etc.}$$

Each denominator is the number subject to first appearance at the specified age, i.e., the number at risk.

Estimating P on the basis of juvenile court records for a single year (say 1960) is somewhat more complicated, although the structure of the estimate is the same. Let

$N_6^{(i)}$ = number who entered population at age 6 who were i years of age in 1960 (i = 6, . . . , 17)

n_i = number who appeared for the first time in 1960 who were i years of age.

Estimates of the age specific rates are then

$$p_6 = \frac{n_6}{N_6^{(6)}},$$

$$p_7 = \frac{n_7}{(1-p_6)N_6^{(7)}} = \frac{n_7}{N_7^{(7)}},$$

$$p_8 = \frac{n_8}{(1-p_6)(1-p_7)N_6^{(8)}} = \frac{n_8}{N_{(8)}^{8}}, \text{ etc.}$$

and

$$P = \frac{n_6}{N_6^{(6)}} + \frac{n_7}{N_6^{(7)}} + \cdots + \frac{n_{17}}{N_6^{(17)}}$$

The numbers $N_6^{(i)}$ can be obtained from census tabulations under the mobility assumption made above, correcting for deaths if necessary.

For the Fayette County data for boys in Table 1–6, $N_6^{(6)} = 1306$, $N_6^{(7)} = 1279$, etc. That is, we assume that there were 1279 boys who

were first subject to the rate for 6 year olds and then to the rate for 7 year olds, etc.

To estimate the standard error of P we note that in the last expression for the P the n_i are independent, being the number of first court appearances in each age group for a given year. Then the variance of n_i is, by the usual formula for the sum of binomial variates,

$$\text{var}(n_i) = N_i^{(i)} p_i (1 - p_i)$$

and the variance of P is

$$\text{var}(P) = \sum_{i=6}^{17} \frac{N_i^{(i)} P_i (1-p_i)}{\left(N_6^{(i)}\right)^2}$$

The standard error of P is $\sqrt{\text{var}(P)}$. The standard error of the rate 20.71 in Table 1–6 is 1.50, and for 5.21 the standard error is 0.76.

Thus, the total risk of court appearance before age 18—prevalence as here defined—is a summation of the age specific risks. The additive prevalence figure assumes that these rates are fairly constant, or, more precisely, that according to 1960 specific age-sex first delinquency rates, the prevalence is 20.7 per cent for boys and 5.2 per cent for girls. This construction is comparable to that followed in determining life expectancy rates.

INTERPRETATION OF RESULTS

Comparison of the incidence and prevalence statistics reveals that the prevalence of juvenile delinquency is nine times the yearly incidence for boys and ten times the yearly incidence for girls (2.3 vs. 20.7 per cent, and 0.5 vs. 5.2 per cent), in this metropolitan area. This *ratio* is primarily affected by the extent of juvenile recidivism in a given jurisdiction, since multiple offenses increase incidence but not prevalence. It may therefore prove to be a useful index of the persistence of delinquency.

The incidence and prevalence data presented here unquestionably underestimate the extent of recorded delinquency among the youth of this metropolitan area. This is due to the rigid criterion of delinquency here employed: official appearance before the juvenile court.[6] Not included are arrests by the police, offenses recorded by educational or other authorities, or "conference" cases handled by the court. These additional sources of information would probably affect incidence more than prevalence rates, but this must remain conjecture until such computations are undertaken.[7]

---

[6]Courtlandt C. Van Vechten, "Differential Criminal Case Mortality in Selected Jurisdictions," *American Sociological Review* 7 (December, 1942): 833–39; Edwin H. Sutherland and Donald R. Cressey, *Principles of Criminology,* 5th ed. (New York: J. B. Lippincott Co., 1955), chap. 2.

[7]Computation of recidivism rates in a given juris-

SUMMARY

Juvenile court data from a metropolitan area were used to compute incidence and prevalence rates of delinquency for the year 1960. The incidence of delinquency varied markedly with age and sex; the highest incidence (7 per cent) was among 17 year old boys. On the basis of prevalence rates of delinquency for this metropolitan area, it was estimated that 20.7 per cent of the boys and 5.2 per cent of the girls would appear in court before age 18.

---

diction would involve additional considerations, since the effect of mobility could not be assumed to be negligible.

4.

WILLIAM R. ARNOLD

CONTINUITIES IN RESEARCH: SCALING DELINQUENT BEHAVIOR

One of the more recent efforts to refine data relative to juvenile delinquency has been aimed at the development of unilinear scales to measure the degree of delinquency of youths. These efforts have been largely applied to data provided by self-reports of delinquent acts by adolescents. Short and Nye developed a set of items, each relating to a different delinquent act, from which they selected seven items to form an "omnibus" scale which did not differentiate among types of delinquency.[1] F. R. Scott de-

veloped two scales, one of acts against relatively impersonal objects or unknown persons and one of acts against persons or objects owned by persons known to the actors.[2] Dentler and Monroe developed a scale of items relating only to theft. Dentler and Monroe conclude their discussion by suggesting that "the next step in this project is creation of Guttman scales for the four most common types of juvenile offenses, truancy, vandalism, injury to persons and theft, using more precise items and a sample of urban youth."[3] Clark and Wenninger did carry out research on self-reported delinquency in an urban setting, but, while they recognized the

---

SOURCE: William R. Arnold, "Continuities in Research: Scaling Delinquent Behavior," *Social Problems,* 13, no. 1 (Summer, 1965): 59–66. Reprinted by Permission of the author and The Society for the Study of Social Problems.

[1]F. Ivan Nye and James F. Short, Jr., "Scaling Delinquent Behavior," *American Sociological Review,* 22 (June, 1957): 326–31; F. Ivan Nye, *Family Relationships and Delinquent Behavior* (New York: John Wiley & Sons, Inc., 1958), esp. chap. 2; James F. Short, Jr. and F. Ivan Nye, "Reported Behavior as a Criterion of Deviant Behavior," *Social Problems* 5 (Winter, 1957): 207–13.

[2]John Finley Scott, "Two Dimensions of Delinquent Behavior," *American Sociological Review* 24 (April, 1959): 240–43.

[3]Robert A. Dentler and Lawrence J. Monroe, "Social Correlates of Early Adolescent Theft," *American Sociological Review* 26 (October, 1961): 743.

desirability of separating types of delinquency,[4] they did not scale their findings or categorize them systematically into types of delinquency.

DATA COLLECTION

In response to the suggestions of these earlier works, research on self-reported delinquency was undertaken, with one goal being the development of scales for attacks against persons, for vandalism, and theft. Defenses for the use of self-reported data have been presented by other researchers and need not be repeated here. The overall design of the present research calls for getting responses from a variety of settings ranging from metropolitan to rural. The scaling reported here, however, is based on data acquired in a middle-sized city of nearly 200,000, essentially an urban but not metropolitan setting. In this and future reports, this community will be called Lake City.

The procedure followed for the research in Lake City differed from that used elsewhere in two regards:

1. The questionnaires were administered by university students who were students in my criminology or juvenile delinquency classes at the time of the administration.

2. The forms were administered to 100 percent of the sophomore class of the six high schools in Lake City, thus providing a larger body of data for analysis and eliminating any possible bias in selecting a sample. The sophomore class was chosen, like the 15 year upper age limit used by Short and Dentler and Monroe, to eliminate, as much as possible, the problem of school drop-outs. The administration of the forms to only one age group simplifies the contemplated task of comparing official delinquency rates with those developed from self-reports, a task not yet undertaken.

The administration procedure was in other regards both like and unlike these past studies. As in the Short study, the respondents were asked to report all their delinquent acts since they had started to school. Since committing

delinquent acts so often begins before adolescence, the longer time span seems to make up in comprehensiveness what it loses in precision. The questionnaires were self-administered, and the instructions stressed the anonymity of the responses and the necessity of honest reporting. Criteria similar to those used by Short and Nye will be applied to discarding responses.[5] These criteria seemed to call for discarding the data from twelve respondents out of the 200 whose answers were selected to develop the scales presented here. Incomplete responses rather than any apparent attempt to falsify answers accounted for most of the discarded responses. The respondents were told simply that we wanted to know about the opinions and behavior of high school sophomores. The answer categories to the questions were the same for all the questions about all types of delinquency—none, one or two times, three or four times, five to ten times, and more than ten times. The instrument was pretested for clarity of questions and time of administration in my juvenile delinquency classes. The proportion of the high school sophomores who failed to finish the form in the allotted class period was small in view of the fact that all classes, including those of remedial level, were used as respondents.

SCALING OF RESPONSES

The form included 13 items relating to attacks against persons, 13 items relating to vandalism, and six items relating to theft, including the five items in Dentler and Monroe's theft scale. The wording of these five items was slightly changed after the pretest. Scalogram analysis (Cornell technique) was undertaken on these items using the answers from a randomly selected sample of 200 responses from Lake City. Ford's "Tabulating Procedure for Determining Scalability of More Than Six Questions"[6] was used on all three sets of items. The data on males and females were combined in hopes

---

[4]John P. Clark and Eugene P. Wenninger, "Socio-Economic Class and Area as Correlates of Illegal Behavior among Juveniles," *American Sociological Review* 27 (December, 1962): 831.

[5]Nye and Short, op. cit., p. 327.
[6]Robert N. Ford, "A Rapid Scoring Procedure for Scaling Attitude Questions," in *Sociological Studies in Scale Analysis,* ed. Matilda White Riley, John W. Riley, Jr., and Jackson Toby (New Brunswick, N.J.: Rutgers University Press, 1954), pp. 298–305.

of developing scales which could be used for both sexes.

The scaling procedure used validated the Dentler and Monroe five-item theft scale for the population studied, but the positive responses on the item added in this research—relating to check forgery—were so few that this item had to be eliminated. The overall reproducibility of the remaining five items was 93.9 percent. The maximum marginal reproducibility[7] was .73 and the coefficient of scalability[8] was .66. The scale thus meets all these criteria for an acceptable scale. This validation suggests that defenses others have given for the utility of their self-reported data apply to this research as well.

Scaling proved to be somewhat more difficult for the other two scales. Three of the thirteen questions about vandalism had to be eliminated immediately because of insufficient positive response. These three related to cutting tires on vehicles, breaking up tools or equipment, and tearing up furnishings in a house. The remaining ten items had an overall reproducibility coefficient of only 83.5 percent, and there was over 15 percent error on four of the items. Following Short and Nye's lead, image analysis was undertaken on these ten items. One of the ten items did not legitimately seem to fit into any image, and image analysis of another did not improve its reproducibility. The reproducibility of the remaining eight items after image analysis, however, was 92 percent. Despite the fact that the meanings of maximum marginal reproducibility and coefficient of scalability are not altogether clear for scales that have been subjected to image analysis, these tests of scalability were undertaken for the scales of vandalism and attacks against persons. For the vandalism scale, the skew of the responses in the negative direction produced a maximum marginal reproducibility of .79 and a coefficient of scalability of .55, both of which are on the borderline of acceptability.

The scale of attacks against persons also reached acceptable levels of reproducibility only

after image analysis. Two of the thirteen items received too few positive responses to be used as scale items. These two related to hitting your mother, father, or older relative and to physically hurting another person just for fun. The remaining eleven questions had an overall reproducibility of only 78 percent, and nine of the eleven had over 15 percent error. Three of the items with the most errors did not materially improve in reproducibility under image analysis. The remaining eight items had a reproducibility of 94.2 percent after image analysis. This somewhat remarkable improvement seems to have resulted from the presence of two fairly distinct images in the questions—one relating to refusal to obey and one relating to fighting. These images suggest that my category of "attacks against persons" might bear further subdivision in future research. The maximum marginal reproducibility of the eight-item attacks against persons scale was .64, and the coefficient of scalability was .66, both of which are quite acceptable.

It is necessary, of course, to raise and answer the question of the statistical separateness of these three scales. The correlation of the scores on these scales is quite high. The product moment correlation for the relation of the scales of vandalism and attacks against persons is .57; for the relation of the vandalism and theft scales, .62; and for the relation of the attacks against persons and the theft scale, .08. The first two of these three correlations are significant at the .05 level. The third of these product moments is not significant. Even the two significant correlations may be interpreted, however, as meaning that the score on one scale can only explain 32 percent and 38 percent of the variance of the scores on the other scale in its respective pair.

However, as Dentler and Monroe point out with regard to Scott's data,[9] product moment correlation analysis is not appropriate for analyzing the correlation of delinquency scores which are almost bound to be skewed in the direction of negative responses. This skewness prohibits our assuming that we are dealing with normal distributions. For the three scales developed in

---

[7]Allen Edwards, *Techniques of Attitude Scale Construction* (New York: Appleton-Century-Crofts, 1957), pp. 191–93.

[8]Herbert Menzel, "A New Coefficient for Scalogram Analysis," *Public Opinion Quarterly* 17 (Summer, 1953): 268–80.

[9]Dentler and Monroe, op. cit., pp. 742–43.

this study, for example, the distribution around the mean score has a generally normal form for the vandalism scale but is so skewed as to suggest a J curve for the other two scales. Spearman's rank order correlation (using scores "uniformized" into ranks) gives us a correlation of .665 for the vandalism and attacks against persons scales, a correlation of .631 for the vandalism and theft scales, and a correlation of .518 for the attacks against persons and theft scales. All three of these correlations are significant at the .001 level. There is a certain abstract similarity between my attacks against persons scale and Scott's scale of theft from persons known to the thief, and there is some similarity between the Dentler and Monroe theft scale and Scott's scale of theft from impersonal entities. The fact that the product moment between the attacks against persons scores and the theft scores is quite low while the Spearman correlation between these two sets of scores is quite significant suggests that a Spearman correlation of the scores on Scott's two scales might reveal considerably more relation between the two than his reported product moment of .17 would suggest.

Dentler and Monroe pointed out, however, that we are not as interested in overall correlations between types of delinquency as we are in the capacity of a score relative to one type of delinquency to predict a score relative to another type of delinquency.[10] If we arbitrarily say that scores on the two scales within one scale point of each other constitute "good" predictors of each other, we have another possible measure of the utility of these scales as separate indicators of behavior. To make this comparison for the scales here, we must weight the scores on the theft scale so that they fall on a range from zero to eight. By this criterion, vandalism and attacks against persons are "good" predictors of each other 57 percent of the time (an improvement of 19 percentage points over pure chance), vandalism and theft scores are good predictors of each other 54 percent of the time (an improvement of only 16 percentage points over chance), and attacks against persons and theft scores are good pre-

dictors of each other 37 percent of the time (an improvement of only 10 percentage points over chance). On the grounds, then, that the scores as derived do not serve as good predictors of each other nor account for large proportions of the variance of each other, it appears that we may use them as separate indicators of behavior. In doing so, however, it should be borne in mind that we are dealing with related phenomena.

One or two further questions about the validity of the scales developed here can be best raised only after the scale items have been presented. The vandalism scale consisted of the following eight items listed, with modes of scoring, in order of decreasing proportions of positive responses.

1. Walked on some grass, yards, or fields where you weren't supposed to: none *0*; one or two times *1*; three or four times *1*; five to ten times *1*; more than ten times *1*.
2. Marked with a pen, pencil, knife, or chalk on walls, sidewalks, or desks: none *0*; one or two times *0*; three or four times *1*; five to ten times *1*; more than ten times *1*.
3. Thrown eggs, tomatoes, garbage, or anything else like this at any person, house, or building: none *0*; one or two times *1*; three or four times *1*; five to ten times *1*; more than ten times *1*.
4. Broken out any windows: none *0*; one or two times *1*; three or four times *1*; five to ten times *1*; more than ten times *1*.
5. Broken down anything such as fences, or a flower bed, or a clothes line: none *0*; one or two times *1*; three or four times *1*; five to ten times *1*; more than ten times *1*.
6. Put paint on anything you weren't supposed to be painting: none *0*; one or two times *1*; three or four times *1*; five to ten times *1*; more than ten times *1*.
7. Broken out any light bulbs on the street or elsewhere: none *0*; one or two times *1*; three or four times *1*; five to ten times *1*; more than ten times *1*.
8. Let the air out of somebody's tires: none *0*; one or two times *1*; three or four times *1*; five to ten times *1*; more than ten times *1*.

The items selected for the scale of attacks against persons and the mode of scoring these items were as follows:

1. Disobeyed your parents: none *0*; one or two times *0*; three or four times *0*; five to ten times *0*; more than ten times *1*.

---

[10] *Ibid.*

2. Purposely said mean things to someone to get back for something they had done to you: none *0*; one or two times *0*; three or four times *1*; five to ten times *1*; more than ten times *1*.
3. Had a fight with one other person in which you hit each other or wrestled: none *0*; one or two times *0*; three or four times *1*; five to ten times *1*; more than ten times *1*.
4. Disobeyed teachers, school officials, or others who told you what to do: none *0*; one or two times *1*; three or four times *1*; five to ten times *1*; more than ten times *1*.
5. Defied your parents' authority to their face: none *0*; one or two times *0*; three or four times *1*; five to ten times *1*; more than ten times *1*.
6. Made anonymous phone calls just to annoy the people you called: none *0*; one or two times *0*; three or four times *1*; five to ten times *1*; more than ten times *1*.
7. "Beat up" anybody in a fight: none *0*; one or two times *1*; three or four times *1*; five to ten times *1*; more than ten times *1*.
8. Signed somebody's name other than your own name an excuse for absence from school: none *0*; one or two times *1*; three or four times *1*; five to ten times *1*; more than ten times *1*.

The frequency of the positive responses was the same for items five and six and for items seven and eight on this scale. The items used in the theft scale are already familiar to those who have read the Dentler and Monroe article but are presented here to indicate the relative numbers of positive responses on the items, again in order of decreasing frequency of these positive responses.

1. Taken little things (worth less than $2) that you were not supposed to take: none *0*; one or two times *1*; three or four times *1*; five to ten times *1*; more than ten times *1*.
2. Taken things from someone else's desk or locker at school that the person would not want you to take: none *0*; one or two times *1*; three or four times *1*; five to ten times *1*; more than ten times *1*.
3. Taken things of value (between $2 and $50) that you were not supposed to take: none *0*; one or two times *1*; three or four times *1*; five to ten times *1*; more than ten times *1*.
4. Taken a car for a ride without the owner's permission: none *0*; one or two times *1*; three or four times *1*; five to ten times *1*; more than ten times *1*.
5. Taken things of large value (over $50): none *0*; one or two times *1*; three or four times *1*; five to ten times *1*; more than ten times *1*.

One of the questions that must be raised about the scales as presented relates to their face validity. The face validity of the theft scale is almost unquestionable. The vandalism scale items beyond item two clearly refer to behavior which is illegal, destruction of property which could result in apprehension and a court appearance if it persisted. However, with regard to the attacks against persons scale, the items seem to deal largely with antisocial behavior which is less serious than the crimes normally called attacks against persons. This is partly a result of the fact that all questions about sex offenses had to be deleted from the original form to make it acceptable to the Lake City schools. Further, the more violent crimes against persons were omitted because I supposed, based on Short's experience, that such items would receive so few positive responses that they could not be used as acceptable scale items. The resulting scale, however, does not seem to be so much an attacks against persons scale as it seems to be a scale of authority protest or, perhaps, hostility. In any case, the scale seems to measure a kind of antisocial behavior which differs in nature from vandalism and from theft. As such, it seems to be useful regardless of the label we apply to it.

It should be noted that the scales developed here are not so much scales of the volume of delinquency committed as of the variety of types of delinquent acts the respondents have committed. Preliminary analysis of the data suggests, however, that committing the more serious acts is associated with committing the less serious acts more frequently.

There are several uses to which these scales and their resulting scores for individuals may be put. In the research for which this paper is an initial report, the primary focus will be on the differential distribution of these three types of antisocial acts at various socio-economic levels of society. If the Clark and Wenninger conclusion—that the rate of commission of antisocial acts in the various classes is uniform in small communities but not in metropolitan areas —is correct, the Lake City study will help to delineate the size of community at which this change in distribution takes place. Furthermore, the data will permit us to validate or lay to rest the impression which law enforcement officials seem to have that theft is characteristic of lower class areas while vandalism is more common in middle class areas.

The use of these scales in analyzing delinquency in the various socio-economic levels may be illustrated by the data in Table 1-7. It should be noted that the socio-economic levels are here represented only by occupational groupings. More refined analysis of class position using the prestige ratings of the North-Hatt rankings and Index of Status Position scores will be undertaken and reported elsewhere. Only the responses received from the sample selected for scaling are reported here. The frequencies of the occupational groups in the sample correspond quite closely to the distribution of the occupational groupings in Lake City as reported in the census data for that city.

It will be noted that the findings as reported here are somewhat anomalous. The slight variation in the N's was brought about by non-responses on any one item used to develop a scale score. The inconsistency between the chi-square and gamma measures on the first two parts of the table suggests that the small sample for which data are presented here do not permit any quick generalization of the findings. While these data suggest that delinquency is more widespread in the higher socio-economic levels than in the lower levels, the weakness of the associations does not permit us to reject or revise the Short and Dentler and Monroe conclusions that there is no association between delinquency and class position. The conclusion of the earlier

research may prove valid even when different types of delinquency are measured.

The questionnaire responses also contain data relative to the nature of peer group associations of the respondents, the respondents' role models, and the degree to which the respondents perceive adolescence as a time of preparing for adulthood as opposed to a time of simple freedom from responsibility. These three types of responses obviously relate, respectively, to the differential association, role model, and indefiniteness of adolescent status theories of delinquency. These responses, coupled with the scores on the three scales of antisocial behavior, should help answer questions about the possible differences in the causation of different types of delinquency.

Finally, the responses received should permit us to make some comparison between self-reported rates of commission of either particular delinquent acts or types of acts and official rates of commission of these same acts or types of acts. Ball, Ross, and Simpson have used a relatively simple system for estimating the prevalence of officially known delinquency for a given age group by reviewing police records of first offenses for each succeeding year into the past.[11] If this official data could be analyzed by school districts and compared with the self-reported data by school districts, we might be able to approach some estimate of the propor-

---

[11]John C. Ball, Alan Ross, and Alice Simpson, "Incidence and Estimated Prevalence of Recorded Delinquency in a Metropolitan Area," *American Sociological Review* 29 (February, 1964): 90–93.

TABLE 1-7.

THE ASSOCIATION OF OCCUPATIONAL CLASSIFICATION OF HEADS OF HOUSEHOLDS WITH DELINQUENCY SCALE SCORES OF RESPONDENTS

Occupational Level	Scores on Vandalism Scale			Scores on Attacks against Persons Scale			Scores on Theft Scale		
	0-1	2-3	4-8	0-1	2-4	5-8	0	1	2-5
Professional, Technical, Managerial Levels	15	24	23	17	21	27	18	23	24
Clerical and Sales Levels	15	9	20	12	12	14	15	11	18
Skilled and Unskilled Workers	31	23	20	29	29	16	29	29	25

$N = 180$ $\chi^2 = 8.87$ (sig. at .09 level) gamma $= -.17$

$N = 177$ $\chi^2 = 7.05$ (not sig.) gamma $= -.27$

$N = 183$ $\chi^2 = 3.29$ (not sig.) gamma $= -.10$

tion of antisocial behavior which is officially known, using the social class of an area as a crucial variable in the explanation of the variation of these proportions.

It would appear that the scaling of self-reports of delinquency may open up a number of areas for investigation in which we have, to this point, been limited in the measurement of the incidence, causation, and career development of delinquency.

5.

IRVING PILIAVIN AND SCOTT BRIAR

POLICE ENCOUNTERS WITH JUVENILES

ABSTRACT

In an observational study of police officers' contacts with juveniles the authors reached these conclusions: (1) Wide discretion was exercised by policemen in dealing with youthful offenders. (2) The exercise of this discretion was affected by a few readily observable criteria, including boys' prior offense records, race, grooming, and demeanor. Among first offenders particularly, but to some degree among all offenders, a youth's demeanor was a major criterion for determining what police disposition he would be given. Officers estimated that 50-60 per cent of first offense dispositions were based on this criterion. (3) The differential in arrest and apprehension rates between Negroes and whites was not simply a consequence of a greater offense rate among the former or police bias. To some extent this differential was due to the fact that Negroes more often than Caucasians exhibited those aspects of demeanor associated by officers with "true" delinquent boys.

As the first of a series of decisions made in the channeling of youthful offenders through the agencies concerned with juvenile justice and corrections, the disposition decisions made by police officers have potentially profound consequences for apprehended juveniles. Thus arrest, the most severe of the dispositions available to police, may not only lead to confinement of the suspected offender but also bring him loss of social status, restriction of educational and employment opportunities, and future harassment by law-enforcement personnel.[1] According to

some criminologists, the stigmatization resulting from police apprehension, arrest, and detention actually reinforces deviant behavior.[2] Other authorities have suggested, in fact, that this stigmatization serves as the catalytic agent initiating delinquent careers.[3] Despite their presumed significance, however, little empirical analysis has been reported regarding the factors influencing, or consequences resulting from, police actions with juvenile offenders. Furthermore, while some studies of police encounters with adult offenders

SOURCE: Irving Piliavin and Scott Briar, "Police Encounters with Juveniles," *American Journal of Sociology* 70, no. 2 (September, 1964): 206–14, Copyright 1964 by the University of Chicago. Reprinted by permission of the authors and the journal.

This study was supported by Grant MH-06328-02, National Institute of Mental Health, United States Public Health Service.

[1] Richard D. Schwartz and Jerome H. Skolnick, "Two Studies of Legal Stigma," *Social Problems* 10 (April, 1962): 133–42; Sol Rubin, *Crime and Juvenile Delinquency* (New York: Oceana Publications, Inc., 1958); B. F. McSally, "Finding Jobs for Re-

leased Offenders," *Federal Probation* 24 (June, 1960): 12–17; Harold D. Lasswell and Richard C. Donnelly, "The Continuing Debate over Responsibility: An Introduction to Isolating the Condemnation Sanction," *Yale Law Journal* 68 (April, 1959): 869–99.

[2] Richard A. Cloward and Lloyd E. Ohlin, *Delinquency and Opportunity* (New York: The Free Press, 1960), pp. 124–30.

[3] Frank Tannenbaum, *Crime and the Community* (New York: Columbia University Press, 1936), pp. 17–20; Howard S. Becker, *Outsiders: Studies in the Sociology of Deviance* (New York: The Free Press, 1963), chaps. 1 and 2.

have been reported, the extent to which the findings of these investigations pertain to law-enforcement practices with youthful offenders is not known.[4]

The above considerations have led the writers to undertake a longitudinal study of the conditions influencing, and consequences flowing from, police actions with juveniles. In the present paper findings will be presented indicating the influence of certain factors on police actions. Research data consist primarily of notes and records based on nine months' observation of all juvenile officers in one police department.[5] The officers were observed in the course of their regular tours of duty.[6] While these data do not lend themselves to quantitative assessments of reliability and validity, the candor shown by the officers in their interviews with the investigators and their use of officially frowned-upon practices while under observation provide some assurance that the materials presented below accurately reflect the typical operations and attitudes of the law-enforcement personnel studied.

The setting for the research, a metropolitan police department serving an industrial city with approximately 450,000 inhabitants, was noted within the community it served and among law-enforcement officials elsewhere for the honesty and superior quality of its personnel. Incidents involving criminal activity or brutality by members of the department had been extremely rare during the ten years preceding this study; personnel standards were comparatively high; and

an extensive training program was provided to both new and experienced personnel. Juvenile Bureau members, the primary subjects of this investigation, differed somewhat from other members of the department in that they were responsible for delinquency prevention as well as law enforcement, that is, juvenile officers were expected to be knowledgeable about conditions leading to crime and delinquency and to be able to work with community agencies serving known or potential juvenile offenders. Accordingly, in the assignment of personnel to the Juvenile Bureau, consideration was given not only to an officer's devotion to and reliability in law enforcement but also to his commitment to delinquency prevention. Assignment to the Bureau was of advantage to policemen seeking promotions. Consequently, many officers requested transfer to this unit, and its personnel comprised a highly select group of officers.

In the field, juvenile officers operated essentially as patrol officers. They cruised assigned beats and, although concerned primarily with juvenile offenders, frequently had occasion to apprehend and arrest adults. Confrontations between the officers and juveniles occurred in one of the following three ways, in order of increasing frequency: (1) encounters resulting from officers' spotting officially "wanted" youths; (2) encounters taking place at or near the scene of offenses reported to police headquarters; and (3) encounters occurring as the result of officers' directly observing youths either committing offenses or in "suspicious circumstances." However, the probability that a confrontation would take place between officer and juvenile, or that a particular disposition of an identified offender would be made, was only in part determined by the knowledge that an offense had occurred or that a particular juvenile had committed an offense. The bases for and utilization of non-offenses related criteria by police in accosting and disposing of juveniles are the focuses of the following discussion.

SANCTIONS FOR DISCRETION

In each encounter with juveniles, with the minor exception of officially "wanted" youths,[7] a central

---

[4]For a detailed accounting of police discretionary practices, see Joseph Goldstein, "Police Discretion Not to Invoke the Criminal Process: Low Visibility Decisions in the Administration of Justice," *Yale Law Journal* 69 (1960): 543–94; Wayne R. LaFave, "The Police and Non-enforcement of the Law: Part I," *Wisconsin Law Review*, January, 1962, 104–37; S. H. Kadish, "Legal Norms and Discretion in the Police and Sentencing Processes," *Harvard Law Review* 75 (March, 1962): 904–31.

[5]Approximately thirty officers were assigned to the Juvenile Bureau in the department studied. While we had an opportunity to observe all officers in the Bureau during the study, our observations were concentrated on those who had been working in the Bureau for one or two years at least. Although two of the officers in the Juvenile Bureau were Negro, we observed these officers on only a few occasions.

[6]Although observations were not confined to specific days or work shifts, more observations were made during evenings and weekends because police activity was greatest during these periods.

[7]"Wanted" juveniles usually were placed under

task confronting the officer was to decide what official action to take against the boys involved. In making these disposition decisions, officers could select any one of five discrete alternatives:

1. outright release
2. release and submission of a "field interrogation report" briefly describing the circumstances initiating the police-juvenile confrontation
3. "official reprimand" and release to parents or guardian
4. citation to juvenile court
5. arrest and confinement in juvenile hall.

Dispositions 3, 4, and 5 differed from the others in two basic respects. First, with rare exceptions, when an officer chose to reprimand, cite, or arrest a boy, he took the youth to the police station. Second, the reprimanded, cited, or arrested boy acquired an official police "record," that is, his name was officially recorded in Bureau files as a juvenile violator.

Analysis of the distribution of police disposition decisions about juveniles revealed that in virtually every category of offense the full range of official disposition alternatives available to officers was employed. This wide range of discretion resulted primarily from two conditions. First, it reflected the reluctance of officers to expose certain youths to the stigmatization presumed to be associated with official police action. Few juvenile officers believed that correctional agencies serving the community could effectively help delinquents. For some officers this attitude reflected a lack of confidence in rehabilitation techniques; for others, a belief that high case loads and lack of professional training among correctional workers vitiated their efforts at treatment. All officers were agreed, however, that juvenile justice and correctional processes were essentially concerned with apprehension and punishment rather than treatment. Furthermore, all officers believed that some aspects of these processes (e.g., judicial definition of youths as delinquents and removal of delinquents from the community), as well as some of the possible consequences of these processes (e.g., intimate institutional

contact with "hard-core" delinquents, as well as parental, school, and conventional peer disapproval or rejection), could reinforce what previously might have been only a tentative proclivity toward delinquent values and behavior. Consequently, when officers found reason to doubt that a youth being confronted was highly committed toward deviance, they were inclined to treat him with leniency.

Second, and more important, the practice of discretion was sanctioned by police-department policy. Training manuals and departmental bulletins stressed that the disposition of each juvenile offender was not to be based solely on the type of infraction he committed. Thus, while it was departmental policy to "arrest and confine all juveniles who have committed a felony or misdemeanor involving theft, sex offense, battery, possession of dangerous weapons, prowling, peeping, intoxication, incorrigibility, and disturbance of the peace," it was acknowledged that "such considerations as age, attitude and prior criminal record might indicate that a different disposition would be more appropriate."[8] The official justification for discretion in processing juvenile offenders, based on the preventive aims of the Juvenile Bureau, was that each juvenile violator should be dealt with solely on the basis of what was best for him.[9] Unofficially, administrative legitimation of discretion was further justified on the grounds that strict enforcement practices would overcrowd court calendars and detention facilities, as well as dramatically increase juvenile crime rates—consequences to be avoided because they would expose the police department to community criticism.[10]

In practice, the official policy justifying use of discretion served as a demand that discretion be exercised. As such, it posed three problems for juvenile officers. First, it represented a departure from the traditional police practice with which the juvenile officers themselves were

---

arrest or in protective custody, a practice which in effect relieved officers of the responsibility for deciding what to do with these youths.

[8]Quoted from a training manual issued by the police department studied in this research.

[9]Presumably this also implied that police action with juveniles was to be determined partly by the offenders' need for correctional services.

[10]This was reported by beat officers as well as supervisory and administrative personnel of the juvenile bureau.

identified, in the sense that they were expected to justify their juvenile disposition decisions not simply by evidence proving a youth had committed a crime—grounds on which police were officially expected to base their dispositions of non-juvenile offenders[11]—but in the *character* of the youth. Second, in disposing of juvenile offenders, officers were expected, in effect, to make judicial rather than ministerial decisions.[12] Third, the shift from the offense to the offender as the basis for determining the appropriate disposition substantially increased the uncertainty and ambiguity for officers in the situation of apprehension because no explicit rules existed for determining which disposition different types of youths should receive. Despite these problems, officers were constrained to base disposition decisions on the character of the apprehended youth, not only because they wanted to be fair, but because persistent failure to do so could result in judicial criticism, departmental censure, and, they believed, loss of authority with juveniles.[13]

DISPOSITION CRITERIA

Assessing the character of apprehended offenders posed relatively few difficulties for officers in the case of youths who had committed serious crimes such as robbery, homicide, aggravated assault, grand theft, auto theft, rape, and arson. Officials generally regarded these juveniles as confirmed delinquents simply by virtue of their involvement in offenses of this magnitude.[14] However, the infraction committed did not always suffice to determine the appropriate dis-

position for some serious offenders;[15] and, in the case of minor offenders, who comprised over 90 per cent of the youths against whom police took action, the violation per se generally played an insignificant role in the choice of disposition. While a number of minor offenders were seen as serious delinquents deserving arrest, many others were perceived either as "good" boys whose offenses were atypical of their customary behavior, as pawns of undesirable associates or, in any case, as boys for whom arrest was regarded as an unwarranted and possibly harmful punishment. Thus, for nearly all minor violators and for some serious delinquents, the assessment of character—the distinction between serious delinquents, "good" boys, misguided youths, and so on—and the dispositions which followed from these assessments were based on youths' personal characteristics and not their offenses.

Despite this dependence of disposition decisions on the personal characteristics of these youths, however, police officers actually had access only to very limited information about boys at the time they had to decide what to do with them. In the field, officers typically had no data concerning the past offense records, school performance, family situation, or personal adjustment of apprehended youths.[16] Furthermore, files at police headquarters provided data only about each boy's prior offense record. Thus both the decision made in the field—whether or not to bring the boy in—and the decision made at the station—which disposition to invoke—were based largely on cues which emerged from the interaction between the officer and the youth, cues from which the officer inferred the youth's character. These cues included the youth's group

---

[11]In actual practice, of course, disposition decisions regarding adult offenders also were influenced by many factors extraneous to the offense per se.

[12]For example, in dealing with adult violators, officers had no disposition alternative comparable to the reprimand-and-release category, a disposition which contained elements of punishment but did not involve mediation by the court.

[13]The concern of officers over possible loss of authority stemmed from their belief that court failure to support arrests by appropriate action would cause policemen to "lose face" in the eyes of juveniles.

[14]It is also likely that the possibility of negative publicity resulting from the failure to arrest such violators—particularly if they became involved in further serious crime—brought about strong administrative pressure for their arrest.

[15]For example, in the year preceding this research, over 30 per cent of the juveniles involved in burglaries and 12 per cent of the juveniles committing auto theft received dispositions other than arrest.

[16]On occasion, officers apprehended youths whom they personally knew to be prior offenders. This did not occur frequently, however, for several reasons. First, approximately 75 per cent of apprehended youths had no prior official records; second, officers periodically exchanged patrol areas, thus limiting their exposure to, and knowledge about, these areas; and third, patrolmen seldom spent more than three or four years in the juvenile division.

affiliations, age, race, grooming, dress, and demeanor. Older juveniles, members of known delinquent gangs, Negroes, youths with well-oiled hair, black jackets, and soiled denims or jeans (the presumed uniform of "tough" boys), and boys who in their interactions with officers did not manifest what were considered to be appropriate signs of respect tended to receive the more severe dispositions.

Other than prior record, the most important of the above clues was a youth's *demeanor*. In the opinion of juvenile patrolmen themselves the demeanor of apprehended juveniles was a major determinant of their decisions for 50–60 per cent of the juvenile cases they processed.[17] A less subjective indication of the association between a youth's demeanor and police disposition is provided by Table 1–8, which presents the police dispositions for 66 youths whose encounters with police were observed in the course of this study.[18] For purposes of this

analysis, each youth's demeanor in the encounter was classified as either co-operative or unco-operative.[19] The results clearly reveal a marked association between youth demeanor and the severity of police dispositions.

The cues used by police to assess demeanor were fairly simple. Juveniles who were contrite about their infractions, respectful to officers, and fearful of the sanctions that might be employed against them tended to be viewed by patrolmen as basically law-abiding or at least "salvageable." For these youths it was usually assumed that informal or formal reprimand would suffice to guarantee their future conformity. In contrast, youthful offenders who were fractious, obdurate, or who appeared nonchalant in their encounters with patrolmen were likely to be viewed as "would-be tough guys" or "punks" who fully deserved the most severe sanction: arrest. The following excerpts from observation notes illustrate the importance attached to demeanor by police in making disposition decisions.

TABLE 1-8.

SEVERITY OF POLICE DISPOSITION
BY YOUTH'S DEMEANOR

Severity of Police Disposition	Youth's Demeanor		
	Co-op-erative	Unco-op-erative	Total
Arrest (most severe)	2	14	16
Citation or official reprimand	4	5	9
Informal reprimand	15	1	16
Admonish and release (least severe)	24	1	25
Total	45	21	66

---

[17]While reliable subgroup estimates were impossible to obtain through observation because of the relatively small number of incidents observed, the importance of demeanor in disposition decisions appeared to be much less significant with known prior offenders.

[18]Systematic data were collected on police encounters with 76 juveniles. In 10 of these encounters the police concluded that their suspicions were groundless, and consequently the juveniles involved were exonerated; these 10 cases were eliminated from this analysis of demeanor. (The total number of encounters observed was considerably more than 76, but systematic data-collection procedures were not instituted until several months after observations began.)

1. The interrogation of "A" (an 18-year-old upper-lower-class white male accused of statutory rape) was assigned to a police sergeant with long experience on the force. As I sat in his office while we waited for the youth to arrive for questioning, the sergeant expressed his uncertainty as to what he should do with this young man. On the one hand, he could not ignore the fact that an offense had been committed; he had been informed, in fact, that the youth was prepared to confess to the offense. Nor could he overlook the continued pressure from the girl's father (an important political figure) for the police to take severe action against the youth. On the other hand, the sergeant had formed a low opinion of the girl's moral character, and he considered it unfair to charge "A" with statutory rape when the girl was a willing partner to the offense and might even have been the instigator of it. However, his sense of injustice concerning "A" was tempered by his image of the youth as a "punk," based, he explained, on information he had received that the youth belonged to a cer-

---

[19]The data used for the classification of demeanor were the written records of observations made by the authors. The classifications were made by an independent judge not associated with this study. In classifying a youth's demeanor as co-operative or unco-operative, particular attention was paid to: (1) the youth's responses to police officers' questions and requests; (2) the respect and deference—or lack of these qualities—shown by the youth toward police officers; and (3) police officers' assessments of the youth's demeanor.

tain gang, the members of which were well known to, and disliked by, the police. Nevertheless, as we prepared to leave his office to interview "A," the sergeant was still in doubt as to what he should do with him.

As we walked down the corridor to the interrogation room, the sergeant was stopped by a reporter from the local newspaper. In an excited tone of voice, the reporter explained that his editor was pressing him to get further information about this case. The newspaper had printed some of the facts about the girl's disappearance, and as a consequence the girl's father was threatening suit against the paper for defamation of the girl's character. It would strengthen the newspaper's position, the reporter explained, if the police had information indicating that the girl's associates, particularly the youth the sergeant was about to interrogate, were persons of disreputable character. This stimulus seemed to resolve the sergeant's uncertainty. He told the reporter, "unofficially," that the youth was known to be an undesirable person, citing as evidence his membership in the delinquent gang. Furthermore, the sergeant added that he had evidence that this youth had been intimate with the girl over a period of many months. When the reporter asked if the police were planning to do anything to the youth, the sergeant answered that he intended to charge the youth with statutory rape.

In the interrogation, however, three points quickly emerged which profoundly affected the sergeant's judgment of the youth. First, the youth was polite and co-operative; he consistently addressed the officer as "sir," answered all questions quietly, and signed a statement implicating himself in numerous counts of statutory rape. Second, the youth's intentions toward the girl appeared to have been honorable; for example, he said that he wanted to marry her eventually. Third, the youth was not in fact a member of the gang in question. The sergeant's attitude became increasingly sympathetic, and after we left the interrogation room he announced his intention to "get 'A' off the hook," meaning that he wanted to have the charges against "A" reduced or, if possible, dropped.

2. Officers "X" and "Y" brought into the police station a seventeen-year-old white boy who, along with two older companions, had been found in a home having sex relations with a fifteen-year-old girl. The boy responded to police officers' queries slowly and with obvious disregard. It was apparent that his lack of deference toward the officers and his failure to evidence concern about his situation were irritating his questioners. Finally, one of the officers turned to me and, obviously angry, commented that in his view the boy was simply a "stud" interested only in sex, eating, and sleeping. The policemen conjectured that the boy "probably already had knocked up half a dozen girls." The boy ignored these remarks, except for an occasional

impassive stare at the patrolmen. Turning to the boy, the officer remarked, "What the hell am I going to do with you?" And again the boy simply returned the officer's gaze. The latter then said, "Well, I guess we'll just have to put you away for a while." An arrest report was then made out and the boy was taken to Juvenile Hall.

Although anger and disgust frequently characterized officers' attitudes toward recalcitrant and impassive juvenile offenders, their manner while processing these youths was typically routine, restrained, and without rancor. While the officers' restraint may have been due in part to their desire to avoid accusation and censure, it also seemed to reflect their inurement to a frequent experience. By and large, only their occasional "needling" or insulting of a boy gave any hint of the underlying resentment and dislike they felt toward many of these youths.[20]

PREJUDICE IN APPREHENSION AND DISPOSITION DECISIONS

Compared to other youths, Negroes and boys whose appearance matched the delinquent stereotype were more frequently stopped and interrogated by patrolmen—often even in the absence of evidence that an offense had been committed[21]—and usually were given more severe

---

[20]Officers' animosity toward recalcitrant or aloof offenders appeared to stem from two sources: moral indignation that these juveniles were self-righteous and indifferent about their transgressions, and resentment that these youths failed to accord police the respect they believed they deserved. Since the patrolmen perceived themselves as honestly and impartially performing a vital community function warranting respect and deference from the community at large, they attributed the lack of respect shown them by these juveniles to the latters' immorality.

[21]The clearest evidence for this assertion is provided by the overrepresentation of Negroes among "innocent" juveniles accosted by the police. As noted, of the 76 juveniles on whom systematic data were collected, 10 were exonerated and released without suspicion. Seven, or two-thirds of these 10 "innocent" juveniles, were Negro, in contrast to the allegedly "guilty" youths, less than one-third of whom were Negro. The following incident illustrates the operation of this bias: One officer, observing a youth walking along the street, commented that the youth "looks suspicious" and promptly stopped and questioned him. Asked later to explain

dispositions for the same violations. Our data suggest, however, that these selective apprehension and disposition practices resulted not only from the intrusion of long-held prejudices of individual police officers but also from certain job-related experiences of law-enforcement personnel. First, the tendency for police to give more severe dispositions to Negroes and to youths whose appearance corresponded to that which police associated with delinquents partly reflected the fact, observed in this study, that these youths also were much more likely than were other types of boys to exhibit the sort of recalcitrant demeanor which police construed as a sign of the confirmed delinquent. Further, officers assumed, partly on the basis of departmental statistics, that Negroes and juveniles who "look tough" (e.g., who wear chinos, leather jackets, boots, etc.) commit crimes more frequently than do other types of youths.[22] In this sense, the police justified their selective treatment of these youths along epidemiological lines: that is, they were concentrating their attention on those youths whom they believed were most likely to commit delinquent acts. In the words of one highly placed official in the department:

If you know that the bulk of your delinquent problem comes from kids who, say, are from 12 to 14 years of age, when you're out on patrol you are much more likely to be sensitive to the activities of juveniles in this age bracket than older or younger groups. This would be good law enforcement practice. The logic in our case is the same except that our delinquency problem is largely found in the Negro community and it is these youths toward whom we are sensitized.

As regards prejudice per se, 18 of 27 officers interviewed openly admitted a dislike for Negroes. However, they attributed their dislike to

experiences they had, as policemen, with youths from this minority group. The officers reported that Negro boys were much more likely than non-Negroes to "give us a hard time," be uncooperative, and show no remorse for their transgressions. Recurrent exposure to such attitudes among Negro youth, the officers claimed, generated their antipathy toward Negroes. The following excerpt is typical of the views expressed by these officers:

They (Negroes) have no regard for the law or for the police. They just don't seem to give a damn. Few of them are interested in school or getting ahead. The girls start having illegitimate kids before they are 16 years old and the boys are always "out for kicks." Furthermore, many of these kids try to run you down. They say the damnedest things to you and they seem to have absolutely no respect for you as an adult. I admit I am prejudiced now, but frankly I don't think I was when I began police work.

IMPLICATIONS

It is apparent from the findings presented above that the police officers studied in this research were permitted and even encouraged to exercise immense latitude in disposing of the juveniles they encountered. That is, it was within the officers' discretionary authority, except in extreme limiting cases, to decide which juveniles were to come to the attention of the courts and correctional agencies and thereby be identified officially as delinquents. In exercising this discretion policemen were strongly guided by the demeanor of those who were apprehended, a practice which ultimately led, as seen above, to certain youths (particularly Negroes[23] and boys dressed in the style of "toughs") being treated more severely than other juveniles for comparable offenses.

But the relevance of demeanor was not limited only to police disposition practices. Thus, for example, in conjunction with police crime statistics the criterion of demeanor led police to concentrate their surveillance activities in areas frequented or inhabited by Negroes. Further-

---

what aroused his suspicion, the officer explained, "He was -a Negro wearing dark glasses at midnight."

[22] While police statistics did not permit an analysis of crime rates by appearance, they strongly supported officers' contentions concerning the delinquency rate among Negroes. Of all male juveniles processed by the police department in 1961, for example, 40.2 per cent were Negro and 33.9 per cent were white. These two groups comprised at that time, respectively, about 22.7 per cent and 73.6 per cent of the population in the community studied.

[23] An unco-operative demeanor was presented by more than one-third of the Negro youths but by only one-sixth of the white youths encountered by the police in the course of our observations.

more, these youths were accosted more often than others by officers on patrol simply because their skin color identified them as potential troublemakers. These discriminatory practices—and it is important to note that they are discriminatory, even if based on accurate statistical information—may well have self-fulfilling consequences. Thus it is not unlikely that frequent encounters with police, particularly those involving youths innocent of wrongdoing, will increase the hostility of these juveniles toward law-enforcement personnel. It is also not unlikely that the frequency of such encounters will in time reduce their significance in the eyes of apprehended juveniles, thereby leading these youths to regard them as "routine." Such responses to police encounters, however, are those which law-enforcement personnel perceive as indicators of the serious delinquent. They thus serve to vindicate and reinforce officers' prejudices, leading to closer surveillance of Negro districts, more frequent encounters with Negro youths, and so on in a vicious circle. Moreover, the consequences of this chain of events are reflected in police statistics showing a disproportionately high percentage of Negroes among juvenile offenders, thereby providing "objective" justification for concentrating police attention on Negro youths.

To a substantial extent, as we have implied earlier, the discretion practiced by juvenile officers is simply an extension of the juvenile-court philosophy, which holds that in making legal decisions regarding juveniles, more weight should be given to the juvenile's character and life-situation than to his actual offending behavior. The juvenile officer's disposition decisions—and the information he uses as a basis for them—are more akin to the discriminations made by probation officers and other correctional workers than they are to decisions of police officers dealing with non-juvenile offenders. The problem is that such clinical-type decisions are not restrained by mechanisms comparable to the principles of due process and the rules of procedure governing police decisions regarding adult offenders. Consequently, prejudicial practices by police officers can escape notice more easily in their dealings with juveniles than with adults.

The observations made in this study serve to underscore the fact that the official delinquent, as distinguished from the juvenile who simply commits a delinquent act, is the product of a social judgment, in this case a judgment made by the police. He is a delinquent because someone in authority has defined him as one, often on the basis of the public face he has presented to officials rather than of the kind of offense he has committed.

6.

MAYNARD L. ERICKSON AND LAMAR T. EMPEY

COURT RECORDS, UNDETECTED DELINQUENCY AND DECISION-MAKING

There is almost universal dissatisfaction with the accuracy of official records on delinquency.[1] Yet, at present, there are few realistic alternatives. Official records must be used, not only to provide statistical information on delinquent trends, but to act as an information base on the qualitative characteristics (i.e., delinquent types) of offenders. It is this base upon which many important practical and theoretical decisions are presently dependent. A host of provocative problems relative to each of these uses merits serious attention. Two are discussed below.

The first has to do with the currently increasing emphasis on preventing delinquency.[2] If prevention is to be successful, it must forestall delinquent behavior before it becomes a matter of official record. But how much is known about the whole body of delinquent acts which do not become a matter of official concern? How accurately do official statistics reveal the *actual* extent and types of offenses committed? Answers to these questions are needed before revisions in control strategies can proceed rationally toward desired goals.

At present most control decisions are without the benefit of answers to important questions. Most people are left in a quandary as to whether official records understate or overstate the problem. For example, as a result of finding a vast number of undetected violations in their study, Murphy, Shirley and Witmer concluded that "even a moderate increase in the amount of attention paid to [them] by law-enforcement authorities could create a semblance of a 'delinquency wave' without there being the slightest change in adolescent behavior."[3]

SOURCE: Maynard L. Erickson and Lamar T. Empey, "Court Records, Undetected Delinquency and Decision-Making," *Journal of Criminal Law, Criminology and Police Science* 54, no. 4 (December, 1963): 456–69.
Reprinted by Special Permission of the *Journal of Criminal Law, Criminology and Police Science* (Northwestern University School of Law), Copyright © 1963.
Mr. Erickson was Research Director of the Provo Experiment in Delinquency Rehabilitation, Brigham Young University. Mr. Empey was Director of the Provo Experiment.
Grateful acknowledgement is expressed by the authors to Monroe J. Paxman for his cooperation and support and to the Ford Foundation for the grant under which this research was conducted. Appreciation is also extended to Stanton Wheeler, Peter Garabedian, and James Short for their helpful criticisms.

[1]Discussions and criticisms are legion. A sample might include: Donald R. Cressey, "The State of Criminal Statistics," *National Probation and Parole Association Journal* 3 (1957): 230; Albert J. McQueen, "A Comparative Prospective on Juvenile Delinquency," in *A Symposium on Delinquency: Patterns, Causes and Cures* (1960), pp. 1–21; Thorsten Sellin, "The Basis of a Crime Index," *Journal of Criminal Law and Criminology* 22 (1931): 335; Edwin H. Sutherland, *Principles of Criminology* (Philadelphia: J. B. Lippincott Company, 1947), pp. 29-30; Taft, *Criminology* (New York: Macmillan, 1956), pp. 61–65; and C. Van Vechten, "Differential Criminal Case Mortality in Selected Jurisdictions," *American Sociological Review* 7 (1942): 833.
On the other hand, Perlman and Schwartz, noting a high degree of agreement in trends between police and court records on juveniles, feel the two are subject to common determining factors. See I. Richard Perlman, "The Meaning of Juvenile Delinquency Statistics," *Federal Probation* 13 (September, 1949): 63. See also Perlman, "Reporting Juvenile Delinquency," *National Probation and Parole Association Journal* 3 (1957): 242; and Richard D. Schwartz, "Statistics of Juvenile Delinquency in the United States," *Annals* 261 (1949): 9.

[2]A good example is President Kennedy's creation of the President's Committee on Juvenile Delinquency and Youth Crime; see Executive Order 10940, and The Federal Delinquency Program Objective and Operation under the President's Committee on Juvenile Delinquency and Youth Crime, and the Juvenile Delinquency and Youth Offenses Control Act of 1961 (1962).
[3]Fred J. Murphy, Mary M. Shirley, and Helen L. Witmer, "The Incidence of Hidden Delinquency," *American Journal of Orthopsychiatry* 16 (1946):

Therefore, perhaps even more basic than deciding what should be done, we need more information in deciding whether, to what extent, or along what dimensions anything needs to be done. A greater knowledge of the nature of *undetected offenses* among the adolescent population might be important in determining prevention (and treatment) strategies.

A second problem has to do with the research on delinquency. Few authorities would dispute the value of using legal norms, in contrast to diffuse moral or extralegal concepts, to define a delinquent act. But the extension of this use to practical purposes often results in the development of extreme, either-or dichotomies: delinquent or nondelinquent, institutionalized or noninstitutionalized.

It is an obvious oversimplification to believe in the validity of such dichotomies. Delinquent behavior is not an attribute—something which one either is or is not, such as male or female, plant or animal. It is "a more or less thing,"[4] possibly distributed along one or more continua.

Even so, many sophisticated efforts to develop specific criminal or delinquent typologies based on this premise must still depend on the either-or nature of official records as the major criterion for selecting samples for study.

Once this is done, analyses tend to proceed in one of two directions: (1) either to rely further upon official records for specific information on such things as offense patterns; or (2) to reject as unimportant the official offense pattern in favor of psychological, cultural, or interactional factors.[5] This latter action is usually taken on the premise that the delinquent act is merely a symptom of some more basic cause and that to understand or perhaps remove the cause is what is important. But, in either case, the paradox remains: the court record serves as the basic criterion for sample selection.[6] Any strong bias in it will likely color what is found. Thus, it may be that refined analyses based upon official samples are based also upon a rather questionable foundation.

So long as samples are selected on this basis, there is a possibility that important information is being excluded. What of the possibility, for example, that there are patterns of delinquent activity which are etiologically distinct?[7] What of the possibility that the search for different configurations of variables has been inadequate because of the incompleteness of official records on delinquent activity? Even further, what of the possibility that official records do not even reveal the pattern of offenses which most commonly characterizes an offender?

The fact that many studies have found age and sex to be more highly correlated with delinquency than a host of other supposedly more important etiological variables,[8] suggests the need to explore these questions. The addition of information on the actual, not official, amount and type of delinquency in which an individual has been involved might be an aid in filling many of the gaps which exist. One important gap would have to do with the extent to which, and under what circumstances, the delinquent offense pattern should be treated as an *independent* rather than as a dependent variable. What might be revealed if it were viewed as a variable which helps to explain rather than one which is always explained by other factors?

---

696. See also **Austin** L. Porterfield, *Youth in Trouble* (Austin, Tex.: Leo Potishman Foundation, 1946); and a summary of studies in Cohen, *Delinquent Boys: The Culture of the Gang* (Glencoe, Ill.: The Free Press, 1955), pp. 36–44.

[4] James F. Short, Jr., "The Sociological Context of Delinquency," *Crime and Delinquency* 6 (1960): 365, 366.

[5] For excellent summaries and bibliographies on typological developments in criminology, see: Don C. Gibbons and Donald L. Garrity, "Some Suggestions for the Development of Etiological and Treatment Theory in Criminology," *Social Forces* 38 (1960): 51; M. Q. Grant, "Inquiries Concerning Kinds of Treatment for Kinds of Delinquents," *California Board of Corrections Monograph No. 2* (1961), p. 5.

[6] For example, such diverse typologies as those produced by Clyde Sullivan, Douglas Grant, and Marguerite Grant in "The Development of Interpersonal Maturity: Applications to Delinquency," *Psychiatry* 20 (1957): 373, and Gresham Sykes, in *The Society of Captives* (Princeton: Princeton University Press, 1958), must still rely upon official definition for their basic samples of offenders.

[7] This question has been raised in Don C. Gibbons and Donald L. Garrity, op. cit. supra n. 5, p. 51; Short, op. cit. supra n. 4, p. 366.

[8] James F. Short, Jr., "The Study of Juvenile Delinquency by Reported Behavior: An Experiment in Method and Preliminary Findings" (Paper read at the annual meeting of the American Sociological Association, 1955), p. 12.

THE PRESENT RESEARCH

This research is a modest attempt to provide some information on the questions just raised:

1. What is revealed about the total volume of delinquency when undetected offenses are enumerated? What offenses are most common?

2. To what degree do violations go undetected? To what extent do they go unacted upon in the courts?[9]

3. Do non-official delinquents—young people that have never been convicted—commit delinquencies equal in number and seriousness to those committed by officially designated offenders?[10]

4. How useful are traditional dichotomies—delinquent or nondelinquent, institutionalized or noninstitutionalized—in distinguishing groups of offenders one from another?

5. How valid are court records as an index of the total volume and types of offenses in which individuals are most commonly involved?

In seeking answers to such questions as these, this research sought: (1) to examine reported lawbreaking across an adolescent continuum extending from those who had never been officially declared delinquent, through those who had appeared in court once, to those who were "persistent" offenders; and (2) to question adolescent respondents across the whole spectrum of legal norms for which they might have been taken to court. In all, they were asked about 22 violations.[11]

THE SAMPLE

The sample included only males, ages 15–17 years. It was made up of four subsamples:

1. A subsample of 50 randomly selected high school boys who had never been to court.

2. A subsample of 30 randomly selected boys who had been to court once.[12]

3. A subsample of 50 randomly selected, repeat offenders who were on probation. The respondents in this sample were assigned to a special community treatment program. If the program had not existed, 32 percent of these offenders would have been incarcerated, and 68 percent on regular probation.[13]

4. A subsample of 50 randomly selected, incarcerated offenders. Subsamples 1, 2, and 3 were drawn from the same community population. Subsample 4 was drawn from a statewide population of incarcerated offenders.

It was necessary to keep the number of respondents relatively small because each respondent was questioned at length about the whole spectrum of legal norms for which he might have been taken to court—22 different violations in all. As will be seen, the questioning resulted in the accumulation of a large mass of data which turned out to be expensive and difficult to handle.

DATA COLLECTION

All respondents were contacted in person by the authors. The study was explained to them and they were asked to participate. There were no refusals. Data were gathered by means of a detailed interview which was conducted as follows:

---

[9]For studies dealing with the problem of undetected delinquency, see: Fred J. Murphy, Mary M. Shirley, and Helen L. Witmer, op. cit. supra n. 3; James Wallerstein and Clement Wyle, "Our Law-Abiding Lawbreakers," *Federal Probation* 25 (April, 1947): 110; O. W. Wilson, "How to Measure the Extent of Juvenile Delinquency," *Journal of Criminal Law and Criminology* 41 (1950): 435.

[10]Austin L. Porterfield's work, op. cit. supra n. 3, throws some light on this question; however, the evidence is not conclusive.

[11]Unfortunately, no data on sex violations can be presented. Two things stood in the way. The first was a general policy of high school administrators against questions on sex. The second had to do with possible negative reactions by parents against questions because of the brutal sex slaying of an 11-year-old girl and several attacks on women which occurred at the very time we began our study. For these reasons we did not attempt to gather these data for fear they might endanger the whole study.

[12]Since this study was part of a larger study comparing persistent delinquents—incarcerated and unincarcerated—with nondelinquent high school students, data were not collected initially from one-time offenders. Consequently, they had to be collected especially for this group. However, time and budgetary considerations required that the sample of one-time offenders be limited to 30.

[13]They are assignees to the Provo Experiment in Delinquency Rehabilitation. All assignees are, by design, persistent offenders. Assignment is made on a random basis and includes both offenders who might otherwise be left on regular probation and offenders who might otherwise be incarcerated in the State Industrial School. See Lamar T. Empey and Jerome Rabow, "The Provo Experiment in Delinquency Rehabilitation," *American Sociological Review* 26 (1961): 693.

First, each of the 22 offenses was described in detail. For example, under the section regarding breaking and entering, it is not enough to ask a boy, "Have you ever broken into a place illegally?" He wants to know what constitutes "a place": a car, a barn in the country, an unlocked garage? All of these had to be defined.

Second, after the act was defined, the respondent was asked if he had ever committed the offense. In judging his response, attention was paid to nonverbal cues—blushes, long pauses, nervousness—as well as to verbal cues. These cues served as guides to further questions, probes and reassurances.

Third, if the respondent admitted having committed the offense, he was asked how many times he had done so. Again, considerable time and effort were spent in obtaining an estimate, the idea being that the greater accuracy could be obtained by this means than by fitting answers to a predetermined code or having him respond to such general categories as "none," "a few times," or "a great many times." In the case of habitual offenders, however, it was necessary on some offenses to have them estimate a range—15–20 times, 200–250 times—rather than a specific number.

Finally, the respondent was asked if he had ever been *caught, arrested,* or *to court* for each type of offense. If so, he was asked how many times this had occurred.

METHODOLOGICAL PROBLEMS

Beside the methodological problems inherent in any reported data, there are others peculiar to the nature of this type of study.[14] Perhaps the most important has to do with the method of obtaining data. An extended pilot study[15] and pretests, using both interviews and questionnaires, suggested that interviews could provide more complete and reliable data. Two main considerations led to this conclusion.

The first had to do with the lack of literacy skills among persistent delinquents. Two 15-year-olds in this study could neither read nor write; others had great trouble with simple instructions and questions. In our opinion, therefore, an interview was the only alternative for the delinquent subsamples.

Second, in addition to the need for comparable data, our pilot studies indicated that high school samples had trouble understanding specific questions and supplying the data wanted. Therefore, the value of using an interview for this group, as for delinquents, seemed to outweigh the virtues of an anonymous questionnaire.

We did not find the confrontation of an interview to be generally harmful. By using only three skilled interviewers, it became possible to anticipate recurring difficulties and to deal more effectively with them. These interviewers encountered two types of problems.

The first was the resistance on the part of high school students to revealing offenses. Patience, skepticism regarding replies, probes, and reassurances seemed to encourage candor. The second was a memory problem. Habitual offenders were not so reluctant to admit offenses, but they had often committed them so frequently that they could make an easy estimate neither as to number nor the age at which they began. Probes and extended discussions helped considerably here in settling upon a reasonable estimate.

One possible problem regarding the validity of these data has to do with the perceptions of respondents regarding the "social desirability" of answering questions according to social expectation. What is each respondent's reference group? How does he perceive the interviewer? Are his responses biased by special perceptions of each?

For example, if, among delinquents, it is desirable to exhibit extensive delinquent behavior, then, at least up to a certain point, the less delinquent an individual is, the more likely he may be to inflate his own actual violations. The converse might also be true for the conventional boy. Actually, as will be seen later, our findings tended to question the premise that social expectation influences boys' answers (or

---

[14] See James F. Short, Jr., op. cit. supra n. 8; and James F. Short, Jr., and F. Ivan Nye, "Reported Behavior as a Criterion of Deviant Behavior," *Social Problems* 5 (Winter, 1957-1958): 210.

[15] Maynard Erickson, "An Experiment To Determine the Plausibility of Developing an Empirical Means of Differentiating between Delinquents and Nondelinquents without Consideration to Involvement in Legal Process" (Master's Thesis, Brigham Young University, 1960).

at least they failed to establish its validity). Nondelinquents reported so much delinquent behavior that it became difficult to assess the extent to which official delinquents, by contrast, might have inflated their own illegal behavior.

By way of determining validity, the names of all respondents were run through court records. None of those who had been to court failed to say so in the interview, nor did anyone fail to describe the offense(s) for which he was charged.

Few responses were so distorted as to be questionable. For example, no one maintained complete detachment from lawbreaking; no one admitted having committed all offenses. These findings tended to parallel the experience of Short and Nye in this regard.[16]

FINDINGS

1. *What is revealed about the total volume of delinquency when undetected offenses are enumerated? What offenses are most common?*

The number of violations which respondents admitted having committed was tremendous. So great was the volume that it posed some difficulty for display and analysis. A comprehensive table, Table 1–9, was prepared for use throughout the paper. The reader's patience is requested in referring to it.

The first two columns of Table 1–9 deal with the total volume of reported delinquency. These columns rank types of offenses in terms of the total frequency with which they were reported by all four samples. The frequencies reported for one-time offenders (N = 30) have been inflated by two-fifths in order to make them comparable to the other subsamples (N = 50). This inflation is also reflected in the *totals column* of Table 1–9 for the entire sample.[17]

[16]Short and Nye, op. cit. supra n. 14, p. 211.

[17]It is impossible to assess any increase in error which might have resulted from this inflation. If there is bias in the sample of 30, it will have been magnified. See Morris H. Hansen, William N. Hurwitz, and William G. Madow, *Sample Survey Method and Theory* (New York: John Wiley & Sons, 1953). Insofar as sample size, per se, is concerned, error would not have been significantly decreased had this sample of 30 been increased to

(Many other refinements and differences among subsamples in this comprehensive table will be discussed later.)

Three types of offenses were most common: theft (24,199)—especially of articles worth less than $2 (15,175)—, traffic (23,946), and the purchase and drinking of alcohol (21,698). ·

Grouped somewhat below these three were open defiance of authority—parents and others— (14,639); violations of property, including breaking and entering (12,278); retreatist activities such as running away (9,953); offenses against person (9,026); and finally such offenses as gambling (6,571). In the case of smoking, the total number of respondents who smoke habitually, rather than the estimated number of times all have smoked, was obtained. Of the 200, 86 reported smoking habitually.

2. *To what degree do violations go undetected? To what extent do they go unacted upon in the courts?*

The reader is again referred to Table 1–9 where, along with the volume of delinquent violations, the percentage of each of those violations which went (1) *undetected* and (2) *unacted upon* in court is presented.

With regard to detection, respondents were asked after each reported violation to tell whether they had been *caught by anyone*: parents, police, or others. With regard to court action, they were asked to report *any* appearance, *formal or informal*, before *any* officer of the court: judge, referee, or probation officer. (It was this question which served as an outside check on reliability. As noted above, respondents were generally very accurate.)

More than nine times out of ten—almost ten times out of ten—most offenses go *undetected* and *unacted upon*. This is especially true with respect to so-called minor violations: traffic offenses, theft of articles worth less than $50, buying and drinking liquor, destroying property, skipping school, and so on.

As might be expected, the picture changes with respect to more serious violations—theft of articles worth more than $50, auto theft, breaking and entering, forgery, and so on. Fewer

50. Both (N = 30) and (N = 50) are very small proportions of the total population of one-time offenders.

TABLE 1-9.

EXTENT OF VIOLATIONS AND PER CENT UNDETECTED AND UNACTED UPON

Offense	Rank	Entire Adolescent Sample[1]			Non-Delinquents[2]			One-Time Offenders[3]			Delinquents Community[4]			Delinquents Incarcerated[5]		
		Total Offenses	% Undetected	% Unacted Upon	Total Offenses	% Undetected	% Unacted Upon	Total Offenses	% Undetected	% Unacted Upon	Total Offenses	% Undetected	% Unacted Upon	Total Offenses	% Undetected	% Unacted Upon
Traffic Offenses	1															
Driving without License		11,796	98.9	99.7	1,845	99.6	100.0	512	98.7	98.7	2,386	98.0	99.1	7,053	99.1	99.9
Traffic Viol. (not lic.)		12,150	98.2	99.3	2,040	98.3	99.9	2,142	98.4	98.7	3,068	96.8	98.4	4,900	99.0	98.8
Total		23,946	98.6	99.5	3,885	98.9	100.0	2,654	98.4	98.6	5,454	97.3	98.7	11,953	99.0	99.8
Theft	2															
Articles Less Than $2		15,175	97.1	99.8	966	91.7	100.0	1,738	96.5	99.6	7,886	98.6	99.8	4,585	95.6	99.8
Articles Worth $2 to $50		7,396	97.1	99.1	60	83.3	100.0	80	93.8	95.8	4,671	98.5	99.2	2,585	94.8	99.1
Articles More Than $50		294	71.0	92.8	1	100.0	100.0	2	100.0	100.0	90	66.7	91.1	201	72.6	93.5
Auto Theft		822	88.9	95.5	4	100.0	100.0	0	0.0	0.0	169	84.6	93.5	649	90.0	96.0
Forgery		512	93.4	97.5	0	0.0	0.0	0	0.0	0.0	60	70.0	90.0	452	96.5	98.5
Total		24,199	96.3	99.3	1,031	91.3	100.0	1,820	96.3	99.4	12,876	98.0	99.4	8,472	94.5	99.0
Alcohol and Narcotics	3															
Buying Beer or Liquor		8,890	99.6	99.9	18	100.0	100.0	57	94.1	100.0	1,453	99.6	100.0	7,362	99.6	99.9
Drinking Beer or Liquor		12,808	98.8	99.8	219	100.0	100.0	270	100.0	100.0	4,173	99.0	99.7	8,146	98.6	99.8
Selling Narcotics		1	100.0	100.0	0	0.0	0.0	0	0.0	0.0	0	0.0	0.0	1	100.0	100.0
Using Narcotics		74	100.0	100.0	0	0.0	0.0	0	0.0	0.0	3	100.0	100.0	71	100.0	100.0
Total		21,773	99.1	99.9	237	100.0	100.0	327	99.0	100.0	5,629	99.1	99.8	15,580	99.1	99.9
Open Defiance of Authority	4															
Defying Parents		8,142	99.7	99.9	138	100.0*	100.0	128	100.0*	100.0	4,804	99.7*	99.9	3,072	99.9*	99.9
Defying Others		6,497	99.4	99.7	124	100.0*	100.0	170	100.0*	100.0	1,478	99.3*	99.3	4,725	99.5*	99.9
Total		14,639	99.5	99.9	262	100.0*	100.0	298	100.0*	100.0	6,282	99.6*	99.8	7,797	99.6*	99.9

	[1]			[2]			[3]			[4]			[5]		
	No.	%	%	No.	%	%	No.	%	%	No.	%	%	No.	%	%
Property Violations .. 5															
Breaking and Entering	1,622	85.6	94.4	67	94.0	100.0	102	98.4	100.0	527	84.4	93.5	926	84.9	94.2
Destroying Property	10,645	98.5	99.7	477	97.1	100.0	800	98.5	99.7	4,927	98.7	99.6	4,441	98.7	99.4
Setting Fires (Arson)	11	40.0	90.0	2	0.0	0.0	2	0.0	100.0	0	0.0	0.0	7	100.0	100.0
Total	12,278	96.8	99.0	546	96.7	100.0	904	96.5	99.6	5,454	97.3	99.0	5,374	96.4	98.5
Retreatist Activities .. 6															
Running Away from Home	578	86.8	94.7	19	100.0	100.0	19	100.0	100.0	103	75.0	87.4	437	89.0	96.1
Skipping School	9,375	93.9	99.8	377	94.7	100.0	698	93.1	100.0	3,478	93.2	99.8	4,822	94.4	99.8
Total	9,953	93.5	99.5	396	94.9	100.0	717	93.2	100.0	3,581	92.6	99.5	5,259	94.0	99.5
Offenses against Person 7															
Armed Robbery	46	80.4	91.3	0	0.0*	0.0	0	0.0*	0.0	22	68.2	90.9	24	91.7	91.7
Fighting, Assault	8,980	99.7	99.9	354	100.0*	100.0	103	100.0*	100.0	2,207	99.9*	99.8	6,316	99.6*	99.9
Total	9,026	99.6	99.9	354	100.0*	100.0	103	100.0*	100.0	2,229	99.6*	99.7	6,340	99.5*	99.9
Others .. 8															
Gambling	6,571	99.9	99.8	1,185	100.0	100.0	2,400	100.0	100.0	1,186	99.3	99.5	2,800	99.9	100.0
Smoking (habitually)	86	87.1	91.8	1	.*	100.0	3	50.0	100.0	39	.*	94.9	43	.*	88.4

*Because of their nature, these offenses almost never remain undetected by someone in authority. Thus, these figures refer to per cent unarrested, rather than *undetected.*

[1]Number of Respondents = 180, except on Arson (N = 136) and Gambling (N = 171).

[2]N = 50.

[3]Actual N = 30. However, figures in this column have been inflated as though N = 50. This was done to make frequencies comparable with other subsamples.

[4]N = 50, except on Arson (N = 15) and Gambling (N = 41).

[5]N = 50, except on Arson (N = 41).

of these offenses went undetected and unacted upon. Yet, even in these cases, eight out of ten reported that their violations went undetected and nine out of ten did not result in court action.

3. *Do nonofficial delinquents—young people who never have been convicted—commit delinquencies equal in number and seriousness to those committed by officially designated offenders?*

The answer to this question illustrates the extreme importance of distinguishing between the *frequency* with which a given norm or set of norms is violated by two different samples and the proportion of respondents in each sample who report having violated them. The distinction helps to avoid the pitfall of concluding that, because large *proportions* of two different samples—i.e., students and institutionalized delinquents—have committed various offenses, the samples are equally delinquent in terms of total volume. Because of early studies, this impression regarding the total volume of delinquency in different samples has become almost traditional, even though it was not embraced by the authors of these studies.[18] The fact is that the *frequency*, as well as the types of offenses, with which individuals violated certain statutes turns out to be vitally important.

By way of example, consider Table 1–10. It presents the *proportions* of respondents in the four different samples who reported committing various offenses. On some offenses—theft of articles worth less than $2, traffic violations, and destroying property—there is little to choose among the four samples. Most young people in each sample reported having committed them.

The proportions of all 180 boys who reported committing various offenses were as follows: petty theft (93%), gambling (85%), driving without a license (84%), skipping school (83%), destroying property (80%), other traffic offenses (77%), drinking (74%), fighting (70%), defying others (64%), and thefts of from $2 to $50 (59%).

However, it would be premature and superficial to conclude that, because large *proportions* of the entire sample have committed these offenses, the subsamples are equally delinquent.

On only two offenses—gambling and traffic—did the proportions of nondelinquents exceed those of the delinquent subsamples. (However, the proportions for the nondelinquents and one-time offenders were very much the same.)

Furthermore, a re-examination of Table 1–9 reveals that the *frequency* with which official offenders violate the law is in excess of the *frequency* with which non-official offenders violate it. (Again, however, non-official and one-time offenders differ very little. More will be said on them later.) The chief distinctions were between non- and one-time offenders, on the one hand, and the two subsamples of persistent offenders on the other.

If non- and one-time offenders are combined —because of their similarity—the cumulative violations of persistent offenders exceed their violations by thousands: thefts, excluding forgery (20,836 vs. 2,851); violations of property (10,828 vs. 1,450); violations of person (8,569 vs. 457); and violations involving the purchase and drinking of alcohol (21,134 vs. 564).

In addition, as shown in Table 1–10, far smaller proportions of non- and one-time offenders committed offenses of a "serious" nature than did persistent offenders: theft of articles worth more than $50 (2% vs. 50%), auto theft (2% vs. 52%), forgery (0% vs. 25%), and armed robbery (0% vs. 9%).

The significance of these data, then, seems to be that one should guard against the use of *proportions* of total populations as a measure of delinquent involvement without also taking into account the *frequency* with which these proportions commit violations. Although in two cases proportionately fewer of the delinquent samples had committed certain violations, those who had committed them did so with much greater *frequency* than official nondelinquent samples.

4. *How useful are traditional dichotomies—delinquent or nondelinquent, institutionalized or noninstitutionalized—in distinguishing groups of offenders one from another?*

A series of tests was run, beginning on the non-delinquent end of the continuum, to discover where, if any, there were discriminating dichotomies on the volume of delinquent offenses, either between delinquent and nondelin-

---

[18]See Austin Porterfield, op. cit. supra n. 3.

TABLE 1–10.

PROPORTION OF RESPONDENTS COMMITTING OFFENSES

Offense	Per Cent of Rank Total[1]	Subsamples			
		Non-Delinquents[2]	One-Time Offenders[3]	Delinquents Community[4]	Delinquents Incarcerated[5]
Theft 1					
Less Than $2	93	92	98	96	86
Worth $2 to $50	59	22	36	78	90
More Than $50	26	2	2	46	54
Auto Theft	29	2	2	54	60
Forgery	13	0	0	16	34
Others 2					
Gambling	85	90	100	56	72
Smoking (habitually)	42	2	4	76	86
Traffic Offenses 3					
Driving without License	84	72	78	94	92
Traffic Viol. (not lic.)	77	84	84	72	66
Retreatist Activities 4					
Running Away from Home	38	22	24	46	60
Skipping School	83	66	68	96	100
Property Violations 5					
Breaking and Entering	59	32	46	74	84
Destroying Property	80	66	84	86	84
Setting Fires (Arson)	6	2	2	0	8
Alcohol and Narcotics 6					
Buying Beer or Liquor	29	4	8	46	58
Drinking Beer or Liquor	74	52	66	84	94
Selling Narcotics	0.5	0	0	0	2
Using Narcotics	4	0	0	2	12
Offenses against Person 7					
Armed Robbery	5	0	0	4	14
Fighting, Assault	70	52	60	82	86
Open Defiance of Authority 8					
Defying Parents	53	40	44	64	64
Defying Others	64	52	54	72	78

[1]Number of Respondents = 200, except on Arson (N = 156) and Gambling (N = 191).
[2]N = 50.
[3]N = 30.
[4]N = 50, except on Arson (N = 15) and Gambling (N = 41).
[5]N = 50, except on Arson (N = 41).

quent subsamples or between institutionalized and noninstitutionalized offenders.

Chi Square was used as a test of significance. This test examines the possibility that any difference between groups could have occurred by chance. If differences are so great as to suggest that factors other than chance are responsible, it then suggests the confidence one might have in making that assumption.

To lend further refinement, a measure of association (T) was used to indicate the degree of relationship, when any difference was significant,[19] between official status and total volume of delinquency. For example, if Chi Square indicated that a delinquent and nondelinquent sample differed significantly on a given offense, the measure of association (T) suggests the power

[19]Margaret J. Hagood and Daniel O. Price, *Statistics for Sociologists* (1952), pp. 370–71.

of that offense to distinguish between these two samples.

An effort was made to increase the validity of all comparisons by diminishing the impact of the large number of offenses committed by a few individuals. Thus, instead of making a gross comparison between two samples on the total number of times an offense was committed, respondents in each sample were ordered according to the number of times they reported committing an offense (i.e., 1–3 times, 4–6 times, etc.). Comparisons were then made between the number of respondents from each sample found in each category.

The wisdom of doing this can be illustrated by examining Table 1–9. Persistent delinquents in the community reported having committed more petty theft than institutionalized offenders, while the reverse is true for auto theft. But these differences were largely due to the excessive activities of a few individuals. By taking them into account, the tests could more accurately reflect real, overall differences. If we had not accounted for them, excessively large differences between samples might have been suggested when, in fact, they did not exist.

Official Nondelinquents vs. Official One-time Offenders. The first comparison was between the subsamples of 50 high school boys who had *no* court record and the 30 one-time offenders.[20] In this particular comparison, only one significant difference past the .05 level of confidence was found; the offense was *destruction of property.* Official offenders were more likely to have been involved.

Comparisons on such offenses as stealing articles worth more than $50, auto theft, armed robbery, forgery, etc., were meaningless because they were seldom, if ever, reported by either group. This in itself tells us much about the similarity of these two groups.

This dichotomy, then—official nondelinquent

vs. one-time offenders—did not prove to be discriminating.

Official One-time vs. Persistent Offenders. The second comparison was between one-time offenders and the subsample of 50 boys who were non-incarcerated persistent offenders. Differences between these two on most offenses were marked.

Persistent offenders were significantly—that is, 99 times out of 100—more inclined than one-time offenders, as a group, to have stolen expensive and inexpensive items, skipped school, defied parents, bought and drunk liquor, smoked regularly, stolen autos, fought, and driven without a license. There was also a significant difference past the .05 level with regard to forgery.

They did not differ significantly from one-time offenders on such things as running away from home, breaking and entering, destroying property, or committing most types of traffic violations. They could not be compared on such offenses as armed robbery, arson, or selling and using narcotics because of the small number of violations by both groups, but especially by one-time offenders.

This dichotomy, then—*one-time* vs. *persistent* offenders in the community—was generally discriminating.

Institutionalized vs. Noninstitutionalized Offenders. The final comparisons had to do with the institutionalized vs. noninstitutionalized dichotomy. First, the sample of institutionalized offenders (Subsample 4) was compared with those noninstitutionalized offenders who had been to court *once* (Subsample 2). As might be expected, differences were significant on virtually all offenses. The samples seemed to represent two different populations because of the much heavier involvement of the institutionalized offenders (Subsample 4) in delinquency.

Second, institutionalized offenders (Subsample 4) were compared with the subsample of persistent offenders who had not been institutionalized (Subsample 3). The two did not differ significantly.

Persistent institutionalized offenders as a group reported having committed more traffic offenses, forgeries, auto thefts, offenses involving alcohol, and fights than persistent noninstitutionalized offenders. The latter, meanwhile, re-

---

[20]This and other comparisons have the serious weakness of dealing with only a limited number of boys. But, at the same time, two things must be recalled: (1) that such comparisons involve an enumeration of violations which, in most cases, was very large; and (2) that it was necessary to limit the number of respondents because of the time and money involved in gathering and analyzing data on such a large number of violations.

ported considerably more petty thefts, thefts of items worth up to $50, defying parents, and destruction of property. But these differences were due largely to a few extreme individuals. Consequently, as explained earlier, when tests of significance took this fact into account, the modal behavior of boys in the two samples tended to be very much the same.

Consequently, the only significant difference between these two subsamples was on habitual smoking; more boys in the reformatory smoked regularly. Otherwise, the two samples might be taken as representative of the same population insofar as the modal volume and nature of their offenses were concerned.

The significance of this finding is diluted somewhat by the fact that only two-thirds of the noninstitutionalized group (Subsample 3) would have been on probation (and free in the community) had they not been attending a special rehabilitative program. Nevertheless, the findings strongly support the idea that a dichotomy which distinguishes, without qualification, between *institutionalized* and *noninstitutionalized* offenders may not be valid. *Persistency* rather than institutionalization seems to be the more important variable in distinguishing groups. In this study, for example, the clearest distinction among official offenders was between *one-time* offenders, on one hand, and persistent offenders —whether institutionalized or noninstitutionalized—on the other.

This finding suggests that where persistent offenders are involved, the decision to incarcerate one group and to leave the other in the community may be highly subjective. Factors other than the extent and seriousness of these offenses seem to determine whether they are incarcerated or not.

Because of the significance of this finding, both samples of persistent offenders were combined and compared with the two subsamples on the nondelinquent end of the continuum (Subsamples 1 and 2, the official nondelinquents and one-time offenders) which likewise had been found not to differ. By combining samples in this way, comparisons could be made more reliable because of larger numbers with which to work. The results are displayed in Table 1–11.

Differences were strong and striking. On vir-

TABLE 1–11.

COMPARISON OF OFFICIAL NON- AND ONE-TIME OFFENDERS WITH PERSISTENT OFFENDERS

Offense	Probability That Differences Could Be Due to Chance	Degree of Association between Volume and Official Classification
Theft		
Articles Less Than $2..	.001	.28
Articles Worth $2 to $50	.001	.46
Articles More Than $50.	.001	.45
Auto Theft	.001	.45
Forgery	.001	.31
Property Violations		
Breaking and Entering..	.001	.34
Destroying Property ...	.001	.24
Setting Fires (Arson) ..	*	
Offenses against Person		
Armed Robbery	*	
Fighting, Assault	.001	.41
Open Defiance of Authority		
Defying Parents	.001	.27
Defying Others	.001	.34
Retreatist Activities		
Running Away from Home	.001	.32
Skipping School	.001	.50
Traffic Offenses		
Driving without License	.001	.36
Traffic Viol. (not lic.)..	.05	.17
Alcohol and Narcotics		
Buying Beer or Liquor..	.001	.40
Drinking Beer or Liquor	.001	.42
Selling Narcotics	*	
Using Narcotics .....·.	*	
Others		
Gambling	.001	.29
Smoking (habitually) ..	.001	.78

*Offense not committed enough times to test differences.

tually all offenses, the chances were less than one in a thousand that they could have occurred by chance (see Table 1–11). Furthermore, all relationships were positive as indicated by the measures of association (T). This means that persistent offenders report having committed more of virtually every offense. Those offenses which best distinguished them from official non- or one-time offenders were smoking regularly (T = .78), skipping school (T = .50), theft of articles worth $2 to $50 (T = .46), theft of articles worth more than $50 (T = .45), auto theft (T = .45), and drinking alcohol (T = .42).

This finding re-emphasizes the idea that the old dichotomies may be misleading. Persistency is the most distinguishing variable.

To what extent this finding may be generalized is hard to say. Many of the most significant differences—smoking regularly, all kinds of theft, drinking, fighting, and skipping school—are associated with behavior often thought to be more characteristic of the lower than the middle class. Other offense patterns may have been characteristic of their setting in a Mormon subculture. However, such offenses as auto theft, forgery, breaking and entering, or stealing items worth more than $50 were also highly discriminating between these two samples and are likely to draw strong official reaction anywhere.

The implication of these findings for both practice and research seems to be that the unqualified use of traditional dichotomies—i.e., delinquent vs. nondelinquent or institutionalized vs. noninstitutionalized—may be unreliable. A further examination of undetected offenses on other populations, to test the validity of these dichotomies, might be an important prerequisite to their future use as an important source of data.

5. *How valid are court records as an index of the total volume and types of offenses which are committed?*

Court Records as an Index of Volume. Evidence presented earlier indicated that the great majority of all delinquent offenses remain undetected and unacted upon. It might be concluded, therefore, that official records do not accurately reflect the total volume of delinquency. However, this might not be true.

It may be that official records are useful in reflecting volume by (1) distinguishing between those who have been heavily delinquent and those who have not; and/or (2) reflecting a tiny but consistently accurate portion of all offenses.

One method of treating these possibilities is to calculate the correlation between the actual number of court appearances for a given population and the number of violations it reports having committed. This calculation was made.

A coefficient of correlation was calculated for all 180 respondents. To do this and still maintain specificity, court appearances were broken into 9 categories—never been to court, been to court one time, two times, three times . . . nine or more times. The total number of reported violations was broken into 11 categories—never, 1–50, 51–100, 101–150 . . . 501 or more. The degree of association between these two variables was then calculated.

A correlation of .51 was obtained. This coefficient is statistically significant, indicating the existence of a relationship between appearing in court and the total number of violations one has committed; that is, the greater the number of reported violations, the greater likelihood that an individual will have appeared in court.

On one hand, this coefficient leaves much to be desired in terms of accurate predictability. A coefficient of .51 means that 26 percent of the variation in the number of court appearances among the 180 respondents could be associated with variations in the number of delinquent offenses they reported having committed.

When only 26 percent of the variation in violation rates, using specific categories, is explained in terms of court appearances, the ability of these appearances to supply a good index of the actual number of violations may be highly questionable.

To further illustrate this point we found a correlation of .56 between dropping out of school and the number of reported violations. This suggested that whether or not individuals had dropped out of school was as accurate or possibly more accurate a predictor of reported violations than court records. (For those respondents incarcerated in the Utah State Industrial School, this meant dropping out of school prior to incarceration, not because of incarceration.)

One would not expect official delinquency rates to be an exact match of the volume of delinquency. Seriousness is also very important. Society demands that stronger measures be taken for serious violations.

In order to examine its significance, correlation coefficients were run between court appearance and a series of single violations, extending all the way from misdemeanors to felonies. The results are displayed in Table 1–12.

TABLE 1–12.

CORRELATION COEFFICIENT BETWEEN COURT
APPEARANCES AND REPORTED NUMBER
OF VIOLATIONS

Offense	Correla-tion	Percentage of Variation Explained
Misdemeanors		
A. Taken Singly		
Skipping School	.17	.03
Theft (less than $2)..	.19	.04
Theft ($2 to $50) ...	.20	.04
Traffic Violations		
(all types)	.18	.03
B. Combined	.15	.02
Felonies*		
A. Taken Singly		
Theft (more than $50)	.25	.06
Auto Theft	.43	.18
Breaking and Entering	.40	.15
Forgery	.05	.003
B. Combined	.29	.08

*Armed robbery, arson and the selling and use of narcotics were not included because the number reporting such violations was small.

As might be expected, reported felonies correlated more highly with court appearances than did reported misdemeanors. However, taken singly, the correlation between any one of the felonies (theft of articles worth more than $50, auto theft, breaking and entering, and forgery)[21] was not so high as that between the total *volume* of violations and court appearance.

Furthermore, even though the total number of reported violations for the four felonies, when they were combined and then correlated with court appearance, produced a higher coefficient (.29) than did the combined misdemeanors (.15), this correlation (.29) was considerably lower than the correlation (.51) between the total volume of offenses and court appearance.

This finding raises questions regarding the traditional assumption that the court record is a better index of serious violations than it is of the total number of offenses an individual has committed. One might speculate, however, that the finding is due to the inaccuracy of reported data. But if one were to discard these reported data as inaccurate, he would have to ignore the

[21]Armed robbery, arson, and the selling and use of narcotics were not included in this analysis because the number reporting such violations was small.

fact that, except for seriousness, these findings met other assumptions rather consistently regarding distinctions between persistent and nonpersistent offenders, as to both frequency and seriousness. And they also seemed capable of making more precise distinctions in the direction of theoretical expectations among various dichotomies than court records.

Thus, these findings also raise important questions regarding the accuracy of official records as an index of volume and seriousness. But it is difficult either to assess the amount of combined error inherent in these court and reported data or to generalize from this to other police and court jurisdictions.

Court Records and Types of Offenses. One of the major problems raised in the introduction had reference to the adequacy of official records for the purpose of conducting typological research. There are at least two different levels of complication.

The first has to do with the validity of the official dichotomies—delinquent or nondelinquent, institutionalized or noninstitutionalized—which are used as the major criteria for distinguishing groups and setting up research samples. The foregoing analysis has already suggested some possible difficulties. It suggests that important qualifications may be needed.

The second level of complications comes in specific attempts to establish delinquent typologies based not only upon basic dichotomies but upon the offense patterns which are revealed by court records. To be accurate, these records would have to reflect reliably an individual's major offense pattern, with respect to both number and seriousness. Some test of their ability to do so was made.

The first part of the analysis was concerned with volume. It sought to determine how well the court record reflected, without special regard to seriousness, the offense which each respondent reported having committed *most often.* The court record proved to be a fair index for offenders who had been to court only once. Sixteen of 30, half of them, had appeared in court for the types of offenses they reported having committed most often.

But this was not the case for the more persistent offenders. The more delinquent they tended to be, the less predictive the court record was of their most commonly reported violations. For example, only 26 of the 100 official, persistent delinquents had appeared in court more often for their major areas of offense than for other offenses. Nineteen of the 100 had *never* appeared in court for their reported major areas of offense. Thus, if these reported data are valid, the court record for this latter group would not give any clues as to the types of offenses they reported having committed most frequently.

In between these two extremes were 55 other boys, all of whom had been to court for their major patterns of offense, but they had also been there equally as often for other offenses. Consequently, even for them court records would fail to provide a clear picture of the most commonly reported offense patterns.

With regard to seriousness, the foregoing analysis has already suggested that court records may be a relatively poor index of the total number of *serious* violations. But what of individual offenders rather than their total offenses? How well does the court record eventually select boys who report having committed *serious* violations?

Answers to such questions are important. Although an offender may have a long record of petty violations, his commission of a serious offense, such as breaking and entering, will more likely type him as a burglar than a petty thief.

In order to examine this dimension, a crude "seriousness" classification was established. Five judges and five chief probation officers from Utah's six juvenile judicial districts[22] were asked to rank 25 offenses according to seriousness. The first ten of these offenses were then selected to serve as the *serious* criterion. They were:

1. Rape[23]
2. Selling narcotics
3. Arson
4. Using narcotics
5. Armed robbery
6. Breaking and entering
7. Forgery
8. Auto theft
9. Homosexuality[23]
10. Theft of items worth more than $50

Two specific questions were examined: (1) How accurate is the court record in reflecting the most *serious* offense each respondent has committed (in terms of the hierarchy of eight serious violations)? (2) How accurate is the court record in reflecting each offender's most frequently committed *serious* violation?

For a relatively large group, the court record could supply no information regarding these questions. This group was comprised primarily of the official nondelinquents and one-time offenders. Twenty-three of the 50 nondelinquents (46%) and 14 of the 30 one-time offenders (47%) had committed one or more of the serious violations, but none had ever been to court for any of them. (The close similarity between the nondelinquents and one-time offenders in this study is again illustrated.)

By contrast, a much higher proportion of the two most delinquent samples had not only committed serious offenses—i.e., 88 of 100—but had also been to court for committing them—i.e., 77 of the 88 (or 88%).

Upon reading such information one might conclude that official records are likely biased against persistent offenders. It should be recalled from Table 1–9, however, that respondents in the two most delinquent samples reported having committed many more serious offenses than the less delinquent subsamples. Court records, therefore, may simply reflect the greater probability of being caught because of excessive violations.

For this group of 77 persistent offenders who had been to court, the court record was accurate for 65 percent of them in reflecting the most serious offense they had committed. It said nothing of the remaining 35 percent. If, therefore, the premise is accepted that an offender would likely be typed on the basis of his most serious known offense, the court record would be accurate approximately two-thirds of the time for this select group. This is encouraging in some ways because it is persistent of-

---

[22]Utah has one of the two State Juvenile Court Systems in the United States. Connecticut has the other. Judges are appointed for six-year terms; they must be members of the bar. Chief probation officers

are selected on the basis of a state merit system examination and training and experience in correctional work.

[23]It will be recalled that data on rape and homosexuality are not presented in this paper. Therefore, the seriousness classification includes the eight remaining offenses.

fenders with whom officials and researchers have been most concerned.

On the other hand, the large proportion of juveniles whose serious offenses remained undetected might easily have been typed in the same way had they been apprehended. Yet, without official action, many of them apparently make a reasonable, conventional adjustment.

A second qualification has to do with the ability of the court record to reflect not only an individual's most *serious* violation, but the type(s) of *serious* violation(s) he commits most frequently. Another premise might be that an individual should be typed on the basis of frequency of seriousness rather than extremity of seriousness. For example, it may be preferable to type an individual as an auto thief for having been to court three times for auto theft than to type him as an armed robber for having been to court once for armed robbery.

The court records were somewhat less accurate in this regard. About half (39) of the 77 persistent offenders who had appeared in court for serious violations had appeared there more often for the types of *serious* violations they reported committing most often than for any other *serious* violation. However, the picture for this group of 39 was muddied somewhat because 52 percent of them had appeared in court just as often, or more often, for other offenses not considered serious.

For the other half of the 77 offenders who had not been to court more often for their most common serious violation, 20 (26%) had *never* been to court for their most common *serious* offense. And 18 (23%) had been to court just as often for other *serious* offenses. In these cases, the court record would not be an accurate means for typing an individual according to *serious* offense.

CONCLUSION

In conclusion, official records seemed more accurate in reflecting an individual's single most *serious* violation than the pattern of offenses, either *serious* or *nonserious*, which he most commonly commits.

On the surface, these findings may seem more encouraging from the treatment and control, than the research, standpoints. That is, court records, when compared with reported behavior, did distinguish persistent offenders (with whom officials are most concerned) from one-time offenders or nondelinquents, in terms of both number and seriousness of violation. Furthermore, they seemed quite efficient in indicating the most *serious* violations which persistent offenders had committed.

However, a great deal of refined information regarding types of offenders is needed if treatment and control strategies are to be effective. And, even though such information may be most needed for the persistent offender, it cannot be supplied, even for him, until more is known about two things: (1) about any differences or similarities between him and those juveniles who, if they were apprehended, might be typed the same way; and (2) about the offense patterns of him and others who, though they are apprehended, often remain largely unincorporated into the official record. Varying degrees of such information are needed no matter what theoretical orientation one takes towards developing typologies for treatment and control purposes.

Obviously, the findings which led to these conclusions must be qualified because of the data from which they were derived and the methodological problems inherent in obtaining them. Yet, even if they are only partially correct, they indicate one possible reason why we have encountered so much difficulty in pinpointing important etiological and treatment variables.

If different patterns of delinquency have important significance for the administration of justice, for prevention and treatment strategies, and for research purposes, data which could be used to supplement official records seem needed. At least it would seem important to explore the possibility that reported data on undetected offenses might be helpful in understanding delinquency.

The methods for obtaining such data need not be greatly different from those which are used in a variety of other areas, clinical and scientific. Possible legal and constitutional questions would have to be explored. Yet, we are not without precedent in the clinical field where the communication of important information is privileged.

Furthermore, reported data might also open avenues to more detailed examination of the circumstances surrounding the commission of delinquent acts: Who is present? How are the acts carried out? What social and psychological variables seem to be operating? And then attempts might be made to relate such questions to court, control, and research strategies.

7.

STANTON WHEELER

CRIMINAL STATISTICS: A REFORMULATION OF THE PROBLEM

The history of papers on criminal statistics is rather discouraging. The basis for pessimism lies not in the papers themselves, for there have been many useful, clearly formulated analyses. I need point only to the number and range of contributions by Sellin,[1] the recent work by Sellin and Wolfgang,[2] to Wolfgang's own systematic critique of uniform crime reports,[3] to Ronald Beattie's review of the uses of criminal statistics in the United States,[4] and to discussions by Donald Cressey,[5] Dan Glaser,[6] and many others —not to mention important contributors from other countries. Many relevant problems in the use and interpretation of criminal statistics have been raised, so that we are aware of the shortcomings, the unreliability and lack of uniformity, and hence of the hazards in making valid inferences about crime from the criminal statistics.

The cause for pessimism, therefore, does not lie with the absence of intelligent critical work. Rather, there is an absence of any follow-through that attempts to solve the problems pointed up in the various critiques. Many of the criticisms have been known for a long time, as a recent detailed historical review of the literature of criminal statistics shows. In this paper I want to suggest that our inability to utilize and interpret criminal statistics is a result not of the technical deficiencies that have been pointed to before, but rather is a result of the way in which the original problem has been put. My suggestion is that we need a reformulation of the problem, rather than further refinements in the technology of crime reporting.

The problem has to do with the underlying conception of crime, and therefore with the nature of the materials that are gathered as a result of this underlying conception. Put briefly, the underlying conception is that *the data of criminal statistics are mere records of response to the actions of criminals.* A person commits an act that is defined as illegal by statute. When the police department is notified of the act we have an offense known to police. If the

SOURCE: Stanton Wheeler, "Criminal Statistics: A Reformulation of the Problem," *Journal of Criminal Law, Criminology and Police Science* 58, no. 3 (1967): 317–24. Reprinted by Special Permission of the *Journal of Criminal Law, Criminology and Police Science* (Northwestern University School of Law), Copyright © 1967.

[1] Thorsten Sellin, "The Basis of a Crime Index," *Journal of Criminal Law and Criminology* 22 (1931): 335.
[2] Thorsten Sellin and Marvin E. Wolfgang, *The Measurement of Delinquency* (1964).
[3] Marvin E. Wolfgang, "Uniform Crime Reports: A Critical Appraisal," *University of Pennsylvania Law Review* 111 (1963): 608.
[4] Ronald H. Beattie, "Criminal Statistics in the United States: 1960," *Journal of Criminal Law, Criminology and Police Science* 51 (1960): 49.
[5] Donald Cressey, "The State of Criminal Statistics," *National Probation and Parole Association Journal* 3 (1957): 230.
[6] Daniel Glaser, *The Effectiveness of a Prison and Parole System* (Indianapolis: The Bobbs-Merrill Company, Inc., 1964). Also see Glaser, "Criminal Career Statistics," 1957 Proceedings of the American Correctional Association, p. 103, and Glaser, "Released Offender Statistics: A Proposal for a New National Program," *American Journal of Correction* 19 (1957): 15-17, 25.

department also finds someone and arrests him for the act we have a unit that enters arrest statistics. In either case the assumption is that the units reflect the passive responses of officials to the active behavior of criminals. Differential tendencies to report crimes, or failures to catch offenders, are seen as mere unreliability, and efforts may be made to stamp out such problems, since unreliability is bad. Efforts are made to achieve uniformity in crime reporting, to assure that all officials are handling the acts in similar ways. And efforts are made to improve the efficiency and reliability of the actual coding and classifying operations themselves, through the work of the research bureau of the police department, of those processing the data at the FBI or elsewhere.

Is it feasible, however, to sustain this conception of the nature of criminal statistics? The assumptions hold true only in very important but extremely rare limiting cases. We can treat the record of criminal acts as the record of criminals only when we have indeed achieved a precise uniformity in the reporting of such acts to the police, and in the processing of such acts by the police. Now, of course, we approach this ideal more or less closely with differing types of crime, as the early classification into part 1 and part 2 offenses by the FBI suggests. But the important point is that there is still great room for variability in reporting and processing, and the ideal is only rarely approached. Thus the conception of criminal statistics solely as records of response to the actions of criminals may not be the most useful way to conceive of the underlying problem.

The alternative is to conceive of three elements as *inherently* a part of the rate producing process, and of the resulting rate as an interaction of all three. The three categories include: (1) the offender who commits an act specified by statute to be illegal, (2) pool of citizens who may be either victims or reporters of the acts of the offenders, and (3) officers of the law who are formally charged with the obligation to respond to the action. We would then express offenses as a function of the interaction of these three elements, any one of which might be more or less important in a particular instance.

It should be noted immediately that this is in no way a radical reformulation of the problem. All who work with criminal statistics are aware of the great sources of variability that lie in differential values of the community and in differential police actions. This proposed change simply introduces these concerns as a legitimate and inherent part of the model of criminal statistics, rather than conceiving of them as external and unwanted sources of error and unreliability. The principal gain from making this transition is that variations in citizen and police actions become important events to be explained, just as we make efforts to explain why some commit crimes and some do not.

Each of these three categories can be looked at both individually and collectively. Thus we have single criminals, or in some cases criminal organizations. We can conceive of the police system as a whole as the responding agency, where variation in police policies, technology, and so forth are the relevant aspects. Or we could concentrate on individual officers, relating their characteristics to their arrest behavior just as we now relate the offender's characteristics to his criminal behavior. Finally, we can think of the community as a pool of separate residents or as an organized whole with shared sentiments in response to crime. But before passing to several specific consequences that would flow from such a reformulation, more should be said by way of an operational and theoretical justification for this shift.

THE OPERATIONAL JUSTIFICATION

Consider how the records of crime are in fact produced. In most cases they do indeed begin with an act of an offender, but they never end there. As is obviously the case, they must be reported by someone or they never end up in our statistics. We have usually assumed, as indicated in a quote by Sellin which is perhaps the most oft-quoted remark about criminal statistics: "the value of a crime rate for index purposes decreases as the distance from the crime itself, in terms of procedure, increases."[7] But

[7] Thorsten Sellin, "The Basis of a Crime Index," *Journal of Criminal Law and Criminology* 22 (1931): 346.

as that very wording suggests, even the immediate reports themselves may be subject to great error, and it is that error which is so troublesome to those who wish to use official data to test theories of crime causation. While there is certainly no reason to quarrel with the general wisdom of Sellin's statement, neither should we let it hide the fact that the greatest gap of all is likely to occur between the crime itself and the initiating procedure.

There are very few detailed accounts of the actual procedures used by police agencies in the processing of cases and the reporting of crime statistics. Where there are really full and detailed statements (as in the recent Sellin and Wolfgang volume where a full chapter is devoted to the method of reporting delinquency by a division of the Philadelphia police),[8] two things seem abundantly clear.

First, standardizing decision-making at the initial stage, particularly in areas such as delinquency, is very difficult and requires a great deal of effort and attention to detail. For example, cases may come to the attention of a juvenile bureau either directly in the course of the juvenile officer's duties, or indirectly by referral. In addition to possible effects of these differences, there are different criteria used in the decision to arrest or report. In Philadelphia these include the juvenile's previous contacts with police, the type of offense, the attitude of the complainant, the offender's family situation, and potential community sources. It seems quite evident that individual officers might resolve these matters in somewhat different ways, despite a good deal of training.

The second point, however, is more important. These are procedures worked out by the Philadelphia department for the processing of Philadelphia cases. Quite clearly other principles may be utilized in other cities. How, then, are we to compare the figures in any sensible way? Even though each department may end up with reasonably uniform data for its area, comparability across towns, cities, or regions will be missing, as will comparability over time in the same jurisdiction if any further changes occur.

The operational justification, then, is that these sources of variability appear built into the problem. It seems a wise course of action to attempt to understand them, since we are unlikely to get rid of them.

THE THEORETICAL JUSTIFICATION

The theoretical justification for treating crime statistics as a result of three-way interaction between an offender, victims or citizens, and official agents, is that deviation itself is increasingly recognized as a social process that depends heavily on social definition.[9] Acts become deviant when they are so defined by members of the collectivities in which they occur. Whether a given pattern of behavior will be labeled deviant is itself problematic, and is likely to vary from community to community, or from policeman to policeman, at least within certain fairly broad limits. Why emphasize only the person who might commit an act, and not those who might label it as deviant, or those who might officially respond?

The concept here is close to that suggested decades ago by VanVechten: The tolerance quotient of a community.[10] This has to do with how much "trouble" the community will put up with before it acts, or in other words how much deviant behavior it will permit before either citizens or official agents take offense and respond in some systematic way.

Evidence in support of this orientation is found increasingly in the study of forms of deviation close to but not identical with criminality. Consider, for example, mental retardation. A recent study shows that the mentally retarded from families with lower educational background spend a shorter time in institutions and are released more readily than are those from higher educational background.[11] This is

[8]Thorsten Sellin and Marvin E. Wolfgang, *The Measurement of Delinquency* (New York: John Wiley & Sons, Inc., 1964), pp. 82–114.

[9]This orientation is most fully stated in Howard S. Becker, *Outsiders* (Glencoe, Ill.: Free Press, 1964), and in John Kitsuse and Aaron Cicourel, "A Note on the Uses of Official Statistics," *Social Problems* 11 (1963): 131.

[10]C. VanVechten, "The Tolerance Quotient as a Device for Defining Certain Social Concepts," *American Journal of Sociology* 46 (1940): 35–42.

[11]Jane Mercer, "Social System Perspective and Clinical Perspective: Frames of Reference for Understanding Career Patterns of Persons Labelled

true even when they are matched carefully by IQ. The suggested explanation is that families of lower educational level are less likely to define their offspring as mentally retarded, and are therefore more ready to accept them back into the home. A related study shows that families of higher socio-economic status are able to get their children accepted into institutions for the mentally retarded more quickly than are those of lower socio-economic status, and this appears in part to be because they are more insistent about the need of the child in question.[12] In other words, they think of this behavior as more deviant than do those of lower socio-economic levels. It appears likely that both entry and release from the hospital are functions of the social characteristics of those who are attempting to get them in or out, and are not mere reflections of intelligence as measured by standardized tests.

Consider further some of the evidence regarding mental illness. Several recent studies suggest that rates of commitment bear a close correspondence to the paths of entry to hospitals. In one instance, that of a child guidance clinic where the concern is for which children are accepted among all those referred, the evidence is that those referred by doctors are more likely to be accepted than those referred by family members.[13] The further evidence is that the acceptance is more closely related to the source of referral than to the nature of the symptoms of the individual who is being referred.

In these areas of social deviation, therefore, it makes good sense to think of the deviation itself as a social process involving not only the person who commits deviant acts, but also those who choose to label them as deviant and those who are officially charged with acting upon them as such. Indeed, a full understanding of rates of institutionalization or rates of retardation and illness seems to require that we consider more than simply the mental or intellectual status of the person in question.

THE SPECIAL CASE OF CRIME

It can be argued that a mistake is made in attempting to treat crime in the same category as the foregoing forms of deviance. The criminal law is primarily statutory law, and the specification of conditions necessary to convict one of the commission of the crime is certainly more detailed and specific than is the case for mental subnormality or mental illness. Criminal statutes typically specify in some detail the nature of the offense, and we have well worked out techniques which, in the case of pleas of not guilty, may be utilized by juries to assess guilt or innocence. Therefore, we might expect somewhat more objectivity in the collection and analysis of data on crime than is true for other forms of deviation.

This argument is certainly true to a point, and it would be a mistake to equate crime overly readily with other forms of deviation. There is a sizeable difference between the behavioral specification of acts, for example, of burglary or arson, and the much more general, abstract, and judgmental character of the process of diagnosis of a person as psychotic. But again, two features of crime remain important to note in this context. First, enforcement of all statutes is not attempted. Diligence in some areas is matched by negligence in others. In fact, our policing and detection policies introduce new sources of variation that are not encompassed in the definition of the statutes, as Daniel Bell's article on the myths of crime waves reminds us.[14] Policies to "crack down" on all narcotics users or pushers, while "tolerating" organized prostitution, are likely to be found within the same police jurisdiction. This simply indicates that the clarity of the specification of law-violating behavior in the statutes is often not repeated by the policies in fact enforced by the policing agencies.

as Mentally Retarded," *Social Problems* 13 (1965): 18.

[12]Georges Sabagh, Richard Eyman, and Donald Cogburn, "The Speed of Institutionalization: A Study of a Preadmission Waiting List Cohort in an Institution for the Retarded" (unpublished manuscript).

[13]James E. Teele and Sol Levine, "The Acceptance of Emotionally Disturbed Children by Psychiatric Agencies," in *Controlling Delinquents*, ed. Stanton Wheeler (New York: John Wiley & Sons, Inc., 1967), chap. 5.

[14]Daniel Bell, ed., "The Myth of Crime Waves," in *The End of Ideology* (Glencoe, Ill.: The Free Press, 1960), pp. 137–58.

Even more important than this, however, is the fact that some of the forms of crime that are becoming increasingly important no longer have the clear-cut statutory form of definition. A principal case, of course, is delinquency. Most legal definitions of delinquency are so broad and vague as to make it roughly synonymous with juvenile trouble making. In addition to including offenses that also hold for adults, there are such things as being truant, willful disobeying of parental commands, and staying out after curfew. The lack of specification in these instances approaches that of the case of mental illness, which of course is not surprising in that many see forms of delinquency and forms of mental illness as synonymous.

For these reasons, I think it can be effectively argued that a model stressing the social definition of crime, and especially the actions of other social agents as well as those of presumed offenders, is pragmatically useful as well as being highly realistic.

SOME PRACTICAL CONSEQUENCES

The most immediate effect that would flow from adoption of this rationale is that we might be able to learn something more about systematic variations in the crime rate than we learn by examination of the characteristics of criminals. Consider each of the following four consequences:

1. *Improved Understanding of Police and Official Agents.* Remembering the distinction between the collective and individual forms, and beginning with the collective, we might ask: What are characteristics of *police systems* where high crime or arrest rates prevail? Here is a problem eminently worthy of study, and we might almost refer to it, especially in the context of recent events, as the Los Angeles police problem. Some years ago Ronald Beattie wanted to argue that the high rate of offenses known to the police in Los Angeles was a result, not of the law-violating behavior of Angelenos, but of the good deeds of Chief Parker and his force. The Los Angeles police department, he argued, was a superior force in terms of efficiency and dedication. The high rate of arrests was a result

of efficiency, rather than the result of a high rate of offenses. This example at least suggests that we should be able to find some stable and reliable differences between police departments that report high rates of offenses and those that report relatively low rates. What are those differences? Suppose we introduce controls for the nature of the social composition of the community, would we still find stable differentials based upon differences in the police function?

Clearly, to answer these questions requires that we work hard to establish differential degrees of police efficiency in crime reporting, and differentials in types of police organization. Conceivably the arrest rate is a function of the number of motorcycles versus police cars on the road, a function of the proportion of the total police force that is civilian, a function of the average educational attainment of the individual officers, a function of whether or not there is a police academy that serves to train policemen for this particular department, and so on. The whole point is that introducing the official actions of the police, not as mere passive response to the criminal, but rather as an inherent part of the production of a crime rate, forces us to ask these questions, and hence ultimately to understand better the workings of police organization.

I shall cite two studies, of radically different styles, where this sort of contribution seems to be forthcoming. One is interesting work by the political scientist James Q. Wilson.[15] Wilson has compared a relatively non-professionalized police force in an Eastern city with a highly professionalized force in a West Coast city. His interest was in seeing whether the nature of the professional organization of the police is related to modes of handling delinquents and to the rate of arrest of juvenile offenders; and his findings suggest that it is indeed. The old-line force, fraternal in organization, recruits its members largely on grounds of locale, provides little training for them, and little professional esprit. The result is that while they are punitive

[15]James Q. Wilson, "The Police and the Delinquent in Two Cities," in *Controlling Delinquents,* ed. Stanton Wheeler (New York: John Wiley & Sons, Inc., 1967), chap. 2.

toward youthful offenders, there is no strong sense of urgency about police work and hence relatively low rates of official actions with regard to youthful offenders. The force in the West Coast city, in contrast, is one that is recruited nationwide, places a high premium on education, pays better, and in other ways appears to fit the model of a professional as distinguished from fraternal system. In the West Coast city youths are more likely to be picked up for minor offenses, minor offenses are more likely to be treated as major infractions, and the arrest rate tends to be much higher than in the East Coast city. This example merely serves to illustrate that the crime rate may vary in close correspondence with the nature of police organization, and conceivably quite independently from the nature of delinquent activity.

The second example comes from an ecological study by W. F. Greenhaigh of the British Home Office.[16] He had the wisdom to include as a relevant variable in his analysis the number of police per capita in various social units. He finds that the number of officers is related to the number of offenses reported, and while this of course raises a neat problem as to cause and effect, it serves to emphasize the potential role of the structure of the police systems themselves.

We may also find important sources of variation in individual differences *within* police departments. There is certainly good reason to imagine that there are sizeable differences in policemen in terms of the number of individuals they arrest or take official action upon. A police officer who has had many years of experience once related to me an incident from one of his early days on the force. He was in a squad car when they received a radio call from central headquarters to proceed rapidly to the scene of a particular offense. He was driving the car with his partner in the automobile, a much older and wiser policeman, sitting next to him. As my young, "gung ho" friend roared to the scene of the crime with the siren wailing, his older colleague turned to him and said "For

crying out loud, slow down and turn off the siren. You're makin me noivous." The point is fairly clear: there is little more reason to expect age, training, ethnic background, and other characteristics to be irrelevant in this context than there is to expect them to disappear when we study offenders.

The necessary first step is to begin collecting data on policemen and police departments similar in form if not in content with what we gather on criminals. This is already done to some extent by the FBI, which annually publishes, for example, the list of the number of uniformed and civilian police employees for every reporting city over 2,500 population. Because this is thought to be relevant for policing, but not for crime, there have been no analyses, to my knowledge, of the possible correlation between number of police and either the number of criminals, or the number of offenses cleared by arrest.

The chief practical consequence of adopting a new rationale is that we would begin to understand the dynamics of police systems in relation to offenders. So long as we treat the police as mere reactors to the actions of criminals, this whole area will remain hidden from our view. My argument is simply that if we transform the degree of police efficiency into a variable to be explained, rather than one to be eliminated by the production of uniformity in procedure, we will enhance our understanding of crime.

2. *Improved Understanding of Citizens and Social Control.* The pool of conventional persons in the community, either victims of crimes or citizens who observe them, often initiate the production of crime rates by being the first reporters of criminal events. There appear to be relatively vast community-wide differences in the rate at which persons call the police for help with problems. In Nathan Goldman's study of differential selection of juvenile offenders for court appearance, he suggests that official agents are highly responsive to the definition of deviation on the part of the citizens of the community, and that some of his communities have high rates of delinquency because the officials feel that the citizens will complain if they do

---

[16]W. F. Greenhaigh, "A Town's Rate of Serious Crime against Property and Its Association with Some Broad Social Factors," Home Office, Scientific Advisers Branch, February, 1964.

not take official action, whereas other ones have low rates because the citizens simply do not complain.[17]

Another example of the possibilities here is provided in a study by Eleanor Maccoby and others.[18] They interviewed members of two communities, one of which had a high rate of delinquency and the other a low rate, where socio-economic characteristics were held constant insofar as possible. One of the things they found is that the community that had a low rate of official offenses had a high rate of community cohesion. That is, friends, neighbors and others would intervene when they saw kids getting into trouble. In the community with the high official delinquency, there was very little interaction among members, and little intervention at these early stages. The strong suggestion here is that informal social controls operate effectively in one community to obviate the need for official actions, whereas in the other they did not. The low official rates were due to prompt intervention in cases of incipient deviation; in the other community incipient deviation was not responded to at all, and it grew in seriousness until official actions occurred.

Although the evidence in these two cases is not entirely clear, the general point is certainly not to be debated: different types of neighborhoods and communities may respond to deviant behavior in radically different ways, and their responses become the initiation of the official reporting system. Unless we understand them we will not be led to a full understanding of the rate production process.

As in the case of police systems, we may find individual variation within the neighborhood or community, just as we find systematic variations between them. Either as victim or as observer, we are likely to find many important differences in the role of the citizenry in the production of crime rates. There are of course several studies focusing on the victim, but usually these have been separate investigations that have little relation to routine police reporting. And there

is folk knowledge, though little systematic evidence, of individual differences in willingness to report offenses to the police. Older single women living alone are thought by some to be inordinately observant of potential criminal situations. One police captain once told me that the rate of telephone calls reporting crimes in progress dropped substantially with the growth of television. The implication was that people who used to mind others' business, and hence keep their eyes on the street below, were now absorbed watching crime dramas on TV and did not see the real thing anymore.

Although these examples may be of dubious validity, they serve to illustrate the main point: whether a person gets treated officially as an offender depends on which citizen he happened to meet and which community he happened to be in when the act occurred; and our explanation of variations in crime rates will have to do in part with area variations in the nature of communities and their law-abiding citizens.

3. *The Development of Consumer-Oriented Crime Statistics.* A third practical consequence is that we could begin to express crime rates in ways that would have more meaning for the public. The police system itself exists for the protection of the community, but so far we have done extremely little to provide data that is directly relevant to community members. This is apparent by examining the denominators that typically are used in construction of crime rates. If one is diligent, one can find arrest rates for Negroes, for Puerto Ricans, for whites. Or one can find age-specific rates of offense. In a handful of cases, one can find cohort analysis tables indicating the probability that a person will ever be arrested between, say, ages 7 to 18.

All of these figures have a curious cast. They tell us much more about who commits the offense than about the person against whom it is committed. Yet if we think now as citizens, and not as persons interested solely in offenders or policing, it seems that we might ask rather different questions. Personally, I am more concerned whether my wife and children are likely to be assaulted at all, than whether, if the deed is done, they are assaulted by a Caucasian, a Puerto Rican, or a Negro. Yet I can find figures on the latter topic but not on the former. Sim-

[17]Nathan Goldman, "The Differential Selection of Juvenile Officers for Court Appearance," National Council on Crime and Delinquency, 1963.

[18]Eleanor Maccoby et al., "Community Integration and the Social Control of Juvenile Delinquency," *Journal of Social Issues* 3 (1958): 38.

ilarly, one may wonder what New York City residents would make of the fact that the reportedly rising crime rate in the City could be explained as a function of the increased number of persons of juvenile age, which is of course the age at which most crimes are committed (so far as we can tell from official statistics). Certainly it is important theoretically to understand that the rising rate does not appear to be a response to new forces and fears in mass society, but rather can be explained fairly directly as a function of the age structure of the population. But for the typical resident, the important question would seem to be whether or not the rate has gone up for victims in his category.

This is simply to suggest that a useful way of reporting crime data would be to use as a denominator not some characteristic that might describe offenders, but one that will describe their victims. Apartment dwellers might well want to know what the probability is that their apartment will be burgled within the next five years. Others might want to know what the probability is that they will be robbed. In principle, it should not be difficult to prepare such statistics. We take the number of offenses appearing in a particular area against a particular type of victim, and express it as a proportion of all persons who have the social characteristics that the victim happens to hold. In this way we have victim-specific rather than offender-specific crime rates—in effect, a box score which the citizen can use to keep tabs on differing areas in his community, and hopefully on differing communities. It would become abundantly clear, for example, which areas of the city are most dangerous at night, and for what categories of persons they are most dangerous. Such consumer-oriented statistics would seem to be more important as a public service than are offender-oriented statistics such as those we now produce.

The issues are clearly more complicated than suggested here. One problem is the necessity of correcting for the daytime and nighttime populations of the areas. And in order to get detailed victim-specific rates, we would have to learn more now than we normally do about the nature of the victim. In the latest *Uniform Crime Report* available to me (for the year 1963) only one out of some 49 tables tells us anything about the victim. This one has to do with the victims of homicides, and classifies the victims according to their age, sex, and race.[19] At least, I would argue, it is an effort in a much needed direction.

4. *Improved Understanding of Criminals and Criminal Acts.* The fourth and final consequence is that adopting the frame of reference outlined here might enable us to approach what we have always traditionally desired, namely, better descriptive and explanatory accounts of the actions of criminals. Paradoxically, it is only by first directing our attention to the citizens and the police that we can begin making headway on the initial problem of sources of variation in crime rates.

At the moment, any community-wide comparisons of crime data are subject to possible unreliability, and certainly debatable as to the interpretation of meaning, because of possible differentials in the functioning of the citizens and the police. A higher rate of crime for community A than for community B cannot be guaranteed to tell us something about the actual level of law violations in the two communities, for all the reasons we have already reviewed. Any efforts aimed at assessing the actual rate of legal violations, or differentials in the rate that are related to differential characteristics of the offenders, must of necessity take into account the variation due to citizens and policing. We can do so, of course, only if we have studied such variations and have evidence with regard to them.

THE NECESSARY FIRST STEP

The most essential first step is that there must be new sources of input to the official collections of data. If the position argued here is correct, it will no longer be enough for the established reporting agencies such as the FBI to collect data simply on the number of crimes reported in the various jurisdictions. It will be essential that they also collect systematic data on (a) the complaining witness, (b) the social characteristics of the community, (c) the reporting

---

[19] *Uniform Crime Reports*, 1963, Table 18, p. 102.

or arresting officer, and (d) the nature of the police system as a whole. Just as there is a reporting form for crime, there must be a reporting form for complaints, for the community, for officers, and for police departments. This would enable us to gather systematic data on the other possible sources of variation in crime rates. The details for such reporting forms would of course have to be worked out, and problems of uniformity would be sure to arise. But there is no reason why they should be any more severe than those now plaguing the reporting of crimes. Also, it would be necessary for us to think about more creative denominators for crime rates, along the lines suggested above. But here too, the technical task is not overwhelming, and much of the work has already been done by the Bureau of the Census.

If prestigious organizations such as the FBI were to begin collecting such data routinely, we could begin to close in on the haunting problems of biases in criminal statistics. We could at least compare jurisdictions whose police procedures were roughly similar, and where the types of complaining witnesses were not simply a function of the demographic structure of the community. More importantly, we could begin to examine the interactions between the three major sources of variation: the offender, the citizenry, and the police system.

CONCLUSION

Most of the questions raised here concern the uses of crime rate data. Implicit throughout is the question: what is a useful rate? Assuming the crimes or arrests enter the numerators, the question concerns the sorts of denominators that are most important and relevant. The suggestion is that the received wisdom, so far, leads us to construct denominators reflecting the nature of the crime-committing person. The principal suggestion of this paper is that we ought to broaden the conception of the relevant denominators to include characteristics of the police system and the nature of victims or the citizen population. To adopt such a view systematically would, I feel, greatly broaden the richness and relevance of our understanding of crime and its control, and would have the further advantage of making more meaningful the very data we now complain about in our critiques of criminal statistics.

CHAPTER II

On the Labelling of Behavior

EDITOR'S INTRODUCTION

A GOOD MANY YEARS AGO Frank Tannenbaum speculated about the process by which a delinquent is created by society.[1] Tannenbaum's articulation focused especially, it seems, on what has since come to be called secondary deviation, i.e., the individual's subsequent response to society's reaction to his earlier condition or behavior. Thus, Tannenbaum deals with both the process by which the individual's self-image comes to be the self-image of a deviant and the process by which society became convinced of an individual's "delinquent nature." More recently, social scientists have referred to these processes as some of the hypothetical effects of labelling, a matter which several of the authors of papers in this section consider.

The first paper in this section, however, by Kai Erikson, considers the effects of labelling individuals only secondarily. Erikson is primarily concerned with understanding deviance as a *societal need*, i.e., a precious resource which is guarded and maintained by social systems. Developing his approach out of Durkheim's sociological thought, Erikson suggests that deviance serves the function of boundary-setting in the regulation of behavior and as such is vital to all social systems. The implications of Erikson's conclusions for sociological theory are substantial, to say the least. Thus, if deviance is important to societies, then the role of social audiences in the imputation of deviance must be examined.

---

[1]Frank Tannenbaum, *Crime and the Community* (New York: Columbia University Press, 1938).

J. L. Simmons, in his paper with Hazel Chambers, "Public Stereotypes of Deviants," shows one way in which the audience may be studied. These authors investigated public attitudes towards deviant behavior, utilizing a study group of persons mixed on age, sex, education, race and other attributes. The fact that this is the only research paper in this section is a reflection of the fact that studies designed to test notions about the process and the effects of labelling are lacking.[2] Indeed, labelling theory itself is said to be in its infancy.

Two papers which point to some of the problems and precautions which labelling theorists and researchers will have to take under consideration follow the paper by Simmons. The first of these two papers, by R. Akers, is entitled "Problems in the Sociology of Deviance: Social Definitions and Behavior." Taking a cue from the conflict criminologist, George Vold,[3] Akers states that the sociological "goal is not to account for *either* social definitions *or* deviant behavior, but rather to account for both and ultimately to specify the interaction and integrate explanations of behavior and social definitions." Thus, while not minimizing the task for sociologists of explaining how society is implicated in the labelling of individuals and more particularly in secondary deviation, Akers emphasizes that sociologists need not and should not forsake the task of explaining deviant behavior, especially primary deviation. The second of these two papers focusing on future directions of labelling theorists and researchers is by J. DeLamater, "On The Nature Of Deviance." DeLamater, although focusing also on the effects of labelling, is much more concerned with the manner in which initial deviant behavior occurs. He draws the distinction between individuals whose initial socialization is in terms of conventional norms and those whose early socialization is based on deviant norms. DeLamater's analysis of the socialization process in deviance leads him to conclude that for individuals whose initial socialization was conventional, the costs associated with labelling are likely to be much higher than for those whose initial socialization was deviant. In focusing on socialization processes, DeLamater also introduces the student to the theme which will be dealt with in Chapter Three of this book, namely, the explanation of delinquency.

In the final paper in Chapter Two, Howard Becker considers one of the main issues which confront social scientists engaged in research on deviance, viz., how can they assure their audience that their reporting is unbiased when the report seems to take the side of the deviant? Becker wonders why the issue of bias is not raised more often when the report seems to take the side of the officials involved. He introduces the dis-

---

[2]The student is reminded, however, that the paper on the police by Piliavin and Briar in chapter one is a research paper which is directly relevant to the issue of labelling.

[3]George Vold, *Theoretical Criminology* (New York: Oxford University Press, 1958).

tinction between apolitical and political contexts in pondering these questions.[4] Although Becker's paper is useful in exploring some of the considerations which may affect the choice and conduct of research studies by social scientists, it is also useful in focusing on the role of power in the definition of behavior, a matter which is most basic to labelling theory.

---

[4]For a view which takes issue with Becker's and similar analyses, see Alvin Gouldner, "The Sociologist as Partisan: Sociology and the Welfare State," *The American Sociologist* 3 (May, 1968): 103–16.

8.

KAI T. ERIKSON

NOTES ON THE SOCIOLOGY OF DEVIANCE

It is general practice in sociology to regard deviant behavior as an alien element in society. Deviance is considered a vagrant form of human activity, moving outside the more orderly currents of social life. And since this type of aberration could only occur (in theory) if something were wrong within the social organization itself, deviant behavior is described almost as if it were leakage from machinery in poor condition: it is an accidental result of disorder and anomie, a symptom of internal breakdown.

The purpose of the following remarks will be to review this conventional outlook and to argue that it provides too narrow a framework for the study of deviant behavior. Deviation, we will suggest, recalling Durkheim's classic statement on the subject, can often be understood as a normal product of stable institutions, a vital resource which is guarded and preserved by forces found in all human organizations.[1]

I

According to current theory, deviant behavior is most likely to occur when the sanctions governing conduct in any given setting seem to be contradictory.[2] This would be the case, for example, if the work rules posted by a company required one course of action from its employees and the longer-range policies of the company

required quite another. Any situation marked by this kind of ambiguity, of course, can pose a serious dilemma for the individual: if he is careful to observe one set of demands imposed upon him, he runs the immediate risk of violating some other, and thus may find himself caught in a deviant stance no matter how earnestly he tries to avoid it. In this limited sense, deviance can be regarded a "normal" human response to "abnormal" social conditions, and the sociologist is therefore invited to assume that some sort of pathology exists within the social structure whenever deviant behavior makes an appearance.

This general approach is clearly more concerned with the *etiology* of deviant behavior than with its continuing social *history*—and as a result it often draws sociological attention away from an important area of inquiry. It may be safe to assume that naive acts of deviance, such as first criminal offenses, are provoked by strains in the local situation. But this is only the beginning of a much longer story, for deviant activities can generate a good deal of momentum once they are set into motion: they develop forms of organization, persist over time, and sometimes remain intact long after the strains which originally produced them have disappeared. In this respect, deviant activities are often absorbed into the main tissue of society and derive support from the same forces which stabilize other forms of social life. There are persons in society, for example, who make career commitments to deviant styles of conduct, impelled by some inner need for continuity rather than by any urgencies in the immediate social setting. There are groups in society which actively encourage new deviant trends, often prolonging them beyond the point where they represent an adaptation to strain. These sources of support for deviant behavior are difficult to visualize when we use terms like "strain,"

SOURCE: Kai T. Erikson, "Notes on the Sociology of Deviance," *Social Problems* 10, (Spring, 1962): 307–14. Reprinted by Permission of the author and The Society for the Study of Social Problems.

Paper read at the 55th annual meetings of the American Sociological Association, New York, 1960.
[1]Emile Durkheim, *The Rules of Sociological Method,* trans. S. A. Solovay and J. H. Mueller (New York: The Free Press, 1958).

[2]The best known statements of this general position, of course, are by Robert K. Merton and Talcott Parsons. Merton, *Social Theory and Social Structures* rev. ed. (New York: The Free Press, 1957); and Parsons, *The Social System* (New York: The Free Press, 1951).

"anomie," or "breakdown" in discussions of the problem. Such terms may help us explain how the social structure creates fresh deviant potential, but they do not help us explain how that potential is later shaped into durable, persisting social patterns.[3] The individual's need for self continuity and the group's offer to support are altogether normal processes, even if they are sometimes found in deviant situations; and thus the study of deviant behavior is as much a study of social organization as it is a study of *disorganization* and anomie.

II

From a sociological standpoint, deviance can be defined as conduct which is generally thought to require the attention of social control agencies —that is, conduct about which "something should be done." Deviance is not a property *inherent in* certain forms of behavior; it is a property *conferred upon* these forms by the audiences which directly or indirectly witness them. Sociologically, then, the critical variable in the study of deviance is the social *audience* rather than the individual *person*, since it is the audience which eventually decides whether or not any given action or actions will become a visible case of deviation.

This definition may seem a little indirect, but it has the advantage of bringing a neglected sociological issue into proper focus. When a community acts to control the behavior of one of its members, it is engaged in a very intricate process of selection. Even a determined miscreant conforms in most of his daily behavior— using the correct spoon at mealtime, taking good care of his mother, or otherwise observing the mores of his society—and if the community elects to bring sanctions against him for the occasions when he does act offensively, it is responding to a few deviant details set within a vast context of proper conduct. Thus a person may be jailed or hospitalized for a few scattered moments of misbehavior, defined as a fulltime deviant despite the fact that he had supplied the community with countless other indications that he was a decent moral citizen. The screening device which sifts these telling details out of the individual's over-all performance, then, is a sensitive instrument of social control. It is important to note that this screen takes a number of factors into account which are not directly related to the deviant act itself: it is concerned with the actor's social class, his past record as an offender, the amount of remorse he manages to convey, and many similar concerns which take hold in the shifting moods of the community. This is why the community often overlooks behavior which seems technically deviant (like certain kinds of white collar graft) or takes sharp exception to behavior which seems essentially harmless (like certain kinds of sexual impropriety). It is an easily demonstrated fact, for example, that working class boys who steal cars are far more likely to go to prison than upper class boys who commit the same or even more serious crimes, suggesting that from the point of view of the community lower class offenders are somehow more deviant. To this extent, the community screen is perhaps a more relevant subject for sociological research than the actual behavior which is filtered through it.

Once the problem is phrased in this way, we can ask: how does a community decide what forms of conduct should be singled out for this kind of attention? And why, having made this choice, does it create special institutions to deal with the persons who enact them? The standard answer to this question is that society sets up the machinery of control in order to protect itself against the "harmful" effects of deviance, in much the same way that an organism mobilizes its resources to combat an invasion of germs. At times, however, this classroom convention only seems to make the problem more complicated. In the first place, as Durkheim pointed out some years ago, it is by no means clear that all acts considered deviant in a culture are in fact (or even in principle) harmful to group life.[4] And in the second place, specialists in crime and mental health have long suggested that deviance can play an important role in keeping the social order intact—again a

---

[3] Cf. Daniel Glaser and Kent Rice, "Crime, Age, and Employment," *American Sociological Review* 24 (1959): 679–86.

[4] Emile Durkheim, *The Division of Labor in Society,* trans. George Simpson (New York: The Free Press, 1952). See particularly chap. 2, bk. 1.

point we owe originally to Durkheim.[5] This has serious implications for sociological theory in general.

III

In recent years, sociological theory has become more and more concerned with the concept "social system"—an organization of society's component parts into a form which sustains internal equilibrium, resists change, and is boundary maintaining. Now this concept has many abstract dimensions, but it is generally used to describe those forces in the social order which promote a high level of uniformity among human actors and a high degree of symmetry within human institutions. In this sense, the concept is normatively oriented since it directs the observer's attention toward those centers in social space where the core values of society are figuratively located. The main organizational principle of a system, then, is essentially a centripetal one: it draws the behavior of actors toward the nucleus of the system, bringing it within range of basic norms. Any conduct which is neither attracted toward this nerve center by the rewards of conformity nor compelled toward it by other social pressures is considered "out of control," which is to say, deviant.

This basic model has provided the theme for most contemporary thinking about deviance, and as a result little attention has been given to the notion that systems operate to maintain boundaries. Generally speaking, boundaries are controls which limit the fluctuation of a system's component parts so that the whole retains a defined range of activity—a unique pattern of constancy and stability—within the larger environment.[6] The range of human behavior is potentially so great that any *social* system must make clear statements about the nature and location of its boundaries, placing limits on the flow of behavior so that it circulates within a given cultural area. Thus boundaries are a crucial point of reference for persons living within any system, a prominent concept in the group's

special language and tradition. A juvenile gang may define its boundaries by the amount of territory it defends, a professional society by the range of subjects it discusses, a fraternal order by the variety of members it accepts. But in each case, members share the same idea as to where the group begins and ends in social space and know what kinds of experience "belong" within this domain.

For all its apparent abstractness, a social system is organized around the movements of persons joined together in regular social relations. The only material found in a system for marking boundaries, then, is the behavior of its participants; and the form of behavior which best performs this function would seem to be deviant almost by definition, since it is the most extreme variety of conduct to be found within the experience of the group. In this respect, transactions taking place between deviant persons on the one side and agencies of control on the other are boundary maintaining mechanisms. They mark the outside limits of the area in which the norm has jurisdiction, and in this way assert how much diversity and variability can be contained within the system before it begins to lose its distinct structure, its unique shape.

A social norm is rarely expressed as a firm rule or official code. It is an abstract synthesis of the many separate times a community has stated its sentiments on a given issue. Thus the norm has a history much like that of an article of common law: it is an accumulation of decisions made by the community over a long period of time which gradually gathers enough moral influence to serve as a precedent for future decisions. Like an article of common law, the norm retains its validity only if it is regularly used as a basis for judgment. Each time the community censures some act of deviance, then, it sharpens the authority of the violated norm and re-establishes the boundaries of the group.

One of the most interesting features of control institutions, in this regard, is the amount of publicity they have always attracted. In an earlier day, correction of deviant offenders took place in the public market and gave the crowd a chance to display its interest in a direct, active way. In our own day, the guilty are

[5]Emile Durkheim, *The Rules of Sociological Method*, op. cit.

[6]Cf. Talcott Parsons, *The Social System*, op. cit.

no longer paraded in public places, but instead we are confronted by a heavy flow of newspaper and radio reports which offer much the same kind of entertainment. Why are these reports considered "newsworthy" and why do they rate the extraordinary attention they receive? Perhaps they satisfy a number of psychological perversities among the mass audience, as many commentators have suggested, but at the same time they constitute our main source of information about the normative outlines of society. They are lessons through which we teach one another what the norms mean and how far they extend. In a figurative sense, at least, morality and immorality meet at the public scaffold, and it is during this meeting that the community declares where the line between them should be drawn.

Human groups need to regulate the routine affairs of everyday life, and to this end the norms provide an important focus for behavior. But human groups also need to describe and anticipate those areas of being which lie beyond the immediate borders of the group—the unseen dangers which in any culture and in any age seem to threaten the security of group life. The universal folklore depicting demons, devils, witches and evil spirits may be one way to give form to these otherwise formless dangers, but the visible deviant is another kind of reminder. As a trespasser against the norm, he represents those forces excluded by the group's boundaries: he informs us, as it were, what evil looks like, what shapes the devil can assume. In doing so, he shows us the difference between kinds of experience which belong within the group and kinds of experience which belong outside it.

Thus deviance cannot be dismissed as behavior which *disrupts* stability in society, but is itself, in controlled quantities, an important condition for *preserving* stability.

IV

This raises a serious theoretical question. If we grant that deviant behavior often performs a valuable service in society, can we then assume that society as a whole actively tries to promote this resource? Can we assume, in other words, that some kind of active recruitment process is

going on to assure society of a steady volume of deviance? Sociology has not yet developed a conceptual language in which this sort of question can be discussed without a great deal of circularity, but one observation can be made which gives the question an interesting perspective—namely, that deviant activities often seem to derive support from the very agencies designed to suppress them. Indeed, the institutions devised by human society for guarding against deviance sometimes seem so poorly equipped for this task that we might well ask why this is considered their "real" function at all.

It is by now a thoroughly familiar argument that many of the institutions built to inhibit deviance actually operate in such a way as to perpetuate it. For one thing, prisons, hospitals, and other agencies of control provide aid and protection for large numbers of deviant persons. But beyond this, such institutions gather marginal people into tightly segregated groups, give them an opportunity to teach one another the skills and attitudes of a deviant career, and even drive them into using these skills by reinforcing their sense of alienation from the rest of society.[7] This process is found not only in the institutions which actually confine the deviant, but in the general community as well.

The community's decision to bring deviant sanctions against an individual is not a simple act of censure. It is a sharp rite of transition, at once moving him out of his normal position in society and transferring him into a distinct deviant role.[8] The ceremonies which accomplish this change of status, usually, have three related phases. They arrange a formal *confrontation* between the deviant suspect and representatives of his community (as in the criminal trial or psychiatric case conference); they announce

[7] For a good description of this process in the modern prison, see Gresham Sykes, *The Society of Captives* (Princeton, N.J.: Princeton University Press, 1958). For views of two different types of mental hospital settings, see Erving Goffman, "The Characteristics of Total Institutions," *Symposium on Preventive and Social Psychiatry* (Washington, D.C.: Walter Reed Army Institute of Research, 1957); and Kai T. Erikson, "Patient Role and Social Uncertainty: A Dilemma of the Mentally Ill," *Psychiatry* 20 (1957): 263–74.

[8] Talcott Parsons, op. cit., has given the classical description of how this role transfer works in the case of medical patients.

some *judgment* about the nature of his deviancy (a "verdict" or "diagnosis," for example); and they perform an act of social *placement,* assigning him to a special deviant role (like that of "prisoner" or "patient") for some period of time. Such ceremonies tend to be events of wide public interest and ordinarily take place in a dramatic, ritualized setting.[9] Perhaps the most obvious example of a commitment ceremony is the criminal trial, with its elaborate ritual and formality, but more modest equivalents can be found almost anywhere that procedures are set up for judging whether or not someone is officially deviant.

An important feature of these ceremonies in our culture is that they are almost irreversible. Most provisional roles conferred by society—like those of the student or citizen soldier, for instance—include some kind of terminal ceremony to mark the individual's movement back out of the role once its temporary advantages have been exhausted. But the roles allotted to the deviant seldom make allowance for this type of passage. He is ushered into the special position by a decisive and dramatic ceremony, yet is retired from it with hardly a word of public notice. As a result, the deviant often returns home with no proper license to resume a normal life in the community. From a ritual point of view, nothing has happened to cancel out the stigmas imposed upon him by earlier commitment ceremonies: the original verdict or diagnosis is still formally in effect. Partly for this reason, the community is apt to place the returning deviant on some form of probation within the group, suspicious that he will return to deviant activity upon a moment's provocation.

A circularity is thus set into motion which has all the earmarks of a "self-fulfilling prophecy," to use Merton's fine phrase. On the one hand, it seems obvious that the apprehensions of the community help destroy whatever chances the deviant might otherwise have for a successful return to society. Yet, on the other hand, everyday experience seems to show that these apprehensions are altogether reasonable, for it is a well-known and highly publicized fact that

most ex-convicts return to prison and that a large proportion of mental patients require additional treatment after once having been discharged. The community's feeling that deviant persons cannot change, then, may be based on a faulty premise, but it is repeated so frequently and with such conviction that it eventually creates the facts which "prove" it correct. If the returned deviant encounters this feeling of distrust often enough, it is understandable that he too may begin to wonder if the original verdict or diagnosis is still in effect—and respond to this uncertainty by resuming deviant activity. In some respects, this solution may be the only way for the individual and his community to agree what forms of behavior are appropriate for him.

Moreover, this prophecy is found in the official policies of even the most advanced agencies of control. Police departments could not operate with any real effectiveness if they did not regard ex-convicts as an almost permanent population of offenders, a constant pool of suspects. Nor could psychiatric clinics do a responsible job if they did not view former patients as a group unusually susceptible to mental illness. Thus the prophecy gains currency at many levels within the social order, not only in the poorly informed attitudes of the community at large, but in the best informed theories of most control agencies as well.

In one form or another, this problem has been known to Western culture for many hundreds of years, and this simple fact is a very important one for sociology. For if the culture has supported a steady flow of deviant behavior throughout long periods of historical evolution, then the rules which apply to any form of functionalist thinking would suggest that strong forces must be at work to keep this flow intact. This may not be reason enough to assert that deviant behavior is altogether "functional"—in any of the many senses of that term—but it should make us reluctant to assume that the agencies of control are somehow organized to prevent deviant acts from occurring or to "cure" deviant offenders of their misbehavior.[10]

This in turn might suggest that our present models of the social system, with their clear

---

[9]Cf. Harold Garfinkel, "Successful Degradation Ceremonies," *American Journal of Sociology* 61 (1956): 420–24.

[10]Albert K. Cohen, for example, speaking for most sociologists, seems to take the question for

emphasis on harmony and symmetry in social relations, only do a partial job of representing reality. Perhaps two different (and often conflicting) currents are found within any well-functioning system: those forces which promote a high over-all degree of conformity among human actors, and those forces which encourage some degree of diversity so that actors can be deployed throughout social space to mark the system's boundaries. In such a scheme, deviant behavior would appear as a variation on normative themes, a vital form of activity which outlines the area within which social life as such takes place.

As Georg Simmel wrote some years ago:

An absolutely centripetal and harmonious group, a pure "unification," not only is empirically unreal, it could show no real life process. . . . Just as the universe needs "love and hate," that is, attractive and repulsive forces, in order to have any form at all, so society, too, in order to attain a determinate shape, needs some quantitative ratio of harmony and disharmony, of association and competition, of favorable and unfavorable tendencies. . . . Society, as we know it, is the result of both categories of interaction, which thus both manifest themselves as wholly positive.[11]

V

In summary, two new lines of inquiry seem to be indicated by the argument presented above.

First, this paper attempts to focus our attention on an old but still vital sociological question: how does a social structure communicate its "needs" or impose its "patterns" on human actors? In the present case, how does a social structure enlist actors to engage in deviant activity? Ordinarily, the fact that deviant behavior is more common in some sectors of society than in others is explained by declaring that something called "anomie" or "disorganization" prevails at these sensitive spots. Deviance leaks out where the social machinery is defective; it occurs where the social structure *fails* to communicate its needs to human actors. But if we consider the possibility that deviant persons are responding to the same social forces that elicit conformity from others, then we are engaged in another order of inquiry altogether. Perhaps the stability of some social units is maintained only if juvenile offenders are recruited to balance an adult majority; perhaps some families can remain intact only if one of their members becomes a visible deviant or is committed to a hospital or prison. If this supposition proves to be a useful one, sociologists should be interested in discovering how a social unit manages to differentiate the roles of its members and how certain persons are "chosen" to play the more deviant parts.

Second, it is evident that cultures vary in the way they regulate traffic moving back and forth from their deviant boundaries. Perhaps we could begin with the hypothesis that the traffic pattern known in our own culture has a marked Puritan cast: a defined portion of the population, largely drawn from young adult groups and from the lower economic classes, is stabilized in deviant roles and generally expected to remain there for indefinite periods of time. To this extent, Puritan attitudes about predestination and reprobation would seem to have retained a significant place in modern criminal law and public opinion. In other areas of the world, however, different traffic patterns are known. There are societies in which deviance is considered a natural pursuit for the young, an activity which they can easily abandon when they move through defined ceremonies into adulthood. There are societies which give license to large groups of persons to engage in deviant behavior for certain seasons or on certain days of the year. And there are societies in which special groups are formed to act in ways "contrary" to the normal expectations of the culture. Each of these patterns regulates deviant traffic differently, yet all of them provide some institutionalized means for an actor to give up a deviant "career" without permanent stigma. The problem for sociological theory in general might be to learn whether or not these varying patterns are functionally equivalent in some meaningful sense; the problem for applied sociology might be to see if we have anything to learn from those cultures which permit re-entry into normal social life to persons who have spent a period of "service" on society's boundaries.

granted: "It would seem that the control of deviant behavior is, by definition, a culture goal." "The Study of Social Disorganization and Deviant Behavior," in *Sociology Today*, ed. Merton et al. (New York: Basic Books, Inc., 1959), p. 465.

[11]Georg Simmel, *Conflict*, trans. Kurt H. Wolff (New York: The Free Press, 1955), pp. 15–16.

9.

J. L. Simmons with assistance from Hazel Chambers

PUBLIC STEREOTYPES OF DEVIANTS

The idea that publics "create" deviance through the same symbolic processes by which they invent "baseball," "flags," and "niggers" existed *passim* in the writings of Durkheim[1] and has recently been set forth in a more explicit and systematic manner by Lemert,[2] Erikson,[3] Kitsuse,[4] and Becker,[5] among others. Put simply, the assertion is that "deviance" is not an intrinsic attribute of any behavior, but is instead the distilled result of a social process of labelling.[6]

One of the most provocative outgrowths of this approach is that it has focused attention upon the labelling and imputing social audience as well as on the deviate himself. But the approach still remains a promising orientation rather than a full-blown theory.[7] With a few notable exceptions,[8] there has been remarkably little explicit investigation of public attitudes toward deviant behavior. And for almost all the questions arising from this perspective, we have little more than intelligent guesses as answers.

This paper is a report on four pilot studies which were carried out as an attempt to provide a more empirical grounding for the perspective sketched above. The aim was to explore this labelling process and its consequences by modifying techniques previously developed for studying attitudes toward racial and cultural minorities. These studies yielded some preliminary and "soft" data on the following questions: (1) How much agreement is there about what is deviant? (2) Does the public hold stereotyped images of deviants? (3) If so, what are some of the consequences? Some differences between those who stereotype and those who don't will also be noted.

PUBLIC CONSENSUS ON WHAT IS DEVIANT

In the first pilot study the following question was asked of one hundred and eighty subjects selected by a quota formula designed to produce variation in age, sex, education, occupation, religion, race, and census region within the sample:[9]

In the following spaces please list those things or types of persons whom you regard as deviant.

In response, the 180 subjects listed a total of 1,154 items (mean of 6.4 responses per subject). Even with a certain amount of grouping and collapsing, these included no less than 252 different acts and persons as "deviant." The sheer range of responses included such expected

Source: J. L. Simmons, "Public Stereotypes of Deviants," *Social Problems* 13, no. 2 (Fall, 1965): 223–32. Reprinted by Permission of the author and The Society for the Study of Social Problems.

This research was carried out under a grant from the University Research Board, Graduate College, University of Illinois. The writer is indebted to Daniel Glaser for his advice and constructive criticism.

[1] See especially, Emile Durkheim, *The Rules of Sociological Method* (New York: The Free Press, 1938).

[2] Edwin Lemert, *Social Pathology* (New York: McGraw-Hill Book Company, 1951), pp. 3–101.

[3] Kai Erikson, "Notes on The Sociology of Deviance," *Social Problems* 9 (Spring, 1962): 307–14.

[4] John Kitsuse, "Societal Reactions to Deviant Behavior," *Social Problems* 9 (Winter, 1962): 247–57.

[5] Howard S. Becker, *Outsiders* (New York: The Free Press, 1963).

[6] This does not mean there is "really" no such thing as deviance, or that society is the villain and the deviate an innocent bystander.

[7] This is, of course, also true of most other "theories" in sociology. Cf. Hans Zetterberg, *On Theory and Verification in Sociology* (Totowa, N.J.: The Bedminster Press, Inc., 1963).

[8] Kitsuse, op. cit., and Thomas Sheff, "The Societal Reaction to Deviance: Ascriptive Elements in the Psychiatric Screening of Mental Patients in a Midwestern State," *Social Problems* 11 (Spring, 1964): 401–13.

[9] The questionnaires were administered by members of an advanced research methods class who had been previously trained in interviewing.

items as homosexuals, prostitutes, drug addicts, beatniks, and murderers; it also included liars, democrats, reckless drivers, atheists, self-pitiers, the retired, career women, divorcees, movie stars, perpetual bridge-players, prudes, pacifists, psychiatrists, priests, liberals, conservatives, junior executives, girls who wear makeup, and know-it-all professors.

The most frequently mentioned acts or persons, together with the per cent of respondents who mentioned them, are given in Table 2–1. No type was mentioned by as many as half of the subjects, and only 14 of the 252 different types were mentioned by as many as 10% of the sample. Examination of the percentages in Table 2–1 shows, further, that the proportion *spontaneously* subscribing to a given thing as deviant falls off sharply.

TABLE 2–1.

MOST FREQUENT RESPONSES TO THE QUESTION "WHAT IS DEVIANT?"

$N = 180$

Response	%
Homosexuals	49
Drug Addicts	47
Alcoholics	46
Prostitutes	27
Murderers	22
Criminals	18
Lesbians	13
Juvenile Delinquents	13
Beatniks	12
Mentally Ill	12
Perverts	12
Communists	10
Atheists	10
Political Extremists	10

But the data from this study must be interpreted in the light of the weaknesses inherent in all open-ended responses. We can more or less assume that the respondent means what he *says*, but we can assume nothing about what he happened *not* to say. For instance, we can assume that at least 47% of the subjects regard drug addiction as deviant, but it does not follow that the other 53% do not. Given a list, we would expect 80% or 90% of a sample to check drug addiction as deviant.[10] When you

ask persons to list "what is deviant," you get primarily the denotative definition of a word.

In light of this qualification, the data from this study suggest that there is wide consensus that some types of acts and persons are deviant, but also that a tremendous variety of things are considered deviant by at least some people.

The respondents were subdivided by age, sex, and education but there were few significant differences between these subgroups in frequency of mentioning types. Thirty-six per cent of the females, as opposed to 18% of the males, mentioned prostitute; 54% of those with some college, as opposed to 34% of those who had finished high school or less, mentioned drug addicts; and 19% of those over 40 years old, as opposed to 7% of those under 40, said beatniks were deviant. But all other subgroup variations were too slight to be reliable. Thus, no clear between-group differences emerged, at least with these variables, and within-group variations remained very high.

Because of sample inadequacies[11] the data from this pilot study must be regarded as tentative and exploratory, but they do suggest and lend support to the following generalizations. The facts that even this small number of respondents—all contemporary Americans—named so many different things as deviant, and that there was much within-group variation even among those with the same social background, suggest that almost every conceivable dimension of human behavior is considered deviant from the normative perspective of some existing persons and groups. A fascinating corollary of this is that most individuals would be labelled deviant from someone's point of view.

The range of items mentioned seems to defy content analysis; that is, the items do not seem to have any characteristics in common except that they are regarded as deviant by someone. Thus, *there may be only one sense in which all deviants are alike: very simply, the fact that*

---

[10]A further study using a list to be checked deviant-nondeviant would be useful in providing more accurate data on percentages of respondents who regarded various acts as deviant.

[11]Actually, since such quota samples almost always underrepresent the heterogeneity of the population from which it is drawn, a representative sample would, almost certainly, produce even greater variation of response on what is deviant. Also, response biases—tendencies not to write down "unspeakable" things and tendencies to omit one's more idiosyncratic dislikes—would lead to a spurious reduction in variation of response.

some social audience regards them and treats them as deviant.

A further implication of the above variation in responses is that, by embracing and conforming to the normative standards of some groups, the individual will *automatically* be violating the standards of other groups and persons. To the extent that this is true, questions of deviance and conformity become questions of intergroup divergence and conflict. And to the extent that the individual is mobile he will tend to experience normative cross-pressures. Hence, as mobility rates increase within a pluralistic society, the amount of such cross-pressures and the amount of ambivalence resulting from it will likely increase. As one of our informants said: "I'm not sure what's right anymore so how can I say who's doing wrong?"

This may indeed be one important sense in which our society and perhaps other modern industrial societies are "pluralistic." It seems that there are not one but several publics and normative standards. As a result, societal definitions of deviance become somewhat blurred and standards of right and wrong become issues in themselves. This would seem to call into question the assumption, so pervasive among "social structure" theorists, that American society is composed of a large majority who more or less conform to a broad normative standard and a fraction of "boat-rockers" who deviate grossly from this standard. "Social system" is a devised abstraction, several steps removed from concrete social life, and when we observe conflicts and accommodations among groups and cliques in every milieu, the degree of normative integration within society seems quite problematic.

STEREOTYPED CONCEPTIONS OF DEVIANTS

The "overcategorization" of objects seems to be a necessary and ubiquitous aspect of human thought processes—a necessary means of organizing the infinite detail and complexity of the "outside" world.[12] But such coding is neces-sarily a simplification of incoming stimuli, a *selective* simplification in which information is lost, and misinformation may be added. It must be emphasized that such stereotypes about people and things often contain some freight of truth. But they lead to distorted appraisals because they overestimate within-group similarity and between-group differences, and they tend to be unresponsive to objective evidence.

The other three pilot studies were designed to explore the content of public stereotypes of several kinds of deviants, the extent of consensus on these stereotypes, and some possible corollaries of tendency to stereotype. The types chosen were those usually considered deviant by social scientists and laymen, and they were further picked to represent something of a range of behaviors. The research designs were an elaboration of techniques developed by Katz and Braly to explore stereotypes of racial and ethnic groups.[13]

First, we asked a sample of 89 students enrolled in a social problems class to answer the following question with regard to homosexuals, beatniks, adulterers, and marijuana smokers: "Characterize each of the following groups in your own terms."

In response, more than half of the students wrote a highly stereotyped characterization of every deviant type. The responses of those who presented stereotypes were remarkably similar in content; the only major variation among the student protocols was between those who stereotyped and those who didn't. This variation appeared to be something of a natural dichotomy; the former group expressing an image of the deviate as a dark haunted creature beyond the pale of ordinary life, the latter describing deviates as just people. Illustrative of the stereotyped response is the following description of the marijuana smoker by a male sociology major.

. . . a greasy Puerto Rican boy or the shaky little Skid Row bum. . . . As for the life led, it is shiftless, unhappy, dog eat dog for survival. I guess marijuana is used as a means of avoiding reality. The pleasure

---

[12]For an excellent summary of this process see Jerome Bruner, "Social Psychology and Perception," in *Readings in Social Psychology*, 3rd ed., ed. Eleanor Maccoby et al. (New York: Holt, Rinehart & Winston, Inc., 1958), pp. 85–94.

[13]Daniel Katz and Kenneth Braly, "Racial Stereotypes of One Hundred College Students," *Journal of Abnormal and Social Psychology*, October–December, 1933, pp. 280–90.

that comes from the drug outweighs the pleasure of life as it really is.

The following portrayal of homosexuals by a female sophomore illustrates the nonstereotyped responses.

As far as I know the homosexual is not like anything. They are merely people who have different ideas about sex than I do. They probably lead lives which are normal and are different only in the way they receive sexual gratification. They have no distinguishing characteristics.

Emotional reactions toward the deviants ranged from revulsion to benevolent contempt among the stereotyping group, and from mild sympathy to no apparent reaction among the nonstereotypers. The only exceptions were in the responses to beatniks, in which a moderate fraction of both groups expressed some ambivalence.

The two groups of respondents were not distinguishable by any of the social category variables included in the questionnaire. Some other facets of the open-ended responses will be drawn upon in the final section of this paper, dealing with the consequences of stereotypes.

Following the procedures developed by Katz and Braly and similar studies of racial and ethnic stereotypes, we constructed a second questionnaire listing 70 traits extracted from content analysis of the first open-ended questionnaire. The list included a variety of positive, negative, and neutral attributes from which respondents could choose in building their portraits. Respondents were asked to select those words and phrases they considered necessary to adequately characterize each of the following groups: marijuana smokers, adulterers, beatniks, homosexuals, and political radicals. They were encouraged to add any words they considered descriptively important, but only a very few did so. They were asked then to go back and encircle those five words which they considered the most important in describing each group. As with earlier studies, our analysis is based largely on the encircled words, although as a reliability check we analyzed the entire lists chosen, with comparable results.

The questionnaire was administered to a sample of 134 subjects selected again on the basis of a quota sampling formula designed to guarantee variation in age, education, census region, sex, occupation, and race.

The most frequently chosen traits and the proportion who encircled them for each of the five deviant types are presented in Table 2–2. Examination of the table shows that, for each deviant type, a handful of traits accounts for a large proportion of the responses and that a large number of traits were chosen not at all or only once or twice. Thus, as in the open-ended questionnaire, a fair degree of stereotyping is evidenced.

From further examination of the table, we see that the stereotypic portrait of each deviant type is somewhat distinct in content. The marijuana smoker stereotype emerges as an insecure escapist, lacking self-control and looking for kicks; the beatnik is a sloppy, immature nonconformist; the adulterer is immoral, promiscuous, and insecure; the homosexual is perverted and mentally ill; the political radical is ambitious, aggressive, stubborn, and dangerous. The only characteristic imputed frequently to all five types was irresponsible—lacking self-control. All but the radicals were described as lonely and frustrated. Immaturity was encircled by at least some fraction of respondents for each of the types.

The word portraits are almost unequivocally negative for the marijuana smoker, homosexual, and adulterer. The only differences of opinion seem to revolve around whether they should be pitied or condemned. Characterizations of the beatnik and political radical were more ambivalent and respectful. Each was considered clearly beyond the pale of the ordinary citizen, but a number of positive and neutral traits were imputed to each with a good deal of frequency. The beatnik image included artistic, imaginative, and happy-go-lucky, and the radical was considered imaginative and intelligent. Both were conceived as individualistic by over one-fourth of the respondents. But the preponderant image of both these types was also negative; the positive and neutral imputations were only an attenuation of a basically pariah image.

In order to get a more quantitative idea of the degree of agreement among the respondents in

TABLE 2-2.

Traits Encircled as Descriptively Most Important for Each of the Five Deviant Groups

N = 134

Marijuana Smokers	%	Beatniks	%	Adulterers	%	Homosexuals	%	Political Radicals	%
Looking for kicks	59	Sloppy	59	Immoral	57	Sexually abnormal	41	Ambitious	61
Escapist	52	Non-conformist	52	Promiscuous	46	Perverted	36	Aggressive	47
Insecure	49	Escapist	49	Insecure	32	Mentally Ill	34	Stubborn	32
Lacking self-control	41	Immature	41	Lonely	28	Maladjusted	32	Non-conformist	32
Frustrated	34	Individualistic	34	Sinful	27	Effeminate	31	Impulsive	29
Excitement seeking	29	Lazy	29	Self-interested	27	Lonely	29	Dangerous	28
Nervous	26	Insecure	26	Lacking self-control	26	Insecure	28	Individualistic	26
Maladjusted	24	Irresponsible	24	Passionate	20	Immoral	24	Self-interested	23
Lonely	22	Self-interested	22	Irresponsible	18	Repulsive	22	Intelligent	22
Immature	21	False lives	21	Frustrated	16	Frustrated	21	Irresponsible	21
Weakminded	17	Artistic	17	Immature	16	Weakminded	16	Conceited	15
Irresponsible	15	Maladjusted	15	Sensual	14	Lacking self-control	14	Imaginative	14
Mentally Ill	13	Harmless	13	Over-sexed	13	Sensual	13	Excitement-seeking	9
Pleasure-loving	11	Imaginative	11	Sexually abnormal	12	Secretive	12		
Dangerous	11	Lonely	11	Pleasure-loving	11	Over-sexed	12		
		Imitative	10	False lives	11	Dangerous	11		
		Frustrated	10	Maladjusted	10	Sinful	11		
		Happy-go-lucky	9		9	Sensitive	11		

imputing traits to the deviant types, we calculated what proportion of the total encirclings was covered by the one most frequent, by the five most frequent, and by the ten most frequent traits for each deviant type. When there was no agreement, any one word received less than 2% of the responses; any five words accounted for 7% of the responses; and any ten words, for 14%. When there was a completely consensual image, every respondent encircled the same five words, and these would account for 100% of the responses. The results are presented in Table 2–3.

This table shows a fair degree of consensus among the respondents in imputing traits to each deviant type. One-twelfth to one-seventh of all responses were accounted for by the first trait; from a third to half of all responses were covered by the five most frequent traits; and the ten most frequent traits accounted for three-fifths or more of the encirclings. Since a number of the words overlap each other in meaning, the actual degree of consensus among the sample is somewhat higher. That is, if the traits were distinct, the consensus figures would have been even higher.

It appears that the deviant types are far more similar than different in the degree to which a consensual stereotype of them exists. Hence an attempt to rank the types on amount of consensus would be exaggerating the significance of slight variations.

In summary, the data lend preliminary support to the contention that discernible stereotypes of at least several kinds of deviants do exist in our society and that there is a fair amount of agreement on the content of these stereotypes.

SOME CORRELATES OF TENDENCY TO STEREOTYPE

Like the respondents on the open-ended questionnaire, the subjects of the third pilot study seemed to fall into a natural dichotomy of those who stereotyped and those who didn't. We therefore classified the subjects into this high-low dichotomy by the extent to which their encircled words corresponded with the group of most frequently chosen words (those negative words chosen by at least 10% of the respondents). This classification was then run against the other variables in the questionnaire and a fourth pilot study, using exactly the same procedures and based on a judgment sample of 78 students, was conducted to explore the possible correlates of tendency to stereotype deviants.[14]

To see the extent to which stereotyping was a generic tendency, we computed the associations between scores on each possible pairing of deviant types. All ten of the resulting associations (Q) were significant beyond the .001 level, and positive, suggesting that tendency to stereotype deviants is a general characteristic of

[14]As a reliability check, we "intuitively" coded tendencies to stereotype and ran this variable against the others. All associations were as high or higher than those here reported. For example, the gamma between education and this intuitive coding was .75.

TABLE 2–3.

AMOUNT OF AGREEMENT AMONG RESPONDENTS IN
IMPUTING TRAITS TO DEVIANTS
$N = 134$

	% of all Responses Covered by:		
Deviant Type	Most Frequent Trait	Five Most Frequent Traits	Ten Most Frequent Traits
Marijuana Smokers	12	47	71
Adulterers	8	35	60
Beatniks	11	38	59
Homosexuals	14	47	64
Political Radicals	12	40	64
Expected by Chance	1.5	7	14

the appraiser himself. The associations ranged from .80 to .22 and eight of them were above .50.

There was also a rather marked relationship between educational level and tendency to stereotype deviants. When the high-low dichotomy was run against an education trichotomy (less than high school grad, high school grad, some college) the resulting associations (gamma) ranged from .38 to .64. When respondents' scores for each of the five deviant types were summed, the relationship between these composite stereotype scores and education was .63. Thus a strong inverse association between amount of education and tendency to stereotype was found.

But this finding cannot be taken at face value. For one thing, the associations are largely one-way. The majority of even the most highly educated group expressed unequivocally negative stereotypes toward most or all of the deviant types. The associations were produced by the fact that *none* of those low in education scored low in tendency to stereotype. The "success" of education in teaching more thoughtfulness in appraising social objects is therefore only relative.

In the second place, the response protocols suggest that the more educated groups expressed what might be termed a "secondary stereotype" of each deviant type, derived from the currently fashionable psychiatric explanations of human behavior so rampant in the high- and middle-brow mass media. Albeit, these images are more liberal than the traditional stereotypes and psychoanalytic pity is a softer stance than rigid rejection, these protocols suggest that many of the educated are merely more subtle in their stereotyping.

Sex, age, and the other background variables bore no significant relationship to tendency to stereotype deviants.

In the fourth pilot study, stereotyping tendencies were compared with a number of attitudinal variables. Since this study was also a pre-test of other measures and since the sample size was small, analysis problems are complex and only one of the associations will be presented here.[15]

For this student sample, a moderate inverse relationship was found between tendencies to stereotype and a composite liberalism scale.[16] The associations (gamma) between these scores and stereotyping of the specific deviant types ranged from .22 to .58 and the relation between composite liberalism and composite stereotyping tendency was .57. These associations are fairly modest, but unlike the education findings they are more reliable because they are two-way. Liberals stereotyped less and conservatives stereotyped more often than moderates.

CONSEQUENCES OF PUBLIC STEREOTYPES OF DEVIANTS

The major generalization suggested by the data from these pilot studies is that empirically discernible stereotypes of at least several major types of deviance do exist among the populace. But this finding is important only to the extent that it has consequences for deviants or for society, or both. The finding that stereotypes exist immediately poses the question, what effects do they have?

In the first place, it should be noted that stereotypes may provide useful information for evaluating and behaving toward deviants. To the extent that they contain some descriptive validity, they may provide the same kind of utility as generalizations like "policemen can be trusted to help when you're in trouble" or "wildcats are vicious and unfriendly." Stereotypes of deviants probably do contain some fraction of truth; certainly the populace does better than chance in recognizing deviants and predicting their behavior. However, as Merton and others have pointed out,[17] even those aspects of the stereotype which have some *descriptive* validity may be the self-fulfilling result of the stereotype in the first place.

---

[15]The other findings and many details from the

other pilot studies will be presented in J. L. Simmons, *The Deviant in Society*, forthcoming.

[16]The liberalism scale is a composite index including questions pertaining to politics, economics, international affairs, sex, divorce, child rearing, and religion.

[17]Robert Merton, "The Self-fulfilling Prophecy," in *Social Theory and Social Structure*, rev. ed. (New York: The Free Press, 1957), pp. 421–39.

Second, as Becker has suggested,[18] the stereotype is a major mechanism of social control. The baleful image, learned in socialization, prevents a large proportion of the populace from engaging in that type of deviance or even seriously contemplating it. Becker pointed out that this negative stereotype must be overcome before an individual will become a marijuana smoker. And in our open-ended questionnaire, three-fourths of the respondents—enrolled in an advanced sociology course—characterized the marijuana smoker as physiologically enslaved by the drug.

Third, the negative stereotype results in a virtual *a priori* rejection and social isolation of those who are labelled, wrongly or rightly, deviant. In this sense the person so labelled is literally prejudged and is largely helpless to alter the evaluations or treatment of himself. The force of such negative stereotypes is not necessarily attenuated even when the individual is aware that his image is a stereotypic one. As one student wrote in the open-ended questionnaire:

I realize that this is a stereotypical picture, but nevertheless it is my conception. For me homosexuality is repulsive. It is inconceivable to me how anyone can physically love someone of the same sex.

The negative stereotype may imprison or freeze the individual so labelled into willy-nilly adopting and continuing in a deviant role. This "role imprisonment" occurs because the stereotype leads to social reactions which may considerably alter the individual's opportunity structure, notably, impeding his continuation or re-adoption of conventional roles. The reaction of others, based on stereotypes, is thus a major aspect of the link between performing deviant acts and systematically adopting deviant roles.

It should be noted that this reaction may be somewhat realistic in terms of the self-interests of those reacting. Even the enlightened reformer is realistic in hesitating to let his children become involved with youths who have delinquent records, and we cannot entirely damn a businessman for hesitating to hire an ex-mental patient on an important deadline job. But the

sum of these personal behavioral decisions—many of them made by liberal and kindhearted people—is to make it more than ordinarily difficult for one labelled deviant to perform conventional roles.

Finally, among those known to have committed deviant acts, stereotypes have a selective influence upon who is labelled "deviant." Studies have shown[19] that a sizeable proportion of the populace has committed deviant acts, yet only a small fraction of this proportion is labelled deviant. The fraction so labelled is not a random subset of the larger group. With type and frequency of offense held constant, it has been shown that minority groups, lower class persons, and men, for most offenses, are differentially susceptible to the labelling process.[20] Among those who are known to have committed a deviant act, those who seem to possess additional qualities concurring with the stereotypic image of that kind of deviance are far more likely to be labelled and processed as deviate. Again, to the extent that the stereotype is a valid generalization about a class of elements, this labelling by stereotype may have diagnostic and prognostic value. But to the extent that the stereotype is invalid, it serves no useful purpose and does positive damage by imprisoning innocent people, and people no more guilty than a large proportion of the populace, in deviant roles.

We noted earlier that stereotyping, in the broad sense of building up inferential generalizations about classes of phenomena, is an inherent aspect of perception and cognition. In the light of this, an injunction to eliminate stereotypic thinking is facile and impossible, and it is based, if you will, on stereotyped thinking about stereotypes. We are, it would seem, stuck with stereotypes. But stereotypes are variable: at one extreme they may be myths invented from superstition and misinformation; at the other, verified scientific generalizations. They

---

[18]Howard S. Becker, op. cit., pp. 41–78.

[19]For example, see James Wallerstein and Clement Wyle, "Our Law-abiding Law Breakers," *Probation*, April, 1947, pp. 107–12.

[20]For a summary discussion of this point, see the monograph by Donald Cressey, "Crime," in *Contemporary Social Problems*, ed. Robert Merton and Robert Nisbet (New York: Harcourt, Brace and World, Inc., 1961), pp. 21–76.

may be rigid prejudgments immune to reality testing, or they may be tentative appraisals with the built-in notion that their validity and applicability to all class members is problematic.

Rather than try to eliminate stereotypes about deviants and other social objects, it would seem, then, that social scientists should aim at gathering and communicating valid knowledge, in the hope that this knowledge will form the basis for future public attitudes.

10.

RONALD L. AKERS

PROBLEMS IN THE SOCIOLOGY OF DEVIANCE: SOCIAL DEFINITIONS AND BEHAVIOR

ABSTRACT

The sociology of deviance faces two basic and interrelated problems: How and/or why certain kinds of behavior and people get defined and labelled as deviant; how and/or why some people engage in deviant acts. The meaning of these two problems, the nature of theories and research revolving around them, and their implications for the future direction of the sociology of deviance are explored. The goal is not to account for *either* social definitions *or* deviant behavior, but rather to account for *both* and ultimately to specify the interaction and integrate explanations of behavior and social definitions.

The conflict criminologist, George Vold reminded us some years ago that the phenomenon of crime involves two major dimensions—the behavioral and the definitional:

There is, therefore, always a dual problem of explanation—that of accounting for the behavior *as behavior,* and equally important, accounting for *the definitions* by which specific behavior comes to be considered crime or non-crime.[1]

A growing number of criminologists have become aware of the two-sided nature of the problem and suggest that interest be turned increasingly to the study of and accounting for the contents of the criminal law. They have suggested that the legal norms defining certain behavior as crime be subjected to analysis and explanations sought for why some acts are de-

fined as crime and others are not.[2] One has even suggested that this constitutes *the* problem in the sociology of crime.[3]

While directly traceable to a conflict orientation,[4] this newer emphasis on studying the law

SOURCE: Ronald L. Akers, "Problems in the Sociology of Deviance: Social Definitions and Behavior," *Social Forces* 46, no. 4 (June, 1968): 455–65. Version of a paper read at the annual meeting of the Pacific Sociological Association, March, 1967. Reprinted by permission of the author and *Social Forces.*

[1]George Vold, *Theoretical Criminology* (New York: Oxford University Press, 1958), p. vi.

[2]Clarence R. Jeffery, "The Structure of American Criminological Thinking," *Journal of Criminal Law, Criminology, and Police Science* 46 (January–February, 1956): 670–72; "Crime, Law and Social Structure," *Journal of Criminal Law, Criminology, and Police Science* 47 (November–December, 1956): 423–25; and "An Integrated Theory of Crime and Criminal Behavior," *Journal of Criminal Law, Criminology, and Police Science* 49 (March–April, 1959): 441–552. See also Donald J. Newman, "Legal Norms and Criminological Definitions," in *Sociology of Crime,* ed. Joseph S. Roucek (New York: Philosophical Library, Inc., 1961), pp. 56–60; and "Sociology, Criminology, and Criminal Law," *Social Problems* 7 (Summer, 1959): 43–45; and Richard Quinney, "Crime in Political Perspective," *American Behavioral Scientist* 8 (December, 1964): 19; and "Is Criminal Behaviour Deviant Behaviour?" *British Journal of Criminology,* April 1965, pp. 137–39.

[3]Austin Turk, "Prospects for Theories of Criminal Behavior," *Journal of Criminal Law, Criminology, and Police Science* 55 (December, 1964): 454–55; and "Conflict and Criminality," *American Sociological Review* 31 (June, 1966): 338–52.

[4]Vold, op. cit., pp. 203–41; Thorsten Sellin, *Culture Conflict and Crime* (New York: Social Science

itself has also received major impetus from the theoretical issues raised by an interest in white-collar crime. The very differences between the set of laws regulating occupational behavior and other statutes embodying legal proscriptions and sanctions have raised questions about how and why they were enacted—not just why they have been violated.[5] The study of white-collar crime, as Newman says, calls for the investigator ". . . to cast his analysis not only in the framework of those who *break* laws, but in the context of those who *make* laws as well."[6]

In a recent article, Gibbs notes that one of the major questions left unanswered by the "new" labelling conception of deviance is whether the ultimate goal is "to explain deviant behavior or to explain reactions to deviations?"[7] A re-reading of the literature expounding this approach would suggest that the goal is not to account for *either* the behavior *or* the reaction, but *both*. Thus, in a sense, the labellers have illuminated the two-fold problem of explanation in the broader study of deviance just as conflict and white-collar crime perspectives have done in the narrower field of criminology.

These, then, are the two basic problems facing the sociology of deviance: How and/or why certain kinds of behavior and people get defined and labelled as deviant. How and/or why some people engage in deviant acts. Our research must provide data on and our theories should explain *both* social definitions and behavior. The purpose of this paper is to explore the meaning of these two problems, the *nature of*

theories and research revolving around them, and their implications for the future direction of the sociology of deviance.

THE BEHAVIORAL QUESTIONS

The explanation of deviant behavior must address itself to two interrelated problems: (a) accounting for the group and structural variations in rates of deviancy, and (b) describing and explaining the process by which individuals come to commit acts labelled deviant. Cressey, following Sutherland, refers to them as the problems of epidemiology and individual conduct.[8] Other terms could be used, but I prefer to talk about structural and processual questions. Some want to speak of them as the sociological and psychological "levels" of explanations.[9] Reference to the two problems of behavioral explanation in these terms continues the old Durkheimian polemic designed to assure sociologists that they have a unique discipline. This polemic in intellectual imperialism is probably no longer meaningful or necessary; but if it is, it is not relevant to this distinction between structural and processual explanations of deviant behavior, for both can be sociological.[10]

Research Council, 1938); and Richard C. Fuller, "Morals and the Criminal Law," *Journal of Criminal Law and Criminology* 32 (1942): 624–30.

[5]Vilhelm Aubert, "White Collar Crime and Social Structure," *American Journal of Sociology* 58 (1952): 264.

[6]Donald J. Newman, "White Collar Crime," *Law and Contemporary Problems* 23 (1958): 746. See also Frank Hartung, "White Collar Crime: Its Significance for Theory and Practice," *Federal Probation* 17 (1953): 31; Donald Cressey, "Foreword" to Edwin H. Sutherland, *White Collar Crime* (New York: Holt, Rinehart & Winston, Inc., 1961), p. xiii; and Earl R. Quinney, "The Study of White Collar Crime: Toward a Reorientation in Theory and Research," *Journal of Criminal Law, Criminology, and Police Science* 55 (June, 1964): 214.

[7]Jack P. Gibbs, "Conceptions of Deviant Behavior: The Old and the New," *Pacific Sociological Review* 9 (Spring, 1966): 14.

[8]Donald R. Cressey, "Epidemiology and Individual Conduct: A Case from Criminology," *Pacific Sociological Review* 3 (Fall, 1960): 47–58.

[9]Albert K. Cohen, "The Study of Social Disorganization and Deviant Behavior," in *Sociology Today*, ed. Robert K. Merton et al. (New York: Basic Books, Inc., 1959), p. 461; *Deviance and Control* (Englewood Cliffs, N.J.: Prentice-Hall, Inc., 1966), pp. 41–47; and "Review of Hermann Mannheim, Comparative Criminology," *Social Forces* 45 (December, 1966): 298-99.

[10]Homans seems to think that the argument is meaningful, although he offers a different answer from the "levels" solution. See George C. Homans, "Bringing Men Back In," *American Sociological Review* 29 (December, 1964): 808–18. He resolves the issue by arguing that there are no general "sociological" propositions which cannot be derived from "psychological" principles. Thus, he feels that the two are not "levels" of independent analytic status. This is somewhat unenlightening, however, because by "psychological" Homans means simply propositions about men's observable behavior, and this is not what is usually meant by "psychological." The fact that Homans sees these propositions coming from the work of psychologists such as Skinner does not *ipso facto* make them psychological. Whether a theoretical framework be labelled sociological or psychological, then, is a definitional

The theoretical emphasis in the sociology of deviance has been on structural explanations, however, and we have some fairly sophisticated notions about the kinds of structures and environments which produce certain kinds of deviancy. But this emphasis should be balanced by an increased concern with the process by which these environments do so. Although there are excellent miniature theories of embezzlement, drug addiction, marihuana use, and check forgery, little recently has been done to reconstruct the process of coming to commit various kinds of deviant behavior.[11] Moreover, there have been virtually no efforts to locate the common elements in these separate explanations toward the end of testing or constructing a general processual theory.

Sutherland's differential association theory is notable for standing nearly alone as a general processual theory of criminal behavior.[12] Sutherland recognized that while theories addressed to structural and processual questions may be different, the two must be consistent.[13] Not only should they be consistent, but, as Cressey notes, they should be integrated.[14] This integration is

possible because in the final analysis both kinds of theory propose answers to the *same overall* question of why some people come to commit deviant acts and others do not. The structural theories contend that more people in certain groups, located in certain positions in, or encountering particular pressures created by the social structure, will engage in deviancy than those in other groups and locations.[15] In a sense, they explain between-group variations. But in so doing, they implicitly or explicitly posit processes by which these structural conditions produce higher probabilities of deviancy. Processual theories explain within-group variation. They say that the individual commits deviancy because he has encountered a particular life history. But in so doing, they are also saying something about the deviancy-producing groups, structures, and circumstances he must encounter to increase the probability of his becoming and remaining deviant.[16]

---

problem. I would agree with this concept: If the explanatory variables and processes in propositions about behavior are those contained in or arising out of social interaction (as contrasted, for instance, with intrapsychic, individual constitutional, personality, or unconscious variables) then one is justified in naming them sociological. If the independent variables are social-environmental, then we have a sociological theory whether the dependent variables be individual or collective behavior. It is in this sense that both structural and processual theories can be sociological.

[11]Donald Cressey, *Other People's Money* (New York: The Free Press, 1953); Alfred R. Lindesmith, *Opiate Addiction* (Bloomington, Indiana: Principia Press, 1947); Howard S. Becker, *Outsiders* (New York: The Free Press, 1963), chaps. 3 and 4; and Edwin M. Lemert, "An Isolation and Closure Theory of Naive Check Forgery," *Journal of Criminal Law, Criminology, and Police Science* 44 (September–October, 1953): 296–307. Quinney has presented a miniature "structural" theory of a form of white-collar crime. Earl R. Quinney, "Occupational Structure and Criminal Behavior: Prescription Violations by Retail Pharmacists," *Social Problems* 11 (Fall, 1963): 179–85.

[12]Edwin H. Sutherland and Donald R. Cressey, *Principles of Criminology*, 6th ed. (Philadelphia: J. B. Lippincott Co., 1960), pp. 77–79.

[13]Ibid., p. 80.

[14]Donald R. Cressey, "The Theory of Differential Association: An Introduction, *Social Problems* 8 (Summer, 1960): 5.

[15]Most other sociological perspectives are primarily structural in emphasis. The ones that have exerted the most influence are disorganization-anomie and conflict theory. Although there are now a number of variations on the disorganization-anomie theme, they all derive ultimately from Durkheim. The following are among the more careful and systematic statements on variants of this approach: Robert K. Merton, *Social Theory and Social Structure* (New York: The Free Press, 1957), pp. 131–94; Albert K. Cohen, *Delinquent Boys* (New York: The Free Press, 1955); Richard Cloward and Lloyd Ohlin, "Illegitimate Means, Anomie, and Deviant Behavior," *American Sociological Review* 24 (April, 1959): 164–77, and *Delinquency and Opportunity* (New York: The Free Press, 1961); Arnold Rose, *Theory and Method in the Social Sciences* (Minneapolis: University of Minnesota Press, 1954), chap. 1; Albert Cohen, "Study of Social Disorganization and Deviant Behavior"; Albert Cohen, "The Sociology of the Deviant Act: Anomie Theory and Beyond," *American Sociological Review* 30 (February, 1965): 9–14; Marshall B. Clinard, ed., *Anomie and Deviant Behavior* (New York: The Free Press, 1964); Clifford Shaw and Henry D. McKay, *Juvenile Delinquency and Urban Areas* (Chicago: University of Chicago Press, 1942); and Bernard Lander, *Towards an Understanding of Juvenile Delinquency* (New York: Columbia University Press, 1954). For the most thorough analysis, critique, and modification of that variant of anomie theory which emphasizes delinquent subcultures, see David Downes, *The Delinquent Solution* (New York: The Free Press, 1966). Conflict theories are found in Vold, op. cit.; Sellin, op. cit.; and Solomon Kobrin, "The Conflict of Values in Delinquency Areas," *American Sociological Review* 16 (October, 1951): 653–61.

[16]Other theories which attempt to answer the

The differential association-reinforcement theory formulated by Burgess and Akers avoids some of the problems of Sutherland's original formulation and describes the general process (consistently and integrally with a broader theory of behavior) of deviant behavior.[17] It is capable of identifying the common elements in the separate processual theories and provides the groundwork for integrating structural and processual explanations. By conceptualizing groups and social structure as learning environments which structure the patterns of associations and reinforcement, a long step is taken in the direction of bringing the two together. Differential association-reinforcement spells out the *mechanisms* by which environmental stimuli produce and maintain behavior and the structural theories explicate the type of *environments* most likely to sustain norm and law-violating behavior.

But before we will learn which theory or combination of theories turns out to be our best explanation of deviance, we must broaden our data-gathering technology beyond the traditional research strategies. Compared to those in other sociological specialties, students of deviancy have relatively ready access to regularly compiled data on behavior that has come to the attention of official agencies. Nevertheless, we still do not know very much about even the official distribution and variations in rates of some kinds of deviancy and are practically ignorant of the true distribution of nearly every type of deviant behavior. To test theories adequately, we need to utilize as broad a range of research techniques and as representative data as possible. This means that we must be more imaginative in ferreting out other sources of data beyond the usual official statistics, records, and populations of apprehended offenders to get a better idea of the distribution of rates of deviant behavior. More precise knowledge of the behavioral process in deviancy not only awaits more systematic and extensive use of case histories and analytic inductive techniques, but requires greater utilization of laboratory experimentation.

Reliable and valid techniques of studying delinquency in representative samples of the general adolescent population are being developed, and these could be extended into other fields.[18]

---

essentially processual questions of why particular individuals commit deviancy, although the "process" is not explicit in each case are self-concept and role-commitment theories. The self-concept theory of Reckless and his associates and students at Ohio State is essentially a social control theory containing both structural and individual components, but the burden of this perspective is borne by the conceptualization of one's self-image as an individual selective mechanism which accounts for differential response to environment. Walter Reckless, "A New Theory of Delinquency and Crime," *Federal Probation* 25 (December, 1961): 42–46; "The Self Component in Potential Delinquency and Potential Non-Delinquency," *American Sociological Review* 22 (October, 1957): 566–70; "Self Concept as an Insulator Against Delinquency," *American Sociological Review* 21 (December, 1956): 744–46; and "The Good Boy in a High Delinquency Area," *Journal of Criminal Law, Criminology, and Police Science* 48 (August, 1960): 18–26; Frank R. Scarpitti et al., "Good Boy in a High Delinquency Area: Four Years Later," *American Sociological Review* 25 (August, 1960): 555–58. Role-commitment theories can be found in Howard S. Becker, "Notes on the Concept of Commitment," *American Journal of Sociology* 66 (July, 1960): 32–40; David Matza, *Delinquency and Drift* (New York: John Wiley & Sons, Inc., 1964); Richard Korn and Lloyd W. McCorkle, *Criminology and Penology* (New York: Holt Rinehart & Winston, Inc., 1959), pp. 327–53; and Scott Briar and Irving Piliavin, "Delinquency, Situational Inducements, and Commitment to Conformity," *Social Problems* 13 (Summer, 1965): pp. 35–45. Of course, the impact of labelling conceptions also can be seen to be perspectives on role-commitment. One should also view Short and Strodtbeck's conceptions of gang delinquency as explanations of individual actions. James F. Short, Jr. and Fred L. Strodtbeck, *Group Process and Gang Delinquency* (Chicago: University of Chicago Press, 1965). All of these are consistent with a general learning perspective. I omit multicausation, psychiatric, personal pathology, and other personality theories from discussion.

[17]Robert L. Burgess and Ronald L. Akers, "A Differential Association-Reinforcement Theory of Criminal Behavior," *Social Problems* 14 (Fall, 1966): 128–47.

[18]Of a 32-item bibliography of studies using unofficial measures of delinquency I have collected, the following are cited: Ronald L. Akers, "Socioeconomic Status and Delinquent Behavior: A Re-Test," *Journal of Research in Crime and Delinquency* 1 (January, 1964): 38–46; John P. Clark and Eugene P. Wenninger, "Goal Orientations and Illegal Behavior Among Juveniles," *Social Forces* 42 (October, 1963): 49–60; Robert A. Dentler and Lawrence J. Monroe, "Social Correlates of Early Adolescent Theft," *American Sociological Review* 26 (October, 1961): 733–43; Maynard L. Erickson and LaMar T. Empey, "Court Records, Undetected Delinquency, and Decision-Making," *Journal of Criminal Law, Criminology, and Police Science* 54

Of course, there is much yet to be done even in the restricted area of delinquency, and it could be argued that these techniques are simply inappropriate to some types of deviancy. But the spirit, if not the substance, of the developing technology of unofficial measures of delinquency could be applied to some adult violations. This could be combined with the utilization of official and semi-official compilations. We have not yet realized the full implications of the pioneering work of Sutherland, Clinard, and Hartung on white-collar offenses.[19] There is a whole class of research sites of which we have thus far little availed ourselves—the files and records of private police, detective, security and similar agencies, insurance and management consultant firms, and business and occupational control boards and commissions.[20] Also, we are just beginning to recognize the importance and potential impact on sociology of the very effective experimental technology developing in the operant conditioning tradition.[21]

SOCIAL DEFINITIONS

In the broadest sense, the problem of explaining social definitions is that of accounting for why people come to have the values and norms they do. But more specifically the problem is to learn how the prevailing conceptions of what behavior constitutes the major forms of deviancy in society have come to be established. This entails examining two related processes: (a) establishing the rules, definitions, norms, and laws the infraction of which constitutes deviance, and (b) reacting to people who have or are believed to have violated the norms by applying negative sanctions and labels to them (and applying deviant labels to others not because of their actions but because they possess some physical characteristic or disability). We are infinitely more knowledgeable about both the behavioral questions than either of these two aspects of the defining and labelling process.

Those criminologists who have given thought to the problem of why certain behavior is defined as criminal offer explanations that converge on a group-conflict theme—what becomes defined as illegal is related to the ability of certain groups in society to have their values, norms, and interests incorporated into or reflected in the law and its administration even against the interests of other groups and the general public.[22] Thus, they have been led to recognize the political nature of crime and a well-documented observation concerning politics in democratic

(December, 1963): 456-69; Martin Gold, "Undetected Delinquent Behavior," *Journal of Research in Crime and Delinquency* 3 (January, 1966): 27–46; David E. Hunt and Robert H. Hardt, "Developmental Stage, Delinquency, and Differential Treatment," *Journal of Research in Crime and Delinquency* 2 (January, 1965): 20–31; Jay Lowe, "Prediction of Delinquency with an Attitudinal Configuration Model," *Social Forces*, 45 (September, 1966): 106–13; F. Ivan Nye and James Short, "Scaling Delinquent Behavior," *American Sociological Review* 22 (June, 1957): 326–31; Austin Porterfield, "Delinquency and Its Outcome in Court and College," *American Journal of Sociology* 49 (September, 1943): 199–204; John Finley Scott, "Two Dimensions of Delinquent Behavior," *American Sociological Review* 24 (April, 1959): 240 43; James F. Short, Jr., " Differential Association with Delinquent Friends and Delinquent Behavior," *Pacific Sociological Review* 1 (Spring, 1958): 20–25; James F. Short, Jr. and F. Ivan Nye, "Extent of Unrecorded Delinquency: Tentative Conclusions," *Journal of Criminal Law, Criminology, and Police Science* 49 (November–December, 1958): 296–302; James F. Short, Jr., Ray A. Tennyson and Kenneth I. Howard, "Behavior Dimensions of Gang Delinquency," *American Sociological Review* 28 (June, 1963): 411–28; and Harwin L. Voss, "Socioeconomic Status and Reported Delinquent Behavior," *Social Problems* 13 (Winter, 1966): 314–24.

[19]Sutherland, op. cit.; Marshall B. Clinard, *The Black Market* (New York: Holt, Rinehart & Winston, Inc., 1952); and Frank Hartung, "White Collar Offenses in the Wholesale Meat Market Industry in Detroit," *American Journal of Sociology* 56 (November, 1950): 325–42.

[20]Mary O. Cameron, *The Booster and the Snitch: Department Store* (New York: The Free Press, 1964) makes use of department store detective files. James E. Price utilizes insurance statistics in "A Test of the Accuracy of Crime Statistics," *Social Problems* 14 (Fall, 1966): 214–21. An imaginative combination of interview data and data from the records of drug law enforcement agencies is found in Earl Quinney, "Occupational Structure and Criminal Behavior." In addition, see the rich, but unsystematically reported, cases taken from the files of his management consultant firm by Norman Jaspan, *The Thief in the White Collar* (Philadelphia: J. B. Lippincott Co., 1960).

[21]Robert L. Burgess and Ronald L. Akers, "Prospects for an Experimental Analysis in Criminology" (paper read at the annual meeting of the American Sociological Association, August, 1966).

[22]Richard Quinney, "Crime in Political Perspective," pp. 19–21; Vold, op. cit., pp. 207–09; Sellin, op. cit.; Clinard, *The Black Market*, p. 153; and F. James Davis et al., *Society and the Law* (New York: The Free Press, 1962), pp. 69–71.

society: the passage and content of nearly all laws, the formulation of nearly all public policy, and nearly every public decision, including court decisions, are in some measure the outcome of the direct or indirect political influence of competing interest groups.[23]

Investigation of the political process by which the criminal label is established and applied remains a neglected area, however. What literature there is on this point has been largely suggestive and programmatic, with little in the way of research.[24] We will have to scrutinize more carefully the process by which the criminal law is formed and enforced in a search for those variables which determine what of the total range of behavior becomes prohibited and which of the total range of norms become a part of the law. Certainly these variables would include not only the activities of political-interest groups but also a range of factors in the changing social, economic, political, and normative structures of society, its historical development, legal traditions, governmental forms, and the general political process.

It is the politically dominant subunits of society that at any given time can see to it that public policy reflects their interests, whether these be whole classes or segments, major vested interests, more specialized private groups, or even agencies of the government itself which exert influence in the law-making and enforcing processes. However, the law reflects not only the interests of particular segments but also

the changing needs and functions of the whole society. The extent to which public policy is the result of the victories, compromises, and resolutions of group conflict is an empirical question that must be answered for the specific form of deviancy in question. Empirical research on this question may take the form of longitudinal or current study of some policy-in-the-making or historical reconstruction of the way the policy came into being. Such research is already available on theft law,[25] vagrancy law,[26] public policy on drugs,[27] prohibition,[28] and legal regulation of certain professional practices.[29] But the surface has just been scratched. The field is wide open for sociological research in the process of legislation, the content of laws, and the operation of administrative agencies, courts, police,[30] and other agents of formal social control as well as the operation and function of private police and detectives as more informal enforcement agencies.

Conflict explanation and research into the degree to which group interests form a part of the total political process is only a start. If differences in the power of interest groups accounts for some differences in the laws and public policy, what makes for power?[31] What differentials in organizational and other group properties account for differential political influence? Sociological theory has been nearly mute and systematic research almost nonexistent on this problem.[32]

This type of research should be complemented by research into the variables operative in the

---

[23]Of the vast literature that could be cited on this point, these are among the best: David Truman, *The Governmental Process,* 8th ed. (New York: Alfred A. Knopf, Inc., 1962); Earl Latham, *The Group Basis of Politics* (New York: Octagon Books, Inc., 1965); Harmon Ziegler, *Interest Groups in American Society* (Englewood Cliffs, N.J.: Prentice-Hall, Inc., 1964); V. O. Key, *Politics, Parties, and Pressure Groups* (New York: Thomas Y. Crowell Company, 1958), and *Public Opinion and American Democracy* (New York: Alfred A. Knopf, Inc., 1961), 500–31; Henry W. Ehrmann, ed., *Interest Groups of Four Continents* (Pittsburgh: University of Pittsburgh Press, 1958); Donald C. Blaisdell, ed., "Unofficial Government: Pressure Groups and Lobbies," Special Issue of *Annals of the American Academy of Political and Social Science* 319 (September, 1958); and Lester W. Milbrath, *The Washington Lobbyists* (Chicago: Rand McNally & Co., 1963).

[24]Turk, "Prospects for . . . Criminal Behavior"; Richard Quinney, "Crime in Political Perspective," 19; Jeffery, "Structure of American Criminological Thinking," pp. 663-67; and Jeffery, "An Integrated Theory of Crime and Criminal Behavior," p. 534.

[25]Jerome Hall, *Theft Law and Society* (Indianapolis: The Bobbs-Merrill Co., Inc., 1952).

[26]William Chambliss, "A Sociological Analysis of the Law of Vagrancy," *Social Problems* 12 (Summer, 1964): 67–77.

[27]Becker, *Outsiders,* pp. 135–46; Alfred R. Lindesmith, "Federal Law and Drug Addiction," *Social Problems* 7 (Summer, 1959): 48–57.

[28]Peter Odegard, *Pressure Politics: The Story of the Anti-Saloon League* (New York: Columbia University Press, 1928).

[29]Ronald L. Akers, "Professional Organization, Political Power, and Occupational Laws" (Ph.D. diss., University of Kentucky, 1966).

[30]Jerome Skolnick, *Justice without Trial* (New York: John Wiley & Sons, Inc., 1966).

[31]Truman, op. cit., p. 13; Marian D. Irish and James W. Prothro, *The Politics of American Democracy* (Englewood Cliffs, N.J.: Prentice-Hall, Inc., 1959), p. 336.

[32]Akers, "Professional Organization, Political Power and Occupational Laws."

defining and reacting to deviance by more informal social audience than those connected with the formulation and implementation of the law. The significant theoretical problem here is the relationship between prevailing moral sentiments of the society and the normative stances incorporated into public policy. This concern with the overlap of current public opinion and the contents of the law is part of the old question of whether the law always flows from or can induce changes in the folkways and mores. The reasonable answer, of course, is that law is both an independent and dependent variable in society, but research and theoretical perspectives are needed which define when and under what conditions it is one or the other.[33] Some research has always been reported which utilizes survey data on public views of certain kinds of deviancy and public policy,[34] and "impact" studies have been conducted or are underway in the sociology of law.[35] This sort of research could be combined with studies of the similarities in the norms of specialized groups and particular legal norms.[36] Research of this nature

may not tell us anything about the basic process by which norms are formed and social control is exercised, however. We may have to have recourse to historical, cross-cultural, and small-group experimental studies to get at this question.[37]

LABELLING AND DEVIANT BEHAVIOR

The professors of the labelling perspective contend that the important questions concerning deviancy are: Who applies the deviant label to whom? Whose rules shall prevail? Under what circumstances is the label successfully and unsuccessfully applied? How does a community decide what forms of conduct should be singled out for this kind of attention?[38] These kinds of questions do not exclude a concern with deviant behavior, but they do give it secondary importance. One would expect, then, that this approach offers a valuable balance to exclusive concern with the causes of deviation and the characteristics of deviants. Indeed, some of the research alluded to above has been generated by this perspective. However, the theoretical contribution of this approach to the problem of social definitions has not been as great as its promise.

Today only the most unregenerate biological or constitutional determinist would quibble with the basic contention of this school that the deviant nature of acts resides not in the acts or the person committing them, but rather in group definitions and reactions. Certainly, it has been a long time since sociologists have said otherwise. It is true that in the past we have sometimes forgotten the basically social nature of deviance, and in an effort to untangle the etiology, we have become overly concerned with the conditions and characteristics of the deviants themselves. But this is just another way of saying that we have devoted most of our energy to the behavioral question and have implicitly accepted, as given, the established

---

[33]William M. Evan, "Law as an Instrument of Social Change," *Estudio de Sociologia* 2 (1962): 167–75.

[34]John I. Kitsuse, "Societial Reaction to Deviant Behavior: Problems of Theory and Method," *Social Problems* 9 (Winter, 1962): 247–56; Elizabeth A. Rooney and Don C. Gibbons, "Social Reactions to 'Crimes without Victims,'" *Social Problems* 13 (Spring, 1966): 400–10; J. L. Simmons, "Public Stereotypes of Deviants," *Social Problems* 13 (Fall, 1965): 223–32; Donald J. Newman, "Public Attitudes toward a Form of White Collar Crime," *Social Problems* 4 (1957): 228–32; Edwin M. Schur, "Attitudes towards Addicts: Some General Observations and Comparative Findings," *American Journal of Orthopsychiatry* 34 (January, 1964): 80–90; and Arnold Rose and Arthur E. Prell, "Does the Punishment Fit the Crime? A Study of Social Valuation," *American Journal of Sociology* 24 (September, 1955): 247–59. For a historical treatment see Harris Isbell, "Historical Development of Attitudes toward Opiate Addiction in the U. S." in *Conflict and Creativity,* ed. Seymour Farber and Roger Wilson (New York: McGraw-Hill Book Company, 1963), pp. 154–70.

[35]Harry V. Ball, "Social Structure and Rent Control Violations," *American Journal of Sociology* 65 (May, 1960): 598–604; Richard Lempert, "Strategies of Research Design in the Legal Impact Study," *Law and Society Review* 1 (November, 1966): 111–32; and N. Walker and M. Argyle, "Does the Law Affect Moral Judgment?" *British Journal of Criminology* 4 (October, 1964): 570–81.

[36]Earl Quinney, "The Study of White Collar Crime," pp. 210–12.

[37]See Paul Secord and Carl Backman, *Social Psychology* (New York: McGraw-Hill Book Company, 1964), pp. 323–51.

[38]Becker, *Outsiders,* pp. 1–18; Howard S. Becker, ed., *The Other Side* (New York: The Free Press, 1964), p. 3; Kai T. Erikson, "Notes on the Sociology of Deviance," in Becker, *The Other Side,* p. 12; Kitsuse, op. cit., p. 247.

norms defining various kinds of behavior as deviant. Nonetheless, this in no way implies that sociologists thought that there was something inherently evil or deviant about the behavior itself. Not since Garofalo have we attempted to erect universal or natural categories of inherently criminal behavior, and certainly since Durkheim we have been cognizant of the centrality of social definitions to the conception of criminal and deviant behavior. Yet, much of the effort expended by the writers in the labelling tradition has been to exorcise this nonexistent fallacy.

The labelling approach does rightly emphasize, neither wholly originally nor uniquely, the importance of studying social definitions and the process by which acts and people get labelled as deviant. But when labelling theorists have attempted to answer questions about social definitions, they say little more than what conflict theorists have been saying for some time, i.e., the dominant groups in society will have their norms and values prevail, will successfully apply their conceptions of who are the deviants and become more or less official definers of deviancy.[39] In fact, the most sophisticated statement (going much beyond this) about the determinants of one type of labelling, "criminalization," is in a recent article written from an avowedly conflict perspective, not a stigma or labelling perspective.[40] Rather, although those of this school come dangerously close to saying that the actual behavior is unimportant, their contribution to the study of deviancy comes precisely in their conception of the impact of labelling on behavior. One sometimes gets the impression from reading this literature that people go about minding their own business, and then—"wham"—bad society comes along and slaps them with a stigmatized label. Forced into the role of deviant the individual has little choice but to be deviant. This is an exaggeration, of course, but such an image can be gained easily from an overemphasis on the impact of labelling. However, it is exactly this image, toned down and made reasonable, which is the central contribution of the labelling school to the sociology of deviance.

Thanks to this image, we are now more appreciative of the impact of norm enforcement in the furtherance of deviancy. Societal reaction may deter individuals from engaging in further deviant behavior, but it may not effectively reduce the behavior it was designed to combat. In fact, it may play a role in setting up conditions conducive to subsequent and other deviancy. The stigmatization of deviance may have an impact such that the deviant comes to view himself as irrevocably deviant, becomes more committed to a deviant role, or becomes involved in deviant groups; this influences his future deviance and may force him to participate in various kinds of secondary deviance.[41]

---

[39]Becker, *Outsiders*, pp. 15–18. One example of what more is said about social definitions is Eliot Friedson, "Disability as Social Deviance," in *Sociology and Rehabilitation*, ed. Marvin R. Sussman (Washington, D.C.: American Sociological Association 1966), pp. 71–99. Friedson addresses the difficult problems of illness, disability, and handicaps as bases for labelling as a deviant. He offers a framework that could be applied not only to mental illness which has long been of interest to students of deviance but also to physical illness which has not received much attention. No special mention of the problem of illness as deviance has been made here, but it should be evident that this is another area awaiting further investigation. One can be socially defined as sick but not all sick roles are stigmatized. Friedson suggests that the curability of the illness and the extent to which the ill person is believed responsible for his disability or illness need to be considered in connection with stigmatized and non-stigmatized sick roles. Thus, he opens the way for research into the relationships among these variables and the question of why some illnesses are stigmatized and others are not. Another area of research which should prove profitable is deviation from the expectations of the sick role itself. Certainly, being sick or handicapped may prevent one from fulfilling his other role expectations, but it is also an acceptable excuse for doing so and may forestall sanctions for deviations from other roles. The question is what kinds of deviations from the norms of sickness, or under what conditions such deviations, are stigmatized or negatively sanctioned whether or not the person is labelled as a deviant.

[40]Turk, "Conflict and Criminality."

[41]Becker, *Outsiders*, pp. 31–39; Edwin M. Lemert, *Social Pathology* (New York: McGraw-Hill Book Company, 1951); Edwin M. Schur, *Narcotic Addiction in Britain and America: The Impact of Public Policy* (Bloomington: Indiana University Press, 1962); Harold Garfinkel, "Successful Degradation Ceremonies," *American Journal of Sociology* 61 (January, 1956): 420–24; Richard D. Schwartz and Jerome H. Skolnick, "Two Studies of Legal Stigma," in Becker, *The Other Side*, pp. 103–17; Marsh B. Ray, "The Cycle of Abstinence and Relapse," in Becker, ibid., pp. 163–79; Erikson, op. cit., pp. 16–

This perspective has also generated some ideas about what kinds of deviancy are likely to be affected in this way.[42]

When carried too far, however, this insight serves as a blinder. The labelling creates the deviance, yes, and often operates to increase the probability that certain stigmatized persons will commit future deviancy, and to promote deviant behavior that might not have occurred otherwise. But the label does not create the behavior in the *first place*. People can and do commit deviant acts because of the particular contingencies and circumstances in their lives, quite apart from or in combination with the labels others apply to them.[43] The labelling process is not completely arbitrary and unrelated to the behavior of those detected and labelled. Although errors are made and criteria extraneous to behavior are used, we do not react to others as homosexuals unless they exhibit behavior believed to be indicative of homosexuality, and the courts do not stigmatize with the label of criminal until it has been legally determined that criminal acts have been committed. There were addicts loose in the land long before Anslinger and the Narcotics Bureau were let loose on the addicts. Obviously, the behavior is not itself deviant; it is only because others have defined it so. But once defined, aside from questions of secondary deviations, the behavior is prior to the labelling reaction. One may say that, in this sense, the behavior creates the label.

Such statements do not go far enough, however. Neither behavior nor its social definitions

occur in a vacuum; they are mutually influencing. A given class of behaviors and those performing them may carry no particular stigma or at best be mildly disapproved by the norm-enforcing and conventional segments of society until such time as they become more widespread, visible, and offensive to extant notions of propriety. There is certainly some question about the deviancy of taking *LSD-25* and similar drugs until some and then many began this practice. Who, just a few months ago, would have condemned the smoking of the baked parts of the inside of banana skins? There surely were those who made regular use of certain drugs before that use became proscribed. But that use began to violate other norms regarding drug "abuse," became offensive to large parts of the population, partly because it was by those already considered deviant on other counts, and was stigmatized to some degree. Once the behavior was proscribed and deviant labels attached to those engaging in this behavior, these users became more committed deviants, subcultural support for the behavior evolved, and various forms of secondary deviancy emerged. This then evoked stronger prohibitions and more stigmatized and even criminal labels, which then turned some off and others on the drugs. The theoretical problem, then, becomes one of specifying the ways and under what conditions such an interactive process involving both behavior and definitions will take place. What determines when a behavior pattern not previously specifically stigmatized will become defined as deviant and when labelling increases or decreases the probability of further involvement in that behavior pattern?

17; Alfred R. Lindesmith and John Gagnon, "Anomie and Drug Addiction," in Clinard, *Anomie and Deviant Behavior,* pp. 158–88; and Edwin M. Schur, *Crimes Without Victims* (Englewood Cliffs, N.J.: Prentice-Hall, Inc., 1965), pp. 1–7. For discussion of the impact of stigmatized physical characteristics on behavior of the stigmatized see Fred Davis, "Deviance Disavowal: The Management of Strained Interaction by the Visibly Handicapped," in Becker, *The Other Side,* pp. 119–38; and Erving Goffman, *Stigma* (Englewood Cliffs, N.J.: Prentice-Hall, Inc., 1963).

[42]Schur, *Crimes without Victims.*

[43]Lemert, of course, does recognize this point and consistently maintains the distinction between primary and secondary deviance. Edwin Lemert, *Human Deviance, Social Problems and Social Control* (Englewood Cliffs, N.J.: Prentice-Hall, Inc., 1967), pp. 40–64.

CONCLUSIONS

The two major problems of accounting for behavior and definitions are of equal importance, but both criminology and the broader field of the sociology of deviance have tended to give short shrift to explaining social definitions of deviancy. We have tended to see our job nearly exclusively as the study of those who break the laws and violate the norms. The time is here for increased theoretical and research interest in the making and enforcing of the laws and norms.

Conflict theorists, those criminologists interested in white-collar crime, and those in the labelling school of deviance have been more alert to the problem than have those operating from other perspectives. But we are in the beginning stage of mapping out the parameters and still know very little about the determining variables in the social defining and reacting process.

To give more complete answers to the questions about deviant behavior, increased attention needs to be turned to explicating the process by which individuals come to commit deviant acts, and eventually we must integrate processual and structural explanations. We are not likely to come up with a complete explanation of deviant behavior in general until we tie it into a general theory of social behavior. By the same token, the study of societal control of deviance must be tied to the larger study and theory of conflict, power, and norm formation and enforcement.

Finally, the ultimate goal should be to specify the interaction and integrate explanations of behavior and social definitions. Jeffery has attempted something similar to this regarding crime and the law.[44] His formulation is not entirely satisfactory as a broader solution, however, mainly because it is too narrowly concerned with these rather than the whole problem of behavior and social definitions. It should be said, by no means originally and at the risk of sounding trite and mouthing platitudes, that the solution will need to be general enough that the sociology of deviance becomes simply sociology. Patterned social behavior, both conforming and nonconforming, is the stuff of which society is made, and social definitions is just another term for normative and value patterns, i.e., culture. The study of society *and* culture, of course, is the stuff of which sociology is made.

[44] Jeffery, "An Integrated Theory of Crime and Criminal Behavior."

11.

JOHN DELAMATER

ON THE NATURE OF DEVIANCE

ABSTRACT

This paper attempts a conceptual clarification of several issues surrounding sociological and social psychological analyses of deviant behavior. A basic distinction is made between individuals whose initial socialization is in terms of conventional norms and values, and those whose early socialization is based on deviant norms and values. The implications of this distinction for the manner in which initial deviant behavior occurs, the rewards and costs the deviant experiences, and the effects of labelling upon him, are drawn.

This paper is concerned with the processes by which an individual becomes deviant. Specifically, the focus is on (a) two ways in which an individual may become *deviant* and (b) the *reward-cost* balance experienced by the person who violates strongly-sanctioned social norms.

Reward-cost, or "economic man," formulations

of social behavior[1] are beset by a number of conceptual problems, such as the specification of what is rewarding to given persons. Typically, limited to broad generalizations, applicable to most people in the long run, these statements are more useful in *post hoc* applications than in predictive ones. At the same time, however, it seems clear that, unless forced to do so, most

SOURCE: John DeLamater, "On the Nature of Deviance," *Social Forces* 46, no. 4 (June, 1968): 445–55. Reprinted by permission of the author and *Social Forces*.

[1] See, for example, John Thibaut and Harold Kelley, *The Social Psychology of Groups* (New York: John Wiley & Sons, Inc., 1959).

people will not repeatedly engage in behavior that has unpleasant consequences. It appears, therefore, that people do employ a dimension of anticipated pleasantness of consequences in selecting behavioral alternatives. Further, these alternatives are usually selected so as to optimize the reward-cost consequences of behavior (as opposed to the maximization of rewards independently of costs); this is a basic assumption in the analysis which follows.

It is also assumed that this principle is equally applicable to deviant and "normal" or socially-approved behavior. Many psychological and some sociological analyses of deviance seem to be trapped by its negative social and moral connotations. Since deviance is bad, disruptive, etc., it follows (in these conceptions) that it is caused by other abnormalities ("evil causes evil"). Thus, dope addiction, alcoholism, and prostitution are attributed to abnormal personalities, and crime to the fact that "racketeers" (who are psychopathic) force others to commit crimes under threat of violence.

The analysts' values have interfered with objectivity in another way. To the extent that one wishes to reduce or eliminate deviance, it is difficult to recognize that such behavior may be highly rewarding. If the causes are also viewed as negative, one simply needs to focus on and remove these; the admission into conceptualization of rewards which can maintain deviant behavior complicates both the analysis and the solution. In any case, the potential rewards of deviance have, by and large, been neglected. What attention has been given them has been scattered and unsystematic. It is the purpose of this paper to indicate what these may be, and an approach to their analysis.

Following Erikson[2] a distinction will be made between behavior that violates norms and the labelling by society of the violator as "deviant." The former will be referred to as *deviance* or *deviant behavior,* and is the major concern of this paper. The *labelling* is taken as problematic; it may or may not occur, and an additional concern is the effects of labelling on the deviator's reward-cost balance.

The types of deviance of concern here are limited to those which society (or social scientists?) deems of enough importance to label "social problems." Thus, this analysis focuses on criminal and delinquent behavior, alcoholism, dope addiction, mental illness, etc. This is not to say that the same principles are not applicable to less significant deviations; this is an empirical question and will be left for others to resolve.

In the analysis of deviance, there appear to be at least four distinct questions. (1) The first is the genesis of a given behavioral alternative or deviant role in the social structure; such questions include "What produced prostitution in Western societies?" and "Why did delinquent subcultures develop?" (2) The second addresses itself to the factors that maintain or change that alternative or role in the contemporary social structure; these factors may not have any direct relation to those which caused its initial development. These two are structural or organizational questions. The other two are analogous questions, but refer to the individual and are at the social psychological level. (3) Why did person X initially select a deviant role or behavior, and (4) What maintains his deviance at the present time? Again, the answer to the latter may bear only an indirect relation to the answer to the former.

The distinction between the two levels of the same question is often overlooked. Many authors seem to confuse the historical question of the genesis of the role with that of why current holders of the role have adopted it. Thus, limited access to cultural goals by legitimate means[3] may explain the development of deviant subcultures, but it can explain current delinquent behavior only by assuming that each delinquent was frustrated in his attempts to achieve goals by such means. The latter seems questionable in view of the fact that many youths are delinquent before they make any serious attempt to achieve success goals. Each question is legitimate in its own right; a problem arises only if one confuses the levels of analysis involved.

[2]Kai Erikson, "Notes on the Sociology of Deviance," in *The Other Side,* ed. Howard Becker (New York: The Free Press, 1964), pp. 9–22.

[3]Cf. Robert Merton, *Social Theory and Social Structure,* rev. ed. (New York: The Free Press, 1957). Also Richard Cloward and Lloyd Ohlin, *Delinquency and Opportunity* (New York: The Free Press, 1960).

Extant analyses of deviance[4] appear to be primarily relevant to the two social organizational questions: why deviant roles developed and what maintains them. The emphasis in what follows is on the social psychological questions, why a person selects an existing deviant alternative, and what maintains his commitment to it once selected. These questions will be considered in this order.

TWO PROCESSES OF BECOMING A DEVIANT

Many theoretical analyses of deviant behavior begin with the assumption that each member of society learns the conventional norms and values.[5] Given this assumption, a whole series of problems arises in attempting to explain deviance from these norms: what led the deviant to "neutralize" these norms, with what did he replace them, and how does he maintain his commitment to deviance in the face of strong sanctions? Thus, Cloward and Ohlin[6] develop an elaborate conception of the withdrawal of attributions of legitimacy to conventional standards; Sykes and Matza[7] discuss "techniques of neutralization" of conventional norms, etc. Certainly, this assumption and these resultant processes are validly applied to some deviants, and this process-type will be discussed below.

On the other hand, this assumption is perhaps not applicable to a large percentage of deviants. It appears that many deviants never learned or were never committed to conventional norms. Often, the initial socialization of people who subsequently become deviants appears to have been in terms of deviant norms and standards in that area of behavior. A distinction can thus be made between deviants whose original socialization is in terms of deviant norms and

attitudes and those who are originally socialized into conventional society. Although implicit in some conceptualizations,[8] this distinction has never been explicitly made, nor have its implications been detailed. The process of becoming a deviant appears to be very different in these two cases.

DEVIANT SOCIALIZATION

If one analyzes the background of many deviants, it appears that they were *not originally* socialized into conventional society. In some cases, childhood socialization occurred in a deviant subculture, and was explicitly in terms of deviant (i.e., contraconventional) norms and values. For example, some prostitutes are the children of prostitutes, and their mothers made no attempt to hide this deviant behavior from the child. Harris[9] reports such cases; often the girls learned at least attitudes and expectations supportive of prostitution "at their mothers' knees." Thus, they learned that "men are interested only in sex, and you'd better make them pay for it."

More frequently, the potential deviant's socialization as a child was simply inadequate or lacking. Either the parents made no attempt to systematically train the child to any set of norms, or there were no parents or other adults available to serve as effective socializing agents (e.g., with children who are raised in institutions). Cohen and Short[10] report cases of the former among delinquents, where the child was left to shift for himself at an early age, with little or no training or control exercised over him by parents. Harris[11] discusses prostitutes with similar backgrounds. Here, there is simply a failure in socialization; the individual is not exposed to either conventional or deviant norms and values.

In either case, there is no initial commitment to conventional norms and values. As the individual's self-image or identity develops, therefore, it will not be in terms of these, but rather

[4]For example, Albert Cohen, "The Study of Social Disorganization and Deviant Behavior," in *Sociology Today*, ed. Robert Merton, et. al. (New York: Basic Books, Inc., 1959), pp. 461–84; Richard Cloward, "Illegitimate Means, Anomie and Deviant Behavior," *American Sociological Review* 24 (April, 1959): pp. 164–76; and Merton, op. cit.
[5]Ibid.
[6]Cloward and Ohlin, op. cit.
[7]Gresham Sykes and David Matza, "Techniques of Neutralization," *American Sociological Review* 22 (December, 1957): 664–70.

[8]Albert Cohen and James Short, "Juvenile Delinquency," in *Contemporary Social Problems*, ed. Robert Merton and Robert Nisbet (New York: Harcourt, Brace & World, Inc., 1961).
[9]Sara Harris, *Nobody Cries for Me* (New York: Signet Books, 1958).
[10]Cohen and Short, op. cit.
[11]Harris, op. cit.

in terms of the standards of those around him.[12] In the first case, parents will be specifically reinforcing an identity based on deviant evaluative standards. In the second, the child's peers become of crucial importance, since they will be the primary determinants of both socialization and self-image. In both cases, as the child grows, peers become increasingly important in providing the child with behavioral alternatives and evaluative standards on which to base his identity. If the individual lives within a deviant subculture peer influences will, in all likelihood, be in the direction of deviance.

Therefore, many persons who become deviant appear to have learned contraconventional means and/or goals and supporting attitudes in their initial socialization. This occurs through the normal process of social learning, and, as suggested by the differential association theory,[13] probably includes the learning of attitudes, values and motivations supportive of deviance. To the extent that these become part of the individual's identity, he will have a fairly strong commitment to their maintenance. This type of learning and socialization prepares the individual for deviant behavior fairly directly; it removes the necessity for him to neutralize conventional norms or withdraw legitimacy attributions from them, eliminates the possibility of guilt feelings with which he would have to deal, etc.

With the exception of isolated cases, this type of learning is most likely to occur in "lower-class" or slum subcultures, for several reasons. First, there is some evidence that these groups do have norms and values which differ from conventional ones and support deviance.[14] Here, the socialization of children will be in terms of these norms and values. Second, as Gibbs[15]

points out, all types of deviant behavior—prostitution, crime, addiction, suicide, etc.—are prevalent in such areas, providing greatly increased opportunities for learning such deviance from adult role models. Third, both Clinard[16] and Finestone[17] point out that it is precisely in these areas that conventional normative institutions—such as churches and schools—fail, either by neglect or withdrawal. This failure removes them as potentially effective socializing agents.

In short, considerable deviant behavior can probably be traced to the transmission, through early socialization, of such behavior and supporting attitudes, motivations, etc., in areas (or from parents) characterized by such patterns. There are few, if any, informal reactive sanctions (i.e., those from peers, parents, etc.) in these cases for deviance, and such behavior is quite consistent with the individual's identity. The only potential negative sanction would be through action by formal agencies of social control. To the extent that the deviant can prevent detection and/or punishment by such agencies, or to the extent that they "overlook" the deviance, the rewards (whose specific nature is considered below) will regularly exceed the deprivations resulting from the deviance. Deviant behavior should thus be quite stable and difficult to change.

DEVIANT RESOCIALIZATION

The deviant resocialization process is the one implied in most existing analyses. Here, the individual is assumed to be initially socialized into conventional or "middle-class" society. He learns socially-approved norms, values and motivations. (Whether he "internalizes" them or not is a moot question.) Similarly, his self-image or identity will be based on conventional standards and evaluations, since it is derived from the reactions of parents and peers who employ these in their evaluations of him.[18] On the basis of this socialization, he behaves more or less conventionally during the period prior to the deviance.

The process by which he becomes deviant

[12]Cf. Tamotsu Shibutani, "Reference Groups and Social Control," in Arnold Rose, ed., *Human Behavior and Social Processes* (Boston: Houghton Mifflin Company, 1962), pp. 128–47.

[13]Donald Cressey, "Role Theory, Differential Association and Compulsive Crimes," in ibid., pp. 443–67.

[14]Edwin Lemert, *Social Pathology* (New York: McGraw-Hill Book Company, 1951); and Walter Miller, "Lower Class Culture as a Generating Mechanism of Gang Delinquency," *Journal of Social Issues* 14 (1958): 5–19.

[15]Jack Gibbs, "Suicide," in Merton and Nisbet, op. cit.

[16]Marshall Clinard, *Sociology of Deviant Behavior*, rev. ed. (New York: Holt, Rinehart & Winston, Inc., 1963).

[17]Harold Finestone, "Cats, Kicks and Color," in Becker, op. cit., pp. 281–97.

[18]Shibutani, op. cit.

begins with some event or experience which leads him to commit the initial deviant act or rule-breaking behavior. Any number of experiences may lead to this initial act. First, he may, in fact, be frustrated in attempts to achieve his goals by conventional means. For example, he may find that he cannot get steady employment because of his race[19] or some socially-devalued physical defect,[20] etc. *Streetwalker*[21] is the autobiography of a girl who became a prostitute partly because of the failure of her marriage and her inability to find conventional employment. Similarly, the person may be incapable of meeting conventional standards due to personal or intellectual deficiency. Thus, a mentally retarded person may not have access to conventional economic roles or sexual outlets, and thus be forced to adopt deviant ones. Third, the initial deviance may occur in a situation of intense role or value conflict;[22] by definition, such a conflict can only be resolved by deviating from one, or both, set(s) of standards.

Various psychological motivations may also lead to an initial deviant act. One such factor may be a strong desire to obtain status or acceptance in some group.[23] Thus, a "middle-class" youth may steal in order to win acceptance by members of his peer group. Similarly, Greenwald[24] found that some girls become sexually promiscuous due to an intense desire for affection(?). Winick[25] reports that a number of physicians become drug addicts due to overwork and the excessive demands placed on them. Such a desire to escape from various role and personal pressures seems to be responsible for a good deal of alcoholism as well as addiction. Finally, as Becker[26] points out, the initial act may be unintended; the individual may be unaware that he is violating conventional norms by performing some act.

There are thus any number of conditions or experiences which can lead to the initial deviance. Some of these, such as role conflict or differential access to legitimate means, are a direct consequence of social structural arrangements. Others, however, such as the various psychological motivations, inability to meet role demands, etc., are primarily a function of the individual and his interaction with society. Although all of these might be characterized as "failure to achieve goals by conventional means" at one level of abstraction, this overlooks the fact that very different rewards will be involved in deviance due to the different sources.

Given some motivating condition, the deviant alternatives which are available are culturally determined.[27] Further, as Cloward[28] points out, not all possible alternatives are equally available; the individual's access to illegitimate means may be limited.

The initial deviant act is primarily an individual rather than a social occurrence.[29] Due to some experience like those discussed above, the individual commits the deviance, either alone or in the presence of a very few others. During the period following the act, the deviance is often tentative and secret. The person is not committed to it, and if he engages in it again, he does so in such a way that those around him who represent conventional standards are unaware of it. During this period, therefore, he will not experience any negative sanctions from either his primary relations or control agencies. Thus, the rewards will far exceed the costs of the deviance. This is the period which Lemert[30] characterizes as "primary deviation," during which the deviant behavior has had relatively little impact on his identity or role organization. During this time, both the behavior and his interactions are very tentative;[31] each time he engages in the deviance he carefully gauges the reactions of those around him.

This initial phase may have one of at least three outcomes. First, the person may eschew

---

[19]Finestone, op. cit.

[20]Lemert, op. cit.

[21]Anonymous, *Streetwalker* (New York: Viking Press, Inc., 1960).

[22]Shibutani, op. cit.

[23]Cohen and Short, op. cit.

[24]Harold Greenwald, *The Call Girl* (New York: Ballantine Books, Inc., 1958).

[25]Charles Winick, "Physician Narcotic Addicts," in Becker, op. cit., pp. 261–80.

[26]Howard Becker, *Outsiders* (New York: The Free Press, 1963).

[27]Lemert, op. cit.

[28]Cloward, op. cit.

[29]Becker, op. cit.

[30]Lemert, op. cit.

[31]Albert Cohen, "The Sociology of the Deviant Act: Anomic Theory and Beyond," *American Sociological Review*, vol. 30 (February, 1965).

further deviant behavior. This can occur if those with whom he has primary relations discover the deviance and threaten or induce strong sanctions, or if he finds the deviant behavior itself unrewarding. This is possible because he has not committed himself to the deviance; it has not affected his self-image.[32] Second, if he finds the deviance mildly rewarding, and can keep it secret, he may continue to perform it occasionally, when conditions enable him to do so without discovery.[33] This is probably the adaptation which occurs with many types of "individual" deviance, those which can be secretly engaged in by a single person—e.g., alcoholism, fetishism, when the deviant desires to maintain his primary ties with conventional society.

If, however, the deviance itself is very rewarding and/or difficult to keep secret, the person may begin to commit himself to a deviant "career." This decision may be precipitated by either (1) discovery and negative sanctions from those persons with whom he has primary relations in society, or (2) strong pressure from those with whom he has been engaging in the deviance. (Note that this does not refer to formal labelling by society.) Thus, whether the deviance continues depends on the responses of others, both deviants and primary relations, and the reward-cost balance which the individual experiences. If the person decides to adopt the deviance on a regular basis, it then becomes necessary for him to neutralize or remove the control ties preventing it.[34]

An essential part of neutralization, as a number of authors have stressed,[35] is that of changing normative orientation. The individual must replace conventional norms with deviant ones, or develop justification for violating the conventional ones. This is necessary primarily to protect his self-image or identity. If he can justify his deviance, e.g., through "techniques of neutralization,"[36] he can prevent the negative self-evaluation which would occur if he applied conventional standards to his behavior. Similarly, he may adopt a set of deviant attitudes and standards by changing his "normative reference group."[37] Due to the new standards, his identity will change but remain a positive one even though he engages in the deviant behavior. Either of these adjustments will solve what Cohen[38] refers to as "the moral problem."

In one of these two ways, the person must neutralize the conventional norms and values at some point, nullify them as evaluative criteria for his behavior. The rationalization method is the easier of the two, since it is primarily a matter of cognitive learning. It provides (1) reasons why conventional norms and standards are inapplicable in the situation where the deviance occurs, and (2) justifications for the specific deviant behavior which does occur. The latter may include learning the motivations for that behavior[39] as well as the nature of the rewards which can be obtained from it.[40] These learnings may be enough to allow the person to engage in the deviance without precipitating a negative evaluation. Note that this neutralization is highly selective, referring to specific situations and justifying only specific behaviors as acceptable in that situation. It is only through such specificity, perhaps, that either a reorganization of identity or internal conflicts can be prevented.

When such cognitive learning is not enough to solve the problem of negative self-evaluation due to the deviance, the person will have to change a number of his evaluative standards and withdraw his commitment to conventional norms in order to maintain the deviance. He must adopt a set of alternative norms and standards which will both justify the deviance and provide him with a positive self-evaluation. This is a much more extensive process, requiring a change in "normative reference groups,"[41] "status reference groups,"[42] and a reorganization of one's identity. The individual must also break his ties with those persons who represent conventional society in order for this process to occur.[43]

Which of these occurs is perhaps a function of

[32]Lemert, op. cit.; Becker, op. cit.

[33]Becker, op. cit., describes this outcome in addicts.

[34]Ibid.

[35]For example, Cloward and Ohlin, op. cit., and Cohen, in Merton, op. cit.

[36]Sykes and Matza, op. cit.

[37]Shibutani, op. cit.

[38]Cohen, in Merton, op. cit.

[39]Cf. Cressey, op. cit.

[40]Cf. Becker, op. cit.

[41]Shibutani, op. cit.

[42]Cohen and Short, op. cit.

[43]Becker, op. cit.

how extensive a readjustment is necessitated by engaging regularly in the deviance. For example, adolescents studied by Reiss[44] were able to rationalize their homosexual activity and did not experience major changes in identity; at the same time, this behavior occurred only intermittently, and the boys knew it was only temporary. Similarly, "white-collar criminals" probably learn a number of such rationalizations, and thereby maintain their old self-image. On the other hand, a drug addict probably experiences a reorganization of his identity and roles when he becomes committed to addiction, since it influences his behavior in other roles and he must orient himself toward maintaining a constant supply. Such a reorganization produces what Lemert[45] refers to as "secondary deviation"—a relatively complete commitment to the deviance. This reorganization leads to the adoption of a deviant "career." (It is this type of commitment that characterizes the first class of deviants, those who learn the deviant standards initially.)

If one of these two adjustments does not occur, the person will either relinquish the deviant behavior, retreat to conventional society and conform,[46] or evidence considerable ambivalence and vacillate back and forth. Lofland[47] describes the case of a young man who wanted to join a deviant religious sect, but whose ties with his wife were strong enough that she was able to persuade him not to. Ray[48] discusses the fluctuations between being cured and returning to addiction of drug addicts who have not been able to break their ties with home and family. One force in their conflict is the desire to reestablish positive, stable relations with primary relations. Finestone[49] describes a similar pattern in some of the addicts he studied.

Thus, a strong force[50] in preventing deviance is the response or anticipated response of those with whom one has primary relationships. It is for this reason that deviant behavior is facilitated when it can be performed outside of their

surveillance. Similarly, this perhaps accounts for the high proportion of "anomic" or "unattached" persons found in deviant subcultures. Many of the prostitutes described by Greenwald[51] and Harris[52] had no such primary relationships. Similarly, such ties are weak or nonexistent for a large percentage of chronic alcoholics.[53] In some cases, such relationships never existed; in others, they were weakened or broken during the onset of the deviance.

Another characteristic noted by several authors is that, between the initial deviant act and commitment to a deviant career, many individuals drift into the "grey areas" of society—such areas as the slums or central city where deviance is prevalent. Thus, a number of the call girls studied by Greenwald[54] were recruited in such areas, having come there by themselves from more "conventional" environments. Clausen[55] notes a similar phenomenon among drug addicts. This geographical movement typically follows (or effects) the cutting of primary ties, and the withdrawal of legitimacy from conventional norms. This relocation provides the link between initial socialization into conventional norms and values, and peer group support of deviance. A potential prostitute, drug addict, homosexual, etc., who comes from a "middle-class" background must move into a new environment if he is to obtain access to these illegitimate means and opportunities, to find support from others for such deviance, since it is only in these areas that learning structures and opportunities to play such roles exist.

One can speculate that this necessity of movement plays a part in reducing the number of those found in deviant subcultures who come from conventional backgrounds. Having committed the initial deviant act, and having at least neutralized conventional norms, such a person must still find access to the deviant role before he can commit himself to the behavior. Also, lacking peer support for the deviance in

---

[44]Albert Reiss, "The Social Integration of Peers and Queers," in Becker, op. cit., pp. 181–210.
[45]Lemert, op. cit.
[46]Cohen, in Merton, op. cit.
[47]John Lofland, personal communication, 1965.
[48]Marsh Ray, "The Cycle of Abstinence and Relapse among Heroin Addicts," in Becker, op. cit., pp. 163–77.
[49]Finestone, op. cit.
[50]Perhaps the only major one; cf. Becker, op. cit.

[51]Greenwald, op. cit.
[52]Harris, op. cit.
[53]Earl Rubington, " 'Failure' as a Heavy Drinker; The Case of the Chronic-Drunkenness Offender on Skid Row," in *Society, Culture and Drinking Patterns*, ed. David Pittman and Charles Snyder (New York: John Wiley & Sons, Inc., 1962), pp. 146-53.
[54]Greenwald, op. cit.
[55]John Clausen, "Drug Addiction," in Merton and Nisbet, op. cit., pp. 181–221.

his conventional environment, any negative sanctions applied through primary relations will be more powerful; this itself may prevent further deviance. If it does not, the difficulties of movement to a grey area may serve as a further barrier to the continuation of the deviance, in that the person must know where to go and what to do when he gets there. Finally, once arriving there, he must gain access to the appropriate role structure. Call girls recall having spent a number of days or weeks in places where prostitutes and pimps spend time (such as certain bars) before anyone approached them about the possibility of becoming a call girl.[56]

This analysis, therefore, argues that one reason why deviance rates are not as high among those with middle-class backgrounds is low access to deviant learning and opportunity structures. Again, we see that access to such structures is much higher in central city and slum areas. Those who are born and socialized into such areas have ready access to deviant roles; those who are not must move there. (A number of authors have presented good analyses as to why deviance is higher in these areas.[57] These will not be repeated here.) This also suggests the hypothesis that conventionally-socialized persons are more likely to adopt individual types of deviance which can be maintained without peer support.

Most contemporary writers on deviance agree that peer support for deviant behavior is an important precondition.[58] A number of factors contribute to its importance. First, deviant behavior and supporting norms, attitudes and motivations are learned, just as conventional ones are.[59] In many cases, this learning occurs through contact with peers. Second, some deviant roles exist and can be played only in an organized role structure, with established and controlled relations to other supporting roles. Thus, Becker[60] points out that an individual can become an addict only if he has a stable, dependable relation to a supplier of the drug.

Similarly, a prostitute has to have a pimp, primarily to protect her from incursions by police and other criminals.[61] Third, peers provide primary relations (or replace broken ones) from which the individual can gain a positive identity and self-esteem. They accept him as a person and support his deviant behavior.[62] Peers are thus a powerful source of interpersonal rewards for the deviant, and, in addition, often provide him with the materials necessary to continue in his deviant role.

These considerations are particularly relevant to deviants who come from conventional backgrounds. They need new definitions, social support, and access to the deviant role structure, whereas those socialized into deviance initially may be able to maintain the role without such support. These comments are also more relevant to certain types of deviancy than others; some deviant behavior—e.g., sexual crimes, alcoholism—are more readily performed alone. Such individual deviance appears to be maintained by using other deviants as a reference group, although some studies indicate that such "loners" are more likely to be apprehended by formal control agencies.

REWARDS IN DEVIANCE

As noted earlier, the rewards in deviance are only indirectly related to the factors which produce the initial deviance. Where initial socialization is deviant, deviant behavior occurs "naturally," so to speak. Many of the alternative behaviors which the individual has learned are deviant to a greater or less degree. It therefore requires no special rewards (or failures) to account for the occurrence of such behavior. However, it is maintained over time by several types of rewards which may accrue to the deviant.

Where original socialization is conventional, on the other hand, some positive or negative experience does not appear to be necessary to explain the onset of the deviance. A number of possible ones were considered above. Thus, deviance may result from failure in or lack of

---

[56]Greenwald, op. cit.
[57]For example, Clinard, op. cit.
[58]For example, Becker, op. cit.; Clinard, op. cit.
[59]Edwin Sutherland and Donald Cressey, *Principles of Criminology*, 6th ed. (New York: J. B. Lippincott Co., 1960).
[60] Becker, op. cit.

---

[61]Greenwald, op. cit.
[62]Cohen and Short, op. cit.

access to conventional means of goal achievement, various kinds of role or value conflicts, or other social structural factors. The initial deviant act may also occur due to internal psychological conditions; thus, a desire for status and acceptance, the need to escape from role or other pressures with which the person cannot cope, or the "anomie" produced by the loss of one's ties to conventional society—through death, divorce, etc.—may all produce initial deviance. Given these precipitating events, it would seem that the person will try that deviant alternative(s) which is available *and* which he views as potentially providing an optimal reward-cost balance. Costs here include one's ability to neutralize conventional norms, the amount of "guilt" involved, time and effort necessary, etc.

Once committed to the deviance, through either of the processes described above, the principal rewards which serve to maintain the deviant behavior seem to be the same for both types. Which ones are of most importance in a given case depend on the reasons for the initial deviance, as well as on the type of deviance and the person himself. Thus, different persons may obtain different types of gratification through the same deviant behavior, or the same gratification from different types of deviance. In the discussion which follows, it is not assumed that the deviant himself is consciously aware of these obtained rewards; whether he is is an empirical question.

In any type of group deviance, such as delinquent subcultures, criminal gangs, some dope addiction, etc., where the deviant associates with a number of others, one of the strongest rewards is the status and self-esteem which the deviant achieves.[63] The group typically develops a culture, a set of values, ideals and attitudes, which provide status to those engaged in the deviance.[64] With this status and associated positive evaluations from peers, the deviant can develop a positive identity and high self-esteem. He often has friendship if not close personal ties with the members of the group, and also finds these rewarding. Such achieved status and identity may be of primary importance where the initial deviance was caused by a failure to achieve status through conventional means. The deviant behavior itself is of only secondary importance in these cases; the direct rewards are from one's peers and associates rather than from the behavior itself. Any other behavioral route to status might be equally acceptable to the persons involved. These rewards can be self-provided where the initial socialization was deviant, since the individual's own (internalized?) standards provide him with esteem for the deviant behavior.

A related type of reward is derived from deviant behavior which allows the individual to resolve status or identity problems. Here, the behavior itself is of somewhat greater importance, since it bears a fairly direct relation to the status problem which initiated it. Thus, teenage drinking may be the result of adolescents' attempts to relate to the adult world. Similarly, sexual promiscuity, before or after marriage, may be due to the person's attempts to prove that he or she is a "man" or a "woman."[65] In these cases, the status rewards accrue as a result of the successful performance of the behavior. Such success is typically culturally defined as an attribute of the desired role or identity (e.g., adulthood or masculinity), as opposed to the first case where the attributes and ideals are defined by the deviant group itself.[66]

A third type of reward is the achievement of various material and success goals. These rewards are probably the principal ones in property crimes and delinquency. Thus, robbery, burglary, confidence games, gambling[67] and prostitution,[68] and some homosexual behavior[69] are all primarily oriented toward the material and monetary gains which can be derived from them. It is to this type of deviance that Merton's conception of deviance as the result of failure or inability to attain such goals by legitimate means is most relevant. Here, the specific behavior is of intermediate importance, and is primarily determined by the differential in access to illegitimate means which the individual

[63] Ibid.
[64] Ibid; see also Clinard, op. cit.
[65] Cf. Greenwald, op. cit.
[66] Cf. Finestone, op. cit.
[67] Irving Zola, "Observations on Gambling in a Lower-Class Setting," in Becker, op. cit., pp. 247–60.
[68] Cf. Anonymous, op. cit.
[69] Reiss, op. cit.

has. To the extent that the rewards sought by the deviant are solely material ones, this type of deviance can occur on an individualistic basis. Where the initial socialization is deviant, these may be the only means to material and success goals which the individual has learned.

A fourth class of rewards is the escape from role or value pressures which some types of deviance provide. This is probably the primary reward in most chronic alcoholism,[70] some dope addiction,[71] and the psychogenic mental illnesses. With regard to the latter, psychology and psychiatry have long recognized what are termed the "secondary gains" of mental illness.[72] The person who can lay claim to such a condition is excused for past misbehaviors, relieved of many or all role demands, and thus has a much less demanding environment with which to cope. Sampson et al.[73] found that a group of married women performed aberrant behaviors and were diagnosed as mentally ill and hospitalized precisely at a point where their marriages were about to break up; upon return to their families, the relationship often readjusted and became stable again. Here, the behavior is of critical importance, since it must relieve the pressures that precipitated the deviance. Also, it typically is an individual deviation, performed without direct peer support.

These, then, appear to be the four primary classes of potential rewards in deviance. They vary as to whether they are derived from the deviance itself or relations with other deviants, and with the type of deviance involved. It is probable that a given person obtains more than one of these from his deviance, in varying combinations and to varying degrees. Thus, the addicts studied by Finestone[74] not only achieved status within the group but also escaped from the pressures of conventional values through their addiction. Similarly, prostitution is not only a means to economic goals for women with no occupational skills but may also be an extreme solution to problems of feminine identity. An interesting aspect on which there is no good evidence is whether or not the individual deviant derives status rewards from a psychological attachment to a deviant reference group.

THE LABELLING OF THE DEVIANT

Just as the various types of rewards are of differential importance to the two types of deviant, labelling the individual as deviant has differential effects on the two types. Labelling as used here refers to action by a formal agency of social control; the effects of knowledge of the deviance by members of his primary group have been discussed above.

Labelling an individual whose initial socialization was into deviance, and who is thus committed to deviance as a way of life, probably has little effect on him other than to add more or less serious costs to his balance. These costs are primarily associated with deprivation of freedom and other unpleasant aspects of arrest and trial, or hospitalization, etc. The person's socialization has probably insulated him against any rehabilitative effects these costs might have; he will probably view society's reaction as unjustified, and maintain his commitment to the behavior.

With an individual whose initial socialization was conventional, however, the costs associated with labelling may be much higher. The labelling may end the secrecy of his deviance, and thus his primary relations may be disrupted by it.[75] Second, it may close conventional behavioral alternatives for him; e.g., once it is known that he is an addict, he may be unable to find employment. These two effects, the cutting of primary ties with conventional society and the closing of legitimate alternatives, may produce severe psychological effects for the deviant. In addition, they create a "self-fulfilling prophecy." Without primary relations as a deterrent (or a potential reward) and unable to achieve goals by conventional means, the person may be forced into a deviant career.[76] Also, if

[70]Rubington, op. cit.

[71]Finestone, op. cit.; Winick, op. cit.

[72]Ronald White, *The Abnormal Personality*, 2d ed. (New York: The Ronald Press, 1956).

[73]Harold Sampson et al., "The Mental Hospital and Marital Family Ties," in Becker, op. cit., pp. 139–62.

[74]Finestone, op. cit.

[75]Lemert, op. cit.

[76]Becker, op. cit.

the person cannot neutralize conventional norms and standards, he may label himself as a deviant; as a result, he will incur a negative self-evaluation and may perceive his primary relations as being disrupted. Such self-labelling may produce as much of a self-fulfilling prophecy as does labelling by society's agents.

Particularly for the former "middle-class" person, these severe costs that occur when he is labelled may shift his overall balance to one of predominantly costs. The rewards achieved through the deviance may not be sufficient to balance the loss of friends and personal ties which occurs. (The latter may also reintegrate negative self-evaluations.) At the same time, however, the loss of these ties and access to legitimate alternatives can prevent him from relinquishing the deviance; he may be forced to remain in it in order to obtain the rewards of association with others, and perhaps access to money and material goods. To the degree that society refuses to allow him to "repent" and return to conventional life, he will be caught in a situation where the costs far outweigh the rewards. Thus, *Streetwalker*[77] describes a girl who hated prostitution, but had to remain in it in order to live; she was unable to get any other type of job. Also, there may be explicit costs, in the form of norms and negative sanctions, associated with leaving the deviance when it is within a deviant subculture.

Thus, labelling seems to have the principal effect of forcing the person to remain deviant in order to obtain even minimal rewards. In some cases, it may cause the person to return (or enter) conventional society, but this can occur only when access to conventional alternatives and primary support for doing so are provided the former deviant. Interestingly, the major route out of prostitution and perhaps other types of deviance as well is the same as the route for the initially conventional person —geographic relocation, usually to another city.[78]

CONCLUSIONS

It is hoped that this analysis has clarified some of the issues involved in conceptualizations of deviant behavior, as well as some of the processes operative in becoming and remaining a deviant. The principal difficulty in such analyses is the paucity of good descriptive material about the everyday life and backgrounds of persons defined by society as deviant. Much of the material which is available is obscured by theoretical selection and interpretation which is imposed on the descriptive data. Hopefully, analyses such as the present one and better data will, in appropriate combinations, produce a conceptualization of deviant behavior which will accord better with reality than those currently available.

[77]Anonymous, op. cit.

[78]Greenwald, op. cit.

12.

HOWARD S. BECKER

WHOSE SIDE ARE WE ON?

To have values or not to have values: the question is always with us. When sociologists undertake to study problems that have relevance to the world we live in, they find themselves caught in a crossfire. Some urge them not to take sides, to be neutral and do research that is technically correct and value free. Others tell them their work is shallow and useless if it does not express a deep commitment to a value position.

This dilemma, which seems so painful to so many, actually does not exist, for one of its horns is imaginary. For it to exist, one would have to assume, as some apparently do, that it is indeed possible to do research that is uncontaminated by personal and political sympathies. I propose to argue that it is not possible and, therefore, that the question is not whether we should take sides, since we inevitably will, but rather whose side we are on.

I will begin by considering the problem of taking sides as it arises in the study of deviance. An inspection of this case will soon reveal to us features that appear in sociological research of all kinds. In the greatest variety of subject matter areas and in work done by all the different methods at our disposal, we cannot avoid taking sides, for reasons firmly based in social structure.

We may sometimes feel that studies of deviance exhibit too great a sympathy with the people studied, a sympathy reflected in the research carried out. This feeling, I suspect, is entertained off and on both by those of us who do such research and by those of us who, our work lying in other areas, only read the results. Will the research, we wonder, be distorted by that sympathy? Will it be of use in

SOURCE: Howard S. Becker, "Whose Side Are We On?" *Social Problems* 14, no. 3 (Winter, 1967): 239–47. Reprinted by Permission of the author and The Society for the Study of Social Problems. Presidential address, delivered at the annual meeting of the Society for the Study of Social Problems, Miami Beach, August, 1966.

the construction of scientific theory or in the application of scientific knowledge to the practical problems of society? Or will the bias introduced by taking sides spoil it for those uses?

We seldom make the feeling explicit. Instead, it appears as a lingering worry for sociological readers, who would like to be sure they can trust what they read, and a troublesome area of self-doubt for those who do the research, who would like to be sure that whatever sympathies they feel are not professionally unseemly and will not, in any case, seriously flaw their work. That the worry affects both readers and researchers indicates that it lies deeper than the superficial differences that divide sociological schools of thought, and that its roots must be sought in characteristics of society that affect us all, whatever our methodological or theoretical persuasion.

If the feeling were made explicit, it would take the form of an accusation that the sympathies of the researcher have biased his work and distorted his findings. Before exploring its structural roots, let us consider what the manifest meaning of the charge might be.

It might mean that we have acquired some sympathy with the group we study sufficient to deter us from publishing those of our results which might prove damaging to them. One can imagine a liberal sociologist who set out to disprove some of the common stereotypes held about a minority group. To his dismay, his investigation reveals that some of the stereotypes are unfortunately true. In the interests of justice and liberalism, he might well be tempted, and might even succumb to the temptation, to suppress those findings, publishing with scientific candor the other results which confirmed his beliefs.

But this seems not really to be the heart of the charge, because sociologists who study deviance do not typically hide things about the people they study. They are mostly willing to grant that there is something going on that put the deviants in the position they are in, even if they are not willing to grant that it is what the people they studied were originally accused of.

A more likely meaning of the charge, I think, is this. In the course of our work and for who knows what private reasons, we fall into deep sympathy with the people we are studying, so that while the rest of the society views them as unfit in one or another respect for the deference ordinarily accorded a fellow citizen, we believe that they are at least as good as anyone else, more sinned against than sinning. Because of this, we do not give a balanced picture. We focus too much on questions whose answers show that the supposed deviant is morally in the right and the ordinary citizen morally in the wrong. We neglect to ask those questions whose answers will show that the deviant, after all, has done something pretty rotten and, indeed, pretty much deserves what he gets. In consequence, our overall assessment of the problem being studied is one-sided. What we produce is a whitewash of the deviant and a condemnation, if only by implication, of those respectable citizens who, we think, have made the deviant what he is.

It is to this version that I devote the rest of my remarks. I will look first, however, not at the truth or falsity of the charge, but rather at the circumstances in which it is typically made and felt. The sociology of knowledge cautions us to distinguish between the truth of a statement and an assessment of the circumstances under which that statement is made; though we trace an argument to its source in the interests of the person who made it, we have still not proved it false. Recognizing the point and promising to address it eventually, I shall turn to the typical situations in which the accusation of bias arises.

When do we accuse ourselves and our fellow sociologists of bias? I think an inspection of representative instances would show that the accusation arises, in one important class of cases, when the research gives credence, in any serious way, to the perspective of the subordinate group in some hierarchical relationship. In the case of deviance, the hierarchical relation-

ship is a moral one. The superordinate parties in the relationship are those who represent the forces of approved and official morality; the subordinate parties are those who, it is alleged, have violated that morality.

Though deviance is a typical case, it is by no means the only one. Similar situations, and similar feelings that our work is biased, occur in the study of schools, hospitals, asylums and prisons, in the study of physical as well as mental illness, in the study of both "normal" and delinquent youth. In these situations, the superordinate parties are usually the official and professional authorities in charge of some important institution, while the subordinates are those who make use of the services of that institution. Thus, the police are the superordinates, drug addicts are the subordinates; professors and administrators, principals and teachers, are the superordinates while students and pupils are the subordinates; physicians are the superordinates, their patients the subordinates.

All of these cases represent one of the typical situations in which researchers accuse themselves and are accused of bias. It is a situation in which, while conflict and tension exist in the hierarchy, the conflict has not become openly political. The conflicting segments or ranks are not organized for conflict; no one attempts to alter the shape of the hierarchy. While subordinates may complain about the treatment they receive from those above them, they do not propose to move to a position of equality with them, or to reverse positions in the hierarchy. Thus, no one proposes that addicts should make and enforce laws for policemen, that patients should prescribe for doctors, or that adolescents should give orders to adults. We can call this the *apolitical* case.

In the second case, the accusation of bias is made in a situation that is frankly political. The parties to the hierarchical relationship engage in organized conflict, attempting either to maintain or change existing relations of power and authority. Whereas in the first case subordinates are typically unorganized and thus have, as we shall see, little to fear from a researcher, subordinate parties in a political situation may have much to lose. When the situation is political, the researcher may accuse himself or be accused of bias by someone else when he gives credence to the perspective of either party to the political conflict. I leave the political for later and turn now to the problem of bias in apolitical situations.[1]

We provoke the suspicion that we are biased in favor of the subordinate parties in an apolitical arrangement when we tell the story from their point of view. We may, for instance, investigate their complaints, even though they are subordinates, about the way things are run just as though one ought to give their complaints as much credence as the statements of responsible officials. We provoke the charge when we assume, for the purposes of our research, that subordinates have as much right to be heard as superordinates, that they are as likely to be telling the truth as they see it as superordinates, that what they say about the institution has a right to be investigated and have its truth or falsity established, even though responsible officials assure us that it is unnecessary because the charges are false.

We can use the notion of a *hierarchy of credibility* to understand this phenomenon. In any system of ranked groups, participants take it as given that members of the highest group have the right to define the way things really are. In any organization, no matter what the rest of the organization chart shows, the arrows indicating the flow of information point up, thus demonstrating (at least formally) that those at the top have access to a more complete picture of what is going on than anyone else. Members of lower groups will have incomplete information, and their view of reality will be partial and distorted in consequence. Therefore, from the point of view of a well socialized participant in the system, any tale told by those at the top intrinsically deserves to be regarded as the most credible account obtainable of the organizations' workings. And since, as Sumner pointed out, matters of rank and status are

contained in the mores,[2] this belief has a moral quality. We are, if we are proper members of the group, morally bound to accept the definition imposed on reality by a superordinate group in preference to the definitions espoused by subordinates. (By analogy, the same argument holds for the social classes of a community.) Thus, credibility and the right to be heard are differentially distributed through the ranks of the system.

As sociologists, we provoke the charge of bias, in ourselves and others, by refusing to give credence and deference to an established status order, in which knowledge of truth and the right to be heard are not equally distributed. "Everyone knows" that responsible professionals know more about things than laymen, that police are more respectable and their words ought to be taken more seriously than those of the deviants and criminals with whom they deal. By refusing to accept the hierarchy of credibility, we express disrespect for the entire established order.

We compound our sin and further provoke charges of bias by not giving immediate attention and "equal time" to the apologies and explanations of official authority. If, for instance, we are concerned with studying the way of life inmates in a mental hospital build up for themselves, we will naturally be concerned with the constraints and conditions created by the actions of the administrators and physicians who run the hospital. But, unless we also make the administrators and physicians the object of our study (a possibility I will consider later), we will not inquire into why those conditions and constraints are present. We will not give responsible officials a chance to explain themselves and give their reasons for acting as they do, a chance to show why the complaints of inmates are not justified.

It is odd that, when we perceive bias, we usually see it in these circumstances. It is odd because it is easily ascertained that a great many more studies are biased in the direction of the interests of responsible officials than the other way around. We may accuse an occasional

---

[1]No situation is necessarily political or apolitical. An apolitical situation can be transformed into a political one by the open rebellion of subordinate ranks, and a political situation can subside into one in which an accommodation has been reached and a new hierarchy been accepted by the participants. The categories, while analytically useful, do not represent a fixed division existing in real life.

[2]William Graham Sumner, "Status in the Folkways," *Folkways* (New York: The New American Library, Inc., 1960), pp. 72–73.

student of medical sociology of having given too much emphasis to the complaints of patients. But is it not obvious that most medical sociologists look at things from the point of view of the doctors? A few sociologists may be sufficiently biased in favor of youth to grant credibility to their account of how the adult world treats them. But why do we not accuse other sociologists who study youth of being biased in favor of adults? Most research on youth, after all, is clearly designed to find out why youth are so troublesome for adults, rather than asking the equally interesting sociological question: "Why do adults make so much trouble for youth?" Similarly, we accuse those who take the complaints of mental patients seriously of bias; what about those sociologists who only take seriously the complaints of physicians, families and others about mental patients?

Why this disproportion in the direction of accusations of bias? Why do we more often accuse those who are on the side of subordinates than those who are on the side of superordinates? Because, when we make the former accusation, we have, like the well socialized members of our society most of us are, accepted the hierarchy of credibility and taken over the accusation made by responsible officials.

The reason responsible officials make the accusation so frequently is precisely because they are responsible. They have been entrusted with the care and operation of one or another of our important institutions: schools, hospitals, law enforcement, or whatever. They are the ones who, by virtue of their official position and the authority that goes with it, are in a position to "do something" when things are not what they should be and, similarly, are the ones who will be held to account if they fail to "do something" or if what they do is, for whatever reason, inadequate.

Because they are responsible in this way, officials usually have to lie. That is a gross way of putting it, but not inaccurate. Officials must lie because things are seldom as they ought to be. For a great variety of reasons, well-known to sociologists, institutions are refractory. They do not perform as society would like them to. Hospitals do not cure people; prisons do not rehabilitate prisoners; schools do not educate

students. Since they are supposed to, officials develop ways both of denying the failure of the institution to perform as it should and explaining those failures which cannot be hidden. An account of an institution's operation from the point of view of subordinates therefore casts doubt on the official line and may possibly expose it as a lie.[3]

For reasons that are a mirror image of those of officials, subordinates in an apolitical hierarchical relationship have no reason to complain of the bias of sociological research oriented toward the interests of superordinates. Subordinates typically are not organized in such a fashion as to be responsible for the overall operation of an institution. What happens in a school is credited or debited to the faculty and administrators; they can be identified and held to account. Even though the failure of a school may be the fault of the pupils, they are not so organized that any one of them is responsible for any failure but his own. If he does well, while others all around him flounder, cheat and steal, that is none of his affair, despite the attempt of honor codes to make it so. As long as the sociological report on his school says that every student there but one is a liar and a cheat, all the students will feel complacent, knowing they are the one exception. More likely, they will never hear of the report at all or, if they do, will reason that they will be gone before long, so what difference does it make? The lack of organization among subordinate members of an institutionalized relationship means that, having no responsibility for the group's welfare, they likewise have no complaints if someone maligns it. The sociologist who favors officialdom will be spared the accusation of bias.

And thus we see why we accuse ourselves of bias only when we take the side of the subordinate. It is because, in a situation that is not openly political, with the major issues defined as arguable, we join responsible officials and the man in the street in an unthinking acceptance

---

[3] I have stated a portion of this argument more briefly in "Problems of Publication of Field Studies," in *Reflections on Community Studies,* ed. Arthur Vidich, Joseph Bensman, and Maurice Stein (New York: John Wiley and Sons, Inc., 1964), pp. 267–84.

of the hierarchy of credibility. We assume with them that the man at the top knows best. We do not realize that there are sides to be taken and that we are taking one of them.

The same reasoning allows us to understand why the researcher has the same worry about the effect of his sympathies on his work as his uninvolved colleague. The hierarchy of credibility is a feature of society whose existence we cannot deny, even if we disagree with its injunction to believe the man at the top. When we acquire sufficient sympathy with subordinates to see things from their perspective, we know that we are flying in the face of what "everyone knows." The knowledge gives us pause and causes us to share, however briefly, the doubt of our colleagues.

When a situation has been defined politically, the second type of case I want to discuss, matters are quite different. Subordinates have some degree of organization and, with that, spokesmen, their equivalent of responsible officials. Spokesmen, while they cannot actually be held responsible for what members of their group do, make assertions on their behalf and are held responsible for the truth of those assertions. The group engages in political activity designed to change existing hierarchical relationships and the credibility of its spokesmen directly affects its political fortunes. Credibility is not the only influence, but the group can ill-afford having the definition of reality proposed by its spokesmen discredited, for the immediate consequence will be some loss of political power.

Superordinate groups have their spokesmen too, and they are confronted with the same problem: to make statements about reality that are politically effective without being easily discredited. The political fortunes of the superordinate group—its ability to hold the status changes demanded by lower groups to a minimum—do not depend as much on credibility, for the group has other kinds of power available as well.

When we do research in a political situation we are in double jeopardy, for the spokesmen of both involved groups will be sensitive to the implications of our work. Since they propose openly conflicting definitions of reality, our statement of our problem is in itself likely to call into question and make problematic, at least for the purposes of our research, one or the other definition. And our results will do the same.

The hierarchy of credibility operates in a different way in the political situation than it does in the apolitical one. In the political situation, it is precisely one of the things at issue. Since the political struggle calls into question the legitimacy of the existing rank system, it necessarily calls into question at the same time the legitimacy of the associated judgments of credibility. Judgments of who has a right to define the nature of reality that are taken for granted in an apolitical situation become matters of argument.

Oddly enough, we are, I think, less likely to accuse ourselves and one another of bias in a political than in an apolitical situation, for at least two reasons. First, because the hierarchy of credibility has been openly called into question, we are aware that there are at least two sides to the story and so do not think it unseemly to investigate the situation from one or another of the contending points of view. We know, for instance, that we must grasp the perspectives of both the resident of Watts and of the Los Angeles policeman if we are to understand what went on in that outbreak.

Second, it is no secret that most sociologists are politically liberal to one degree or another. Our political preferences dictate the side we will be on and, since those preferences are shared by most of our colleagues, few are ready to throw the first stone or are even aware that stone-throwing is a possibility. We usually take the side of the underdog; we are for Negroes and against Fascists. We do not think anyone biased who does research designed to prove that the former are not as bad as people think or that the latter are worse. In fact, in these circumstances we are quite willing to regard the question of bias as a matter to be dealt with by the use of technical safeguards.

We are thus apt to take sides with equal innocence and lack of thought, though for different reasons, in both apolitical and political situations. In the first, we adopt the commonsense view which awards unquestioned credibility to the responsible official. (This is not to deny that a few of us, because something in our experience has alerted them to the possibility, may question the conventional hierarchy of credibility in the special area of our expertise.) In the second case, we take our politics so for granted that it supplants convention in dictating whose side we will be on. (I do not deny, either, that some few sociologists may deviate politically from their liberal colleagues, either to the right or the left, and thus be more liable to question that convention.)

In any event, even if our colleagues do not accuse us of bias in research in a political situation, the interested parties will. Whether they are foreign politicians who object to studies of how the stability of their government may be maintained in the interest of the United States (as in the *Camelot* affair)[4] or domestic civil rights leaders who object to an analysis of race problems that centers on the alleged deficiencies of the Negro family (as in the reception given to the Moynihan Report),[5] interested parties are quick to make accusations of bias and distortion. They base the accusation not on failures of technique or method, but on conceptual defects. They accuse the sociologist not of getting false data but of not getting all the data relevant to the problem. They accuse him, in other words, of seeing things from the perspective of only one party to the conflict. But the accusation is likely to be made by interested parties and not by sociologists themselves.

What I have said so far is all sociology of knowledge, suggesting by whom, in what situations and for what reasons sociologists will be accused of bias and distortion. I have not yet addressed the question of the truth of the accusations, of whether our findings are distorted by our sympathy for those we study. I have implied a partial answer, namely, that there is no position from which sociological research can be done that is not biased in one or another way.

We must always look at the matter from someone's point of view. The scientist who proposes to understand society must, as Mead long ago pointed out, get into the situation enough to have a perspective on it. And it is likely that his perspective will be greatly affected by whatever positions are taken by any or all of the other participants in that varied situation. Even if his participation is limited to reading in the field, he will necessarily read the arguments of partisans of one or another side to a relationship and will thus be affected, at least, by having suggested to him what the relevant arguments and issues are. A student of medical sociology may decide that he will take neither the perspective of the patient nor the perspective of the physician, but he will necessarily take a perspective that impinges on the many questions that arise between physicians and patients; no matter what perspective he takes, his work either will take into account the attitude of subordinates, or it will not. If he fails to consider the questions they raise, he will be working on the side of the officials. If he does raise those questions seriously and does find, as he may, that there is some merit in them, he will then expose himself to the outrage of the officials and of all those sociologists who award them the top spot in the hierarchy of credibility. Almost all the topics that sociologists study, at least those that have some relation to the real world around us, are seen by society as morality plays and we shall find ourselves, willy-nilly, taking part in those plays on one side or the other.

There is another possibility. We may, in some cases, take the point of view of some third party not directly implicated in the hierarchy we are investigating. Thus, a Marxist might feel that it is not worth distinguishing between Democrats and Republicans, or between big business and big labor, in each case both groups being equally inimical to the interests of the workers. This would indeed make us neutral with respect to the two groups at hand, but would only mean that we had enlarged the scope of the political conflict to include a party not ordinarily brought in whose view the sociologist was taking.

We can never avoid taking sides. So we are left with the question of whether taking sides means that some distortion is introduced into

---

[4]See Irving Louis Horowitz, "The Life and Death of Project Camelot," *Transaction* 3 (November–December, 1965): 3–7, 44–47.

[5]See Lee Rainwater and William L. Yancey, "Black Families and the White House," ibid. 3 (July–August, 1966): 6–11, 48–53.

our work so great as to make it useless. Or, less drastically, whether some distortion is introduced that must be taken into account before the results of our work can be used. I do not refer here to feeling that the picture given by the research is not "balanced," the indignation aroused by having a conventionally discredited definition of reality given priority or equality with what "everyone knows," for it is clear that we cannot avoid that. That is the problem of officials, spokesmen and interested parties, not ours. Our problem is to make sure that, whatever point of view we take, our research meets the standards of good scientific work, that our unavoidable sympathies do not render our results invalid.

We might distort our findings, because of our sympathy with one of the parties in the relationship we are studying, by misusing the tools and techniques of our discipline. We might introduce loaded questions into a questionnaire, or act in some way in a field situation such that people would be constrained to tell us only the kind of thing we are already in sympathy with. All of our research techniques are hedged about with precautionary measures designed to guard against these errors. Similarly, though more abstractly, every one of our theories presumably contains a set of directives which exhaustively covers the field we are to study, specifying all the things we are to look at and take into account in our research. By using our theories and techniques impartially, we ought to be able to study all the things that need to be studied in such a way as to get all the facts we require, even though some of the questions that will be raised and some of the facts that will be produced run counter to our biases.

But the question may be precisely this. Given all our techniques of theoretical and technical control, how can we be sure that we will apply them impartially and across the board as they need to be applied? Our textbooks in methodology are no help here. They tell us how to guard against error, but they do not tell us how to make sure that we will use all the safeguards available to us. We can, for a start, try to avoid sentimentality. We are sentimental when we refuse, for whatever reason, to investigate some matter that should properly be regarded as

problematic. We are sentimental, especially, when our reason is that we would prefer not to know what is going on, if to know would be to violate some sympathy whose existence we may not even be aware of. Whatever side we are on, we must use our techniques impartially enough that a belief to which we are especially sympathetic could be proved untrue. We must always inspect our work carefully enough to know whether our techniques and theories are open enough to allow that possibility.

Let us consider, finally, what might seem a simple solution to the problems posed. If the difficulty is that we gain sympathy with underdogs by studying them, is it not also true that the superordinates in a hierarchical relationship usually have their own superordinates with whom they must contend? Is it not true that we might study those superordinates or subordinates, presenting their point of view on their relations with their superiors and thus gaining a deeper sympathy with them and avoiding the bias of one-sided identification with those below them? This is appealing, but deceptively so. For it only means that we will get into the same trouble with a new set of officials.

It is true, for instance, that the administrators of a prison are not free to do as they wish, not free to be responsive of the desires of inmates, for instance. If one talks to such an official, he will commonly tell us, in private, that of course the subordinates in the relationship have some right on their side, but that they fail to understand that his desire to do better is frustrated by his superiors or by the regulations they have established. Thus, if a prison administrator is angered because we take the complaints of his inmates seriously, we may feel that we can get around that and get a more balanced picture by interviewing him and his associates. If we do, we may then write a report which *his* superiors will respond to with cries of "bias." They, in their turn, will say that we have not presented a balanced picture, because we have not looked at *their* side of it. And we may worry that what they say is true.

The point is obvious. By pursuing this seemingly simple solution, we arrive at a problem of infinite regress. For everyone has someone standing above him who prevents him from doing things just as he likes. If we question the superiors of the prison administrator, a state department of corrections or prisons, they will complain of the governor and the legislature. And if we go to the governor and the legislature, they will complain of lobbyists, party machines, the public and the newspapers. There is no end to it and we can never have a "balanced picture" until we have studied all of society simultaneously. I do not propose to hold my breath until that happy day.

We can, I think, satisfy the demands of our science by always making clear the limits of what we have studied, marking the boundaries beyond which our findings cannot be safely applied. Not just the conventional disclaimer, in which we warn that we have only studied a prison in New York or California and the findings may not hold in the other forty-nine states—which is not a useful procedure anyway, since the findings may very well hold if the conditions are the same elsewhere. I refer to a more sociological disclaimer in which we say, for instance, that we have studied the prison through the eyes of the inmates and not through the eyes of the guards or other involved parties. We warn people, thus, that our study tells us only how things look from that vantage point—what kinds of objects guards are in the prisoners' world—and does not attempt to explain why guards do what they do or to absolve the guards of what may seem, from the prisoners' side, morally unacceptable behavior. This will not protect us from accusations of bias, however, for the guards will still be outraged by the unbalanced picture. If we implicitly accept the conventional hierarchy of credibility, we will feel the sting in that accusation.

It is something of a solution to say that over the years each "one-sided" study will provoke further studies that gradually enlarge our grasp of all the relevant facets of an institution's operation. But that is a long-term solution, and not much help to the individual researcher who has to contend with the anger of officials who feel he has done them wrong, the criticism of those of his colleagues who think he is presenting a one-sided view, and his own worries.

What do we do in the meantime? I suppose the answers are more or less obvious. We take sides as our personal and political commitments dictate, use our theoretical and technical resources to avoid the distortions that might introduce into our work, limit our conclusions carefully, recognize the hierarchy of credibility for what it is, and field as best we can the accusations and doubts that will surely be our fate.

CHAPTER III

On Theories Relating to the Explanation of Delinquency

A. SUBCULTURAL DELINQUENCY

EDITOR'S INTRODUCTION

T HE CONTRIBUTIONS to Chapter Three all bear on the task of explaining delinquent behavior. These selections are rather roughly divided and presented in two sub-sections. Sub-section A includes papers which bear primarily on the explanation of subcultural (i.e., gang or group) delinquency. The papers in sub-section B emphasize the relationship of background and situational factors to *individual* delinquency. Papers in sub-section A are more theoretical than the papers in sub-section B which tend to be more research oriented; this difference in emphasis reflects, perhaps, a greater difficulty involved in carrying out research on gangs.

The first paper in sub-section A is by Rodman and Grams who differentiate three types of *delinquents:* the occasional delinquent, the gang delinquent, and the maladjusted delinquent. These authors then suggest that there are three dimensions of *delinquency* and describe these dimensions as: occasional delinquency–habitual delinquency, gang delinquency–lone delinquency, and maladjusted delinquency–adjusted delinquency. They then list and discuss the possible interrelationships among these dimensions of delinquency. Next in this section is a paper by Albert Cohen and James Short, "Research in Delinquent Subcultures." The authors, in this paper, take a backward look upon the classic by Cohen, *Delinquent Boys: The Culture of the Gang.*[1] Cohen and Short discuss the kinds of theoretical and research work which social scientists should

---

[1] Albert K. Cohen, *Delinquent Boys: The Culture of the Gang* (New York: The Free Press, 1955).

subsequently engage in. They also respond to the Sykes-Matza criticism of Cohen's thesis that working-class delinquency is based on a set of peer-group norms antithetical to those of the dominant culture and which derive their content through a process of hostile and negativistic reaction against the dominant culture.[2]

The third paper in this section is by Walter B. Miller who also takes issue with Cohen's thesis concerning the negativistic and reactive nature of lower class gang culture. Instead, Miller attempts to show that lower class gang delinquency is customary behavior—that is to say that it is behavior which arises out of the typical values and forms of behavior which exist in the lower class community rather than behavior which arises from the pressure of a delinquent subculture, itself the product of conflict with middle class culture. In this paper, the student will find Miller's well-known discussion of the concept of *focal concerns* of lower class culture, briefly identified as trouble, toughness, smartness, excitement, fate and autonomy.

Following Miller's paper, a selection from the classic book by Richard Cloward and Lloyd Ohlin is presented.[3] This piece, taken from their chapter on "Goals, Norms, and Anomie," states one of the major differences between these authors' views and those of Cohen. The latter postulates that lower class youth who are dissatisfied with their position and internalize middle class values form the core of the delinquent subculture; Cloward and Ohlin, however, argue instead that it is those lower class boys who wish only to better their position within the lower class who are discontented and go on to form a delinquent subculture. Cloward and Ohlin, in this selection, discuss the relationship between type of aspiration, orientation toward class membership, and orientation toward economic position among lower class youth.

In the next paper in this section, Bordua undertakes an analysis of the differences (and similarities) among the theories of Cohen, Miller, Cloward and Ohlin, and Thrasher. Bordua notes what he considers to be strengths and weaknesses of the various positions taken. For example, Bordua suggests that the most serious weakness in Cloward and Ohlin's book is the absence of life histories of their delinquents: "Cloward and Ohlin's delinquents seem suddenly to appear on the scene sometime in adolescence, to look at the world, and to discover, 'Man, there's no opportunity in my structure.'"

The next two papers in this section, by Wolfgang and by Matza and Sykes, question a facile use of the term "delinquent subculture," so notably

[2]G. Sykes and D. Matza, "Techniques of Neutralization: A Theory of Delinquency," *American Sociological Review*, 1957, pp. 664–70.
[3]Richard Cloward and Lloyd Ohlin, *Delinquency and Opportunity* (New York: The Free Press, 1961).

used by sociologists. Wolfgang focuses on the similarity and differences between the youth subculture and the larger culture, noting that there is a substantial number of shared values between the parent culture and various tolerated youth subcultures. He notes Yinger's use of the concept of contraculture to refer to subcultural groups that are at considerable variance with the larger culture. To Wolfgang, the term "delinquent subculture" means a subculture that is much more than merely different from the parent culture, being antithetical to the social system in which it operates. He calls for more research and theory on the similarities and differences between the value content of the parent culture and the subculture as well as on the varieties of youth subculture within the social system.

Matza and Sykes strongly argue that the delinquent's values are far less deviant from the parent cultural values than commonly portrayed and "that the faulty picture is due to an erroneous view of the middle class value system." They elaborate on the notion that a number of leisure class values may be converted into delinquent behavior, such as the search for thrills and excitement.

The following paper, by Albert Reiss and A. Lewis Rhodes, reports the results of a test of Sutherland's differential association hypothesis. This paper also relates closely both to the earlier call by Wolfgang for research on the values of members of youth subcultures and to the different types of delinquents described by Rodman and Grams. The focus of the paper by Reiss and Rhodes is to test the effect of intensity of association (as called for by Sutherland), but using data on the actual *types* of delinquent behavior reported by a boy and his best friends. These authors discuss the need to operationalize Sutherland's hypothesis so as to "test the relationship of association with delinquent others through time"—a matter not yet accomplished by social scientists.

The final paper in this section, by Paul Lerman, also deals with the theoretical and empirical issues involved in the description of subcultural values. Lerman argues that the term "subcultural delinquency" has too many different usages to permit proper evaluation of the various theories purporting to explain subcultural delinquency. He argues, therefore, that descriptive issues must be resolved before explanatory issues are considered. His paper deals mainly with some of the descriptive issues involved in defining subcultural delinquency. He also presents data designed to resolve some of the disputes which have arisen over the perception, the versatility, and the consistency of subcultural values. In doing so, he considers some of the points of difference among Cohen and Short, Cloward and Ohlin, Miller, Matza and Sykes, and others.

13.

HYMAN RODMAN AND PAUL GRAMS

TYPES OF DELINQUENTS

Many studies of juvenile delinquents and their families and peers have pointed to the fact that there seem to be several fairly well-defined types of delinquents. These various groups can be differentiated in many ways—by type of offense, family background, residence, peer-group relations, personality characteristics, and psychiatric measures such as the development of the ego and superego. Some of the subculture theorists, Cloward and Ohlin (1960) especially, have given much attention to the formation of gangs composed of similar delinquent types. Other writers have pointed to the importance of different treatments for different types of delinquents (Jenkins and Hewitt, 1944). A recent statement by Gibbons (1965) makes a strong case for both the etiological and treatment importance of a typology of delinquency.

Another reason for focusing on delinquent types is to be able to put studies which have dealt solely with one type of delinquent into correct perspective. Any comparison of the findings of the Gluecks (1950) and Nye (1958), for instance, must take into account the fact that the Gluecks studied lower class incarcerated delinquents while Nye studied a sample of schoolchildren who were rated "most" or "least" delinquent from their responses to a self-report questionnaire.

The number of types delineated by theorists varies. Some make two divisions: gang boys and nongang boys (Wattenberg and Balistrieri, 1950); property offenders and personal offenders (Ferdinand, 1964; Scott, 1959); boys and girls (Wattenberg and Saunders, 1954). Most studies, however, have pointed to three types of juvenile delinquents and three general types will be discussed here.

SOURCE: Excerpts from Hyman Rodman and Paul Grams, "Juvenile Delinquency and the Family: A Review and Discussion," 1967 President's Committee Task Force Report (Washington, D.C.: Government Printing Office), pp. 203–206.

One important point must be kept in mind. This discussion of delinquent types will be largely a comparison of various findings and theories of sociologists, psychologists, and psychiatrists. The basis for comparing these studies is the striking similarities in personal characteristics and family backgrounds which they assign to the different delinquent types. The seriousness of criminal participation by the delinquents varies greatly from study to study. It seems that this variation is largely a result of community differences; perhaps the seriousness of the delinquent behavior is more strongly influenced by the community environment while the extent of participation in delinquency is more strongly influenced by the adolescent's family experiences and his personality. Community variations might be ascribed to the "toleration level" of the neighborhoods, i.e., some delinquent acts may be considered serious in some communities and not so serious in others.

THE OCCASIONAL DELINQUENT

Probably the largest subgroup among delinquents appearing before juvenile court or having police contact is one-time offenders charged with minor violations. Usually these delinquents have participated in acts of vandalism or petty theft, generally in a group. These "normal" or casual delinquents have been discussed by several commentators. Reiss (1952), for instance, in one of the earliest sociological studies of delinquent types, found 730 of 1,110 delinquent probationers examined by Cook County court psychiatrists to be "relatively integrated." John W. Kinch (1962), in a more recent study of Washington, D.C., delinquents, called his group of casual delinquents "prosocial." The similarities in the family backgrounds of these delinquents are noticeable. Reiss' "integrated" delinquents came from unbroken homes in which there was little family tension, had average school records and adjustments, and had short, recent court records. Kinch's "prosocial" delinquents came from unbroken, harmonious homes and described themselves as "friendly," "warmhearted," "courteous," and so on. Moreover, Wattenberg and Balistrieri (1952), in a Detroit study of juvenile auto theft (a "middle class delinquency"), found that these delinquents usually came from intact homes and had strong peer-group ties with a gang dedicated to having fun.

Several writers have pointed to types of delinquents in many ways analogous to this description of the occasional delinquent. Cloward and Ohlin (1960), for instance, explain how adolescents in a slum where racketeering or organized gambling flourishes often become assimilated into the existing adult criminal subculture, a process which usually involves normal boys from intact homes. These boys, although delinquent in a legal sense, are not considered as such by the norms of the neighborhood. Spergel (1964) found several of these "organized" slums in New York, and Drake and Cayton (1962) have vividly described the slum rackets and "policy" games of Chicago. Another picture of the occasional delinquent is given by William F. Whyte in "Street Corner Society" (1943), a study of a lower class Italian slum. Whyte's "corner boys" were well socialized to the society they lived in, and although they engaged in occasional "binges" and minor delinquencies, they were usually nondelinquent.

THE GANG DELINQUENT

Most studies of the different types of delinquency have concentrated on the habitual rather than the occasional delinquent. This is the delinquent who generally commits the most serious infractions, is most often sent to a correctional institution, and most often continues in a pattern of semiprofessional criminal behavior as an adult. Once again, the studies by Kinch and Reiss give the best picture of this general type. Reiss (1952) describes the habitual offender as one with a "weak superego." They are loyal gang members from poor residential areas; their families more often are large and broken and contain other delinquent members; they do

poorly in school; they have the highest rate of recidivism of the three types Reiss studied. Kinch (1962) termed these delinquents "antisocial" and also found them to be urban gang members coming from large families with lax discipline techniques. Their siblings were often delinquent. The "antisocial" delinquents had records of poor achievement and truancy in school. On a self-description inventory, they described themselves as "smart," "excitable," "stubborn," and not "warmhearted." Kinch indicates the similarity of these self-descriptions to Miller's description (1958) of the "focal concerns" of the lower class—excitement, smartness, toughness and autonomy—and, indeed, probably the best way to describe the habitual delinquent is as a "lower class gang delinquent." Also in keeping with Miller's position is Reiss' (1952, p. 717) description of this delinquent type: "The defective superego type does not internalize the norms of conventional society, and experiences little sense of guilt over his delinquent acts. Rather, he accepts the content of, and membership in, a delinquent peer culture."

The habitual delinquent has also been identified by other theorists and researchers, although generally in different terms. Lees and Newson (1954), studying the effect of ordinal position in the family on a child's delinquency, discovered a great many intermediates in the delinquent group, most of them gang members. Scott (1959) reported that in his study of delinquency he found two unrelated scales, one of which involved offenses against "anonymous persons or impersonal property," a form which Scott suggested resulted from "normal" socialization to a deviant peer-group.

The property offense–personal offense difference has led some commentators to delineate two kinds of habitual delinquents. Cloward and Ohlin (1960), for example, distinguish between a conflict-oriented and a criminal subculture. Spergel (1964) found two kinds of serious delinquent gangs in New York City slums—a conflict-oriented gang and a theft-oriented gang. Short and Strodtbeck (1965) reported similar kinds in Chicago. Jenkins and Hewitt (1944), in an early psychiatric study of Michigan child guidance clinic patients, divided the serious delinquents into three groups, two of which were the "pseudosocial" gang offender and the "unsocialized" aggressive offender. Both groups suffered from superego defects, but the "pseudosocial" group refrained from conflicts within the gang, and were only aggressive toward outsiders, while the "unsocialized" group had no such inhibitions. And finally, Yablonsky (1962) made a similar distinction when he discussed the "delinquent" (theft-oriented) gang and the "violent" (conflict-oriented) gang.

THE MALADJUSTED DELINQUENT

The third type of delinquent usually identified is a maladjusted one. His criminal activity stems from personality disturbance rather than gang activity or slum residence. Reiss (1952) called this type the "weak ego" delinquent and reported the most significant characteristics of this type to be high-tension homes, small families, much school retardation, and "lone" delinquencies. Kinch (1962), naming his maladjusted group "asocial," found its major characteristic to be "early and severe parental rejection." These delinquents also had very poor peer relations and suffered general social isolation. On the self-description inventory that Kinch administered, the "asocial" group saw themselves as "disorderly," "nervous," "confused," and "not dependable," adjectives highly suggestive of pathological disturbance. Other studies have found similar patterns of maladjustment among delinquents. Jenkins and Hewitt (1944) labeled their third group of delinquents "neurotic" and found much parental repression and lack of warmth in the background of the boys of this group. Scott's second dimension of delinquent behavior included offenses against persons who were known to the delinquent, and his explanation of this dimension of delinquency was that it was due to the "abnormal" socialization of children in disturbed families (Scott, 1959). The study by Lees and Newson (1954) found a large number of eldest and only children in the group of serious, lone offenders, and Reiss' study (1952) also found that many of the "weak ego" delinquents were eldest children from small families. An explanation for this finding may be found in Reiss' suggestion that these eldest delinquents

are the scapegoats for parental anxieties or marital tensions.

Furthermore, theoretical and observational work done by several "subculture" writers has indicated that there may be a form of delinquent subculture analogous to the maladjusted, individual delinquent. Both Cohen and Short (1958) and Cloward and Ohlin (1960) identify a "retreatist" or drug-using subculture which they suggest arises when adolescents, out of frustration or lack of opportunity, seek to escape reality. Although Spergel (1964) was unable to find a "retreatist" gang in his New York City survey, Short and Strodtbeck (1965) did find one in Chicago.

Understanding that several general types of delinquents exist makes it easier to understand the differences in the various theories that have been offered to explain delinquency. Psychiatric theories, for instance, are particularly relevant to the development of the maladjusted delinquent. The subcultural theories apply primarily to the habitual gang delinquent. Some idea of the proportions of types involved can be found in Reiss' study (1952)—there were 730 "relatively integrated," 135 "weak superego," and 245 "weak ego" delinquents in a group of 1,110 brought before the Cook County Juvenile Court. However, it seems likely from the descriptions Reiss gave that the 135 "weak superego" delinquents are the most serious and persistent of the group. In the relative absence of studies dealing with types of delinquencies, their extensiveness, and related antecedent variables, however, it is extremely difficult to say which group presents the most serious problem to a community interested in reducing delinquency. Further research is needed dealing with delinquency types as variables in order to sift out the varying etiological factors that are involved in different kinds of delinquency.

DIMENSIONS OF DELINQUENCY

The three types of delinquents discussed above —the occasional delinquent, the gang delinquent, and the maladjusted delinquent—are not based upon a single dimension. There are, rather, three different dimensions involved, and it is worth spelling these out in order to demonstrate that there are some very rough edges to any classification of delinquent types. Delinquents can be distinguished along at least the following three dimensions: (1) Occasional delinquency-habitual delinquency; (2) gang delinquency-lone delinquency; (3) maladjusted delinquency-adjusted delinquency. The simple classification into occasional, gang, and maladjusted delinquent types makes a number of assumptions about the interrelationships of the three dimensions—for example, that the occasional delinquent is relatively adjusted or that the gang delinquent is a habitual and a relatively adjusted delinquent. But some of the data published about delinquency suggest that matters are not quite so simple. The Yablonsky (1962) material suggests that some gang delinquents may be maladjusted; some accounts of gangs, such as those by Thrasher (1927) and Whyte (1943), suggest that some gang delinquency is occasional. If we therefore decide to use the three dimensions to generate delinquent types, we come up with eight types. Since practically no research has been directed at the etiology of delinquency that fits any of these types, we will do little more than list them. Further, it should be understood that these are merely logical types and are not derived from empirical data.

Type 1. Adjusted-Occasional-Gang Delinquent: The gang consists of members showing relatively good personality adjustment, and the major activities of the gang are nondelinquent. Nevertheless, their activities are occasionally delinquent. William F. Whyte (1943) has described a gang of this type.

Type 2. Adjusted-Habitual-Gang Delinquent: The members of the gang show relatively good personality adjustment; their behavior is frequently or habitually delinquent. The accounts by Miller (1958) and Cloward and Ohlin (1960) of gangs manifesting lower class "focal concerns" or oriented to a "criminal subculture" are closely related to this type.

Type 3. Adjusted-Occasional-Lone Delinquent: This type refers to the relatively adjusted adolescent who occasionally engages in delinquency on his own. Many of the delinquents that are turned up on a self-report questionnaire are probably of this type (see Nye, 1958).

Type 4. Adjusted-Habitual-Lone Delinquent: The delinquent is relatively well adjusted and engages in delinquent behavior largely on his own. The "precocious delinquent" who has taken over a "rational" criminal career would fall into this type.

Type 5. Maladjusted-Occasional-Gang Delinquent: This delinquent, as an individual, may have difficulty remaining a member within a delinquent gang of relatively well adjusted boys; delinquent behavior therefore takes place only occasionally. His maladjustment would show up in other areas of behavior more than it does in delinquent behavior.

Type 6. Maladjusted-Habitual-Gang Delinquent: The members of the gang show relatively poor personality adjustment; their behavior is habitually delinquent. The "retreatist subculture" described by Cloward and Ohlin (1960) or the gang as a near-group described by Yablonsky (1962) would fit this pattern.

Type 7. Maladjusted-Occasional-Lone Delinquent: The personality disturbance ordinarily manifests itself in nondelinquent ways and occasionally in lone delinquent acts.

Type 8. Maladjusted-Habitual-Lone Delinquent: Personality maladjustment habitually manifests itself in some type of lone delinquent behavior.

Since relatively little research has been done on the etiology of different types of delinquency, it is easy to be optimistic about the possible gains from further research which does focus upon delinquency types. There are several reasons for tempering such optimism, however. First of all, some of the research done in the past, while it may not have dealt deliberately with delinquent types as a variable, actually did study delinquents of a particular type because of the manner in which the samples were selected. It therefore remains to be seen whether a more deliberate treatment of delinquency types as a variable will lead to a substantial increase in our knowledge of delinquency causation. Secondly, there are many other dimensions of delinquency in addition to the 3 we have elaborated here; adding a fourth dimension would permit us to generate 16 types of delinquency; adding a fifth would lead to 32 types. This would undoubtedly lead to an interesting exercise in classification and naming, but it might not contribute very much to our ability to predict and control delinquency. Thirdly, each of the dimensions represents a continuum, and the typology therefore involves sacrificing the variability in the various dimensions of delinquency. Finally, several research studies cited by Quay (1965, pp. 162–165) suggest that it is necessary to deal with personality dimensions that are related to delinquency rather than with delinquency types. This is because the studies could not place an appreciable number of delinquents into clearly delineated types. In short, focusing upon the existence of delinquency types might add some clarity to past and future research on delinquency, but it remains to be seen whether it will also add to our ability to predict and control delinquency.

REFERENCES

CLOWARD, RICHARD A., AND OHLIN, LLOYD E. (1960), *Delinquency and Opportunity.* New York: The Free Press.

COHEN, ALBERT K., AND SHORT, JAMES F., JR. (1958), "Research in Delinquent Subcultures." *Journal of Social Issues,* 14:20–36.

DRAKE, ST. CLAIR, AND CAYTON, HORACE R. (1962), *Black Metropolis,* rev. and enl. ed. New York: Harper & Row, Publishers.

FERDINAND, THEODORE N. (1964), "The Offense Patterns and Family Structures of Urban, Village and Rural Delinquents." *Journal of Criminal Law, Criminology, and Police Science,* 55:86–93.

GIBBONS, DON C. (1965), *Changing the Lawbreaker.* Englewood Cliffs, N.J.: Prentice-Hall, Inc.

GLUECK, SHELDON, AND GLUECK, ELEANOR (1950), *Unraveling Juvenile Delinquency.* New York: Commonwealth Fund.

JENKINS, R. L., AND HEWITT, LESTER (1944), "Types of Personality Structure Encountered in Child Guidance Clinics." *American Journal of Orthopsychiatry,* 14:84–94.

KINCH, JOHN W. (1962), "Self-Conceptions of Types of Delinquents." *Sociological Inquiry,* 32:228–234.

LEES, J. P., AND NEWSON, L. J. (1954), "Family or Sibship Position and Some Aspects of Juvenile Delinquency." *British Journal of Delinquency,* 5:46–65.

MILLER, WALTER B. (1958), "Lower Class Culture as a Generating Milieu of Gang Delinquency." *Journal of Social Issues,* 14:5–19.

NYE, F. IVAN (1958), *Family Relationships and Delinquent Behavior.* New York: John Wiley & Sons, Inc.

QUAY, HERBERT C., ed. (1965), "Personality and Delinquency," in *Juvenile Delinquency: Research and Theory.* Princeton, N.J.: D. VanNostrand, pp. 139–166.

REISS, ALBERT J., JR. (1952), "Social Correlates of Psychological Types of Delinquency." *American Sociological Review,* 17:710–718.

SCOTT, JOHN FINLEY (1959), "Two Dimensions of Delinquent Behavior." *American Sociological Review,* 24:240–243.

SHORT, JAMES F., JR., AND STRODTBECK, FRED L. (1965), *Group Process and Gang Delinquency.* Chicago: University of Chicago Press.

SPERGEL, IRVING (1964), *Racketville, Slumtown, Haulburg.* Chicago: University of Chicago Press.

THRASHER, FREDERIC M. (1927), *The Gang.* Chicago: University of Chicago Press.

WATTENBERG, WILLIAM W., AND BALISTRIERI, JAMES J. (1950), "Gang Membership and Juvenile Misconduct." *American Sociological Review,* 15:744–752.

WATTENBERG, WILLIAM W., AND BALISTRIERI, JAMES, J. (1952), "Automobile Theft: A 'Favored Group' Delinquency." *American Journal of Sociology,* 57:575–579.

WATTENBERG, WILLIAM W., AND SAUNDERS, FRANK (1954), "Sex Differences among Juvenile Offenders." *Sociology and Social Research,* 39:24–31.

WHYTE, WILLIAM FOOTE (1943), *Street Corner Society.* Chicago: University of Chicago Press.

YABLONSKY, LEWIS (1962), *The Violent Gang.* New York: Crowell Collier & Macmillan, Inc.

14.

ALBERT K. COHEN AND JAMES F. SHORT, JR.

RESEARCH IN DELINQUENT SUBCULTURES

This paper is a backward look upon the book *Delinquent Boys: The Culture of the Gang* (2), and a look ahead to the kinds of theoretical and research work which it is hoped and anticipated will soon make this book obsolete.

Without trying to summarize the argument of this book, let us indicate what it tried to do. It proceeded from the premise that much delinquency—probably the vast bulk of it—represents participation in a delinquent subculture. Much of the sociological literature on juvenile delinquency has been concerned with demonstrating that this is so, and with formulating the processes whereby this subculture is taken over by the individual. *Delinquent Boys* posed the problem: Why is the delinquent subculture there in the boys' milieu to be taken over? More specifically, why is there a subculture with this specific content, and distributed in this particular way within the social system? Secondly, it set forth a general theory of subcultures, on the methodological premise that the explanation of any phenomenon consists of a demonstration that it conforms to a general theory applicable to all phenomena of the same class. Thirdly, it formulated an explanation of the delinquent subculture. In brief, it explained the delinquent subculture as a system of beliefs and values generated in a process of communicative interaction among children similarly circumstanced by virtue of their positions in the social structure, and as constituting a solution to problems of adjustment to which the established culture provided no satisfactory solutions. These problems are largely problems of status and self-respect arising among working-class children as a result of

socially structured inability to meet the standards of the established culture; the delinquent subculture, with its characteristics of non-utilitarianism, malice, and negativism, provides an alternative status system and justifies, for those who participate in it, hostility and aggression against the sources of their status frustration.

The nature of the theoretical issues raised by this book will be clearer if we pause to consider a thoughtful critique by Gresham Sykes and David Matza. These authors dispute the proposition, central to the argument of *Delinquent Boys*, that delinquency is based on a set of norms antithetical to those of the dominant culture and, indeed, deriving their content by a process of hostile and negativistic reaction against the dominant culture. They offer, in turn, what they describe as "a possible alternative or modified explanation for a large portion of juvenile delinquency." (18, p. 664) They present impressive evidence that the delinquent is by no means immune or indifferent to the expectations of respectable society, that he has internalized the respectable value system, and that in many ways he appears to recognize its moral validity. They go on to say that "the theoretical viewpoint that sees juvenile delinquency as a form of behavior based on the values and norms of a deviant sub-culture in precisely the same way as law-abiding behavior is based on the values and norms of the larger society is open to serious doubt. Instead, the juvenile delinquent would appear to be at least partially committed to the dominant social order in that he frequently exhibits guilt or shame when he violates its proscriptions . . ." (18, p. 666). They then proceed to argue that much delinquency is based on a set of justifications for deviance that are seen as valid by the delinquent but not by the legal system or society at large; that is, on a set of techniques for neutralizing the internal and external demands for conformity, deriving from

SOURCE: Albert K. Cohen and James F. Short, Jr., "Research in Delinquent Subcultures," *Journal of Social Issues* 14, no. 3 (1958): 20–37. Permission to reprint granted by publisher and author.

This is a revision of a paper read at the annual meeting of the American Sociological Society, August, 1958.

values whose legitimacy is at least on some level recognized. These techniques of neutralization are then set forth in considerable and convincing detail.

With all of this we have no quarrel. The analysis of the techniques of neutralization, in fact, we would regard as an important elaboration of the argument of *Delinquent Boys*. It is not clear, however, that this analysis provides an *alternative* explanation of delinquent behavior. The notion that the delinquent boy has internalized the respectable value system, *is* therefore profoundly ambivalent about his own delinquent behavior, and must contend continuously with the claims of the respectable value system is one of the central propositions of *Delinquent Boys*. Although *Delinquent Boys* does not mention the techniques of neutralization enumerated by Sykes and Matza (and the failure to do so constitutes a significant omission), it strongly emphasizes the part played by the mechanism of reaction-formation, one of the most elementary techniques of neutralization. Reaction-formation is stressed because it is not only a way of coming to terms with one's delinquent impulses; it helps to account for the nature of the delinquent behavior itself. To quote *Delinquent Boys*: ". . . we would expect the delinquent boy who, after all, has been socialized in a society dominated by middle-class morality and who can never quite escape the blandishments of middle-class society, to seek to maintain his safeguards against seduction. Reaction-formation, in his case, should take the form of an 'irrational,' 'malicious,' 'unaccountable' hostility to the enemy within the gates as well as without: the norms of respectable middle-class society." (2, p. 133) As a final commentary on the paper by Sykes and Matza, we would add this: The formation of a subculture is itself probably the most universal and powerful of techniques of neutralization, for nothing is so effective in allaying doubts and providing moral reassurance against a gnawing superego as the repeated, emphatic, and articulate support and approval of other persons.

Wilensky and Lebeaux (21) are concerned with other limitations of *Delinquent Boys*. The most obvious of these limitations is the fact that there is not *one* delinquent subculture but a *variety* of delinquent subcultures. This is suggested in the book but not developed there. Although there does not as yet exist a real comparative sociology of juvenile delinquency, evidence from other countries suggests that some of the features of delinquent behavior which in this country are so pervasive that we have come to take them for granted as inherent in the very idea of delinquency may be absent elsewhere (27). It is probable that delinquent subcultures have distinct emphases in different societies and that these can be related to differences in the respective social systems of which they are the products. Comparative research in the sociology of delinquent subcultures is to be most strongly encouraged, for it is bound to highlight aspects of delinquent behavior in the American scene which we are prone to overlook, and to make them the object of theoretical concern. Furthermore, the comparative study of delinquency in different national settings will undoubtedly focus attention on hitherto neglected aspects of the relationship of delinquency to the overall structure of society and may clarify some of the present confusion regarding *individual* and *socially structured* motivations for delinquency. These questions tend to become clouded by a sort of "cultural blindness" when we restrict our observations to our own society.

However, we need not await such national culture comparative data before embarking on a comparative sociology of juvenile delinquency. There is ample variation in such behavior within the bounds of our own national society—variation which has not adequately been taken into account by existing etiological theory and research. Before we proceed to enumerate some of these delinquent subcultures and the problems they raise, let us consider what is involved in the explanation of a delinquent subculture.

The first task is descriptive; to establish the facts the theory must fit. These facts are of two orders. First, we need detailed descriptions of the content of these subcultures. American delinquency studies, particularly psychological and psychiatric, have long emphasized that delinquency may be variously motivated, that similar overt behavior may proceed from a variety of etiologies. Delinquency studies have not been so quick to appreciate the theoretical implications of the fact that delinquency does not even look the same, that the diversity of content is itself enormous and requires explanation. More than this, however, we suggest that careful attention to the diversity of content will itself provide fertile clues for theory. An apposite illustration is the work of Grosser (10), which takes as its point of departure the characteristic differences between male and female delinquency and leads to important new insights into the ways in which delinquency is determined by the role structure of society.

Another limitation of American delinquency studies has been the tendency, with some notable exceptions among the sociologists, to conceive of variations in delinquency as variations solely in the behavior of individuals rather than variations in cultural patterns and collective behavior. This way of conceiving and describing delinquency is implicit in the dominant methodological model, which compares an experimental group of delinquents with a control group of non-delinquents, or a group of one-time offenders with a group of recidivists and attempts to relate these differences in individual behavior to differences in situational or developmental backgrounds. This model is appropriate to certain kinds of problems, **but it** cannot yield descriptions of delinquent subcultures, for these are social phenomena *sui generis* and must be described on their own level. Cultural patterns are inferred from the observation of groups as wholes, of the social relationships among their members, of what happens when the members of the group are together and what happens when they are apart, of the order, the sequence, the variety of the group's activities, delinquent and non-delinquent, of the interaction between the group and other groups and the larger community as well. Such patterns do not emerge from a table of individual differences.

The second order of descriptive data relates to the distribution of these patterns in the social system, that is to their distribution by age, sex, class, ethnic group, ecological area, etc. Again, on the one hand our theories must make sense of these distributions and, on the other hand, these distributions provide clues

to the social structuring of the patterns, for the distributions must in some way be a function of correlates of their positional coordinates. We already have a lot of data on the social distribution of delinquency, but it is not very useful for our purposes. Most of our distributional studies treat delinquency as though it were homogeneous. With the exception of comparisons by sex, most of our distributional data consist of simple frequency distributions of delinquent acts. We have few studies mapping out the distribution of different kinds of delinquency, much less different kinds of delinquent subcultures.

These data specify what is to be explained. The explanation sets forth the manner in which the content and distribution are socially structured, that is, are functions of the structure of the larger social system. Such an explanation necessarily implies a general theory of subcultures, for explanation of any phenomenon consists in a demonstration that that phenomenon is consistent with a general theory applicable to the entire class of which the phenomenon in question is a special case. The general theory of subcultures is presently in a rather crude and undeveloped state. Parallel with our efforts to explain particular subcultures, therefore, must be continuing efforts at the further development and refinement of the general theory so that it will be adequate to all its special applications.

In the following discussion, we present a list of the principal varieties of delinquent subcultures which can be tentatively differentiated at the present time, some descriptive notes, etiological speculations, and some problems for theory and research suggested by this discussion. Certain general observations are in order before we set forth our typology. The concrete variability of delinquent subcultures must be assumed to be almost infinite. These subcultures, therefore, will exhibit a range of variation that cannot be encompassed by any empirical typology. The subcultures listed here are those which, although they shade off into one another, stand out in the literature as conspicuously differentiated trends or, on theoretical ground, seem likely to represent etiologically differentiated entities. It would seem to be a logical goal for theory to work toward a conceptual scheme consisting of a set of variables or dimensions of variation, on both the descriptive and etiological levels, in terms of which we can state the essential features, on both these levels, of any concrete variant.

Delinquent or any other subcultures are to be defined, like clinical entities in medicine, in terms of variations in their manifest content and their etiology. The terminology of sex and social class roles, which we have found convenient in *naming* the varieties of delinquent subcultures, do not stand for these *defining attributes* but for the *positional coordinates* of these subcultures. Research will undoubtedly reveal that other positional variables such as age, ethnicity, and ecological location and combinations of these variables also correspond to differences in life conditions which give rise to distinctive subcultural variants. Some of the ways in which these other positional variables may be relevant are suggested in the pages which follow. However, it is not to be assumed *a priori* that every way of mapping social space is also a way of mapping delinquent subcultures, nor that to every social position there corresponds a distinctive variety of delinquent subculture. Positional data and data relating to content and etiology are of two different, although related, orders. Some of the variants we describe here may yet be discovered to occur in other regions of social space as well as those in which we have located them. It is a task for research to determine which variations in position are linked to variations in life conditions which make for significant differences in the defining attributes of delinquent subcultures.

DELINQUENT SUBCULTURES: MALE

1. *The parent male subculture.* This is what the book, *Delinquent Boys,* calls "the" delinquent subculture. It has been described as non-utilitarian, malicious, negativistic, versatile, and characterized by short-run hedonism and group autonomy. We refer to it as the parent subculture because it is probably the most common variety in this country—indeed, it might be called the "garden variety" of delinquent subculture—and because the characteristics listed above seem to constitute a common core shared by other important variants. However, in addi-

tion, these variants possess distinctive attributes or emphases which are not fully accounted for by the argument of *Delinquent Boys.* We believe the parent subculture is a working-class subculture. This position, however, is open to question and we shall consider the matter further in our discussion of the middle-class subculture.

2. *The conflict-oriented subculture.* This is the subculture most prominent in the news today and is probably regarded by many laymen as the typical form which delinquency takes. In its highly developed forms it has the following characteristics. It is a culture of large gangs, whose membership numbers ordinarily in the scores and may run into the hundreds; in this respect contrasting to the parent subculture, whose members consist of small gangs or cliques. These gangs have a relatively elaborate organization, including such differentiated roles as president, vice-president, war-chief, and armorer. The gang may be subdivided into sub-gangs on an age or territorial basis and may have alliances with other gangs. These gangs have names, a strong sense of corporate identity, a public personality or "rep" in the gang world. The gang is identified with a territory or "turf" which it tries to defend or to extend. The status of the gang is largely determined by its toughness, that is, its readiness to engage in physical conflict with other gangs and its prowess in intergang "rumbles." Although fighting occupies but a small portion of the gang's time, "heart" or courage in fighting is the most highly prized virtue and the most important determinant of the position of gang members within the gang as well as that of the gang among other gangs. Fighting within the gang is regulated by a code of fairness; gang members, however, are relatively unconstrained by any concepts of chivalry or fairness in warfare with other gangs. To demonstrate "heart" it is not necessary to give the other fellow a decent chance or to show forbearance toward an outnumbered or defeated enemy. There is evident ambivalence about fighting; it is not a simple outpouring of accumulated aggression. Members are afraid of rumbles, and are frequently relieved when police intervention prevents a scheduled rumble, but the ethic of the gang requires the suppression

of squeamishness, an outward demeanor of toughness, and a readiness to defend turf and rep with violence and even brutality. In their other activities, these gangs exhibit the general characteristics of the delinquent subculture. Drinking, sex, gambling, stealing, and vandalism are prominent. Such gangs include a wide age range. They are concentrated in sections of the city that are highly mobile, working-class, impoverished, and characterized by a wide variety of indices of disorganization.

This is the full-blown conflict gang. Although large conflict gangs may be found in many cities, it is doubtful that the degree of organization, including the officers and functionaries, found in the New York gangs is to be found elsewhere. Probably more common than the type of gang described here is a form intermediate between the conflict gang and the parent subculture: a loosely organized and amorphous coalition of cliques with only a vague sense of corporate identity, coalescing sporadically and frequently for displays of open violence. But the reality of gangs in New York and in other cities, similar to those we have described, cannot be doubted.

3. *The drug addict subculture.* What we know of this subculture is derived primarily from two large-scale research projects conducted in New York and Chicago respectively. Although these studies do not agree in all respects, especially with reference to etiological questions, it is clear that the subculture which centers around the use of narcotic drugs provides a markedly distinct way of life. Both studies are agreed that drug addiction and criminality go hand-in-hand, that addiction arises in communities where delinquency is already endemic, that most juvenile addicts—although not all— were delinquent prior to their addiction. They are agreed that the addict eschews the more violent forms of delinquency—rape, assault, gang warfare, "general hell-raising"—and prefers income-producing forms of delinquency, which are essential to the support of a drug habit in a society in which drugs are obtainable only in an illegal market and at great cost. The addict subculture, therefore, in contrast to the parent and the conflict gang cultures, has a marked utilitarian quality, but this utilitarianism

is in support of and a precondition of the addict way of life.

The kinship of the addict and other delinquent subcultures is brought out in the finding of the New York study that addicts are usually members of organized gangs and share the general philosophy of those gangs. After the onset of addiction, however, their participation in the more violent and disorderly activities of the gangs is reduced and they tend to cluster in cliques on the periphery of the gangs. There is little moral disapproval of drug use on the part of gang members, but it is usually discouraged and the status of the addict within the larger gang is lowered on the practical grounds that addiction lowers the value of the addict to the group. The reports of the Chicago investigators, however, suggest that they were studying a more "mature" addict subculture, one that is not peripheral to more "conventional" subcultures and in a merely tolerated status, but one that has achieved a higher degree of autonomy, with a loose and informal but independent organization, enjoying a relatively high status in the communities within which it flourishes. The Chicago addict, as described, is not a hanger-on of a conflict gang but moves proudly in the world of the "cats." The characteristics of the cat culture are suggested in the reports of the New York study, but are elaborately and richly described in the Chicago reports. Central to the cat culture is the "kick," defined by Finestone as "any act tabooed by 'squares' that heightens and intensifies the present moment of experience and differentiates it as much as possible from the humdrum routine of daily life," and the "hustle," defined as "any non-violent means of making some bread (money) which does not require work." Heroin is "the greatest kick of them all"; pimping, conning, pickpocketing, and such are approved and respectable hustles. Both the kick and the hustle, notes Finestone, are in direct antithesis to the central values of the dominant culture. The cat cultivates an image of himself as "cool," self-possessed, assured, and quietly competent, places great value upon the esthetic amenities of clothes and music, and possesses a discriminating and critical taste.

Both studies locate the addict subculture in

those areas of the city which are most deprived, of the lowest socio-economic status, most lacking in effective adult controls—characterized by extensive family disorganization, high mobility, and recently arrived populations. Addiction characteristically occurs after the age of 16 and is most heavily concentrated among the most-discriminated-against minority groups, especially Negroes.

4. *Semi-professional theft.* The word "professional" is not intended to connote the "professional thief" of Sutherland's description. The latter represents the elite of the criminal underworld, skilled, sophisticated, nonviolent, specialized. It is intended to suggest, rather, a stage in a life history which has been described by Sutherland and Cressey as proceeding "from trivial to serious, from occasional to frequent, from sport to business, and from crimes committed by isolated individuals or by very loosely organized groups to crime committed by rather tightly organized groups." (17) This sequence appears to characterize especially "persons who in young adult life become robbers and burglars." The earlier stage of this sequence describes what we have called the parent subculture. Most participants in this subculture appear to drop out or to taper off after the age of 16 or 17. A minority, however, begin to differentiate themselves from their fellows, at about this age, and to move in the direction of more utilitarian, systematic, and pecuniary crime—what we are calling "semi-professional theft."

Systematic research on this pattern, as a differentiated variant or offspring of the parent subculture, is scanty. However, an unpublished study on the amount of admitted delinquency among boys of juvenile court age in high delinquency areas of Chicago supports this conception of a subculture of semi-professional theft.[1] The detailed statistical findings will be presented in a later report. Preliminary analysis strongly suggests that the following characteristics, all presumptive evidence of a strong utilitarian emphasis, tend to go together with the later stages of a long history of frequent stealing which began at an early age:

a. The use of strong-arm methods (robbery) of obtaining money.

b. The *sale* of stolen articles, *versus* using for oneself, giving or throwing away, or returning stolen articles.

c. Stating, as a reason for continued stealing, "want things" or "need money" *versus* stealing for excitement, because others do it, because they like to, or for spite.

In the areas studied, this semi-professional stealing appears to be more of a differentiation of emphasis within a more diversified climate of delinquency than an autonomous subculture independently organized. Boys who show the characteristics listed above commonly participate in non-utilitarian delinquency as well; e.g., giving or throwing away stolen articles or indicating that they steal for excitement, because they like to, or for spite. Furthermore, they belong to gangs the majority of whose members may engage in predominantly non-utilitarian delinquency. It seems probable, although it has not been demonstrated, that the semi-professional thieves constitute cliques within the larger gangs and that they are differentiated from other delinquents in the same gangs with respect to other characteristics than patterns of stealing alone. We would surmise that, to the degree to which stealing becomes rational, systematic, deliberate, planned, and pursued as a primary source of income, it becomes incompatible with anarchic, impulsive, mischievous, and malicious characteristics of non-utilitarian delinquent subcultures and that its practitioners tend to segregate themselves into more professionally oriented and "serious-minded" groups. This, however, is speculation and is a subject for further research.

5. *The middle-class delinquent subculture.* Thus far we have distinguished subcultures primarily on empirical grounds; that is, investigators have observed the differences we have described. Middle-class delinquency commonly takes a subcultural form as well, but there is as yet no firm basis in research for ascribing to it a different content from that of the parent male subculture (13, 19). We distinguish it rather on theoretical grounds; since none of the problems of adjustment to which the working-class subcultures seem to constitute plausible and intelligible responses appear to be linked

---

[1] This study was conducted under the auspices of the Illinois Institute for Juvenile Research and the immediate direction of Mr. Guy Procaccio.

with sufficient frequency to middle-class status, we assume that middle-class subcultures arise in response to problems of adjustment which are characteristic products of middle-class socialization and middle-class life situations. The notion that different patterns of behavior may be "functionally equivalent" solutions to the same or similar problems is familiar. We are suggesting that the same or similar patterns of behavior may be "functionally versatile" solutions to different problems of adjustment. However, we are persuaded that further research will reveal subtle but important differences between working-class and middle-class patterns of delinquency. It seems probable that the qualities of malice, bellicosity, and violence will be underplayed in the middle-class subcultures and that these subcultures will emphasize more the deliberate courting of danger (suggested by the epithet "chicken") and a sophisticated, irresponsible, "playboy" approach to activities symbolic, in our culture, of adult roles and centering largely around sex, liquor, and automobiles.

DETERMINANTS OF THE MALE SUBCULTURES

A fully satisfactory theory of delinquent subcultures must specify the different problems of adjustment to which each of these subcultures is a response, and the ways in which the social structure generates these problems of adjustment and determines the forms which the solutions take.

Definitive theory can grow only out of research specifically concerned with differences among these subcultures. Such research is in its infancy. For example, it is not possible to determine from the published literature what are the characteristics of the cities in which the conflict gangs appear and of those in which it does not; the specific characteristics which differentiate urban areas in which delinquency assumes this form and those in which it does not; or the specific characteristics of the children who become involved in this sort of delinquency and of those who do not. There is a literature, most of it growing out of the work of the New York City Youth Board, which is valuable and suggestive (5, 15, 22, 24, 25, 26, 28). Little of this literature, however, employs a systematic comparative perspective designed to throw light on the *differential* characteristics of this subculture and its social setting. With respect to the conditions which favor the emergence of a semi-professional subculture, the literature is practically silent. On the matter of middle-class delinquency, there is an enormous emotional to-do and vocal alarm, but little more. There is a great need of case studies of middle-class delinquent groups, including detailed descriptions of the specific quality of their delinquencies and the behavioral context and community settings of these delinquencies. It is interesting that some of our most adequate and illuminating research concerns the drug addict subculture, which is numerically perhaps the least significant delinquent subculture and is restricted to a few sections of our larger cities, although where it appears it is a grave social problem and is most ominous for the young people who are caught up in it.

To us, the subculture of the conflict gang is the most baffling. Several years ago Solomon Kobrin suggested, on the basis of his intimate knowledge of delinquency in Chicago, the differential characteristics of areas in which delinquency assumes the semi-professional form, and of those in which it assumes a violent, "hoodlum," conflict form. These differences he described as differences in the degree of integration between the conventional and criminal value systems. In areas in which adults are engaged in consistently profitable and highly organized illegal enterprises and also participate in such conventional institutions as churches, fraternal and mutual benefit societies, and political parties, criminal adult role models have an interest in helping to contain excesses of violence and destructiveness; in these areas youngsters may perceive delinquency as a means to the acquisition of skills which are useful to the achievement of conventional values and which may, as a matter of fact, lead to a career in the rackets, and to prestige in the community. Here delinquency tends to assume a relatively orderly, systematic, rational form. We suspect that this type of area is relatively rare and that the pattern of semi-professional theft is correspondingly rare, as compared with the occurrence of the parent and hoodlum-type patterns. In a contrasting type of area adults may violate the law, but this violation is not systematic and organized, and the criminal and conventional value systems do not mesh through the participation of criminals in the conventional institutions. "As a consequence, the delinquency in areas of this type tends to be unrestrained by controls originating *at any point* in the adult social structure." (12, p. 658) Delinquency takes on a wild, untrammeled, violent character. "Here groups of delinquents may be seen as excluded, isolated conflict groups dedicated to an unending battle against all forms of restraint." (12, p. 659)

This is the kind of provocative formulation of which we stand much in need. However, Kobrin's formulations have not, to our knowledge, led to research to test their validity. Furthermore, although this formulation specifies the kind of breakdown of controls under which a conflict subculture can flourish, it does not account for the positive motivation to large-scale organized gangs, the warlike relationships between gangs, and the idealization of toughness, relatively unregulated by an intergang code of chivalry and fairness. It is a defect of many of our theories of delinquency that they try to account for delinquency by demonstrating the absence of effective restraints. Delinquency, however, and certainly this particular form of delinquency, cannot be assumed to be a potentiality of human nature which automatically erupts when the lid is off. Nor do we believe that the emphasis on conflict can be explained as a way of expressing and channelizing aggression accumulated through a variety of frustrations. We do not deny either the frustrations or the aggression of many of the youngsters in this subculture. But it is apparent from the reports of workers that the violence we see is as much a matter of conformity, sometimes in the face of great fear and reluctance, to a highly compulsive group-enforced ideal of toughness as it is a simple outburst of pent-up hostility. We will not at this point add our own speculations to those of others. It is our purpose here merely to indicate the nature of the problem.

It is a matter for further research to determine the extent to which the patterns we have described, and other patterns, are *variants* of a common subculture or subcultures, with qualitatively distinct etiologies, or *quantitative extremes* of the common subculture with the same variables accounting for their existence and their extremity. In this paper we have chosen to describe these patterns as variants. The description of these variants, and their accounting, in etiological research and theory, is the major task of the larger project of which this paper is a partial report.

With respect to the drug addict subculture, the New York and Chicago investigators present different interpretations, and it is an interesting challenge to theory to account for these differences or to reconcile them. The New York investigators state unequivocally that "All juvenile drug addicts are severely disturbed individuals," and that "adolescents who become addicts have deep-rooted, major personality disorders." (1, pp. 59–60) Specifically, they suffer from a weak ego, an inadequately functioning superego, and inadequate masculine identification. These defects, in turn, can be traced to family experiences. Up to the age of 16 or so these boys do not behave very differently from the ordinary gang delinquent. At about this age the emotionally healthy youngsters develop a new conception of themselves consistent with age-graded role definitions and expectations in our culture. The gang activities become kid stuff, the gang begins to break up, the boy begins to organize his life around a job, his girl, his future. "It is at this stage that those members or hangers-on who are too disturbed emotionally to face the future as adults find themselves seemingly abandoned by their old cronies and begin to feel increasingly anxious." (1, p. 62) They take to the use of drugs because drugs help to reduce anxieties resulting from personal incapacity and because they make it easy to deny and to avoid facing deep-seated personal problems (14).

The Chicago investigators, on the contrary, question the concept of the addict as a "sick person," whose addiction is a symptom of personality defects (8). They emphasize, on the one hand, the breakdown of controls which occurs in areas which "are characterized by a high density of a recently arrived and largely unsettled population" (23), and whose residents cannot mobilize effectively to secure law enforcement against even that behavior which offends their own standards. They emphasize, on the other hand, the problems of adjustment which are a function of the social position of the populations within those areas, the problems, that is, of the most depressed sectors of the most disadvantaged minority groups, who are increasingly sensitized to the value, goals, and conceptions of success of the dominant social order but who are categorically excluded from the opportunity for legitimately achieving them. Since they are denied participation, except in a servile and unrewarding capacity, in those activities which are defined by the dominant institutional order as the legitimate, "serious," and really important activities, these groups turn their back on this order and the sober virtues which it enjoins, and make a virtue and an ideal of "play," of irresponsible, autonomous, hedonically oriented activity which seeks its consummation and reward in the extraction of the maximum "kick" from the present moment. The problems of adjustment to which the cat culture is a response are not a function of a pathological character structure; they are socially structured strains endemic in the lower-class urban Negro and other minority group populations.

How are we to account for the contrast between the two interpretations? It is possible that one or the other represents faulty speculation which is not in keeping with the data and which is a product of a sociologistic or psychologistic bias. However, both grow out of responsible, systematic research and neither can be lightly dismissed as an autistic distortion of the plain facts. It is possible that the two populations studied cannot be equated, that we are dealing with two different addict subcultures. It is possible, also, that the cat culture described by the Chicago researchers is a logical extreme of the gradual isolation from the more conventional gangs which is documented by the New York studies. This still does not explain the differences noted in the two studies, however. It is further possible that the two sets of conclusions are not mutually exclusive. With respect to the Chicago study we may make two observations: (1) it is always a minority of young people in any given area who become addicts, and therefore there must be selective processes at work in addition to those stressed by the Chicago investigators; (2) the methods of the Chicago study were not designed to reveal the kinds of data concerning personality structure to which the New York investigators attach such importance. It may well be that, without regard to individual peculiarities and abnormalities, the social setting described in the Chicago reports is one in which the addict subculture is attractive and possible, but that, within this general setting, the attractiveness of this response is further enhanced for those with the character structure described in the New York reports. Furthermore, it is possible that this kind of character structure occurs with exceptionally high frequency in lower-class Negro areas. A family constellation of floating, irresponsible males centering around a hard-working, overburdened mother is common in this segment of the Negro population, and it is the sort of constellation that might be expected to produce the weak ego, inadequately functioning superego, and inadequate masculine identification that are ascribed to the addict's personality. In short, it is possible, although it is still speculative, that the methods of the two studies illuminate different aspects of the same reality.

In *Delinquent Boys*, it was suggested that the middle-class delinquent subculture is a response to ambivalence and anxiety in the area of sex-role identification, aggravated by the prolonged dependence of the boy upon his family, and the indefinite postponement of adult self-sufficiency and self-determination. This interpretation has been questioned by Wilensky and Lebeaux (21) who argue that anxiety about male identity is greater in the *lower class*. The working-class delinquent subculture, therefore, is determined by both status anxiety and sex-role anxiety; the middle-class subculture is determined by anxiety about becoming a man, an adult. Wilensky and Lebeaux conclude that this theory would predict even sharper contrasts between working-class and middle-class delinquency than the official statistics would show.

A recent study (13) based on self-reported behavior of western and mid-western high school students does not support this prediction or suggest that there is any significant difference in middle-class and working-class delinquency rates in the several communities studied. The same findings might not obtain in large urban areas or non-caucasian populations, which were not studied, but at least in this one respect the findings are not consistent with inference from the Wilensky and Lebeaux hypothesis. This argument does not lack plausibility, however, and research is obviously necessary to decide between what are, at this point, rival speculations.

In an effort to account for the apparent increase in middle-class delinquency, Cohen (4) suggested that, as a result of changes in the structure of our economy, labor market, and school system, the traditional deferred gratification pattern of the middle-class boy is breaking down. In an economy of scarcity this pattern of deferred gratification did, as a matter of fact, "pay off." It was a prerequisite to movement through the schools and to the economic opportunities to which the schools were an avenue. Furthermore, middle-class parents could point to the obviously greater economic affluence of themselves in contrast to the unskilled and generally unprotected mass of working-class people. Thus, with support from parents, the economy, and the school, the "college boy" way of life, to use Whyte's felicitous phrase (20), was inculcated in middle-class children and in working-class children who aspired to "better themselves." This pattern was incompatible with commitment to a delinquent way of life.

What has happened to this picture? Again very briefly, we find that the labor market no longer requires large numbers of unskilled workers and that organized labor does not welcome teen-aged competitors for a limited supply of jobs. The demand is, on the contrary, that the school hold on to young people as long as possible and keep them off the labor market. The school is compelled to retain and to promote "college boy" and "corner boy" alike, to adopt a child-centered philosophy, to minimize invidious distinctions and differential rewards for working-class and middle-class ways of life. The structural supports of a pattern of deferred gratification are therefore weakened. Incentive for this pattern is further weakened by the relatively greater economic strides made by organized labor. The child can see all of this and, as a consequence, is likely to find the college boy way of life less attractive—this, in spite of the fact that a college education can be *statistically* demonstrated to be "worth" a considerable sum!

Sociologists have pointed out that our society provides no well-defined roles for adolescence (21), a period in the child's life when the problem of establishing his personal identity becomes especially crucial. With the weakening of the deferred gratification pattern, the choice among alternatives as the boy seeks to fill this status void is more likely to become a delinquent choice. When he tries to establish his identity as an adult, or as a man, he finds the "conventional," the "respectable," the "responsible" criteria of adult status denied him. Hence, he tends to symbolize his adulthood by irresponsible, hedonically oriented behavior involving the courting of danger, liquor, sex, cars, etc.

Still other changes in society and in child rearing patterns, especially among middle-class parents, may have contributed to an increase in delinquency in this class of youngsters. These changes have to do with the relatively greater independence from each other of family members as a result of the economic changes we have talked about, the democratization of family relations, vacillation in child rearing philosophy as a result of increasing concern with what the "experts" in the field have to say (together with vacillation on the part of the latter), and the "cult of youth" which holds that all pain, especially psychic pain, is injurious to children and that it is the responsibility of parents to minimize pain and frustration for their children. All of these things require documentation in the form of carefully conducted research. All, however, appear to weaken the deferred gratification pattern of socialization and the authority of parental figures, to retard the internalization of authority, to reduce the ability to tolerate frustration, and to contribute to an increase in delinquency among middle-class children.

This is, perhaps, more than enough speculation on the conditions which might facilitate the formation of middle-class delinquent subcultures. The saddest commentary, however, is that we are faced with a poverty of speculation, without which there can be no meaningful research, without which, in turn, there can be no conclusions that are more than speculation.

DELINQUENT SUBCULTURES: FEMALE

With a very few exceptions, (e.g. 9, 11) the professional literature on female delinquency is of little help in determining how, in what ways, and to what extent that delinquency is subculturally patterned. There is little on what this delinquency actually consists of, other than that it usually involves sexual misconduct of some kind; or on the relationships of the girls to the boys and men with whom they are involved, and how these relationships, as well as the girls' relationships to other peers of both sexes, are affected by their sexual behavior; or on the contexts of other activities; or on other characteristics of the social settings within which sexual episodes occur. It is our position that the meaning and function, for the persons concerned, of any form of delinquent behavior can only be inferred from rich and detailed descriptive data about the behavior itself, about its position in a larger context of interaction, and about how it is perceived and reacted to by the actor himself and by other participants in that interactive context. These data are largely lacking for female delinquency.

In *Delinquent Boys* Cohen suggested the socially structured motivations to participation in what might be called a female parent delinquent subculture. He argues that a girl's status depends largely upon the status of the males with whom she is identified; that, in order to achieve respectability, a girl must be able to attract the "honorable" attentions of respectable and responsible males; that many girls, especially of lower socio-economic status, have not been trained in the arts and graces and lack the material means necessary for competing successfully for such attentions; that such girls, despairing of respectable marriage and social mobility, are inclined to seek reassurance of their sense of adequacy *as girls* by abandoning their

reputation for chastity, which has proven, for them, an unrewarding virtue, and by making themselves sexually available; that they gain, thereby, the assurance of male attention and male favors, albeit within transitory and unstable relationships which further lower their value on the marriage market. Like its male counterpart, this pattern represents the rejection of conventional and respectable but unattainable status goals and the disciplines which lead to them, and the substitution therefor of the satisfactions to be obtained in the immediate present with the resources presently available. The complete mechanism whereby the social structure generates this subculture is surely much more complex than this, but the argument is intended only to suggest a common core of motivation which goes far to explain the characteristic sexual content of this subculture and, indeed, of female delinquency in general.

Not only is little known about this parent subculture. With perhaps one exception, still less is known about the numerous varieties of female delinquent subcultures, except that they exist. There are gangs of girls organized for and around sexual activities; there are mixed groups of middle- and upper-middle-class boys and girls organized as sex gangs, with an emphasis on refinement, gentility, and sophistication; and there are gangs of girls strongly resembling the male hoodlum gang. At the present time little can be said, even in a descriptive way, about any of these.

It is possible to say a little more about the female drug addict subculture, on the basis of our analysis of interview material gathered in the course of the Chicago drug use study, and of material in preparation for a Master's degree thesis at the University of Chicago (16). The observations to be set forth here are tentative and will be more fully elaborated in a later publication.

The girls whose interviews we have read are predominantly Negro, of low social status, and located in the same type of area as that from which the male addicts characteristically come. However, some of them come from relatively respectable and well-off Negro families and there are no strikingly obvious common patterns, sequences, or problems of adjustment exhibited by all the cases. However, certain features recur with impressive frequency. Almost all of these girls have had difficulty in establishing satisfactory relationships with the other sex, although for divers reasons. A theme which runs through history after history is isolation from the main stream of normal, relaxed, boy-girl relationships, loneliness, depression, and a pathetic yearning for marriage to a stable, responsible, respectable man. These girls appear to fall prey easily to exploitative and irresponsible men, who exercise extraordinary power over them apparently because of the girls' need for male companionship and love, or a simulacrum thereof. Pregnancy, desertion, and "hustling" occur with monotonous regularity. The girl may be introduced to opiate drugs by other girls, by male companions, or in mixed groups of "fast" company. The nature of these circumstances is such that the girls often find themselves isolated, depressed, and threatened. These conditions heighten their dependence on the drug and upon social contacts which assure the completion of the cycle.

After addiction, hustling on a full time basis in order to support her habit and sometimes her lover's habit is almost invariable. During the period of addiction her range of associates is almost entirely narrowed to other addicts and prostitutes, but her relationships with even these people are likely to be tangential and incidental to the procurement of the drug, and to her profession. A vicious cycle is characteristic of all the histories we have read: addiction and prostitution lead to a further isolation from respectable society and a lowering of status; these, in turn, increase loneliness and depression and the girl's vulnerability to exploitation by men; and these, in turn, encourage continuation in or relapse into the use of drugs.

Although these girls move on the fringes of the cat culture, they do not, we think, participate fully in it. They are not "fast, noisy, aggressive cats," seeking status among other cats through their kicks and their hustle. They are not proud of their habit and their hustle is strictly business, frequently a distasteful one. Without exception, these girls express a desire for respectability, but they find it difficult to escape from the vicious circle in which they have become entrapped.

SUMMARY

It is apparent that we have barely stepped over the threshold of the study of delinquent subcultures. The purpose of this paper has been to enumerate some of the principal varieties of these subcultures, to describe or to suggest some of their important features, to speculate on their origins, to indicate the types of research and theoretical work which are most needed, and to provide some suggestive hypotheses to be tested or revised by later research.

REFERENCES

1. CHEIN, ISIDOR, AND ROSENFELD, EVA, "Juvenile Narcotics Use," *Law and Contemporary Problems*, 1957, 22, 52–68.
2. COHEN, ALBERT K., *Delinquent Boys: The Culture of the Gang*. New York: The Free Press, 1955.
3. COHEN, ALBERT K., "Sociological Research in Juvenile Delinquency," *American Journal of Orthopsychiatry*, 1957, 27, 781–88.
4. COHEN, ALBERT K., "Middle-class delinquency and the social structure," paper read at the annual meeting of the American Sociological Society, 1957.
5. CRAWFORD, PAUL L., MALAMUD, DANIEL L., AND DUMPSON, JAMES R. *Working with Teen-Age Gangs*. New York: Welfare Council of New York City, 1950.
6. EISENSTADT, S. N., "Delinquent Group-Formation Among Immigrant Youth," *British Journal of Delinquency*, 1951, 2, 34–45.
7. FINESTONE, HAROLD, "Cats, Kicks and Color," *Social Problems*, 1957, 5, 3–13.
8. FINESTONE, HAROLD, "Narcotics and Criminality," *Law and Contemporary Problems*, 1957, 22, 69–85.
9. GREEN, ARNOLD, "The 'Cult of Personality' and Sexual Relations," *Psychiatry*, 1941, 4, 344–48.
10. GROSSER, GEORGE. "Juvenile delinquency and contemporary American sex roles," Ph.D. dissertation, Harvard University, 1952.
11. JEPHCOTT, A. P., AND CARTER, M. P. *The Social Background of Delinquency*, University of Nottingham, 1955.
12. KOBRIN, SOLOMON, "The Conflict of Values in Delinquency Areas," *American Sociological Review*, 1951, 16, 653–61.
13. NYE, F. IVAN, SHORT, JAMES F. JR., AND OLSON, VIRGIL J., "Socio-economic Status and Delinquent Behavior," *The American Journal of Sociology*, 1958, 63, 381–89.
14. ROSENFELD, EVA, "Social Research and Social Action in Prevention of Juvenile Delinquency," *Social Problems*, 1957, 4, 138–48.

15. SALISBURY, HARRISON E., "The Shook-up Generation," a series of articles from *The New York Times*, March 24–30, 1958.
16. SHYPPER, MIRIAM. "The 'career' of opiate addiction," Master's thesis, University of Chicago, 1953.
17. SUTHERLAND, EDWIN H. *Principles of Criminology* (5th edition), reviewed by Donald R. Cressey. Chicago: J. B. Lippincott Co., 1955.
18. SYKES, GRESHAM M., AND MATZA, DAVID, "Techniques of Neutralization: A Theory of Delinquency," *American Sociological Review*, 1957, 22, 664–70.
19. WATTENBERG, WILLIAM, AND BALISTRIERI, JAMES, "Automobile Theft: A 'Favored-Group' Delinquency," *The American Journal of Sociology*, 1952, 57, 575–79.
20. WHYTE, WILLIAM F. *Street Corner Society.* Chicago: University of Chicago Press, 1955.
21. WILENSKY, HAROLD L., AND LEBEAUX, CHARLES N. *Industrial Society and Social Welfare.* New York: The Russell Sage Foundation, 1958.
22. "The Cherubs Are Rumbling," *The New Yorker*, September 21, 1957.
23. *Drug Addiction Among Young Persons in Chicago.* A Report of a Study Conducted by the Illinois Institute for Juvenile Research and The Chicago Area Project, issued October, 1953.
24. *Notes on the Gates-Tompkins Chaplains.* Research Department, Bedford Stuyvesant Unit, Council of Social and Athletic Clubs, Brooklyn, New York, January, 1958.
25. *Reaching the Group: An Analysis of Group Work Methods Used with Teen-Agers.* New York City Youth Board, Monograph No. 4, April, 1956.
26. *Reaching the Unreached.* New York City Youth Board, 1952.
27. Vagrant Children, *Problems in Education Series*, No. 3. UNESCO Publication 644, Paris, 1951.
28. *Who Killed Michael Farmer?* Verbatim transcript (mimeographed) of a broadcast over the Columbia Broadcasting System Radio Network, Monday, April 21, 1958.

15.

WALTER B. MILLER

LOWER CLASS CULTURE AS A GENERATING MILIEU OF GANG DELINQUENCY

The etiology of delinquency has long been a controversial issue, and is particularly so at present. As new frames of reference for explaining human behavior have been added to traditional theories, some authors have adopted the practice of citing the major postulates of each school of thought as they pertain to delinquency, and going on to state that causality must be conceived in terms of the dynamic interaction of a complex combination of variables on many levels. The major sets of etiological factors currently adduced to explain delinquency are, in simplified terms, the physiological (delinquency results from organic pathology), the psychodynamic (delinquency is a "behavioral disorder" resulting primarily from emotional disturbance

generated by a defective mother-child relationship), and the environmental (delinquency is the product of disruptive forces, "disorganization," in the actor's physical or social environment).

This paper selects one particular kind of "delinquency"[1]—law-violating acts committed by members of adolescent street corner groups in lower class communities—and attempts to show that the dominant component of motivation underlying these acts consists in a directed at-

[1]The complex issues involved in deriving a definition of "delinquency" cannot be discussed here. The term "delinquent" is used in this paper to characterize behavior or acts committed by individuals within specified age limits which if known to official authorities could result in legal action. The concept of a "delinquent" individual has little or no utility in the approach used here; rather, specified types of *acts* which may be committed rarely or frequently by few or many individuals are characterized as "delinquent."

SOURCE: Walter B. Miller, "Lower Class Culture as a Generating Milieu of Gang Delinquency," *Journal of Social Issues* 14, no. 3 (1958): 5–19. Permission to reprint granted by publisher and author.

tempt by the actor to adhere to forms of behavior, and to achieve standards of value as they are defined within that community. It takes as a premise that the motivation of behavior in this situation can be approached most productively by attempting to understand the nature of cultural forces impinging on the acting individual as they are perceived *by the actor himself*—although by no means only that segment of these forces of which the actor is consciously aware—rather than as they are perceived and evaluated from the reference position of another cultural system. In the case of "gang" delinquency, the cultural system which exerts the most direct influence on behavior is that of the lower class community itself—a long-established, distinctively patterned tradition with an integrity of its own—rather than a so-called "delinquent subculture" which has arisen through conflict with middle class culture and is oriented to the deliberate violation of middle class norms.

The bulk of the substantive data on which the following material is based was collected in connection with a service-research project in the control of gang delinquency. During the service aspect of the project, which lasted for three years, seven trained social workers maintained contact with 21 corner group units in a "slum" district of a large eastern city for periods of time ranging from 10 to 30 months. Groups were Negro and white, male and female, and in early, middle, and late adolescence. Over 8,000 pages of direct observational data on behavior patterns of group members and other community residents were collected; almost daily contact was maintained for a total time period of about 13 worker years. Data include workers' contact reports, participant observation reports by the writer—a cultural anthropologist—and direct tape recordings of group activities and discussions.[2]

FOCAL CONCERNS OF LOWER CLASS CULTURE

There is a substantial segment of present-day American society whose way of life, values, and characteristic patterns of behavior are the product of a distinctive cultural system which may be termed "lower class." Evidence indicates that this cultural system is becoming increasingly distinctive, and that the size of the group which shares this tradition is increasing.[3] The lower class way of life, in common with that of all distinctive cultural groups, is characterized by a set of focal concerns—areas or issues which command widespread and persistent attention and a high degree of emotional involvement. The specific concerns cited here, while by no means confined to the American lower classes, constitute a distinctive *patterning* of concerns which differs significantly, both in rank order and weighting from that of American middle class culture. Table 3–1 presents a highly schematic and simplified listing of six of the major concerns of lower class culture. Each is conceived as a "dimension" within which a fairly wide and varied range of alternative behavior patterns may be followed by different individuals under different situations. They are listed roughly in order of the degree of *explicit* attention accorded each, and, in this sense represent a weighted ranking of concerns. The "perceived alternatives" represent polar positions which define certain parameters within each dimension. As

gories. Analysis of these data aims to ascertain the actual nature of customary behavior in these areas, and the extent to which the social work effort was able to effect behavioral changes.

[3] Between 40 and 60 percent of all Americans are directly influenced by lower class culture, with about 15 percent, or 25 million, comprising the "hard core" lower class group—defined primarily by its use of the "female-based" household as the basic form of child-rearing unit and of the "serial monogamy" mating pattern as the primary form of marriage. The term "lower class culture" as used here refers most specifically to the way of life of the "hard core" group; systematic research in this area would probably reveal at least four to six major subtypes of lower class culture, for some of which the "concerns" presented here would be differently weighted, especially for those subtypes in which "law-abiding" behavior has a high overt valuation. It is impossible within the compass of this short paper to make the finer intracultural distinctions which a more accurate presentation would require.

[2] A three year research project is being financed under National Institutes of Health Grant M–1414, and administered through the Boston University School of Social Work. The primary research effort has subjected all collected material to a uniform data-coding process. All information bearing on some 70 areas of behavior (behavior in reference to school, police, theft, assault, sex, collective athletics, etc.) is extracted from the records, recorded on coded data cards, and filed under relevant cate-

TABLE 3–1.

FOCAL CONCERNS OF LOWER CLASS CULTURE

Area	Perceived Alternatives (*state, quality, condition*)	
1. Trouble: . . . . law-abiding behavior	law-violating behavior
2. Toughness: . . . . physical prowess, skill; "masculinity"; fearlessness, bravery, daring	weakness, ineptitude; effeminacy; timidity, cowardice, caution
3. Smartness: . . . . ability to outsmart, dupe, "con"; gaining money by "wits"; shrewdness, adroitness in repartee	gullibility, "con-ability"; gaining money by hard work; slowness, dull-wittedness, verbal maladroitness
4. Excitement: . . . . thrill; risk, danger; change, activity	boredom; "deadness," safeness; sameness, passivity
5. Fate: . . . . favored by fortune, being "lucky"	ill-omened, being "unlucky"
6. Autonomy: . . . . freedom from external constraint; freedom from superordinate authority; independence	presence of external constraint; presence of strong authority; dependency, being "cared for"

will be explained in more detail, it is necessary in relating the influence of these "concerns" to the motivation of delinquent behavior to specify *which* of its aspects is oriented to, whether orientation is *overt* or *covert, positive* (conforming to or seeking the aspect), or *negative* (rejecting or seeking to avoid the aspect).

The concept "focal concern" is used here in preference to the concept "value" for several interrelated reasons: (1) It is more readily derivable from direct field observation. (2) It is descriptively neutral—permitting independent consideration of positive and negative valences as varying under different conditions, whereas "value" carries a built-in positive valence. (3) It makes possible more refined analysis of subcultural differences, since it reflects actual behavior, whereas "value" tends to wash out intracultural differences since it is colored by notions of the "official" ideal.

Trouble. Concern over "trouble" is a dominant feature of lower class culture. The concept has various shades of meaning; "trouble" in one of its aspects represents a situation or a kind of behavior which results in unwelcome or complicating involvement with official authorities or agencies of middle class society. "Getting into trouble" and "staying out of trouble" represent major issues for male and female, adults and children. For men, "trouble" frequently involves fighting or sexual adventures while drinking; for women, sexual involvement with disadvantageous consequences. Expressed desire to avoid behavior which violates moral or legal norms is often based less on an explicit commitment to "official" moral or legal standards than on a desire to avoid "getting into trouble," e.g., the complicating consequences of the action.

The dominant concern over "trouble" involves a distinction of critical importance for the lower class community—that between "law-abiding" and "non-law-abiding" behavior. There is a high degree of sensitivity as to where each person stands in relation to these two classes of activity. Whereas in the middle class community a major dimension for evaluating a person's status is "achievement" and its external symbols, in the lower class, personal status is very frequently gauged along the law-abiding—non-law-abiding dimension. A mother will evaluate the suitability of her daughter's boyfriend less on the basis of his achievement potential than on the basis of his innate "trouble" potential. This sensitive awareness of the opposition of "trouble-producing" and "non-trouble-producing" behavior represents both a major basis for deriving status distinctions, and an internalized conflict potential for the individual.

As in the case of other focal concerns, which of two perceived alternatives—"law-abiding" or "non-law-abiding"—is valued varies according to the individual and the circumstances; in many instances there is an overt commitment to the "law-abiding" alternative, but a covert commitment to the "non-law-abiding." In certain situations, "getting into trouble" is overtly recognized as prestige-conferring: for example, membership in certain adult and adolescent primary groupings ("gangs") is contingent on having demonstrated an explicit commitment to the law-violating alternative. It is most important to note that the choice between "law-abiding" and "non-law-abiding" behavior is still a choice *within* lower class culture; the distinction between the policeman and the criminal, the outlaw and the sheriff, involves primarily this one dimension; in other respects they have a high community of interests. Not infrequently brothers raised in an identical cultural milieu will become police and criminals respectively.

For a substantial segment of the lower class population "getting into trouble" is not in itself overtly defined as prestige-conferring, but is implicitly recognized as a means to other valued ends, e.g., the covertly valued desire to be "cared for" and subject to external constraint, or the overtly valued state of excitement or risk. Very frequently "getting into trouble" is multi-functional, and achieves several sets of valued ends.

Toughness. The concept of "toughness" in lower class culture represents a compound combination of qualities or states. Among its most important components are physical prowess, evidenced both by demonstrated possession of strength and endurance and athletic skill; "masculinity," symbolized by a distinctive complex of acts and avoidances (bodily tattooing; absence

of sentimentality; non-concern with "art," "literature," conceptualization of women as conquest objects, etc.); and bravery in the face of physical threat. The model for the "tough guy" —hard, fearless, undemonstrative, skilled in physical combat—is represented by the movie gangster of the thirties, the "private eye," and the movie cowboy.

The genesis of the intense concern over "toughness" in lower class culture is probably related to the fact that a significant proportion of lower class males are reared in a predominantly female household, and lack a consistently present male figure with whom to identify and from whom to learn essential components of a "male" role. Since women serve as a primary object of identification during pre-adolescent years, the almost obsessive lower class concern with "masculinity" probably resembles a type of compulsive reaction-formation. A concern over homosexuality runs like a persistent thread through lower class culture. This is manifested by the institutionalized practice of baiting "queers," often accompanied by violent physical attacks, an expressed contempt for "softness" or frills, and the use of the local term for "homosexual" as a generalized pejorative epithet (e.g., higher class individuals or upwardly mobile peers are frequently characterized as "fags" or "queers"). The distinction between "overt" and "covert" orientation to aspects of an area of concern is especially important in regard to "toughness." A positive overt evaluation of behavior defined as "effeminate" would be out of the question for a lower class male; however, built into lower class culture is a range of devices which permit men to adopt behaviors and concerns which in other cultural milieux fall within the province of women, and at the same time to be defined as "tough" and manly. For example, lower class men can be professional short-order cooks in a diner and still be regarded as "tough." The highly intimate circumstances of the street corner gang involve the recurrent expression of strongly affectionate feelings towards other men. Such expressions, however, are disguised as their opposite, taking the form of ostensibly aggressive verbal and physical interaction (kidding, "ranking," rough-housing, etc.).

Smartness. "Smartness," as conceptualized in lower class culture, involves the capacity to outsmart, outfox, outwit, dupe, "take," "con" another or others, and the concomitant capacity to avoid being outwitted, "taken," or duped oneself. In its essence, smartness involves the capacity to achieve a valued entity—material goods, personal status—through a maximum use of mental agility and a minimum use of physical effort. This capacity has an extremely long tradition in lower class culture, and is highly valued. Lower class culture can be characterized as "non-intellectual" only if intellectualism is defined specifically in terms of control over a particular body of formally learned knowledge involving "culture" (art, literature, "good" music, etc.), a generalized perspective on the past and present conditions of our own and other societies, and other areas of knowledge imparted by formal educational institutions. This particular type of mental attainment is, in general, overtly disvalued and frequently associated with effeminancy; "smartness" in the lower class sense, however, is highly valued.

The lower class child learns and practices the use of this skill in the street corner situation. Individuals continually practice duping and outwitting one another through recurrent card games and other forms of gambling, mutual exchanges of insults, and "testing" for mutual "conability." Those who demonstrate competence in this skill are accorded considerable prestige. Leadership roles in the corner group are frequently allocated according to demonstrated capacity in the two areas of "smartness" and "toughness"; the ideal leader combines both, but the "smart" leader is often accorded more prestige than the "tough" one—reflecting a general lower class respect for "brains" in the "smartness" sense.[4]

The model of the "smart" person is represented in popular media by the card shark, the professional gambler, the "con" artist, the promoter. A conceptual distinction is made between two kinds of people: "suckers," easy marks,

"lushes," dupes, who work for their money and are legitimate targets of exploitation; and sharp operators, the "brainy" ones, who live by their wits and "getting" from the suckers by mental adroitness.

Involved in the syndrome of capacities related to "smartness" is a dominant emphasis in lower class culture on ingenious aggressive repartee. This skill, learned and practiced in the context of the corner group, ranges in form from the widely prevalent semi-ritualized teasing, kidding, razzing, "ranking," so characteristic of male peer group interaction, to the highly ritualized type of mutual insult interchange known as "the dirty dozens," "the dozens," "playing house," and other terms. This highly patterned cultural form is practiced on its most advanced level in adult male Negro society, but less polished variants are found throughout lower class culture—practiced, for example, by white children, male and female, as young as four or five. In essence, "doin' the dozens" involves two antagonists who vie with each other in the exchange of increasingly inflammatory insults, with incestuous and perverted sexual relations with the mother a dominant theme. In this form of insult interchange, as well as on other less ritualized occasions for joking, semi-serious, and serious mutual invective, a very high premium is placed on ingenuity, hair-trigger responsiveness, inventiveness, and the acute exercise of mental faculties.

Excitement. For many lower class individuals the rhythm of life fluctuates between periods of relatively routine or repetitive activity and sought situations of great emotional stimulation. Many of the most characteristic features of lower class life are related to the search for excitement or "thrill." Involved here are the highly prevalent use of alcohol by both sexes and the widespread use of gambling of all kinds —playing the numbers, betting on horse races, dice, cards. The quest for excitement finds what is perhaps its most vivid expression in the highly patterned practice of the recurrent "night on the town." This practice, designated by various terms in different areas ("honky-tonkin'"; "goin' out on the town"; "bar hoppin'"), involves a patterned set of activities in which alcohol, music, and sexual adventuring are major compo-

---

[4]The "brains-brawn" set of capacities are often paired in lower class folk lore or accounts of lower class life, e.g., "Brer Fox" and "Brer Bear" in the Uncle Remus stories, or George and Lennie in *Of Mice and Men.*

nents. A group or individual sets out to "make the rounds" of various bars or night clubs. Drinking continues progressively throughout the evening. Men seek to "pick up" women, and women play the risky game of entertaining sexual advances. Fights between men involving women, gambling, and claims of physical prowess, in various combinations, are frequent consequences of a night of making the rounds. The explosive potential of this type of adventuring with sex and aggression, frequently leading to "trouble," is semi-explicitly sought by the individual. Since there is always a good likelihood that being out on the town will eventuate in fights, etc., the practice involves elements of sought risk and desired danger.

Counterbalancing the "flirting with danger" aspect of the "excitement" concern is the prevalence in lower class culture of other well established patterns of activity which involve long periods of relative inaction, or passivity. The term "hanging out" in lower class culture refers to extended periods of standing around, often with peer mates, doing what is defined as "nothing," "shooting the breeze," etc. A definite periodicity exists in the pattern of activity relating to the two aspects of the "excitement" dimension. For many lower class individuals the venture into the high risk world of alcohol, sex, and fighting occurs regularly once a week, with interim periods devoted to accommodating to possible consequences of these periods, along with recurrent resolves not to become so involved again.

Fate. Related to the quest for excitement is the concern with fate, fortune, or luck. Here also a distinction is made between two states—being "lucky" or "in luck," and being unlucky or jinxed. Many lower class individuals feel that their lives are subject to a set of forces over which they have relatively little control. These are not directly equated with the supernatural forces of formally organized religion, but relate more to a concept of "destiny," or man as a pawn of magical powers. Not infrequently this often implicit world view is associated with a conception of the ultimate futility of directed effort towards a goal: if the cards are right, or the dice good to you, or if your lucky number comes up, things will go your way; if luck is

against you, it's not worth trying. The concept of performing semi-magical rituals so that one's "luck will change" is prevalent; one hopes that as a result he will move from the state of being "unlucky" to that of being "lucky." The element of fantasy plays an important part in this area. Related to and complementing the notion that "only suckers work" (Smartness) is the idea that once things start going your way, relatively independent of your own effort, all good things will come to you. Achieving great material rewards (big cars, big houses, a roll of cash to flash in a fancy night club), valued in lower class as well as in other parts of American culture, is a recurrent theme in lower class fantasy and folk lore; the cocaine dreams of Willie the Weeper or Minnie the Moocher present the components of this fantasy in vivid detail.

The prevalence in the lower class community of many forms of gambling, mentioned in connection with the "excitement" dimension, is also relevant here. Through cards and pool which involve skill, and thus both "toughness" and "smartness"; or through race horse betting, involving "smartness"; or through playing the numbers, involving predominantly "luck," one may make a big killing with a minimum of directed and persistent effort within conventional occupational channels. Gambling in its many forms illustrates the fact that many of the persistent features of lower class culture are multi-functional—serving a range of desired ends at the same time. Describing some of the incentives behind gambling has involved mention of all of the focal concerns cited so far—Toughness, Smartness, and Excitement, in addition to Fate.

Autonomy. The extent and nature of control over the behavior of the individual—an important concern in most cultures—has a special significance and is distinctively patterned in lower class culture. The discrepancy between what is overtly valued and what is covertly sought is particularly striking in this area. On the overt level there is a strong and frequently expressed resentment of the idea of external controls, restrictions on behavior, and unjust or coercive authority. "No one's gonna push *me* around," or "I'm gonna tell him he can take the job and shove it. . . ." are commonly expressed sentiments. Similar explicit attitudes are maintained to systems of behavior-restricting rules, insofar as these are perceived as representing the injunctions, and bearing the sanctions of superordinate authority. In addition, in lower class culture a close conceptual connection is made between "authority" and "nurturance." To be restrictively or firmly controlled is to be cared for. Thus the overtly negative evaluation of superordinate authority frequently extends as well to nurturance, care, or protection. The desire for personal independence is often expressed in such terms as "I don't need *nobody* to take care of me. I can take care of myself!" Actual patterns of behavior, however, reveal a marked discrepancy between expressed sentiment and what is covertly valued. Many lower class people appear to seek out highly restrictive social environments wherein stringent external controls are maintained over their behavior. Such institutions as the armed forces, the mental hospital, the disciplinary school, the prison or correctional institution, provide environments which incorporate a strict and detailed set of rules defining and limiting behavior, and enforced by an authority system which controls and applies coercive sanctions for deviance from these rules. While under the jurisdiction of such systems, the lower class person generally expresses to his peers continual resentment of the coercive, unjust, and arbitrary exercise of authority. Having been released, or having escaped from these milieux, however, he will often act in such a way as to insure recommitment, or choose recommitment voluntarily after a temporary period of "freedom."

Lower class patients in mental hospitals will exercise considerable ingenuity to insure continued commitment while voicing the desire to get out; delinquent boys will frequently "run" from a correctional institution to activate efforts to return them; to be caught and returned means that one is cared for. Since "being controlled" is equated with "being cared for," attempts are frequently made to "test" the severity or strictness of superordinate authority to see if it remains firm. If intended or executed rebellion produces swift and firm punitive sanctions, the individual is reassured, at the same time that

he is complaining bitterly at the injustice of being caught and punished. Some environmental milieux, having been tested in this fashion for the "firmness" of their coercive sanctions, are rejected, ostensibly for being too strict, actually for not being strict enough. This is frequently so in the case of "problematic" behavior by lower class youngsters in the public schools, which generally cannot command the coercive controls implicitly sought by the individual.

A similar discrepancy between what is overtly and covertly desired is found in the area of dependence-independence. The pose of tough rebellious independence often assumed by the lower class person frequently conceals powerful dependency cravings. These are manifested primarily by obliquely expressed resentment when "care" is not forthcoming rather than by expressed satisfaction when it is. The concern over autonomy-dependency is related both to "trouble" and "fate." Insofar as the lower class individual feels that his behavior is controlled by forces which often propel him into "trouble" in the face of an explicit determination to avoid it, there is an implied appeal to "save me from myself." A solution appears to lie in arranging things so that his behavior will be coercively restricted by an externally imposed set of controls strong enough to forcibly restrain his inexplicable inclination to get in trouble. The periodicity observed in connection with the "excitement" dimension is also relevant here; after involvement in trouble-producing behavior (assault, sexual adventure, a "drunk"), the individual will actively seek a locus of imposed control (his wife, prison, a restrictive job); after a given period of subjection to this control, resentment against it mounts, leading to a "break away" and a search for involvement in further "trouble."

FOCAL CONCERNS OF THE LOWER CLASS ADOLESCENT STREET CORNER GROUP

The one-sex peer group is a highly prevalent and significant structural form in the lower class community. There is a strong probability that the prevalence and stability of this type of unit is directly related to the prevalence of a stabilized type of lower class child-rearing unit— the "female-based" household. This is a nuclear kin unit in which a male parent is either absent from the household, present only sporadically, or, when present, only minimally or inconsistently involved in the support and rearing of children. This unit usually consists of one or more females of child-bearing age and their offspring. The females are frequently related to one another by blood or marriage ties, and the unit often includes two or more generations of women, e.g., the mother and/or aunt of the principal child-bearing female.

The nature of social groupings in the lower class community may be clarified if we make the assumption that it is the *one-sex peer unit* rather than the two-parent family unit which represents the most significant relational unit for both sexes in lower class communities. Lower class society may be pictured as comprising a set of age-graded one-sex groups which constitute the major psychic focus and reference group for those over 12 or 13. Men and women of mating age leave these groups periodically to form temporary marital alliances, but these lack stability, and after varying periods of "trying out" the two-sex family arrangement, gravitate back to the more "comfortable" one-sex grouping, whose members exert strong pressure on the individual *not* to disrupt the group by adopting a two-sex household pattern of life.[5] Membership in a stable and solidary peer unit is vital to the lower class individual precisely to the extent to which a range of essential functions —psychological, educational, and others, are not provided by the "family" unit.

The adolescent street corner group represents the adolescent variant of this lower class structural form. What has been called the "delinquent gang" is one subtype of this form, defined on the basis of frequency of participation in law-violating activity; this subtype should not be considered a legitimate unit of study per se, but rather as one particular variant of the adolescent street corner group. The "hanging" peer group is a unit of particular importance

for the adolescent male. In many cases it is the most stable and solidary primary group he has ever belonged to; for boys reared in female-based households the corner group provides the first real opportunity to learn essential aspects of the male role in the context of peers facing similar problems of sex-role identification.

The form and functions of the adolescent corner group operate as a selective mechanism in recruiting members. The activity patterns of the group require a high level of intra-group solidarity; individual members must possess a good capacity for subordinating individual desires to general group interests as well as the capacity for intimate and persisting interaction. Thus highly "disturbed" individuals, or those who cannot tolerate consistently imposed sanctions on "deviant" behavior cannot remain accepted members; the group itself will extrude those whose behavior exceeds limits defined as "normal." This selective process produces a type of group whose members possess to an unusually high degree both the *capacity* and *motivation* to conform to perceived cultural norms, so that the nature of the system of norms and values oriented to is a particularly influential component of motivation.

Focal concerns of the male adolescent corner group are those of the general cultural milieu in which it functions. As would be expected, the relative weighting and importance of these concerns pattern somewhat differently for adolescents than for adults. The nature of this patterning centers around two additional "concerns" of particular importance to this group—concern with "belonging," and with "status." These may be conceptualized as being on a higher level of abstraction than concerns previously cited, since "status" and "belonging" are achieved *via* cited concern areas of Toughness, etc.

Belonging. Since the corner group fulfills essential functions for the individual, being a member in good standing of the group is of vital importance for its members. A continuing concern over who is "in" and who is not involves the citation and detailed discussion of highly refined criteria for "in-group" membership. The phrase "he hangs with us" means "he is accepted as a member in good standing by current consensus"; conversely, "he don't hang

---

[5]Further data on the female-based household unit (estimated as comprising about 15 per cent of all American "families") and the role of one-sex groupings in lower class culture are contained in Walter B. Miller, "Implications of Urban Lower Class Culture for Social Work," *Social Service Review*, vol. 33, no. 3 (1959).

with us" means he is not so accepted. One achieves "belonging" primarily by demonstrating knowledge of and a determination to adhere to the system of standards and valued qualities defined by the group. One maintains membership by acting in conformity with valued aspects of Toughness, Smartness, Autonomy, etc. In those instances where conforming to norms of this reference group at the same time violates norms of other reference groups (e.g., middle class adults, institutional "officials"), immediate reference group norms are much more compelling since violation risks invoking the group's most powerful sanction: exclusion.

Status. In common with most adolescents in American society, the lower class corner group manifests a dominant concern with "status." What differentiates this type of group from others, however, is the particular set of criteria and weighting thereof by which "status" is defined. In general, status is achieved and maintained by demonstrated possession of the valued qualities of lower class culture—Toughness, Smartness, expressed resistance to authority, daring, etc. It is important to stress once more that the individual orients to these concerns *as they are defined within lower class society*; e.g., the status-conferring potential of "smartness" in the sense of scholastic achievement generally ranges from negligible to negative.

The concern with "status" is manifested in a variety of ways. Intra-group status is a continued concern, and is derived and tested constantly by means of a set of status-ranking activities; the intra-group "pecking order" is constantly at issue. One gains status within the group by demonstrated superiority in Toughness (physical prowess, bravery, skill in athletics and games such as pool and cards), Smartness (skill in repartee, capacity to "dupe" fellow group members), and the like. The term "ranking," used to refer to the pattern of intra-group aggressive repartee, indicates awareness of the fact that this is one device for establishing intra-group status hierarchy.

The concern over status in the adolescent corner group involves in particular the component of "adultness," the intense desire to be seen as "grown up," and a corresponding aversion to "kid stuff." "Adult" status is defined less in terms

of the assumption of "adult" responsibility than in terms of certain external symbols of adult status—a car, ready cash, and, in particular, a perceived "freedom" to drink, smoke, and gamble as one wishes and to come and go without external restrictions. The desire to be seen as "adult" is often a more significant component of much involvement in illegal drinking, gambling, and automobile driving than the explicit enjoyment of these acts as such.

The intensity of the corner group member's desire to be seen as "adult" is sufficiently great that he feels called upon to demonstrate qualities associated with adultness (Toughness, Smartness, Autonomy) to a much greater degree than a lower class adult. This means that he will seek out and utilize those avenues to these qualities which he perceives as available with greater intensity than an adult and less regard for their "legitimacy." In this sense the adolescent variant of lower class culture represents a maximization or an intensified manifestation of many of its most characteristic features.

Concern over status is also manifested in reference to other street corner groups. The term "rep" used in this regard is especially significant, and has broad connotations. In its most frequent and explicit connotation, "rep" refers to the "toughness" of the corner group as a whole relative to that of other groups; a "pecking order" also exists among the several corner groups in a given interactional area, and there is a common perception that the safety or security of the group and all its members depends on maintaining a solid "rep" for toughness vis-a-vis other groups. This motive is most frequently advanced as a reason for involvement in gang fights: "We *can't* chicken out on this fight; our rep would be shot!"; this implies that the group would be relegated to the bottom of the status ladder and become a helpless and recurrent target of external attack.

On the other hand, there is implicit in the concept of "rep" the recognition that "rep" has or may have a dual basis—corresponding to the two aspects of the "trouble" dimension. It is recognized that group as well as individual status can be based on both "law-abiding" and "law-violating" behavior. The situational resolution of the persisting conflict between the "law-abiding" and "law-violating" bases of status comprises a vital set of dynamics in determining whether a "delinquent" mode of behavior will be adopted by a group, under what circumstances, and how persistently. The determinants of this choice are evidently highly complex and fluid, and rest on a range of factors including the presence and perceptual immediacy of different community reference-group loci (e.g., professional criminals, police, clergy, teachers, settlement house workers), the personality structures and "needs" of group members, the presence in the community of social work, recreation, or educational programs which can facilitate utilization of the "law-abiding" basis of status, and so on.

What remains constant is the critical importance of "status" both for the members of the group as individuals and for the group as a whole insofar as members perceive their individual destinies as linked to the destiny of the group, and the fact that action geared to attain status is much more acutely oriented to the fact of status itself than to the legality or illegality, morality or immorality of the means used to achieve it.

LOWER CLASS CULTURE AND THE MOTIVATION OF DELINQUENT BEHAVIOR

The customary set of activities of the adolescent street corner group includes activities which are in violation of laws and ordinances of the legal code. Most of these center around assault and theft of various types (the gang fight; auto theft; assault on an individual; petty pilfering and shoplifting; "mugging"; pocketbook theft). Members of street corner gangs are well aware of the law-violating nature of these acts; they are not psychopaths, nor physically or mentally "defective"; in fact, since the corner group supports and enforces a rigorous set of standards which demand a high degree of fitness and personal competence, it tends to recruit from the most "able" members of the community.

Why, then, is the commission of crimes a customary feature of gang activity? The most general answer is that the commission of crimes by members of adolescent street corner groups

is motivated primarily by the attempt to achieve ends, states, or conditions which are valued, and to avoid those that are disvalued within their most meaningful cultural milieu, through those culturally available avenues which appear as the most feasible means of attaining those ends.

The operation of these influences is well illustrated by the gang fight—a prevalent and characteristic type of corner group delinquency. This type of activity comprises a highly stylized and culturally patterned set of sequences. Although details vary under different circumstances, the following events are generally included. A member or several members of group A "trespass" on the claimed territory of group B. While there they commit an act or acts which group B defines as a violation of its rightful privileges, an affront to their honor, or a challenge to their "rep." Frequently this act involves advances to a girl associated with group B; it may occur at a dance or party; sometimes the mere act of "trespass" is seen as deliberate provocation. Members of group B then assault members of group A, if they are caught while still in B's territory. Assaulted members of group A return to their "home" territory and recount to members of their group details of the incident, stressing the insufficient nature of the provocation ("I just *looked* at her! Hardly even said anything!"), and the unfair circumstances of the assault ("About *twenty* guys jumped just the *two* of us"). The highly colored account is acutely inflammatory; group A, perceiving its honor violated and its "rep" threatened, feels obligated to retaliate in force. Sessions of detailed planning now occur; allies are recruited if the size of group A and its potential allies appears to necessitate larger numbers; strategy is plotted, and messengers dispatched. Since the prospect of a gang fight is frightening to even the "toughest" group members, a constant rehearsal of the provocative incident or incidents and the essentially evil nature of the opponents accompanies the planning process to bolster possibly weakening motivation to fight. The excursion into "enemy" territory sometimes results in a full scale fight; more often group B cannot be found, or the police appear and stop the fight, "tipped off" by an anonymous informant. When this occurs, group members express disgust and disappointment; secretly there is much relief; their honor has been avenged without incurring injury; often the anonymous tipster is a member of one of the involved groups.

The basic elements of this type of delinquency are sufficiently stabilized and recurrent as to constitute an essentially ritualized pattern, resembling both in structure and expressed motives for action classic forms such as the European "duel," the American Indian tribal war, and the Celtic clan feud. Although the arousing and "acting out" of individual aggressive emotions are inevitably involved in the gang fight, neither its form nor motivational dynamics can be adequately handled within a predominantly personality-focused frame of reference.

It would be possible to develop in considerable detail the processes by which the commission of a range of illegal acts is either explicitly supported by, implicitly demanded by, or not materially inhibited by factors relating to the local concerns of lower class culture. In place of such a development, the following three statements condense in general terms the operation of these processes:

1. Following cultural practices which comprise essential elements of the total life pattern of lower class culture automatically violates certain legal norms.

2. In instances where alternate avenues to similar objectives are available, the non-law-abiding avenue frequently provides a relatively greater and more immediate return for a relatively smaller investment of energy.

3. The "demanded" response to certain situations recurrently engendered within lower class culture involves the commission of illegal acts.

The primary thesis of this paper is that the dominant component of the motivation of "delinquent" behavior engaged in by members of lower class corner groups involves a positive effort to achieve states, conditions, or qualities valued within the actor's most significant cultural milieu. If "conformity to immediate reference group values" is the major component of motivation of "delinquent" behavior by gang members, why is such behavior frequently referred to as negativistic, malicious, or rebellious? Albert Cohen, for example, in *Delinquent Boys*

(New York: The Free Press, 1955) describes behavior which violates school rules as comprising elements of "active spite and malice, contempt and ridicule, challenge and defiance." He ascribes to the gang "keen delight in terrorizing 'good' children, and in general making themselves obnoxious to the virtuous." A recent national conference on social work with "hard-to-reach" groups characterized lower class corner groups as "youth groups in conflict with the culture of their [*sic*] communities." Such characterizations are obviously the result of taking the middle class community and its institutions as an implicit point of reference.

A large body of systematically interrelated attitudes, practices, behaviors, and values characteristic of lower class culture are designed to support and maintain the basic features of the lower class way of life. In areas where these differ from features of middle class culture, action oriented to the achievement and maintenance of the lower class system may violate norms of middle class culture and be perceived as deliberately non-conforming or malicious by an observer strongly cathected to middle class norms. This does not mean, however, that violation of the middle class norm is the dominant component of motivation; it is a by-product of action primarily oriented to the lower class system. The standards of lower class culture cannot be seen merely as a reverse function of middle class culture—as middle class standards "turned upside down"; lower class culture is a distinctive tradition many centuries old with an integrity of its own.

From the viewpoint of the acting individual, functioning within a field of well-structured cultural forces, the relative impact of "conforming" and "rejective" elements in the motivation of gang delinquency is weighted preponderantly on the conforming side. Rejective or rebellious elements are inevitably involved, but their influence during the actual commission of delinquent acts is relatively small compared to the influence of pressures to achieve what is valued by the actor's most immediate reference groups. Expressed awareness by the actor of the element of rebellion often represents only that aspect of motivation of which he is explicitly conscious; the deepest and most compelling components of motivation—adherence to highly meaningful group standards of Toughness, Smartness, Excitement, etc.—are often unconsciously patterned. No cultural pattern as well-established as the practice of illegal acts by members of lower class corner groups could persist if buttressed primarily by negative, hostile, or rejective motives; its principal motivational support, as in the case of any persisting cultural tradition, derives from a positive effort to achieve what is valued within that tradition, and to conform to its explicit and implicit norms.

16.

Richard A. Cloward and Lloyd E. Ohlin

SOCIAL CLASS, ASPIRATIONS, AND ANOMIE

SUCCESS VALUES IN AMERICAN LIFE

We have noted that the success-goals toward which Americans are enjoined to orient themselves are not class-bounded; that is, people are not, so the ideology goes, forever restricted to the station into which they were born or even to the one above. But to what extent are success values internalized by people in different parts of the society? Precisely what is it that people aspire toward?

The Class Distribution of Aspirations

We have hypothesized that adolescents feel pressures for deviant behavior when they experience marked discrepancies between their aspirations and opportunities for achievement. To support our assumption that delinquent subcultures arise primarily among lower-class adolescent males in large cities, we must, therefore, demonstrate that these youngsters are exposed to greater discrepancies between aspirations and opportunities than are persons located elsewhere in the social structure. Before we review some of the relevant evidence, an important distinction should be made. "Aspiration" may be defined in at least two ways. First, we may ask: How

high does the individual aspire, *irrespective of his present position?* We may also ask: How high does he aspire *in relation to his present position?*

Absolute Aspirations. In a recent article, Hyman assembled an array of evidence on aspirations in American society, culled principally from public-opinion surveys.[1] In general, these data reveal differences in absolute aspiration among persons in various social strata. For example, when respondents in a national survey were asked to express their preference for one of three types of job ("a low income but secure job; a job with good pay but with a 50-50 risk of losing it; or a job with extremely high income and great risk"), the responses differed markedly by class. With each upward step in the social hierarchy, the proportion who chose the high-income but great-risk alternative increased. Only 14 per cent of youth from laboring families chose this alternative as contrasted with 31 per cent from executive and professional families. This general finding, confirmed by the results of several other studies, led Hyman to suggest that "the poor cannot accept the risk involved in becoming less poor." The results of a study of high school seniors conducted by

Source: Richard A. Cloward and Lloyd E. Ohlin, "Goals, Norms, and Anomie," *Delinquency and Opportunity: A Theory of Delinquent Gangs* (New York: The Free Press, 1960), 86–107. Permission granted by publisher and authors.

[1] H. H. Hyman, "The Value Systems of Different Classes: A Social-Psychological Contribution to the Analysis of Stratification," in *Class, Status and Power,* ed. Reinhard Bendix and S. M. Lipset (New York: The Free Press, 1953), pp. 432–34.

Empey support this conclusion.[2] Empey asked members of his sample to state the occupations that they hoped to enter. When their choices were ranked on the basis of generally accepted criteria of occupational status in American society, the aspirations of middle- and upper-class respondents were found to be consistently higher than those of seniors from lower-class families.

It should be noted that our hypothesis does not depend upon showing that a *large proportion* of persons in the lower class exhibit a high level of aspiration; it is sufficient to show that a *significant number* of lower-class members aspire beyond their means if it can also be demonstrated that these same persons contribute disproportionately to the ranks of delinquent subcultures. In this connection, the conclusions of several studies might be cited. In a comparative study of drug-users and nonusers, Gerard and Kornetsky concluded:

Regardless of the actual familial socioeconomic status, familial needs for high attainment in education and vocational areas play very important roles in the developmental experiences of many of the addict patients. Their families inculcated high levels of aspiration and expectation into them, yet failed to strengthen their capacities to attain their goals through realistic appraisal of their environments and acceptance of the need to work toward subordinate goals in the paths to their more final objectives. Denial of personal limitations, wish-fulfilling distortions of reality, and status-orientation at the expense of satisfaction are some of the prominent features of the family backgrounds of the adolescent addicts which are plausibly related to their aspiration-achievement discrepancies. . . . Unrealistic and excessive aspirations are likely to be a heavy burden for even the most intact ego.[3]

Finestone drew similar conclusions from studies of drug addicts in Chicago. He noted that addiction among lower-class Negro adolescents "represents a reaction to a feeling of exclusion from access to the means toward the goals of our society."[4] These observations suggest that youngsters who participate in delinquent subcultures may experience serious discontent with their position in the social structure.

Relative Aspirations. The studies we have cited support the general conclusion that there are class differentials in absolute level of aspiration. We get a rather different picture of the relationship between social class and aspirations if we look at the height to which people aspire in relation to the point from which they start.

The results of several studies tend to confirm the hypothesis that most Americans, whatever their social position, are dissatisfied with their income. There are, however, social-class differences in the degree of dissatisfaction. In general, the poor desire a proportionately larger increase in income than do persons in higher strata. As Hyman says, "*Relatively* speaking, the wealthier need and want less of an increase. . . . As one goes up in the economic ladder, the increment of income desired decreases."[5] The absolute or dollar increase in income sought is far greater among the wealthy than among the poor, but the proportion of current income that this increment represents decreases with each upward step in the scale. Empey reports a similar finding: almost all the seniors in his sample hoped to improve their position over that of their father, but the degree of relative occupational aspiration decreased significantly with each upward step in the social scale.[6] Thus we may conclude that persons in the lower reaches of society experience a relatively greater sense of position discontent despite the fact that their absolute aspirations are less lofty.

The concept of relative aspirations gives us a better gauge of position discontent than can be derived by comparing the heights to which people in various social classes aspire. And it is position discontent that is of greatest relevance to our theory. If, as we have suggested, lower-class persons experience relatively greater dissatisfaction with their present position and also have fewer legitimate ways of changing their

---

[2]L. T. Empey, "Social Class and Occupational Aspiration: A Comparison of Absolute and Relative Measurement," *American Sociological Review* 21, no. 6 (December, 1956): 706.

[3]D. L. Gerard and Conon Kornetsky, "Adolescent Opiate Addiction—A Study of Control and Addict Subjects," *Psychiatric Quarterly* 29 (April, 1955): 483.

[4]Harold Finestone, "Cats, Kicks, and Color," *Social Problems* 5, no. 1 (July, 1957): 13.

[5]Hyman, op. cit., pp. 435–36.

[6]Empey, op. cit., pp. 706–07.

status, then they should experience greater pressures toward deviant behavior.

TYPES OF ASPIRATION

It is somewhat misleading to assert, as we have done, that there are class differences in level of aspiration, for this implies that all members of a given class share the same goals. In this section, therefore, we shall try to qualify this implication by developing a typology of goals within the lower class. Our typology is limited to the lower class because, as we have pointed out, this is the primary locus of delinquent subcultures.

In his classic study of life in an urban slum, William F. Whyte divided lower-class male adolescents into two broad categories: the "college boys," who are "primarily interested in social advancement," and the "corner boys," who are "primarily interested in their local community."[7] The two groups, in other words, are differentiated essentially in terms of aspirations. The college boys identify with the middle-class style of life; the corner boys, on the other hand, are relatively content with their lower-class life-style. The "social advancement" sought by the college boys therefore means rising into the middle class.

Since Whyte's study, other writers also have assumed that "ambitious" lower-class youth wish to rise into the middle class. Bloch and Niederhoffer, for example, take this view: "The lower-class boy . . . absorbs dominant middle-class values which set goals for him."[8] Cohen's recent work on delinquency also assumes that many lower-class youth seek to affiliate with the middle class: "It is a plausible assumption . . . that the working-class boy whose status is low in middle-class terms cares about that status, that this status confronts him with a general problem of adjustment."[9] Indeed Cohen suggests that delinquency results when access to this goal is limited: "The delinquent subculture, we sug-

gest, is a way of dealing with . . . status problems: certain children are denied status in the respectable society because they cannot meet the criteria of the respectable status system. The delinquent subculture deals with these problems by providing criteria of status which these children *can* meet."[10] Using Whyte's classification of "corner boys" and "college boys" as a starting point, Cohen adds the category of "delinquent boys." He describes these three modes of adaptation as follows:

(1) A certain proportion of working-class boys [the "college boys"] accept the challenge of the middle-class status system and play the status game by the middle-class rules. . . .

(2) Another response, perhaps the most common, is what we may call the "stable corner-boy response." It represents an acceptance of the corner-boy way of life and an effort to make the best of a situation. . . .

(3) The delinquent response . . . differs from the stable corner-boy response. The hallmark of the delinquent subculture is the explicit and wholesale repudiation of middle-class standards and the adoption of their very antithesis. *The corner-boy culture is not specifically delinquent . . . ;* [it] temporizes with middle-class morality; the full-fledged delinquent subculture does not.[11]

The assumption that many lower-class youth seek to affiliate with the middle class has come under sharp attack by other students of delinquency. Kitsuse and Dietrick, for example, question whether available evidence supports this contention:

Cohen's image of the working-class boy . . . standing alone to face humiliation at the hands of middle-class agents is difficult to comprehend. To add to this picture of the pre-teen and teen-ager an intense desire to gain status in the middle-class system, which when frustrated provides sufficient basis for a reaction-formation response, is to overdraw him beyond recognition.[12]

Cohen's tendency to equate high levels of aspiration among lower-class youth with an orientation toward the middle class implies that lower-class youth who are dissatisfied with their position (1) internalize middle-class values and

[7]W. F. Whyte, *Street Corner Society: The Social Structure of an Italian Slum,* enl. ed. (Chicago: The University of Chicago Press, 1955), p. 97.

[8]Herbert Bloch and Arthur Niederhoffer, *The Gang: A Study in Adolescent Behavior* (New York: Philosophical Library, Inc., 1958), p. 109.

[9]A. K. Cohen, *Delinquent Boys: The Culture of the Gang* (New York: The Free Press, 1955), p. 129.

[10]Ibid., p. 121.

[11]Ibid., pp. 128–30.

[12]J. I. Kitsuse and D. C. Dietrick, "Delinquent Boys: A Critique," *American Sociological Review* 24, no. 2 (April, 1959): 211–12.

(2) seek to leave their class of origin and affiliate with the carriers of middle-class values. We submit, however, that this may be true of *some* discontented lower-class youth but not of all. It is our view that many discontented lower-class youth do not wish to adopt a middle-class way of life or to disrupt their present associations and negotiate passage into middle-class groups. The solution they seek entails the acquisition of higher position in terms of lower-class rather than middle-class criteria.

Our point may be illustrated by referring again to Miller's typology of lower-class adolescents (pp. 72–73). He describes boys of type 1 as "'stable' lower-class [members] who, for all practical purposes, do not aspire to higher status." This category thus seems to be identical with what Whyte and Cohen refer to as "corner boys."[13] According to Miller, "There is evidence that type 1, the 'nonaspiring' lower-class youngster, is far more common than generally supposed, and that this group does not seem to be getting smaller, and may be getting larger."[14] As it turns out, however, Miller's own data raise serious question about whether a category of stable, nonaspiring lower-class youth exists at all. Consider only the following description of this category:

In common with most adolescents in American society, the lower-class corner group manifests a dominant concern with "status." What differentiates this type of group from others, however, is the particular set of criteria and weighting thereof by which "status" is defined. In general, status is achieved and maintained by demonstrated possession of the valued qualities of lower-class culture. . . . It is important to stress once more that the individual orients to [success-goals] as they are defined within lower-class society.[15]

Thus Miller, despite his clear recognition of the importance of status striving among corner boys, tends to classify lower-class youth as "nonaspiring" if they do not orient themselves toward the middle class. Once we recognize that lower-class youngsters may experience intense position discontent without being oriented toward the middle class, we can classify lower-class youth to distinguish between boys who define success-goals in essentially lower-class terms and those who define them in essentially middle-class terms.

Evidence from studies of social stratification suggests that the criteria people use to rank one another vary depending upon social-class position.[16] That is, there is not uniform agreement throughout the class structure as to the basis for invidious distinctions. The upper-class person tends to rank others primarily in terms of style of life and ancestry; the middle-class person, in terms of money and morality; the lower-class person, in terms of money alone. Except for the lower class, money is a significant but not a sufficient criterion of high rank; it must be translated into a way of life that symbolizes such things as "respectability." The lower class, by contrast, appears to make fewer distinctions in terms of life-style and social reputation. For many lower-class members, society is divided into two general categories of persons: those who have money, and those who do not. In this respect as in others, however, the lower class is extremely heterogeneous: money may be an important criterion of success for some but not for all. To many, the middle-class style of life may be the controlling model; the goal of such persons would be to rise into the middle class. Success within the lower-class world is doubtless the chief goal for many others, however; these persons are interested in maintaining their general membership affiliations but wish to rise within that structure.

What we are here suggesting is that types of aspiration can be classified on the basis of

---

[13] See Miller's comments in W. C. Kvaraceus and W. B. Miller, *Delinquent Behavior: Culture and the Individual* (Washington, D.C.: National Education Association, 1959), p. 72.

[14] Ibid., p. 73.

[15] W. B. Miller, "Lower Class Culture as a Generating Milieu of Gang Delinquency," *Journal of Social Issues* 14, no. 3 (1958): 15.

[16] See, e.g., W. L. Warner and P. S. Lunt, *The Social Life of a Modern Community*, Yankee City Series, vol. 1 (New Haven, Conn.: Yale University Press, 1941), p. 91. The fact that socioeconomic position influences perceptions of the number of ranks and the criteria distinguishing ranks is evident from the data gathered by Warner and Lunt, although they did not stress this point. It remained for various critics of the Yankee City Series to emphasize the importance of class differentials in perceptions of social divisions. For a summary of these criticisms, see Ruth Rosner Kornhauser, "The Warner Approach to Social Stratification," in op. cit., ed. Bendix and Lipset, pp. 224–55.

whether or not the aspirer envisages a change in membership group. For the lower-class boy who seeks to change his economic position without shifting his style of life or associations, his membership group—the lower class—continues to be his primary reference group. However, lower-class youth in the "college boy" category envisage a definite change in membership group. They take the style of life of the middle-class world as a frame of reference and are oriented toward eventual affiliation with the carriers of middle-class values. Furthermore, for some of these boys the anticipated shift in membership group may assume greater importance than political shifts in economic position. There are doubtless many "college boys" who, if faced with a choice between a high-paying position as a master craftsman (or a racketeer) and a low-paying position as a teacher, would choose the latter, for these youngsters are seeking a new way of life, a new definition of reputability, a new set of associations. Hence they tend to devalue their membership group and to seek acceptance in a group that is less invidiously defined, if less well remunerated. Members of lower-middle-class professions—teachers, for example—probably accord higher value to respectability and life-style than to money as such. This is not to say that they would not like to improve their financial positions, but they probably would not relinquish their style of life and social position in order to maximize financial gain (for example, by entering a manual occupation that is more highly remunerated than teaching).

Once we recognize that level of aspiration may entail a change in economic position or in reference group or both, we can then classify lower-class youth as follows:

TABLE 3–2.

ORIENTATION OF LOWER-CLASS YOUTH

Categories of Lower-Class Youth	Toward Membership in Middle Class	Toward Improvement in Economic Position
Type I	+	+
Type II	+	—
Type III	—	+
Type IV	—	—

Types I and II are composed of the "college boys" so vividly portrayed by Whyte. Those of type I place *equal* emphasis on change in economic position and in reference group. Youth of type II regard a change in membership group as a more important goal than a change in economic position. Youth of type III are oriented toward a definition of success that stresses a change in economic position, but they do not seek to change their style of life or to affiliate with the carriers of middle-class values. Those of type IV are genuinely nonaspiring, for they do not exhibit serious distress about remaining in their present membership-group position *and* their present economic status. These four categories, then, are distinguished by the criteria of success that they employ. All these criteria define ends that come within the scope of "culturally approved goals," although the particular goals vary.

One potential value of this typology is that it may correlate with a typology of delinquent behavior. Youngsters of types I and II may react to status discontent differently from those of type III. For example, it may be that property destruction is a type of delinquency that is characteristic of types I and II, according to Cohen's contention that youngsters who are thwarted in the quest for middle-class status may, by a process of reaction-formation, come to devalue what they secretly prize. The members of certain esoteric adolescent cults, such as the "hipster" groups which emphasize jazz and sex, may also be frustrated aspirants for middle-class status; although not specifically delinquent, these cults are on the borderline between tolerated and illegal behavior. However, we do not think that the seriously delinquent constituents of the criminal, conflict, and retreatist subcultures are drawn from types I and II. It is our view that they are more likely to be from type III, and that the process by which such persons become delinquent has less to do with reaction-formation than with the selective withdrawal or qualification of sentiments supporting the legitimacy of institutional norms. The literature on lower-class delinquent subcultures is replete with references to the conspicuous consumption of wealth: delinquents repeatedly remark that they want "big cars," "flashy clothes," and "swell dames." These symbols of success, framed primarily in economic terms rather than in terms of middle-class life-styles, suggest to us that the participants in delinquent subcultures are seeking higher status within their own cultural milieu. If legitimate paths to higher status become restricted, then the delinquent subculture provides alternative (albeit illegal) avenues. Our discussion . . . is therefore concerned primarily with type III youth, for these, we believe, are the principal constituents of delinquent subcultures.

This typology, it might also be noted, can also be used in respecifying the much discussed conflict between lower-class youth and carriers of middle-class values—a conflict which is often said to have a direct bearing upon the etiology of delinquency. Youths of types I and II, who aspire to enter the middle class, exhibit values that are essentially congruent with those of the middle-class carriers with whom they come in contact in school and settlement houses. Value differences are therefore not a source of conflict for these adolescents. If pressures for deviant behavior do arise among such boys, the reason may be, as Cohen argues, that many of them lack the skills and attitudes that make conformity with middle-class values possible. Hence they are led to devalue what they secretly desire but cannot achieve.

Type III youth, we contend, experience the greatest conflict with middle-class carriers, who not only devalue the lower-class style of life and seek to induce a desire for change in membership group but also devalue the materialistic success-goals toward which type III adolescents orient themselves. Type III youth, in short, are looked down upon both for what they do *not* want (i.e., the middle-class style of life) and for what they *do* want (i.e., "crass materialism").

Unlike type III youth, who are devalued because they want the "wrong" things, type IV youth—the "corner boys," who are not strongly oriented toward social mobility in any sphere—are criticized principally because they are "unmotivated." They doubtless resent the invidious definition of their way of life implicit in their contacts with middle-class agents, but this resentment can be largely managed by minimizing interaction. Thus the corner boy plays hookey from school and avoids the settlement house.

Note that our hypothesis challenges the view that the school participates in producing delinquency by imposing middle-class success-goals which lower-class youth cannot achieve. Type III youth are alienated from the school because of a conflict regarding *appropriate* success-goals; this conflict simply reinforces their own definitions of criteria of success. If these youngsters subsequently become delinquent, it is chiefly because they anticipate that legitimate channels to the goals they seek will be limited or closed.

BARRIERS TO LEGITIMATE OPPORTUNITY

"Education," Lipset and Bendix have remarked, "has become the principal avenue for upward mobility in most industrial nations," particularly in the United States. The number of nonmanual occupations that can be fruitfully pursued without extensive educational background is diminishing and will doubtless continue to do so as our occupational structure becomes increasingly technical and specialized.[17] This being the case, we might focus our discussion of barriers to opportunity on the question of barriers to education.

It should be pointed out, however, that educational attainment does not necessarily enable the lower-class person to overcome the disadvantages of his low social origins.

Thus workers' sons with "some college" education are about as well off [financially] as a group as the sons of nonmanual fathers who have graduated from high school but not attended college. Similarly, high school graduation for the sons of workers results in their being only slightly better off than the sons of nonmanual workers who have not completed high school.[18]

To the extent that one's social origins, despite education, still constitute a restraining influence on upward movement, we may assume that other objective consequences of social position intervene, such as the ability of one's family to give

[17]S. M. Lipset and Reinhard Bendix, *Social Mobility in Industrial Society* (Berkeley and Los Angeles, Calif.: University of California Press, 1959), p. 91.

[18]Ibid., p. 99.

one a start in a business or profession by supplying funds or influential contacts. Nevertheless, the lower-class boy who fails to secure an education is likely to discover that he has little chance of improving his circumstances. Hence acute discontent may be generated, leading in turn to aberrant behavior.

Although education is widely valued in our society, it is not equally valued among the several social classes. Hyman has summarized a national survey in which a sample of 500 youths was asked: "About how much schooling do you think most young men need these days to get along well in the world?" The results are shown in Table 3–3.

TABLE 3–3.

Class Differentials in Emphasis on the Need for College Education
(201 Males Aged 14 to 20)

Socioeconomic Position of Family	Per Cent Recommending a College Education	Number of Respondents
Wealthy and prosperous	74	39
Middle class	63	100
Lower class	42	62

Source: H. H. Hyman, "The Value Systems of Different Classes: A Social-Psychological Contribution to the Analysis of Stratification," in *Class, Status and Power,* ed. Reinhard Bendix and S. M. Lipset (New York: The Free Press, 1953), p. 432.

Table 3–3, like others that Hyman presents, shows that a sizable proportion of persons at each point in the social structure consider a college education desirable. Even in the lowest level of society, the proportion who emphasize the need for education is not small. But it is also true that there are strong differences from one stratum to another. In general, the proportion recommending higher education increases with each upward step in the socioeconomic hierarchy.

Given the fundamental importance of education to social advancement, how are we to account for these class differentials in emphasis on the value of education? Why is it that a substantial proportion of lower-class males aged 14 to 20 do *not* orient themselves toward acquiring higher education?

CULTURAL BARRIERS

The lower class is still influenced to some extent by the persistence of values brought to our shores by immigrants from various peasant cultures in which education was not greatly stressed or was even devalued. Toby has remarked on this point in his comparison of Jewish and Italian immigrants and their descendants.[19]

Jews and Italians came to the United States in large numbers at about the same time—the turn of the century—and both settled in urban areas. There was, however, a very different attitude toward intellectual accomplishment in the two cultures. Jews from Eastern Europe regarded religious study as the most important activity for an adult male. The rabbi enjoyed great prestige because he was a scholar, a teacher, a logician. . . . Life in America gave a secular emphasis to the Jewish reverence for learning. Material success is a more important motive than salvation for American youngsters, Jewish as well as Christian, and secular education is better training for business and professional careers than Talmudic exegesis. Nevertheless, intellectual achievement continued to be valued by Jews—and to have measurable effects. Second-generation Jewish students did homework diligently, got high grades, went to college in disproportionate numbers, and scored high on intelligence tests. Two thousand years of preparation lay behind them.

[19]See Jackson Toby, "Hoodlum or Businessman: An American Dilemma," in *The Jews: Social Patterns of an American Group,* ed. Marshall Sklare (New York: The Free Press, 1958), pp. 548–50, from which the excerpts that follow are taken. There are, of course, other features of lower-class socialization that inhibit mobility. Such traits as the inability to defer gratification, the unwillingness to postpone marriage and family, the lack of readiness to minimize obligations to family of orientation and to maximize investment in occupational preparation, and the inability to sever peer ties and to move easily into new groups are apparently more characteristic of the lower than of the middle class. A number of studies have shown that the capacity to defer gratification, for example, is stressed by middle-class parents to a greater extent than by lower-class parents. Similarly, middle-class youth are encouraged if not expected to minimize kinship ties and to devote their energies to occupational achievement, whereas among certain groups in the lower class young people are expected to maintain close ties with the family. These kinship obligations often interfere with occupational obligations and thus detract from occupational achievement. In these respects, then, the lower-class child is not so well prepared as his middle-class counterpart to take advantage of traditional avenues to higher position. For a review of studies bearing upon class-related attitudes and values influencing mobility patterns, see Lipset and Bendix, op. cit.

Immigrants from Southern Italy, on the other hand, tended to regard formal education either as a frill or as a source of dangerous ideas from which the minds of the young should be protected. They remembered Sicily, where a child who attended school regularly was a rarity. In the United States, many Southern Italian immigrants maintained the same attitudes. They resented compulsory school-attendance laws and prodded their children to go to work and become economic assets as soon as possible. They did not realize that education has more importance in an urban-industrial society than in a semi-feudal one. . . . [Children] accepted their parents' conception of the school as worthless and thereby lost their best opportunity for social ascent.

Second-generation Italian youngsters, having failed in school, tended to quit and go to work. But employment opportunities for the uneducated do not usually afford much chance for advancement. Consequently, according to Toby, frustrations increased and the young turned to illegitimate activities.

Second-generation Italian boys became delinquent in disproportionately large numbers. In New York City, 39 per cent of the white delinquents of foreign-born parents in 1930 were of Italian origin, although less than 22 per cent of the white families with foreign-born heads were of that ethnic group. In Chicago, second-generation Italian boys in the years of 1927–33 had an appearance rate in the Cook County Juvenile Court twice as high as white boys generally.

The figures for Jewish adolescents were quite different:

Second-generation Jewish youths had less reason to become hoodlums . . . for their chances in the marketplace were excellent. . . . In New York City, for example, Jewish youngsters constituted in 1930 about a quarter of the white delinquents—although the Jewish population at large was estimated to be about a third of the total white population of the city. . . . Crude though these data are, they show that the probability of becoming a hoodlum was not the same for second-generation Jews and second-generation Italians.

Toby concludes that "some youths become hoodlums instead of businessmen, not because they lack the ability to succeed legitimately . . . but because they find out too late the relationship between school adjustment and [upward social mobility]."[20]

[20]Whyte made much the same point in his study of lower-class youth (op. cit., p. 273): "Our society

STRUCTURAL BARRIERS

Despite their importance, these cultural barriers, we contend, do not fully account for class differentials in the values placed on education. Success-themes, as we have noted, are widely diffused throughout our society. In fact, there is reason to think that lower-class persons experience a *relatively* greater sense of position discontent than persons higher in the social structure. By the same token, it is doubtful that lower-class persons are unaware of the general importance assigned to education in our society or of the relationship between education and social mobility. But they are probably also very much aware of their limited opportunities to secure access to educational facilities. Educational achievement is not just a matter of favorable attitudes; opportunities must be available to those who seek them. For many members of the lower class, struggling to maintain a minimum level of subsistence, the goal of advanced education must seem remote indeed. In a family that can scarcely afford food, shelter, and clothing, pressure is exerted upon the young to leave school early in order to secure employment and thereby help the family. In a recent study of an extensive sample of adolescents in Nashville, Tennessee, Reiss and Rhodes found that most adolescents who quit school did so not because they devalued education but because they wanted to go to work immediately. Quitting school, their data show, is not necessarily a negative or rebellious response to compulsory-attendance laws but may be a necessary response to economic pressures.[21]

places a high value upon social mobility. . . . To get ahead, the Cornerville man must move either in the world of business and Republican politics or in the world of Democratic politics and the rackets. He cannot rise in both worlds at once. . . . If he advances in the first world, he is recognized by society at large as a successful man, but he is recognized in Cornerville only as an alien to the district. If he advances in the second world, he achieves recognition in Cornerville but becomes a social outcast to the respectable people elsewhere. The entire course of the corner boy's training in the social life of his district prepares him for a career in the rackets or in Democratic politics."

[21]A. J. Reiss and A. L. Rhodes, "Are Educational Norms and Goals of Conforming and Delinquent Adolescents Influenced by Group Position in American Society?" *Journal of Negro Education* (Summer, 1959), pp. 262–66.

In the past few decades, a variety of studies have concluded that there are marked class differentials in access to educational facilities.[22] The lower the social position of one's father, the less likely that one can take advantage of educational opportunities. Furthermore, class differentials in access to educational facilities are not explained by differences in intelligence. If children from various social classes who have the same general intelligence are compared, differentials in chances to acquire an education still obtain.

The influence of economic barriers to education can be inferred from studies of situations in which these barriers have been temporarily relaxed. Warner and his associates, for example, observed a "sharp increase in college and high school enrollment [resulting from] the establishing of the National Youth Administration student-aid program in 1935."[23] In a more recent study, Mulligan examined the proportions of students from various socioeconomic strata enrolled in a Midwestern university before and during the G. I. Bill of Rights educational program. Not surprisingly, his data show that as a result of the government-aid program a larger proportion of students was drawn from the lower echelons of the society. This strongly suggests that the lower class contains many persons who desire higher education but cannot ordinarily afford to acquire it.[24]

It is our view that class differentials in the value placed on education reflect in large part differentials in the availability of educational opportunities. What we are suggesting is that lower-class attitudes toward education are adaptive; that is, expectations are scaled down to accord with the realistic limitations on access to educational opportunities. Educational attainment and related forms of goal-striving are thus eschewed not so much because they are inherently devalued as because access to them is relatively restricted. Although these cultural orientations, once crystallized, persist as major obstacles to the utilization of opportunity, it should be remembered that they emerged initially as adaptive responses to socially structured deprivations.[25]

ALTERNATIVE AVENUES TO SUCCESS-GOALS

If traditional channels to higher position, such as education, are restricted for large categories of people, then pressures will mount for the use of alternative routes. Studies have shown that some lower-class persons orient themselves toward occupations in the field of entertainment and sports.[26] People of modest social origins who have been conspicuously successful in these spheres often become salient models for the

[22]See W. L. Warner, R. J. Havighurst, and M. B. Loeb, *Who Shall Be Educated: The Challenge of Unequal Opportunities* (New York: Harper & Row, Publishers, 1944); Lipset and Bendix, op. cit.; Elbridge Sibley, "Some Demographic Clues to Stratification," *American Sociological Review* 7 (June, 1942): 322–30; and George F. Zuok, "The Findings and Recommendations of the President's Commission on Higher Education," *Bulletin of the American Association of University Professors* 35 (Spring, 1949): 17–22.

[23]W. L. Warner, R. J. Havighurst, and M. B. Loeb, op. cit., p. 53. Commenting on financial barriers to high-school attendance, Warner and his associates note: "There is a substantial out-of-pocket cost attached to attendance at a 'free' high school. . . . Students can go to school and spend little or no money. But [the poor] are barred from many of the school activities; they cannot even take regular laboratory courses, and they must go around in what is to high-school youngsters the supremely embarrassing condition of having no change to rattle in their pockets, no money to contribute to a party, no possibility of being independent in their dealings with their friends" (pp. 53–54). For a further discussion of these and related matters, see A. B. Hollingshead, *Elmtown's Youth* (New York: John Wiley & Sons, Inc., 1949).

[24]R. A. Mulligan, "Socio-Economic Background and College Enrollment," *American Sociological Review* 16, no. 2 (April, 1951): 188–96.

[25]In this connection, Hyman (op. cit., p. 437) summarizes data which show that there are distinct differentials by class in judgments regarding the accessibility of success-goals. Thus 63 per cent of one sample of persons in professional and managerial positions felt that the "years ahead held good chances for advancement" while only 48 per cent of a sample of factory workers gave this response. Furthermore, the factory workers were more likely to think that "getting along well with the boss" or being a "friend or relative of the boss" were important determinants of mobility; professional and executive personnel were more likely to stress "quality of work" and "energy and willingness." Such findings suggest that lower-class persons perceive differentials in opportunity associated with social origins. . . .

[26]Ibid., p. 437.

young in depressed sectors of the society. The heavyweight champion, the night-club singer, the baseball star—these symbolize the possibility of achieving success in conventional terms despite poor education and low social origins. The businessman, the physicist, and the physician, on the other hand, occupy roles to which the lower-class youngster has little access because of his limited educational opportunities. By orienting himself toward occupations which offer some hope of success in spite of poor social origins and education, the lower-class boy follows a legitimate alternative to traditional avenues to success-goals.

But the dilemma of many lower-class people is that their efforts to locate alternative avenues to success-goals are futile, for these alternatives are often just as restricted as educational channels, if not more so. One has only to think of the many lower-class adolescents who go into the "fight game," hoping to win great social rewards —money and glamor—by sheer physical exertion and stamina. A few succeed, but the overwhelming majority are destined to fail. For these lower-class youth there seems no legitimate way out of poverty. In a society that did not encourage them to hold high aspirations, to devalue their station in life, to set their sights high, they might adjust more easily to their impoverished circumstances; but since social worth is so closely identified with social position in our society, discontent and frustration pervade the lower reaches of the social order.[27]

When pressures from unfulfilled aspirations and blocked opportunity become sufficiently intense, many lower-class youth turn away from legitimate channels, adopting other means, beyond conventional mores, which might offer a possible route to success-goals. As Merton suggests, "It is only when a system of cultural values extols, virtually above all else, certain *common* success-goals *for the population at large* while the social structure rigorously restricts or completely closes access to approved modes of reaching these goals *for a considerable part of*

the same population, that deviant behavior ensues on a large scale."[28] Discrepancies between aspirations and legitimate avenues thus produce intense pressures for the use of illegitimate alternatives. Many lower-class persons, in short, are the victims of a contradiction between the goals toward which they have been led to orient themselves and socially structured means of striving for these goals. Under these conditions, there is an acute pressure to depart from institutional norms and to adopt illegitimate alternatives. Merton puts this theory as follows:

Of those located in the lower reaches of the social structure, the culture makes incompatible demands. On the one hand, they are asked to orient their conduct toward the prospect of large wealth . . . and on the other, they are largely denied effective opportunities to do so institutionally. The consequence of this structural inconsistency is a high rate of deviant behavior. The equilibrium between culturally designated ends and means becomes highly unstable with progressive emphasis on attaining the prestige-laden ends by any means whatsoever.[29]

What we have been saying only points up all the more the fallacy of attributing delinquent responses in the lower class to inadequate socialization or simply to conformity with lower-class values. One can accept these perspectives only if it is assumed either that the lower class is highly disorganized and demoralized or that a large number of lower-class persons are unacculturated to the system of norms that prevails in our society generally. We contend, on the other hand, that widespread tendencies toward delinquent practices in the lower class are modes of adaptation to structured strains and inconsistencies within the social order.[30] These modes of adaptation are then passed on from one generation to another.

Although we have been focusing upon class differentials in pressures toward deviant behavior, it should also be noted that these pres-

[27]Poverty alone, as Durkheim, Merton, and others have made abundantly clear, is not necessarily a source of deviant behavior. But poverty coupled with culturally approved high aspirations under conditions of limited opportunity can be an important source of pressures toward deviance.

[28]Robert K. Merton, *Social Theory of Social Structure,* rev. and enlarged ed. (Glencoe, Ill.: The Free Press, 1957), p. 146.

[29]Ibid.

[30]For a further discussion of adaptations to limited opportunity, see Oscar Handlin, *The Newcomers: Negroes and Puerto Ricans in a Changing Metropolis* (Cambridge, Mass.: Harvard University Press, 1959), chap. 4.

sures affect males more than females and adolescents more than younger or older people. It is primarily the male who must go into the marketplace to seek employment, make a career for himself, and support a family. It is during adolescence that decisions regarding occupational selection and routes to occupational success must be made. The adolescent male in the lower class is therefore most vulnerable to pressures toward deviance arising from discrepancies between aspirations and opportunities for achievement. If educational facilities appear beyond his financial reach, life may seem to hold very few prospects for him. The "permanent" quality of this dilemma makes it all the more acute. If the problem were simply one of achieving adult status, it would be less severe, for adolescents are well aware that adult status will be accorded them eventually. But improving one's lot in life constitutes a more enduring problem. We suggest that many lower-class male adolescents experience desperation born of the certainty that their position in the economic structure is relatively fixed and immutable—a desperation made all the more poignant by their exposure to a cultural ideology in which failure to orient oneself upward is regarded as a moral defect and failure to become mobile as proof of it.

Delinquent subcultures, we believe, represent specialized modes of adaptation to this problem of adjustment. Two of these subcultures—the criminal and the conflict—provide illegal avenues to success-goals. The retreatist subculture consists of a loosely structured group of persons who have withdrawn from competition in the larger society, who anticipate defeat and now seek escape from the burden of failure.

17.

David J. Bordua

A CRITIQUE OF SOCIOLOGICAL INTERPRETATIONS OF GANG DELINQUENCY

The problem of group delinquency has been a subject of theoretical interest for American sociologists and other social observers for well over a half century. In the course of that period, the group nature of delinquency has come to be a central starting point for many theories of delinquency, and delinquency causation has been seen by some sociologists as pre-eminently a process whereby the individual becomes associated with a group which devotes some or all of its time to planning, committing, or celebrating delinquencies and which has elaborated a set of lifeways—a subculture—which encourages and justifies behavior defined as delinquent by the larger society.

In addition to the processes whereby an individual takes on the beliefs and norms of a pre-existing group and thereby becomes delinquent —a process mysterious enough in itself in many cases—there is the more basic, and in many respects more complex, problem of how such groups begin in the first place. What are the social conditions that facilitate or cause the rise of delinquency-carrying groups? What processes of planned social control might be usable in preventing the rise of such groups or in redirecting the behavior and moral systems of groups already in existence? All these questions and many others have been asked for at least two generations. Within the limits of this brief paper, it is impossible to present and analyze

SOURCE: David J. Bordua, "A Critique of Sociological Interpretations of Gang Delinquency," *The Annals of the American Academy of Political and Social Science* 338 (November, 1961): 120–36. Permission granted by publisher and author.

in detail the many answers to these questions which have been put forward by social scientists. What I can do is single out a few of the major viewpoints and concentrate on them.

In its more well-developed and extreme forms, gang or subcultural delinquency has been heavily concentrated in the low status areas of our large cities. The theoretical interpretations I will discuss all confine themselves to gang delinquency of this sort.

THE CLASSICAL VIEW

Still the best book on gangs, gang delinquency, and—though he did not use the term—delinquent subcultures is *The Gang* by Frederick M. Thrasher, and his formulations are the ones that I have labeled "the classical view." Not that he originated the basic interpretative framework, far from it, but his application of the theoretical materials available at the time plus his sensitivity to the effects of social environment and his willingness to consider processes at all behavioral levels from the basic needs of the child to the significance of the saloon, from the nature of city government to the crucial importance of the junk dealer, from the consequence of poverty to the nature of leadership in the gang still distinguish his book.[1]

Briefly, Thrasher's analysis may be characterized as operating on the following levels. The ecological processes which determine the structure of the city create the interstitial area characterized by a variety of indices of conflict, disorganization, weak family and neighborhood controls, and so on. In these interstitial areas, in response to universal childhood needs, spontaneous play groups develop. Because of the relatively uncontrolled nature of these groups— or of many of them at least—and because of the presence of many attractive and exciting opportunities for fun and adventure, these groups engage in a variety of activities, legal and illegal, which are determined, defined, and directed by the play group itself rather than by conventional adult supervision.

The crowded, exciting slum streets teem with such groups. Inevitably, in a situation of high population density, limited resources, and weak social control, they come into conflict with each other for space, playground facilities, reputation. Since many of their activities, even at an early age, are illegal, although often not feloniously so—they swipe fruit from peddlers, turn over garbage cans, stay away from home all night and steal milk and cakes for breakfast, play truant from school—they also come into conflict with adult authority. Parents, teachers, merchants, police, and others become natural enemies of this kind of group and attempt to control it or to convert it to more conventional activities. With some groups they succeed, with some they do not.

If the group continues, it becomes part of a network of similar groups, increasingly freed from adult restraint, increasingly involved in intergroup conflict and fighting, increasingly engaged in illegal activities to support itself and to continue to receive the satisfactions of the "free" life of the streets. Conflict, especially with other groups, transforms the play group into the gang. Its illegal activities become more serious, its values hardened, its structure more determined by the necessity to maintain eternal vigilance in a hostile government.

By middle adolescence, the group is a gang, often with a name, usually identified with a particular ethnic or racial group, and usually with an elaborate technology of theft and other means of self-support. Gradually, the gang may move in the direction of adult crime, armed robbery, perhaps, or other serious crimes.

Prior to that time, however, it is likely to have engaged in much stealing from stores, railroad cars, empty houses, parents, drunks, almost anywhere money or goods are available. The ready access to outlets for stolen goods is of major importance here. The junk dealer, especially the junk wagon peddler, the convenient no-questions-asked attitudes of large numbers of local adults who buy "hot" merchandise, and the early knowledge that customers are available all help to make theft easy and profitable as well as morally acceptable.[2]

---

[1]Frederick M. Thrasher, *The Gang* (Chicago: University of Chicago Press, 1927).

[2]One of the charms of Thrasher's old-time sociology is the fashion in which fact intrudes itself upon the theorizing. For example, he tells us that there were an estimated 1,700 to 1,800 junk wagon

Nonutilitarian?

It is appropriate at this point to deal with a matter that has become important in the discussion of more recent theories of group delinquency. This is Albert K. Cohen's famous characterization of the delinquent subculture as nonutilitarian, by which he seems to mean that activities, especially theft, are not oriented to calculated economic ends.[3]

Thrasher makes a great point of the play and adventure quality of many illegal acts, especially in the pregang stages of a group's development, but he also describes many cases where theft has a quite rational and instrumental nature, even at a fairly early age.

The theft activities and the disposition of the loot make instrumental sense in the context of Thrasher's description of the nature of the group or gang. Much theft is essentially for the purpose of maintaining the group in a state of freedom from adult authority. If a group of boys lives days or weeks away from home, then the theft of food or of things which are sold to buy food is hardly nonutilitarian. If such a group steals from freight cars, peddles the merchandise to the neighbors for movie money, and so on, this can hardly be considered nonutilitarian. The behavior makes sense as instrumental behavior, however, only after one has a picture of the general life led by the group. Boys who feed themselves by duplicating keys to bakery delivery boxes, creep out of their club rooms right after delivery, steal the pastry, pick up a quart of milk from a doorstep, and then have breakfast may not have a highly developed sense of nutritional values, but this is not nonutilitarian.

Such youngsters may, of course, spend the two dollars gained from selling stolen goods entirely on doughnuts and gorge themselves and throw much of the food away. I think this largely

indicates that they are children, not that they are nonutilitarian.[4]

Let us look a little more systematically at the Thrasher formulations, however, since such an examination can be instructive in dealing with the more recent theories. The analysis proceeds at several levels, as I have mentioned.

Levels of Analysis

At the level of the local adult community, we may say that the social structure is permissive, attractive, facilitative, morally supportive of the gang development process.

It is permissive because control over children is weak; attractive because many enjoyable activities are available, some of which are illegal, like stealing fruit, but all of which can be enjoyed only if the child manages to evade whatever conventional controls do exist.

In another sense, the local environment is attractive because of the presence of adult crime of a variety of kinds ranging from organized vice to older adolescents and adults making a living by theft. The attraction lies of course, in the fact that these adults may have a lot of money and live the carefree life and have high status in the neighborhood.

The local environment is facilitative in a num-

---

men in Chicago, most of whom were suspected of being less than rigid in inquiring about the source of "junk." Ibid., p. 148. He also does some other things that seem to have gone out of style, such as presenting information on the age and ethnic composition of as many of the 1,313 gangs as possible. Ibid., pp. 73, 74, 191–93.

[3] Albert K. Cohen, *Delinquent Boys: The Culture of the Gang* (New York: The Free Press, 1955), pp. 25, 26.

[4] The examples cited above are all in Thrasher along with many others of a similar nature. In general, views of the nature of gang activity have shifted quite fundamentally toward a more irrationalist position. Thus, the gang's behavior seems to make no sense. Underlying this shift is a tendency to deal almost entirely with the gang's subculture, its values, beliefs, and the like, to deal with the relationships between this subculture and presumed motivational states which exist in the potential gang members before the gang or protogang is formed, and to deal very little with the developmental processes involved in the formation of gangs. Things which make no sense without consideration of the motivational consequences of gang membership are not necessarily so mysterious given Thrasher's highly sensitive analysis of the ways in which the nature of the gang as a group led to the development—in relation to the local environment—of the gang subculture. Current theory focuses so heavily on motive and culture to the exclusion of group process that some essential points are under-emphasized. It would not be too much of a distortion to say that Thrasher saw the delinquent subculture as the way of life that would be developed by a group becoming a gang and that some recent theorists look at the gang as the kind of group that would develop if boys set about creating a delinquent subculture.

ber of ways. There are things readily available to steal, people to buy them, and places to hide without adult supervision.

The environment is morally supportive because of the presence of adult crime, as previously mentioned, but also for several additional reasons. One is the readiness of conventional adults to buy stolen goods. Even parents were discovered at this occasionally. The prevalence of political pull, which not only objectively protected adult crime but tended to undercut the norms against crime, must be mentioned then as now. The often bitter poverty which turned many situations into matters of desperate competition also contributed.

Additionally, many gang activities, especially in the protogang stage, are not seriously delinquent and receive adult approval. These activities include such things as playing baseball for "side money" and much minor gambling such as penny pitching. Within limits, fighting lies well within the local community's zone of tolerance, especially when it is directed against members of another ethnic group.

At the level of the adolescent and preadolescent groups themselves, the environment is essentially coercive of gang formation. The presence of large numbers of groups competing for limited resources leads to conflict, and the fullfledged adolescent gang is pre-eminently a conflict group with a high valuation of fighting skill, courage, and similar qualities. Thus, the transition from spontaneous group to gang is largely a matter of participating in the struggle for life of the adolescent world under the peculiar conditions of the slum.

At the level of the individual, Thrasher assumes a set of basic needs common to all children. He leans heavily on the famous four wishes of W. I. Thomas, security, response, recognition, and new experiences, especially the last two. Gang boys and boys in gang areas are, in this sense, no different from other boys. They come to choose different ways of satisfying these needs. What determines which boys form gangs is the differential success of the agencies of socialization and social control in channeling these needs into conventional paths. Thus, due to family inadequacy or breakdown or school difficulties, coupled with the ever present temp-

tations of the exciting, adventurous street as compared to the drab, dull, and unsatisfying family and school, some boys are more available for street life than others.

Finally, it should be pointed out that the gang engages in many activities of a quite ordinary sort. Athletics are very common and highly regarded at all age levels. Much time is spent simply talking and being with the gang. The gang's repertory is diverse—baseball, football, dice, poker, holding dances, shooting the breeze, shoplifting, rolling drunks, stealing cars.

This is more than enough to give the tenor of Thrasher's formulations. I have purposely attempted to convey the distinctive flavor of essentially healthy boys satisfying universal needs in a weakly controlled and highly seductive environment. Compared to the deprived and driven boys of more recent formulations with their status problems, blocked opportunities (or psychopathologies if one takes a more psychiatric view), Thrasher describes an age of innocence indeed.

This is, perhaps, the most important single difference between Thrasher and some—not all —of the recent views. Delinquency and crime were attractive; being a "good boy" was dull. They were attractive because they were fun and were profitable and because one could be a hero in a fight. Fun, profit, glory, and freedom is a combination hard to beat, particularly for the inadequate conventional institutions that formed the competition.

WORKING CLASS BOY AND MIDDLE CLASS MEASURING ROD

If Thrasher saw the gang as being formed over time through the attractiveness of the free street life and the unattractiveness and moral weakness of the agencies of social control, Albert K. Cohen sees many working class boys as being driven to develop the delinquent subculture as a way of recouping the self-esteem destroyed by middle-class-dominated institutions.

Rather than focusing on the gang and its development over time, Cohen's theory focuses on the way of life of the gang—the delinquent subculture. A collective way of life, a subculture, develops when a number of people with a common problem of adjustment are in effective interaction, according to Cohen. The bulk of his basic viewpoint is the attempted demonstration that the common problem of adjustment of the lower class gang boys who are the carriers of the delinquent subculture derives from their socialization in lower class families and their consequent lack of preparation to function successfully in middle class institutions such as the school.

The institutions within which the working class boy must function reward and punish him for acceptable or unacceptable performance according to the child-assessing version of middle class values. The middle class value pattern places great emphasis on ambition as a cardinal virtue, individual responsibility (as opposed to extreme emphasis on shared kin obligations, for example), the cultivation and possession of skills, the ability to postpone gratification, rationality, the rational cultivation of manners, the control of physical aggressions and violence, the wholesome and constructive use of leisure, and respect for property (especially respect for the abstract rules defining rights of access to material things).[5]

The application of these values adapted to the judgment of children constitutes the "middle class measuring rod" by which all children are judged in institutions run by middle class personnel—the school, the settlement house, and the like. The fact that working class children must compete according to these standards is a consequence of what Cohen, in a most felicitous phrase, refers to as the "democratic status universe" characteristic of American society. Everyone is expected to strive, and everyone is measured against the same standard. Not everyone is equally prepared, however, and the working class boy is, with greater statistical frequency than the middle class boy, ill prepared through previous socialization.

CULTURAL SETTING

Social class for Cohen is not simply economic position but, much more importantly, a set of more or less vertically layered cultural settings which differ in the likelihood that boys will be

[5] Albert K. Cohen, op. cit., pp. 88–93.

taught the aspirations, ambitions, and psychological skills necessary to adjust to the demands of the larger institutions.

Cohen goes on to describe this predominantly lower working class cultural setting as more likely to show restricted aspirations, a live-for-today orientation toward consumption, a moral view which emphasizes reciprocity within the kin and other primary groups and correlatively less concern with abstract rules which apply across or outside of such particularistic circumstances. In addition, the working class child is less likely to be surrounded with educational toys, less likely to be trained in a family regimen of order, neatness, and punctuality. Of particular importance is the fact that physical aggression is more prevalent and more valued in the working class milieu.

When a working class boy thus equipped for life's struggle begins to function in the school, the settlement, and other middle-class-controlled institutions, and encounters the middle class measuring rod, he inevitably receives a great deal of disapproval, rejection, and punishment. In short, in the eyes of the middle class evaluator, he does not measure up. This is what Cohen refers to as the problem of status deprivation which constitutes the fundamental problem of adjustment to which the delinquent subculture is a solution.

SELF-DEROGATION

But this deprivation derives not only from the negative evaluations of others but also from self-derogation. The working class boy shares in this evaluation of himself to some degree for a variety of reasons.[6] The first of these is the previously mentioned democratic status universe wherein the dominant culture requires everyone

[6] In presenting the theoretical work of someone else, it is often the case that the views of the original author are simplified to his disadvantage. I have tried to guard against this. At this point in Cohen's formulation, however, I may be over-simplifying to his benefit. In view of the considerable struggle over the matter of just what the working class boy is sensitive to, I should point out that Cohen is less than absolutely clear. He is not as unclear, however, as some of his critics have maintained. For the best statement in Cohen's work, see *Delinquent Boys*, pp. 121–28.

to compete against all comers. Second, the parents of working class boys, no matter how adjusted they seem to be to their low status position, are likely to project their frustrated aspirations onto their children. They may do little effective socialization to aid the child, but they are, nevertheless, likely at least to want their children to be better off than they are. Third, there is the effect of the mass media which spread the middle class life style. And, of course, there is the effect of the fact of upward mobility as visible evidence that at least some people can make the grade.

In short, the working class boy is subjected to many social influences which emphasize the fact that the way to respect, status, and success lies in conforming to the demands of middle class society. Even more importantly, he very likely has partly accepted the middle class measuring rod as a legitimate, even superior, set of values. The profound ambivalence that this may lead to in the individual is simply a reflection of the fact that the larger culture penetrates the lower working class world in many ways.

Thus, to the external status problem posed by devaluations by middle class functionaries is added the internal status problem of low self-esteem.

This, then, is the common problem of adjustment. Given the availability of many boys similarly situated, a collective solution evolves, the delinquent subculture. This subculture is characterized by Cohen as nonutilitarian, malicious, and negativistic, characterized by versatility, short-run hedonism, and an emphasis on group autonomy, that is, freedom from adult restraint.

These are, of course, the direct antitheses of the components of the middle class measuring rod. The delinquent subculture functions simultaneously to combat the enemy without and the enemy within, both the hated agents of the middle class and the gnawing internal sense of inadequacy and low self-esteem. It does so by erecting a counterculture, an alternative set of status criteria.

GUILT

This subculture must do more than deal with the middle-class-dominated institutions on the one hand and the feelings of low self-esteem on the other. It must also deal with the feelings of guilt over aggression, theft, and the like that will inevitably arise. It must deal with the fact that the collective solution to the common problem of adjustment is an illicit one in the eyes of the larger society and, certainly, also in the eyes of the law-abiding elements of the local area.

It must deal, also, with the increasing opposition which the solution arouses in the police and other agencies of the conventional order. Over time, the subculture comes to contain a variety of definitions of these agents of conventionality which see them as the aggressors, thus legitimating the group's deviant activities.

Because of this requirement that the delinquent subculture constitute a solution to internal, psychological problems of self-esteem and guilt, Cohen sees the group behavior pattern as being overdetermined in the psychological sense and as linking up with the mechanism of reaction formation.

Thus, the reason for the seeming irrationality of the delinquent subculture lies in the deeply rooted fears and anxieties of the status deprived boy. I have already discussed the shift from Thrasher's view of delinquency as attractive in a situation of weak social control to the views of it as more reactive held by some modern theorists. Cohen, of course, is prominent among these latter, the irrationalists. It is extremely difficult to bring these viewpoints together at all except to point out that Cohen's position accords well with much research on school failure and its consequences in damaged self-esteem. It does seem unlikely, as I will point out later in another connection, that the failure of family, school, and neighborhood to control the behavior of Thrasher's boys would result in their simple withdrawal from such conventional contexts without hostility and loss of self-regard.

Cohen emphasizes that not all members of an ongoing delinquent group are motivated by this same problem of adjustment. Like any other protest movement, the motives which draw new members at different phases of its development will vary. It is sufficient that a core of members share the problem.

The analysis of the delinquent subculture of urban working class boys set forth in *Delinquent Boys* has been elaborated and supplemented in a later article by Cohen and James F. Short.[7]

OTHER DELINQUENT SUBCULTURES

Responding to the criticism that there seemed a variety of kinds of delinquent subcultures, even among lower class urban youth, Cohen and Short distinguish the parent-male subculture, the conflict-oriented subculture, the drug addict subculture, and a subculture focused around semiprofessional theft.[8]

The parent subculture is the now familiar subculture subscribed in *Delinquent Boys*. Cohen and Short describe it as the most common form.[9]

We refer to it as the parent sub-culture because it is probably the most common variety in this country—indeed, it might be called the "garden variety" of delinquent sub-culture—and because the characteristics listed above seem to constitute a common core shared by other important variants.

In discussing the conditions under which these different subcultures arise, Cohen and Short rely on a pivotal paper published in 1951 by Solomon Kobrin.[10] Dealing with the differential location of the conflict-oriented versus the semiprofessional theft subculture, Kobrin pointed out that delinquency areas vary in the degree to which conventional and criminal value systems are mutually integrated. In the integrated area, adult criminal activity is stable and organized, and adult criminals are integral parts of the local social structure—active in politics, fraternal orders, providers of employment. Here delinquency can form a kind of apprenticeship for adult criminal careers with such careers being relatively indistinct from conventional careers. More importantly, the interests of organized criminal groups in order and a lack of police attention would lead to attempts to prevent the wilder and more untrammeled forms of juvenile violence. This would mean, of course, that crime in these areas was largely of the stable, profitable sort ordinarily associated with the rackets.

LOWER CLASS BOY AND LOWER CLASS CULTURE

The interpretation of the delinquent subculture associated with Albert Cohen that I have just described contrasts sharply in its main features with what has come to be called the lower class culture view associated with Walter B. Miller.[11] Miller disagrees with the Cohen position concerning the reactive nature of lower class gang culture.[12]

In the case of "gang" delinquency, the cultural system which exerts the most direct influences on behavior is that of the lower class community itself —a long-established, distinctively patterned tradition with an integrity of its own—rather than a so-called delinquent sub-culture which has arisen through conflict with middle class culture and is oriented to the deliberate violation of middle class norms.

What, then, is the lower class culture Miller speaks of and where is it located? Essentially Miller describes a culture which he sees as emerging from the shaking-down processes of immigration, internal migration, and vertical mobility. Several population and cultural streams feed this process, but, primarily, lower class culture represents the emerging common adaptation of unsuccessful immigrants and Negroes.

---

[7]Albert K. Cohen and James F. Short, Jr., "Research in Delinquent Sub-Cultures," *Journal of Social Issues* 14 (1958): 20–36.

[8]For criticism in this vein as well as for the most searching general analysis of material from *Delinquent Boys*, see Harold L. Wilensky and Charles N. Lebeaux, *Industrial Society and Social Welfare* (New York: Russell Sage Foundation, 1958), chap. 9.

[9]Cohen and Short, op. cit., p. 24. The characteristics are those of maliciousness and so on that I have listed previously.

[10]Solomon Kobrin, "The Conflict of Values in Delinquency Areas," *American Sociological Review* 16 (October, 1951): 653–61.

[11]See the following papers, all by Walter B. Miller: "Lower Class Culture as a Generating Milieu of Gang Delinquency," *Journal of Social Issues* 14 (1958): 5–19; "Preventive Work with Street Corner Groups: Boston Delinquency Project," *The Annals of the American Academy of Political and Social Science* 322 (March, 1959), 97–106; "Implications of Urban Lower Class Culture for Social Work," *The Social Service Review* 33 (September, 1959), 219–36.

[12]Walter B. Miller, "Lower Class Culture as a Generating Milieu of Gang Delinquency," pp. 5, 6.

It is the thesis of this paper that from these extremely diverse and heterogeneous origins (with, however, certain common features), there is emerging a relatively homogeneous and stabilized native-American lower class culture; however, in many communities the process of fusion is as yet in its earlier phases, and evidences of the original ethnic or locality culture are still strong.[13]

In his analysis, Miller is primarily concerned with what he calls the hard core group in the lower class—the same very bottom group referred to by Cohen as the lower-lower class. The properties of this emerging lower class culture as described by Miller may be divided into a series of social structural elements and a complex pattern of what Miller calls focal concerns.

FOCAL CONCERNS

The first of the structural elements is what Miller calls the female-based household, that is, a family form wherein the key relationships are those among mature females (especially those of different generations but, perhaps, also sisters or cousins) and between these females and their children. The children may be by different men, and the biological fathers may play a very inconsistent and unpredictable role in the family. Most essentially, the family is not organized around the expectation of stable economic support provided by an adult male.

The relationship between adult females and males is characterized as one of serial mating, with the female finding it necessary repeatedly to go through a cycle of roles of mate-seeker, mother, and employee.

Closely related to and supportive of this form of household is the elaboration of a system of

one-sex peer groups which, according to Miller, become emotional havens and major sources of psychic investment and support for both sexes and for both adolescents and adults. The family, then, is not the central focus of primary, intimate ties that it is in middle class circles.

In what is surely a masterpiece of cogent description, Miller presents the focal concerns of lower class culture as trouble, toughness, smartness, excitement, fate and autonomy. His description of the complexly interwoven patterns assumed by these focal concerns cannot be repeated here, but a brief discussion seems appropriate.[14]

Trouble is what life gets you into—especially trouble with the agents of the larger society. The central aspect of this focal concern is the distinction between law-abiding and law-violating behavior, and where an individual stands along the implied dimension either by behavior, reputation, or commitment is crucial in the evaluation of him by others. Toughness refers to physical prowess, skill, masculinity, fearlessness, bravery, daring. It includes an almost compulsive opposition to things seen as soft and feminine, including much middle class behavior, and is related, on the one hand, to sex-role identification problems which flow from the young boy's growing up in the female-based household and, on the other hand, to the occupational demands of the lower class world. Toughness, along with the emphasis on excitement and autonomy, is one of the ways one gets into trouble.

Smartness refers to the ability to "con," outwit, dupe, that is, to manipulate things and people to one's own advantage with a minimum of conventional work. Excitement, both as an activity and as an ambivalently held goal, is best manifested in the patterned cycle of the week end night-on-the-town complete with much drink and sexual escapades, thereby creating the risk of fighting and trouble. Between week ends, life is dull and passive. Fate refers to the perception by many lower class individ-

---

[13]Walter B. Miller, "Implications of Urban Lower Class Culture for Social Work," p. 225. Miller seems to be saying that the processes of sorting and segregating which characterized American industrial cities in the period referred to by Thrasher are beginning to show a product at the lower end of the status order. In this, as in several other ways, Miller is much more the inheritor of the classical view, as I have called it, than are Cohen or Cloward and Ohlin. Miller shows much the same concern for relatively wholistic description of the local community setting and much the same sensitivity to group process over time. Whether his tendency to see lower class culture in terms of a relatively closed system derives from differences in fact due to historical change or primarily to differences in theoretical perspective is hard to say.

[14]This description of the focal concern is taken from Walter B. Miller, "Lower Class Culture as a Generating Milieu of Gang Delinquency," especially chart 1, 7. In this case especially, the original should be read.

uals that their lives are determined by events and forces over which they have little or no control. It manifests itself in widespread gambling and fantasies of "when things break for me." Gambling serves multiple functions in the areas of fate, toughness, smartness, and excitement.

The last focal concern described by Miller is that of autonomy—concern over the amount, source, and severity of control by others. Miller describes the carrier of lower class culture as being highly ambivalent about such control by others. Overtly, he may protest bitterly about restraint and arbitrary interference while, covertly, he tends to equate coercion with care and unconsciously to seek situations where strong controls will satisfy nurturance needs.

Growing Up

What is it like to grow up in lower class culture? A boy spends the major part of the first twelve years in the company of and under the domination of women. He learns during that time that women are the people who count, that men are despicable, dangerous, and desirable. He also learns that a "real man" is hated for his irresponsibility and considered very attractive on Saturday night. He learns, too, that, if he really loves his mother, he will not grow up to be "just like all men" but that, despite her best efforts, his mother's pride and joy will very likely turn out to be as much a "rogue male" as the rest. In short, he has sex-role problems.

The adolescent street group is the social mechanism which enables the maturing boy to cope with a basic problem of feminine identification coupled with the necessity of somehow growing up to be an appropriately hated and admired male in a culture which maximizes the necessity to fit into all male society as an adult. The seeking of adult status during adolescence, then, has a particular intensity, so that manifestations of the adult culture's focal concerns tend to be overdone. In addition, the street group displays an exaggerated concern with status and belongingness which is common in all adolescent groups but becomes unusually severe for the lower class boy.

The street group, then, is an essential transition mechanism and training ground for the lower class boy. Some of the behavior involved is delinquent, but the degree to which the group engages in specifically delinquent acts, that is, constructs its internal status criteria around the law-violating end of the trouble continuum, may vary greatly depending on local circumstances. These include such things as the presence and salience of police, professional criminals, clergy, functioning recreational and settlement programs, and the like.

Like Thrasher, Miller emphasizes the wide range of activities of a nondelinquent nature that the gang members engage in, although, unlike Thrasher's boys, they do not do so because of poor social control, but because of the desire to be "real men."

Participation in the lower class street group may produce delinquency in several ways:[15]

1. Following cultural practices which comprise essential elements of the total pattern of lower class culture automatically violates certain legal norms.
2. In instances where alternative avenues to similar objectives are available, the non-law-abiding avenue frequently provides a greater and more immediate return for a relatively smaller investment of energy.
3. The "demanded" response to certain situations recurrently engendered within lower class culture involves the commission of illegal acts.

Impact of Middle Class Values

Miller's approach, like the approaches of Thrasher and Cohen, has its strengths and weaknesses. Miller has not been very successful in refuting Cohen's insistence on the clash between middle class and lower class standards as it affects the sources of self-esteem. To be sure, Cohen's own presentation of just what the lower class boy has or has not internalized is considerably confused. As I have remarked elsewhere, Cohen seems to be saying that a little internalization is a dangerous thing.[16] Miller seems to be saying that the involvements in lower class culture are so deep and exclusive

[15] Walter B. Miller, "Lower Class Culture as a Generating Milieu of Gang Delinquency," p. 18.
[16] David J. Bordua, "Sociological Theories and Their Implications for Juvenile Delinquency," *Facts and Facets*, No. 2, Children's Bureau, Juvenile Delinquency (Washington, D.C.: Government Printing Office, 1960), pp. 9–11.

that contacts with agents of middle class dominated institutions, especially the schools, have no impact.

Actually, resolution of this problem does not seem so terribly difficult. In handling Cohen's formulations, I would suggest that previous internalization of middle class values is not particularly necessary, because the lower class boys will be told about them at the very time they are being status-deprived by their teachers and others. They will likely hate it and them (teachers and values), and the process is started. On the other hand, it seems unlikely that Miller's lower class boys can spend ten years in school without some serious outcomes. They should either come to accept middle class values or become even more antagonistic or both, and this should drive them further into the arms of lower class culture.

This would be especially the case because of the prevailing definition of school work as girlish, an attitude not at all limited to Miller's lower class culture. With the sex-role identification problems Miller quite reasonably poses for his boys, the demands of the middle class school teacher that he be neat and clean and well-behaved must be especially galling.[17] In short, it seems to me inconceivable that the objective conflict between the boys and the school, as the most crucial example, could end in a simple turning away.

Miller also seems to be weak when he insists upon seeing what he calls the hard core of lower class culture as a distinctive form and, at the same time, must posit varieties of lower class culture to account for variations in behavior and values. This is not necessarily a factually untrue position, but it would seem to underemphasize the fluidity and variability of American urban life. It is necessary for him to point out that objectively low status urban groups vary in the degree to which they display the core features of lower class culture, with

Negroes and Irish groups among those he has studied displaying it more and Italians less.

VALIDITY OF FEMALE BASE

Miller seems so concerned that the features of lower class culture, especially the female-based household, not be seen as the disorganization of the more conventional system or as signs of social pathology that he seems to overdo it rather drastically. He is very concerned to show that lower class culture is of ancient lineage and is or was functional in American society. Yet, at the same time, he says that lower class culture is only now emerging at the bottom of the urban heap. He also forgets that none of the low status groups in the society, with the possible exception of low status Negroes, has any history of his female-based household, at least not in the extreme form that he describes.[18]

A closely related problem is posed by Miller's citation of cross-cultural evidence, for example, "The female-based household is a stabilized form in many societies—frequently associated with polygamy—and is found in 21 per cent of world societies."[19] I do not doubt that figure, but I question the implication that the female-based household as the household form, legitimated and normatively supported in societies practicing polygamy, can be very directly equated with a superficially similar system existing on the margins of a larger society and clearly seen as deviant by that larger society. Surely, in primitive societies, the household can count on the stable economic and judicial base provided by an adult male. The very fact that such a household in the United States is under continuous and heavy pressure from the law, the Aid to Dependent Children worker, and nearly all other agents of the conventional order must make for a very different situation than in societies where it is the accepted form. In such societies, would mothers generally regard men as "unreliable and untrustworthy" and would the statement "all men are no good" be common?[20]

---

[17]For evidence that lower class Negro girls seem to do much better than boys in adjusting to at least one middle class institution, see Martin Deutsch, *Minority Group and Class Status as Related to Social and Personality Factors in School Achievement*, Monograph No. 2, The Society for Applied Anthropology (Ithaca, New York: The Society, 1960).

[18]E. Franklin Frazier, *The Negro Family in the United States* (Chicago: University of Chicago Press, 1939).

[19]Walter B. Miller, "Implications of Urban Lower Class Culture for Social Work," p. 225, n.

[20]Ibid., p. 226.

Surely, such an attitude implies some awareness that things should be otherwise.

All this is not to argue that tendencies of the sort Miller describes are not present nor to underestimate the value of his insistence that we look at this way of life in its own terms—a valuable contribution indeed—but only to ask for somewhat greater awareness of the larger social dynamics that produce his lower class culture.

Danger of Tautology

Finally, a last criticism of Miller's formulations aims at the use of the focal concerns material. There seems more than a little danger of tautology here if the focal concerns are derived from observing behavior and then used to explain the same behavior. One would be on much safer ground to deal in much greater detail with the structural roots and reality situations to which lower class culture may be a response. Thus, for example, Miller makes no real use of the vast literature on the consequences of prolonged instability of employment, which seems to be the root of the matter.

These criticisms should not blind us to very real contributions in Miller's position. Most importantly, he tells us what the lower class street boys are for, rather than just what they are against. In addition, he deals provocatively and originally with the nature of the adult culture which serves as the context for adolescent behavior. Finally, he alerts us to a possible historical development that has received relatively little attention—the emergence of something like a stable American lower class. This possibility seems to have been largely neglected in studies of our increasingly middle class society.

SUCCESS GOALS AND OPPORTUNITY STRUCTURES

The last of the major approaches to the problem of lower class delinquency to be considered here is associated with Richard A. Cloward and Lloyd E. Ohlin.[21] Stated in its briefest form, the theory

is as follows: American culture makes morally mandatory the seeking of success goals but differentially distributes the morally acceptable means to these success goals, the legitimate opportunities that loom so large in the approach.[22]

This gap between culturally universalized goals and structurally limited means creates strain among lower class youths who aspire to economic advancement. Such strain and alienation leads to the formation of delinquent subcultures, that is, normative and belief systems that specifically support and legitimate delinquency, among those boys who blame the system rather than themselves for their impending or actual failure. The particular form of delinquent subculture—conflict, criminal, or retreatist (drug-using)—which results depends on the nature of the local neighborhood and, especially, on the availability of illegitimate opportunities, such as stable crime careers as models and training grounds.

The criminal subculture develops in stable neighborhoods with much regularized crime present; the conflict form develops in really disorganized neighborhoods where not even illegitimate opportunities are available; the retreatist, or drug-use, subculture develops among persons who are double failures due either to internalized prohibitions against violence or theft or to the objective unavailability of these solutions.

Intervening between the stress due to blocked aspirations and the creation of the full-fledged subculture of whatever type is a process of collectively supported "withdrawal of attributions of legitimacy from established social norms."

This process, coupled with the collective development of the relevant delinquent norms, serves to allay whatever guilt might have been felt over the illegal acts involved in following the delinquent norms.

Since the argument in *Delinquency and Opportunity* is, in many ways, even more compli-

---

[21]The full statement of the approach is in Richard A. Cloward and Lloyd E. Ohlin, *Delinquency and*

Opportunity (New York: The Free Press, 1960); see also Richard A. Cloward, "Illegitimate Means, Anomie and Deviant Behavior," *American Sociological Review* 24 (April, 1959): 164–76.

[22]For the original version of this formulation, see Robert K. Merton, *Social Theory and Social Structure* rev. and enl. (New York: The Free Press, 1951), chaps. 4, 5.

cated than those associated with Cohen, Short, and Miller, I will discuss only a few highlights.[23]

POTENTIAL DELINQUENTS

On the question of who aspires to what, which is so involved in the disagreements between Cohen and Miller, Cloward and Ohlin take the position that it is not the boys who aspire to middle class status—and, therefore, have presumably partially internalized the middle class measuring rod—who form the raw material for delinquent subculture, but those who wish only to improve their economic status without any change in class membership. Thus, it is appropriate in their argument to say that the genitors of the delinquent subcultures are not dealing so much with an internal problem of self-esteem as with an external problem of injustice. Cohen says, in effect, that the delinquent subculture prevents self-blame for failure from breaking through, the reaction formation function of the delinquent subculture. Cloward and Ohlin say that the delinquent norm systems are generated by boys who have already determined that their failures, actual or impending, are the fault of the larger social order.[24]

This insistence that it is the "system blamers" who form the grist for the subcultural mill leads Cloward and Ohlin into something of an impasse, it seems to me. They must, of course, then deal with the determinants of the two types of blame and choose to say that two factors are primarily relevant. First, the larger culture engenders expectations, not just aspirations, of success which are not met, and, second, there exist highly visible barriers to the fulfillment of these expectations, such as racial prejudice, which are defined as unjust.

These do not seem unreasonable, and, in fact, in the case of Negro youth, perhaps, largely fit the case. Cloward and Ohlin, however, are forced for what seems overwhelmingly polemical reasons into a position that the feeling of injustice must be objectively correct. Therefore, they say (1) that it is among those actually fitted for success where the sense of injustice will flourish and (2) that delinquent subcultures are formed by boys who do not essentially differ in their capacity to cope with the larger institutions from other boys. This point deserves some attention since it is so diametrically opposed to the Cohen position which states that some working class boys, especially lower working class boys, are unable to meet the demands of middle-class dominated institutions.

It is our impression that a sense of being unjustly deprived of access to opportunities to which one is entitled is common among those who become participants in delinquent subcultures. Delinquents tend to be persons who have been led to expect opportunities because of their potential ability to meet the formal, institutionally-established criteria of evaluation. Their sense of injustice arises from the failure of the system to fulfill these expectations. Their criticism is not directed inward since they regard themselves in comparison with their fellows as capable of meeting the formal requirements of the system. It has frequently been noted that delinquents take special delight in discovering hypocrisy in the operation of the established social order. They like to point out that it's "who you know, not what you know" that enables one to advance or gain coveted social rewards. They become convinced that bribery, blackmail, fear-inspiring pressure, special influence, and similar factors are more important than the publicly avowed criteria of merit.[25]

DELINQUENTS AND NONDELINQUENT PEERS

On the same page in a footnote, the authors go on to say that the research evidence indicates "the basic endowments of delinquents, such as intelligence, physical strength, and agility, are the equal of or greater than those of their nondelinquent peers."

The material in these quotations is so riddled with ambiguities it is difficult to know where to begin criticism, but we can at least point out the following. First, Cloward and Ohlin seem to be confusing the justificatory function of delinquent

---

[23]Large segments of *Delinquency and Opportunity* are devoted to refutations of others' positions, especially those of Cohen and Miller. I felt that, at least for the present paper, criticizing in detail other people's refutations of third parties might be carrying the matter too far. It should be pointed out, however, that the tendency to take extreme positions as a consequence of involvement in a polemic which is apparent in Miller's work seems even more apparent in the Cloward and Ohlin book.

[24]Richard A. Cloward and Lloyd E. Ohlin, *Delinquency and Opportunity.* For the problem of types of aspiration and their consequences, see, especially, pp. 86–97. For the matter of self-blame and their system blame for failure, see pp. 110–26.

[25]Ibid., p. 117.

subcultures with their causation. All of these beliefs on the part of gang delinquents have been repeatedly reported in the literature, but by the very argument of *Delinquency and Opportunity*, it is impossible to tell whether they constitute compensatory ideology or descriptions of objective reality.

Second, Cloward and Ohlin seem to be victims of their very general tendency to ignore the life histories of their delinquents.[26] Thus, there is no way of knowing really what these subcultural beliefs may reflect in the experience of the boys. Third, and closely related to the ignoring of life history material, is the problem of assessing the degree to which these gang boys are in fact prepared to meet the formal criteria for success. To say they are intelligent, strong, and agile is to parody the criteria for advancement. Perhaps Cohen would point out that intelligent, agile, strong boys who begin the first grade using foul language, fighting among themselves, and using the school property as arts and crafts materials do not meet the criteria for advancement.

It is quite true that members of highly sophisticated delinquent gangs often find themselves blocked from whatever occupational opportunities there are, but this seems, often, the end product of a long history of their progressively cutting off opportunity and destroying their own capacities which may begin in the lower class family, as described by either Cohen or Miller, and continue through school failure and similar events. By the age of 18, many gang boys are, for all practical purposes, unemployable or need the support, instruction, and sponsorship of trained streetgang workers. Participation in gang delinquency in itself diminishes the fitness of many boys for effective functioning in the conventional world.[27]

If, indeed, Cloward and Ohlin mean to include the more attitudinal and characterological criteria for advancement, then it seems highly unlikely that any large number of boys trained and prepared to meet these demands of the occupational world could interpret failure exclusively in terms which blame the system. They would have been too well socialized, and, if they did form a delinquent subculture, it would have to perform the psychological function of mitigating the sense of internal blame. This, of course, would make them look much like Cohen's boys.

In short, Cloward and Ohlin run the risk of confusing justification and causation and of equating the end with the beginning.

All of this is not to deny that there are real obstacles to opportunity for lower class boys. There are. These blocks on both the performance and learning sides, are a major structural feature in accounting for much of the adaption of lower class populations. But they do not operate solely or even primarily on the level of the adolescent. They create a social world in which he comes of age, and, by the time he reaches adolescence, he may find himself cut off from the larger society. Much of the Cloward and Ohlin approach seems better as a theory of the origins of Miller's lower class culture. Each generation does not meet and solve anew the problems of class structure barriers to opportunity but begins with the solution of its forebears.[28] This is why reform efforts can be so slow to succeed.

---

[26]This is the most fundamental weakness in the book. The delinquents in Thrasher, Cohen, and Miller were, in varying degrees, once recognizably children. Cloward and Ohlin's delinquents seem suddenly to appear on the scene sometime in adolescence, to look at the world, and to discover, "Man, there's no opportunity in my structure." It is instructive in this connection to note that the index to *Delinquency and Opportunity* contains only two references to the family. One says that the family no longer conducts occupational training; the other criticizes Miller's ideas on female-based households.

[27]Here, again, Thrasher seems superior to some of the modern theorists. He stressed the fact that

long-term involvement in the "free, undisciplined" street life with money at hand from petty theft and with the days devoted to play was not exactly ideal preparation for the humdrum life of the job. Again, Thrasher's sensitivity to the attitudinal and subcultural consequences of the gang formation and maintenance process truly needs reintroduction.

[28]Parenthetically, the Cloward and Ohlin position has great difficulty in accounting for the fact that lower class delinquent subculture carriers do not avail-themselves of opportunities that do exist. The mixed success of vocational school training, for example, indicates that some fairly clear avenues of opportunity are foregone by many delinquent boys. For Negro boys, where avenues to the skilled trades may indeed be blocked, their argument seems reasonable. For white boys, I have serious question. In fact, the one really convincing case they make on the aspiration-blockage, system-blame side is for Negroes.

SOME INSIGHTS

The positive contributions of the Cloward-Ohlin approach seem to me to lie less on the side of the motivational sources of subcultural delinquency, where I feel their attempts to clarify the ambiguities in Cohen have merely led to new ambiguities, but more on the side of the factors in local social structure that determine the type of subcultural delinquency.

The major innovation here is the concept of illegitimate opportunities which serves to augment Kobrin's almost exclusive emphasis on the differentially controlling impact of different slum environments. I do think that Cloward and Ohlin may make too much of the necessity for systematic, organized criminal careers in order for the illegitimate opportunity structure to have an effect, but the general argument has great merit.

In addition to the concept of illegitimate opportunities and closely related to it is the description, or speculation, concerning historical changes in the social organization of slums. Changes in urban life in the United States may have truly produced the disorganized slum devoid of the social links between young and old, between children and older adolescents which characterized the slums described by Thrasher. Certainly, the new conditions of life seem to have created new problems of growing up, though our knowledge of their precise impact leaves much to be desired.

CONCLUSION

This paper should not, I hope, give the impression that current theoretical interpretations of lower class, urban, male subcultural delinquency are without value. Such is far from the case. Many of my comments have been negative since each of the theorists quite ably presents his own defense, which should be read in any case. In fact, I think that this problem has led to some of the most exciting and provocative intellectual interchange in all sociology in recent years. I do believe, however, that this interchange has often been marred by unnecessary polemic and, even more, by a lack of relevant data.

As I have indicated, there have been some profound changes in the way social theorists view the processes of gang formation and persistence. These, I believe, derive only partially, perhaps even unimportantly, from changes in the facts to be explained. Indeed, we must wait for a study of gangs which will approach Thrasher's in thoroughness before we can know if there are new facts to be explained. Nor do I believe that the changes in viewpoint have come about entirely because old theories were shown to be inadequate to old facts. Both Cohen and Cloward and Ohlin feel that older theorists did not deal with the problem of the origins of delinquent subcultures, but only with the transmission of subculture once developed.[29] A careful reading of Thrasher indicates that such is not the case.

All in all, though, it does not seem like much fun any more to be a gang delinquent. Thrasher's boys enjoyed themselves being chased by the police, shooting dice, skipping school, rolling drunks. It was fun. Miller's boys do have a little fun, with their excitement focal concern, but it seems so desperate somehow. Cohen's boys and Cloward and Ohlin's boys are driven by grim economic and psychic necessity into rebellion. It seems peculiar that modern analysts have stopped assuming that "evil" can be fun and see gang delinquency as arising only when boys are driven away from "good."[30]

---

[29]Albert K. Cohen, *Delinquent Boys,* p. 18; Richard A. Cloward and Lloyd E. Ohlin, *Delinquency and Opportunity,* p. 42.

[30]For a more thorough commentary on changes in the view of human nature, which, I think, partly underlie the decline of fun in theories of the gang, see Dennis Wrong, "The Oversocialized View of Man," *American Sociological Review* 26 (April, 1961): 183–93.

18.

MARVIN E. WOLFGANG

THE CULTURE OF YOUTH

THE SUBCULTURE OF YOUTH

The first issue confronted in discussing youth is whether social analysts may validly refer to a given age group as constituting a culture or a subculture. The term "culture" has gone through many definitional forms since E. B. Tylor's famous statement in 1871 defining it as ". . . that complex whole which includes knowledge, belief, art, morals, law, custom, and any other capabilities and habits acquired by man as a member of society."[1]

By 1962, A. L. Kroeber and Clyde Kluckhohn had analyzed 160 definitions in English by anthropologists, sociologists, and others, and offered a synthesis that embodied the elements accepted by most contemporary social scientists: "Culture consists of patterns, explicit and implicit, by symbols, constituting the distinctive achievements of human groups, including their embodiment in artifacts; the essential core of culture consists of traditional (i.e., historically derived and selected) ideas and especially their attached values; culture systems may, on the one hand, be considered as products of action, on the other as conditioning elements of further action."[2]

In discussing the elements of culture, social scientists usually refer to life style, prescribed ways of behaving, norms of conduct, beliefs, values, behavior patterns and uniformities, as well as the artifacts which these "nonmaterial" aspects create. The writings of Franz Boas,

Ralph Linton, Otto Klineberg, Pitirim Sorokin, Robert MacIver, and Leslie White are only a few examples among the many important contributions to the embellishment of the meaning of culture.[3]

More recently, A. L. Kroeber and Talcott Parsons have provided a meaningful distinction between "society" and "culture" in the following way: "We suggest that it is useful to define the concept 'culture' for most usages more narrowly than has been generally the case in American anthropological tradition, restricting its reference to transmitted and created content and patterns of values, ideas and other symbolic-meaningful systems as factors in the shaping of human behavior and the artifacts produced through behavior. On the other hand, we suggest that the term "society" or, more generally, "social system" be used to designate the specifically relational system of interaction among individuals and collectivities."[4]

The term "subculture," although not the concept, did not become common in social science literature until after World War II. Alfred Mc-

SOURCE: Marvin E. Wolfgang, "The Culture of Youth," *President's Commission on Law Enforcement and Administration of Justice: Task Force Report on Juvenile Delinquency and Youth Crime* (Washington, D.C.: Government Printing Office, 1967), pp. 145–54.

[1]E. B. Tylor, *Primitive Culture* (London: John Murray, 1871), p. 1.

[2]A. L. Kroeber and Clyde Kluckhohn, "A Critical Review of Concepts and Definitions." Papers of the Peabody Museum of American Archeology and Ethnology, vol. 47, no. 1, 1952.

[3]Typical statements of these authors may be found in Franz Boas, "Anthropology," in *Encyclopedia of the Social Sciences*, ed. E. R. A. Seligman (New York: Crowell Collier & Macmillan, Inc., 1930), 11:79; Ralph Linton, *The Study of Man* (New York: Appleton-Century, 1936), p. 78; Otto Klineberg, *Race Differences* (New York: Harper & Row, Publishers, 1935), p. 255; Pitirim Sorokin, *Society, Culture and Personality* (New York: Harper & Row, Publishers, 1947), p. 313; Robert M. MacIver, *Social Causation* (Boston: Ginn and Company, 1942), pp. 269–90; Robert M. MacIver and Charles H. Page, *Society: An Introductory Analysis* (New York: Holt, Rinehart & Winston, Inc., 1949), pp. 498 ff.; Leslie White, *The Science of Culture* (New York: Farrar, Straus & Giroux, Inc., 1949), p. 25.

[4]A. L. Kroeber and Talcott Parsons, "The Concepts of Culture and of Social Systems." *American Sociological Review* 23 (October, 1958): 582–83. See also the seminal article by Gertrude Jaeger and Philip Selznick, "A Normative Theory of Culture," *American Sociological Review*, October, 1964.

Clung Lee[5] made use of the term in 1945; Milton Gordon in 1947 defined subculture as " . . . a subdivision of the natural culture, composed of a combination of factorable social situations such as class status, ethnic background, regional and rural or urban residence, and religious affiliation, but forming in their combination a functional unity which has an integrated impact on the participating individual."[6]

In sociological criminology, Albert Cohen,[7] in his *Delinquent Boys*, describes the term by referring to the following items: The cultural patterns of subgroups; the emergence of subcultures "only by interaction with those [persons] who already share and embody, in their belief and action, the culture pattern"; the psychogenic situation of physical limitations in problems requiring solution; the fact that human problems are not randomly distributed among the roles that make up the social system; reference groups for interaction, for the sharing of values, and as the means of achieving status, recognition, and response.

Even before the publication of Richard Cloward and Lloyd Ohlin's *Delinquency and Opportunity*,[8] with its significant breakdown into criminal, conflict, and retreatist subcultures, Milton Yinger[9] noted over 100 books and articles that made some use of the idea of "subculture." After a comprehensive review of such terms as "situation," "anomie," and "role," which should not, he says, be confused with the meaning of "subculture," Yinger introduced the concept of "contraculture" to refer to those subcultural groups that are at considerable variance with the larger culture.

It is not our purpose to try to add new clarity, precision, or quantifiable parameters to the meaning of "subcultures."[10] We are drawing attention to the generally communicative meaning of "subculture" in order to indicate that youth represent a separate subculture in society. We do assume, however, that not all values, beliefs, or norms in a society have equal status, that some priority allocation of them is made which the persons in a subculture partially accept and partially deny. The representatives of a subculture may even construct antitheses to elements of the central or dominant values while still remaining within the larger cultural system.

These assumptions lead us to assert that a "subculture" implies that there is a cluster of value judgments, or a social value system, which is both apart from and a part of the central value system. From the viewpoint of the larger, dominant culture, the values of the subculture set the latter apart and prevent total integration, occasionally causing open or covert conflicts. The dominant culture may directly or indirectly promote this apartness, and the degree of reciprocal integration may vary, but whatever the reason for the difference, some normative isolation and solidarity of the subculture result. There are, thus, shared values that are learned,

[5]Alfred McClung Lee, "Levels of Culture as Levels of Social Generalization," *American Sociological Review* 10 (August, 1945): 485–95; "Social Determinants of Public Opinion," *International Journal of Opinion and Attitude Research* (March, 1947): 12–29; "A Sociological Discussion of Consistency and Inconsistency in Inter-group Relations," *Journal of Social Issues* 5 (1949): 12–18.

[6]Milton M. Gordon, "The Concept of the Sub-Culture and Its Application," *Social Forces* 26 (October, 1947): 40. For additional discussions by Gordon, using the term "subculture," see also "A System of Social Class Analysis," Drew University Studies, No. 2 (August, 1951), pp. 15–18; *Social Class in American Sociology* (Durham, N. C.: Duke University Press, 1958), pp. 252–56; "Social Structure and Goals in Group Relations," in *Freedom and Control in Modern Society*, ed. Morroe Berger, Theodore Abel, and Charles H. Page (New York: D. Van Nostrand Co., Inc., 1954). In these references, Gordon uses the term to refer to subsociety as well.

Gordon has recently gone further and proposes a new term, "ethclass," to refer to "the subsociety created by the intersection of the vertical stratifications of ethnicity with the horizontal stratifications of social class. . . ." *Assimilation in American Life* (New York: Oxford University Press, 1964), p. 51.

[7]Albert K. Cohen, *Delinquent Boys* (New York: The Free Press, 1955).

[8]Richard Cloward and Lloyd Ohlin, *Delinquency and Opportunity* (New York: The Free Press, 1960).

[9]Milton Yinger, "Contraculture and Subculture," *American Sociological Review* 25 (October, 1960): 625–35.

[10]An effort to show how parameters of subcultures might be designed appears in Marvin E. Wolfgang and Franco Ferracuti, *Subculture of Violence* (London: Tavistock Publications, 1967). Some of the notions expressed in this section of the paper are contained in more detail in the Wolfgang-Ferracuti book. See also Thorsten Sellin, *Culture Conflict and Crime* (New York: Social Science Research Council, Bulletin 41, 1938) for some of the provocative theoretical antecedents to current ideas about subcultures; and Leslie T. Wilkins, *Social Deviance* (London: Tavistock Publications, 1964).

adopted, and even exhibited by participants in the subculture, and these values differ in quantity and quality from the dominant culture.

A subculture is, then, only partly different from the parent culture, the larger culture from which subcultural elements have stemmed as different offshoots of its own value system. But there must be a sufficient number and variety of significant values commonly shared between "parent" and "child" if the latter is to retain its theoretical attribution of subculture. Some of the values of a subculture may, however, be more than different from the larger culture; they may be in conflict or at wide variance with the latter. Thus, a delinquent subculture represents a contractual system that is more than merely different from the parent culture, for in its dysfunctional character it is also antithetical to the broader social system. To be part of the larger culture implies that some values related to the ends and means of the whole are shared by the part. The subculture that is only different is a tolerated deviation; what we generally refer to as the youth subculture is in fact a tolerated form of variation from the parent culture. Values shared in the subculture are often made evident in terms of conduct that is expected, ranging from permissible to required expectations in certain kinds of life situations. These conduct norms generated by the value content of the subculture (indeed, of any subculture) have not yet been subjected to much quantified measurement.

It is difficult to discuss subcultures and conduct norms without reference to social groups, for values are shared by individuals, and individuals sharing values make up groups. In most cases, when we refer to subcultures we are thinking of individuals who share common values and who socially interact in some limited geographical or residential isolation. However, value sharing does not necessarily require direct or primary social interaction. Consequently, a subculture may exist widely distributed spatially and without interpersonal contact among individuals or whole groups of individuals. Several delinquent gangs, for example, may be spread throughout a city and rarely, if ever, have contacts; yet, they are referred to collectively as the "delinquent subculture," and properly so,

for otherwise each gang would have to be considered as a separate subculture.

If a subculture, like a culture, is composed of values, conduct norms, social situations, role definitions and performances, sharing, transmission, and learning of values, then there is sufficient reason to speak of the subculture of youth in American society. We have said that the degree of concordant and tolerated, as well as discordant and untolerated, values of various segments of youth are related to the dominant culture themes of American society. A detailed analysis of the establishment and measurement of the parameters of the youth subculture would seem to be necessary in order to establish exactly where the values vary, to measure the intensity or strength of these values among youth, and to determine the degree of commitment or allegiance that youth has to certain values that when clustered together, may be called the value system of youth. It may be contended that an age group roughly embracing 12 to 20 years represents a subcultural system, although there are, of course, other subcultures, or other transmittable value systems, within which youth functions.

Without appropriate measurements of values and value systems, it is difficult to indicate exactly where subcultures blend into one another. However, the subculture of the lower class poor, of a Negro subsociety, delinquent subcultures, and other varieties of subcultural affiliations may be assumed to have groups of individuals who represent not only separate subcultures, but also conclaves where these various subcultures overlap. The descriptive characteristics of the generic term "youth" are often of little help to the social analysts or the consumers of social observations who wish to understand the variety of youth problems. Our attention, therefore, should be drawn not merely to the ways in which an age group called "youth" fits functionally into the larger culture system created and maintained by adults; what is needed beyond these age-graded and age-linked descriptive features is some notion of how several subcultures combine with youth. In a more elaborate treatise, the linkages should contain an interwoven thread of theory and be embraced by meaningful sociological conceptualisms. One of the main conceptual propositions to be employed later in this paper includes protest against the lack of, and request or even demand for more power and for participation in the larger culture system and its processes.

An interesting feature in the present generation that contributes to this age-graded subculture we call "youth" is the massive network of communication. Instant awareness of news and the rapid spread of innovations in dress, dancing, and dating habits quickly unify people and make rapid the sharing of values and norms across the entire country. The structure of our mass communication functions to make elements in the youth subculture quickly reinforced by supportive acts and attitudes on a numerically larger scale and spatially wider arena than ever before. For example, a university sit-in protest is known abroad even while it happens, and repetitive reinforcement readily appears in other universities. The transistor radio carried by a West Berlin teenager reports the same musical styles heard in Boise, Idaho. Thus, the contraction of time and the extension of space for spreading the elements attractive to and shared by youth combine to create a firm subculture of their own.

It should be remembered, however, that more new things lasting shorter periods of time create only an illusion of diversity. The young listeners to television and transistors, more sensitive than their elders to innovation, fads, and fashion, do not have alternatives of action that correspondingly increase with the number of changes they witness. Their repertoire of response may even be reduced as the youth culture grows stronger. Deviance from adult models may be more evident now, but the more committed the youth become to their own subculture, the more captive they become to their conformity. The more they strive to be recognized, loved, wanted, and feared within their own group culture, the more they contribute to their own captivity. The shared mass media of magazines and electronics probably produce greater homogenization among the young than among adults, and within the youth subculture of today more than during any previous period. This generalization is applicable to the considerable variability that exists in the youth subculture, ranging from Saturday afternoon dance clubs to Florida and Bermuda springtime frolics, the free university students, the Berkeley free speech movement, and the local drugstore crowd of the "Street Corner Society."[11]

EXTENDED SOCIALIZATION AND DEPENDENCY STATUS

Gertrude Stein is alleged to have said that the United States is the oldest country in the world because it has had the most experience with modern industrial society and its complex consequences. With similar perception, Dwight Macdonald[12] has said that the United States was the first to develop the concept of the teenager, a concept which is still not well accepted in Europe, and that we have had the longest experience with the subculture of youth. The way we handle a nearly "overdeveloped" society with transportation, bureaucratization, impersonal, automated living, and the way we learn to understand the new problems of youth and the existence of poverty to remind us of our social imperfection, will be lessons of value to underdeveloped or newly developed countries. Despite our longer experience with modernity and the teenage subculture, we still have lessons to learn about the problems created by both, and the particular interrelation of modern youth and modern poverty is especially important and striking in many ways.

Our youth in general are richer today than they have ever been and have more alternatives of action and more privileges. The list of privileges usurped by youth has not only increased but has shifted downward in age. The high school student of today has the accoutrements of the college student of yesteryear—cars, long pants, money, and more access to girls. This downward shift in privileges, precocious to younger ages, is a phenomenon well known to

---

[11]William Foot Whyte, *Street Corner Society* (Chicago: University of Chicago Press, 1943 and 1955).

[12]Dwight Macdonald, "Profile," *The New Yorker,* November 22, 1957. Both this reference and the remark by Gertrude Stein are cited in Reuel Denney, "American Youth Today: A Bigger Case, A Wider Screen," in *The Challenge of Youth,* ed. Erik H. Erikson (Garden City, N.Y.: Doubleday and Company, Inc., Anchor Books, 1965), pp. 155–79.

every parent whose own youth subculture was devoid of them.

Not only are our youth more privileged and richer, but they have for some time constituted an increasingly significant portion of American purchasing power. The statistics of consumption of lipstick and brassieres, even by 12- and 13-year-olds, are well known, as are those of records, used cars, popular magazines, and transistor radios. The magnified purchasing power of young teenagers is one of the factors that tends to make them want to grow up faster or not at all, which is suggestive of Reuel Denney's credit-card viewpoint of "grow up now and pay later."[13]

The ambivalence of the analyzers regarding whether our youth become adultlike too early or behave as adolescent children too long is a scholastic debate that has not yet been resolved by empirical data. Moreover, a valid appraisal of the "youth problem" is also made difficult by the existence of conflicting cultural prescriptions for youth. We appear to want teenagers to act like young adults in our society, yet we are increasingly stretching the whole socialization process from childhood to adulthood. And the number of people involved in the subculture stretch is increasingly large. There are nearly 70 million persons in the United States under 18 years of age, or nearly one-third of the Nation's population.[14]

The number reaching age 18 each year has, however, doubled within a decade. There were 2 million in 1956 and 4 million in 1965, the result of the "baby boom" of the late forties. Of the more than 1.5 million who graduate from high school, about half will register for college, and the 25 percent of the 16–24 age group now in college will increase. One could say with Denney[15] that the age of extended socialization is already in full swing.

It is of correlative interest that the public has become disturbed by the announced figure of 7.5 million school dropouts during the 1960's, despite some queries about whether we really want to or can prevent all school dropouts. The middle-class and middle-aged producers of prescriptions for youth want to keep them in, or return them to school for reasons that extend from a genuine belief that all youth should benefit from more formal education to fears that dropout youths inundate the labor market and thereby contribute to delinquency and crime. Our society would apparently like more children to go to college, often without commensurate concern for how the extended period of dependency, socialization, and an indiscriminate density of college population may contribute to producing mediocrity of educational standards. Yet, without continued education, the dropouts are commonly dependent in other ways. As Lucius Cervantes has very recently pointed out, although the dropout group cuts

---

Teenager (Indianapolis: The Bobbs-Merrill Co., Inc., 1957); Edgar Z. Friedenberg, *The Vanishing Adolescent* (Boston: Beacon Press, 1959); Paul Goodman, *Growing Up Absurd* (New York: Random House, Inc., 1960); Jessie Bernard, ed. "Teen-Age Culture," *Annals of the American Academy of Political and Social Science* (November, 1961), p. 338; J. S. Coleman, *The Adolescent Society* (New York: The Free Press, 1961); Lee G. Burchinal, ed., "Rural Youth in Crisis: Facts, Myths, and Social Change," Proceedings of A National Conference on Rural Youth in a Changing Environment, Stillwater, Okla., 1963 (Washington, D.C.: Government Printing Office, 1965); David Gottlieb and J. Reeves, *Adolescent Behavior in Urban Areas* (New York: Crowell Collier & Macmillan, Inc., 1963); Orville G. Brin, Jr., "Adolescent Personality as Self-Other Systems," *Journal of Marriage and the Family* 27 (May, 1965): 156–62; Erik H. Erikson, ed., *The Challenge of Youth* (Garden City, N.Y.: Doubleday and Company, Inc., Anchor Books, 1965); David Gottlieb, "Youth Subculture: Variations on a General Theme," in *Problems of Youth: Transition to Adulthood in a Changing World*, ed. Muzafer W. Sherif and Carolyn Sherif (Chicago, Aldine Publishing Company, 1965), pp. 28–45; Kenneth Keniston, *The Uncommitted: Alienated Youth in American Society* (New York: Harcourt Brace and World, Inc., 1965); John Barron Mays, *The Young Pretenders: A Study of Teenage Culture in Contemporary Society* (London: Michael Joseph, 1965); Blaine R. Porter, "American Teen-Agers of the 1960's: Our Despair or Hope?" *Journal of Marriage and the Family* 27 (May, 1965): 139–47; Graham B. Blaine, Jr., *Youth and the Hazards of Affluence* (New York: Harper and Row, Publishers, 1966).

---

[13]Reuel Denney, op. cit.

[14]We might parenthetically remind ourselves that at the time of the signing of the Declaration of Independence, about one-half of the Nation was under 18 years of age.

[15]Denney, op. cit. For other detailed descriptions of adolescents, teenagers, the youth subculture, etc., see the following useful examples: F. Elkin and W. Westley, "The Myth of Adolescent Culture," *American Sociological Review* 20 (1955): 680–84; Hermann H. Remmers and D. H. Radler, *The American*

across social class, ethnic, and geographic lines, most come from the blue- and lower white-collar economic classes. In summarizing, he says: "The dropout rate nationally is between 30 and 40 percent. The rate is higher in the South than in the North; higher among boys than girls (53 percent versus 47 percent); higher in the slums than in the suburbs. Most dropouts withdraw from school during or before their sixteenth year. There is 10 times the incidence of delinquency among the dropouts as there is among the stayins. In view of society's educational expectations for modern youth and dropout youth's inability to get a job while 'just waiting around for something to happen,' the very state of being a dropout has all but become by definition a condition of semidelinquency."[16]

On the one hand, then, the privileges and age roles are being extended by being lowered, and young teenagers are as sophisticated or cynical, as fantasy-filled and joyriding as our older teenagers used to be. On the other hand, and at the other end of the range of the youth age, the period of their not moving into adult roles is also being extended.

This extended socialization is accompanied by the problem of poor adult models. Throughout the social classes, it appears that the search for the adult to be emulated is often a desperate and futile quest. Part of the reason for this futility is due to the very rapid social and technological changes occurring in our society which make it more difficult for the adult to perform his traditional role of model and mentor to youth. Social change is so rapid, says Kenneth Keniston,[17] that growing up no longer means learning how to fit into society because the society into which young people will someday fit has not yet been developed or even, perhaps, cannot properly be imagined. Many youth feel forced into detachment and premature cynicism because society seems to offer youth today so little that is stable, relevant, and meaningful. They often look in vain for values, goals, means, and institutions to which they can be committed

because their thrust for commitment is strong. Youth can be a period of fruitful idealism, but there are few of what Erik Erikson[18] would call "objects of fidelity" for our youth; so that "playing it cool," is more than an ephemeral expression—it becomes a way of avoiding damaging commitments to goals and life styles of the parent generation which may be outmoded tomorrow. Times and viewpoints shift rapidly, and many of our children resemble world-weary and jaded adults at age 14. The social isolation, social distance, alienation, and retreat from the adult world are increased by many social and technological mechanisms operating to encourage a youth subculture. As the numbers and intensity of value sharing in the youth subculture increase, the process of intergenerational alienation also escalates. Parents have almost always been accused of not understanding their children. What may be new is that more parents either do not care that they do not understand, or that it is increasingly impossible for them to understand. Perhaps, then, it is not that parents are poor models for the kinds of lives that the youths will lead in their own mature years; parents may simply be increasingly irrelevant models for their children. So rapid is current social change that the youth of today have difficulty projecting a concept of themselves as adults.

This double stretch in that band of the life cycle we call youth has systemic effects on definitions and dependency. As the period of socialization extends further for more people, the concept of youth embraces later ages. When to this conceptual change is added the fact of greater life expectancy and a larger proportion of our population living longer, the social and perhaps physical meaning of middle age has changed, likewise moving upward. Our society has created linguistic support for this notion by its references to young adults, older youth, young or junior executives when referring to men who are in their midthirties or early forties.

The conceptual extension of what being young means is also reflected in the perpetuation of a dependency status started in youth (that is,

[16]Lucius F. Cervantes, *The Dropout* (Ann Arbor: University of Michigan Press, 1965), p. 197.

[17]Kenneth Keniston, "Social Change and Youth in America," in *The Challenge of Youth*, ed. Erik H. Erikson (Garden City, N.Y.: Doubleday and Co., Inc., 1965), pp. 191–222.

[18]Erik H. Erikson, "Youth: Fidelity and Diversity," in ibid., pp. 1–28.

during late adolescence and early adulthood). The child from an economically deprived family, the dropout who becomes, like his parents, economically dependent on welfare benefits, remains in his dependency condition throughout much or most of his life. Others, mostly from the middle class, shift their extended dependency from being supported by parents or educational grants to being dependent on bureaucratic systems which continue the socialization process that often leads to the pathos of the organization man.

THE MASCULINE PROTEST AND ITS TRANSFORMATION

Social scientists have long stressed the importance of the theme of masculinity in American culture and the effect that this image of the strong masculine role has had on child rearing and the general socialization process. The inability of the middle-class male child to match himself to this masculine model and the neuroticism that is the consequence of this increasingly futile struggle was vividly brought to our attention years ago by Arnold Green.[19] The continuity of this masculine role in the lower classes has often been asserted and was made one of the "focal concerns" in Walter B. Miller's[20] profile of the lower class milieu. There is reason to believe, however, that this once dominating culture theme is dissipating, especially in the central or middle-class culture, and that this dissipation is diffusing downwards through the lower classes via the youth subculture. It may be argued that in the United States, while the status of the sexes in many social spheres of activity has been approaching equality, there has been an increasing feminization of the general culture. Instead of females becoming more like males, males have increasingly taken on some of the roles and attributes formerly assigned to females. It is not so much that maleness is reduced as a goal motivating young boys; rather, physical aggressiveness, once the manifest feature of maleness, is being reduced and the meaning of masculinity is thereby being changed to more symbolic forms. The continued diminution of the earlier frontier mores which placed a premium on male aggressiveness has been replaced by other attributes of masculinity. The gun and fist have been substantially replaced by financial ability, by the capacity to manipulate others in complex organizations, and by intellectual talents. The thoughtful wit, the easy verbalizer, even the striving musician and artist are, in the dominant culture, equivalents of male assertiveness where broad shoulders and fighting fists were once the major symbols. The young culture heroes may range from Van Cliburn to the Beatles, but Billy the Kid is a fantasy figure from an earlier history.

It may well be true that in many lower class communities violence is associated with masculinity and may not only be acceptable but admired behavior. That the rates of violent crimes are high among lower class males suggests that this group still strongly continues to equate maleness with overt physical aggression. In the Italian slum of the Boston West End, Herbert Gans[21] describes families dominated by the men and where mothers encourage male dominance. On the other hand, lower class boys who lack father or other strong male figures, as is the case with many boys of Negro families, have a problem of finding models to imitate. Rejecting female dominance at home and at school, and the morality which they associate with women, may be the means such boys use to assert their masculinity, and such assertion must be performed with a strong antithesis of femininity, namely by being physically aggressive. Being a bad boy, Parsons[22] has said, can become a positive goal if goodness is too closely identified with femininity.

Whatever the reasons for this stronger masculine role among lower class youth, its retention will continue to result in violence, because the young male is better equipped physically to

---

[19]Arnold W. Green, "The Middle Class Male Child and Neurosis," *American Sociological Review* 11 (February, 1946): 31–41.

[20]Walter B. Miller, "Lower Class Culture as a Generating Milieu of Gang Delinquency," *Journal of Social Issues* 14 (1958): 5–19.

[21]Herbert J. Gans, *The Urban Villages* (New York: The Free Press, 1962).

[22]Talcott Parsons, "Certain Primary Sources and Patterns of Aggression in the Social Structure of the Western World," *Psychiatry* 10 (May, 1947): 167–81.

manifest this form of masculinity than the very young, the middle-aged, or the very old. Because he needs no special education to employ the agents of physical aggression (fists, feet, agility), and because he seeks, as we all do, reinforcement from others for his ego and commitment, in this case to the values of violence, a youth often plays violent games of conflict within his own age-graded violent subcultural system. So do others play games, of course; the artist when he competes for a prize, the young scholar for tenure, the financier for a new subsidiary, and a nation for propaganda advantage. But the prescribed rules for street fighting produce more deadly quarrels with weapons of guns and knives than do competitions among males who use a brush, a dissertation, or a contract.

Jackson Toby[23] has recently suggested that if the compulsive masculinity hypothesis has merit, it ought to generate testable predictions about the occurrence of violence. He lists the following: "(1) Boys who grow up in households headed by women are more likely to behave violently than boys who grow up in households headed by a man. . . . (2) Boys who grow up in households where it is relatively easy to identify with the father figure are less likely to behave violently than boys in households where identification with the father figure is difficult. . . . (3) Boys whose development toward adult masculinity is slower than their peers are more likely to behave violently than boys who find it easy to think of themselves as 'men'. . . . (4) Masculine ideals emphasize physical roughness and toughness in those populations where symbolic masculine power is difficult to understand. Thus, middle-class boys ought to be less likely than working class youngsters to idealize strength and its expression in action and to be more likely to appreciate the authority over other people exercised by a physician or a business executive."[24] As Toby indicates, it is unfortunate that evidence at present is so fragmentary that these predictions are not subject to rigorous evaluation.

The male self-conception is both important and interesting. Recently Leon Fannin and Marshall Clinard[25] tested for differences between lower class and middle class boys through informal depth interviewing and by forced-choice scales. While self-conceptions were quite similar, lower class boys felt themselves to be tougher, more powerful, fierce, fearless, and dangerous than middle class boys. "It was unexpected," claim the authors, "that they (the lower class boys) did not feel themselves to be significantly more violent, hard, and pugilistic." The middle class boys conceived themselves as being more clever, smart, smooth, bad, and loyal. The self-conceptions were also related to specific types of behavior, for the "tough guys" significantly more often "committed violent offenses, fought more often and with harsher means, carried weapons, had lower occupational aspirations, and stressed toughness and related traits in the reputation they desired and in sexual behavior."[26]

Should the lower classes become more like the middle class in value orientation, family structure, and stability, there is reason to believe the emphasis on masculine identification through physical prowess and aggression will decline. The need to prove male identity may not disappear, but even being "bad" in order to sever the linkage of morality and femininity may become increasingly difficult to perform in a purely masculine way. And if there are available, as some believe, new and alternative models for demonstrating masculinity, ways that may be neither "bad" nor physically aggressive, then we should expect masculine identity to be manifested differently, that is symbolically, even by lower class boys. As the larger culture becomes more cerebral, the refined symbolic forms of masculinity should be more fully adopted. And as the disparity in life style, values, and norms between the lower and middle classes is reduced, so too will be reduced the subculture of violence that readily resorts to violence as an expected form of masculine response to certain situations.

---

[23]Jackson Toby, "Violence and the Masculine Ideal: Some Qualitative Data," in "Patterns of Violence," ed. Marvin E. Wolfgang, *The Annals of the American Academy of Political and Social Science* 364 (March, 1966): 19–27.

[24]Ibid., pp. 21–22.

[25]Leon F. Fannin and Marshall B. Clinard, "Differences in the Conception of Self as a Male among Lower and Middle Class Delinquents," *Social Problems* 13 (Fall, 1965): 205–14.

[26]Ibid., p. 214.

If this social prognosis proves correct, there may not always be functional and virtuous expertise in the masculine symbolism. We could witness, for example, a shift from direct physical violence to detached and impersonalized violence or to corruption. The dominant, middle class culture has a considerable tolerance for distant and detached violence expressed in ways that range from dropping heavy bombs on barely visible targets, to the stylized, bloodless violence of film and television heroes, and to the annual slaughter of 50,000 persons on our highways. This same culture, for reasons too complex to detail here, not only tolerates but sometimes creates structural features in its social system that seem to encourage corruption, from tax evasion to corporate crime.[27] To transform the theme of male aggressiveness may mean assimilation with the larger culture, but this may merely increase the distance between the user and consumer of violence, and increase the volume of contributors to corruption. It may be hoped, of course, that changes in the current direction of the dominant culture may later produce a more sanguine description of this whole process.

YOUTH AND VIOLENT CRIME

There is little more than faulty and inadequate official delinquency statistics to answer basic questions about the current extent and character of youth crime. Recording techniques have changed, more juvenile police officers are engaged in handling young offenders, more methods are used for registering such minor juvenile status offenses as running away from home, being incorrigible, or truant. For over a decade most city police departments have used a dichotomy of "official-nonofficial arrest" or "remedial-arrest" or "warned-arrest" for apprehending juveniles, but not for adults. Yet both forms of juvenile disposition are recorded and rates of delinquency are computed in the total. Separate treatises have been written on these matters[28] which we cannot pursue here in detail.

The public image of a vicious, violent juvenile population producing a seemingly steady increase in violent crime is not substantiated by the evidence available. There may be more juvenile delinquency recorded today, but even that is predominantly property offenses. Rather consistently we are informed by the *Uniform Crime Reports,* published by the Federal Bureau of Investigation, that two-thirds of automobile thefts and about one-half of all burglaries and robberies are committed by persons under 18 years of age. Among crimes of personal violence, arrested offenders under age 18 are generally low; for criminal homicide they are about 8 percent; for forcible rape and aggravated assault, about 18 percent.

What this actually means is not that these proportions of these crimes are committed by juveniles, but that among persons who are taken into custody for these offenses, these proportions hold. Most police officers agree that it is easier to effect an arrest in cases involving juveniles than in cases involving adults. Most crimes known to the police, that is, complaints made to them or offenses discovered by them, are not "cleared by arrest," meaning cleared from their records by taking one or more persons into custody and making them available for prosecution. The general clearance rate is roughly 30 percent. Thus, the adult-juvenile distribution among 70 percent of so-called major crimes (criminal homicide, forcible rape, robbery, aggravated assault, burglary, larceny over $50, auto theft) is not known and cannot safely be projected from the offenses cleared or the age distribution of offenders arrested.

In addition, very often the crude legal labels attached to many acts committed by juveniles

---

[27]We have borrowed from a quite different context in which Georges Sorel expressed similar ideas about the shift from force to fraud, from violence to corruption as the path to success and privilege. The first edition of *Reflexions sur la violence* appeared in 1906; also, Paris: M. Riviere, 1936. For additional reference to this work, see Marvin E. Wolfgang, "A Preface to Violence," in "Patterns of Violence," *The Annals of the American Academy of Political and Social Science* 364 (March, 1966): 1–7.

[28]See for example, Thorsten Sellin and Marvin E. Wolfgang, *The Measurement of Delinquency* (New York: John Wiley and Sons, Inc., 1964). A new summary of these problems from around the world may be found in T. C. N. Gibbens, and R. A. Ahrenfeldt, eds., *Cultural Factors in Delinquency* (London: Tavistock Publications, 1966).

give a false impression of the seriousness of their acts. For example, a "highway robbery" may be a $100-theft at the point of a gun and may result in the victim's being hospitalized from severe wounds. But commonly, juvenile acts that carry this label and are used for statistical compilation are more minor. Typical in the files of a recent study were cases involving two nine-year-old boys, one of whom twisted the arm of the other on the school yard to obtain 25 cents of the latter's lunch money. This act was recorded and counted as "highway robbery." In another case, a nine-year-old boy engaged in exploratory sexual activity with an eight-year-old girl on a playlot. The girl's mother later complained to the police, who recorded the offense as "assault with intent to ravish."

Nothing now exists in the official published collection of crime statistics to yield better information about the qualitative variations of seriousness. Weighted scores of seriousness are possible and available for producing a weighted rate of crime and delinquency, much like the operating refinements in fertility and mortality rates or in econometric analyses.[29] Without a weighted system, it is only the incautious observer who is willing to assert that youth crime is worse today than a generation or even a decade ago.

Moreover, computing rates of crime or delinquency per 100,000 is an extremely unsatisfactory and crude technique. Even a rate for all persons under 18 years of age fails to account for the bulges in specific ages like 14, 15, 16, 17, 18 that have occurred because of high fertility rates shortly after World War II. Without age-specific rates, most criminologists are reluctant to make assertions about trends or even the current amount of juvenile crime and violence. Research is now underway that hopefully will provide new and more meaningful age specific rates. It would not be unexpected if, when these rates are computed, much of any recorded increase in violent juvenile crime for the past eight years or so could be attributed to standard statistical error.

By making certain gross assumptions about the proportion of juvenile population between the meaningful ages of 10 and 17 for the population in cities of 2,500 and over included in the survey areas of the *Uniform Crime Reports* from 1958 to 1964,[30] it has been possible to provide some juvenile rates for violent or assaultive crimes against the person. Computations were performed in the following way: the population of all cities of 2,500 inhabitants and more, included in the Uniform Crime Reporting area, was summed for each of the seven years from 1958 through 1964. (1958 was a year of important revisions in the UCR classification system, hence a safe year with which to begin the analysis.) The total populations of the United States and of the children from ages 10 through 17 were obtained for each of the seven years from reports of the Bureau of the Census. The respective proportions of the 10- to 17-year-old population for each year were readily obtained from these census reports and then applied to the UCR survey population. The number of juveniles under 18 years of age arrested for specific offenses, divided by the population of persons aged 10 to 17, multiplied by 100,000, yielded a rate for each of the years. Table 3–4 shows these rates.[31]

[29]For details of one such weighting system, see Sellin and Wolfgang, op. cit.

[30]*Uniform Crime Reports* (Washington, D.C.: Federal Bureau of Investigation, Department of Justice, 1958 to 1964). See also the report of the New York Division of Youth on this period, "Youth Crime: A Leveling Off?", *Youth Services News* 17 (Spring, 1966): 3–5, and the succinct analysis of UCR and California data, found in Ronald H. Beattie and John P. Kenney, *The Annals of the American Academy of Political and Social Science* 364 (March, 1966): 73–85.

[31]The following data were used for computing the rates:
The UCR survey population of cities of 2500 and more inhabitants, for the years 1958 through 1964, was: for 1958—52,329,497; 1959—56,187,181; 1960—81,660,735; 1961—85,158,360; 1962—94,014,000; 1963—94,085,000; 1964—99,326,000 (Source: UCR Reports, Tables, 18, 17, 18, 21, 21, 28, 27 for the respective years.)
The U.S. population for the years 1959–64 was: 171,882,000; 177,830,000; 180,684,000; 183,756,000; 186,591,000; 189,417,000; 192,119,000. (Source: Estimate of the Bureau of the Census, Department of Commerce, Current Population Reports, Series P-25, No. 314, August, 1965).
The percentages which the UCR survey population represented of the total U.S. population were: 29, 31, 45, 46, 50, 50, and 52 percent. (Computed.)
The U.S. child population aged 10-17 for the

TABLE 3–4.

URBAN RATES OF CRIMES OF VIOLENCE FOR PERSONS ARRESTED, AGED 10–17

	1958	1959	1960	1961	1962	1963	1964
Criminal homicide: murder and nonnegligent manslaughter	1.9	2.3	3.0	3.2	2.9	2.9	3.1
Negligent manslaughter ..	1.15	0.98	1.10	0.96	0.79	1.00	0.87
Forcible rape	10.0	9.8	10.9	11.4	11.2	10.3	10.0
Aggravated assault	34.4	35.8	53.2	60.1	61.6	63.0	74.5
Other assaults	95.9	118.0	118.7	126.0	139.2	153.7	163.6

Caution must be applied to these figures because of two major assumptions that had to be made: That the UCR survey population contained roughly the same proportion of persons aged 10–17 as the general population of the United States; that the overwhelming bulk of arrests of juveniles under 18 years of age, for offenses against the person, involved offenders no younger than age 10. It is assumed that little error is involved in this latter assumption because most juvenile court statutes with a lower age limit do not go below ages 6 or 7, and very few of these offenses are ever recorded for ages below 10. Moreover, computing a rate based on the entire population under 18 years would continue the unsatisfactory practice of including in the denominator preschool and infant children.

With this caution and these assumptions, the table can nevertheless be said to show substantially the same rates in 1964 as in 1960 for murder and nonnegligent manslaughter and for rape. Murder and nonnegligent manslaughter reached a peak rate in 1961 of 3.2, was under

years 1958–64 was: 23,443,000; 24,607,000; 25,364,-000; 26,023,000; 27,983,000; 29,119,000. (Source: Estimates of Bureau of Census, Department of Commerce, Current Population Reports, Series P-25.) The UCR child population aged 10–17 for the years 1958–64 was: 6,798,470; 7,625,170; 11,413,800; 13,-468,000; 13,999,150; 15,141,880. (Assumed and computed).

The number of persons under 18 years of age arrested for each of the five offenses over each of the 7 years may be found on the specific tables in the UCR annual reports.

In gathering and computing these data, the author had the assistance of Bernard Cohen, Research Assistant, Center of Criminological Research, University of Pennsylvania.

a rate of 3.0 per 100,000 in 1962 and 1963, and was 3.1 in 1964. These slight variations are of no statistical consequence, considering the operation of chance errors.

Negligent manslaughter was highest in 1958 (1.15), had no statistically significant increase in the years since then, and in 1964 was down to 0.87. This offense mostly refers to automobile deaths, and despite the fact that more teenagers are driving today, the rate has not increased. Forcible rape has not significantly changed over the seven years: the high was 11.4 in 1961 and has dropped to 10.3 in 1963 and 10.0 in 1964. Aggravated assault jumped from 34.4 in 1958 to 53.2 in 1960, had a relatively stable rate of 60.1 to 63.0 between 1961 and 1963, and then rose to 74.5 in 1964. Other assaults (not part of the UCR index offenses) climbed steadily from 95.9 in 1958 to 163.6 in 1964.

There is little in these figures of criminal homicide or rape that should cause alarm. Assaults appear to be the main area of violence that should cause concern. But not until better data are available from some of the studies previously mentioned can we make proper conclusions and interpretations.

Among city gangs selected for their reputation for toughness and studied in detail by detached workers, the amount of violent crime, reports Walter B. Miller, is surprisingly low. Twenty-one groups, numbering about 700 members, yielded cumulative figures of 228 known offenses committed by 155 boys during a 2-year period and 138 court charges for 293 boys during a 12-year span. Miller remarks that ". . . violence appears neither as a dominant preoccupation of city gangs nor as a dominant form of criminal activity,"[32] for even among these toughest of gang members, the yearly rate of assault charges per 100 individuals per year of age was only 4.8 at age 15, 7.2 at 16, 7.2 at 17, and 7.8 at 18, after which the rates dropped through the early twenty's. Violent crimes were committed by only a small minority of these gang members, represented a transient phenomenon, were mostly unarmed physical encounters between combatting males, did not victimize adult females, and were not ideological forms of behavior.[33]

It should be mentioned also that the increasingly methodologically refined studies of hidden delinquency have not clearly and consistently reported a significant reduction in the disparity of social classes for crimes of violence.[34] The incidence and frequency of crimes of violence appear to remain considerably higher among boys from lower social classes when the appropriate questions are asked about these offenses over specific periods of time. In their recent study of delinquents, Fannin and Clinard reported: "One of the more important of the tests was a comparison of the frequency with which reported and unreported robberies and assaults were committed by members of the two class levels (middle and lower). The vast majority of all lower class delinquents, 84 percent, had committed at least one such offense compared to 28 percent of the middle class (probability

less than 0.01); 28 percent of the lower and 8 percent of the middle class had committed 10 or more violent offenses. Class level was also related to the frequency of fighting with other boys. Lower class delinquents fought singly and in groups significantly more often (probability less than 0.05) than middle class delinquents, with 20 percent of them averaging five or more fights per month compared to 4.0 percent."[35]

It should also be kept in mind that the proportion of the entire juvenile population under 18 years of age that, in any calendar year, is processed by the police and juvenile court is generally no higher than 3 to 5 percent. There are, however, several factors denied clarity by this kind of commonly reported statistic: (1) Arrest or juvenile-court-appearance statistics include duplicate counting of the same juveniles who have run away, been truant, or committed malicious mischief more than once during the year, and for some types of offenses this amount of duplication can be sizable; (2) the figure ignores the fact that children have been delinquent during preceding years, and that in many census tracts throughout large cities as many as 70 percent or more of all juveniles under 18 years, at one time or another during their juvenile-court-statute ages, may have been delinquent. Solomon Kobrin[36] and others have drawn attention to this perspective; Nils Christie[37] in Norway has done the most elaborate study on the topic by analyzing a birth cohort; and Thorsten Sellin and Marvin Wolfgang[38] are presently engaged in a large-scale research of a birth cohort of approximately 10,000 males in Philadelphia in order to compute a cohort rate of delinquency, examine their cumulative seriousness scores by age and over time, and to provide a prediction model that might aid in decisions about the most propitious time in juvenile life

[32]Walter B. Miller, "Violent Crimes in City Gangs," in "Patterns of Violence," ed. Marvin E. Wolfgang, *The Annals of the American Academy of Political and Social Science* 364 (March, 1966), 96–112.

[33]Ibid. For a new, detailed listing of research and theory in this area, see Dorothy Campbell Tompkins, *Juvenile Gangs and Street Gangs: A Bibliography* (Berkeley Calif.: Institute of Governmental Studies at the University of California, 1966).

[34]See Robert Hardt and George F. Bodine, *Development of Self-Report Instruments in Delinquency Research* (Syracuse, N.Y.: Youth Development Center, Syracuse University, 1965). This item is a conference report on methods of doing research on hidden delinquency and includes a good bibliography of major items in that area. See also Nils Christie, Johs. Andenaes, and Sigurd Skirbekk, "A Study of Self-Reporting Crime," in *Scandinavian Studies in Criminology*, ed. Karl O. Christiansen, vol. 1 (London: Tavistock Publications, 1965); Kerstein Elmhorn, "Study in Self-Reported Delinquency among School-Children in Stockholm," in ibid.

[35]Fannin and Clinard, op. cit., p. 211.

[36]Solomon Kobrin, "The Conflict of Values in Delinquency Areas," *American Sociological Review* 16 (October, 1951): 653–61.

[37]Nils Christie, *Unge norske lovovertrebere* (Oslo, Norway: Institute Criminology, Oslo University, 1960).

[38]Thorsten Sellin and Marvin E. Wolfgang, "The Extent and Character of Delinquency in an Age Cohort," research project of the Center of Criminological Research, University of Pennsylvania, sponsored by the National Institute of Mental Health.

cycles for maximizing the effectiveness of social intervention.

The data needed to describe the volume of youth crime are inadequate at present, but an alarmist attitude does not appear justified. Age-specific and weighted rates are required before trends can be validly presented and analyzed, but because of the known rise in the present adolescent population due to high fertility rates of the late forties, there is reason to suspect that any overall increase in juvenile delinquency can be largely attributed to the population increase in the ages from 14 to 18. The absolute amount of delinquency can be expected to increase for some time, for this same reason, but there is no basis for assuming that rates of juvenile violence will increase.

Moreover, as the suburban population increases, the amount of juvenile delinquency can be expected to rise in these areas even without a rate increase. In addition, as the social class composition of suburbs changes, as it has been, from being predominantly upper class to containing more middle and lower middle class families, the rates of delinquency of the last migrating class will travel with them. And as Robert Bohlke[39] has suggested, what is often viewed as middle class delinquency is not middle class in the sense of the traditional middle class value system or life style but only in terms of a middle income group. There is considerable theoretical merit in this suggestion which should be further explored through empirical research.

Finally, with respect to delinquency, it might be said that a certain amount of this form of deviancy has always existed, will continue to exist, and perhaps should exist. In the sense discussed by Emile Durkheim,[40] crime is normal, and perhaps even, in some quantity, desirable. Not only does the existence of delinquency provide the collective conscience an opportunity to reinforce its norms by applying sanctions, but the presence of deviancy reflects the existence of something less than a total system of control over individuals. Moreover, there appear to be personality traits among many delinquents that could be viewed as virtues if behavior were rechanneled. For instance, Sheldon and Eleanor Glueck noted, in *Unraveling Juvenile Delinquency*,[41] that among 500 delinquents compared to 500 nondelinquents, the delinquent boys were characterized as hedonistic, distrustful, aggressive, hostile and, as boys who felt they could manage their own lives, were socially assertive, and defied authority. The nondelinquents were more banal, conformistic, neurotic, felt unloved, insecure, and anxiety-ridden. The attributes associated with the delinquents sound similar to descriptions of the Renaissance Man who defied the authority and static orthodoxy of the middle ages, who was also aggressive, richly assertive, this-world rather than other-world centered, and was less banal, more innovative, than his medieval predecessors. The Glueck delinquents also sound much like our nineteenth century captains of industry, our twentieth century political leaders and corporation executives. The freedom to be assertive, to defy authority and orthodoxy may sometimes have such consequences as crime and delinquency. But it is well to remember that many aspects of American ethos, our freedom, our benevolent attitude toward rapid social change, our heritage of revolution, our encouragement of massive migrations, our desire to be in or near large urban centers, and many other values that we cherish, may produce the delinquency we deplore as well as the many things we desire.

THE SEARCH FOR POWER AND PARTICIPATION: YOUTH, NEGROES, AND THE POOR

We have said that to speak generically of youth overlooks variability in a pluralistic society, and we have drawn attention to some notable variations between middle class and lower class youth. There are, however, many more versions

[39]Robert H. Bohlke, "Social Mobility, Stratification Inconsistency in Middle Class Delinquency," *Social Problems* 8 (Spring, 1961): 351–63. See also, Ralph W. England, Jr., "A Theory of Middle Class Delinquency," *Journal of Criminal Law, Criminology and Police Science* 50 (April, 1960): 535–40.

[40]Emile Durkheim, *Rules of Sociological Method*, 8th ed., trans. Sarah A. Solvay and John H. Mueller, ed. George E. G. Catlin (New York: The Free Press, 1950), pp. 65–73.

[41]Sheldon and Eleanor Glueck, *Unraveling Juvenile Delinquency* (Cambridge, Mass.: Harvard University Press for the Commonwealth Fund, 1950).

of the concatenation of variables that differentiate youth. Being young, middle class, white, and from an economically secure family generates a quite different image from being young, lower class, poor, and Negro. In sheer absolute numbers, more young people are located in the former group than in the latter and probably suffer fewer strains from culture contradictions, anomie, and psychological deprivation than do the latter. There is likely to be greater conformity to parental prescriptions in the former, more familial transmission of group values, more cohesiveness of the family. The Negro, lower class youth drop out of school and drift into delinquency in greater proportions than do white middle class youth. Class is probably a stronger factor contributing to value allegiance and normative conduct than is race, which is to say that Negro and white middle class youth are more alike than are Negro middle and lower class or white middle and lower class youngsters.

Yet, with all the variabilities that might be catalogued in an empirically descriptive study of youth, there are characteristics of the life stage, status, and style of youth in general which are shared by the status of poverty and the status of being Negro in American society. All may be described as possessing a kind of structural marginality[42] that places them on the periphery of power in our society. When the multiple probabilities of being young, Negro, and poor exist, the shared attributes are more than a summation. The force of whatever problems they represent is more of a multiplicative than an additive function.

Youth, Negroes, and the poor have subcultural value systems different from, yet subsidiary to the larger culture. They often share many features, such as being deprived of certain civil rights and liberties, barred from voting, and denied adequate defense counsel and equality of justice. Their current statuses are frequently subject to manipulation by an enthroned elite and their power to effect change in their futures

may be minimal. They tend to have common conflicts with authority and to be dominated by females in the matriarchial structure of their own social microcosms.

All three groups know the meaning of spatial segregation, whether voluntary or compulsory. For youth, it is in schools, clubs, seating arrangements, occupations, forms of entertainment, and leisure pursuits. For the poor and for Negroes, it may be all of these as well as place of residence and other alternatives of work, play, and mobility opportunities. There are similarities in their subordinate and dependency status, and in having poor, inadequate, or irrelevant role models. The values and behavior of the dominant culture and class in American society, as adopted by Negroes, often reveal a pathetically compulsive quality; the poor have been denied access to the ends to which they subscribe, and youth is, at best, a power-muted microculture. For all three, norms seem to shift and change with more than common frequency or are not clearly designated. All three groups tend to be more romantic, nonrational, impulsive, physically aggressive, more motivated toward immediacy and directness than their counterparts in the dominant culture. There is among youth, Negroes, and the poor more deviant and criminal behavior, and a greater disparity between aspiration and achievement. At times their revolt against authority erupts into violence for which they feel little guilt or responsibility.

Increasingly they are self-conscious, aware of their own collectivities as subcultural systems, partly because their revolt is today a greater threat to the systems which have been established to control, govern, or manipulate them. The poor are being asked for the first time what they want and what they would like to do to help themselves or have done for them. Negroes are acting as advisers and consultants on Federal policy, and young people are being heard when they speak about Vietnam, restrictions on passports, college curricula, faculty appointments, and new notions of freedom and sexual morality.

With more clarity and conscience, the three groups are searching for meaningfulness, identity, and social justice. They are articulating their protest against powerlessness, are seeking par-

---

[42]Tamme Wittermans and Irving Kraus, "Structural Marginality and Social Worth," *Sociology and Social Research* 48 (April, 1964): 348–60. For an excellent summary of theory and research on lower class family life, see the recent work of Suzanne Keller, *The American Lower Class Family* (Albany: New York State Division for Youth, 1965).

ticipation in decision making processes that affect their own life conditions. That some retreat into drugs, alcohol, and other symptoms of alienation is now viewed as dysfunctional by their own majorities as well as by the establishment. That some resort to violence, whether in Watts or in Hampton Beach,[43] is episodic, meant to display boredom with their condition, blatant protest, and latent power. As achievement, as a danger signal, and as a catalyst, violence for them may serve the social functions outlined by Lewis Coser.[44] But their use of violence is end-oriented and cannot be viewed as a cultural psychopathology. They desire to be recognized, not to be forgotten, because they now see themselves for the first time. They are seeking what Edmund Williamson,[45] dean at the University of Minnesota, calls the most important freedom of all—to be taken seriously, to be listened to.

One of the interesting things about American youth today, especially the older student segment, is its activistic character and increasing identification with the poor and with the civil rights movement. There is an intense morality and a demand for clear commitments. In many cases young people are directly involved in working in neighborhoods of poverty or in the Negro struggle in the South, whether in song, march, or litigation. Moreover, the idealism of youth and this identification with the process toward participation in power is being fostered by Federal support of the Peace Corps program, both foreign and domestic, and by much governmental concern and protection of young civil rights workers in the South. But the reference here to identification is not to these overlapping involvements; it is to the means for communicating their lack of participation in formulating the rules of life's games. Impatience, discontent, and dissatisfaction with the state of American so-

ciety[46] become healthy reflections of a new commitment, a commitment to the desire for change and for participating in the direction of change.

Obviously, there are also differences among the three groups, the most striking of which is the fact that youth is a temporary stage in a life cycle and that ultimately the structural marginality and status deprivations are overcome for many by the passage of time. The representatives of the subculture of youth are mobile, eventually leave the subculture, and with age, birth cohorts socially fold into one another. But the status designation of Negro is, except for race crossings, permanent, and the poor commonly have oppressive generational continuity. That youth in its temporariness shares with the major minority groups certain attributes of being and of the struggle for becoming is itself noteworthy, even if the youth were less affected by and conscious of their mutual interests, means, and goals. Perhaps the short sample of time represented by youth will one day be viewed in the long perspective as symbolic of the longer, but also temporary, state of deprivation and disenfranchisement of being poor or of having the status of Negro in American society.

The identity of youth with the protestation process, whether similar to or in common with the poor and the Negro, is, of course, not universal and may not even be a cultural modality. Its expression is, nonetheless, vigorous and viable. It has entered the arena of public attention and functions as a prodder for its concepts of progress. With this identity, the youth of today are unlike the "flaming youth" in the frenetic milieu of the twenties, the youth associated with the political left and the proletarian cult of the thirties, the uninformed youth of the forties, or the passive youth of the fifties. And yet, even with this identity they are without a systematic ideology. Despite the fact that they have come to realize the advantages of collective drives that prick the giants of massive and lethargic organization into action, they have developed no political affiliation. Perhaps the closest these young groups come to a focal con-

---

[43]See the Hampton Beach Project, Paul Estaver, Director, *Project Director's Report* (Hampton Beach, N.H.: Hampton Beach Chamber of Commerce, n.d.)

[44]Lewis A. Coser, "Some Social Functions of Violence," in Marvin E. Wolfgang, ed., "Patterns of Violence," *The Annals of the American Academy of Political and Social Science* 364 (March, 1966): 8–18.

[45]*New York Times*, November 21, 1965, p. 72.

[46]On this point, see Talcott Parsons, "Youth in the Context of American Society," in *The Challenge of Youth*, ed. Erik H. Erikson, pp. 110–41.

cern is in their alerting their peers and adults to the ethical conflicts and issues embraced by society's increasing ability to reduce individual anonymity and to manipulate lives. In one sense it could be said that they jealously guard the constraints a democratic society ideologically imposes on overcontrol, invasion of privacy, and overreaction to deviancy.

There are fringes to most movements, and there are parasites attached to the youth we have been describing as healthier segments of society. Frequently the fringe looms larger than the core in the public image of youth and an excessive degree of rebelliousness is conveyed. The bulk of our youth are not engaged in a rebellion against adults, and the degree of dissimilarity between the generations has often been overstressed, as some authors have recently asserted.[47] Rather than rejecting most parental norms, the majority of those in the youth subculture are eager to participate in the larger society. Individuals resisting specific authority patterns do not constitute group rejection of dominant social norms.

Moreover, except for those suppressed beyond youth by their status of being poor or being Negro, achievement comes with aging and that convergence often leads to the collapse of a once fiery, romantic drive. And, as Peter Berger[48] has eloquently remarked, with success, prophets become priests and revolutionaries become administrators.

The gravity of time pulls hard on our muscles and ideals and too often the earlier triumph of principle gives way to the triumph of expedience. The once lambent minds of youth are frequently corroded by conformity in adulthood, and a new flow of youth into the culture is needed to invoke their own standards of judgment on our adult norms.

[47]Robert C. Bealer, Fern K. Willits, and Peter R. Maida, "The Myth of a Rebellious Adolescent Subculture: Its Detrimental Effects for Understanding Rural Youth," in *Rural Youth in Crisis*, ed. Lee G. Burchinal, Proceedings of a National Conference on Rural Youth in a Changing Environment, Stillwater, Okla., 1963 (Washington, D.C.: Government Printing Office, 1965).

[48]Peter Berger, *An Invitation to Sociology: A Humanistic Perspective* (New York: Doubleday & Company, Inc., Anchor Book, 1963).

19.

DAVID MATZA AND GRESHAM M. SYKES

JUVENILE DELINQUENCY AND SUBTERRANEAN VALUES

Current explanations of juvenile delinquency place a heavy stress on the delinquent's deviance, not only with regard to his behavior but also with regard to his underlying values. It can be argued, however, that the delinquent's values are far less deviant than commonly portrayed and that the faulty picture is due to an erroneous view of the middle-class value system. A number of supposedly delinquent values are closely akin to those embodied in the leisure activities of the dominant society. To view adolescents in general and delinquents in particular as members of the last leisure class may help us explain both the large amount of unrecorded delinquency and the occurrence of delinquency throughout the class structure.

Current explanations of juvenile delinquency can be divided roughly into two major types.

SOURCE: David Matza and Gresham M. Sykes, "Juvenile Delinquency and Subterranean Values," *American Sociological Review* 26 (October, 1961): 712–19. Reprinted by Permission of the authors and the American Sociological Association.

On the one hand, juvenile delinquency is seen as a product of personality disturbances or emotional conflicts within the individual; on the other hand, delinquency is viewed as a result of relatively normal personalities exposed to a "disturbed" social environment—particularly in the form of a deviant sub-culture in which the individual learns to be delinquent as others learn to conform to the law. The theoretical conflict between these two positions has been intensified, unfortunately, by the fact that professional pride sometimes leads psychologists and sociologists to define the issue as a conflict between disciplines and to rally behind their respective academic banners.

Despite many disagreements between these two points of view, one assumption is apt to elicit common support. The delinquent, it is asserted, is deviant; not only does his behavior run counter to the law but his underlying norms, attitudes, and values also stand opposed to those of the dominant social order. And the dominant social order, more often than not, turns out to be the world of the middle class.

We have suggested in a previous article that this image of delinquents and the larger society as antagonists can be misleading.[1] Many delinquents, we argued, are essentially in agreement with the larger society, at least with regard to the evaluation of delinquent behavior as "wrong." Rather than standing in opposition to conventional ideas of good conduct, the delinquent is likely to adhere to the dominant norms in belief but render them ineffective in practice by holding various attitudes and perceptions which serve to neutralize the norms as checks on behavior. "Techniques of neutralization," such as the denial of responsibility or the definition of injury as rightful revenge, free the individual from a large measure of social control.

This approach to delinquency centers its attention on how an impetus to engage in delinquent behavior is translated into action. But it leaves unanswered a serious question: What makes delinquency attractive in the first place? Even if it is granted that techniques of neutralization or some similar evasions of social controls pave the way for overt delinquency, there remains the problem of the values or ends underlying delinquency and the relationship of these values to those of the larger society. Briefly stated, this paper argues that (a) the values behind much juvenile delinquency are far less

deviant than they are commonly portrayed; and (b) the faulty picture is due to a gross oversimplification of the middle-class value system.

THE VALUES OF DELINQUENCY

There are many perceptive accounts describing the behavior of juvenile delinquents and their underlying values, using methods ranging from participant observation to projective tests.[2] Although there are some important differences of opinion in the interpretation of this material, there exists a striking consensus on actual substance. Many divisions and sub-divisions are possible, of course, in classifying these behavior patterns and the values on which they are based, but three major themes emerge with marked regularity.

First, many observers have noted that delinquents are deeply immersed in a restless search for excitement, "thrills," or "kicks." The approved style of life, for many delinquents, is an adventurous one. Activities pervaded by displays of daring and charged with danger are highly

---

[1]Gresham M. Sykes and David Matza, "Techniques of Neutralization," *American Sociological Review* 22 (December, 1957): 664–70.

[2]Frederic M. Thrasher, *The Gang* (Chicago: University of Chicago Press, 1936); Clifford R. Shaw and Maurice E. Moore, *The Natural History of a Delinquent Career* (Chicago: University of Chicago Press, 1931); Albert K. Cohen, *Delinquent Boys: The Culture of the Gang* (New York: The Free Press, 1955); Albert K. Cohen and James F. Short, Jr., "Research in Delinquent Subcultures," *Journal of Social Issues* 14 (1958): 20–37; Walter B. Miller, "Lower Class Culture as a Generating Milieu of Gang Delinquents," *Journal of Social Issues* 14 (1958): 5–19; Harold Finestone, "Cats, Kicks, and Color," *Social Problems* 5 (July, 1957): 3–13; Solomon Kobrin, "The Conflict of Values in Delinquent Areas," *American Sociological Review* 16 (October, 1951): 653-61; Richard Cloward and Lloyd Ohlin, "New Perspectives on Juvenile Delinquency," unpublished manuscript; Dale Kramer and Madeline Karr, *Teen-Age Gangs* (New York: Holt, Rinehart & Winston, Inc., 1953); Stacey V. Jones, "The Cougars: Life with a Delinquent Gang," *Harper's*, November, 1954; Harrison E. Salisbury, *The Shook-Up Generation* (New York: Harper and Row, Publishers, 1958); William C. Kvaraceus and Walter B. Miller, eds., *Delinquent Behavior: Culture and the Individual* (Washington, D.C.: National Education Association of the United States, 1959); Herbert A. Bloch and Arthur Niederhoffer, *The Gang* (New York: Philosophical Library, Inc., 1958); Beatrice Griffith, *American Me* (Boston: Houghton Mifflin Company, 1948); Sheldon Glueck and Eleanor Glueck, *Unraveling Juvenile Delinquency* (New York: Commonwealth Fund, 1950).

valued in comparison with more mundane and routine patterns of behavior. This search for excitement is not easily satisfied in legitimate outlets such as organized recreation, as Tappan has indicated. The fact that an activity involves breaking the law is precisely the fact that often infuses it with an air of excitement.[3] In fact, excitement or "kicks" may come to be defined with clear awareness as "any act tabooed by 'squares' that heightens and intensifies the present moment of experience and differentiates it as much as possible from the humdrum routines of daily life."[4] But in any event, the delinquent way of life is frequently a way of life shot through with adventurous exploits that are valued for the stimulation they provide.

It should be noted that in courting physical danger, experimenting with the forbidden, provoking the authorities, and so on, the delinquent is not simply enduring hazards; he is also creating hazards in a deliberate attempt to manufacture excitement. As Miller has noted, for example, in his study of Roxbury, for many delinquents "the rhythm of life fluctuates between periods of relatively routine and repetitive activities and sought situations of greater emotional stimulation."[5] The excitement, then, that flows from gang rumbles, games of "chicken" played with cars, or the use of drugs is not merely an incidental by-product but may instead serve as a major motivating force.

Second, juvenile delinquents commonly exhibit a disdain for "getting on" in the realm of work. Occupational goals involving a steady job or careful advancement are apt to be lacking, and in their place we find a sort of aimless drifting or grandiose dreams of quick success. Now it takes a very deep faith in the maxims of Benjamin Franklin—or a certain naiveté, perhaps—to believe that hard work at the lower ranges of the occupational hierarchy is a sure path to worldly achievement. The delinquent is typically described as choosing another course, rationally or irrationally. Chicanery or manipulation, which may take the form of borrowing from social workers or more elaborate modes

of "hustling"; an emphasis on "pull," frequently with reference to obtaining a soft job which is assumed to be available only to those with influential connections: all are seen as methods of exploiting the social environment without drudgery, and are accorded a high value. Simple expropriation should be included, of course, in the form of theft, robbery, and the rest; but it is only one of a variety of ways of "scoring" and does not necessarily carry great prestige in the eyes of the delinquent. In fact, there is some evidence that, among certain delinquents, theft and robbery may actually be looked down upon as pointing to a lack of wit or skill. A life of ease based on pimping or the numbers game may be held out as a far more admirable goal.[6] In any event, the delinquent is frequently convinced that only suckers work and he avoids, if he can, the regimen of the factory, store, and office.

Some writers have coupled the delinquent's disdain of work with a disdain of money. Much delinquent activity, it is said, is non-utilitarian in character and the delinquent disavows the material aspirations of the larger society, thus protecting himself against inevitable frustration. Now it is true that the delinquent's attacks against property are often a form of play, as Cohen has pointed out, rather than a means to a material end.[7] It is also true that the delinquent often shows little liking for the slow accumulation of financial resources. Yet rather than saying that the delinquent disdains money, it would seem more accurate to say that the delinquent is deeply and constantly concerned with the problem of money in his own way. The delinquent wants money, probably no less than the law-abiding, but not for the purposes of a careful series of expenditures or some long-range objective. Rather, money is frequently desired as something to be squandered in gestures of largesse, in patterns of conspicuous consumption. The sudden acquisition of large sums of money is his goal—the "big score"—and he will employ legal means if possible and illegal means if necessary. Since legal means are likely to be thought of as ineffective, it is far from acci-

---

[3]Paul Tappan, *Juvenile Delinquency* (New York: McGraw-Hill Book Company, 1949), pp. 148–154.
[4]Finestone, op. cit.
[5]Miller, op. cit.

---

[6]Finestone, op. cit.
[7]Cohen, op. cit.

dental that "smartness" is such an important feature of the delinquent's view of life: "Smartness involves the capacity to outsmart, outfox, outwit, dupe . . ."[8]

A third theme running through accounts of juvenile delinquency centers on aggression. This theme is most likely to be selected as pointing to the delinquent's alienation from the larger society. Verbal and physical assaults are a commonplace, and frequent reference is made to the delinquent's basic hostility, his hatred, and his urge to injure and destroy.

The delinquent's readiness for aggression is particularly emphasized in the analysis of juvenile gangs found in the slum areas of large cities. In such gangs we find the struggles for "turf," the beatings, and the violent feuds which form such distinctive elements in the portrayal of delinquency. As Cloward and Ohlin have pointed out, we can be led into error by viewing these gang delinquents as typical of all delinquents.[9] And Bloch and Niederhoffer have indicated that many current notions of the delinquent gang are quite worn out and require reappraisal.[10] Yet the gang delinquent's use of violence for the maintenance of "rep," the proof of "heart," and so on, seems to express in extreme form the idea that aggression is a demonstration of toughness and thus of masculinity. This idea runs through much delinquent activity. The concept of *machismo*, of the path to manhood through the ability to take it and hand it out, is foreign to the average delinquent only in name.

In short, juvenile delinquency appears to be permeated by a cluster of values that can be characterized as the search for kicks, the disdain of work and a desire for the big score, and the acceptance of aggressive toughness as proof of masculinity. Whether these values are seen as pathological expressions of a distorted personality or as the traits of a delinquent subculture, they are taken as indicative of the delinquent's deviation from the dominant society. The delinquent, it is said, stands apart from the dominant society not only in terms of his illegal behavior but in terms of his basic values as well.

DELINQUENCY AND LEISURE

The deviant nature of the delinquent's values might pass unquestioned at first glance. Yet when we examine these values a bit more closely, we must be struck by their similarity to the components of the code of the "gentleman of leisure" depicted by Thorstein Veblen. The emphasis on daring and adventure; the rejection of the prosaic discipline of work; the taste for luxury and conspicuous consumption; and the respect paid to manhood demonstrated through force—all find a prototype in that sardonic picture of a leisured elite. What is *not* familiar is the mode of expression of these values, namely, delinquency. The quality of the values is obscured by their context. When "daring" turns out to be acts of daring by adolescents directed against adult figures of accepted authority, for example, we are apt to see only the flaunting of authority and not the courage that may be involved. We suspect that if juvenile delinquency were highly valued by the dominant society—as is the case, let us say, in the deviance of prisoners of war or resistance fighters rebelling against the rules of their oppressors—the interpretation of the nature of delinquency and the delinquent might be far different.[11]

In any event, the values of a leisure class seem to lie behind much delinquent activity, however brutalized or perverted their expression may be accounted by the dominant social order. Interestingly enough, Veblen himself saw a similarity between the pecuniary man, the embodiment of the leisure class, and the delinquent. "The ideal pecuniary man is like the ideal delinquent," said Veblen, "in his unscrupulous conversion of goods and services to his own ends,

---

[8]Miller, op. cit.
[9]Cloward and Ohlin, op. cit.
[10]Bloch and Niederhoffer, op. cit.

[11]Merton's comments on in-group virtues and out-group vices are particularly germane. The moral alchemy cited by Merton might be paraphrased to read:

> I am daring
> You are reckless
> He is delinquent

Cf. Robert K. Merton, *Social Theory and Social Structure* (New York: The Free Press, 1957), pp. 426–30.

and in a callous disregard for the feelings and wishes of others and of the remoter effects of his actions."[12] For Veblen this comparison was probably no more than an aside, a part of polemical attack on the irresponsibility and pretensions of an industrial society's rulers. And it is far from clear what Veblen meant by delinquency. Nonetheless, his barbed comparison points to an important idea. We have too easily assumed that the delinquent is deviant in his values, opposed to the larger society. This is due, in part, to the fact that we have taken an overly simple view of the value system of the supposedly law-abiding. In our haste to create a standard from which deviance can be measured, we have reduced the value system of the whole society to that of the middle class. We have ignored both the fact that society is not composed exclusively of the middle class and that the middle class itself is far from homogeneous.[13]

In reality, of course, the value system of any society is exceedingly complex and we cannot solve our problems in the analysis of deviance by taking as a baseline a simplicity which does not exist in fact. Not only do different social classes differ in their values, but there are also significant variations within a class based on ethnic origins, upward and downward mobility, region, age, etc. Perhaps even more important, however, is the existence of subterranean values —values, that is to say, which are in conflict or in competition with other deeply held values

but which are still recognized and accepted by many.[14] It is crucial to note that these contradictions in values are not necessarily the opposing viewpoints of two different groups. They may also exist within a single individual and give rise to profound feelings of ambivalence in many areas of life. In this sense, subterranean values are akin to private as opposed to public morality. They are values that the individual holds to and believes in but that are also recognized as being not quite *comme il faut*. The easier task of analysis is to call such values deviant and to charge the individual with hypocrisy when he acts on them. Social reality, however, is somewhat more intricate than that and we cannot take the black and white world of McGuffey's Readers as an accurate model of the values by which men live.

Now the value of adventure certainly does not provide the major organizing principle of the dominant social order in modern, industrial society. This is especially true in the work-a-day world where so much activity is founded on bureaucratization and all that it implies with regard to routinization, standardization, and so on. But this is not to say that the element of adventure is completely rejected by the society at large or never appears in the motivational structure of the law-abiding. Instead, it would appear that adventure, i.e., displays of daring and the search for excitement, is acceptable and desirable but only when confined to certain circumstances such as sports, recreation, and holidays. The last has been frequently noted in the observation that conventions are often viewed as social events in which conventional canons of conduct are interpreted rather loosely. In fact, most societies seem to provide room for Saturnalias in one form or another, a sort of periodic anomie in which thrill-seeking is allowed to emerge.

In other words, the middle class citizen may seem like a far cry from the delinquent on the prowl for "thrills," but they both recognize and share the idea that "thrills" are worth pursuing and often with the same connotation of throwing over the traces, of opposing "fun" to the routine.

[12]T. Veblen, *The Theory of the Leisure Class* (Modern Library, Inc., 1934), pp. 237–38.

[13]Much of the current sociological analysis of the value systems of the different social classes would seem to be based on a model which is closely akin to an out-moded portrayal of race. Just as racial groups were once viewed as a clustering of physical traits with no overlapping of traits from one group to the next (e.g., Caucasians are straight-haired, light-skinned, etc., whereas Negroes are kinky-haired, dark-skinned, etc.), so now are the value systems of social classes apt to be seen as a distinct grouping of specific values which are unique to the social class in which they are found. The model of the value systems of the different social classes we are using in this paper is more closely allied to the treatment of race presently used in anthropology, i.e., a distribution of frequencies. Most values, we argue, appear in most social classes; the social classes differ, however, in the frequency with which the values appear.

[14]Robert S. Lynd, *Knowledge for What* (Princeton, N.J.: Princeton University Press, 1948).

As members of the middle class—and other classes—seek their "kicks" in gambling, night-clubbing, the big night on the town, etc., we can neither ignore their use of leisure nor claim that it is based on a markedly deviant value. Leisure class values have come increasingly to color the activities of many individuals in the dominant society, although they may limit their expression more sharply than does the delinquent. The search for adventure, excitement, and thrills, then, is a subterranean value that now often exists side by side with the values of security, routinization, and the rest. It is not a deviant value, in any full sense, but it must be held in abeyance until the proper moment and circumstances for its expression arrive. It is obvious that something more than the delinquent's sense of appropriateness is involved, but it is also clear that in many cases the delinquent suffers from bad timing.

Similarly, to characterize the dominant society as being fully and unquestioningly attached to the virtue of hard work and careful saving is to distort reality. Notions of "pull" and the soft job are far from uncommon and the individual who entertains such notions cannot be thrust beyond the pale merely because some sociologists have found it convenient to erect a simplified conception of *the* work values of society. As Chinoy and Bell, and a host of other writers have pointed out, the conditions of work in modern society have broken down earlier conceptions of work as a calling and there are strong pressures to define the job as a place where one earns money as quickly and painlessly as possible.[15] If the delinquent carries this idea further than many of society's members might be willing to do, he has not necessarily moved into a new realm of values. In the same vein it can be argued that the delinquent's attachment to conspicuous consumption hardly makes him a stranger to the dominant society. Just as Riesman's "inside dopester," Whyte's "organization man," and Mills' "fixer" have a more authentic ring than an obsolete Weberian image in many instances, the picture of the delinquent as a spender seems more valid than a picture of him as an adolescent who has renounced material aspirations. The delinquent, we suggest, is much more in step with his times. Perhaps it is too extreme to say with Lowenthal[16] that "the idols of work have been replaced by the idols of leisure," but it appears unquestionable that we are witnessing a compromise between the Protestant Ethic and a Leisure Ethic. The delinquent conforms to society, rather than deviates from it, when he incorporates "big money" into his value system.[17]

Finally, we would do well to question prevalent views about society's attitudes toward violence and aggression. It could be argued, for one thing, that the dominant society exhibits a widespread taste for violence, since fantasies of violence in books, magazines, movies, and television are everywhere at hand. The delinquent simply translates into behavior those values that the majority are usually too timid to express. Furthermore, disclaimers of violence are suspect not simply because fantasies of violence are widely consumed, but also because of the actual use of aggression and violence in war, race riots, industrial conflicts, and the treatment of delinquents themselves by police. There are numerous examples of the acceptance of aggression and violence on the part of the dominant social order.

Perhaps it is more important, however, to recognize that the crucial idea of aggression as a proof of toughness and masculinity is widely accepted at many points in the social system. The ability to take it and hand it out, to defend one's rights and one's reputation with force, to prove one's manhood by hardness and physical courage—all are widespread in American culture. They cannot be dismissed by noting the equally valid observation that many people will declare that "nice children do not fight." The use of aggression to demonstrate masculinity is, of course, restricted by numerous prohibitions against instigating violence, "dirty" fighting,

---

[15]Daniel Bell, *Work and Its Discontents* (Boston: Beacon Press, 1956); Ely Chinoy, *Automobile Workers and the American Dream* (Garden City, N.Y.: Doubleday and Company, Inc., 1955).

[16]Leo Lowenthal, "Historical Perspectives of Popular Culture," in *Mass Culture: The Popular Arts in America*, ed. Bernard Rosenberg and David M. White (New York: The Free Press, 1957).

[17]Arthur K. Davis, "Veblen on the Decline of the Protestant Ethic," *Social Forces* 22 (March, 1944): 282–86.

bullying, blustering, and so on. Yet even if the show of violence is carefully hedged in by both children and adults throughout our society, there is a persistent support for aggression which manifests itself in the derogatory connotations of labels such as "sissy" or "fag."[18]

In short, we are arguing that the delinquent may not stand as an alien in the body of society but may represent instead a disturbing reflection or a caricature. His vocabulary is different, to be sure, but kicks, big-time spending, and rep have immediate counterparts in the value system of the law-abiding. The delinquent has picked up and emphasized one part of the dominant value system, namely, the subterranean values that coexist with other, publicly proclaimed values possessing a more respectable air. These subterranean values, similar in many ways to the values Veblen ascribed to a leisure class, bind the delinquent to the society whose laws he violates. And we suspect that this sharing of values, this bond with the larger social order, facilitates the frequently observed "reformation" of delinquents with the coming of adult status.[19] To the objection that much juvenile behavior other than simply delinquent behavior would then be analyzed as an extension of the adult world rather than as a product of a distinct adolescent subculture we can only answer that this is precisely our thesis.

DELINQUENCY AND SOCIAL CLASS

The persistence of the assumption that the juvenile delinquent must deviate from the law-abiding in his values as well as in his behavior can be traced in part, we suspect, to the large number of studies that have indicated that delinquents are disproportionately represented in the lower classes. In earlier years it was not too difficult to believe that the lower classes were set off from their social superiors in most attributes, including "immorality," and that this taint produced delinquent behavior. Writers of more recent vintage have avoided this reassuring

error, but, still holding to the belief that delinquency is predominantly a lower class phenomenon, have continued to look for features peculiar to certain segments of the lower class that would create values at variance with those of the rest of society and which would foster delinquency.

Some criminologists, however, have long expressed doubts about the validity of the statistics on delinquency and have suggested that if all the facts were at hand the delinquency rate of the lower classes and the classes above them would be found to be far less divergent than they now appear.[20] Preferential treatment by the police and the courts and better and more varied means for handling the offender may have led us to underestimate seriously the extent to which juvenile delinquency crops up in what are euphemistically termed "relatively privileged homes."

Given the present state of data in this field, it is probably impossible to come to any firm conclusion on this issue. One thing, however, seems fairly clear: juvenile delinquency does occur frequently in the middle and upper classes and recent studies show more delinquency in these groups than have studies in the past. We might interpret this as showing that our research methods have improved or that "white-collar" delinquency is increasing—or possibly both. But in any event, the existence of juvenile delinquency in the middle and upper classes poses a serious problem for theories which depend on status deprivation, social disorganization, and similar explanatory variables. One solution has been to change horses in the middle of the stratification system, as it were, shifting from social environment to personality disturbances as the causative factor as one moves up the social ladder. Future research may prove that this shift is necessary. Since juvenile delinquency does not appear to be a unitary phenomenon we might expect that no one theoretical approach will be adequate. To speak of juvenile delinquency in general, as we have done in this paper, should not obscure the fact that there are different types of delinquency and the differences among them cannot be ignored. Yet

18Albert Bandura and Richard Haig Walters, *Adolescent Aggression* (New York: The Ronald Press Company, 1959), chap. 3.

19See, for example, William McCord, Joan McCord, and Irving K. Zola, *Origins of Crime* (New York: Columbia University Press, 1939), p. 21.

20Milton L. Barron, *The Juvenile in Delinquent Society* (New York: Alfred A. Knopf, Inc., 1954).

it seems worthwhile to pursue the idea that some forms of juvenile delinquency—and possibly the most frequent—have a common sociological basis regardless of the class level at which they appear.

One such basis is offered, we believe, by our argument that the values lying behind much delinquent behavior are the values of a leisure class. All adolescents at all class levels are to some extent members of a leisure class, for they move in a limbo between earlier parental domination and future integration with the social structure through the bonds of work and marriage.[21] Theirs is an anticipatory leisure, it is true, a period of freedom from the demands for self-support which allows room for the schooling enabling them to enter the world of work. They thus enjoy a temporary leisure by sufferance rather than by virtue of a permanent aristocratic right. Yet the leisure status of adolescents, modified though it may be by the discipline of school and the lack of wealth, places them in relationship to the social structure in a manner similar to that of an elite which consumes without producing. In this situation, disdain of work, an emphasis on personal qualities rather than technical skills, and a stress on the manner and extent of consumption all can flourish. Insofar, then, as these values do lie behind delinquency, we could expect delinquent behavior to be prevalent among all adolescents rather than confined to the lower class.

CONCLUSION

This theory concerning the role of leisure in juvenile delinquency leaves unsolved, of course, a number of problems. First, there is the question why some adolescents convert subterranean values into seriously deviant behavior while others do not. Even if it is granted that many adolescents are far more deviant in their behavior than official records would indicate, it is clear that there are degrees of delinquency and types of delinquency. This variation cannot be explained simply on the basis of exposure to leisure. It is possible that leisure values are typically converted into delinquent behavior when such values are coupled with frustrations and resentments. (This is more than a matter of being deprived in socio-economic terms.) If this is so, if the delinquent is a sort of soured sportsman, neither leisure nor deprivation will be sufficient by itself as an explanatory variable. This would appear to be in accordance with the present empirical observations in the field. Second, we need to know a good deal more about the distribution of leisure among adolescents and its impact on their value systems. We have assumed that adolescents are in general leisured, i.e., free from the demands for self-support, but school drop-outs, the conversion of school into a tightly disciplined and time-consuming preparation for a career, the facilities for leisure as opposed to mere idleness will all probably have their effect. We suspect that two variables are of vital importance in this area: (a) the extent of identification with adult symbols of work, such as the father; and (b) the extent to which the school is seen as providing roles to enhance the ego, both now and in the future, rather than as an oppressive and dreary marking of time.

We conclude that the explanation of juvenile delinquency may be clarified by exploring the delinquent's similarity to the society that produced him rather than his dissimilarity. If his values are the subterranean values of a society that is placing increasing emphasis on leisure, we may throw new light on Taft's comment that the basic values in our culture are accepted by both the delinquent and the larger society of which he is a part.[22]

---

[21]Reuel Denney, *The Astonished Muse* (Chicago: University of Chicago Press, 1957). See also Barbara Wooton, *Social Science and Social Pathology* (New York: Crowell Collier & Macmillan, Inc., 1959); Austin L. Porterfield, *Youth in Trouble* (Austin, Tex.: Leo Potishman Foundation, 1946).

[22]Donald R. Taft, *Criminology* (New York: Crowell Collier & Macmillan, Inc., 1950).

whose activities and traditions were delinquent in character, and that he was never implicated in any offense with more than three delinquents.[14] Recognizing that current best friends are not necessarily companions from past delinquent association, it seems consistent with differential association theory to argue that, if current best friends comprise a salient primary group, and if past behavior serves as a basis for mutual communication and action within it (which it need not), then boys currently in intense association with one another should show similar patterns of delinquency. Assuming that specific techniques for committing delinquent acts are communicated in primary association, it follows that all, or none, of the boys in close friendship triads should report committing a given kind of offense. Within a triadic friendship group, there should be no dyads committing a given type of offense, since group constraint should produce homogeneity in behavior. It should be clear that whether or not boys in close friendship groups show similarity in delinquent behavior because they select one another on this basis, or as a result of association, failure to show that delinquency histories of boys in close friendship groups are the same casts doubt at least upon the *specificity* of any learned delinquent behavior in intense association with others. Since Sutherland did not restrict his hypothesis to lower class delinquents, behavioral homophily should hold regardless of social class.[15]

To show that one's close friends are also delinquent is not to show that they have an effect on all of one's delinquent activity. Shaw and McKay early showed that stealing is more likely to be a group offense than are offenses against the home and school.[16] Enyon and Reckless have gone further to show that companionship characterizes first participation in some kinds of offenses more than in others. Companions were present in 100 per cent of boys' first involvement in gang fights but only 56 per cent of the cases of first running away from home.[17] While our study cannot demonstrate the precise effect of friendship on delinquency patterns, it investigates the extent to which there is covariation in a boy's delinquent behavior and that of his friends for different kinds of delinquent behavior.

Sociological theories on delinquent subcultures that are consistent with Sutherland's differential association hypothesis postulate that members of delinquent subcultures become highly dependent upon one another, particularly for status gratification. As Short points out, it follows that members of such groups, having a more intense association with one another, should show greater similarity in their patterns of delinquency than do members of other delinquent groups.[18] Cohen's general theory of delinquent subcultures holds that subcultural delinquent groups should be homogeneous in behavior for a variety of delinquent offenses against property and persons. It is implicit in his theory that middle class boys will show less similarity and versatility in their delinquency.[19] Miller holds that delinquency is endemic in lower class culture. It would be consistent with his theory to argue that delinquent behavior of lower class boys is independent of the commission of the act by other members of the group.[20]

THE INVESTIGATION

The investigation was designed to gather information on the actual delinquent behavior of boys in close friendship cliques. A sample of 378 boys was drawn from a base population of all white males between the ages of 12 and 16 who were registered in one of 45 public, private or parochial junior or senior high schools in Davidson County, Tennessee, during the 1957 school year. Strata were designed so as to

---

[14]Clifford R. Shaw and Henry D. McKay, op. cit., p. 221.

[15]Albert Cohen, Alfred Lindesmith, and Karl Schuessler, op. cit., pp. 15, 32–33 and 58–59.

[16]Clifford R. Shaw and Henry D. McKay, op. cit., pp. 195–96.

[17]Thomas G. Enyon and Walter C. Reckless, op. cit., Table 3, p. 170.

[18]James F. Short, Jr., op. cit., p. 17.

[19]Albert K. Cohen, *Delinquent Boys: The Culture of the Gang* (New York: The Free Press, 1955), pp. 157–69.

[20]Walter Miller, "The Impact of a 'Total Community' Delinquency Control Project," *Social Problems* 10 (Fall, 1962): 169-91.

select disproportionately lower- and middle-class delinquent boys.[21]

Each clique is a triad composed of a boy selected in the stratified probability sample of 378 boys and his two closest friends. Given a large population from which the sample of boys was drawn, only a few sample cases chose the same "closest" friend. Effects of overlapping friendship choice or of pyramiding therefore are negligible. Information was gathered for 299 triads and 79 dyads. The dyads are pairs where a boy selected only one "best friend." Data are presented in this paper only for the 299 triads. Each step was replicated for the 79 dyads and the results are similar where the number of dyads makes comparison possible.

The index person in each triad was classified into one of seven conforming or delinquent types.[22] The career-*oriented delinquent* is the most delinquent person in the classification schema. He is oriented toward the adult criminal world and maintains contact with adult criminals. The largest group of delinquents are *peer-oriented* and directed in their goals and behavior. The lone delinquent is our *nonconforming isolate*. There are four types of conforming boys. The *conforming nonachiever* is comparable to William Whyte's "corner boy" and the *conforming achiever* to his "college boy," if social class attributes are disregarded.[23] The *hyperconformer* disregards conventional for strict conformity while the *conforming isolate* is outside the clique system. Peer-oriented delinquents, conforming nonachievers, and achievers are divided into white-collar and blue-collar status based on father's occupation.[24]

The dependent variable, self-reported delinquent behavior, was measured by asking each boy how often he had done any of the following things, whether alone or with others, and by inquiring about the conditions related to it: taken little things worth less than $2? $2 to $50? more than $50? purposely damaged or destroyed property? taken a car without the owner's permission or knowledge? beat up somebody badly enough to be arrested?[25] Self-reports include virtually all cases of officially recorded delinquency. Only delinquent acts committed after age 10 are data for this paper.

Self-reported delinquent acts were tabulated for each of the six categories of delinquent act for the 299 triads arranged in the 10 types of conforming-delinquent, SES groups.[26] This tabulation provided information on kind of delinquent behavior reported by none, one, two or all members of the triad in each of the 10 conforming-delinquent groups. A model was then constructed to give the expected delinquent behavior composition of the triad, using the actual rate of delinquency for the sample of boys for estimation purposes. The model is based on the expansion of the binomial.[27] Our use of the binomial ignores variability in response patterns by friendship choice, e.g. + (original) − (first best friend) + (second best friend) and + + − or − + + are all treated as two boys expected (or actual) to commit the act. This disregard of response order seems warranted for we cannot determine whether the original subject models his behavior on that of his two closest friends, or whether he chooses friends who have similar behavior, or whether they copy his behavior.

The observed distribution of boys in triads

[21]This is a more efficient sample design inasmuch as delinquency is a relatively low incidence phenomenon in the general population. The methodological problems encountered in dealing with a low incidence phenomenon in a population have been discussed in Daniel Glaser, "Differential Association and Criminological Prediction," *Social Problems* 8 (Summer, 1960): 7, and Albert J. Reiss, Jr., "Unraveling Juvenile Delinquency II: An Appraisal of the Research Methods," *American Journal of Sociology* 57 (September, 1951): 118–19.

[22]Albert J. Reiss, Jr. and A. Lewis Rhodes, "The Distribution of Juvenile Delinquency in the Social Class Structure," *American Sociological Review* 26 (October, 1961), chart I.

[23]William F. Whyte, *Street Corner Society* (Chicago: University of Chicago Press, 1937).

[24]Albert J. Reiss, Jr. and A. Lewis Rhodes, op. cit., pp. 721–22.

[25]Readers will note the similarity of these questions with the Nye-Short delinquency scale items: Ivan F. Nye and James F. Short, Jr., "Scaling Delinquent Behavior," *American Sociological Review* 22 (June, 1957): 326–31.

[26]The authors express their appreciation to NAL, State University of Iowa for use of the IBM 650. A special program for rapid tabulation of response patterns in triads was developed for this study.

$$[27] f(x) = \left(\frac{3!}{x!(3-x)!} \right) p^x (q)^{3-x}$$

where x is the number of boys expected to commit the act (0, 1, 2 or 3); p is the proportion of the subgroup reporting commission of the acts; q is the proportion of the subgroup not reporting commission of the act.

reporting they committed an act of delinquency is then compared with the expected distribution. The chi square test of goodness of fit is used to test the significance of the departure of the observed measure from the hypothetical one of the binomial.[28] Occasionally, the conventional test of the significance of difference between two proportions is used to test whether there is any significant difference in the number of observed and expected triads where all members of the triad reported committing the act.

Very briefly, this paper attempts to shed light on three closely related questions that are germane to propositions about the group nature

of delinquency and the empirical testing of differential association theory: (1) Does the probability of an individual committing kinds of delinquent acts depend upon his close friends committing these acts? (2) Is there variation in dependence upon friends committing delinquent acts among different kinds of delinquent behavior? (3) Is the probability of committing a delinquent act less dependent upon one's friends committing the act in some kinds of conforming or delinquent groups than in others?

FINDINGS

Boys generally choose boys as close friends whose law-abiding or delinquent behavior is similar to their own. Table 3–5 answers our

[28]No test was made if the expected frequency in any cell was less than two or less than five in two cells of a 2 × 3 table.

TABLE 3–5.

Observed (f), Expected (f_e)[a] and Sum of Expected $(f\Sigma)$[a] for Conforming-Delinquent Subgroups

Number of White Male Triads Classified by Number of Males in Each Triad Who Reported Delinquent Behavior One or More Times for Six Kinds of Delinquent Behavior

Kind of Delinquent Behavior	Per Cent Reporting Behavior	Number in Triad Reporting Delinquent Behavior				Number of Triads	$P(\chi^2)$[b]
		0	1	2	3		
Auto theft	12						<.001
f_e		204	83	11[d]	1[d]	299	
f		229	42	17	11	299	
$f\Sigma$		227	43	19	10	299	
Theft over $50	12						<.001
f_e		204	84	11[d]	1[d]	299	
f		236	31	18	14	299	
$f\Sigma$		232	37	19	11	299	
Theft: $2–$50	18						<.001
f_e		111	130	51	7	299	
f		161	65	36	37	299	
$f\Sigma$		150	78	44	27		
Assault	28						<.001
f_e		168	107	23[d]	2[d]	299	
f		200	61	18	20	299	
$f\Sigma$		189	74	26	10	299	
Vandalism[c]	—[c]						<.001
f_e		44	116	103	31	294	
f		75	84	78	57	294	
$f\Sigma$		60	103	86	45	294	
Theft under $2[c]	—[c]						<.001
f_e		27	98	120	49	294	
f		52	80	77	85	294	
$f\Sigma$		42	88	97	67	294	

[a]Expected frequencies are calculated for the binomial using the proportion of boys in the sample who reported committing each kind of delinquency.
[a]Expected frequencies were calculated for the binomial for each of 10 conforming-delinquent subgroups. The sum of these expected values is reported here.
[b]χ^2 computed for actual (f) with expected (f_e) values only.
[c]Offense committed two or more times.
[d]Cell frequencies combined for computation of χ^2.

first question in comparing reported delinquent behavior of boys in triads with that expected from the proportion of boys in the sample who reported committing specific kinds of delinquency. For each kind of delinquent behavior, *the probability of an individual committing a specific delinquent act depends upon the commission of the act by other members of the friendship triad.* More of the triads in Table 3–5 than expected from the binomial are made up of boys, all or none of whom engaged in the same kind of delinquent act. The more serious the offense, the greater the difference between observed and expected proportions of triads where *all* of the boys committed the same kind of delinquent offense. Confidence in the finding that the probability for a boy committing a delinquent act is not independent of the behavior of his close friends is increased with the observation that fewer of the triads than expected have only one boy reporting he engaged in the delinquent activity. Table 3–6 restates the conclusion in a way that aids the interpretation. For each kind of act, significantly more of the original sociometric subjects who reported the

offense, than of those who did not, have friends who also committed the act.

Nonetheless, Tables 3–5 and 3–6 make apparent considerable variation in delinquent behavior homophily of close friendship triads. Of the triads in Table 3–5 where at least one boy reported committing auto theft or assault, three-fifths have only one boy reporting he committed the act. By way of contrast, but one-fourth of the triads where at least one boy committed an act of vandalism and one in five for petty larceny are made up of boys where only one reported committing the act. Original sociometric subjects in Table 3–6 are more likely to choose boys as friends who also committed acts of vandalism or theft under two dollars than they are to have chosen boys as friends who also committed acts of auto larceny or assault, when they report having done these things. We must conclude in answer to our second question that although, in the aggregate, commission of a kind of delinquent act is not independent of the commission of the act by other members of a close friendship triad, the correlation varies with kind of delinquent behavior and is far from perfect for any kind.

We know from previous studies that roughly four-fifths of all boys arrested for delinquency had associates in the offense for which they were arrested, and that at least that high a proportion of delinquent boys have as close friends boys who have committed some kind of delinquent act. We must conclude then, that close friendship choices are more closely correlated with delinquency *per se* than with specialization or engagement in all specific kinds of delinquency.

Attention has been called to the ambiguity in formulation of Sutherland's differential association theory rendering difficult both operationalization of the theory and deductions from it. An altogether literal deduction from Sutherland's theory, though he never made it, is that either all or none of the boys in a close friendship triad should report committing the same kind of offense. It is immediately apparent from inspection of Tables 3–5 and 3–6 that there is a substantial number of triads where only one or two members of the triad committed the same kind of delinquent act, thereby calling into question any postulate about the homo-

TABLE 3–6.

PER CENT OF TRIADS WITH NUMBER OF FRIENDS COMMITTING DELINQUENT ACT BY ORIGINAL SUBJECT'S DELINQUENT BEHAVIOR, FOR SIX KINDS OF DELINQUENT BEHAVIOR

Original Subject's Delinquent Act	Number of Friends Committing Same Kind of Act				$P(\chi^2)$
	0	1	2	Total	
Auto theft					
Yes	45	28	27	40	.001
No	88	9	3	259	
Theft over $50					
Yes	29	29	42	34	.001
No	89	8	3	265	
Theft: $2–$50					
Yes	24	32	44	84	.001
No	75	21	4	215	
Assault					
Yes	35	27	38	52	.001
No	81	17	2	247	
Vandalism					
Yes	16	41	43	134	.001
No	47	39	14	160	
Theft under $2					
Yes	9	37	54	158	.001
No	38	48	14	136	

geneity of law-violative behavior in triads through differential association. Let us assume, however, as does a variant of coalition theory, that when two members of a triad engage in a given kind of behavior, the third member is under strong pressure to do likewise.[29] We would expect, then, that there should be relatively few, if any, close friendship triads with only two members engaging in delinquent behavior. Expressing the triads where *all* members commit the same kind of delinquent act as a per cent of all triads where two or three members commit the act, the following distribution results; auto theft (65 per cent); theft over $50 (64 per cent); theft $2–$50 (80 per cent); assault (83 per cent); vandalism (71 per cent); theft under $2 (82 per cent). The distribution supports the contention that there is pressure toward uniformity of behavior in these triads. In two-thirds or more of the triads, for each kind of delinquent offense, all members report they committed the act, i.e., if more than one did it, it was probably three. There remained, nonetheless, a substantial minority of triads in which only two members committed the same kind of delinquency. The more serious offenses are least likely to show triadic uniformity.

Thus far two main ways of accounting for the observed distribution of delinquent associates in close friendship triads have been introduced. We first examined whether the sample of triads was a sample drawn from a binomial based on the rate of a specified kind of delinquency, and we concluded that the departure of the observed distribution from the binomial exceeded that ordinarily encountered in random sampling. The probability of an individual committing a specific kind of delinquent act depends upon the commission of the act by other members of the friendship triad. We then examined whether the sample of triads conformed to predictions from Sutherland's differential association theory or coalition theory. Inasmuch as there was a substantial number of triads with only one or two members reporting they engaged in a specific kind of delinquent behavior, we are led to question the postulate that differential association is a necessary and sufficient condi-

tion explaining delinquency. Table 3–7 summarizes these comparisons and is a convenient way of raising the further question whether the observed distribution of triads departs more from the random distribution than the expected one based on the differential association hypothesis. Although no test of statistical significance is employed, it seems clear that the observed distribution is closer to the binomial than to the expected distribution based on the differential association hypothesis.

The reciprocation of sociometric choices, the delinquency orientation and behavior of boys chosen as close friends, and the content and seriousness of a boy's delinquent offenses were

TABLE 3–7.

COMPARISON OF REPORTED BEHAVIOR IN 299 DELINQUENT TRIADS (f) WITH RANDOM EXPECTATION (f_e) AND NUMBER EXPECTED UNDER DIFFERENTIAL ASSOCIATION EFFECT ON BEHAVIOR OF ORIGINAL MEMBER OF SOCIOMETRIC TRIAD (f_d)[a] FOR SIX KINDS OF DELINQUENT BEHAVIOR

Type of Delinquency and Number in Triad Committing Act	f_e[*]	f	f_d[a]
Auto theft			
3	—[b]	11	40
2 or 1	95	59	0
0	204	229	259
Theft over $50			
3	—[b]	14	34
2 or 1	95	49	0
0	204	236	265
Theft: $2–$50			
3	7	37	84
2 or 1	181	101	0
0	112	161	215
Assault			
3	2	20	52
2 or 1	129	79	0
0	168	200	247
Vandalism			
3	121	138	220
2 or 1	172	151	0
0	5	10	79
Theft under $2			
3	49	85	158
2 or 1	218	157	0
0	27	52	136

[*]The proportion of boys in the sample who reported each kind of delinquency is used to set up the binomial of triads.
[a]The expected values for differential association are the marginal frequencies of original subjects committing and not committing a specific kind of delinquent act.
[b]Less than one case.

[29]See n. 13.

the main criteria in classifying a boy into a particularly conforming or delinquent type in our study. The *type* and *content* of the delinquent offenses of his close friends were not used as criteria in classifying a boy into a particular group. Although classification of a boy and his friends into a conforming or delinquent subtype then is not independent of classification by type of delinquent behavior, there still can be considerable variation in the delinquent behavior among the members of a triad within any kind of delinquent group. Given the possibility of variation in type and content of delinquent offense within a triad, we compared the triads in each subtype of conforming or delinquent group to see whether boys in each subtype chose as close friends boys who committed acts of delinquency similar to their own. Table 3–8 compares the reported behavior of boys in each subtype of conforming or delinquent triad with the behavior expected from the proportion of boys in each type who reported committing each kind of act. Such comparisons should permit us to learn whether membership in a specific kind of conforming or delinquent group has any effect upon one's delinquent behavior independent of the rate of delinquency within that type of group.

Inspection of Table 3–8 shows that there is little significant variation between observed and expected values for any of the conforming-delinquent groups. The answer to our third question then is that selection of close friends who commit a specific kind of act within a given type of conforming-delinquent group is largely a function of the rate of that kind of delinquency within each group. The more boys there are committing any kind of offense in a type of group, the more likely one is to have groups in which all members commit that kind of offense. Put in another way, our classification of boys into conforming and delinquent types of groups accounts in large part for the tendency for boys to choose as close friends boys who commit delinquent acts similar to their own. This can be seen by turning again to Table 3–5 where we observe that the sum of the expected values for the conforming-delinquent subgroups is remarkably like that observed for all triads, particularly for the serious offenses of auto theft

and theft over $50. These two types of offenses are more clearly concentrated in the career- and peer-oriented delinquent types, of course. The similarity between the sum of the expected values for subgroups and the actual behavior reported within triads is less marked for the less serious offenses, offenses which occur quite frequently in most conforming and delinquent groups.

These observations (a summary of which is aided by comparing the f and fΣ values in Table 3–5) suggest that a model of random selection accounts for subcultural or career-oriented delinquents associating most frequently with boys who commit delinquent acts similar to their own, given our classification of them into that type of delinquent group. This finding, of course, should not obscure the fact that the classification system does discriminate among types of conforming and delinquent boys. Career-oriented delinquents are easily distinguished from all other types by the fact that for every kind of offense, at least two-thirds of the triads are made up of boys who committed the same kind of offense. There are significantly more career-oriented triads in which all members engaged in every kind of offense than in any other type of delinquent group except that peer-oriented white-collar delinquents have significantly more triads in which all members committed theft under two dollars.

We have shown that for each kind of delinquent behavior reported in this study, the probability of an individual committing a specific act of delinquency is dependent upon the commission of the act by other members of the triad. Except for Sutherland's original formulation of differential association theory, most contemporary sociological theories emphasize a qualitative difference between middle and lower class delinquency. In Table 3–9 we ask whether the finding that a boy's delinquent behavior depends upon his close friends engaging in it is independent of the social class status of the boys. It clearly is not for all types of offenses. Among blue-collar boys, the probability of a boy engaging in any specific kind of delinquency depends upon his close friends engaging in it but among white-collar boys this is true only for theft involving amounts of less than $50 or for vandalism.

TABLE 3-8.

Observed (f) and Expected (f_e)[b] Number of White Male Triads Classified by Number of Males in Each Triad Who Reported Delinquent Behavior for Each of Six Kinds of Delinquency in Each Type of Conforming-Delinquent Subgroup

Kind of Delinquent Act and Number in Triad Reporting Committing Act

Type of Conforming or Delinquent Group		Theft under $2 More Than Once				Vandalism More Than Once				Theft: $2–$50 Once or More				Assault Once or More				Theft over $50 Once or More				Auto Theft Once or More			
		0	1	2	3	0	1	2	3	0	1	2	3	0	1	2	3	0	1	2	3	0	1	2	3
Career oriented: B.C.	f_e	—*	3	12	17[a]	—*	4	13	15	—*	2	11	19	1	7	14	10[a]	1	6	14	11	1	8	14	9
	f	1	4	7	20	3	2	9	18	—*	3	10	19	2	9	7	14	2	6	11	13	4	5	12	11
Peer oriented: B.C.	f_e	1	7	19	16	2	12	19	10	7	19	16	4	22	19	5	—*	27	16	3	—*	29	14	2	—*
	f	1	10	13	19	4	8	22	9	9	18	12	7	24	15	5	2	28	15	2	1	28	17	1	0
Peer oriented: W.C.	f_e	0	0	0	9	—*	0	2	6	—*	2	4	3	3	4	2	—*	3	4	2	—*	5	3	1	—*
	f	0	0	0	9	0	0	3	6	1	1	3	4	3	4	2	0	4	1	4	0	5	3	1	0
Conf. Non-achv: B.C.	f_e	10	29	27	8	16	32	21	5	42	27	6	—*	55	18	2	—*	69	6	—*	—*	69	6	—*	—*
	f	15	23	24	12	19	29	18	8	45	22	5	3	59	12	2	2	70	4	1	0	68	6	1	0
Conf. Non-achv: W.C.	f_e	1	4	12	12	1	8	13	7	9	13	6	1	18	9	2	—*	27	2	—*	—*	18	9	2	—*
	f	1	4	11	13	2	9	9	9	12	9	4	4	21	5	1	2	27	2	0	0	19	8	2	0
Nonconf. isolate	f_e	1	2	3	1	1	3	2	1	6	1	0	0	4	2	1	0	7	0	0	0	7	0	0	0
	f	1	4	1	2	2	2	2	1	6	1	0	0	5	1	1	0	7	0	0	0	7	0	0	0
Conf. achiever: B.C.	f_e	8	10	4	—*	10	9	3	—*	19	3	—*	—*	17	5	0	0	22	0	0	0	22	0	0	0
	f	8	9	4	1	11	8	2	1	20	1	1	0	17	5	0	0	22	0	0	0	22	0	0	0
Conf. achiever: W.C.	f_e	10	21	16	4[a]	17	23	10	1	40	10	1	0	45	6	0	0	49	2	0	0	48	3	—*	—*
	f	14	17	12	8	22	16	8	5	41	9	1	0	45	6	0	0	49	2	0	0	48	3	0	0
Conf. isolate	f_e	6	8	3	0	6	8	3	0	17	1	0	0	15	3	0	0	17	1	0	0	18	0	0	0
	f	7	6	3	1	6	6	5	0	17	1	0	0	15	3	0	0	17	1	0	0	18	0	0	0
Hyperconformer	f_e	5	4	1	0	7	3	0	0	10	0	0	0	9	1	0	0	10	0	0	0	10	0	0	0
	f	5	3	2	0	6	4	0	0	10	0	0	0	9	1	0	0	10	0	0	0	10	0	0	0

*Expected frequency is less than one case.

[a]Null hypothesis rejected for this comparison: $P(x^2) < .05$.

[b]The proportion of boys in each conforming-delinquent subgroup who reported each kind of delinquency is used to set up binomial of triads for each subgroup.

TABLE 3–9.

OBSERVED (f) AND EXPECTED (f$_e$)[a] NUMBER OF WHITE MALE TRIADS CLASSIFIED BY NUMBER OF MALES IN EACH TRIAD WHO REPORTED DELINQUENT BEHAVIOR FOR SIX KINDS OF DELINQUENT BEHAVIOR, CONTROLLING ON SOCIAL CLASS OF ORIGINAL SUBJECT IN EACH TRIAD

Kind of Delinquent Behavior	Number in Triad Reporting Delinquent Behavior by Social Class									
	White Collar Triads					Blue Collar Triads				
	0	1	2	3	$P(\chi^2)$	0	1	2	3	$P(\chi^2)$
Done One or More Times										
Auto theft										
f$_e$	72	16	1	—*		100	61	13	1	
f	72	14	3	0	p > .90	122	28	14	11	p < .001
Theft over $50										
f$_e$	76	12	1	—*		96	64	14	1	
f	80	5	4	0	p > .20	122	25	14	14	p < .001
Assault										
f$_e$	65	22	2	—*		80	72	21	2	
f	69	15	3	2	p > .30	102	41	14	18	p < .001
Theft: $2–$50										
f$_e$	42	36	10	1		46	77	44	8	
f	54	19	8	8	p < .001	74	44	28	29	p < .001
Done More than Once										
Vandalism										
f$_e$	13	36	31	9		22	64	64	21	
f	24	25	20	20	p < .001	37	47	51	36	p < .001
Theft under $2										
f$_e$	6	27	38	18		13	52	73	33	
f	15	21	23	30	p < .001	25	46	48	52	p < .001

*Expected frequency is less than one case.

[a]The proportion of boys in each social class subgroup who reported committing each kind of delinquency is used to set up the binomial of triads for each social class subgroup.

Apparently when middle class delinquent boys engage in serious delinquent behavior it is relatively independent of their close friendship choices.

Our interviews with subjects were structured so as to avoid mention by name of close friends in delinquency. To do so would violate peer norms about "squealers" and at times jeopardize rapport. Many respondents nevertheless volunteered names of their co-participants for delinquent acts in which they had associates and these were usually persons mentioned as "closest friends." Each respondent was explicitly asked for each reported delinquent offense whether he was (always, usually, sometimes or never) alone (or with one or more persons) when committing it. Table 3–10 presents this information only for those triads in which all members reported committing a specific kind of delinquent act. The objective is to investigate whether unanimous reporting of engaging in a kind of delinquent behavior in a triad means they engaged in the behavior as group activity. Evidently this is not always the case. It is apparent that, for close friendship groups where all members committed the same kind of act, participants are most likely to report vandalism as group activity and least likely to report theft under $2 as group activity. This finding is consistent with that of Enyon and Reckless on the percentage of cases in which companions were present at first occurrence of admitted delinquency, it being higher for acts

TABLE 3–10.

PER CENT OF TRIADS WHERE ALL BOYS ADMIT DELINQUENT ACTS IN WHICH ALL BOYS ALSO
INDICATE COMMISSION OF ACT WITH SOMEONE ELSE, BY KIND OF ACT AND TYPE OF TRIAD

Type of Conforming or Delinquent Triad	Kind of Delinquent Act											
	Theft <$2 Once or More		Vandalism Once or More		Theft: $2–$50 Once or More		Assault Once or More		Theft > $50 Once or More		Auto Theft Once or More	
	Per Cent	Number	Per Cent	Number	Per Cent	Number	Per Cent	Number	Per Cent	Number	Per Cent	Number
Career Oriented: B.C.	45	22	86	21	74	19	79	14	100	13	82	11
Peer Oriented: B. C.	45	29	74	19	43	7	50	2	0	1	—	0
Peer Oriented: W.C.	22	9	100	7	75	4	—	0	—	0	—	0
Conf. non-achv: B.C.	32	25	80	20	67	3	0	2	—	0	—	0
Conf. non-achv: W.C.	42	19	92	13	100	4	50	2	—	0	—	0
Non-conf. isolate	20	5	100	3	—	0	—	0	—	0	—	0
Conf. achiever: B.C.	0	6	80	5	—	0	—	0	—	0	—	0
Conf. achiever: W.C.	5	19	80	10	—	0	—	0	—	0	—	0
Conf. isolate	25	4	100	2	—	0	—	0	—	0	—	0
Hyperconformer	—	0	—	0	—	0	—	0	—	0	—	0

of vandalism (91 per cent) than for taking things under $2 (69 per cent).[30]

If attention is directed to variation in group involvement in delinquency among our conforming-delinquent types of triads, there is substantial evidence that only career-oriented delinquents report group involvement for all types of offense other than theft under $2. The career-oriented delinquent is apparently most likely to commit his offenses with accomplices.

SUMMARY AND CONCLUSIONS

The main question for this paper was whether boys in close friendship groups have the same specific patterns of delinquent behavior. The reported delinquent behavior of boys in close friendship triads was compared with that expected for six kinds of delinquent behavior. Two different ways of accounting for the observed distribution were examined.

The first compares the observed delinquent behavior of boys in triads with a binomial based on the rate for each kind of delinquency in the population. We concluded that the probability for an individual committing a specific kind of delinquent act depends upon the commission

[30]Thomas G. Enyon and Walter C. Reckless, op. cit., Table 4.

of the act by other members of the triad. This dependence upon close friends engaging in delinquent activity is not independent of the social class status of boys for all kinds of offenses, however. Among blue-collar boys, the probability of a boy engaging in any of the six kinds of delinquency depends upon his close friends engaging in it but among white-collar boys this is true only for the less serious offenses.

The second comparison asks whether the behavior of boys in triads departs from predictions from Sutherland's differential association theory or coalition theory that there be uniform conformity in conforming groups and uniformity of specific kinds of delinquent behavior in delinquent groups. We concluded there is considerable departure from this explanatory model even when only those groups are considered where at least two boys engaged in the same kind of delinquency. The observed distribution of delinquency in close friendship triads departs somewhat less from the random than the differential association model, at least for the more serious offenses.

There is in fact considerable variation in the delinquent behavior homophily of friendship triads. The degree to which commission of a kind of delinquent act depends upon its commission by other members of the triad varies considerably by type of delinquency. Vandalism and petty larceny, the more common offenses, are commonly committed by two or three members of the triad while a majority of the triads where at least one member committed auto theft or assault are made up of only one member committing the offense. Behavioral homophily in triads does not mean that boys always or usually commit these offenses together, since there is evidence that theft under $2 is least likely to involve group activity. Two things seem evident from these findings, that delinquent behavior homophily in close friendship triads does not necessarily involve association in the commission of offenses and that some offenses are more clearly group activity than others.

Our classification of boys into conforming and delinquent subgroups accounts in large part for the selection of close friends who commit delinquent acts similar to one's own. While career-oriented delinquent boys generally have the highest proportion of triads where boys commit the same kind of delinquent act, they also have the highest overall rate of delinquency for each kind of act. The main problem is to account for the higher rate of delinquency among these boys. Certainly the effect of one's close friends on delinquency does not appear to be a sufficient reason to account for this higher rate since a substantial minority of career-oriented delinquent boys are in close friendship triads where at least one other boy does not commit the same kind of offense and the convergence of boys who commit the same kind of delinquent act in close friendship triads is not greater than that one would expect from the rate of delinquency among these boys.

This study cannot be construed as a test of the genetic formulation of the differential association hypothesis. To the extent that the findings of this study are valid and our logical inferences correctly drawn, however, they may be disappointing to proponents of differential association theory. The association of boys with the *same kind* of delinquent behavior in close friendship triads while somewhat greater than chance is well below what one would expect from the learning hypothesis in differential association theory and the results are not independent of social class. Close friendship choices are more closely correlated with delinquency *per se* than

with participation in specific patterns of delinquency presumably learned from others.

The results also cannot be interpreted as clearly supporting one of the major theories of delinquent behavior over that of another, though some postulates in these theories seem supported over others. The main sociological theories of subcultural delinquency such as those of Cohen and Walter Miller postulating differences between lower and middle class gang behavior find some support in this study. Delinquency among middle class boys, particularly for the more serious delinquent offenses, is independent of friendship choices while among lower class boys the probability of committing any kind of delinquent activity is related to the delinquent activity of one's close friends. The fact that selection of close friends who commit specific kinds of delinquency within each type of conforming-delinquent group is largely a function of the rate of delinquency within each group lends support to Walter Miller's contention that delinquency is endemic in lower class culture. Nonetheless, if Miller is correct, convergence of delinquent patterns of behavior in friendship groups should not exceed chance since he argues that the pressures toward deviance come from outside the immediate peer group. The fact that the probability of a lower class boy's committing any specific kind of delinquency is dependent upon the commission of the act by other members of the group therefore is at odds with Miller's formulation. The model of differential association seems even a less powerful one in accounting for our observed patterns of behavior in close friendship triads than does Miller's formulation, however.

The fact that a substantial proportion of career-oriented delinquent boys do show a marked similarity in delinquent activity, particularly for the more serious offenses, is consistent with Cohen's formulation emphasizing the versatility of delinquency among subcultural delinquents. That some of these groups may be specialized in specific kinds of delinquent activity was not investigated.

This study perhaps only serves to emphasize the difficulty in testing inferences from differential association theory. It perhaps is unnecessary to repeat what is already well stated, that we need to operationalize the hypothesis in such a way as to test the relationship of association with delinquent others through time. Of considerable importance, however, in future research would be an investigation of the "deviant" cases which do not conform to expectations of the differential association model. How can one account for the fact that all members of delinquent groups do not conform to the same patterns of delinquency? Why are some members of close friendship groups delinquent and not others? What are the patterns of recruitment to peer groups and how stable is peer group structure?

21.

Paul Lerman

INDIVIDUAL VALUES, PEER VALUES, AND SUBCULTURAL DELINQUENCY

It is difficult to evaluate competing theories of subcultural delinquency when the dependent variable differs from one theory to another. Descriptive issues must, therefore, be resolved before explanatory issues are engaged. Shared values, language, and behavior are basic "elements" of the subculture; this article focuses on theoretical and empirical issues involved in describing subcultural values. Various formulations are evaluated with the use of data. The use of "tension states" sociological theories is questioned in favor of values competing for the allegiance of youths.

For many years, sociologists have stressed the importance of understanding the peer aspects of the bulk of adolescent delinquency. Since the publication of Cohen's *Delinquent Boys*,[1] this kind of juvenile misconduct has been referred to as "subcultural delinquency." Currently there are various theoretical writings that attempt to describe and explain this phenomenon.[2] It is difficult, however, to evaluate these theories when the dependent variable differs from one to another. There exists a need to describe subcultural delinquency adequately so that the object of the explanation is similar for all theories. Descriptive issues must, therefore, be resolved before explanatory issues are engaged. This article is an attempt to translate theoretical disagreements into new empirical issues that can be resolved with data. In the main, only descriptive issues will be addressed.

In earlier articles[3] we provided evidence in support of the view that the minimal "elements" comprising a subcultural pattern consisted of language, values, and behavior. From this perspective, a subculture is hypothesized to exist

Source: Paul Lerman, "Individual Values, Peer Values, and Subcultural Delinquency," *American Sociological Review* 33, no. 2 (April, 1968): 219–35. Reprinted by Permission of the author and the American Sociological Association. Adapted from Paul Lerman, *Issues in Subcultural Delinquency* (doctoral diss., Columbia University, 1966). The study was conducted under the auspices of the Columbia University School of Social Work, Mobilization for Youth Research Project, Dr. Richard A. Cloward, Project Director. It was funded by the National Institute of Mental Health (Contract MH-01178).

[1] Albert K. Cohen, *Delinquent Boys* (New York: The Free Press, 1955).

[2] In addition to the previously cited work by Cohen, the following are major statements: Albert K. Cohen and James F. Short, Jr., "Research in Delinquent Subcultures," *Journal of Social Issues* 14 (Summer, 1958): 20–37; Walter B. Miller, "Lower Class Culture as a Generating Milieu of

Gang Delinquency," ibid., pp. 5–19; Richard A. Cloward and Lloyd E. Ohlin, *Delinquency and Opportunity* (New York: The Free Press, 1960); and David Matza and Gresham M. Sykes, "Juvenile Delinquency and Subterranean Values," *American Sociological Review* 26 (October, 1961): 712–20.

[3] Paul Lerman, "Argot, Symbolic Deviance and Subcultural Delinquency," *American Sociological Review* 32 (April, 1967): 209–24; "Gangs, Networks, and Subcultural Delinquency," *American Journal of Sociology* 73 (July, 1967): 63–72; and the reply to the critical comments of James F. Short, Jr., concerning "Gangs, Networks and Subcultural Delinquency," *American Journal of Sociology* 73 (January, 1968): 515–17.

if indicators of illegal behavior are significantly related to and consonant with shared symbols, i.e., argot and values. Specifically, this implies the following:

1. Values are deviant from the actor's point of view and can be shared with peers;

2. Linguistic usage is demonstrated by knowledge of argot words used in speaking rather than in writing;

3. Youths scoring high on shared deviant values also score high on argot knowledge, and there is a sense of consonance about the relationship;

4. Youths classified by both their knowledge of argot and shared deviant values can be categorized as *high in shared symbols;* these youths are the most likely to report consonant illegal acts and to be noticed by the police;

5. The interrelationship of deviant values, argot, and illegal behavior constitutes the minimal subpattern that must be demonstrated if a subculture can be posited to exist, and all three variables have to be simultaneously related;

6. The cultural and social boundaries of a deviant youth culture have distinct referents, and the social unit of a subculture is most accurately described as a network of pairs, triads, groups with names, and groups without names.

With each of the "elements" of a subculture there are distinctive issues that can be examined. In the next section we will discuss some of the issues generated by focusing on "values"; data will then be presented relevant to these issues. The findings reported are based on a survey of youths residing in randomly selected households in a portion of New York City's Lower East Side. The original target group consisted of 706 boys and girls aged 10 to 19 years; interviews were completed with 555 youngsters, a rate of 79 percent.

Processing of the entire sample through the official police files disclosed that interviewed boys, even with age controlled, were as likely to be "delinquent" as their non-cooperative peers.[4]

---

[4]Although this finding is important, it is still possible that the non-interviewed boys would have responded differently to the survey's questions. The non-interviewed boys tend to be older; within this age-range they also tend to come from the economically more advantaged households of this low-

DISTINGUISHING BETWEEN THE ACTOR'S AND THE OBSERVER'S POINT OF VIEW

In describing patterns of values, it is important to recognize that they can be assessed from either the actor's or the observer's frame of reference. But if one adopts the observer's point of view, how does one avoid the danger that the values inferred will be operationally of little relevance to the actor? If one adopts the actor's point of view, how does one avoid the danger of not being able to infer patterns of values?

This is the central concern in Miller's criticism of Cohen's formulation of the "spirit" of subcultural delinquency. To Cohen, the illegal actions of youths are stimulated by "non-utilitarian," "malicious," and "negativistic" values.[5] From Miller's point of view, these values are not those of the youthful actor but those of adult observers.[6] He argues that youths have certain "focal concerns" which impart quite different meanings to their illegal behavior. It is not necessary to accept Miller's list of "focal concerns" or to agree that these concerns form a lower-class pattern transmitted by adults; these are issues that can be settled empirically. However, it does seem useful to remember that judgments concerning values can vary; therefore, it is important to know who the value-definer is.

In assessing illegal behavior, it may be necessary for us to accept definitions based on the actual operating (discretionary) criteria of the police. In assessing non-standard values, we have no official system to use as a conventional benchmark. Each theorist can set up his own idealized conception of standard values—without, however,

income area, as well as from non-minority backgrounds. The relationships discussed in this paper are not affected by measures of social class and minority-group status; age, however, is a potent variable. Analysis of the relationship between age and official police contact among boys indicates that the non-interviewed respondents yield a positive, strong relationship—as do the interviewed boys. We assume, therefore, that the *relationships* presented in the following tables hold for both the interviewed and the non-interviewed portion of the sample. For further details about the neighborhood, the sample, and a copy of the questionnaire used, see *A Proposal for the Prevention and Control of Delinquency by Expanding Opportunities* (New York: Mobilization for Youth, Inc., December 9, 1961), Appendices R4, R5.

[5]Cohen, op. cit.

[6]Miller, op. cit.

any guarantee that the actors will feel fairly presented. For example, a recent study attempted to apply Cohen's characterization of deviant values in a survey using youthful respondents (including officially known delinquents). The authors concluded: ". . . The study design operationalized each of these characteristics of the subculture but the measures generally failed to achieve sufficient discrimination to isolate such a subtype."[7]

In this study, we attempted to offset potential observer bias by asking survey respondents to indicate what they regarded as the most important of several "deviant" and "conforming" value statements. An attempt was made to present the items in a neutral manner. Values presumed to be deviant referred to toughness, "kicks," outsmarting others, making a "fast buck," keeping one's mouth shut to the cops, and connection with a racket; conforming values referred to school and work. If the actors and the observer operated within a similar framework with regard to classifying values, the conforming values should have received the largest proportion of responses as "the most important."

Our approach differs from the Cloward-Ohlin approach to "delinquent norms"[8] in that we do not assume that those who are classified as guided by "deviant values" are also interested in violating legal codes. Violation of legal statutes may in many instances be a tolerated consequence of pursuing desired ends. In other words, boys are not *required* to act illegally on behalf of their values; however, they may tolerate illegal behavior if it is consonant with their values.[9]

SHARED VALUES AND INDIVIDUAL VALUES

A major assumption of the subcultural theorists is that the youthful actors share a common set of values. One empirical test of this assumption might require that values be measured from the perspective of the individual and that of his associates. Assessing individual values is not

difficult, but measuring the values of the individual's companions poses problems. In this survey we inferred friends' values from the respondent's report of the abilities (values) admired by his associates. To the degree that the individual's value choices and his perceptions of his friends' values are congruent, it is possible to regard the peer values as shared.

THE CONTENT OF DEVIANT VALUES: VERSATILE OR SPECIALIZED?

In the past few years sociological theorists have debated whether the male delinquent subculture is one or many.[10] Do given neighborhoods tend to specialize in certain types of deviant pattern, or is subcultural delinquency versatile in orientation at the outset, with possible differentiation by age?

The findings on illegal behavior (not reported here) strongly support the contention that, in terms of age sequence, a variety of types of action are quite compatible.[11] Analyses of argot responses, both within an age-grade and between ages, also support the view of versatile deviance.[12] Regarding shared values, the findings should be consonant with those of the behavior and argot analyses. Although major theorists might agree with this assumption, they differ on the values they deem important and on which values "go together."

According to Cloward and Ohlin,[13] delinquent subcultures can be categorized by whether the "dominant orientation" stresses "heart," "kicks," or "scores." Bopping youngsters value "heart," and engage in gang conflicts to maintain their "rep" and to defend their "turf" from invaders. Drug-using "retreatists" seek "kicks" through a "high" via "the needle," eschew violence, and steal only to support their "habit." Criminalistic youth disdain work and seek to "score" by a disciplined, rational approach to conventional crime, or by exploiting their "connections" with

---

[7]Albert J. Reiss, Jr., and Albert L. Rhodes, "Delinquency and Social Class Structure," *American Sociological Review* 26 (1961): 730.

[8]Cloward and Ohlin, op. cit.

[9]For a parallel point of view regarding values see David Matza, *Delinquency and Drift* (New York: John Wiley and Sons, Inc., 1964), esp. pp. 37–40.

[10]See Cohen and Short, op. cit.; and Cloward and Ohlin, op. cit., pp. 161–86.

[11]Paul Lerman, *Issues in Subcultural Delinquency* (doctoral diss., Columbia University, 1966), chap. 3.

[12]Lerman, "Argot, Symbolic Deviance, and Subcultural Delinquency," op. cit.

[13]Op. cit.

the "syndicate." All three types devalue school as well as work, although this is not stressed as part of the explicit characterizations.

Cohen and Short,[14] on the other hand, suggest that subcultures are *not* specialized at the outset but may become so at a later age. In value terms, undifferentiated youth subcultures can be characterized as malicious, hedonistic, negativistic, non-utilitarian, and autonomous. When these values are stripped of invidious connotations, the subcultures can be redefined as aggressive, thrill-seeking, tending to disobey adult rules, and regarding play or kicks as an end. The characterization "autonomous" can be accepted as is, since it is non-invidious to the actor. Cohen also suggests that delinquent boys are ambivalent about school and work, and not alienated from the dominant value system.

Miller,[15] a trained anthropologist, attempts to avoid such invidious terms as "malicious" and "retreatist." He hypothesizes that the values of deviant youths in low-income areas are no different from the values of adults in those milieus. Youth is merely a time when the everyday "focal concerns" of lower-class culture are enacted in an exaggerated fashion by slum boys. These focal concerns are: fatalism, toughness, keeping out of trouble, smartness, autonomy, and excitement. For Miller, and for Cohen as well, toughness, excitement, and autonomy are part of a larger pattern; Cloward and Ohlin use only toughness and excitement, but these are perceived as independent dominant patterns.

One of the broadest attempts to link deviant youth values and the less idealistic everyday values held by many adults in the larger society is the work of Matza and Sykes.[16] They hypothesize that "the delinquent has picked up and emphasized one part of the dominant value system," namely "the subterranean values that coexist with other, publicly proclaimed values possessing a more respectable air." The "cluster of values" permeating delinquent subcultures are: the search for kicks, disdain for work, desire for the "big score," and acceptance of aggressive toughness as proof of masculinity. Matza and Sykes suggest that these values, when examined

more closely, are strikingly similar to the code of the "gentleman of leisure," as portrayed by Thorstein Veblen, with its emphasis on daring and adventure, rejection of the prosaic discipline of work, taste for luxury and conspicuous consumption, and respect paid to manhood demonstrated through force.

The areas of agreement and contention among these theorists will become clearer when we examine the eight value items that were actually used in this study to measure individual and shared orientations.

1. *The ability to keep one's mouth shut to the cops.* This value is implicit in Cloward and Ohlin as cross-cutting all three subcultures; it is explicit in Miller's framework as part of the concern for keeping out of trouble; it is probably implicit in the thinking of both Cohen and Matza-Sykes.

2. *The ability to be hard and tough.* This value is explicitly found in all four theories, but Cloward and Ohlin treat it independently as an aspect of the "conflict" subculture.

3. *The ability to find kicks.* This value also is explicit in all the theories, but Cloward and Ohlin treat it independently in the "retreatist" subculture.

4. *The ability to make a "fast buck."* This value is at variance with Cohen's non-utilitarian approach; it is implicit in Miller's work; Matza-Sykes and Cloward-Ohlin explicitly refer to making a "big score," but the latter treat this value independently in the "criminal" subculture.

5. *The ability to outsmart others.* Matza and Sykes, borrowing explicitly from Miller, conceive of this value as part of the disdain for work; for Cohen it is in contradiction to an emphasis on hedonism and non-utilitarianism; it is restrictively used by Cloward and Ohlin in summarizing the "cool" drug user.[17]

6. *The ability to make connections with a racket.* This value is central to the Cloward-Ohlin description of the criminal type; it plays a part in the Matza-Sykes elaboration of the disdain for work, where they emphasize making a score in the numbers or by pimping; this

---

[14]Op. cit.
[15]Op. cit.
[16]Op. cit.

[17]First portrayed by Harold Finestone in "Cats, Kicks, and Color," *Social Problems* 5 (July, 1957); 3–13.

kind of rationalistic approach to illegal gain is, of course, at variance with Cohen; it appears to be irrelevant to Miller's concerns.

7. *The ability to get good grades.* Cohen suggests that delinquent youths are ambivalent toward this value, whereas Cloward-Ohlin and Miller claim flatly that delinquent boys reject school; Matza and Sykes do not utilize school in their conception of subterranean values, although they imply that differential commitment to school may be related to a strong attraction to subterranean values.

8. *The ability to do well in the job world.* Again Cohen suggests that youths are ambivalent in this regard; the other theorists are quite explicit about youthful alienation from the world of work.

The first six items listed are intended as deviant; the last two are conventional. Except for item 6, the deviant orientations are not explicitly illegal. Worded so as to avoid invidious or unlawful connotations, these items can be used to provide information regarding the types of values that are regarded as part of a pattern by theorists. For example, we could question the creditability of the descriptive models offered by Cohen and by Cloward and Ohlin if the following results were obtained.

1. All of the first six values were interrelated (thus implying a versatile combination of items deemed incompatible by Cohen and regarded as independent entities by Cloward-Ohlin);

2. Boys scoring high on the six interrelated values were also more likely to engage in illegal behavior (thus implying that orientations do not have to be explicitly "delinquent" or in direct opposition to the middle-class ethic); and

3. A majority of boys at all ages were attracted, in some degree, to these interrelated values (thus implying that delinquent actors differ from their peers in the *degree* to which they cherish youthful values, and not in the content of their values).

If these three results were obtained, then the deviant value perspectives advanced by Miller and Matza-Sykes would gain in creditability. This seems paradoxical, since Miller views these orientations as part of broader lower-class focal concerns while Matza and Sykes argue that they are extensions of unofficial, subterranean values

permeating all sectors of society (albeit in varying degree). Although the present sample may not contain the broad cross-section of youths necessary to test these competing viewpoints, an assessment will be attempted.

Categorizing actors by their individual and shared orientations toward school and the job world can also be useful in assessing the theorists' descriptions. If youths who score high on deviant values are alienated from school and work, then all theorists except Cohen gain in creditability. If, however, youths who score high on deviant values also share orientations toward school or work that are neither totally accepting nor totally rejecting, then the Cohen thesis of ambivalence regarding dominant values is supported. A finding that deviant youths are ambivalent toward, rather than alienated from, school or work would cause the most difficulty for the Miller and Cloward-Ohlin models; Miller posits that lower-class culture is distinctively different from the dominant value orientations, and Cloward and Ohlin view alienation and repudiation of "legitimate means to success" as precursors to involvement in a deviant youth culture.

SEX DIFFERENCES

The findings concerning illegal behavior and argot, reported in previous articles, have indicated clear differences between the sexes. The sharing of deviant values should also, therefore, be related to sex. The findings that boys and girls differ in this respect would not only lend creditability to the measures of values but also highlight the fact that the values refer mainly to *masculine* interests.

AGE DIFFERENCES AND VALUE CONSISTENCY

Analysis of self-reports of misconduct indicates that all but two of the ten most often admitted items of misbehavior had a relatively early age of onset. However, older boys engage in a greater number of misbehaviors with greater frequency and greater behavioral consistency.[18] This suggests that not only can peer support of behavior via shared values be hypothesized to occur at an early age; it is also likely that older

[18]Lerman, *Issues in Subcultural Delinquency,* chap. 3.

boys will reveal a more consistent pattern of shared values. Such an increase in value consistency would be in harmony with the behavioral data and with general developmental differences between adolescents and younger boys.

A basic age difference in cognitive functioning has been noted in the child-development literature, but has apparently been overlooked by subcultural theorists. Ausubel, for example, notes, "In comparison with childhood, the cognitive life of adolescence is considerably more dominated by symbolization and abstraction. . . ."[19] He comments that this increased level of cognitive functioning has profound implications for the value and behavior consistency of individuals:

Growth in cognitive capacity alone accounts for several significant changes in character organization. For one thing, moral concepts, like all other concepts, become more abstract. This enables moral behavior to acquire greater generality and consistency from situation to situation, since abstraction presupposes the identification of essential common elements. Hartshorne and May, for example, using objective tests of character traits, found a significant trend with increasing age toward greater consistency of moral behavior. . . .[20]

Other psychologists have also concluded that adolescents are capable of being more abstract and consistent in their cognitions than younger children. Kuhlen, for example, explicitly links the ability to conceptualize abstractly to actual behavioral consistency:

It would be expected that, as age increases and broader concepts of honesty are developed, individuals would tend to become more consistent in their behavior; that is, they would tend to operate honestly (or dishonestly) in a broader variety of situations, and prediction of them would be easier. . . .[21]

However, Kuhlen adds, even at the level of individual functioning there has been "little systematic research on the matter."

Regarding greater value consistency for ideas shared by peers, the literature is virtually silent. Yet if consistency in shared values is dependent on the ability of individuals to engage in more abstract cognitive behavior, then a fully elaborated subculture cannot be evolved and sustained without such a development. In short, we suggest that *full participation in a shared way of life is not likely to occur until the actor has reached an adolescent level of cognitive growth.* The anthropologist's notions about "culture pattern" and the sociologist's assumptions about a "strain toward consistency" are most relevant and appropriate when a sufficient number of individuals have reached an abstract and consistent cognitive level of functioning. Tribal initiation rites, for example, may symbolize the attainment of this cognitive as well as sexual maturity.

PERCEPTIONS OF PEER ORIENTATIONS TOWARD ILLEGAL BEHAVIOR

Theories of subcultural delinquency assume that peers offer the individual actors not only value support but also behavioral support through their examples of illegal conduct. Therefore, merely showing that *individual* misconduct is more likely to occur in a climate of shared deviant values is not a conclusive basis for accepting a subcultural approach. It is important also to demonstrate that different shared-value climates provide a differential likelihood that *peers* are also engaged in illegal behavior.

One way of testing the existence of peer misbehavior is to ask respondents to indicate agreement or disagreement with the statement: "Most teenagers you know are tempted to break the law." A logical inference from this result would be that the differential beliefs about peer temptations are related to actual differences among respondents in the behavior of their associates.

Depending on their associates, youths ought to be in a differential social position to perceive actual differences in behavior; on the basis of their differential perceptions, they ought to differentially *believe* that their associates are likely to be tempted. Although the statement is in the form of a belief (it is doubtful whether youths perceive the temptations *per se*), it seems reasonable to assume that different social realities yield variations in perceptions of misbehavior; this, in turn, would give rise to different rates of agreement with this statement of belief.

This line of analysis might lend credence to

[19]David P. Ausubel, *Theory and Problems of Adolescent Development* (New York: Grune and Stratton, Inc., 1954), p. 285.

[20]Ibid., p. 249.

[21]Raymond G. Kuhlen, *The Psychology of Adolescent Development* (New York: Harper & Row, Publishers, 1952), p. 426.

the views of Sykes and Matza concerning a "technique of neutralization" used by delinquent actors to fend off invidious definitions from adults. These authors have suggested that blaming outside forces—denying personal responsibility—is a potent means of escaping guilt definitions:

From a psychodynamic viewpoint, this orientation toward one's own actions may represent a profound alienation from self, but it is important to stress the fact that interpretations of responsibility are cultural constructs and not merely idiosyncratic beliefs.[22]

Sykes and Matza offer no evidence concerning the shared "constructs," but the outcome of the analysis of shared values and beliefs about peer temptation can be of help in this regard. Although our analysis is not meant to suggest that belief about peer temptation is *actually* used as a technique of neutralization, it is possible to infer under which condition this technique *might* be so used. If there are differences among value climates regarding belief in peer temptations, then it seems likely that this technique would not be a personal idiosyncrasy but would have peer support. That the technique would be based on a probable shared perception would remove it even further from the realm of strictly individualistic interpretations. As anthropologists have long known, what seems to be a "psychological defense" to outside observers may be shared perceptual reality to the participants.[23]

INDIVIDUAL VALUES: EMPIRICAL FINDINGS

THE ACTOR'S PERCEPTION OF DEVIANT VALUES

Respondents were presented with the list of eight "abilities" and asked to choose the one they most admired now and the one they had "looked up to" most two or three years ago.

The list, as we have noted, included six deviant and two conforming values.

Regarding the ability most admired *now,* both boys and girls clearly indicated by their choices that they were sensitive to the value connotations of the question. As a matter of fact, the boys seemed so eager to present themselves in a favorable light that they differed only slightly from the girls in the percentage choosing any of the deviant values (15 percent vs. 8 percent). The major value difference between boys and girls concerned the choice of doing well in school: 64 percent of the girls and 54 percent of the boys regarded this as the most admirable ability.

As might be expected, more respondents were willing to admit attraction to one of the deviant values in the past. The selection of a deviant value increased from 15 percent to 26 percent for boys and from 8 percent to 13 percent for girls when they were asked which ability they had admired most "two or three years ago." The conforming value of good grades remained the dominant choice for both sexes, but girls exceeded boys by a wider margin (71 percent vs. 51 percent).

The shift in the time perspective of the question elicited differences between boys and girls in the rank ordering of the values. For boys, school ranked first at both times, but the second most admired choice "two or three years ago" was one of the deviant values, whereas success in the job world ranked second "now." For girls, too, school ranked first at both times, but deviant values and the job world competed virtually equally as the second most admired ability in the recent past. Although there is little doubt that deviant abilities appear in a less favorable light than good grades, it is also evident that *both* deviant values and the job world are capable of attracting youth away from their dominant choice, school success. This value competition becomes more apparent in an analysis of age differences.

ESTIMATING AGE DIFFERENCES IN ATTRACTION TO VALUES

In order to understand the relative "pull" of the three types of value orientation competing for the allegiance of youth, particularly boys, a developmental perspective is quite useful. Using

---

[22]Gresham M. Sykes and David Matza, "Techniques of Neutralization: A Theory of Delinquency," *American Sociological Review* 22 (December, 1957): 664–70.

[23]One of the earliest and clearest statements of this point of view can be found in Ruth Benedict, "Anthropology and the Abnormal," *Journal of General Psychology* 10 (1934): 59–79: reprinted in *Readings in Anthropology,* ed. M. Fried, vol. 2 (New York: Thomas Y. Crowell Company, 1956), pp. 497–514.

their self-perceptions in the recent past, Table 3–11 presents the nature of this competition for four age-groups of boys.

As age increases, school declines in attraction, and attraction to the job world increases. However, the appeal of the job world even at 16–19 years does not match that of school success at any age. At the younger ages, deviant values considerably outrank the job world in appeal; in fact, the biggest increase in attraction to deviant values takes place around the age when the appeal of good grades decreases the most, age 12–13. Thus it appears that attraction to deviant values has an early age of onset, as do the most admitted behavior activities.

Assuming that attraction to deviant values is related to illegal behavior, an important question concerning value competition can be posed: Does the decrease in the attraction of school success precede the increase in the attraction of deviant values? If so, then we can describe the dynamic relationship among conforming values, deviant values, and illegal behavior more aptly and also begin to erect a model of explanation in accord with empirical facts. Comparison of the relative stability of the competing value orientations should be of assistance in descriptive and explanatory analysis.

Stability of Value Choices

One means of testing the relative stability of competing value orientations is to cross-tabulate past and present value choices (Table 3–12). Those choices that are most stable are likely to represent values that have been internalized for a relatively long time.

At the younger age-range the responses involving good grades are most stable (81 per-

cent), the job world is next in stability (53 percent), and deviant choices are the least stable (42 percent). This suggests that attraction to school is the value that appears earliest in time. This inference is also supported by the fact that none of the respondents who chose job success in the recent past moved to a present choice of a deviant value.

At the older age-range, the deviant responses are not only the least stable but are less stable than for the younger boys (29 percent vs. 42 percent). The good-grades choices are still relatively stable, but less so than for the younger boys (71 percent vs. 81 percent). For this group, job choices are the most stable. Since this value replaces school as the most stable, and the deviant-value choice decreases in stability, we can infer that at the older age attraction to the job world is a more relevant independent variable. This interpretation is supported by the fact that the highest proportion of older boys whose past choices were deviant now choose job success. The percentages of boys who previously made deviant choices but now choose good grades are the same for the two age groups.

The findings concerning stability of attraction suggest that, on an individual level, the world of relevant choices is perceived quite differently by the two age-ranges. At the younger age-range, school is the major counter-attraction to a deviant choice. As the prospect of entering the job world looms closer, older boys may perceive employment as an additional counter-attraction to a deviant choice. Furthermore, at the older age-range, boys who formerly made deviant choices are capable of shifting to this new, more stable value orientation.

TABLE 3–11.

ABILITY BOYS ADMIRED MOST TWO OR THREE YEARS AGO, BY AGE

Ability Admired 2 to 3 Years Ago	*Age*			
	10–11	*12–13*	*14–15*	*16–19*
Good Grades	63%	52%	47%	41%
Job Success	10	12	23	30
A Deviant Ability	18	31	27	29
DK or NA*	9	5	3	0
N =	(67)	(84)	(62)	(63)

*Don't know or no answer.

TABLE 3–12.

RELATIONSHIP BETWEEN ABILITY BOYS ADMIRED MOST TWO OR THREE
YEARS AGO AND NOW, BY AGE

| | Ability Admired 2 or 3 Years Ago | | | | | |
| | 10–13 Years | | | 14–19 Years | | |
Ability Admired Now	Deviant	Grades	Job	Deviant	Grades	Job
Deviant	42%	9%	0%	29%	9%	6%
Grades	34	81	47	34	71	15
Job	24	9	53	37	20	79
N =	(38)	(86)	(17)	(35)	(55)	(33)

If individual attractions were the only operative variable, then widening conforming attractions might serve as an effective counterpoise to a choice of deviant values. However, like-minded peers associate together and produce socialization experiences that limit individual choices. Before exploring some of the consequences of sharing values with peers, we will consider the relationship of individual values and illegal behavior, to provide assurance that the value choices are relevant.

INDIVIDUAL VALUE CHOICES AND ILLEGAL BEHAVIOR

In Table 3–13 boys are grouped by age and classified into three types: (1) youths guided by a stable good-grades orientation, i.e., youths who choose good grades both now and two or three years ago; (2) youths guided by a stable job orientation or a mixed conforming orientation; and (3) youths guided by a deviant-value orientation, stable or unstable.

The results of Table 3–13, particularly for the older boys, suggest that attraction to a deviant value as "most important," either in the past or at present, is strongly related to the number of deviant acts reported. That is, boys who chose a deviant value were most likely to admit having committed deviant acts at some time in their lives. Among the younger boys, those attracted to a deviant value differ from those with a stable attraction to grades in the number of deviant acts reported, particularly when the last two behavior categories are collapsed (43 percent vs. 25 percent), but there is virtually no difference between the "deviant choice" and

TABLE 3–13.

RELATIONSHIP OF INDIVIDUAL VALUE-CHOICE TYPES AND
BEHAVIOR SUMMARY, BY AGE (BOYS ONLY)

| | Individual Value Choices | | | | | |
| | 10–13 Years | | | 14–19 Years | | |
Life-History Acts Reported*	Stable Grades	Stable Job and Mixed	Any Deviant Choice	Stable Grades	Stable Job and Mixed	Any Deviant Choice
None	16%	4%	2%	3%	7%	2%
Lying–1	58	56	55	65	50	19
2–3	17	30	28	28	25	19
4+	8	11	15	5	18	60
N =	(75)	(27)	(46)	(39)	(44)	(42)

*The self-reports are of a life-history variety, since boys were asked if they had ever done any of a list of activities. Those classified as "none" were unwilling to report that they had "ever told a lie"; the "lying–1" classification refers to boys who admitted to lying and/or one other act; the "2–3" category refers to lying and 2 or 3 other acts; and "4+" refers to lying plus 4 or more acts. Elimination of the "none" category would not affect the findings.

"stable job and mixed" categories (43 percent vs. 41 percent). This finding suggests that at the younger age-range the lack of a stable grade orientation in itself is likely to be related to illegal behavior. In a sense, at this age-range failure to choose good grades consistently may be no less deviant a response than direct attraction to one of the deviant values.

At the older age-range, the behavior differences between those who are or have been attracted to a deviant value and those who favor the other choices are quite clear (60 percent vs. 18 percent and 5 percent at the 4+ category). Although boys who are attracted to a job or to a combination of conforming values are likely to report a higher number of illegal acts than the stable-good-grades boys, they report far fewer than those who are attracted to a deviant choice. Their behavior profile, it is interesting to note, is not very different from that of the younger boys whose orientation is similarly conforming. Apparently a youthful adherence to *any* conforming value—even if the focus shifts—tends to discourage involvement in illegal behavior at an older age.

SHARED VALUES: EMPIRICAL FINDINGS

Our analysis of individual values utilized data elicited by presenting individuals with a forced choice concerning admired abilities. In studying shared values, we asked respondents to indicate whether their group or crowd admired each deviant ability listed "a lot," "some," or "not at all"; they were not asked to choose which ability was most admired by associates or to evaluate the appeal of deviant vs. conforming

values. Since youths as well as adults tend to associate with like-minded persons, it can be inferred that respondents share the degree of value attraction estimated for their intimate peers. In this sense, peer values are likely to be shared values. This assumption can be tested by comparing respondents' individual values with their responses regarding peers. If the relationship is strong, we can conclude that the estimates of the strength of peer attraction to values also refer to the degree to which the respondent shares this attraction. To be attracted to a value with others, of course, is not equivalent to assessing it as most important. These distinctions, and the underlying reasoning, should be kept in mind in the analyses that follow.

THE ATTRACTION OF PEER VALUES

The extent to which youth are attracted to the listed values can be assessed by combining the "some" and "a lot" responses for each ability. When this is done, even with age controlled, it is readily apparent that males view these items as attractive *peer* values. Table 3–14 demonstrates that each deviant ability other than the "connections" one is capable of eliciting more than a 50-percent response of attraction on the part of males.

In comparing boys and girls, it should be remembered that the question did not specify the sex of the peer-friends of respondents. Even though older girls probably associate with boys much more than do girls under 13, there is a surprising similarity between the two age-ranges of females. The major difference appears to be the increased attraction to kicks on the part

TABLE 3–14.

ASSESSMENT OF PEER VALUES BY SEX AND AGE

Ability Admired by Peers "a Lot" or "Some"	10–13 Years		14–19 Years	
	Boys	Girls	Boys	Girls
1. Being Hard and Tough	70%	34%	66%	35%
2. Keeping Mouth Shut to Cops	63	41	66	38
3. Outsmarting Others	62	44	60	44
4. Different Kicks	61	44	62	54
5. Fast Buck	55	29	53	38
6. Connections with Rackets	21	10	21	16
N =	(151)	(147)	(125)	(132)

of associates of the older girls; this is the only value for girls that goes above 51 percent, and it is also quite close to the rate for males. At the older ages, the search for kicks, licit and illicit, may be the common meeting ground for boys and girls.

The biggest value difference between younger boys and girls is in the attraction to being tough and hard. Although the attraction of this ability for boys declines with age, it continues to rank fairly high, whereas for girls at both age-ranges it ranks near the bottom of the list. Being tough and hard is, of course, a value that is quite consonant with the aggressive early-age activities of boys.

In summary, the evidence indicates that associates of both boys and girls have at least some attraction to the deviant values listed, and that there is a strong difference by sex. The values refer mainly to masculine interests. Controlling for age discloses only minor differences for boys. A majority of males perceive that their *friends* appreciate values which, on an *individual* basis, were chosen as if the actors were sensitive to their deviant connotation.

PEER-VALUE PATTERNS

To ascertain whether peer values are independent of one another or form a versatile pattern, each item was intercorrelated with every other item, and coefficients were computed (Table 3–15). The analysis indicates that for males *all* the peer values are intercorrelated in a statistically significant manner and thus cohere as one versatile pattern. The approaches of Matza-

Sykes and Miller receive support from these findings. Although Cohen hypothesized a versatile pattern of values, he did not appreciate that the search for a "fast buck" and the pursuit of "kicks" are compatible in the minds of youth. Cloward and Ohlin recognized the important content of the peer values, but erred in describing them as independent.

These peer values were ordered into an index by weighting "a lot" answers as 2, "some" as 1, and "not at all" as zero, and assigning a score to each respondent. "Don't know" and "no answer" responses were arbitrarily weighted as 1. There were very few such responses, and they do not appreciably influence the resulting measure.

After the sample was scored, the distribution was divided roughly into thirds on the basis of the boys' scores. This procedure yielded a "low" group (scores 0–3) comprised of 36 percent of the boys; a "medium" group (scores 4–6) of 39 percent; and a "high" group (7 or more) of 25 percent. The relevance of the index is indicated by its relationship to the life-history behavior summary. Table 3–16 summarizes the results by age, for boys only.

The relationship between peer values and the behavior summary exists regardless of age, but there is obviously an age factor. The greatest increase in delinquent behavior with age occurs for boys who score medium and high on peer values. Similar results are obtained if past-year self-reports are used as the behavioral measure (data not shown).

The boys who do not admit even to lying do

TABLE 3–15.

PRODUCT-MOMENT CORRELATION COEFFICIENTS OF ABILITIES ADMIRED BY PEERS, BOYS ONLY ($N = 276$)*

	Keep Mouth Shut to Cops	Hard and Tough	Kicks	Fast Buck	Out-smart Others	Connec-tions with Rackets
Keep Mouth Shut to Cops	—	.44	.34	.29	.27	.32
Hard and Tough	—	—	.36	.33	.27	.33
Kicks	—	—	—	.28	.31	.29
Fast Buck	—	—	—	—	.29	.22
Outsmart Others	—	—	—	—	—	.27
Connections with Rackets	—	—	—	—	—	—

*The probability is less than 0.001 that any specific intercorrelation might occur by chance alone.

TABLE 3–16.

RELATIONSHIP BETWEEN PEER-VALUE INDEX AND BEHAVIOR SUMMARY, BY AGE (BOYS ONLY)

	Peer-Value Index					
Life-History	10–13 Years			14–19 Years		
Acts Reported	Low	Medium	High	Low	Medium	High
None	17%	4%	8%	4%	5%	3%
Lying Only	27	27	19	23	15	13
1	29	36	25	33	24	19
2–3	21	22	28	29	22	19
4+	6	10	19	12	34	47
N =	(48)	(67)	(36)	(52)	(41)	(32)

not materially affect the results. Closer analysis indicates that only about one-half of these boys can be classified as associating with hyperconformists (i.e., as having low peer-value scores), and that about one-fifth have peers with high deviant values (i.e., high peer-value scores). This indicates that as a group they cannot be dismissed merely as hyperconformists, as suggested by Dentler and Monroe.[24]

PEER VALUES AND INDIVIDUAL VALUES

Data support the expectation that a boy who chooses a deviant ability will be supported by peers who are attracted to similar values. Peer values appear to be shared values, since 50 percent of the boys who choose a deviant value associate with peers who are high in deviant values, as compared to 19 percent of the boys choosing good grades and 21 percent choosing job success. Age does not alter the relationship; even at the younger age-range (10–13 years), individuals choosing a deviant ability tend to associate with peers who share their values to a high degree.

Although the *proportion* of youths guided by conforming (individual) choices who score high on the peer-value index is much smaller than that of the deviant choosers, there appears to be a large *number* of these boys. If we compare the youths who are guided by conforming choices "now" but who were attracted to deviant abilities "two to three years ago" with boys in the stable conforming category, an interesting finding results. Boys who were attracted to a

deviant ability in the past on an individual basis but who now perceive themselves as conforming tend to continue their rejection of peers who are low on peer values (Table 3–17).

In their unwillingness to associate with boys who are low on peer values, these "reformed" deviants appear to stand midway between the stable conformers and the current deviants. The interpretation that youths tend to seek associates whose current individual values are similar to theirs should be amended to account for the influence of past values. Youths who held deviant values in the past probably associated with peers who shared those values; socialization through association with like-minded peers appears to influence choice of friends in the future —even though individual values may begin to change.

PEER VALUES AND POLICE CONTACT

As an important subcultural element, peer values could also be expected to be related to

[24]Robert A. Dentler and Laurence J. Monroe, "Early Adolescent Theft," *American Sociological Review* 26 (October, 1961): 733–44.

TABLE 3–17.

RELATIONSHIP BETWEEN INDIVIDUAL VALUE CHOICES AND PEER-VALUE INDEX (BOYS ONLY)

	Individual Value Choices		
Current Peer-Value Index	Stable Con-forming	Deviant 2–3 Years Ago, Con-forming Now	Deviant Now
	%	%	%
Low	46	23	10
Medium	37	45	38
High	17	32	52
N =	(185)	(47)	(41)

contacts with the police. Table 3–18 summarizes these findings by age for boys. The relationship between police contact and peer values is consistently large for the older boys, regardless of the measure of police contact used. For the younger boys the relationship is insignificant. Examining age differences in the consistency of peer-value patterns may help to account for age differences in the relationship between peer values and police contact.

AGE DIFFERENCES AND PEER-VALUE PATTERNS

All subcultural models appear to assume implicitly either (1) that adolescence is characterized by increased attraction to deviant values or (2) that adolescents are guided by new deviant values. The findings reported here indicate that adolescence is not characterized by growth in either individual or peer attraction to deviant values. The findings also indicate that the deviant values of adolescents are not new. In this respect, the findings are consonant with our knowledge that delinquency is not an exclusively adolescent phenomenon.

As we have pointed out, a major difference between adolescents and their younger counterparts is the greater propensity toward symbolic behavior and cognitive consistency with age. To be consonant with the findings concerning the greater relationship between values and indices of illegal behavior at the older age-range, there

should also be findings that values form a more consistent pattern during this developmental period. The evidence bears out this expectation, as well as clarifying the versatility-specialization issue.

In Table 3–15 findings were presented concerning the inter-item coefficients of peer values for all boys, regardless of age. In Table 3–19 the same items have been intercorrelated for boys, but with *age controlled*. At the younger age-range, all of the coefficients are in a positive direction, but only three of the six items can be regarded as forming a significant pattern. Starting with the highest intercorrelated items of "keep mouth shut to cops" and "hard and tough," the only other item associated with these two core values is enjoying "kicks." For the older boys, however, not only is the coefficient higher for every pair of items, but *all* of the coefficients are at least 0.29. Older boys are decidedly more consistent in their values shared with peers.

The greater consistency in value patterns at the older-age-range is consonant with the findings that age is related to an increase in the frequency of illegal behavior, the persistence of behavior patterns, the number of illegal acts, and the likelihood of police contact. The relative absence of peer-value specialization is also consonant with the versatile content of the behavior patterns. Viewed from the perspective of age-sequence, the fact that the peer values

TABLE 3–18.

RELATIONSHIP OF PEER-VALUE INDEX AND INDICES OF POLICE CONTACT,
BY AGE (BOYS ONLY)

Police-Contact Measures	Peer-Value Index					
	10–13 Years			14–19 Years		
	Low	Medium	High	Low	Medium	High
Presence in Police Files	8%	6%	6%	6%	20%	34%
Stopped by Police (Self-Reports)	6	6	11	10	15	31
Index of Police Contact*	10	13	14	12	29	50
$N =$	(48)	(67)	(36)	(52)	(41)	(32)

*The "index of police contact" refers to whether boys had an official record in the files of the New York City Police Department and/or admitted to having been stopped by the police for one of the self-report items. It therefore represents the sum of the two measures used with duplications eliminated.

TABLE 3–19.

PRODUCT-MOMENT CORRELATION COEFFICIENTS OF PEER VALUES FOR
TWO AGE-RANGES (BOYS ONLY)

	Keep Mouth Shut to Cops	Hard and Tough	Kicks	Fast Buck	Outsmart Others	Connections[*] with Rackets
	10–13 Years ($N = 151$)					
Keep Mouth Shut to Cops	—	.40	.31	.15	.21	.32
Hard and Tough	—	—	.27	.21	.12	.16
Kicks	—	—	—	.19	.23	.15
Fast Buck	—	—	—	—	.17	.33
Outsmart Others	—	—	—	—	—	.21
Connections with Rackets	—	—	—	—	—	—
	14–19 Years ($N = 125$)					
Keep Mouth Shut to Cops	—	.52	.39	.38	.30	.42
Hard and Tough	—	—	.46	.39	.42	.54
Kicks	—	—	—	.42	.40	.42
Fast Buck	—	—	—	—	.43	.46
Outsmart Others	—	—	—	—	—	.29
Connections with Rackets	—	—	—	—	—	—

[*]All coefficients with "Connections" employ a biserial coefficient because of the small numbers involved; the two categories are "lot-some" vs. "not at all."

refer to the *present* suggests that the behavior patterns are likely to be versatile in content *within a given age-period.*[25]

CONFORMING ABILITIES ADMIRED BY PEERS

On an *individual* level, the relative instability of deviant choices, as well as the dominant preferences for conforming abilities, indicates that adult-sponsored institutional areas are capable of attracting slum youths to a greater degree than values associated with illegal behavior.

On a *peer* level, the evidence is that deviant values are attractive to a majority of youths and their associates. Youths differed mainly on the

[25]A similar conclusion regarding behavior was reached by James F. Short, Jr., and Fred L. Strodtbeck, *Group Process and Gang Delinquency* (Chicago: University of Chicago Press, 1965), p. 13. Their studies of gangs in low-income areas of Chicago used reports of gang workers as primary sources of data. The respondents of our survey are also mainly lower-class youths; in addition, the sample included a variety of ethnic groups that could have yielded the Cloward-Ohlin ideal types. For a detailed discussion of the specialization issue, using the variables of argot, shared peer values, and ethnicity, see Lerman, "Argot, Symbolic Deviance, and Subcultural Delinquency," op. cit., pp. 218–20.

degree to which their friends emphasized these peer values. Analysis of peer support for conforming values reveals similar findings. Only 9 to 10 percent of the boys report that their friends are completely negative concerning school or work.

Cohen's contention that many slum boys are "ambivalent" toward—not alienated from—school and the job world is apparently closer to the mark than the position of any of the other theorists. However, Cohen underestimated the appeal and versatity of deviant values and failed to realize that they compete for the allegiance of pre-adolescent as well as older boys. An analysis of the interaction of peer orientations toward school and deviant values will suggest how this competition can be described.

Table 3–20 categorizes two age-groups of boys by their perception of their peers' admiration for good grades and their peer-value index scores. The responses of "some" and "not at all" were compared to the "a lot" responses. The school variable is treated as independent on the basis of the findings relating to value stability.

The table clearly reveals that association with

TABLE 3–20.

RELATIONSHIP OF PEER ADMIRATION OF
GOOD GRADES AND PEER-VALUE INDEX, BY AGE
(BOYS ONLY)

| Peer-Value Index | Good Grades Admired by Peers | | | |
| | 10–13 Years | | 14–19 Years | |
	A Lot	Ambiva-lent	A Lot	Ambiva-lent
Low	43%	21%	55%	27%
Medium	38	48	35	30
High	18	31	9	43
N =	(76)	(71)	(65)	(60)

TABLE 3–21.

RELATIONSHIP OF INDIVIDUAL VALUE
CHOICES AND PEER-VALUE INDEX FOR BOYS
WHOSE PEERS ADMIRE GOOD GRADES

| Peer-Value Index | Good Grades Admired by Peers | | | |
| | Conforming Individual Values | | Deviant Individual Values | |
	A Lot	Ambiva-lent	A Lot	Ambiva-lent
Low	55%	34%	28%	11%
Medium	36	37	41	43
High	9	29	31	46
N =	(109)	(73)	(32)	(56)

peers who are ambivalent toward the rewards of school is likely to lead to association with peers who are attracted to deviant values. Although the relationship is strong at both ages, there is a greater polarization of peer values at the older age range. Greater consistency among peer values is accompanied by increased consonance between deviant and ambivalent school values.

The importance of assessing the peer orientation toward school in depicting the distribution of peer-value index scores is further highlighted by considering the interaction effect of individual value choices (past and present) and peer orientations toward good grades. Peer orientation toward school is strongly related to both the individual and the peer indices of values.

Table 3–21 categorizes male youth by both classifications and their relationship to attraction toward shared deviant values (all ages included).

It is readily apparent that individual attraction to conforming values (past or present) is *not* the sole condition for the selection of friends who rank low on the peer-value index, but is coupled with association with peers who support attraction to school rewards. In contrast, individual attraction to conforming values, when coupled with association with peers who are ambivalent toward school rewards, yields a peer-value index profile similar to that yielded by a deviant individual choice plus association with peers who admire good grades.

Since individuals who chose a deviant ability were also rejecting a conforming ability (mainly

school), in a sense their association with peers who are ambivalent toward school provides support for their rejection of a conforming value. It is not surprising, therefore, that those who reject a conforming ability and associate with ambivalent peers are likely to have the highest score on the peer-value index. In the everyday world of competing values there tends to be an incompatibility between achievement and peer values.

In this section we have stressed the importance of peer support for school achievement in understanding the value competition confronting youth. Peer support for the job world does not seem to be so important, since boys with friends who admire the job world "a lot" are no less likely to be attracted to a deviant individual value (past/present) than are boys who see their peers as only slightly or not at all attracted to job success. Therefore, it appears safe to conclude that for boys in this sample, low admiration of the job world is probably not part of a *shared* outlook that encompasses deviant values. Low peer orientation toward good grades, on the other hand, tends to be a consistent part of a shared value orientation.

BELIEF IN PEER TEMPTATIONS AND
SHARED VALUES

The foregoing analyses have provided strong evidence that individual choices are associated with perception of peer values and hence that perceived peer orientations are likely to be shared by the respondents. Evidence was also presented that youth who score high on the peer-value index are likely to report the highest number of illegal acts, particularly at the older ages. In order to buttress the inference that associates of the respondents are likely to be providing behavioral as well as value support for the actions of individuals, we propose an additional line of analysis. Boys high on the peer-value index should be more likely to indicate agreement with the statement "Most people you know are tempted to break the law."

The data shown in Table 3–22 suggest that peer values are supportive of illegal behavior for friends as well as self. The relationship is consistent for all ages. It should also be noted that a majority of the "high" boys at both age-ranges believe that people they know are tempted to break the law. This suggests that boys sharing deviant values to a high degree are likely to perceive more lawbreaking and therefore believe that "most people" they know are tempted in this direction.

TABLE 3–22.

AGREEMENT WITH "MOST PEOPLE YOU KNOW ARE TEMPTED TO BREAK THE LAW," BY PEER-VALUE INDEX AND AGE (BOYS ONLY)

| Age | Peer-Value Index | | |
	Low	Med.	High
10–13 Years	29%	40%	58%
	N = (48)	(67)	(36)
14–19 Years	21%	44%	53%
	N = (52)	(41)	(32)

This belief may also be used as a "technique of neutralization" vis-à-vis official definers of illegal acts.[26] The fact that the belief is related to shared values indicates that it is supported by others and is therefore a "cultural construct." It is also probable that youth high on peer values would use this peer-supported means of warding off invidious definitions. The early appearance of this belief indicates that young boys are also perceiving illegal behavior. This supports the findings of early age of onset.

[26]See Matza and Sykes, op. cit.

SUMMARY AND CONCLUSIONS

In a pluralistic society, the worlds of school, work, and peers compete for the allegiance of youth; the consequences of this competition are relevant for understanding both individual value choices and shared peer values. The findings bearing on this competition among value orientations can be summarized as follows:

1. Although all youth report the ability to get good grades as the most important value choice both now and in the recent past, boys are less attracted to this conforming value than are girls, and they are more likely to be attracted to a deviant value.

2. Attraction to a deviant value begins early, increases at 12–13 years of age, and then may persist as a counter-attraction to school and work.

3. On an individual level, attraction to a deviant value is the least stable and is likely to shift to a conforming value.

4. With increasing age, the job world tends to replace school as the most stable value orientation.

5. There is a greater attraction to deviant values on a peer level than on an individual level; this attraction appears to be relatively constant for all ages, but it does not outrank attraction to good grades and the job world.

6. Youths attracted to a deviant value—either past or present—are most likely to seek out peers who are supportive of this orientation.

7. High admissions of life-history acts of misbehavior are most likely to occur among older boys (a) who are or have been attracted to a deviant value (and rejecting of school or work) and (b) whose associates support deviant values and are ambivalent toward good grades.

8. There are no new peer values in adolescence, nor is there an increase in attraction to peer values; rather, it is the increase in patterned consistency that distinguishes older from younger age-groups. This increased consistency in value patterns accounts in part for the relationship between age and illegal behavior.

9. With increased age, peer values that tend to be shared values are more likely to be a versatile than a specialized pattern; they also tend to symbolize masculine interests.

10. Ambivalent peer reactions toward good grades or the job world are related to high scores on the peer-value index, as well as to each other; analysis of the two conforming orientations discloses that reaction to school is more closely related to a shared value pattern.

11. Youths who share peer values are more likely to believe that most people they know are tempted to break the law. This suggests that peers lend behavioral as well as value support to one another.

These findings enable us to evaluate some of the descriptions posited by major theorists of delinquency. The data support Miller's contention that the focal concerns of lower-class youths are versatile in content and patterned with some differences by sex and age. Whatever the attractiveness of peer values in other strata of society, there is little doubt that slum youths perceive that their friends are attracted by an array of versatile deviant values. Miller's view of a distinctively lower-class culture is opened to doubt, however, by the reluctance of slum youth to publicly reject the values of school and work. Ambivalence toward good grades and the job world suggests that slum youths are not totally deaf to the messages of the dominant interest groupings; they appear to be more open to the blandishments of the job world, however, than to the attraction of school values.

Cohen's description of the delinquent subculture is correct in its emphasis on versatility but incorrect in specifying the content of the values that yield versatility. Only at the younger age-range is there an emphasis on toughness and non-utilitarian "kicks." At the older age-range, the subculture does not become specialized (as Cohen and Short posited in a later article); rather, there is a compatibility between "kicks" and utilitarian concerns (the "fast buck" and "connections") as well as inclusion of the rationalistic value of "outsmarting others." Since five of the six peer values are attractive in some degree to a majority of youths, it is *not* necessary to posit an opposition to middle-class values on the part of slum youths; nor is it necessary to assume that these youths share a similar means of defending themselves psychologically via a "reaction formation" against these values. Cohen, though, is the only theorist to stress correctly that slum youths are ambivalent, not rejecting, in their attitude toward the adult-dominated worlds of school and work.

Cloward and Ohlin utilize all of the value orientations in their tripartite typology but err. in assuming that youths are specialized in their value patterns. The compatibility of the various values at the older age-ranges suggests, in fact, that the orientation of youths becomes *more* versatile with age. The fact that increased consistency in the versatile value pattern leads to an increase in illegal behavior suggests, too, that this model's stress on explicit prescriptions in behalf of delinquent behavior is not necessary; attraction to peer values is a matter of degree, and these values are not explicitly illegal (except for connection with a racket). The alienation of their ideal role types is probably overdrawn, since slum youths are not openly rejecting of the worlds of school and work but ambivalent, differing from their conforming peers in degree rather than kind.

Matza and Sykes provide the broadest framework for understanding peer-value patterns. The nonconforming values they select are versatile and consistently patterned, particularly at the older age. However, they appear to underestimate the degree to which "subterranean values" are dominated by masculine interests and are therefore more likely to be shared by males than by females. It also seems likely that to regard these values as non-public may miss the point; these values *are* public for youth, but they are not the *ideal* values set forth by adult mentors. Matza and Sykes are supported in their views about shared techniques of neutralization; they appear to have erred, however, in believing that outright disdain for work is a necessary part of the pattern.

There are other sociologists, not treated at length in this article, whose theoretical perspectives fit in well with the lines of analysis pursued here. Bordua, an important critic of Cohen, Cloward-Ohlin, and Miller, exhibits a keen awareness of the usefulness of employing developmental differences and value competition.[27] He, too, is willing to entertain the idea

---

[27]David J. Bordua, "Some Comments on Theories of Group Delinquency," *Sociological Inquiry* 32

that peer values are potentially attractive to youngsters. Once this perspective is accepted, it is no longer necessary to posit that enactment of deviance must be preceded by a "tension state." Youthful sin, like youthful virtue, can also be fun.

The idea that values are in competition for the allegiance of youths is, of course, also compatible with classical culture-conflict theory.[28] However, in a traditional conflict of conduct codes, it appears that one of the codes *prescribes* explicitly illegal behavior while the other *proscribes* it. The peer values that we emphasize are not explicitly illegal; they do not require illegal behavior. Youngsters may "drift" in and out of delinquent episodes in the company of peers. Given an attraction to these values, situational variables—as described by Short and Strodtbeck—may play a critical role in triggering actual delinquent episodes.[29]

If there is a "pull" toward the "garden-variety" values of toughness, kicks, and making a fast buck, then the search for evidence of "reaction formations" and "strains" may be futile. We might more profitably address the conditions that make these kinds of values so attractive that linquistic and behavioral deviance will occur with a greater frequency. Toby has highlighted one condition that is quite congruent with our data: youth who are unwilling or unable to maintain a consistent commitment to achieving success in school are most likely to be unduly attracted to realizing peer values.[30] Efforts to understand how this adult-sponsored commitment is effectively transmitted and supported could add to our knowledge of all youth, not just the wayward and the disadvantaged.

(Spring, 1962): 245-60; and "Delinquent Subcultures: Sociological Interpretations of Gang Delinquency," *Annals* 338 (November, 1961): 119-36.

[28]See Solomon Kobrin, "The Conflict of Values in Delinquency Areas," *American Sociological Review* 16 (October, 1951): 653-61; and Thorsten Sellin, *Culture Conflict and Crime* (New York: Social Science Research Council, 1938).

[29]James F. Short, Jr., and Fred L. Strodtbeck, op. cit., pp. 185-98 and 248-64.

[30]Jackson Toby's work has consistently had this kind of focus. See the following: Larry Karacki and Jackson Toby, "The Noncommitted Adolescent: Candidate for Gang Socialization," *Sociological Inquiry* 32 (Spring, 1962): 203-15; Jackson Toby and Marcia L. Toby, "Low School Status as a Predisposing Factor in Subcultural Delinquency," mimeographed (New Brunswick, N.J.: Rutgers University, n.d.); Jackson Toby, "Hoodlum or Businessman: An American Dilemma," in *The Jews: Social Patterns of an American Group*, ed. Marshall Sklare (New York: The Free Press, 1958), pp. 540-50; and Jackson Toby, "Affluence and Adolescent Crime," in *Task Force Report: Juvenile Delinquency and Youth Crime*, President's Committee on Law Enforcement and Administration of Justice (Washington, D.C.: Government Printing Office, 1967), Appendix H, pp. 132-45. For a discussion of the work of Toby, see Lerman, *Issues in Subcultural Delinquency*, op. cit., chaps. 8, 9.

B. FACTORS OF FAMILY, RACE, RESIDENCE, SCHOOL, SOCIOECONOMIC STATUS, AND THEIR INTERACTION

EDITOR'S INTRODUCTION

Papers in this section, as noted earlier, emphasize the empirical relationship of background and situational factors to *individual delinquency*. While the majority of the papers in Chapter III Section A focused on theoretical matters, the majority of the papers in this section are tied to data. This distinction does, it seems, reflect a general difference, in the literature, in the manner in which social scientists have approached subcultural and individual delinquency.

The first paper, by Rodman and Grams, considers both the sociological and psychiatric-psychological aspects of the family's role in delinquency. For example, these authors consider one of the central sociological interests: the structure of the family (including broken homes, ordinal position, family size), as well as the psychiatric-psychological literature on maternal deprivation, parental discipline, and parental affection. These authors (Rodman and Grams) also consider research on the interaction of social class and family variables as they relate to delinquency.

The next paper in this section, by Gilbert Geis, suggests that crime statistics possess serious shortcomings—a point made earlier in the paper by Wheeler. Geis adds, however, that the introduction of racial and ethnic categories both compounds these statistical errors and induces antagonism between law enforcement agencies and minority groups.

Following the paper by Geis is one by Reiss and Rhodes on the relationship between ascribed social status and juvenile delinquency. For court-adjudicated delinquents, these authors state that both the social status structure of a residential area and the extent to which delinquency occurs as a cultural tradition affect the life-chances that a boy will be delinquent at all social status levels. When self-reports were employed, Reiss and Rhodes report that the career oriented delinquent was found only among lower class boys.

The next paper, by Robert Stanfield, employing data from the Cambridge-Somerville Study, reports on the author's analysis of the relationship between the family and the gang in the etiology of delinquency. Stanfield found that low social status, erratic or lax discipline by the boy's father, and frequent peer activity were all substantially and statistically related to delinquent status. As a result of his further analysis of the relationship of these three variables to delinquency, Stanfield suggests that predictions based on both interaction and additive effects might be more efficient than predictions based solely on additive effects.

The two papers by Ralph England and by Jackson Toby deal, respectively, with the issue of middle class delinquency and with the role which affluence (in industrial societies) plays in adolescent crime. England's paper echoes suggestions by Wolfgang that subcultural values are related to parent culture values and by Bordua that such youth values often lead to hedonistic or fun-oriented behavior. Toby's paper deals with the fact that crime rates are apparently rising as rapidly in affluent countries as in poor countries. Toby suggests that the resentment of poverty is likely to be greater among the relatively poor in a rich country than among the poor in a poor society. He employs this idea quite creatively in focusing on adolescent crime. He gives considerable attention as well to the fact that, in industrial societies, more youths remain in school rather than go to work, suggesting that staying in school has an inhibiting effect on delinquent activities.

Toby's notion that schooling may tend to depress delinquency rates in industrial society can be compared with the suggestion presented in the excerpts from a paper by Walter Schafer and Kenneth Polk in the next selection: that school conditions often contribute to delinquency. In an interesting long paper which was too lengthy to be reproduced here Schafer and Polk suggest that the way the school reacts to students who get into trouble, the attitudes of teachers and school officials to the learning ability of lower class and of black youth, the irrelevancy of much of the instruction, the use of testing and tracking systems, inappropriateness of teaching methods and the inadequacy of compensatory education are among the school factors which contribute to school failure and to delinquency.

The paper by Erdman Palmore and Phillip Hammond, like the one by Stanfield, also deals with interacting factors in delinquency. In considering the effects of legitimate and illegitimate opportunity structures discussed by Cloward and Ohlin, they include school performance among the relevant variables. Other factors which they include are race, sex, family deviance, and neighborhood deviance.

In their paper, Jon Simpson and Maurice Van Arsdol, Jr., continue this examination of the role of school performance in delinquency. In addition they consider the interaction of residential mobility, educational achievement, and delinquency.

The following paper, by Kenneth Polk, considers the relationship between the economic characteristics of urban areas and the ecological distribution of delinquency. Polk, in this paper, addresses himself to an exploration of the reasons behind the lack of such relationships reported in various studies of urban areas, and draws on data from Portland, Oregon, in his discussion.

The final paper in this section, by Charles Willie, also employs ecological data. The author considers the interaction effects of family stability and economic status for white and non-white areas (with respect to delinquency rates) in Washington, D.C. Like Polk, Willie concludes on the basis of his analysis that not only are the economic characteristics of urban areas related to the ecological distribution of delinquency, but also that economic status and family stability make joint contributions to the delinquency rate.

22.

HYMAN RODMAN AND PAUL GRAMS

FAMILY AND DELINQUENCY

Much research has been done by sociologists, psychologists, and psychiatrists concerning the relationship between family and delinquency variables, and many theories have been advanced to explain the relationships found. Due to a severe lack of interdisciplinary communication, however, few attempts have been made to consider both the sociological and psychiatric-psychological aspects of the family's role in delinquency. Axelrad (1965) has pointed to this problem and argued that sociologists should include psychological variables in their studies, in order to provide a more complete analysis of delinquency causation. He comments on the limitations sociological studies incur by not considering the psychic motivations toward deviancy, the internal dynamics of the delinquent, and his family relations. In this context, it is interesting to note that most sociological studies of the family and delinquency have dealt with the outward structure of the family—whether or not it is broken, how large it is, etc.—and most psychiatric studies have dealt with the internal mechanisms of family relationships as they have been uncovered in clinical treatment.

In order to present a more integrated picture of theory and research about the family and delinquency, we will first consider the empirical findings relating to family structure and juvenile delinquency, and then discuss the various sociological and psychiatric theories which relate to the data.

BROKEN HOMES AND DELINQUENCY

One facet of family structure which has been the subject of many studies is the broken home. Some researchers have found a very high incidence of broken homes among delinquents and have attributed much significance to broken homes as a cause of delinquency. Others have given less direct emphasis to the importance of broken homes and have suggested that the broken home may have a differential effect by variables such as sex, area, or family cohesiveness. The controversy over the effect of broken homes on delinquency began with a paper published by Shaw and McKay (1932), in which they concluded from a study of Chicago school boys and juvenile court cases that only slightly more broken homes appeared in the delinquent group than in the control group (42 percent : 36 percent) and the correlation between high delinquency rate areas and high broken home rate areas was small. The data they presented contradicted several earlier studies, especially one by Burt (1925) in London which had found delinquents coming from broken homes twice as often as nondelinquents.

Shaw and McKay's study was criticized as unrepresentative, since it made no attempt to discover delinquents in the control group, and refutations of it soon appeared. A study by Weeks and Smith (1939) in Spokane, Washington, found that 41.4 percent of the delinquents and only 26.7 percent of the controls came from broken homes; their correlation between delinquency and broken homes by area was considerably higher than Shaw and McKay's. Eleanor and Sheldon Glueck (1950), in their monumental study of 500 matched pairs of delinquents and nondelinquents, found 60.4 percent of the delinquents and 34.2 percent of the nondelinquents with broken homes in their backgrounds. More recently, Monahan (1957) reported that delinquents coming from broken homes were more likely to be recidivists than delinquents from unbroken homes. Browning

SOURCE: Hyman Rodman and Paul Grams, "Family and Delinquency," 1967 *President's Commission on Law Enforcement and Administration of Justice: Task Force Report on Juvenile Delinquency and Youth Crime* (Washington, D.C.: Government Printing Office), pp. 195–202 and 209–11.

(1960) found significantly greater numbers of Los Angeles delinquents coming from "disorganized" homes. Slocum and Stone (1963), using the Nye-Short self-report delinquency technique, found a significant correlation between broken homes and delinquent-type behavior. Peterson and Becker (1965) have referred to other studies that have also found a relationship between broken homes and delinquency.

Many researchers, however, have indicated that broken homes have a differential effect upon children—that the delinquency-producing effect is higher for preadolescents than adolescents and for property offenders than authority offenders. Early studies by Barker (1940) and Weeks and Smith (1939) found significant variations in the correlations between delinquency rates and broken home rates among different areas of a community, and there is similar evidence on rural-urban differences in a study by Ferdinand (1964). But the most common observation about the differential effect of the broken home has been that delinquent girls come from broken homes more often than delinquent boys. An early study by Hodgkiss (1933), which repeated Shaw and McKay's Chicago study on delinquency and broken homes using girls instead of boys, found that 66.8 percent of delinquent girls came from broken homes compared to 44.8 percent of the school girls. Hodgkiss' ratio of 1.49 to 1, delinquent girls to school girls, is considerably higher than the ratio computed by Shaw and McKay (1932) for boys, 1.18 to 1. Wattenberg and Saunders (1954), studying Detroit juvenile delinquents, also found a greater percentage of delinquent girls as compared to delinquent boys coming from broken homes. Monahan (1957) reported much the same results for Philadelphia delinquents—55.4 percent of white girls and 74.3 percent of Negro girls coming from broken homes, compared to 32.2 and 57.9 percent of white and Negro boys, respectively.

Jackson Toby (1957b) has reviewed some of the literature on the differential impact of broken homes, and his paper adds a good deal of clarity to the findings. For example, he introduces age as a differential variable in order to explain the apparent discrepancies between the data of Shaw and McKay and others. He points out that while Shaw and McKay found little overall difference between their delinquent group and control group in the percentage of broken homes, some differences do show up when controlling for age. The delinquents were considerably older than the control group, and it turns out that at the older age groups there is little difference between delinquents and controls in the rate of broken homes, while in the younger age groups there is a good deal of difference. Toby reasons that well-integrated American families generally have less control over their older, adolescent sons. As a result, family disorganization (broken homes) would have its greatest impact upon younger, preadolescent sons, where the well-integrated family could generally exert greater control. Toby's data lend support to the hypothesis of differential impact with age, and a similar differential effect was observed by Lees and Newson (1954) in their study of British delinquents.

Toby also applies the same reasoning to account for the differential impact of broken homes on boys and girls—in general the family exercises more control over girls, hence they are more affected by a broken home. Toby presents data showing that, as predicted, the impact of broken homes is greater for girls than for adolescent boys, and further, that urban areas and Negroes, assumed to be more characterized by family disorganization, have a disproportionate number of female (and preadolescent) delinquents. But Toby does not have data on types of offenses, and it appears that the relationship between sex and rate of broken homes is eliminated when one controls for type of offense. Weeks (1940), for example, suggested that the differential effect of broken homes on boys and girls was due to their differential distribution according to type of offense—most girls are arrested for ungovernability, running away, and sex offenses, while most boys are arrested for vandalism, theft, and assault. Testing his theory on Spokane, Washington, delinquents, Weeks found that when type of offense is held constant, delinquent boys and girls come from broken homes in nearly the same proportions. Other studies, by Nye (1958) using his self-report delinquency scale, and Ferdinand (1964) using

Michigan court data, have also shown that broken home rates vary according to the type of delinquency, being higher for "authority" offenses such as ungovernability and truancy.

ORDINAL POSITION, FAMILY SIZE, AND DELINQUENCY

Another aspect of family structure which has often been related to delinquency is the ordinal position of the child in the family. Lees and Newson (1954) made an extensive study of the differences among delinquents which could be attributed to sibling position. Their study showed that intermediates—children having both older and younger siblings—were significantly over-represented in a group of Nottingham, England, delinquents. The explanation they gave for their findings is that the attention parents often give to oldest and youngest children "squeezes" the intermediates out of the family into the gang. Their study has received some support from the findings of both Nye (1958) and the Gluecks (1950). Nye found both the youngest and inter-mediate children overrepresented in his "most delinquent" group. The Gluecks found that 60 percent of their delinquents were intermediate children, compared to only 47.8 percent of their control group. Thus, there would seem to be greater involvement of middle children in delin-quent activities.

Family size has also been cited as a factor which can differentiate between delinquents and nondelinquents, with delinquents seen as more likely to come from larger families. The Gluecks' study gave definite evidence of this, finding that there was a significant difference between a mean of 6.85 children in the delinquents' fam-ilies and 5.90 in the nondelinquents' families. Nye's "most delinquent" boys were also more often from large families, but he found no such relationship for girls.

This differential in the relationship between family size and delinquency is not restricted to sex differences. Several writers have suggested that large families may have a varying relation-ship to different types of delinquent offenses. Barker and Adams (1963), for example, report a greater incidence of large families in the back-ground of a group of juvenile glue sniffers than

in a control group taken from the general popu-lation of a Colorado correctional institution. Over 50 percent of the glue sniffers came from families with more than eight children, compared to 18 percent in the control group. Furthermore, a study by Reiss (1952) of delinquents exam-ined by psychiatrists attached to the Cook Coun-ty Juvenile Court showed that the psychiatric classifications—integrated, weak ego, weak super-ego—also differentiated the delinquents accord-ing to family size. A greater proportion of weak superego delinquents came from large families.

MATERNAL DEPRIVATION AND DELINQUENCY

One aspect of family structure which has re-ceived a great deal of attention, especially from psychiatrists, is that of mother separation—the absence of the mother for a prolonged period of time when the child is young. Although mother separation is generally regarded as a cause of mental illness, one British psychiatrist, John Bowlby, has also attempted to demonstrate its connection with juvenile delinquency. Studying a group of thieves and controls chosen from pa-tients at a child guidance center, Bowlby (1952) found significantly more mother separation among all the thieves, and the statistical signifi-cance is even more pronounced among those thieves he classified as "affectionless"—children who were unable to enter into a deep affec-tionate relationship with anyone. Other studies, of course, have also shown the association be-tween maternal deprivation and an inability to enter an affectionate relationship (Goldfarb, 1943).

Bowlby, however, has been criticized by sev-eral investigators for putting too much emphasis on a factor which is often outweighed by others in the process of delinquency causation. Naess (1959), for instance, in her detailed commen-tary on Bowlby's efforts, accepts the relationship between mother separation and mental illness, but criticizes Bowlby for generalizing from his limited data on thieves in a psychiatric clinic to his thesis that mother separation is an impor-tant cause of juvenile delinquency generally. Furthermore, she presents evidence from a study of Oslo delinquents and their nondelinquent brothers that no such relationship exists. Robert G. Andry (1957, 1962), the most insistent critic of Bowlby's theory, is unhappy with the emphasis Bowlby gives to the part that mother separation plays in the etiology of delinquency, explaining that the role of the father is of at least equal importance. Michael Hakeem (1958) makes a devastating evaluation of Bowlby's study, criticizing it for a lack of scientific sophistication, for generalizing too much from limited data, and for not attempting to eliminate possible diagnostic biases by proper scientific methods.

In addition, Bowlby also theorized that the younger a child was when he was separated from his mother, the more unfortunate were the effects of that separation; but both Nye (1958) and the Gluecks (1950) found that the child's age at the time of the first break in his home bore no relationship to delinquency. Bowlby's theory of maternal deprivation and delinquency therefore lacks strongly supportive evidence. Maternal deprivation may very well be causally related to delinquency but it is not "foremost among the causes of delinquent character development." (1952, p. 34.) Bowlby himself (Bowlby et al., 1956, p. 242) now speaks more cautiously about the consequences of maternal deprivation.

FAMILY INTERRELATIONSHIPS, FAMILY ADJUSTMENT, AND DELINQUENCY

Studies which have focused upon the internal structure of the family have generally shown greater associations with delinquency than studies focusing upon outward structure. This has led Nye to comment, on the basis of his extensive study of juvenile delinquency, that "the structure of the family 'itself' does not cause delinquency." (1958, p. 34.) Similarly, Browning has concluded, after his study of legally and psychologically broken homes in Los Angeles, that the "broken home, as generally defined, is ineffective and probably meaningless as an indicator of family disorganization and other characteristics of family life known to be associated with deviant behavior. It does not include all homes which are sociologically and psychologically broken nor exclude homes which

are well integrated." (1960, p. 43.) McCord and McCord (1959) have indeed shown that quarrelsome and negligent homes lead to more delinquency than broken homes. Nevertheless, we must be careful not to discount the possible influence of a factor like broken homes. As Hirschi and Selvin (1966) have ably documented, it may be true that a broken home is not a sufficient cause of delinquency; it may also be true that other variables are more strongly related to delinquency than broken homes; but such reasons do not permit us to conclude that broken homes are not causally related to delinquency. As a result, we must use statements such as those by Nye and Browning to alert us to the fact that variables measuring the quality of family relationships may be more important in the etiology of delinquency than variables measuring the outward structure of the family, and not to conclude that the latter variables are of no causal importance.

One of the most important aspects of family relations, closely related to the concept of broken or unbroken homes, is the quality of parental marital adjustment. Browning (1960) dealt with marital adjustment and family solidarity and found that both of these bore a significant relationship to truancy and auto theft, the two types of delinquency he studied. Nye (1958) reported a very strong association between his self-report delinquency scale and the marital happiness of the child's parents. Among boys and girls from "completely happy" homes—23 and 22 percent, respectively, were "most delinquent"; from "unhappy homes"—46 and 49 percent. The Gluecks (1950), in their research, found that significantly more delinquents than nondelinquents had parents with poor conjugal relations (31.2 percent : 14.9 percent). They also found that marked family cohesiveness was present in 61.8 percent of the nondelinquents' homes but in only 16 percent of the delinquents'. Slocum and Stone (1963), in a self-report study of Washington State schoolchildren, report that 52 percent of the "most delinquent" boys called their families uncooperative, compared to 16 percent of the boys in the "conformist" category. The same relationship, although less pronounced, existed for girls. Dentler and Monroe (1961) report that adolescent theft is related to the "quality of interpersonal relations" in the family. Furthermore, Jaffe (1963) found that family "anomie," measured by the amount of disagreement within the family on selected value questions, was correlated with a high score on a "delinquency proneness" scale. In all of these studies, therefore, we find that reported variables such as marital adjustment, family agreement, and family solidarity are significantly related to measures of juvenile delinquency.

PARENTAL DISCIPLINE AND DELINQUENT BEHAVIOR

Probably even more important a factor than parental marital relations in delinquency causation is the quality of parent-child relations. The consistency, "fairness," and strictness of parental discipline are among the most important family variables related to delinquent behavior. As Peterson and Becker (1965) say, "If one endorses the common assumption that capacities for internal control are complexly but closely related to previously imposed external restraints, then parental discipline assumes focal significance as a factor in delinquency."

In the Slocum and Stone study (1963), reported fairness of discipline was significantly associated with conforming behavior for boys and for girls. Nye (1958) found that of the children in his study who considered their father's discipline "always fair," only 30 percent of the boys and 20 percent of the girls fell into the "most delinquent" category, while of those who felt their father's discipline was unfair, 55 percent of the boys and 44 percent of the girls fell into the "most delinquent" category. Nye also showed that a relationship existed for girls with regard to the strictness of the mother's discipline, with reported strictness being related to less delinquency.

The Gluecks (1950) found that lax and erratic disciplinary techniques identified a higher percentage of delinquents than did overstrict techniques, and that firm but kindly techniques were practiced much more frequently by the parents of the nondelinquents. McCord and Mc-Cord (1959), reviewing the information collected by the Cambridge-Somerville project, concluded that consistent discipline by both parents,

whether punitive or love oriented, significantly reduced delinquency. Nye (1958) found that 49 percent of both the boys and girls who reported that their mothers "very often" failed to follow through on threatened punishment were in the "most delinquent" category, compared to 30 percent of the boys and 22 percent of the girls who reported that their mother "never" failed to follow through. The overall relationship is significant for girls but not significant for boys.

Exploring the tendencies for parents to use physical punishment rather than reasoning as a disciplinary method, the Gluecks (1950) found that significantly more parents of delinquents than nondelinquents (mothers, 55.6:34.6 percent; fathers, 67.8:34.7 percent) resorted to physical punishment for discipline, while significantly more parents in the control group than in the delinquent group used reasoning (mothers, 28.2:16.4 percent; fathers, 24.4:11.3 percent). Nye (1958), on the other hand, found no relationship between physical punishment and delinquent behavior. He did, however, find a positive relationship between delinquency and love withdrawal as a disciplinary technique, although this relationship seemed to disappear when the adolescents' feelings of acceptance-rejection were taken into consideration. For example, Nye showed that love withdrawal by mothers made no difference among adolescents when one controlled for their feelings of acceptance or rejection. Since many studies have found a relationship between types of discipline and measures of delinquency, Nye's findings are worth noting. It must be remembered, however, that Nye's study also failed to show the usual relationship between delinquency and low socioeconomic status. Furthermore, Kohn (1963) has questioned the association of class with types of punishment.

In short, the data suggest that the consistency of discipline and its fairness are importantly related to nondelinquency. It must be noted, however, that most of these studies (the report by McCord and McCord, 1959, is a significant exception) are based upon the perception and recollection of delinquents and controls. It is therefore possible that delinquents and controls perceive their parental discipline differently despite similarities in disciplinary techniques; it is also possible that the actual differences in disciplinary techniques are due to the parents' differential responses to delinquent and nondelinquent behavior, such behavior having been triggered by other variables.

A. H. Maslow and R. Diaz-Guerrero (1960) have pointed to another way in which parental roles and the cultural support for discipline may play a part in the etiology of delinquency. Comparing Mexico and the United States, they suggest that delinquency is much more common in the United States (definitive evidence is lacking, however) despite the greater incidence of poverty and family disorganization in Mexico. They attribute this difference to the fact that parental roles within the family, especially the father's role, are clear cut in Mexico, but muddled in the United States. Mexican children are brought up understanding quite clearly the differences between "right" and "wrong," and the father's authoritative and disciplinary role, which the mother supports, fosters the development of strong internal controls in the child which reduce his delinquency. The American father, on the other hand, is faced with a larger number of available roles—friendly, authoritarian, democratic, lenient—and he receives less support from his wife in carrying out his role. As a result, there is more role confusion by the father in the United States, and this creates uncertainty in his children about approved and disapproved behavior. This uncertainty about values, Maslow and Diaz-Guerrero assert, plays a major part in the delinquency of United States adolescents.

AFFECTION, REJECTION, AND DELINQUENCY

A second aspect of parent-child relations which is often associated with juvenile delinquency is a lack of parental affection. The Gluecks (1950) reported that all the affectional patterns of a home—mother-child, father-child, child-parent, and child-child—bore a highly significant relationship to juvenile delinquency. The most important factor, however, seemed to be the father's affection for the boy—40.2 percent of the delinquents but 80.7 percent of the controls had affectionate fathers. Andry (1957) reported a similar finding in his study of London delinquents and schoolboys, with 54 percent of his delinquents but only 7 percent of his controls expressing the opinion that their fathers ought to love them more. Slocum and Stone (1963) found that 52 percent of the boys in their "delinquent" group came from unaffectionate families, compared to only 18 percent in the "conformist" group. Nye (1958), choosing acceptance-rejection rather than affection as a variable, found a significant positive correlation between the parents' rejection of their child and the child's delinquency. When mutual rejection between mother and child occurred, 48 percent of the group fell into the "most delinquent" category; with mutual acceptance, 14 percent. McCord and McCord (1964) found that the presence of at least one loving parent, coupled with consistent parental discipline, was enough to mitigate the delinquency-producing effect of a criminal father. More generally, they report that both paternal rejection and the absence of maternal warmth were significantly related to delinquency.

The interplay of affection and discipline in parent-child relationships has been cited by Weinberg (1958) as most important in affecting the personality of the child and predisposing him to select delinquent associates and participate in delinquency. He quotes the Gluecks' study for evidence and then says that the parents of delinquents by "indifference or hostility hindered their children from acquiring positive attitudes toward authority." (1958, pp. 126–127.) Clark and Wenninger's self-report study (1964) of Illinois schoolchildren's attitudes toward the law provides indirect evidence for such a supposition. They found that favorable attitudes toward legal institutions were more closely related to adjustment to maternal and paternal discipline than to social class factors.

Furthermore, Nye (1958) found a strong relationship between the child's acceptance of parental values and the affection of the parent for the child. Finally, the longitudinal data reported by McCord and McCord (1964) show an interesting interaction effect between discipline and affection. With two loving parents, the type of discipline used has no effect upon the delinquency of sons; but with one loving parent, erratic or lax discipline produces significantly more delinquency than consistent discipline.

One way in which child-rearing practices are seen to have an influence upon delinquency is through fostering the development of an aggressive personality. Studying a group of aggressive delinquents and their families, and comparing them to a group of nondelinquent controls and their families, Albert Bandura and Richard H. Walters (1958, 1959) found that a higher proportion of the parents of the aggressive boys had denied the boys an opportunity to express dependency feelings. Parental punishment of the boys' strivings for dependency gratification, a form of parental rejection, was significantly higher for the group of delinquent boys. Bandura and Walters went on to show that adolescents whose dependency needs had not been met were also less likely to internalize their parents' standards and values. Becker (1964), reviewing the various studies dealing with the personality consequences of different types of child-rearing practices, put Bandura and Walters' findings in a wider context and showed them to be consistent with several other studies.

The importance of affection within the family thus emerges as an important factor in relation to delinquency. The findings of a number of studies point to the significant differences between delinquent and nondelinquent groups in terms of the patterns of affection within the family. In addition, several studies point out that affection is related to the child's internalization of parental values. Assuming that parental values support conventional rather than deviant behavior, it appears that an affectionate parent-child relationship promotes the internalization of conventional values and thus insulates a child against delinquent behavior. Of course, affectionate family patterns may also operate in other ways to reduce delinquent behavior.

SOME PSYCHIATRIC THEORIES OF DELINQUENCY

The problem of relating the wealth of available data on the association between family variables and juvenile delinquency has been approached theoretically in many ways. Psychiatrists, psychologists, and sociologists have all tried their hand at explaining the connection, with differing degrees of success. We will start our discussion by reviewing several psychiatric theories of delinquency.

One theory, the "superego lacunae" theory put forward by Adelaide M. Johnson (1949), considers only the delinquencies "arising in 'apparently normal families of good reputation' unassociated with the influence of sociologic gangs." She suggests that inconsistent discipline in many middle class families deprives children of an important part of their security (Johnson and Burke, 1955). Furthermore, this inconsistency is often the manner in which parents unconsciously foster delinquency in their children. These children grow up with gaps or lacunae in their superego, and play a scapegoat role in their families—the parents project their own problems onto their child, and derive vicarious pleasure from the child's delinquency.

Although the theory may have some validity when it is limited to middle class nongang delinquents, other psychiatrists have extended it almost beyond reason. Ruth S. Eissler (1949), for instance, claimed that not only do the parents of delinquents need and foster delinquency in their children, but also that the whole society needs and fosters such delinquency, as a societal scapegoat. Matza and Sykes (1961) have suggested that many of the values held by delinquents are actually subterranean values held by certain segments of society; but Eissler's extreme position claims that society needs criminal or delinquent scapegoats, that it seduces individuals into delinquent behavior, and that it interferes with programs which promise to prevent delinquency.

Hakeem (1958) has pointed to several weaknesses of the "superego lacunae" theory. He points out that no experimental or predictive studies have tested it and that no scientific evidence has been put forth to support it. It is merely based upon case studies that have been presented by the theorists. Moreover, these case histories usually deal with emotionally disturbed children whose delinquency is a secondary problem.

David Abrahamsen (1949, 1960) has presented another theoretical view of the connection between the family and crime or juvenile delinquency. According to him all delinquents are emotionally disturbed, and their disturbance results from tensions in the family. Although his position has changed somewhat between 1949 and 1960 so that he acknowledges multiple factors in the causation of delinquency and crime, he still stresses deformed character structure as a basic causal factor, whether dealing with individual delinquents or gang delinquents, lower class delinquents or middle class delinquents. There is little evidence to support his position, however. The Gluecks (1950), for instance, found only 36 psychopaths in their group of 500 delinquents. This finding hardly supports the statement, as Abrahamsen (1960, p. 82) suggests it does, that "basically the persistent juvenile delinquent has a deformed character structure." Furthermore, Abrahamsen's own evidence in support of his theory about family tension and emotional disturbance is sketchy and unconvincing. He refers to a comparative study he made of 100 criminals and 100 non-criminals who needed treatment. Using data from psychiatric interviews with the criminals and the controls, along with Rorschach tests administered to 31 criminals and 29 of their family members, he concluded that there was much more family tension in the criminal group than in the control group; moreover, he found that criminals always manifested emotional disturbance. Unfortunately, the author worked with knowledge of who was in the delinquent group and control group; he did not attempt to collect similar information from the two groups; and the representativeness of these clinical groups leaves something to be desired. Finally, the author's acknowledgment that some differences between the groups were not easy to detect except through skilled interviewing and interpretation necessarily puts us on guard about the possible operation of subjective bias.

In general it can be said of the psychiatric theories of delinquency that they are based almost entirely on the subjective clinical experience of the theoretician rather than on objective evidence. Furthermore, they probably apply mainly to that small proportion of the delinquent population which can be termed "psychopathic." Estimates differ on the size of this "psychopathic" group, usually depending upon the diagnostic methods and categories used. As examples, the Gluecks (1950) report 7 percent of their delinquents have serious personality disorders while Reiss (1952) reports over 20 percent with some degree of pathology.

CONTAINMENT AND CONTROL THEORIES

The other set of theories dealing directly with the family and delinquency is sociological in nature, and describes the family's main function as one of control—preventing the child, directly and indirectly, from participating in delinquent acts. Albert J. Reiss, Walter C. Reckless, and F. Ivan Nye are the main proponents of these control theories, but numerous others have also contributed to this line of theoretical development.

Reiss (1951) hypothesized that delinquency is likely to result when personal and social controls break down. He distinguished between delinquent recidivists and nonrecidivists on the basis of various indicators of primary group controls, community and institutional controls, and personal controls. Family's socioeconomic status, parental income, parents' marital status and adjustment, and parental moral ideals and techniques of discipline were used as indicators of primary group controls. The amount of delinquency in the neighborhood, measures of school adjustment, family home ownership, and residential stability were used as indicators of community controls. Finally, psychiatric and casework diagnoses and treatment recommendations were used to classify delinquents as exhibiting either relatively strong ego or superego control, or relatively weak ego or superego control. All of these variables were significantly associated with probation outcome, but the most efficient predictor variables turned out to be the "measures of the adequacy of personal controls of the individual and his relation to social controls in terms of the acceptance of or submission to social control" (1951, p. 206).

Nye (1958) proposed a theory quite similar to Reiss' and then tested it using extensive data from a self-report delinquency study. He suggested that four attitude and behavior patterns are influential in controlling juvenile delinquency: "(1) Direct control imposed from without by means of restriction and punishment, (2) internalized control exercised from within through conscience, (3) indirect control related to affectional identification with parents and other noncriminal persons, and (4) availability of alternative means to goals and values" (1958, p. 5).

Nye differs from Reiss in two important ways. First, he introduces the concept of indirect control, which he defines as the consideration adolescents show their parents or other adults by avoiding activities that would embarrass them. This indirect control is based on an affectional relationship between the adolescent and the adult involved. Nye tested this aspect of control by examining the mutual acceptance-rejection pattern between parents and children. He found an orderly progression from least to most delinquency as the acceptance-rejection matrix went from mutual acceptance to mutual rejection.

Secondly, Nye indicates that adolescents may be motivated toward delinquent behavior because such behavior satisfies certain of their needs. He cites William I. Thomas' list of four needs as good examples of the type that may motivate delinquents: affection, recognition, security, and new experiences. Thus, Nye takes psychological motivations for delinquent behavior into account. In this he differs from most other containment theorists; but he nevertheless does propose that in the absence of controls every child would be "delinquent."

Reckless (1961), in the third edition of *The Crime Problem*, reviewed the work of both Nye (1958) and Reiss (1951), and then, citing work by himself (1956) and by Redl and Wineman (1951), developed his own theory of social and personal control, which he terms "containment theory." He pointed to social disorganization—living in a slum or high-delinquency area or being an immigrant or migrant—as the breakdown of social controls and a cause of delinquency. The absence of effective discipline was an indicator of family disorganization and another form of social control failure. But most of Reckless' emphasis is concerned with the factor of inner control, the development of a child's self-concept and superego. He and various associates have made intensive longitudinal studies of boys in a high delin-

quency slum area who do not become delinquent (Dinitz, et al., 1962; Reckless, et al., 1956; Scarpitti, et al., 1960; Simpson, et al., 1960). These boys, chosen by their teachers, were compared over a period of years with a group of delinquents. The "good" boys, Reckless concluded, were marked especially by an excellent self-concept—they evaluated their families favorably; they evaluated their school experiences favorably; and they were confident of their ability to stay out of trouble.

Reckless also showed how the extensive work reported by Redl and Wineman (1951) on ego and superego development fits in with the "inner control" part of his containment theory. An adequate ego and superego, lacking in the young, hyperaggressive delinquents Redl studied, were considered by Redl to be necessary for good behavior control. Reckless suggests that Redl's psychiatric formulation is equivalent to his own formulation of inner control based upon a good self-concept. Thus, Reckless attempted to show that "containment theory" is amenable to certain psychiatric findings about the nature of juvenile delinquency as well as to sociological ones. Furthermore, Ball (1966), after successfully testing Sykes and Matza's (1957) theory of neutralization techniques, suggested that the use of neutralization by delinquents is symptomatic of the breakdown of internal controls and, in that sense, is a specific instance of the more general "containment theory."

In line with the comments by Ball (1966) and Matza (1964), it is possible to see most of Matza's theory, developed in *Delinquency and Drift*, as another example of a containment theory. Matza explains that the development of neutralizing techniques, learned in an individual's family or social situation, and derived from a sense of injustice common to the lower class, sets the adolescent free from the normal moral ties to conventional behavior. Once the adolescent is in this uncommitted moral position he may drift into delinquency. The formulation presented by Matza assumes that adolescents will vary in the degree to which they have been able to neutralize the conventional norms so as to be available for delinquent acts. This may account for the differential participation in delinquent gangs and in delinquency which Ya-blonsky (1962) reported in his study of the gang as a near-group. Since neutralization techniques have been learned, neutralization theory is also akin to differential association theory, although the former stresses the essential similarity of delinquent and conventional values while the latter stresses their dissimilarity.

One criticism that has been leveled against social control theories is that they take the potential delinquent to the point where he is relatively free of social and personal control, but that they do not actually lead him into delinquent behavior. As Matza puts it, the potential delinquent may be in drift, and not subject to social control, but he need not then engage in delinquent behavior. The actual motivational thrust to delinquency is missing.

Different containment theorists have dealt with this problem in different ways. Nye, aware of this problem, suggested the four wishes of W. I. Thomas as possible examples of the motivational forces leading to delinquency. Reckless does not deal with the problem directly in terms of his containment theory, but rather views his containment theory as a central one within a list of other theoretical approaches, some of which emphasize the inner motivational thrust. Matza resurrects the concept of "will" to provide the element of thrust. According to his formulation, the will to engage in delinquent behavior is activated under two kinds of circumstances: (1) when the adolescent is able to manage both the technical skills and the apprehension associated with a delinquent act; (2) when a sense of desperation, of "being pushed around," heightens the value of a delinquent act—for it can set things in motion and thereby provides the adolescent with a means of demonstrating his potency.

However, there is probably a simpler way of phrasing the problem of motivational thrust. Torgoff (1965), for example, has conceptualized the problem of deviant behavior in terms of the interplay between temptation and control, and this approach provides an answer to the question of motivational thrust that has plagued the social control theorists. According to Torgoff, the situation can be seen in terms of two factors—the strength of the temptations and the strength of the controls. How much of a temptation is the radio in a store window to the adolescent? How strong are the internal and external controls against stealing the radio? Whether or not the adolescent steals the radio is a function of the balance of the forces of temptation and control. The stronger the adolescent's internal moral controls, or the stronger the external social constraints, the less likely is he to succumb to a given level of temptation. Viewed in this way, there is no need to try to bootleg a quantum of motivational thrust into one's control theory; the presence of motivational and control elements can be assumed from the start.

Martin Gold (1963) has also developed a theory of delinquency that is based upon two forces—control forces that inhibit delinquency, and provoking forces that lead toward delinquency. Controlling forces are conceptualized as stemming from the attractions that adolescents have toward individuals and organizations that support conventional norms. Gold's research has underlined the important role of the family in this connection. Provoking forces are seen in terms of the problem of status deprivation, derived from the work of Cohen (1955): "Delinquency is an ideal solution for status deprivation problems because . . . delinquent behavior simultaneously repudiates the societal values by which boys are to regard themselves as failures and wins status for boys among peers who share these status problems" (Gold, 1963, p. 182).

One can readily recast Matza's and Nye's analysis to fit Torgoff's or Gold's analysis. For example, Matza's discussion of "will" contains references to temptations based upon internal personality dynamics and external constraints. Jackson Toby's (1957a) formulation is also related. He provided an early statement of social control theory in which the relative ineffectiveness of parental control and community control were singled out as major causes of lower class delinquency. In addition, he referred to the individual's "stake in conformity" to account for individual differences within a community. For example, a youngster who is doing well in school and looking forward to occupational success has a greater stake in conformity—he has more to lose through delinquent behavior. A youngster doing poorly in school and without hope for any kind of occupational success has less to lose, and might therefore be more tempted to gain prestige within a group of delinquent peers.

In addition to the element of inner motivation, social control theories must also handle the related element of situational context. In other words, delinquency arises out of situations that are conducive to it. Briar and Piliavin (1965) have referred to this as "situational inducement" and suggest that it is an important variable in delinquency causation. Case histories presented by Spergel (1964), Short and Strodtbeck (1965), and Karacki and Toby (1962) appear to bear this out. The nature of the inducement would stem not only from the circumstances of the situation but also from the definition of the situation by the adolescent.

In their critical commentaries on social control theories, Cohen and Short (1958) reject the idea that delinquency is a potential of human nature. Matza (1964) considers the same idea, hesitates, and also rejects it as the answer to the appearance of delinquent behavior. But perhaps the answer to the motivational dilemma of social control theory lies, as suggested above, in a slightly different direction. It is not that "delinquency" is built into human nature; rather, "temptation to commit delinquent acts" is built into the process of interaction between an individual and his environment.

Although there are clearly weaknesses in the various containment or control theories that have been offered, they nevertheless do provide a point of departure for further empirical work. Containment theory, stated very generally, seems to fit a good deal of the empirical evidence of delinquency, and it is unfortunate that the various containment theories have received heretofore relatively little attention compared to other theories on the etiology of delinquency. . . .

SOME CONCLUDING REMARKS

Social Class, Delinquent Gangs, and Family Variables

The review of research makes it clear that many variables are related to delinquency. Family variables, particularly parental affection and parental discipline, are among the most important variables. It is possible, of course, that the rather clouded multicausal picture which emerges from the research may be cleared somewhat by attention to "types" of delinquency rather than through dealing grossly with "delinquency" as a variable. But much further research remains to be done for this kind of clarification to emerge.

The research carried out by the Gluecks (1950) is among the most important in demonstrating the potential etiological importance of family variables. This research has been criticized, however, for its lack of attention to social and cultural variables. Since their design involved matching delinquents and nondelinquents on social class, they were unable to examine the independent contribution that social class variables might make to delinquency. They concentrated upon personality and family variables.

Nye (1958) has also demonstrated the importance of family variables for delinquent behavior, and he carried this out within a study that did include social class as an independent variable. Since he found that social class variables were not related to delinquent behavior—measured from data obtained on self-report questionnaires—his finding that family variables were importantly related to delinquent behavior takes on added weight.

More recently, Gold (1963) has suggested that even Nye's data indicate that there is at least a slight association between social class and delinquent behavior, and Gold also presents his own data to demonstrate such a relationship. At the same time Gold is in agreement with Nye that studies based upon officially adjudicated delinquents exaggerate the relationship between class and delinquency because of the biases operating in police and court procedures. Gold presents data that demonstrate the operation of these biases.

For the most part sociologists and anthropologists have focused upon social class and delinquent gangs as etiological variables, while psychiatrists and psychologists have focused upon family and personality variables. It is curious that the study of the family, which has been primarily pursued by sociologists and anthropologists should so largely be ignored by them in relation to delinquency. The sociologist has generally viewed delinquency as a kind of normal social functioning, and has therefore looked to differential social class or peer group patterns that might support such behavior. He has not been able to turn to the family because there is little evidence suggesting socialization to, or overt support for, delinquent patterns within the family. The psychiatrist, however, has generally viewed delinquency as a kind of disturbed personality functioning, and has looked to early family relationships for the origins of this disturbance. Neither approach by itself is totally adequate, although each may be most relevant for the explanation of certain types of delinquency. But what is of special interest is the recent work of a number of investigators with a social psychological orientation who have been developing a number of related "control" theories of delinquency. These theories focus upon personal and social controls, and are therefore able to give a central place to family relationships and personality functioning as well as to social class and to peer groups.

Many independent variables have been related to measures of delinquency, but a narrow disciplinary orientation and a lack of methodological sophistication have kept the study of the simultaneous effect of two or more variables to a minimum. For example, it is possible that the presence of at least one "control" variable, whether personal or social, would significantly inhibit delinquency; the presence of additional "control" variables have an additive or a multiplicative effect. Information of this sort could have strong practical implications. But the amount of research that remains to be done on the simultaneous effect of different combinations of independent variables upon different measures of delinquency for different groups is enormous.

One study done with a cohort of schoolboys reports an additive effect between social class status and truancy record (Robbins, 1965)—14 percent of the boys who were not of lower class status and who showed no truancy record were delinquent; 25 percent of the boys with either characteristic were delinquent; and 42 percent of the boys with both were delinquent.

School retardation was slightly associated with delinquent behavior, and father's presence or absence was not at all associated with delinquent outcome.

A report by Stanfield (1966) presents some suggestive data on the interaction of several key variables from the Cambridge-Somerville Youth Study. Low social status, erratic or lax discipline by father, and frequent peer activity were all significantly related to delinquency. Examining the combined influence of these variables, taken two at a time, the following interesting interaction effects emerge: (1) Erratic or lax discipline by father is more strongly associated with delinquency in low status than in high status families; (2) frequent peer activity is more strongly associated with delinquency in high status than in low status families; (3) frequent peer activity is more strongly associated with delinquency among those boys where father's discipline is erratic or lax than where it is consistent. Further, in examining the interaction of all three independent variables, it turns out that lower class boys with frequent peer activity who are subjected to consistent discipline by their fathers show a surprisingly low proportion of delinquency. It therefore seems that consistent discipline by the father can offset the influence toward delinquency of low status and high peer activity. Conversely, erratic or lax discipline makes boys of lower status more vulnerable to the influence of a delinquent subculture than boys of higher status.

Palmore and Hammond (1964) also present interesting information on the interaction of variables. Working with a sample of deprived children, they first demonstrated that delinquency was higher for Negroes than whites, for boys than girls, and for those failing at school than for those succeeding. Further, they pointed out the following: "(1) A deviant family background increases Negro, but not white, delinquency. (2) A deviant neighborhood increases male, but not female, delinquency. (3) Either kind of deviant influence increases delinquency more among those failing in school than among those succeeding" (p. 851). Palmore and Hammond point out that these interactive findings lend support to one aspect of the Cloward and Ohlin (1960) delinquency theory on the combined influence of the lack of legitimate, and the availability of illegitimate, opportunities. They suggest that family deviance or neighborhood deviance are indicators of the opportunity to learn illegitimate behavior; that being Negro, or a boy, or showing school failure are indicators of fewer legitimate opportunities. Hence the greater impact of family deviance or neighborhood deviance upon Negroes, upon boys, and upon those failing at school.

A Paradigm for Delinquency

Based upon the theory and research we have reviewed, the following is offered as a schematic paradigm on the etiology of delinquency, particularly of the adjusted-habitual-gang type of delinquency. Although many references would be appropriate at each step of the paradigm, we shall generally content ourselves with listing only a single reference.

1. *The community's limited ability to provide opportunities to achieve in accordance with middle class values.*—Living in a lower class community—

 (a) lessens legitimate opportunities and lessens the possibility of achievement in accordance with middle class values (Cloward and Ohlin, 1960);
 (b) makes illegitimate or "delinquent" behavior likelier (Merton, 1957);
 (c) makes it likelier that groups or gangs will develop in which there is social support for delinquent behavior (Cohen, 1955);
 (d) leads to a discrepancy between middle class values and actual behavior so that pressure is exerted to modify the middle class values in some way; this may take the form of reaction formation (Cohen, 1955), of neutralization (Sykes and Matza, 1957), of value stretch (Rodman, 1963), or of a completely separate lower class culture in which the middle class values are not taken as a baseline (Miller, 1958).

One result is that groups with modified values, such as delinquent gangs, are likelier to arise in lower class communities.

2. *The family's limited ability to maintain ex-*

ternal controls.*—Growing up in a lower class family involves—

 (a) social, economic, and occupational deprivation (by definition);
 (b) lesser attraction for the family, and for one's father, given the emphasis that is placed upon the man's occupational position and earning power (Gold, 1963);
 (c) a lower concept of personal and family worth (Reckless, 1961);
 (d) a lesser ability of parents—stemming from limited resources which make the manipulation of rewards and punishments more difficult—to maintain external controls over their children, especially in anonymous urban areas (Hylan Lewis, 1965; Sherwood and Sherwood, n.d.);
 (e) a lesser degree of attractiveness of community agencies—for example, schools—and therefore their lesser ability to maintain external controls (Toby, 1957a).

One result is that individuals less subject to external controls are likelier to come from lower class families.

3. *The family's limited use of child-rearing techniques that lead to effective internal controls.*—Living in a lower class family involves—

 (a) more family disharmony and instability, stemming from the members', and especially the father's, greater difficulty in fulfilling expected roles;
 (b) a greater likelihood of lax or inconsistent discipline and of discipline focused upon the child's actions rather than intentions —stemming in part from the constraining situation represented by lower class occupations (Kohn, 1963);
 (c) a lesser degree of affection within the family, stemming from the pressures imposed upon the family by the need to adapt to deprived circumstances (Nye, 1958);
 (d) a lesser degree of identification with parents or of internalization of parental norms (McCord and McCord, 1959).

One result is that individuals less subject to conventional internal controls are likelier to come from lower class families.

Thus, according to section (1) of the paradigm, the lower class community's limited ability to provide opportunities to achieve in accordance with middle class values makes it more likely that delinquent gangs with modified values will arise. According to section (2), lower class status directly influences the family's (and the community's) transactions with its children because of the lesser degree of attraction it has for them. According to section (3), lower class status indirectly influences the family's transactions with its children because of its influence over the child-rearing techniques that are used. As a result of the low degree of attraction for the family and of the kind of child-rearing techniques used, a greater proportion of children who grow up in lower class families are less subject to conventional personal and family controls. The overall result is that within the lower class community there are more individuals who frequently interact in gangs, who behave in ways that do not accord with evaluated middle class values, and who have modified the middle class values so that the gang provides support and status for its members.

What we have covered in the above paradigm centers specifically upon lower class families, lower class communities, lower class gangs, and lower class delinquency. It helps us to understand the higher rate of delinquency within the lower class. But it does not specifically address itself to variations within the lower class. It is only by inferring the differential availabilities of opportunities within the lower class, or the differential attractiveness of families or of affection within parent-child relationships, that we can begin to deal with such variations.

The above paradigm also does not address itself directly to middle class delinquency. Gold (1963) has suggested that some of the same factors that lead to lower class delinquency also account for middle class delinquency; this would principally involve the child-rearing variables listed in section (3), although such matters as lax discipline or low affection within middle class families would presumably stem from something other than deprived circumstances.

The paradigm, of course, is highly tentative, and is merely presented as a way of coordinating some of the theories and data we have reviewed. As additional data and theoretical interpreta-tions are made available, modifications will become necessary, and these will hopefully be in the direction of turning the loosely organized paradigm into a more tightly conceived theoretical structure.

REFERENCES

ABRAHAMSEN, DAVID (1949), "Family Tension, Basic Cause of Criminal Behavior," *Journal of Criminal Law, Criminology, and Police Science,* 40:330–343.

ABRAHAMSEN, DAVID (1960), *The Psychology of Crime.* New York: Columbia University Press.

ANDRY, ROBERT G. (1957), "Faulty Paternal and Maternal-Child Relationships, Affection and Delinquency," *British Journal of Delinquency,* 8: 34–48.

ANDRY, ROBERT G. (1962), "Parental Affection and Delinquency," chap. in Wolfgang, Marvin E.; Savitz, Leonard; and Johnston, Norman, eds., *The Sociology of Crime and Delinquency.* New York: John Wiley & Sons, Inc., pp. 342–352.

AXELRAD, SIDNEY (1965), "Juvenile Delinquency: A Study of the Relationship between Psychoanalysis and Sociology," *Smith College Studies in Social Work,* 35:89–109.

BALL, RICHARD A. (1966), "An Empirical Exploration of Neutralization Theory," paper presented at Ohio Valley Sociological Society meeting, Dayton, *Criminologica,* vol. 4, 2:22–32.

BANDURA, ALBERT, AND WALTERS, RICHARD H. (1958), "Dependency Conflicts in Aggressive Delinquents," *Journal of Social Issues,* 4:52–56.

BANDURA, ALBERT, AND WALTERS, RICHARD H. (1959), *Adolescent Aggression.* New York: The Ronald Press Company.

BARKER, GORDON H. (1940), "Family Factors in the Ecology of Juvenile Delinquency," *Journal of Criminal Law, Criminology, and Police Science,* 30:681–691.

BARKER, GORDON H., AND ADAMS, W. THOMAS (1963), "Glue Sniffers," *Sociology and Social Research,* 47:298–310.

BECKER, WESLEY C. (1964), "Consequences of Different Kinds of Parental Discipline," chap. in Hoffman, Martin L., and Hoffman, Lois, eds., *Review of Child Development Research.* New York: Russell Sage Foundation, pp. 169–208.

BOWLBY, JOHN (1952), *Maternal Care and Mental Health.* Geneva: World Health Organization.

BOWLBY, JOHN; AINSWORTH, MARY; BOSTON, MARY; AND ROSENBLUTH, DINA (1956), "The Effects of Mother-Child Separation: A Follow-Up Study," *British Journal of Medical Psychology,* 29:211–247.

BRIAR, SCOTT, AND PILIAVIN, IRVING (1965), "Delinquency, Situational Inducements and Commitment to Conformity," *Social Problems,* 13:35–45.

BROWNING, CHARLES J. (1960), "Differential Impact of Family Disorganization on Male Adolescents," *Social Problems*, 8:37–44.

BURT, CYRIL (1925), *The Young Delinquent*. London: University of London Press.

CLARK, JOHN P., AND WENNINGER, EUGENE P. (1964), "The Attitude of Juveniles toward the Legal Institution," *Journal of Criminal Law, Criminology and Police Science*, 55:482–489.

CLOWARD, RICHARD A., AND OHLIN, LLOYD E. 1960), *Delinquency and Opportunity*. Glencoe, Ill.: The Free Press.

COHEN, ALBERT K. (1955), *Delinquent Boys*. Glencoe, Ill.: The Free Press.

COHEN, ALBERT K., AND SHORT, JAMES F., JR. (1958), "Research in Delinquent Subcultures," *Journal of Social Issues*, 14:20–36.

DENTLER, ROBERT A., AND MONROE, LAWRENCE J. (1961), "Social Correlates of Early Adolescent Theft," *American Sociological Review*, 26:733–743.

DINITZ, SIMON; SCARPITTI, FRANK R.; AND RECKLESS, WALTER C. (1962), "Delinquency Vulnerability: A Cross Group and Longitudinal Analysis," *American Sociological Review*, 27:515–517.

EISSLER, RUTH S. (1949), "Scapegoats of Society," chap. in Eissler, K. R., ed. *Searchlights on Delinquency*. New York: International Universities Press, Inc., pp. 288–305.

FERDINAND, THEODORE N. (1964), "The Offense Patterns and Family Structures of Urban, Village and Rural Delinquents," *Journal of Criminal Law, Criminology, and Police Science*, 55:86–93.

GLUECK, SHELDON, AND GLUECK, ELEANOR (1950), *Unraveling Juvenile Delinquency*. New York: Commonwealth Fund.

GOLD, MARTIN (1963), *Status Forces in Delinquent Boys*. Ann Arbor: University of Michigan Press.

GOLDFARB, W. (1943), "The Effects of Early Institutional Care on Adolescent Personality," *Journal of Experimental Education*, 12:106–129.

HAKEEM, MICHAEL (1958), "A Critique of the Psychiatric Approach," chap. 4 of Roucek, Joseph S., *Juvenile Delinquency*. New York: Philosophical Library, Inc., pp. 79–112.

HIRSCHI, TRAVIS, AND SELVIN, HANAN C. (1966), "False Criteria of Causality in Delinquency Research," *Social Problems*, 13:254–268.

HODGKISS, MARGARET (1933), "The Influence of Broken Homes and Working Mothers," *Smith College Studies in Social Work*, 3:259–274.

JAFFE, LESTER D. (1963), "Delinquency Proneness and Family Anomie," *Journal of Criminal Law, Criminology, and Police Science*, 54:146–154.

JOHNSON, ADELAIDE M. (1949), "Sanctions for Superego Lacunae of Adolescents," in Eissler, K. R., ed., *Searchlights on Delinquency*. New York: International Universities Press, Inc., pp. 225–246.

JOHNSON, ADELAIDE M., AND BURKE, EDMUND C.

(1955), "Parental Permissiveness and Fostering in Child Rearing and Their Relationship to Juvenile Delinquency," *Proceedings of the Staff Meetings of the Mayo Clinic*, 30:557–565.

KARACKI, LARRY, AND TOBY, JACKSON (1962), "The Uncommitted Adolescent Candidate for Gang Socialization," *Sociological Inquiry*, 32:203–215.

KOHN, MELVIN L. (1963), "Social Class and Parent-Child Relationships: An Interpretation," *American Journal of Sociology*, 68:471–480.

LEES, J. P., AND NEWSON, L. J. (1954), "Family or Sibship Position and Some Aspects of Juvenile Delinquency," *British Journal of Delinquency*, 5:46–65.

LEWIS, HYLAN (1965), "Child Rearing among Low-Income Families," in Ferman, Louis A.; Kornbluh, Joyce L.; and Haber, Alan, eds., *Poverty in America: A Book of Readings*. Ann Arbor: University of Michigan Press, pp. 342–353.

McCORD, WILLIAM, AND McCORD, JOAN (1959), with Zola, Irving Kenneth, *Origins of Crime*. New York: Columbia University Press.

McCORD, JOAN, AND McCORD, WILLIAM (1964), "The Effects of Parental Role Model on Criminality," in Cavan, Ruth, ed., *Readings in Juvenile Delinquency*. Philadelphia: J. P. Lippincott Co.

MASLOW, A. H., AND DIAZ-GUERRERO, R. (1960), "Delinquency as a Value Disturbance," chap. in Peatman, John G., and Hartley, Eugene L., eds., *Festschrift for Gardner Murphy*. New York: Harper & Row, Publishers, pp. 228–240.

MATZA, DAVID (1964), *Delinquency and Drift*. New York: John Wiley & Sons, Inc.

MATZA, DAVID, AND SYKES, GRESHAM M. (1961), "Juvenile Delinquency and Subterranean Values," *American Sociological Review*, 26:712–719.

MERTON, ROBERT K. (1957), *Social Theory and Social Structure*, rev. and enl. ed., Glencoe, Ill.: Free Press, chap. 5, pp. 161–194.

MILLER, WALTER B. (1958), Lower Class Culture as a Generating Milieu of Gang Delinquency," *Journal of Social Issues*, 14:5–19.

MONAHAN, THOMAS P. (1958), "Family Status and the Delinquent Child: A Reappraisal and Some New Findings," *Social Forces*, 35:250–258.

NAESS, SIRI (1959), "Mother-Child Separation and Delinquency," *British Journal of Delinquency*, 10:22–35.

NYE, F. IVAN (1958), *Family Relationships and Delinquent Behavior*. New York: John Wiley & Sons, Inc.

PALMORE, ERDMAN B., AND HAMMOND, PHILLIP E. (1964), "Interacting Factors in Juvenile Delinquency," *American Sociological Review*, 29:848–854.

PETERSON, DONALD R., AND BECKER, WESLEY C. (1965), "Family Interaction and Delinquency," chap. in Quay, Herbert C., ed., *Juvenile Delinquency. Research and Theory*. Princeton, N.J.: D. Van Nostrand Co., Inc., pp. 36–99.

RECKLESS, WALTER C. (1961), *The Crime Problem*, 3d ed. New York: Appleton-Century-Crofts.

RECKLESS, WALTER C.; DINITZ, SIMON; AND MURRAY, ELLEN (1956), "Self Concept as an Insulator against Delinquency," *American Sociological Review*, 21:744–746.

REDL, FRITZ, AND WINEMAN, DAVID (1951), *Children Who Hate*. New York: The Free Press.

REISS, ALBERT J., JR. (1951), "Delinquency as the Failure of Personal and Social Controls," *American Sociological Review*, 16:196–207.

REISS, ALBERT J., JR. (1952), "Social Correlates of Psychological Types of Delinquency," *American Sociological Review*, 17:710–718.

ROBBINS, LEE N. (1965), *Assessing the Contribution of Family Structure, Class, and Peer Groups to Juvenile Delinquency*, paper presented at the Fifth International Criminological Congress, Montreal.

RODMAN, HYMAN (1963), "The Lower-Class Value Stretch," *Social Forces*, 42:205–215.

SCARPITTI, FRANK; MURRAY, ELLEN; DINITZ, SIMON; AND RECKLESS, WALTER C. (1960), "The 'Good' Boy in a High Delinquency Area: Four Years Later," *American Sociological Review*, 25:555–558.

SHAW, CLIFFORD R., AND MCKAY, HENRY D. (1932), "Are Broken Homes a Causative Factor in Juvenile Delinquency?" *Social Forces*, 10:514–524.

SHERWOOD, CLARENCE C., AND SHERWOOD, SYLVIA (n.d.) "Deviancy and Family Control," mimeographed.

SHORT, JAMES F., JR., AND STRODTBECK, FRED L. (1965), *Group Process and Gang Delinquency*. Chicago: University of Chicago Press.

SIMPSON, JON E.; DINITZ, SIMON; KAY, BARBARA; AND RECKLESS, WALTER C. (1960), "Delinquency Potential of Pre-Adolescents in High-Delinquency Areas," *British Journal of Delinquency*, 10:211–215.

SLOCUM, WALTER, AND STONE, CAROL L. (1963), "Family Culture Patterns and Delinquent-Type Behavior," *Marriage and Family Living*, 25:202–208.

SPERGEL, IRVING (1964), *Racketville, Slumtown, Haulburg*. Chicago: University of Chicago Press.

STANFIELD, ROBERT EVERETT (1966), "The Interaction of Family Variables and Gang Variables in the Aetiology of Delinquency," *Social Problems*, 13:411–417.

SYKES, GRESHAM M., AND MATZA, DAVID (1957), "Techniques of Neutralization: A Theory of Delinquency," *American Sociological Review*, 22:664–670.

TOBY, JACKSON (1957a), "Social Disorganization and Stake in Conformity: Complementary Factors in the Predatory Behavior of Hoodlums," *Journal of Criminal Law, Criminology, and Police Science*, 48:12–17.

TOBY, JACKSON (1957b), "The Differential Impact of Family Disorganization," *American Sociological Review*, 22:505–512.

TORGOFF, IRVING (1965), *Achievement Motivation, Morality, and Conflict: A Study of Italian Working-Class Apprentices*, presented at the Society for Research in Child Development meetings, Minneapolis.

WATTENBERG, WILLIAM W., AND SAUNDERS, FRANK (1954), "Sex Differences among Juvenile Offenders," *Sociology and Social Research*, 39:24–31.

WEEKS, H. ASHLEY (1940), "Male and Female Broken Home Rates by Types of Delinquency," *American Sociological Review*, 5:601–609.

WEEKS, H. ASHLEY, AND SMITH, MARGARET G. (1939), "Juvenile Delinquency and Broken Homes in Spokane, Washington," *Social Forces*, 18:48–59.

WEINBERG, S. KIRSON (1958), "Sociological Processes and Factors in Juvenile Delinquency," chap. 5 in Roucek, Joseph S., *Juvenile Delinquency*. New York: Philosophical Library, Inc., pp. 113–132.

YABLONSKY, LEWIS (1962), *The Violent Gang*. New York: Crowell, Collier & Macmillan, Inc.

23.

GILBERT GEIS

STATISTICS CONCERNING RACE AND CRIME

Statistics purporting to show the amount of crime in a society possess serious shortcomings as accurate indicators of the item they are measuring. The breakdown of such figures into racial and ethnic categories not only compounds the statistical errors, but also introduces elements of general social concern. Such breakdowns should be eliminated in official reports since they contain, besides their inaccuracy, elements which are socially disruptive and disadvantageous.

Present statistics which pretend to report the criminal behavior of minority ethnic and racial groups both reflect and perpetuate a large number of errors and myths, which can be, in their most innocent form, misleading and, in their least innocent, both vicious and malevolent.

It is traditional for persons who have taken the time for even a cursory examination of the source and the meaning of the rather elaborate statistical documents periodically issued by the nation's police to deplore these documents as indicators of criminal activity. At the same time, it is traditional for the mass media, as well as other agencies and commentators, to ignore the patent inadequacies of such numerical data, to publicize the released figures, to moralize about their presumed meaning, and then to act upon them as if they were reliable.[1] One writer has noted: "After at least a quarter-century of articles [deploring this condition] we are aware that the general statistics on crime are among the most unsatisfactory of all social statistics."[2] A second writer, employing a readily understood simile to convey his ideas on the same subject, says that "crime statistics are as reliable as a woman giving her 'correct' age."[3] And even this

last observation, it should be noted, errs on the side of generosity toward the crime statistics.

The reasons for this state of affairs are not difficult to locate. They exist whether the reporting agency is sinister and self-serving or is pure in heart, painfully accurate in its reporting procedures, and meticulously fair in its enforcement program.

The most basic shortcoming in criminal statistics is that they can never hope to represent with accuracy the behavior that we are really interested in; that is, they cannot tell us the amount of criminal behavior taking place within a given jurisdiction. This point can hardly be sufficiently emphasized. We do not know the real extent of crime and there is little chance that we will soon come to know it. The various indexes of criminal activity relied upon in statistical reports need not and do not bear any discernible relationship to this most basic item, the volume of criminal behavior itself.

Our best measure of actual criminal behavior is a category usually labeled *crimes known to the police*. Innumerable crimes, however, never become known to the police, and the numerical relationship between these and those which do come to the attention of the police has never been established beyond the point of sheer guesswork. Possibly one out of ten crimes committed becomes known to the police; maybe one out of twenty; perhaps one out of a hundred; or, if you would care to, you could easily defend the view that, for each 100,000 criminal acts committed, only one becomes known to the police. The New Jersey Commission on Habitual Sex Offenders once decided, to no one's surprise,

SOURCE: Gilbert Geis, "Statistics Concerning Race and Crime," *Crime and Delinquency*, April, 1965, pp. 142–50. Permission to reprint granted by author and publisher. Revised version of a presentation first made to the California Advisory Committee, United States Commission on Civil Rights, Los Angeles, September 13, 1962.

[1]See for instance, "The Negro Crime Rate: A Failure in Integration," *Time*, April 21, 1958, p. 16.
[2]D. R. Cressey, "The State of Criminal Statistics," *NPPA Journal*, July, 1957, p. 230.
[3]D. Bell, "The Myth of Crime Waves," in *The End of Ideology* (New York: The Free Press, 1960), p. 138.

that there are only twenty convictions for every sixty million homosexual acts performed.[4]

The reasons for these numerical gaps can be grouped under the major headings of *invisibility of the act* and *unwillingness to report it*. Crimes such as those involving concealed weapons will, almost by definition, become known to the police only with extreme infrequency; in the same fashion, sex and family offenses are very rarely reported to or discerned by law enforcement agencies. Many of these crimes, of course, are differentially engaged in by various racial and ethnic groups, and whether or not the acts enter into the official awareness of the police will have considerable bearing on the numerical portrait of these groups' criminal activity. Thus, white-collar crimes, such as embezzlement, committed primarily by whites, are severely underreported, as are several types of criminal acts which appear to be disproportionately committed by members of minority groups. It would be absurd, of course, to presume that these gross discrepancies in any way ultimately balance out or even up, just as it is irresponsible to assume that those statistics which we do have represent a meaningful residue of the total or of the more important aspects of criminal activity.

SOME STATISTICAL CONTAMINANTS

Offenses known to the police may also be influenced by operating definitions, by the exercise of official discretion, and by the vagaries of the human animal. Thus, for example, two Ohio cities (Zanesville and Toledo, if I remember correctly) once employed quite different definitions of "auto theft." Zanesville recorded an offense when it was reported by the victim; Toledo waited twenty-four hours before taking official notice of the absent vehicle. As might be expected, Toledo's official statistical reports showed many fewer instances of auto theft than Zanesville's (whose figures included, it might be noted, a not inconsiderable number of "thefts" which amounted to nothing more sinister than the inability of Saturday night revelers to locate

their automobiles until the sobering influence of Sunday morning had set in). So, too, the official exercise of discretion by the police, on grounds of overriding social importance or merely on the basis of momentary caprice, will be reflected in criminal statistics as will, also, the sometimes curious and always statistically variable tendencies of persons and social groups to report crimes. Indeed, some crimes may become known to the police though they never took place; rape, for example, is notorious for possessing this quixotic little statistical quirk.

Crimes known to the police cannot, of course, be broken down by age, sex, or religious or ethnic identification of the perpetrators unless and until these persons are discovered. Thus, originally inadequate and inaccurate conglomerations of statistics become further distorted, as we shall see, by numerous idiosyncratic procedures. Before this stage, however, attempts sometimes are undertaken to establish some sort of rough indicator of criminal activities of divergent groups on the basis of the crimes known to the police category.

An illustration of one such approach is that found in the Statistical Digest prepared for 1961 by the Los Angeles Police Department.[5] On page 12 of this report we find a rather unique chart which lists, for five specified offenses (robbery, theft from person, murder, aggravated assault, and rape), the sex and the "descent" (i.e., Caucasian, Negro, Latin,[6] Japanese or Chinese, or "Others") of what are called "suspects observed." The report itself offers no help in overcoming the vagueness of the designation "suspects observed," though it is readily apparent that, if nothing else, these subjects are not routinely arrested. In regard to aggravated assault, for instance, there were 12,891 suspects observed during the year, while another section of the report (page 38) indicates a total of 4,243 persons arrested for aggravated assault during the same year—or about one ar-

[4]P. Tappan, ed., *The New Jersey Commission on Habitual Sex Offenders, Report*, 1949, pp. 18–19.

[5]The Los Angeles Police Department stopped including race breakdowns in its annual statistical reports after 1961.

[6]Latins, of course, are regarded as Caucasians in most classifications of the human tribe, and this matter is hardly resolved by use of the term "descent." What is the "descent," for instance, of a person born of a Negro mother and a Caucasian father?

rest for every three "suspects observed."[7] For robbery, the proportion of arrests to "suspects observed" is about one out of two, or 5,130 arrests for 10,270 observed suspects; for rape, the proportion shows a quite different tendency, with three out of five observed suspects (843 of 1,232, or 69 per cent) being arrested.

Whatever the table indicates, it certainly does not show any consistent relationship between itself and the figures for minority groups which appear in the arrest tabulations. In regard to robbery, for instance, 64 per cent of the "observed" Caucasian suspects are ultimately arrested, but only 45 and 46 per cent of the Negro and Latin groups, respectively, while for rape 64 and 68 per cent of the observed suspects among the Negroes and Latins, respectively, are arrested in contrast to 76 per cent of the Caucasians. For aggravated assault, 34 and 26 per cent of the observed Negroes and Latins, respectively, are arrested, in contrast to 36 per cent of the Caucasians. Taking the three crimes together, the statistics show a 35 per cent relationship between suspected and arrested Latins, 40 per cent in the case of Negroes, and a figure of 50 per cent for the Caucasians.

STATISTICS IN CONTEXT

A number of interpretations can be brought to bear on these statistics. They may be telling us that there is an overreporting by minority groups of crimes among them, or that there is an overreporting of crimes allegedly committed by minority group members. The figures may also indicate a disinclination on the part of the police to arrest minority group members as often as persons from other groups, or they may reflect a differential efficiency or effectiveness in resolving, by arrest, crimes committed by members of various subgroups in the society. It is noteworthy as well that the figures provide no clue regarding the involvement of the same person in a series of crimes, and the possible reporting of an individual several times as an observed suspect but only once as an arrested

offender. If we accept any of these possible interpretations, or a combination of them, we must conclude that the tables tell us precious little about the criminal activities of the groups into which their numbers are broken down and that, as the tables stand, they represent little more than exercises in the use and abuse of the talents of an IBM tabulating machine.

This conclusion is fortified, it might be added, if we compare the 1961 statistics with those from earlier periods. The comparison soon discloses that there is no constant relationship over the years between the number of suspects observed and the number of those arrested. In 1956, for instance, 43 per cent and, in 1957, 46 per cent of the observed Negro suspects were arrested, in contrast to 64 per cent of such suspects arrested in 1961. We might also legitimately object, I believe, to the gross reporting in the table of the total number of offenders in contrast to a more sensible procedure which would indicate the percentage of alleged crime in a group in terms of that group's proportion in the general population.[8] In fact, if it were really seeking some semblance of accuracy, the report could refine the figures in terms of the age and sex distributions within the various groups.

USE OF ARREST STATISTICS

Most statistical reports which attempt to convey a picture of the illegal behavior of different segments within a society employ *arrest* statistics for this purpose. We have seen earlier that there is a vast and almost totally unknown and unknowable gap between the reality of crimes committed and the residue involving those which come to the attention of the police. Patent statistical fallacies inevitably arise because of this gap, and these fallacies become even more exaggerated as we move farther away, in terms of procedure, from the behavior which we are trying to measure. Arrest statistics may indicate the efficiency or inefficiency of a police department as much as they may indicate the quantity of crime or the type of criminals within its

[7] We will have to assume here that all or almost all persons arrested are counted earlier as "suspects observed;" otherwise, the "suspects observed" table would be even less meaningful.

[8] See M. E. Wolfgang, "Uniform Crime Reports: A Critical Appraisal," *University of Pennsylvania Law Review*, April, 1963, pp. 708–38.

jurisdiction. Arrest statistics do not, however, unless we resort to the most reckless kind of extrapolation, tell us very much about the criminal activity among minority groups.

This point is worth repetition: Arrest statistics and the detailed characteristics (such as race, sex, and age) of persons arrested are no more than descriptions of the persons who, for a veritably endless array of reasons (many of which are beyond our knowledge), are subjected to arrest. If we find, for example, that 20 per cent of the persons arrested in California are females, this cannot be taken to mean that 20 per cent of the state's criminals are females or that 20 per cent of the offenses known to the police are committed by females, or that 20 per cent of any particular offense, even if this is the figure for arrested females in regard to that offense, are committed by females. It may be that females are either more or less readily apprehended than males in regard to certain offenses; in homicide cases, for example, it has been claimed that males are detected more often than females because of the cruder methods they employ in killing.[9] On the same point, it has been observed that if all the females who submitted to abortion, a crime in California, were arrested, female crime rates would more nearly approximate male crime rates; but the same point could be made about numerous undetected or unarrested forms of male criminal activity. All that can be concluded with safety, it seems apparent, is that a certain percentage of persons arrested are females. If you want to know about the criminal behavior of females, you will not find out about it in the statistical reports of the nation's law enforcement agencies.

Arrest statistics reflect in myriad ways the procedures, paradoxes, and idiosyncracies involved in the business of law enforcement. For instance, an efficient police force will often become aware of a greater number of offenses and will arrest a larger number of persons than will a less efficient police organization. Summary statistical reports, taken at face value (which is the way such reports are almost always taken), imply that a better agency is less effective in reducing

crime than a less capable agency, a curious juxtaposition of the facts of the situation.

The same observation may apply in a different fashion to procedures involving minority groups. A belief, based on real or imagined information, that a particular minority group commits more crime than other groups will often lead to a greater saturation of this group's neighborhoods by police patrol. Such saturation will likely turn up more crime and produce a larger number of arrests of persons belonging to the group, though it will also often inhibit some kinds of criminal activity because of the increased likelihood of apprehension. But it is the police activity and not the behavior of the group itself which is conditioning the group's crime rates as they eventually appear in printed statistics.

ILLUSTRATIVE CASES

I was once walking downtown on Main Street when a patrolman stopped a Mexican boy, nudged him toward the side of the street, and requested that he roll up his sleeves so that it could be determined whether his arms had needle marks. The policeman may have recognized the boy as a possible addict, either through experience or perhaps by the way he walked. (An addict will often swing one arm and hold taut the other into which he has shot the drug because moving it is painful.) Or perhaps the policeman was operating on the assumption that a Mexican boy on this street was much more likely to be a narcotics addict than, say, I was, with my tie and pressed suit. His assumption may have been correct, but it is obvious how readily it becomes self-fulfilling and inflates the "Latin" crime rate through procedural tactics. In the same manner, young Negro boys—and I have listened to them discuss the matter at length in college classes—driving a relatively new and expensive car in an area not populated with Negroes expect as a matter of course to be stopped by the police as potential auto thieves. For whatever reason, the law enforcement agencies have come to the conclusion that young Negroes are more likely than similarly situated whites to be thieves, or at least that they can more readily and with greater impunity be stopped to determine the owner-

---

[9] O. Pollak, *The Criminality of Women* (Philadelphia: University of Pennsylvania Press, 1950), p. 82.

ship of the cars they drive. The procedure obviously serves to increase the number of apprehended and reported Negro car thieves, just as the road blockades during the Christmas season inevitably tend to inflate greatly the total of drunken drivers discovered and arrested.

Many other items serve in similar fashion to cast suspicion on the validity of statistics which might be and are taken to represent the real pattern of criminal activity among different segments of the society. One of the few detailed studies of the nature of such distortion clearly documented how it might operate in the instance of an offense such as shoplifting. Examining the figures for three department stores in Philadelphia, Sellin found that the detectives there had knowledge of shoplifting offenses which exceeded in number the total of all thefts of all types for the entire city of Philadelphia; the shoplifting thefts were simply not reported, except occasionally, to the authorities.[10] And it is worth noting, further, that there was a distinct tendency for the detectives to report offenders to the police when they were Negroes and not to report them when they were not, possibly because they felt the Negro offenders were the more dangerous or were less likely to initiate suits for false arrest, or possibly because they were prejudiced against Negroes. The impact of their policy on the racial components of the larceny statistics in Philadelphia is quite clear.

Nothing in all the foregoing material is meant to indicate that minority groups are either overrepresented or underrepresented in current statistics on their criminal activity. The point is only that they are *mis*represented and that the figures on them tell us little of value concerning an issue surrounded by much emotion and deeply involved in matters of social conscience and social policy. It would certainly be of more value, for example, if we had available statistics controlled for socioeconomic status as part of the subcategory of "descent" so that we could determine whether we were really talking about minority group behavior or the behavior of persons similarly situated in regard to income,

housing conditions, and related items. We might speculate that Negro school teachers and similar minority group members of the middle class commit as little crime of the type recorded in police statistics as whites with the same social standing, but the available statistics shed no light at all that advances us beyond the realm of speculation into the realm of knowledge.

CLOSER LOOK AT ARRESTS

The adult arrest statistics issued by the Los Angeles Police Department may be employed as a basis for closer examination of the deficiencies of such material. We have seen that about half of the suspects observed are eventually arrested, with fewer minority group members being so handled than other persons. Again referring to aggravated assault, rape, and robbery for our calculations, we find a rather low proportion of arrests eventuating in the filing of complaints. For rape, 56 per cent of the arrests ultimately result in the filing of complaints, while for aggravated assault only 15 per cent of the arrests lead to complaints and for robbery only about 20 per cent. For the three offenses together, then, about one out of every four or five persons arrested—and described in the statistics in regard to age, sex, and descent—has a complaint filed against him. This does not tell us, of course, the outcome of the filed complaints; it does not say whether the charge was prosecuted successfully or there was an eventual dismissal or acquittal. It can readily be seen, therefore, that to the extent that no complaint is filed against them an overwhelming majority of the persons arrested for the crimes we have considered can hardly, in fairness, be labeled "guilty offenders" or "criminals." For some other offenses complaints are filed in a much larger percentage of arrests, but these offenses are found in the Part II category, which includes what are considered to be the less serious forms of criminal behavior. More than 90 per cent of the arrests lead to the filing of complaints and in cases involving the violation of motor vehicle laws almost every arrest leads to a filed complaint.

Unfortunately, there is no way of determining on the basis of printed statistics the differen-

[10]T. Sellin, *Research Memorandum on Crime in the Depression* (New York: Social Science Research Council, 1937), p. 69.

tial percentage of complaints filed in terms of the category of "descent" since this category is not reported in connection with complaints filed. It might be thought that a breakdown of the latter category would come closer to presenting a useful (though not very much more useful) summary of criminal activity since here at least we might learn about criminal behavior serious enough to warrant the filing of a complaint, a somewhat more formal process than arrest. It is not the purpose of this survey, it might be noted, to discuss in detail the general problem of the striking gap between the number of arrests and the number of complaints filed. Many persons have fluently argued all sides of this issue; I would be inclined to agree with Professor Remington, who has asked for open discussion of the rules by which the police are expected to operate and evaluation of the precise implications of these rules.[11]

CONCLUSIONS AND RECOMMENDATIONS

Statistical tabulations of the work of a public agency are usually undertaken to provide a reckoning for examination by the citizen taxpayer and to aid the agency itself in performing its job more effectively. Criminal statistics, as they now exist, perform neither of these tasks. The information they supply, I have tried to demonstrate, is misleading and readily subject to misinterpretation. As guides to the most expeditious deployment of police resources, the figures hardly seem worth much, and even if they could be shown to be of some slight importance, an intramural awareness of their general content (in contrast to a public report) would be at least equally satisfactory.

There are other matters of public ethics which should be considered. For example, prior to the 1960 federal decennial census it seemed worthwhile to social scientists that they be able to acquire information about the religious preference and performance of our people. The Government, however, declined to gather such material on the ground that there were con-

siderations of more importance than the needs and interests of social scientists. A parallel situation is the matter under consideration here. Statistics purporting to tell us something about the criminal activities of persons of divergent "descent," whatever dubious value they may possess as an item of social inventory, contain many deleterious aspects that render them of strong potential social harm. To defend themselves against charges of overpolicing certain groups, law enforcement agencies may make use of the figures, with all their shortcomings, though the figures themselves really neither lend support to nor contradict the necessity for the enforcement decisions.

The presence of such statistics also covertly indicates and reinforces a splintering of the society into so-called "descent" groups. Males and females will not likely find it discriminatory if their crime rates are singled out for attention, but minority groups have historically sound reasons to believe, correctly or incorrectly, that something invidious is intended by such distinctions. These fears should not be fed unless there are compelling reasons to do so. Why, for instance, do we not indicate the arrest rates of Baptists or Republicans or of migrants from the South? Any of these tabulations might well provide us data of some value, but presumably not of enough value to make it desirable to differentiate between human beings by singling out particular types for special statistical attention.

The elimination of racial classifications from public criminal statistical reports would probably do much good and little harm. It might allow issues between law enforcement agencies and minority groups to be resolved on grounds more substantial than those provided by rather specious statistics. I recall that when the University of Oklahoma integrated its student body, it was besieged with requests for a statement on the percentage of Negroes enrolled. "We simply do not have such material," those seeking it were told. "We do not request the information at registration and thus have no way of determining the percentage." In this simple fashion much of the latent hostility to integration at the school, finding little numerical fuel upon which to feed its prejudices, collapsed.

[11] F. J. Remington, "The Law Relating to 'On the Street' Detention . . .," *Journal of Criminal Law, Criminology, and Police Science,* November-December, 1960, pp. 386–94.

There is already enough antagonism between law enforcement agencies and minority groups. In *Another Country*, James Baldwin expresses an attitude prevalent among minority groups in a slashing reference to "the white policeman who had taught him how to hate."[12] Some of this antagonism may be unavoidable, but it will

[12]James Baldwin, *Another Country* (New York: The Dial Press, Inc., 1962), p. 6.

not do to play into its hands—and the statistics we have been examining seem to tend toward this end—unless strong reasons exist for such a policy. We should not imitate the ways of the person who, as described by Andrew Lang, a Scottish writer, "uses statistics as a drunken man uses lampposts—for support rather than for illumination."

24.

Albert J. Reiss, Jr. and Albert Lewis Rhodes

THE DISTRIBUTION OF JUVENILE DELINQUENCY IN THE SOCIAL CLASS STRUCTURE

There is no simple relationship between ascribed social status and delinquency. Both the status structure of the residential community and the extent to which delinquency is a function of a cultural tradition in a residential community affect the delinquency life-chances of a boy at each ascribed social class level. The largest proportion of delinquents for any status group comes from the more homogeneous status areas for that group, while the delinquency life-chances of boys in any status group tend to be greatest in the lower status areas and in high delinquency rate areas. Evidence presented in the paper for types of conforming and deviating boys lend support to the conclusions that (1) there is more frequent and serious delinquent deviation in the lower than in the middle stratum when self-reports of delinquent deviation are examined, (2) that the career oriented delinquent is found only among lower class boys, (3) that the major type of lower status boy is a conforming non-achiever while the conforming achiever is the major type in the middle class, (4) that conformers are more likely to be isolates than are non-conformers, and (5) that peer-oriented delinquency is the most common form of delinquent organization at both lower and middle status levels.

A number of theories of deviating behavior and juvenile delinquency posit social class variation in rates of delinquency, particularly gang delinquency, such that the lowest social stratum has the highest delinquency rate.[1] The validity of

Source: Albert J. Reiss, Jr. and Albert Lewis Rhodes, "The Distribution of Juvenile Delinquency in the Social Class Structure," *American Sociological Review* 26, no. 5 (October, 1961): 720–32. Reprinted by permission of the authors and the American Sociological Association.

This paper was read at the American Sociological Association Meetings, New York City, August 29, 1960. The research was performed pursuant to a contract with the United States Office of Education, Department of Health, Education, and Welfare.
[1]William Kvaraceus, "Juvenile Delinquency and Social Class," *Journal of Educational Sociology* 18 (June, 1944): 51–54; Robert K. Merton, *Social Theory and Social Structure* (New York: The Free

this postulate is questioned by some who maintain that middle and high status persons have a much higher rate of delinquency than is shown in a statistical test of the hypothesis.[2] These critics demonstrate that the data of law enforcement or judicial agencies give biased

Press, 1957), pp. 144–45; Albert K. Cohen, *Delinquent Boys* (New York: The Free Press, 1955), pp. 36–44; Walter Miller, "Lower Class Culture as a Generating Milieu of Gang Delinquency," *Journal of Social Issues* 14, no. 3 (1958): 5–19.
[2]Austin Porterfield, *Youth in Trouble* (Fort Worth, Tex.: Leo Potishman Foundation, 1946); James S. Wallenstein and C. J. Wyle, "Our Law Abiding Law Breakers," *National Probation*, March-April, 1947, 107–12; F. Ivan Nye, James F. Short, and V. J. Olson, "Socioeconomic Status and Delinquent Behavior" in *Family Relationships and Delinquent Behavior* (New York: John Wiley & Sons, 1958), pp. 23–33.

estimates of a true rate of delinquency in the population. They suggest that the delinquency life chances are equal for all socioeconomic status groups. The apparently higher rate of the low socioeconomic status group is due solely to the fact that agencies of social control are more likely to classify them as delinquents.[3] This paper is an attempt to shed some light on this disagreement by providing evidence on variation in white male delinquency rates among the social classes of the Nashville, Tennessee, Standard Metropolitan Area.

THE STUDY

Nine thousand two hundred thirty-eight white boys, 12 years old and over, and registered in one of the public, private or parochial junior or senior high schools of Davidson County, Tennessee, during the 1957 school year comprise the base population. Any boy who at some time since his twelfth birthday was referred to the Davidson County Juvenile Court and was adjudged a delinquent by either court referees or the presiding judge is classified as a delinquent in Tables 3–23 through 3–29 of this paper. The time span covered, therefore, during which any boy might have been adjudged a delinquent is the period 1950–58. Information is lacking to calculate an age-specific delinquency rate for all boys in the county, since the in-school population does not include all boys of a given age group and many acts of delinquency never are known to a juvenile court. Neither of these differences is sufficient to obviate the kind of analysis undertaken in this paper, as previous analysis of these data demonstrates.[4]

No attempt, therefore, is made to estimate the absolute rate of delinquency by social classes, since it is demonstrated that social classes are categoric risk groups for selection into a juvenile court population. Although it is

shown that the low status boy is more likely to be apprehended by juvenile authorities, more likely to be held for juvenile court procedures, more likely to have his delinquent act made a matter of court record, and more likely to have an official rather than an unofficial court record, the evidence also supports the contention that there is a greater prevalence of delinquency in the lower class.[5] The focus in this paper is on the more precise description of patterned variation in delinquency rates by social class categories and structures.

Limiting the population of boys to those still in school does not bias our conclusions about differentials in delinquency rates among social categories, but it does not permit us to estimate precisely the magnitude of these differences. The rate of delinquency is higher for out-of-school than for in-school boys since out-of-school boys are on the average older, of lower IQ and social status than are in-school boys. Below it is shown that the rate of delinquency is higher for older boys, lower status boys, and dropouts. The rate for out-of-school boys and hence the rate for all adolescent boys must be higher than the observed rate for in-school boys alone. Confidence in the observed differences presented in this paper is therefore justified since the inclusion of the out-of-school groups would increase the magnitude of the observed differences.

A cross-section sample of boys age 12–16 was also selected, since almost all boys in the county from this age group are still in school. Self reports of delinquent acts were secured from each of these boys by means of a personal interview. A boy from this sample was classified as a delinquent person if on the basis of these self-reports, his acts would have classified him as a delinquent person by juvenile court criteria of delinquency or, if he had been classified as a delinquent person by the court. This cross section sample provides the data for the final section of the paper.

Three status groups were defined in terms of the occupation of the head of the household.

Low Status. All laborers, including farm laborers, operatives and kindred workers, service workers (except protective service workers), and peddlers and door-to-door salesmen.

[3]Walter Reckless maintains, for example, that delinquency rates designate *categoric risks* in the population of being reported to a juvenile court. See Walter C. Reckless, *The Crime Problem* (New York: Appleton-Century-Crofts, 1950), p. 194.

[4]Albert J. Reiss, Jr. and Albert Lewis Rhodes, "A Sociopsychological Study of Conforming and Deviating Behavior among Adolescents," U.S. Office of Education Cooperative Research Project 507, 1959, Chap. 8.

[5]Ibid., Chap. 8.

Middle Status. All craftsmen, foremen and kindred workers, clerical and kindred workers, protective service workers, managers and proprietors of small business, sales workers of wholesale and retail stores, and technicians allied to the professional services.

High Status. All managers, officials, and proprietors, and professional, and semi-professional workers not included in the middle status category, and sales workers in finance, insurance, and real estate.

The number of status positions was restricted to three in order to increase the sampling reliability of within-status group comparisons. In some tables, data are reported for only two status positions to increase the number of cases within subgroups created by the detailed breakdown of other variables cross-classified with status. The dichotomous class of *white collar status* includes all "high status" and "middle status" subjects *except* craftsmen, foremen, and kindred workers and protective service workers while *blue collar status* includes these exceptions plus all "low status" subjects.

Delinquency rates of residential areas were calculated for the in-school population of an area. These delinquency rates are based on the combined total of official and unofficial cases known to the juvenile court.

The social status structure of residential areas in the United States varies considerably. Some are quite homogeneous in class status while others tend to be more representative of the class structure of American society. Residential areas, therefore, vary considerably in opportunities for cross-class contacts, institutional access to legitimate and illegitimate means, and so on. These differences in the status structure of residential areas may mean, in turn, that the effects of a class status position are not uniform from one residential status structure to another. The pressures for conformity on a lower class boy, for example, may be greater in a middle than in a lower class residential area. The independent effects of ascribed social status position and of social status structures on delinquency rates were therefore investigated.

The operational definition of the social status structure of a residential area is the distribution derived from aggregating the data for the as-cribed status position of pupils in schools. Seven types of social status context were defined in this way. More than one school is included within each of the contexts.

1. *Upper and Upper Middle Status Context:* Approximately 60 per cent of all students have fathers classified as old or new professionals, managers, officials and proprietors, and 90 per cent are from white collar origins (6 schools).
2. *Balanced Upper and Lower Middle Status Context:* Approximately 90 per cent are from white collar origins with roughly an equal balance between top and bottom white collar occupations (6 schools).
3. *Crosscuts Social Status Structure:Over-representation at Top Context:* Crosscut criterion,[6] plus 15 per cent more than expected in the top two occupation groups of the six major white-collar occupation groups (7 schools).
4. *Crosscuts Social Status Structure: Over-representation at Center Context:* Crosscut criterion, plus 15 per cent more than expected in the two "center" occupation groups of the six major white-collar occupation categories (4 schools).
5. *Representative of All Schools Context:* Within two per cent of the distribution for all schools (4 schools).
6. *Crosscuts Social Status Structure: Over-representation at Bottom Context:* Crosscut criterion, plus 15 per cent more than expected in the bottom two of the four major blue-collar occupation groups (7 schools).
7. *Lower Social Status Context:* Approximately 75 per cent are in blue-collar occupations with 50 per cent in the lowest of the four major blue-collar occupation groups (5 schools).

VARIATION IN DELINQUENCY RATES BY AGE, IQ, AND ASCRIBED SOCIAL STATUS

There is considerable variation in the rate of court recorded delinquency by age. For the in-school population of white boys, only 2.3 per cent of all boys age 10–13 were known to the court as delinquent while eight per cent of all boys age 16 and over were known as delinquents. The relationship with age is somewhat

---

[6]The "Crosscut" social status structure criterion is defined as follows: The occupational distribution of each occupation group is within five per cent of the distribution for all schools. There are 10 major occupation groups: old and new professions; proprietors; managers and officials; quasi-professions; clerical and kindred workers; sales workers; craftsmen, foremen and kindred workers; protective service workers; operatives and kindred workers; laborers and service workers, except protective service.

more striking when ascribed social status is also considered. The age relationship persists within each ascribed status category but it varies from a low of 0.6 per cent for all high status boys, age 10 to 13, to a high of 10.1 per cent of all low status boys, age 16 and over. Inasmuch as the school dropout rate is highest for the low status boys age 16 and over and lowest among the high status boys age 10 to 13, the inclusion of boys who left school would increase subgroup differences in the delinquency rates of low and high status boys.

Table 3–23 provides information on the rate of delinquency for types of offenders[7] in ascribed

[7]The major types of offenders are defined and rank ordered as to their "seriousness" as follows: *Serious offenses* include assault with a weapon, armed robbery, grand larceny, including larceny of an auto, and burglary. *Petty offenses* including petit larceny, receiving and concealing stolen property, assault, malicious destruction of property, malicious mischief, and loitering, drinking, trespassing, curfew, and breach of peace violations, including disorderly conduct. All runaway and truancy cases for which a petition for a court hearing was entered are called the *truancy offenses*. Drag racing, speeding, reckless driving, and violation of registration and driver's license laws are called *traffic offenses*. Many delinquents of course are brought to court and charged with an offense in more than one of

social status and IQ subgroups. The probability of being classified a serious, petty or truancy offender is greater for the blue-collar than white-collar boys. The relationship holds within each IQ subgroup. But, the probability of being classified a traffic-only violator is greater for white-collar than blue-collar boys and this relationship is also independent of IQ. White-collar boys are more likely to use an automobile regularly than are blue-collar boys and they therefore have a greater opportunity to commit traffic-only offenses. This is not, however, the main reason for their higher incidence of traffic-only offenses. The principal reason for the difference lies in the fact that among blue-collar boys, traffic offenses are more likely to be included among other, more serious offenses. The white-collar boy, therefore, lacking the serious offenses, is more likely to be charged with traffic-only offenses.

There is also a substantial relationship be-

the four offense types. An adolescent who was charged with an offense in more than one of the four types was classified within only one of these four types. The offender was placed in that offense type rated as the "more serious" type of offense, thus the category of truant offenders, for example, does not include all truancy petition cases.

TABLE 3–23.

RATE OF DELINQUENCY PER 100 WHITE SCHOOL BOYS BY IQ AND OCCUPATIONAL STATUS OF FATHER

Occupational Status of Father and Type of Delinquent Offense	IQ						Total[a]	
	Low		Middle		High			
	Number	Rate per 100	Number	Rate per 100	Number	Rate per 100	Number	Rate per 100
White Collar	280	(8.2)	1,263	(6.8)	1,115	(4.6)	3,302	(6.2)
J.C.* serious	10	3.6	15	1.2	5	0.4	42	1.3
J.C. petty	8	2.8	25	2.0	15	1.4	67	2.0
Subtotal	(18)	(6.4)	(40)	(3.2)	(20)	(1.8)	(109)	(3.3)
J.C. truant	1	0.4	1	0.1	—	0.0	4	0.1
J.C. traffic	4	1.4	44	3.5	31	2.8	93	2.8
No J.C. record	257	0.0	1,178	0.0	1,064	0.0	3,096	0.0
Blue Collar	926	(10.9)	2,091	(9.4)	672	(5.2)	4,661	(8.8)
J.C. serious	42	4.5	47	2.2	111	1.7	124	2.7
J.C. petty	48	5.2	85	4.1	115	2.2	174	3.7
Subtotal	(90)	(9.7)	(132)	(6.3)	(26)	(3.9)	(298)	(64)
J.C. truant	10	1.2	11	0.6	2	0.3	33	0.7
J.C. traffic	—	—	53	2.5	7	1.0	81	1.7
No J.C. record	826	0.0	1,895	0.0	637	0.0	4,249	0.0

*J.C. = Juvenile Court.
[a]Includes all cases for which IQ information was not obtained.

tween IQ and rate of delinquency which is independent of ascribed social status. High IQ adolescents have the lowest rate of delinquency within each of the major ascribed status subgroups in Table 3–23. This variation in the rate of delinquency for IQ and ascribed social status subgroups in Table 3–23 holds for the serious, petty and truancy offender subgroups but not for traffic-only cases. The low IQ boys subgroup has the lowest rate of traffic-only cases; the middle IQ subgroup has the highest rate.

VARIATION IN DELINQUENCY RATES BY SOCIAL STATUS STRUCTURES AND RESIDENTIAL RATES OF DELINQUENCY

Sociological theories which maintain that delinquency is primarily a lower class phenomenon differ in their explanatory use of the social class concept. The cultural transmission-differential association theorists view delinquency as behavior which is learned from other delinquents in residential areas where there is an established delinquent culture and organization. Although they usually describe the residential areas supporting a delinquent culture as "lower class," "slum" or "disorganized" areas, it can be inferred from their theory that delinquency rates should be high for *all* social class groups resident in high delinquency areas of a city.[8] Albert K. Cohen defines the social class variable as generating a delinquent gang subculture. His "status frustration" hypothesis holds that subcultural delinquency is a reaction-formation against a middle-class organized status dilemma in which the lower-class boy suffers status frustrations in competition with middle status boys. The delinquent subculture provides a solution to these problems when boys who are similarly frustrated interact together, by conferring status on the frustrated boys.[9] Following Cohen's reasoning, one would deduce that: (1) lower status boys, regardless of their residential location, should generate subcultural delinquency (and

perhaps the highest rate of all delinquency as well) if they interact and, (2) that the rate of subcultural delinquency among low status boys who interact should be higher in areas and schools where they are in direct competition with middle status ones (the competition is presumably more intense) and the lowest in the monolithic low-status area. A test of these hypotheses and the deductions from them is made below.

The effects of social class status stem from two principal sources so far as the adolescent in our society is concerned. One source is the status of his family in the larger society, e.g., whether he is middle or lower class, regardless of where he resides. This is sometimes referred to as his mass society status position. The other major effect of status is the status structure of the school and residential community. It may be one thing to be a low status boy in a primarily low status school or community and quite another to be one in a school which crosscuts the class structure or in one of a primarily high status composition. The first status component is referred to as his *ascribed social status* since his status position is that of the family status in the social structure. The second component is referred to as the *social status structure* of the school (and usually therefore of the residential community in American cities). The purpose of our investigation is to learn whether both of these components independently affect the rate of delinquency consistent with deductions from the Cohen and differential association theories and, in turn, whether the effect of the rate of delinquency of an area is independent of both status components in delinquency.

Variation in delinquency rates for the ascribed social status position of boys and the social status structure of schools is described in Table 3–24. Delinquency rates, in general, vary inversely with the prestige component of the social status structure of the school (except for the Crosscut: Center schools) and by the ascribed social status of the boy. The range of variation of ascribed social status is less (3.9 per cent) than that for variation in status structures of schools (12.4 per cent), suggesting that the status structure of the school exercises a greater

---

[8]This seems to be a valid inference from the Shaw-McKay and Sutherland positions, although it is never quite explicitly formulated in this way.

[9]Albert K. Cohen, *Delinquent Boys,* op. cit., Chap. 5.

TABLE 3–24.

RATE OF DELINQUENCY PER 100 WHITE SCHOOL BOYS CALCULATED SEPARATELY FOR ALL OFFENSES[*] AND ALL OFFENSES WITH TRAFFIC OFFENCES EXCLUDED, BY OCCUPATIONAL STATUS OF FATHER AND STATUS STRUCTURE OF THE SCHOOL

Status Structure of the School	Occupational Status of Father											
	High			Middle			Low			Total[a]		
	Sub-total	All Offenses	Excl. Traffic	Sub-total	All Offenses	Excl. Traffic	Sub-total	All Offenses	Excl. Traffic	Number	All Offenses	Excl. Traf.
Upper & upper middle	292	3.8	0.7	109	2.8	0.0	6	0.0	0.0	434	3.2	0.5
Balanced middle	389	6.2	2.6	310	5.8	2.0	35	0.0	0.0	749	5.6	2.2
Crosscut: top	567	6.5	3.9	1,039	5.9	3.7	372	5.9	4.4	2,119	6.1	3.8
Crosscut: center	117	9.4	6.3	446	10.1	6.0	217	9.6	5.8	797	9.7	5.8
Representative of all	160	2.5	1.9	446	6.3	5.3	294	8.5	6.9	965	6.2	5.2
Crosscut: bottom	237	5.5	3.4	1,026	9.4	7.5	914	9.2	8.4	2,267	8.7	7.3
Lower	52	7.7	6.0	423	15.4	13.5	353	16.4	14.5	847	15.6	13.8
Total	1,814	5.7	3.0	3,799	8.3	5.7	2,191	9.6	7.6	9,238	7.8	5.6

[*]Includes all official and unofficial court cases of delinquency other than minor traffic offenses (violation of registration and driver's license laws).

[a]The number of cases for which information on father's occupation is not reported can be obtained by subtraction from the total column of each school prestige status context.

effect on delinquent behavior than does ascribed social status.[10]

The effect of the occupational status structure of the school on ascribed status position is to alter, for an adolescent in any ascribed status group, the life-chances of becoming a delinquent. The occupational structure of the school "virtually eliminates" the *risk* of being a delinquent of court record for low status boys in schools with a predominantly high status student body and substantially increases the *risk* of a low status boy in a predominantly low status school. The average rate of court recorded delinquency is 9.6 for all low status boys, but in the two top status structures it is zero, while in the lowest one it is over 16 per cent. The effect of the status structure is somewhat less for middle status boys and least marked for high status boys. If all traffic offenses are eliminated, however, the results are as striking for the middle and low status boys and somewhat more clearcut for high status ones. The effect of the social structure of a residential community on the rate of delinquency is virtually to double the rate for any status group in the lowest status context and to bring it to its lowest point (approaching zero) in the highest status context.

Despite the effect which the social structure of the school has on the delinquency *rate* of boys, it nevertheless is true that the majority of delinquents at the high and low status levels come from those schools where the class stratification "favors" their status level. Examining Table 3–25, we can see that 70 per cent of all high status delinquents are residents of the top three contexts while 68 per cent of all lower status delinquents are drawn from the lower two status contexts. The pattern of residential segregation in American cities, of course, exerts this effect on the proportionate distribution of delinquents by social structure.

At each status level delinquents are *over-*represented in some stratification context relative to their representation in that context. Thus,

[10]It should be kept in mind, however, that the defined range of variation is restricted to only three classes for ascribed social status but seven classes of social status structures; some ascribed social status variation probably is lost with fewer classes.

TABLE 3–25.

PERCENTAGE OF JUVENILE COURT DELINQUENTS AND OF NON-DELINQUENTS AT EACH
ASCRIBED STATUS LEVEL FROM EACH TYPE OF STATUS STRUCTURE

Status Structure of the School	Occupational Status of Father							
	High		Middle		Low		Total	
	J.C.*	Not J.C.	J.C.	Not J.C.	J.C.	Not J.C.	J.C.	Not J.C.
Upper & upper middle	10.6	16.4	0.9	3.0	0.0	0.3	2.1	5.6
Balanced middle	23.1	21.3	5.7	8.4	0.0	1.8	6.4	9.4
Crosscut: top	35.6	31.1	19.3	28.1	10.5	17.7	20.0	26.4
Crosscut: center	10.6	6.2	14.2	11.5	10.0	9.9	11.8	9.6
Crosscut: representative of all	3.8	9.1	8.9	12.0	11.9	13.6	9.2	12.0
Crosscut: bottom	12.5	13.1	30.4	26.7	40.0	41.8	30.3	27.5
Lower	3.8	2.8	20.6	10.3	27.6	14.9	20.2	9.5
Total per cent	100.0	100.0	100.0	100.0	100.0	100.0	100.0	100.0
Number	114	1,807	366	3,893	253	2,393	759	8,479

* J.C. = Juvenile Court.

twice as many of the delinquents, as of all boys, are drawn from the low ascribed social status position in the lower status structure context. Correlatively, lower class delinquents are *under-* represented in the top stratification contexts. There are, in fact, proportionally fewer delinquents of all status levels in the upper status contexts than would be expected from their status context distribution. The combined effect of ascribed social status and status context can easily be examined in Table 3–26. The delinquency life-chances of a boy in any ascribed status position also varies with the delinquency rate of the residential area, as examination of

Table 3–27 shows. In both the low and high rate delinquency areas, the probability that a boy will be a delinquent varies inversely with his status position. This means that in low and in high delinquency areas, the low status boy has the greatest chance of becoming delinquent, although, to be sure, his chances are only one in a hundred in the low delinquency area, while they are one in five in the high delinquency areas. The relationship is less clear for the areas with "average" rates of delinquency where the probability of being a delinquent is almost as great for high as low status boys.

The joint effects of the delinquency rate of

TABLE 3–26.

PERCENTAGE OF JUVENILE COURT DELINQUENTS AND OF ALL BOYS IN EACH ASCRIBED
SOCIAL STATUS-SOCIAL STRUCTURE POSITION

Social Structure of School	Occupational Status of Father											
	High				Middle				Low			
	J.C.		All		J.C.		All		J.C.		All	
	N	%	N	%	N	%	N	%	N	%	N	%
Upper & upper middle	11	1.7	292	3.7	3	0.5	109	1.4	—	0.0	6	0.1
Balanced middle	24	3.8	389	5.0	18	2.9	310	4.0	—	0.0	35	0.4
Crosscut: top	37	5.9	567	7.3	61	9.7	1,039	13.3	22	3.5	372	4.8
Crosscut: center	11	1.7	117	1.5	45	7.1	446	5.7	21	3.3	217	2.8
Crosscut: representative of all	4	0.6	160	2.1	28	4.4	446	5.7	25	4.0	294	3.8
Crosscut: bottom	13	2.1	237	3.0	96	15.3	1,026	13.1	84	13.4	914	11.7
Lower	4	0.6	52	0.7	65	10.3	423	5.4	58	9.2	353	4.5

TABLE 3–27.

RATE OF DELINQUENCY* PER 100 WHITE SCHOOL BOYS BY OCCUPATIONAL STATUS OF FATHER AND DELINQUENCY RATE OF RESIDENTIAL AREAS

| Delinquency Rate of Residential Area | Occupational Status of Father | | | | | | | | | | | |
| | High | | | Middle | | | Low | | | Total[a] | | |
	Delinquents	Subtotal	Rate per 100	Delinquents	Subtotal	Rate per 100	Delinquents	Subtotal	Rate per 100	Delinquents	Number	Rate per 100
0.0– 1.9	0	298	0.0	3	354	.8	2	213	.9	6	898	.7
2.0– 3.9	3	184	1.6	14	461	3.0	11	313	3.5	28	999	2.8
4.0– 5.9	10	382	2.6	43	1,075	4.0	47	776	6.1	106	2,358	4.5
6.0– 7.9	12	182	6.6	10	103	9.7	5	80	6.3	28	399	7.0
8.0– 9.9	37	481	7.7	54	726	7.4	30	290	10.3	124	1,564	7.9
10.0–11.9	14	114	12.3	44	424	10.4	30	271	11.1	94	874	10.8
12.0–13.9	15	130	11.5	42	322	13.0	10	103	9.7	69	566	12.2
14.0–15.9	2	34	5.9	25	184	13.6	20	138	14.5	49	374	13.1
16.0–17.9	11	80	13.8	49	308	15.9	40	237	16.9	101	635	15.9
18.0 & Over	3	37	8.1	52	299	17.4	43	222	19.4	101	566	17.8
Total	107	1,922	5.6	336	4,258	7.9	238	2,644	9.0	707	9,238	7.7

*Includes all official and unofficial court cases of delinquency other than minor traffic offenses (violation of registration and driver's license laws).

[a]The number of cases for which information on father's occupation is not reported can be obtained from Table 3-24.

an area and its social status structure on the delinquency rate of ascribed status positions must be investigated to clarify the effect of these variables on the delinquency life-chances of a boy. Table 3–28 provides such a distribution. Within each ascribed status group, the delinquency rate usually rises with the delinquency rate of the area regardless of the social status composition of the area. Using a sign test, the probability is less than .01 that the observed differences in rates for ascribed status groups in Table 3–28 would occur by chance. In every status stratification context, the chances that a high, middle or low status boy will be a delinquent are greater if he resides in a high than in a low delinquency rate area. Both the occupational stratification of the area and the delinquency rate of residential areas, then, are independent sources of variation in the rate of delinquency for ascribed social status groups.

Examination of the percentage distribution in Table 3–29 sheds further light on the effect of these variables on the delinquency life-chances of a boy. It is apparent that boys with a juvenile court record, regardless of their ascribed social status and the social status structure of the area in which they live, come in larger numbers than expected from the high rate delinquency areas.

Given a restricted range of delinquency rate areas for any ascribed status-occupational stratification subgroup, the delinquents in every ascribed status occupational stratification subgroup are, with few exceptions (P<.01), disproportionately drawn from areas with the highest rates. This relationship is, however, less apparent in the lower occupational stratification context than in any other.

One other finding in Table 3–29 is of some interest. With the exception of the preponderantly lower or upper class stratification contexts, a substantial proportion of the delinquents at each ascribed status level comes from areas with "moderate" rates of delinquency within the range for that type of context.

IMPLICATIONS FOR
DELINQUENCY THEORY

At this point we have several empirical findings that may be related to the major theories of delinquency causation. First, it is clear that there is no simple relationship between ascribed social status and delinquency. Both the status structure of an area and the extent to which delinquency occurs as a cultural tradition affect the delinquency life-chances of a boy at each ascribed

TABLE 3–28.

RATE OF DELINQUENCY PER 100 WHITE SCHOOL BOYS BY DELINQUENCY RATE OF RESIDENTIAL AREA, PRESTIGE STATUS CONTEXT OF SCHOOL AND OCCUPATIONAL STATUS OF FATHER*

School Prestige Status Context & Occupational Status of Father	Delinquency Rate of Residential Area										
	0.0 to 1.9	2.0 to 3.9	4.0 to 5.9	6.0 to 7.9	8.0 to 9.9	10.0 to 11.9	12.0 to 13.9	14.0 to 15.9	16.0 to 17.9	18.0 to Over	Total
Upper & upper middle											
High	0.0	—	—	6.8	—	—	—	—	—	—	3.8
Middle	0.0	—	—	8.1	—	—	—	—	—	—	2.8
Low	0.0	—	—	0.0	—	—	—	—	—	—	0.0
Balanced middle											
High	0.0	—	—	8.2	—	—	—	—	—	—	6.2
Middle	0.0	—	—	8.8	—	—	—	—	—	—	5.8
Low	0.0	—	—	0.0	—	—	—	—	—	—	0.0
Crosscut: top											
High	0.0	1.6	3.0	—	10.0	13.4	10.6	—	—	—	6.5
Middle	0.0	2.3	3.7	—	5.8	9.1	13.0	—	—	—	5.9
Low	0.0	2.2	4.9	—	8.3	11.9	9.4	—	—	—	5.9
Crosscut: center											
High	0.0	—	2.0	—	—	—	13.9	—	20.0	—	9.4
Middle	0.0	—	4.8	—	—	—	13.1	—	13.7	—	10.1
Low	0.0	—	3.6	—	—	—	9.9	—	19.6	—	9.7
Crosscut: representative of all											
High	0.0	—	2.5	—	3.6	—	—	5.0	—	—	2.5
Middle	2.7	—	3.6	—	7.8	—	—	16.7	—	—	6.3
Low	0.0	—	8.8	—	15.2	—	—	15.2	—	—	8.5
Crosscut: bottom											
High	0.0	2.9	0.0	—	4.2	9.4	—	—	10.9	—	5.5
Middle	1.6	4.7	6.3	—	7.2	11.3	—	—	17.3	—	9.4
Low	2.5	3.2	3.5	—	10.9	10.8	—	—	16.0	—	9.2
Lower											
High	0.0	—	—	—	—	—	—	7.1	—	8.1	7.7
Middle	0.0	—	—	—	—	—	—	11.6	—	17.4	15.4
Low	0.0	—	—	—	—	—	—	14.3	—	19.4	16.4

*Based on 9,238 cases of white boys.

status level. While the life-chances of low ascribed status boys becoming delinquent are greater than those of high status ones, a low status boy in a predominantly high status area with a low rate of delinquency has almost no chance of being classified a juvenile court delinquent. In this latter situation, the delinquency life-chances of a high status boy are greater than for low status boys.[11]

[11]To some it will seem obvious that low-status boys in high-status areas are not "representative" of low-status boys. The theories do not specify what "lower class criteria" are to be utilized in identifying low-status boys who are "delinquency prone." If class selectivity operates by residential areas, then perhaps no area has a "representative" lower class.

Likewise, there does not seem to be much evidence that the lower class boy is more likely to be delinquent the more he is subjected to pressure from middle-class norms. The more the lower class boy is in a minority in the school and residential community,[12] the less likely is he to become delinquent.[13] What seems more

[12]Sociometric data are available for only a cross-section of boys: These data show however, that lower class boys in middle class areas interact together in that they are most likely to choose, and to have reciprocated the choices of, lower class boys.
[13]Some readers may have discerned that the delinquency rate of Crosscut: center schools is higher than might be expected, given its status composi-

(Footnote Continued)

TABLE 3–29.

PERCENTAGE OF JUVENILE COURT DELINQUENTS AND NON-DELINQUENTS BY DELINQUENCY RATE OF RESIDENTIAL AREA FOR SOCIAL STATUS POSITIONS AND PRESTIGE STATUS CONTEXTS[a]

Prestige Status Context & Social Status Position	Delinquency Rate of Residential Area										Per-cent of Context
	0.0 to 1.9	2.0 to 3.9	4.0 to 5.9	6.0 to 7.9	8.0 to 9.9	10.0 to 11.9	12.0 to 13.9	14.0 to 15.9	16.0 to 17.9	18.0 to Over	
Upper & upper middle											
High: J.C.*	—	—	—	100.0	—	—	—	—	—	—	78.5
High: Not J.C.	46.3	—	—	53.7	—	—	—	—	—	—	71.5
Middle: J.C.	—	—	—	100.0	—	—	—	—	—	—	21.5
Middle: Not J.C.	67.9	—	—	32.1	—	—	—	—	—	—	27.0
Low: J.C.	—	—	—	—	—	—	—	—	—	—	—
Low: Not J.C.	83.3	—	—	16.7	—	—	—	—	—	—	1.5
Balanced middle											
High: J.C.	—	—	—	100.0	—	—	—	—	—	—	57.1
High: Not J.C.	26.8	—	—	73.2	—	—	—	—	—	—	52.7
Middle: J.C.	—	—	—	100.0	—	—	—	—	—	—	42.9
Middle: Not J.C.	35.3	—	—	64.7	—	—	—	—	—	—	42.2
Low: J.C.	—	—	—	—	—	—	—	—	—	—	—
Low: Not J.C.	42.9	—	—	57.1	—	—	—	—	—	—	5.1
Crosscut: top											
High: J.C.	—	5.4	13.5	—	24.3	29.7	27.0	—	—	—	30.8
High: Not J.C.	1.3	24.0	30.2	—	15.3	13.4	15.8	—	—	—	28.6
Middle: J.C.	—	9.8	18.0	—	13.1	26.2	32.8	—	—	—	50.8
Middle: Not J.C.	0.9	25.6	29.7	—	13.4	16.4	13.7	—	—	—	52.5
Low: J.C.	—	9.0	31.8	—	13.6	31.8	13.6	—	—	—	18.4
Low: Not J.C.	2.6	26.0	38.9	—	9.4	14.9	8.3	—	—	—	18.9
Crosscut: center											
High: J.C.	—	—	9.1	—	—	—	45.5	—	45.5	—	14.3
High: Not J.C.	6.6	—	45.3	—	—	—	29.2	—	18.9	—	15.1
Middle: J.C.	—	—	15.6	—	—	—	48.9	—	35.6	—	58.4
Middle: Not J.C.	3.5	—	34.9	—	—	—	36.4	—	25.2	—	57.0
Low: J.C.	—	—	14.3	—	—	—	33.3	—	52.4	—	27.3
Low: Not J.C.	3.6	—	40.8	—	—	—	32.7	—	23.0	—	27.9
Crosscut: rep. of all											
High: J.C.	—	—	50.0	—	25.0	—	—	25.0	—	—	7.0
High: Not J.C.	20.5	—	50.0	—	17.3	—	—	12.2	—	—	18.5
Middle: J.C.	7.1	—	28.6	—	21.4	—	—	42.9	—	—	49.1
Middle: Not J.C.	17.5	—	51.2	—	17.0	—	—	14.4	—	—	49.6
Low: J.C.	—	—	60.0	—	20.0	—	—	20.0	—	—	43.9
Low: Not J.C.	21.6	—	57.6	—	10.4	—	—	10.4	—	—	31.9
Crosscut: bottom											
High: J.C.	—	7.7	—	—	23.0	23.0	—	—	46.2	—	6.7
High: Not J.C.	8.0	14.7	11.6	—	30.8	12.9	—	—	21.9	—	11.3
Middle: J.C.	1.0	5.2	7.3	—	22.9	29.1	—	—	34.4	—	49.7
Middle: Not J.C.	6.8	11.0	11.2	—	30.4	23.7	—	—	17.0	—	46.9
Low: J.C.	2.4	4.8	4.8	—	26.2	27.4	—	—	34.5	—	43.6
Low: Not J.C.	9.4	14.6	13.4	—	21.6	22.8	—	—	18.3	—	41.8
Lower											
High: J.C.	—	—	—	—	—	—	—	25.0	—	75.0	3.1
High: Not J.C.	2.0	—	—	—	—	—	—	27.1	—	70.8	6.8
Middle: J.C.	—	—	—	—	—	—	—	20.0	—	80.0	51.2
Middle: Not J.C.	3.4	—	—	—	—	—	—	27.7	—	69.0	51.1
Low: J.C.	—	—	—	—	—	—	—	25.9	—	74.1	45.7
Low: Not J.C.	8.5	—	—	—	—	—	—	30.5	—	60.7	42.1

*J.C. = Juvenile Court.
[a]Based on 9,238 cases of white boys.

apparent is that the largest proportion of delinquents for any status group comes from the more homogeneous status areas for that group and that the delinquency life-chances of *all* status groups tend to be greatest in the lower status area and in the high delinquency rate areas.

Examination of the data in Tables 3–27, 3–28 and 3–29 lends some support to Miller's thesis that delinquency (violative behavior) is normative in lower class culture while conformity (nonviolative behavior) is normative in middle class culture. Yet a number of facts in these tables do not support Miller's position as he has formulated it.[14] The more important of these are: (1) delinquency does not appear to be normative in all lower class areas if the rate is taken as an indicator of a norm; (2) substantial numbers of delinquents come from residential areas where the majority of residents are from other than the lower class; (3) high status boys in the three top status contexts have somewhat higher delinquency rates than middle or low status boys. It is possible for Miller to rationalize these exceptions with his more general formulation. He holds that lower class culture is seldom found in its pure form in most residential areas. Consequently, the rate in a residential area is not a simple function of class culture, but of both the relative prevalence of the classes in an area and the extent to which the class culture of each is diffused to the other.

The third major conclusion which seems warranted at this point is that the factors related to where a family of a given ascribed status will live are important in predicting the delinquency life-chances of a boy of any ascribed status. The evidence seems to be consistent with what we already know but have not generally incorporated in our theory—that lower class status is not a necessary and sufficient set of conditions in the etiology of any type of delinquency. Rather, we know there are some lower class areas of large American cities that consistently produce a high volume of all delinquency and most of the systematically organized career delinquency, while other lower class areas, particularly rural ones, do not. The theoretical problem is: *why should delinquency be so widespread in some lower class areas, and not in others?* Cloward and Ohlin suggest that variation in the availability of both legitimate and illegitimate opportunity structures is crucial in determining the delinquency orientation of lower class boys in status dilemmas.[15] There probably are other community conditions as well which account for these differences.

SUBCULTURAL DELINQUENCY

Gang delinquency is generally viewed as a lower class phenomenon, although Cohen and Short suggest that only some subcultural forms of gang delinquency are a distinctly lower class phenomenon.[16] An attempt was made to learn whether the "parent delinquent subculture" is largely a lower class phenomenon. It is difficult, however, to test for the hypothesized distribution given lack of precision in the theoretical formulation, for this, in turn, generates problems of operationalization.

A two per cent sample of white boys, ages 10 to 16 (158 cases) and their first two sociometric choices was selected and interviewed intensively on their career orientations and delinquency history. The interview population was classified into seven major types of conforming-deviating behavior using eight major variables: (1) achievement orientation in school and vocational aspirations; (2) conforming or deviating behavior score of sociometric choices; (3) whether or not the sociometric choices were reciprocated; (4) whether or not time was spent with peers in the evening; (5) the quality of supervision

tion. The higher rate here is altogether accounted for by two schools. One of these schools is the vocational high school which tends to selectively recruit boys who are "in trouble" in some other school. The other school serves a very large territorial area made up of relatively homogeneous class areas so that the social structure of each junior high school which "feeds" this high school falls either "above" or "below" the structure of the senior high context.

[14]Walter B. Miller, op. cit.

[15]Richard A. Cloward and Lloyd E. Ohlin, *Delinquency and Opportunity: A Theory of Delinquent Gangs* (New York: The Free Press, 1960).

[16]Cohen and Short distinguish varieties of the "parent male subculture." Most of them are viewed as lower class varieties. Albert K. Cohen and James F. Short, Jr., "Research in Delinquent Subcultures," *Journal of Social Issues* 14, no. 3 (1958): 20–37.

offered in leisure situations; (6) the usual type of delinquent offense committed by the boy and his associates in delinquent acts; (7) the pattern of delinquent activity; (8) the teacher's rating of the boy's behavior in the school and community. Table 3–30 briefly outlines the ideal typical characteristics for defining each of the seven conforming-deviating subtypes.

Cohen characterizes the delinquent subculture as having a non-utilitarian, malicious, and negativistic emphasis. Participants in the gang have a versatile content to their delinquent offenses. The group, rather than the individual, is autonomous. The study design operationalized each of these characteristics of the subculture but the measures generally failed to achieve sufficient discrimination to isolate such a subtype.[17]

The "most delinquent" person in the classification schema developed for this study is based on the conception of the career delinquent as advanced by E. W. Burgess, Clifford Shaw and E. H. Sutherland, among others. The career delinquent is one whose achievement orientation is that of the adult criminal. He is a member of a gang that maintains contacts with adult criminals. Most career oriented delinquents probably would be classified as participants in Cohen's parent delinquent subculture, but the class would not exhaust his subcultural category.

The other major type of group delinquent in this investigation is called the peer oriented delinquent, since these boys are essentially peer oriented and peer directed in their goals and activity. Though the boys do band together in delinquent activity, the delinquency is primarily a consequence of orientation toward other group goals. The "lone delinquent" is classified as a non-conforming isolate.

Conformers are divided into four subtypes; two subtypes are classified primarily on the basis of their achievement orientation, one on the absence of peer affiliation, and a fourth on the basis of overconformity to social norms.

---

[17]Cohen's theory accounts for the origin of delinquent subcultures. It is not altogether clear how one would operationally identify gangs which participate in the parent delinquent subculture or one of its varieties.

The social class distribution of each of the conforming-deviating subtypes is presented below. There is a sizeable sampling error for the estimates, since there are but 158 cases representing a two per cent random sample of the population of boys. Nevertheless, several predicted findings emerge from the data: (1) there is more frequent and serious delinquent deviation in the lower than in the middle stratum when the self-reports of delinquent deviation by boys are examined; this is true in fact for all classes of deviators—career and peer oriented delinquents, nonconforming isolates and conforming nonachievers; (2) the career oriented delinquent is found only among lower class boys; (3) peer oriented delinquency is the most common form of delinquent organization at both status levels; (4) the major type of lower status boy is a conforming nonachiever while the conforming achiever is the major type in the middle class; (5) conformers are more likely to be isolates than are non-conformers; the lone delinquent is infrequent in a population of boys.

Career oriented delinquent	*Per Cent*
Blue-collar	1.3
White-collar	0.0
Peer oriented delinquent	
Blue-collar	4.5
White-collar	1.3
Conforming nonachiever	
Blue-collar	31.3
White-collar	3.3
Conforming achiever	
Blue-collar	12.0
White-collar	29.3
Hyperconformer	
Blue-collar	3.9
White-collar	2.0
Nonconforming isolate	
Blue-collar	0.6
White-collar	0.6
Conforming isolate	
Blue-collar	8.6
White-collar	1.3

One other important finding emerges from these comparisons. Conforming isolates are more

TABLE 3–30.

CLASSIFICATION OF SEVEN TYPES OF CONFORMERS OR DEVIATORS BASED ON EIGHT PRINCIPAL CRITERIA OF CLASSIFICATION

Type of Conformer or Deviator	Achievement Orientation	Sociometric Choices	Reciprocation of Sociometric Choices	Time with Peers in Evening	Leisure Time in Supervised Situations	Usual Delinquent Offenses	Content of Delinquent Offenses	Teacher's Rating
Organized career delinquent	Low	Delinquent peers and adult criminals	Yes	Regularly	None	Serious	Versatile	School behavior problem or trouble maker
Peer oriented delinquent	Low	Delinquent peers	Yes	Regularly	None	Petty (some serious)	Versatile	Poorly motivated and school behavior problem
Conforming nonachiever	Low	Conforming peers	Yes	Occasionally	Mostly	Minor infractions	Conventional infractions	Poorly motivated or conformer
Conforming achiever	High	Conforming peers	Yes	Occasionally	Always	Rare	——	Conformer
Nonconforming isolate	Any Level	Few or none	No reciprocation	Never	Alone or family only	Serious or petty	Specialized or versatile	School behavior problem or trouble maker
Conforming isolate	Any Level	Few or none	No reciprocation	Never	Alone or family only	None	——	Poorly motivated or conformer
Hyperconformer	High	Other hyperconformers	Yes	Rare	Always	None	——	Conformer

frequent in the blue- than in the white-collar stratum. If it is assumed that in many lower class areas, the pressures of groups are toward nonconforming activities then at least in these communities isolation from the group may be a price of social conformity. There is much more support for group organized conventional behavior in middle class areas.

25.

Robert Everett Stanfield

THE INTERACTION OF FAMILY VARIABLES AND GANG VARIABLES IN THE AETIOLOGY OF DELINQUENCY

A sociologist has recently written that "[w]herever one can develop a rationale for predicting interaction, one should make a conscious effort to construct and test theories that explicitly take advantage of interactive effects."[1] In empirical research on opportunity theory in delinquency, some evidence has been presented showing interactive relationships between variables representing availability of both legitimate and illegitimate opportunities.[2] This article is a further effort to press for theory building and testing through the use of statistical interaction in empirical studies.

Over the past decades, two major traditions have emerged in the aetiology of delinquency. These have been variously called the psychogenic and the sociogenic,[3] the psychiatric-psychoanalytic and the sociological,[4] the individual and the collective.[5] The first has traced delinquency to the development of a personality with a disposition toward the violation of law. The second has regarded delinquency as a phenomenon of cultural areas that lack social controls over the violation of law or that have positive supports for delinquent behavior.

Proponents of these traditions have argued whether the family or the gang has the greater importance in determining delinquent behavior. Supporters of the psychogenic tradition have tended to emphasize the association between juvenile crime and certain aspects of family life: rejection or lack of affection by a parent; the laxity, inconsistency, or severity of discipline; the absence or inappropriateness of a parent as a role model.[6] Those that hold the sociogenic view have maintained that delinquent behavior is learned in a gang as a system of preferred behavior that is either a consequence of a dissociation in the social structure

SOURCE: Robert Everett Stanfield, "The Interaction of Family Variables in the Aetiology of Delinquency," *Social Problems* 13, no. 4 (Spring, 1966): 411–17. Reprinted by Permission of the author and The Society for the Study of Social Problems.

Support for this study was given by the Ford Foundation. The facilities of the Computation Center at the Massachusetts Institute of Technology, Cambridge, Massachusetts, were used for the analysis of some of the data.

[1] Hubert M. Blalock, Jr., "Theory Building and the Statistical Concept of Interaction," *American Sociological Review* 30 (June, 1965): 374, also 374–80.

[2] Erdman Palmore and Phillip E. Hammond, "Interacting Factors in Juvenile Delinquency," *American Sociological Review* 29 (December, 1964): 848–54.

[3] Albert K. Cohen, *Delinquent Boys: The Culture of The Gang* (New York: The Free Press, 1955), pp. 11–19.

[4] Marshall B. Clinard, "The Sociology of Delinquency and Crime," in *Review of Sociology: Analysis of a Decade*, ed. Joseph B. Gittler (New York: John Wiley & Sons, Inc., 1957), pp. 465–99.

[5] S. Kirson Weinberg, "Theories of Criminality and Problems of Prediction," *Journal of Criminal Law, Criminology and Police Science* 45 (1954): 412–24.

[6] For example see: Sheldon Glueck and Eleanor Glueck, *Unraveling Juvenile Delinquency* (New York: Commonwealth Fund, 1950); William McCord and Joan McCord, with Irving Kenneth Zola, *Origins of Crime: A New Evaluation of the Cambridge-Somerville Youth Study* (New York: Columbia University Press, 1958).

between culturally prescribed goals and culturally approved means[7] or a result of a conflict of values and norms among the social classes of society.[8]

Theory and research in delinquency have benefited from activity along independent lines of development within these two traditions, but further progress in the field might be achieved by investigating the relationship between the family and the gang in the aetiology of delinquency.

THEORY BUILDING WITH EXPECTATIONS OF STATISTICAL INTERACTION

Some efforts at integrating the two traditions already exist in the literature of social science. Shaw and McKay[9] asserted that delinquent behavior occurs when an individual, disposed toward delinquency by a particular family situation, learns such behavior from a group of peers in a neighborhood that has traditional and positive influences acting in support of such behavior. Tannenbaum[10] described delinquency as the consequence of the gang replacing the family as an individual's primary reference group due to the "inadequacy" of the family. Weinberg[11] proposed that boys become delinquent "when, for individualized purposes of emotional security, self-enhancement, or conflict-resolution, they seek and select accessible associates from whom they learn, accept, and express criminal attitudes." He suggested an empirical test that would utilize, as independent variables, certain aspects of family relations, the capacity for peer relations, and the accessibility of delinquent or nondelinquent peers. Haskell[12] identified the family as a reference group aligned with the dominant cultural system and the peer group as a reference group aligned with a deviant subcultural system. The delinquent boy was an individual who had taken the gang as his primary reference group. Haskell explained the negative case of the nondelinquent gang boy by arguing that satisfying experiences in the family as a normative reference group could overcome the effect of the gang as a delinquent reference group.

There seems implicit in all these attempts at integration an extension of Sutherland's theory of differential association,[13] with the family and the gang regarded as competing groups within which the individual may encounter definitions favorable or unfavorable to the violation of law. The differential frequency, duration, priority, and intensity of interpersonal associations within these groups affect the extent to which the values of the group are accepted by the individual. All these views seem to assume that the family is on the side of conformity with law, that the gang favors violation of law, and that a breakdown of associations within the family virtually assures the victory of a gang.

These assumptions, however, may be questioned. It might be appropriate to leave the culture of the family and the culture of the gang (that is, the values and norms regarding conformity to or violation of law) to be determined empirically. Not all families may favor conformity to law; not all gangs may support violation of law. Further, the consequences of a breakdown of interpersonal associations within the family should be more precisely conceptualized.

Although satisfying experiences may increase receptivity to the culture of the group, dissatisfying experiences do not necessarily result in the adoption of an opposing or conflicting culture. Non-acceptance of the family culture renders an individual more receptive to the culture of

---

[7]For example see: Cohen, op. cit.; Richard A. Cloward and Lloyd E. Ohlin, *Delinquency and Opportunity: A Theory of Delinquent Gangs* (New York: The Free Press, 1960).

[8]Walter B. Miller, "Lower Class Culture as a Generating Milieu of Gang Delinquency," *Journal of Social Issues* 14, no. 3 (1958): 5–18.

[9]Clifford R. Shaw and Henry D. McKay, *Social Factors in Juvenile Delinquency: A Study of the Community, the Family, and the Gang in Relation to Delinquent Behavior* (Washington, D.C.: Government Printing Office, 1931), esp. pp. 383–93.

[10]Frank Tannenbaum, *Crime and the Community* (New York: Columbia University Press, 1951 [originally published 1938]), pp. 12–13. Italics are omitted.

[11]Weinberg, op. cit.

[12]Martin Roy Haskell, "Toward a Reference Group Theory of Juvenile Delinquency," *Social Problems* 8 (1960): 219–30.

[13]Edwin H. Sutherland, *Principles of Criminology*, 5th ed., rev. Donald R. Cressey (Philadelphia: J. B. Lippincott Co., 1955 [originally published in 1927]), pp. 74–81.

other groups within his experience. It is possible that dissatisfying experiences in the home will make a boy more receptive to a gang culture that is not greatly different from his family culture. An encounter with a variant cultural pattern is most likely to occur when the socioeconomic status of the family differs from the socioeconomic status of the area in which it resides.

Satisfying experiences in the home do not diminish to a zero point the influence of the gang, but the boy is likely to select a peer group that has a culture compatible with that of the family. In contrast to Tannenbaum's view of the gang as a substitute for the family, one may see the gang as a group reinforcing the cultural pattern learned from the family. Thus, one may say that satisfying or pleasant experiences in a family increase the intensity of relationships within the family, leading to a greater probability of accepting the cultural pattern of the family. Acceptance of the family culture then tends to produce greater selectivity toward peers, leading toward the choice of a gang that supports the cultural pattern of the family. Unsatisfying or unpleasant experiences in a family, however, reduce the intensity of family relationships, leading to reduced receptivity toward family cultural patterns and susceptibility to outside (though not necessarily conflicting or opposing) cultural influences such as a gang.

These considerations suggest that explanation only in terms of direct causal relationships oversimplifies the situation. Family experiences and gang activity are related to delinquency only when such experiences and such activity occur in a cultural context that supports delinquent behavior. Unsatisfying family experiences are likely to result in delinquency to the degree that there exist in the neighborhood environment cultural definitions favorable to the violation of law. Gang activity is less likely to produce delinquent behavior when the gang does not have a culture providing support for criminal activity.

Confirmation of this view would depend on the empirical demonstration of interactive effects that can be adequately accounted for by these considerations. One may approach data with certain expectations of interactive effects. The

effect of family experiences may vary according to the socioeconomic status of the family. Similarly, gang activity may be more strongly related to delinquency at one level of socioeconomic status than at another. Further, the impact of frequent peer activity may depend on the nature of family experiences.

THEORY TESTING WITH OBSERVATIONS OF STATISTICAL INTERACTION

Appearances in a court for one or more juvenile offenses as a dependent variable show in the Cambridge-Somerville Youth Study[14] a direct relationship with each of the three independent variables being examined here. (See Table 3–31.) The lower the occupational status[15] of the father, the greater the percentage of boys appearing in court as juveniles for theft, assault, or sex offenses. A greater percentage of delinquent boys had fathers who were erratic or lax in discipline rather than consistent in discipline. A greater percentage of those active in gangs were delinquent than were those not active in gangs. In addition to these three direct relationships, one can find three meaningful instances of interaction among these variables.[16]

[14]For background on this study, see: Edwin Powers and Helen Witmer, *An Experiment in the Prevention of Delinquency: The Cambridge-Somerville Youth Study* (New York: Columbia University Press, 1951); McCord and McCord, op. cit.

[15]Measured by a scale of occupational status described in Albert J. Reiss, Jr., with Otis Dudley Duncan, Paul K. Hatt, and Cecil C. North, *Occupations and Social Status* (New York: The Free Press, 1961), pp. 109–61; 263–75.

[16]Although theoretically meaningful, these instances of interaction cannot be tested for the statistical significance of the differences in proportions. The Dorn-Stouffer-Tibbitts technique and its modification by Goodman are applicable for statistical tests of this sort when the data are derived from a large, random sample. The sample used here is neither large nor random. See Leo Goodman, "Modifications of the Dorn-Stouffer-Tibbitts Method for 'Testing the Significance of Comparisons in Sociological Data,'" *American Journal of Sociology* 66 (January, 1961): 355–63. A test for second-order interaction proposed by Goodman produces a statistically significant result in only the second of the three examples of interaction that follow. See Leo Goodman, "On the Multivariate Analysis of Three Dichotomous Variables," *American Journal of Sociology* 71 (November, 1965): 290–301. In Table 2, $W^2 = 0.40$ (n.s.); in Table 3, $W^2 = 4.25$ ($p < .05$); in Table 4, $W^2 = 1.23$ (n.s.). These data, then, should be treated merely as examples rather than as confirmations of hypotheses.

TABLE 3–31.

DIRECT RELATIONSHIPS BETWEEN DELINQUENCY AND DISCIPLINE, SOCIOECONOMIC STATUS, AND PEER INVOLVEMENT

Independent Variable	Percentage Convicted of Delinquency
Father's Occupational Status	
Low	29% (n = 154)
High	18% (n = 99)
	Diff. = 11% $X^2 = 3.52$ p < .10
Father's Discipline	
Erratic or lax	33% (n = 120)
Consistent	15% (n = 86)
	Diff. = 18% $X^2 = 7.13$ p < .01
Peer Activity	
Frequent	30% (n = 132)
Occasional	19% (n = 118)
	Diff. = 11% $X^2 = 3.94$ p < .05

First, the impact of paternal discipline seems clearly to be stronger among families of low socioeconomic status. (See Table 3–32). The difference in the delinquent proportion between those with erratic or lax fathers, and those with consistent fathers, is about twice as great among those from low status families as among those from high status families.

Among families of low socioeconomic status, there is probably greater opportunity for a boy to encounter a cultural pattern outside the family that supports behavior that violates law. If family experiences are of the kind that reduce recep-tivity to the family culture, the boy from a low status family is more likely to come into contact with a delinquency-supporting culture than is a boy from a high status family. Unpleasant family experiences are more likely to produce delinquency in circumstances where there is an alternative cultural pattern that is favorable to the violation of law.

Second, delinquency is more strongly related to the frequency of peer activity among boys from high status families than among those from low status families. (See Table 3–33.) Frequent peer activity produces about the same delinquent

TABLE 3–32.

DELINQUENCY, SOCIOECONOMIC STATUS, AND DISCIPLINE

	Percentage with Convictions for Delinquency	
	Father's Occupation	
	Low Status	High Status
Father's Discipline		
Erratic or lax	39% (n = 77)	21% (n = 43)
Consistent	17% (n = 46)	13% (n = 40)
	Diff. = 22% $X^2 = 5.31$ p < .05	Diff. = 20% $X^2 = 0.54$ p > .60

TABLE 3–33.

DELINQUENCY, SOCIOECONOMIC STATUS, AND PEER INVOLVEMENT

	Percentage with Convictions for Delinquency	
	Father's Occupation	
	Low Status	High Status
Peer Activity		
Frequent	31% (n = 83)	28% (n = 47)
Occasional	27% (n = 67)	8% (n = 51)
	Diff. = 4%	Diff. = 20%
	$X^2 = 0.17$	$X^2 = 5.39$
	$p > .60$	$p < .05$

proportion at both status levels in this study, but infrequent peer activity produces a much smaller proportion of juvenile offenders among those from high status families. The frequency of peer activity makes less difference in low status families.

The opportunities for learning delinquent behavior are less common for boys from high status families unless they spend a considerable amount of time on the street with friends. An individual from a low status family who associates rarely or only occasionally with peers still manages to learn delinquent behavior. The family itself may be the source of such learning. On the other hand, support for delinquency may so pervade the lower status levels that learning such a cultural pattern can be accomplished without frequent interaction with peers.

Third, the difference in the proportion of juvenile offenders between those active with peers and those not active with peers is greater among those with erratic or lax paternal discipline than among those with consistent paternal discipline. (See Table 3–34.) Where paternal supervision is weak, frequent activity with peers tends to be associated with delinquency. Consistent discipline by the father keeps the probability of delinquency low, whether or not the boy is actively involved in a gang. Similarly, frequency of peer activity has a stronger effect when the father rejects the son.

The evidence in regard to the father's discipline suggests that the influence of the gang in producing delinquency is stronger when experiences within the family limit the degree to which an individual learns the family's cultural pattern. Lax or erratic discipline by the father obscures the distinction between approved and disapproved behavior. Paternal rejection leads a boy to seek warmer interpersonal relationships in another context, and, thereby, increases the boy's susceptibility to learning a cultural pattern that supports violation of law.

Although the number of cases in each cell drops rather low, some interesting findings consistent with expectations of interaction emerge

TABLE 3–34.

DELINQUENCY, DISCIPLINE, AND PEER INVOLVEMENT

	Percentage with Convictions for Delinquency	
	Father's Discipline	
	Erratic or Lax	Consistent
Peer Activity		
Frequent	43% (n = 60)	16% (n = 44)
Occasional	23% (n = 57)	14% (n = 42)
	Diff. = 20%	Diff. = 2%
	$X^2 = 4.66$	$X^2 = 0.01$
	$p < .05$	$p > .80$

when one examines the interrelationships among the dependent variables and the three independent variables. (See Table 3–35.) Assuming only additive effects, one would expect outcomes of the sort suggested by the column headed "Expectation of Delinquent Outcome Based on Additive Effects." The actual outcomes are somewhat consistent with those expected outcomes, but two of the outcomes seem somewhat lower than might have been anticipated. The combination of consistent discipline, low socioeconomic status, and active gang participation might have been expected to produce a proportion of delinquents in the 30 to 40 per cent range, consistent with the other combinations that have two of the three variables tending toward delinquency; it is, however, only 14 per cent. Similarly, the combination of erratic or lax discipline, high socioeconomic status, and lack of active gang participation might have been expected to have a percentage greater than nine per cent. These low percentages are consistent with expectations based on the idea of interactive effects.

The low percentage of delinquents among those with consistent discipline, low father's occupational status, and gang activity may demonstrate the efficacy of consistent discipline in forestalling delinquency when the surrounding culture and the extent of peer group participation would suggest a high likelihood of delinquent behavior. The low percentage among those with erratic or lax paternal discipline, high father's occupational status, and infrequent gang activity, similarly, would demonstrate the efficacy of higher socioeconomic status and lack of peer group participation in forestalling delinquency despite the influence of bad discipline.

CONCLUSIONS

Evidence from the Cambridge-Somerville Youth Study gives support to a theoretical formulation of delinquency causation proposed in this paper. The findings of interactive effects demonstrate that explanation in terms of direct causal relationships is inadequate. Delinquent behavior is the consequence of *learning* a pattern of *culture* that supports the violation of law, and there is variation in outcome according to the content of the culture learned, the context in which the culture is learned, and the nature of experiences by which the culture is learned.

The demonstration of interactive effects indicates that the effects of experiences in the family and the gang on the learning of delinquent behavior are contingent upon the socioeconomic status of the group. Culture specifies the conditions under which family and gang experiences have a delinquency-producing impact. Socioeconomic status intensifies the relationship of delinquency to parental rejection and discipline at *lower* status levels. It intensifies the relationship of delinquency with the frequency of peer activity at *higher* status levels.

TABLE 3–35.

DELINQUENCY, DISCIPLINE, SOCIOECONOMIC STATUS, AND PEER INVOLVEMENT

Father's Discipline	Father's Occupation	Peer Activity	Expectation of Delinquent Outcome Based on Additive Effects	Percentage Convicted of Delinquency
Erratic or lax (1)	Low status (1)	Frequent (1) .... 3 Very high		46% (n = 41)
		Occasional (0) .... 2 High		32% (n = 34)
	High status (0)	Frequent (1) .... 2 High		37% (n = 19)
		Occasional (0) .... 1 Low		9% (n = 23)
Consistent (0)	Low status (1)	Frequent (1) .... 2 High		14% (n = 22)
		Occasional (0) .... 1 Low		21% (n = 24)
	High status (0)	Frequent (1) .... 1 Low		18% (n = 22)
		Occasional (0) .... 0 Very low		6% (n = 18)

Further, the nature of family experiences performs a similar function of intensifying the effect of peer activity when discipline is low. Lack of parental supervision increases the influence of companions on the street.

Certain shortcomings of the data from the Cambridge-Somerville Youth Study (the nonrandom basis of selecting the study group, the incompleteness of records in some cases, and the small size and homogeneity of the study group) require that the findings reported here be treated as suggestive rather than conclusive.

Further, caution must be exercised in evaluating these data because perceived interaction among variables may actually be due to random error in one or more of the variables. Blalock[17] points to this problem in developing a theory involving three or more variables.

This demonstration suggests, nevertheless, that deeper understanding of causation and greater accuracy in prediction may be achieved through the investigation of the interaction among independent variables that are statistically associated with a dependent variable. In the identification of the predelinquent, techniques of prediction based on an additive model of the joint effects of related factors may have some success, but prediction might be improved by combining predictive factors in both an additive and an interactive way.

These theoretical considerations have focused on the transmission through the family and the gang of an orientation toward delinquent or nondelinquent behavior rather than on the origin of such an orientation in the culture of the family or the gang.[18] Subsequent studies might attempt to use a similar kind of approach to relate theories of transmission to such theories of origin as that of differential opportunity structures[19] or conflict of independently developed class cultures.[20]

---

[17]Hubert M. Blalock, Jr., "Some Implications of Random Measurement Error for Causal Inferences," *American Journal of Sociology* 71 (July, 1965): 37–47, see particularly 44–45.

[18]Cohen, op. cit., pp. 18–19.
[19]Cloward and Ohlin, op. cit.; see also Palmore and Hammond, op. cit.
[20]Miller, op. cit.

26.

RALPH W. ENGLAND, JR.

A THEORY OF MIDDLE CLASS JUVENILE DELINQUENCY

Since 1948 the number of children aged 10 to 17 coming before juvenile court authorities has more than doubled, while the number of children within these ages in the total population has increased by only 19 percent.[1] Despite the caution with which one must regard juvenile court data, police arrest statistics and the testimony of numerous persons working with youth support the Children's Bureau figures.[2] There exists nonstatistical evidence that an unprecedented share of the apparent increase in delinquency is being contributed by "normal" youngsters from middle class families in communities and neighborhoods lacking previous experience with serious misbehavior among their children.

SOURCE: Ralph W. England, Jr., "A Theory of Middle Class Juvenile Delinquency," *Journal of Criminal Law, Criminology and Police Science* 50, no. 6 (April, 1960): 535–40. Reprinted by Special Permission of the *Journal of Criminal Law, Criminology and Police Science* (Northwestern University School of Law), Copyright © 1960, Volume 50, Number 6.

[1]*Juvenile Court Statistics: 1956*, Children's Bureau Statistical Series, No. 47, U. S. Children's Bureau, Washington, D. C., 1958.

[2]Herbert A. Bloch and Frank T. Flynn, *Delinquency: The Juvenile Offender in America Today* (New York: Random House, 1956), p. 29.

Rowdiness in and out of school, abuse of driving privileges, joy-riding thefts, excessive drinking, vandalism and sexual misconduct are among the principal forms of disapproved acts seemingly becoming more frequent among teenagers from "better" backgrounds. And the problem is not merely a phenomenon of metropolitan areas: towns and smaller cities in which delinquency of any kind was nearly non-existent before the war are reporting similar difficulties.

A number of researches have shown the existence of considerable unrecorded delinquency among socially advantaged youths,[3] but few theoretical attempts have been made to explain such behavior. In an article published in 1942 Talcott Parsons touched briefly upon the existence and nature of a "youth culture":[4]

"Perhaps the best single point of reference for characterizing the youth culture lies in its contrast with the dominant pattern of the adult male role. By contrast with the emphasis on responsibility in this role, the orientation of the youth culture is more or less specifically irresponsible. One of its dominant notes is 'having a good time' in relation to which there is a particularly strong emphasis on social activities with the opposite sex (pp. 606–607).

". . . it is notable that the youth culture has a strong tendency to develop in directions which are either on the borderline of parental approval or beyond the pale, in such matters as sex behavior, drinking and various forms of frivolous and irresponsible behavior (p. 608).

"[The youth culture] shows strong signs of being a product of tensions in the relationships of younger people and adults (p. 608)."

The last sentence foreshadows his later theory that in the process of acquiring a masculine role-identity middle class boys react against the feminine identification of their childhoods by engaging in "masculine protest" behavior of a rough, destructive kind. The relative inability of

youths today to observe directly their fathers' occupational roles, coupled with the ubiquity of feminine roles in the home, forces an eventual rebellion not only against "feminineness" but against the "goodness" which seems to the child an integral part of femininity.[5]

A number of objections to this theory can be raised. (a) In the process of "protesting masculinity" why is the trait of adult male responsibility shunned while other presumed traits of the male (loud, aggressive, rambunctious behavior) are adopted? (b) One can imagine middle class boys who live in dormitory suburbs and large cities having some difficulty picturing their fathers' occupational roles, but this may not be true in smaller cities and in towns where the fathers' places of work are more readily accessible for visits, and where their roles are less likely to be obscured by employment in bureaucratic organizations. (c) How can the participation of girls in the youth culture be explained by Parson's theory? (d) Are mothers' roles especially ubiquitous in communities where commuting time for the father is not so great that he cannot be with his family meaningfully except on weekends? "Catching the 7:05" each morning before the children are up and returning in the evening shortly before their bedtime is a pattern found only in our largest cities. (e) Is it to be assumed that the seeming increase in middle class delinquency since the Second World War is the result of a post-war increase in sons' difficulties in identifying with their fathers' roles, in the absence of basic post-war changes in our society's occupation structure?

The present paper begins with a backtrack on Parson's thinking to his idea that hedonistic irresponsibility characterizes the youth culture of the United States, and a departure from this in another direction from that taken by him. The theory to be presented here is that some middle class delinquency is the result of an interaction between certain aspects of our general cultural system and an emerging teenage system, producing norms entirely functional to the latter but not to the former.

[3]F. Ivan Nye, James F. Short, Jr., and Virgil J. Olson, "Socioeconomic Status and Delinquent Behavior," *American Journal of Sociology* 63 (January, 1958): 381–89, n. 3; Frank E. Hartung, "A Critique of the Sociological Approach to Crime and Correction," *Law and Contemporary Problems* 23 (Autumn, 1958): 730.

[4]Talcott Parsons, "Age and Sex in the Social Structure of the United States," *American Sociological Review* 7 (October, 1942): 604–16.

[5]Talcott Parsons, "Certain Primary Sources and Patterns of Aggression in the Social Structure of the Western World," *Psychiatry* 10 (May, 1947): 167–81.

THE TEENAGE SYSTEM

The groundwork for the emergence of a teenage culture in our society was laid a century and more ago when youngsters were gradually removed from functional roles in the economy through restrictive apprenticeship codes, protective labor legislation, the compulsory education movement, and the withdrawal of children from agricultural activities attendant upon urbanization. However diverse the forces were which led to this removal from productive roles, the result was that for probably the first time a major society deactivated a large and energetic segment of its population without clearly redefining the status and function of that segment. The resulting ambiguity of status, the blurring of the lines separating childhood from youth and youth from adulthood, has been commented upon by many observers; the middle class teenager, with his typically lengthened period of ambiguous status compared with working class youngsters, is faced with contradictory expectations. He is not expected to engage in productive labor, but neither is he encouraged to loaf; he is discouraged from early marriage, but is allowed to engage in proto-courtship; he cannot vote, hold public office, or serve on a jury, but is expected to be civic-minded; he is given many privileges and a large measure of individual freedom, but without the obligatory ties to significant others which, for the adult, help keep privilege and freedom from deteriorating into license.

Bloch and Niederhoffer[6] have recently suggested that certain attributes of adolescent life (tattooing, hazing, the adoption of nicknames, etc.) serve as latter-day rites of passage into adolescence to lessen the anxiety-producing absence of adult-sponsored rites. For several generations the teen years have been a singularly faddist time of life, and peculiarities of dress, speech, values and interests are increasingly conspicuous among this population group. It seems reasonable to presume, as have Bloch and others, that these widely-shared peculiarities are highly functional to teenagers, and are not simply youthful fancies. Some might, indeed, be the equivalent of primitive rites of passage; others might serve to maintain the new status; still others might be the ordinary *impedimenta* of a burgeoning youth cultural system.

It is the writer's contention that certain post-World War II changes—mainly in communications—have speeded the development of long-nascent tendencies arising from the ambiguous status of our teenage population. These changes have had the general, if inadvertent, effect of making teenagers newly aware of themselves as a nation-wide segment of our society by fostering communication within this population group. Probably none of these changes singly could have produced this effect, but their conjuncture following the war provided means for teenagers to enter into at least secondary contact far beyond the pre-war confines of their respective communities.

1. Perhaps basic is the exploitation of an enlarged market for teenage goods and services following our post-war rise in living standards and the consequent possession of large amounts of spending money by youngsters. An estimated nine billion dollars are spent annually by teenagers.[7] National advertising campaigns, many found only in the new teen magazines, publicize products tailored to the interests and needs of this age group: motor scooters, acne creams, portable phonographs and radios, western and rock-and-roll movies, auto accessories, hot-rod conversion kits, unusual clothing, mail-order dance lessons, etc. The wide distribution of these items is contributing to the growth of a nationally shared but age-restricted material culture.

2. Post-war changes in local radio broadcasting with increased reliance on canned material, particularly popular music, has brought into prominence the disc jockey, whose seeming chumminess with entertainers gives him some of the glamour of show business. Despite competition from television the number of operating commercial broadcasting stations increased from 890 to 3,680 between 1945 and 1958,[8] many of

---

[6]Herbert A. Bloch and Arthur Niederhoffer, *The Gang* (New York: Philosophical Library, Inc., 1958), Chap. 5.

[7]"Teen-age Consumers," *Consumer Reports* 22 (March, 1957): 139–42.

[8]*Statistical Abstract of the United States: 1958*, U. S. Bureau of the Census, Washington, D. C., p. 519.

them being located in smaller communities throughout the country. The number of disc jockeys has been estimated at 2,500,[9] compared to a handful before the war, and their audiences apparently are drawn mainly from among persons in their teens and early twenties. The recent disturbance in Boston where a disc jockey was accused of inciting his young followers to riot, and the power of these men to stimulate teenage interest in charity drives, contests and the like, are suggestive of their role in teenage communications.

3. Similar to the above, but with the added element of visual impact, is TV programming of teen dance shows, from Dick Clark's nationally broadcast "American Bandstand" to the one-channel town's airing of the local equivalent with a lone disc jockey providing the recorded music. The particular image of teenage life thus promulgated by many of the country's 544 operating commercial television stations (contrasted with six in 1945[10]) probably reaches a large audience.

4. Young people's magazines have been published for many decades in the United States. With few exceptions, their common stamp was one of staid, moralistic conservatism which viewed adolescence as a period of preparation for an adulthood of similar qualities. Since, 1944, however, when *Seventeen* began publication, a number of magazines have appeared whose kinship to the older *Youth's Companion* and *American Boy* is only faintly discernible. At least 11 of these are currently in the market, led by *Seventeen*, whose monthly circulation is slightly over one million copies. *Co-Ed, 'Teen, Cool, Hep Cats, Modern Teen, Ingenue* and *Dig* have combined circulations of about 1,500,000.[11] These publications are similar in format to movie and TV magazines read by many adults, but their picture stories emphasize younger personnel from the entertainment industry, and they contain a thin scattering of teenage love stories,

youth "forums," puzzles and articles on automobiles and high school sports. In sharp contrast with the moralistic flavor of earlier youth magazines, the post-war group is distinguished by its portrayal of hedonistic values within an essentially amoral setting: the teen years are not ones of preparation for responsible adulthood, but of play and diversion.

5. A final influence contributing to the teenagers' awareness of themselves as a distinct population group may be the very fact that the post-war years have seen public attention directed increasingly toward our youth because of the apparent increase in juvenile problems. Teenagers seem very much aware that such problems exist, even if their outlines are not clear to the youngsters.[12]

Given the existence of a large population segment permeated with anxiety arising from its ill-defined status, and communicating, however imperfectly, on a national scale, one observes elements necessary for the development of something akin to a minority group psychology: a shared sense of grievance and alienation among substantial numbers of persons readily identifiable by some conspicuous trait—in this case, being in the teen years. Listing further points of similarity between minority groups and today's teenagers, one could mention *leaders and spokesmen* in the persons of disc jockeys, young entertainers and some educationists; a distinctive set of material and nonmaterial *culture traits; sentiments of exclusiveness* toward most adults and toward "square" (i.e., adult-oriented) youngsters; and *culture heroes*, selected mainly from among entertainers and athletes.

While the theory being presented here does not hinge on teenagers constituting a true minority group, it does assume that on a national scale there is evolving a complex of attitudes and values tending to control and motivate teenagers in ways consonant with the role implied by their position as a youthful group having leisure, relatively ample spending money

[9]*Newsweek* 49 (April 1, 1957): 104–105.
[10]*Statistical Abstract,* p. 519.
[11]*Consumer Magazine and Farm Publication Rates and Data,* May 27, 1959, pp. 400, 411–19. Circulation figures for *Datebook, Teens Today* and *16* are not currently listed in *Rates and Data.* A "Teensters' Union" has recently been organized by *Modern Teens* magazine, ostensibly "for the improvement of teen-age society."

[12]A crude measure of the increased public attention to our youth can be obtained by a count of *Readers' Guide to Periodical Literature* entries under "Youth: United States." For the respective two-year periods of May, 1945 to April, 1947; April, 1951 to March, 1953; and March, 1957 to February, 1959 the number of entries was 24, 42 and 60.

and few responsibilities. The theme of this emerging culture seems to be one of an increasingly institutionalized but immature and irresponsible hedonism, as Parsons suggested.

It is evident that not all teenagers behave as if they were participants in such a culture. The degree to which any particular youth is controlled and motivated by the norms of the teenage system may be a function of the extent and intensity of his affiliation with youthful autonomous cliques, for these, rather than individuals, appear to be the social units of the teenage world. The relative importance of clique-membership may in turn be inversely related to a teenager's commitment to groups—usually adult-dominated—which purvey conventional normative systems, and which have the inherent disadvantage, in competing for teenagers' loyalties, of requiring accommodation to adult demands.

While strong peer-group appeal is exhibited among both working class and middle class youngsters, there may exist class differences both in the content of the youth culture shared by teenagers from the two strata, and in the duration of the culture's importance in the lives of its followers. Those teenagers currently labeled "hoods" by other youngsters are marked by levis and leather jackets, motorcycles and jalopies, frankly promiscuous girl friends, truculent, aggressive behavior in school, and a sneering avoidance of extracurricular school social activities. For these youngsters delinquent motivations may indeed stem from their experiences with snobbish discrimination within the high school social structure, as Cohen maintains.[13] But their earlier entrance into the labor market and their lower age at marriage enable them to acquire adult roles—and to become saddled with adult responsibilities—sooner than middle class teenagers. By contrast, the middle class "social crowd"—more seemly and fashionably dressed, smoother mannered, driving late-model cars, peopling the parties and proms in their communities, and indulged by their prosperous and permissive parents—constitute the spending market alluded to earlier, and may be proportionately greater participants in the teenage communi-

cations network and in that part of the teenage culture depicted in it.

DELINQUENCY AND THE TEENAGE CULTURE

An ethos of irresponsible hedonism is not in itself productive of delinquent motivations, and I am not suggesting that middle class delinquency is simply a manifestation of unchecked impulses, as the term "irresponsible hedonism" connotes. The relationship between this ethos and delinquency is more complex. If the teenager's urgent need for status affirmation is met by the teenage culture, then it becomes necessary for him to reject influences from the adult world which threaten it, and to accept only those giving it support. The threatening influences are attitudes and values running counter to short-run, irresponsible hedonism, such as hard work, thrift, study, self-denial, etc., while those supportive of it are cultural elements adaptable to it. It is the writer's contention that delinquent motivations among middle class teenagers arise from this adaptive process, in which the teenage world, peopled by immature and inexperienced persons, extracts from the adult world those values having strong hedonistic possibilities, with the result that the values of the teenage culture consist mainly of distorted and caricatured fragments from the adult culture. These highly selected and altered values then serve to motivate and give direction to members of the youth world, sometimes in ways adults define as delinquent. Some examples of such value transformation will make my meaning clear.

1. Abuse of driving privileges by some teenagers is a persisting problem in most communities. Open mufflers, drag-racing, speeding, playing "chicken," or just aimlessly driving about constitute nuisances and sometimes dangers on public streets and highways. To emotionally mature adults automobiles primarily represent—and are operated as—means of transportation, but in the process of adaptation to the adolescent ethos they are redefined as playthings whose important qualities are less those pertaining to getting from place to place than to glitter, power and speed, and teenagers tend to operate them

---

[13] Albert K. Cohen, *Delinquent Boys: The Culture of the Gang* (New York: The Free Press, 1955).

in ways appropriate to these qualities. Youth's intense interest in cars is reflected in the current number of magazines (twenty-one) devoted to the automobile. Eighteen of these were founded since 1945, and fourteen since 1950. Their reported combined monthly circulation is about 2,300,000. *Hot Rod Magazine* leads this group, with about 490,000 paid monthly circulation.[14] Some 2,000 so-called "speed shops" supplied by 100 manufacturers distribute parts and accessories for youthful car enthusiasts.[15]

A more serious problem with respect to automobiles is the increasing number of cars "borrowed" for joy rides by middle class (or at least "favored group") teenagers.[16] Larceny is customarily defined as taking another's property with intent to deprive the owner permanently of its use; joyride thievery seldom involves this criminal intention, and apprehended youngsters are quick to point out—quite accurately—that they were "merely having a little fun." (It is worth noting that cars borrowed for joy rides almost invariably embody qualities extraneous to mere transportation. Flashy convertibles are especially vulnerable.)

2. The competitive spirit, valued in our larger society as a spur to achievement, but hedged about with customary and legal restrictions, becomes productive of bitter and childish rivalries when it is applied to high school intermural contests. The youngsters, aroused by pep committees, coaches and alumni, transform competition into a hedonistic travesty: witness the growing problem of fights, car chases and vandalism attendant on important games.

3. Whether or not we are a sex-obsessed society, as European observers sometimes contend, the meaning of sex to our teenagers is confused and contradictory. On the one hand, pre-marital chastity and forbearance are upheld as prime moral values. On the other, sex is heavily exploited in most of the popular media of entertainment. The image of sex, love and romance presented by these media is one rejected by most adults whose views have been tempered by the realities of life, but the middle class youngsters of the teenage world, bemused by their burgeoning sex drives in the prolonged and presumably chaste interval between puberty and marriage, and betrayed by their inexperience, are inclined to accept this image as valid. More importantly, this image is considerably more congenial to their ethos than one conveying restraint and self-control; sex and love are redefined as ends in themselves, and have acquired sufficient preeminence in the teenage system since 1945 to motivate youngsters of 12 to begin "going steady," and of 16 to contemplate marriage seriously.

4. Among the adult values attractive to the teenage ethos, the use of alcoholic beverages is perhaps the one most readily lending itself to distortion, for the temperate use of alcohol by adults themselves requires a degree of restraint seldom found in youngsters. Normatively, alcohol is utilized by the middle class as a social lubricant and as an adjunct to food, and strong social pressures help limit its use to those functions. By custom (as well as by law) teenagers are forbidden generally to use alcoholic beverages on their own for any purpose. But its fundamental hedonistic quality—its capacity to intoxicate—makes it so highly adaptable to the teenage ethos that when alcohol is used, this quality is emphasized, and drinking to excess becomes the norm. A further difficulty arises from the obligatory secretiveness of teenage middle class drinking: it must be done quite apart from adult eyes in automobiles, public parks, rented cottages and motels where drinking parties can easily get out of hand.

SUMMARY

Post-war changes in communication processes are heightening in-group feelings within a large population segment which, during the last one hundred years, has experienced increased status ambiguity as the productive roles of this group

---

[14]*Rates and Data*, pp. 65–74.

[15]*Consumer Reports*, p. 139.

[16]William A. Wattenberg and James T. Balistrieri, "Automobile Theft: A 'Favored Group' Delinquency," *American Journal of Sociology* 57 (May, 1952): 575–79. In studying 3,900 cases of juvenile auto theft in Detroit, the authors observed that not only were the boys from somewhat better neighborhoods than other delinquents, but were well socialized in their peer-group relationships. The "favored group" characteristic has reportedly been observed also in Britain. See, T. C. N. Gibbens, "Car Thieves," *British Journal of Delinquency*, April, 1958.

have diminished. The intensive preoccupation with play among today's teenagers results from the circumstance that hedonistic pursuits, evoked by the youngsters' present position in the social structure, are becoming the status-defining "function" of this emerging national interest group. In order to retain the need-satisfactions produced by this new status clarification, the group's values and norms must support its play function by constituting a hedonistic ethos, and must neutralize non-hedonistic pressures from the adult world either by denigrating them entirely or by altering them to conform with the teenage culture. Once incorporated into that culture, they become controlling and motivating forces for those teenagers sharing the system, but in directions sometimes inconsistent with adult norms.

27.

Jackson Toby

AFFLUENCE AND ADOLESCENT CRIME

In 1960 a United Nations Congress on "The Prevention of Crime and the Treatment of Offenders" met in London. Delegates from countries on every continent compared notes. The verdict was pessimistic: Crime rates were increasing in nearly all countries, especially among adolescents, and rich countries were having as serious problems as poor countries.[1] In 1964 another United Nations Congress met in Stockholm and came to similar conclusions about adolescent crime. Economic growth, though it raised living standards, did not seem to reduce crime rates. Some criminological experts went further: Affluence was itself a causal factor in the worsening crime problems of contemporary society.

What did these crime problems consist of? Rape? Murder? Assault? From crime reports in the daily newspapers of the large cities of the world—New York, London, Tokyo—one might think that crimes of violence were rising rapidly and constituted a major component of "the crime problem." In some places this was happening, but it was not a consistent trend. For example, in Scotland and in England and Wales, there was a steep rise in the crime rate between 1927 and 1962 (see Figure 3–1), but in neither country were crimes against the person an important factor. In Great Britain, crimes against the person consisted of less than five percent of crime in general. Furthermore, crimes against the person were not increasing faster than all crimes together; in Scotland, crimes against the person rose more slowly. Criminologists who disregarded the selective horror stories of daily newspapers and looked at crime statistics coldly have observed that the crime problem revolved mainly around theft. Insofar as crimes of violence increased, they were mainly crimes like armed robbery rather than rape and murder. This thought may not console the gas station attendant shot during a holdup attempt, but it helps to explain the motivations of people who behave in ways summarized in the unrevealing category, "crime."

CRIME AND THE REVOLUTION OF RISING EXPECTATIONS

The preponderance of crimes against property sheds light on the tendency of crime rates

SOURCE: Jackson Toby, "Affluence and Adolescent Crime," *1967 President's Commission on Law Enforcement and Administration of Justice: Task Force Report on Juvenile Delinquency and Youth Crime* (Washington, D.C.: Government Printing Office), pp. 132–44.

[1] Second United Nations Congress on the Prevention of Crime and the Treatment of Offenders, *Report Prepared by the Secretariat* (New York: Department of Economic and Social Affairs, 1960), pp. 8–18.

FIGURE 3–1.

CRIMES MADE KNOWN (SCOTLAND) AND INDICTABLE OFFENCES MADE KNOWN (ENGLAND AND WALES) RELATED TO POPULATION AGE 8 YEARS AND OVER, 1900–1962

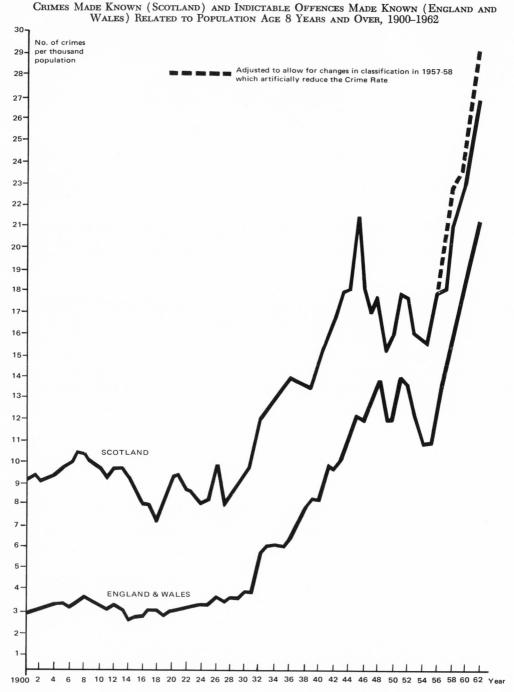

SOURCE: J. V. M. Shields and Judith A. Duncan, *The State of Crime in Scotland* (London: Tavistock Publications, 1964), p. 20.

to rise in the most affluent countries. People steal, not because they are starving, but because they are envious, and they are more likely to be envious of the possessions of others in countries with rising standards of living. Why should this be so? Because the rise in living standards is associated not only with an improvement of the style of life of elite groups; it is associated also with the trickling down of television sets, refrigerators, transistor radios, and automobiles to segments of the population who had not anticipated such good fortune. Industrial societies, which produce the new luxuries, distribute them more democratically than the less affluent agrarian societies did. Paradoxically though, the trend toward increasing equality in the distribution of consumer goods generates expectations of further equality. When expectations are rising faster than the standard of living, the greater availability of consumer goods makes for greater rather than less dissatisfaction. This revolution of rising expectations is both cause and effect of the soaring ownership of automobiles, television sets, and radios not just in the United States or even in Europe but in Africa, Asia, and South America (see Table 3–36). Traffic jams are now fully as serious in Tokyo as they have long been in New York and London; rivers of cars flow toward Tokyo every morning from as far away as Mount Fuji.[2] Suburbanization is no longer an American phenomenon; the automobile has transformed the world.

Table 3–36 reflects the level of affluence in selected countries—at least insofar as radios, television sets, and automobiles can be regarded as indices of affluence. Thus, Table 3–36 shows the United States, Canada, and Sweden to be among the countries of the world rich in durable consumer goods whereas India, Nigeria, and Pakistan are among the poor countries. But for persons interested in the effect of affluence on

[2] In 1964, the number of registered automobiles in Japan was 6,775,971, about 47 times as many as were registered in 1945. The number of traffic deaths in Tokyo was 1,050, about 9.8 per 100,-000 population and about 9.9 per 10,000 registered automobiles. The latter rate is much higher than for large cities in the United States. *Summary of the White Paper on Crime, 1965* (Tokyo: Training and Research Institute, Ministry of Justice, March, 1966), p. 6.

TABLE 3–36.

INDICES OF AFFLUENCE FOR SELECTED COUNTRIES, 1963

Country	Number of Radios per 100 Population	Rank	Number of TV's per 100 Population	Rank	Number of Cars per 100 Population	Rank
U.S.A. ...	97	1	33	1	36	1
Canada ..	48	2	25	2	25	2
Sweden ..	39	3	24	3	20	5
Denmark .	35	4	20	5	13	11
Belgium .	33	5	12	10	11	13
Luxembourg .	33	6	5	21	15	7
West Germany	31	7	15	8	13	9
Finland ..	31	8	10	11	7	19
France ..	30	9	9	12	17	6
United Kingdom	29	10	24	4	14	8
Norway ..	29	11	8	14	10	14
Austria ..	29	12	6	17	9	15
Switzerland ...	28	13	6	18	13	10
Iceland ..	28	14	*–	*–	12	12
Netherlands ..	26	15	13	9	7	18
Argentina	25	16	6	20	3	22
Chile	24	17	0.4	31	1	30
New Zealand .	24	18	6	19	24	3
Israel	24	19	*–	*–	2	25
Panama ..	22	20	4	22	2	26
Australia .	20	21	16	7	23	4
Japan ...	20	22	16	6	1	29
Venezuela	20	23	7	16	4	21
Ireland ..	19	24	7	15	8	16
Italy	19	25	8	13	8	17
Peru	18	26	1	26	1	31
Mexico ..	17	27	3	24	2	28
Jamaica ..	13	28	1	30	3	23
Spain	13	29	3	23	2	27
Portugal .	12	30	1	27	2	24
Greece .	9	31	*–	*–	1	32
Paraguay	9	32	*–	*–	0.4	36
South Africa .	7	33	*–	*–	6	20
U.A.R. ..	7	34	1	29	0.3	39
Ghana ...	7	35	*–	*–	0.4	37
Brazil ...	6	36	2	25	0.1	40
South Korea ..	6	37	a–	34	a–	—
Turkey ...	5	38	a–	35	a–	—
Philippines	4	39	0.2	32	0.3	38
Ceylon ..	4	40	*–	*–	1	33
Iraq	2	41	0.7	28	1	34
Burma ...	1	42	*–	*–	0.1	35
India	1	43	a–	36	0.1	42
Nigeria ..	1	44	a–	33	0.1	45
Pakistan .	0.5	45	*–	*–	0.1	41

*Statistics not available.
aLess than 0.05 per 100 population.
SOURCE: *United Nations Statistical Yearbook, 1964*, New York Statistical Office of the United Nations, 1965, pp. 23–42, 391–398, 714–716.

crime, it is not only the level of affluence that is important, but the rate at which affluence is increasing. Table 3–37 shows that the rate at which affluence is increasing is comparatively slow for the richest countries. Thus, the rate of increase of ownership of radios in the United States and Canada is of the order of 12 percent per year. India's annual rate of increase of radio ownership was 36 percent in the decade 1954–64, and Nigeria's was 89 percent. True, these countries started from very low levels of ownership. Still, if we are interested in the impact of affluence on the revolution of rising expectations, the increases are dramatic. The situation with respect to automobile ownership is somewhat different. The richest countries have a comparatively slow rate of increase in automobile ownership. But it is not the poorest countries that have the fastest rate of increase but countries of the second rank: Italy, Greece, Spain. (Germany and Japan also have high rates of increase, but this can be interpreted as due to "catching up" after the Second World War.) The poorest countries have annual rates of increase only slightly higher than the richest countries, doubtless because an automobile is such a large investment in poor countries. If the increases in ownership of durable consumer goods contribute as much or more to envy as the level of ownership, this would help to explain why crime is increasing in most countries of the world.

Industrialization and suburbanization may be thought of in relation to the world of adults. But the revolution of rising expectations has consequences for the young too. As car registrations grow, so do the desires of adolescents to drive (as well as to own cameras, transistor radios, and new clothes). Few adolescents can get legitimate access to a car, partly because of the age of licensing drivers, partly because of the cost of vehicles. In Japan, for example, the custom is to pay workers in accordance with age as well as skill; so adolescent workers (as well as schoolboys) have almost no chance to buy a car unless they come from rich families. Relative to adults, they are impoverished despite the growing affluence of Japanese society. Interestingly enough, the crime rate in Japan has risen most rapidly for the 14 to 17 age group

TABLE 3–37.

CHANGES IN AFFLUENCE, 1954–64[*]

Country	Percent increase in Radio Ownership per 1,000 Population	Percent increase in Automobile Ownership per 1,000 Population
U.S.A.	134	125
Canada	111	147
Sweden	116	292
West Germany ...	127	469
Argentina	132	136
Japan	155	977
Switzerland	114	296
Italy	175	581
Spain	227	499
Greece	152	457
Philippines	388	165
Ceylon	339	53
Burma	797	184
India	362	172
Nigeria	891	176

[*]For Argentina, Japan, and the United States, the 10-year interval was 1953-63. For Burma and India, the 10-year interval was 1952-62.

SOURCE: Calculated from data in various volumes of *United Nations Statistical Yearbook.*

(see Table 3–38), and has not increased at all for adults.[3] In 1941, the Japanese police apprehended 334,417 suspects of whom seven percent were 14 to 17 years of age; in 1964, 726,910 suspects were apprehended of whom 19 percent were 14 to 17. Although Table 3–38 shows the crime trend for the entire 14 to 17 age group, in 1954 the 14- and 15-year-olds and the 16- and 17-year-olds were separated in Japanese crime statistics, making it possible to study arrest data since then in greater detail.[4] For ages 20 to 24, the crime rate was 17.1 per thousand persons of those ages in 1955, and it was still 17.1 in 1964. For ages 18 and 19, the crime rate increased from 13.1 per thousand persons of those ages in 1955 to 17.8 in 1964. For ages 16 to 17, the crime rate increased from 8.8 per thousand in 1955 to 14.5 per thousand in 1964. For ages 14 and 15, the increase was the greatest of all: From 5.8 thousand persons of those ages in 1955 to 14.1 in 1964.

[3]"Crime rate" refers to the number of persons investigated by the Japanese police for a penal code violation per thousand persons of the base population.

[4]*Summary of the White Paper on Crime, 1965,* p. 18, n. 2.

TABLE 3–38.

INCREASE IN JUVENILE CRIME IN JAPAN

| | Suspects Apprehended by the Japanese Police | | | | | | | | | | |
| | In 1914 | | In 1946 | | In 1951 | | In 1956 | | In 1961 | | In 1964 | |
Age of Suspects	Num- ber	Per- cent	Num- ber	Per- cent	Num- ber	Per- cent	Num- ber	Per- cent	Num- ber	Per- cent	Num- ber	Per- cent
Over 20	281,708	84	333,694	75	452,602	73	427,192	77	422,430	66	488,080	67
18 and 19	19,780	6	51,910	11	58,030	10	48,301	9	62,758	10	55,208	8
14-17	22,731	7	47,479	11	75,626	12	52,457	9	96,126	15	135,334	18
Under 14	10,198	3	12,401	3	32,777	5	26,663	5	57,572	9	48,388	7
Total	334,417	100	445,484	100	619,035	100	554,613	100	638,886	100	727,010	100

SOURCE: *Juvenile Problems in Japan* (Tokyo: Central Council on Juvenile Problems, Prime Minister's Office, 1962), p. 38; *Summary of the White Paper on Crime, 1965* (Tokyo: Training and Research Institute of the Ministry of Justice, March 1966), pp. 17-18.

Can the increase in the crime rate of Japanese 14- and 15-year-olds be fully explained by a desire to share in the new affluence? Probably not. There are other factors, including the decreased authority of adults over children since the defeat of the Japanese in the Second World War. A case history of a Japanese delinquent shows some of these interrelated motivations in vivid form. The following are excerpts from 3 days of conversation with a 19-year-old boy interviewed recently in a training school for delinquents near Tokyo.[5]

At 15, Toshiko graduated from junior high school and enrolled in a vocational school to learn how to drive and repair cars. He stayed six months although the course was supposed to last one year. He said that his friends urged him to quit in order to "live an adult life." He wanted to smoke, to stay out late at night in the entertainment districts of Tokyo, to play *pachinko* [a popular Japanese slot machine game], and to wear fashionable clothing. Before he was imprisoned Toshiko wore bell-bottomed trousers and short jackets, the costume of a *chimpira* gang. He and his friends wished to feel superior to other Japanese and therefore wore what they thought to be American-style clothing. Toshiko's mother disapproved, but his father, a hard-working clerk, did not say anything. Like his friends, Toshiko wore thin underwear instead of the heavy underwear worn by the older generation.

[5]The interviews were conducted in Japanese with the help of a skilled interpreter, Masahiko Kikuchi, during March and April of 1964. The opportunity to visit the training school and interview inmates was graciously provided by the Correction Bureau of the Ministry of Justice and in particular by Director Osawa, Mr. Kakuichiro Ogino, and Mr. Akira Tanigawa.

[There is very little central heating in Japan, and heavy underwear is protection against a cold, damp climate.]

After leaving the vocational school, Toshiko and his friends maintained their interest in cars. They broke into at least 11 cars over a period of several weeks, using a master key to get inside and shorting the ignition wires to start them. They picked up bread in the early morning from in front of grocery stores and ate it while driving around. When the gasoline was used up, they would abandon the cars —first taking care to remove the radios, which they sold for as much as 2,000 yen [$5.50] each.

Toshiko and his friends also broke into shops at night. They would select a little shop without a watchman. It would have to be located where a car, previously stolen for the purpose, could be parked nearby while the break-in was in progress. There were usually three to five in the group, one or two looking out for the police. They would either jimmy the door or apply a chemical paste to a window and set it aflame, enabling it to break easily and quietly.

Sometimes they picked a quarrel with a drunk, beat him up, and went through his pockets. Aside from drunks, however, they did not usually bother conventional people. More usually, they would extort money from members of rival *chimpira* groups. Toshiko would walk down the street until he saw a likely victim. Two confederates would be nearby but not visible. "Hello, fine fellow. Lend me your face." This was a challenge for the victim to go to a less busy place for a fight. Not seeing Toshiko's friends, the victim would agree; he was angry. After the fight started, the confederates would join in, using wooden bats as well as fists. Soon the victim had enough and was willing to agree to give the victors what they wanted. They preferred money. But the victim might not have any. If not, they would take his fountain pen, watch, railroad ticket, and even his clothing. If he had on expensive shoes or a new suit, they might accompany him to a pawn shop where he would exchange these things for old clothes and cash, the latter for Toshiko and his friends. (They would give a small amount to the victim, 10 percent or less).

Since Toshiko was stealing and extorting yen with his friends, he had enough money to spend long evenings in the entertainment districts of Tokyo. Subways and buses stopped running at midnight, whereas he did not usually leave his favorite bars until 2 a.m., so he was forced to pay expensive night rates to taxis in order to get home. This dissatisfied him; he preferred to pay for beer and whiskey or, if he was looking for cut-rate intoxication, for sleeping pills rather than for transportation. He asked his father to buy him a car so that he might drive himself home in the small hours of the morning. His father was outraged. Toshiko did not work; he slept until noon or later every day; he spent his nights in the bars of Shibuya [an entertainment district]; and he had the effrontery to ask his father, a poorly paid clerk, to buy him a car. [His father did not himself have a car.] A violent argument ensued in the course of which his father hit him; he hit his father back.

This blow must have been even more surprising to Toshiko's father than the original request for a car. While paternal authority is not now what it was once in Japan, it is still considerable. In traditional homes, the wife and children do not eat with the father, who is served literally on bended knee. That a son would dare to argue openly with his father is a sign of the increased equality between the generations in urban Japan. That he would hit his father, no matter what the provocation, is, to a Japanese, almost unbelievable.

Toshiko's father ordered him out of the house. He left home and moved in with a friend where he stayed for a week. Then he came home and apologized. His father would not forgive him. For a few weeks he stayed first with one *chimpira* and then with another. As soon as he found a girl who worked in a bar as hostess and could help support him, he rented an apartment. [Such a girl is called *dambe* in Japanese slang, meaning "one who pulls money in on a string."] It was important to him that she not become pregnant because she could not continue to work, so Toshiko was careful to use contraceptives during sexual intercourse. This was not his usual practice with casual pickups.

The significance of Toshiko is not that he is Japanese or even that he is delinquent but that he represents one aspect of the revolution of rising expectations: the dissatisfaction of adolescents with their share in the new affluence. From this point of view, Toshiko is an international phenomenon that can be observed in Stockholm and Tel-Aviv as well as in Tokyo and Newark. Sweden offers an unusual opportunity to observe the effect of affluence on delinquency because circumstances that tend to raise the delinquency rates of other countries are, for the most part, absent from the richest country in Europe. Sweden was not a belligerent during the Second World War and did not suffer the disruptive effects of bombing and population loss, as did Japan. Sweden has no ethnic minorities, except for Lapp reindeer herders in the northern section, and therefore need not be concerned about prejudice and discrimination as a cause of crime. Sweden is culturally homogeneous; except for temporary workers from Latin countries, there has been no large-scale immigration for centuries. In the United States and Great Britain, on the other hand, an appreciable part of the crime problem results from the limited economic and social opportunities of colored persons. In Israel, much crime results from "melting-pot" problems. Since immigrants from the Middle East and Africa are more difficult to educate and to train for industrial occupations than those from Europe and America, young Israeli from "Oriental" backgrounds are more likely to feel materially deprived. Statistics show that Oriental youngsters become delinquent more frequently than European youngsters.[6] The following are excerpts from an interview with a 20-year-old Yemenite prisoner in an Israeli reformatory; they illustrate one byproduct of the revolution of rising expectations in a culturally heterogeneous society:[7]

Happy's parents came to Israel in 1939 from a town in Yemen when they were young adults. Born

[6]Children born in Israel had a delinquency rate in 1960 of 5.6 per thousand of juvenile court age. Children born in Europe or America had exactly the same rate. But children born in Asia had a delinquency rate of 11.4 per thousand in the base population, and children born in Africa a rate of 17.6 per thousand. *Statistical Abstract of Israel, 1963* (Jerusalem: Central Bureau of Statistics, 1963), p. 688.

[7]The interview was conducted in Hebrew with the help of an Israeli colleague, Aryeh Leissner. The opportunity to visit a reformatory and interview prisoners was graciously provided by Dr. Zvi Hermon, Scientific Director, Prison Service of Israel.

in 1944, Happy does not seem to have many pleasant childhood memories. He mentioned two birthday parties when he was very young. I think he mentioned them to suggest how little his parents did for him as he grew older. He stopped going to synagogue at the age of 10. By the age of 15, he began smoking and gambling on the Sabbath. This was shocking behavior to his Orthodox parents, and they objected. "But I did not hear." Happy finished elementary school at 15 and went for a year to a vocational school.

When he was free, he lived in Tel-Aviv. He would wake up about 10:30 a.m. Although his mother was in the house, he would take something to eat for himself. Then he would go to a street with trees and benches where he would meet his friends. If any of the boys had money, they would go to play snooker [a form of pool] or to a day performance in the movies, taking a girl if possible. If there were unaccompanied girls near the meeting place who didn't work and had nothing to do, they might be picked up. If the boys had no money, they sat, talked, got bored, and annoyed people. If there was a plan to steal a car in the evening and break in, they talked about the job. If no job was planned, they talked about girls, about jobs they did pull or would pull.

Happy wanted to be considered *bomba* [tough] rather than *fryer* [a sucker]. A *fryer* wants to be accepted by the gang, but he never succeeds. "This kind of boy hasn't had the kind of childhood we had, and he doesn't know how to take care of himself." He is permitted to associate with the *chevra* [gang] because he gets money [presumably from his parents] for gasoline, for a party, or to pay the bill in a restaurant. A *bomba*, on the other hand, is daring and aggressive. He steals the latest model cars, and he is successful with *fryereet* [girls who are easy to seduce].

The *chevra* gambled three or four evenings a week for about 5 hours at a time, playing poker, rummy, 21, coin tossing, dice, or a game with a numbered board called "7 times 3." Happy was not usually very lucky. He lost as much as $50 in an evening. Gambling usually started on Friday evening, stopped at 2 or 3 a.m. and began again at about 10:30 a.m. on Saturday morning. The gambling stopped by Saturday evening when the *chevra* went to the movies or to a dance club. Sometimes a boy won too much, and the others suspected him of cheating. They might beat him up and take his money.

Happy and his friends drank liquor at every opportunity, sometimes during a card game, sometimes at a coffee shop, sometimes at a party. They drank Stock 84, for which they paid $1.20 to $1.40 for a half pint. When they had little money, they bought a big bottle of medicinal brandy for 70 cents.

Alcohol increased the probability of fights. "When you are a little drunk, sometimes you start pushing someone around." Once Happy kicked a dog when he was "high." The lady who owned the dog shouted at him; he shouted back. The owner's husband joined the argument. Soon the *doda* [literally "aunts" in Hebrew but meaning "police"] were called. But fights occurred for other reasons. Happy recalled one time when he was playing cards out-of-doors on a Saturday afternoon. A member of an extremely Orthodox sect came over to the *chevra* and told them to stop gambling on the Sabbath. In the course of the furious argument that ensued, the Orthodox man threw a nearby bicycle in the middle of the game. They stopped the game and beat him up badly. If members of the *chevra* made remarks about a girl in the movies, and her boyfriend resented them, this could start a fight. Or sometimes a member of the group took a couple of friends and *laredet alay* [literally "went down on" but meaning "beat up"] a boy who was saying insulting things about him or about the group.

On Happy's right hand is a tattoo consisting of a half moon and three stars, which [he said] means, "We are against the law." Although he made this tattoo in the reformatory, this could well have been the motto of his *chevra* in the community. Car thefts were a favorite activity. At first cars were stolen for joyrides. The competition consisted of stealing newer model cars and large cars. "The car is always full—as many as the car will hold." Girls were sometimes reluctant to come for fear of getting involved. Once Happy left his straw hat with a feather in a car he had tried to start unsuccessfully. The gang went back to get the hat after having stolen another car. The *doda* gave chase: but Uri, the driver, outdistanced them. After a while, they decided to use the cars they stole to help in burglaries. For example, they broke into a supermarket through airvents in the back—forcing the grill—and took cigarettes and cognac and chocolate away in the car. Then they went back to the room of one of the boys and had a party.

Once, when they passed a Willys station wagon filled with appliances, they stole them and sold them to a *client* [fence] recommended by a friend. The loot consisted of: Clothes, irons, fans, transistor radios, and electric shavers. Four boys each got $200. Happy hid his share under a tile in the courtyard of his house and continued to ask his mother for a pound or two [33 or 66 cents] for spending money. Happy spent all of his share in a month. (He kept the clothes he bought in a pal's house —so as not to arouse his mother's suspicions.) This success aroused the interest of the *chevra* in transistor radios, and they broke into appliance stores, preferably from the back but sometimes from the front when the street was clear. Sometimes they broke into two stores a week, sometimes none at all. They also broke into dry goods stores—but this was not so profitable. From every car they stole, they took the radio. Sometimes they stripped cars without moving them.

In some ways, the crimes of Happy and his gang are not startling. They remind criminologists of the Irish, Polish, and Italian juvenile gangs in Chicago a half century ago—or of Negro gangs today in Philadelphia, New York, or Cleveland. Gangs consisting of the sons of poverty-stricken migrants to the city are commonplace. But the juvenile gangs of Sweden are less easy to understand because poverty, in the old sense of hunger, ragged clothes, and disease, does not exist in Sweden. As in many countries, there has been a housing shortage in Sweden, especially in the cities; this shortage dates from the post-war rise in the birth rate. But existing housing is modern and pleasant. Slums cannot be the breeding place of crime in Stockholm, Malmö, or Gothenburg, the three largest cities of Sweden, because there are no slums. Nevertheless, delinquency has been a troublesome problem for the Swedes. Table 3–39 shows the rise in adolescent offenders from 1946 to 1955. During those years, the conviction rate rose 38 percent in the age group, 15 to 17; the corresponding rise for the 18 to 20 age group was 57 percent. Note that the increase in Swedish delinquency rates, unlike the increase in Japanese delinquency, was more pronounced among older adolescents. There may be a good ex-planation for this. Sweden is a radically equalitarian country, whereas Japanese tradition stresses the submission of the young to the old. Swedish youngsters, 15 to 17, are the beneficiaries of many governmental services including excellent youth clubs, and they can earn almost as much as adults if they choose to leave school and go to work. So even though they may feel deprived, they are not likely to feel as deprived as Japanese youngsters of the same age.

In spite of these favorable circumstances, Swedish adolescents commit crimes. And in addition to committing crimes, they behave in ways that are, if not illegal, disturbing to adults. For example, in the 1950's gangs of *raggare* (cruisers) drove around the downtown districts of the large cities in American-made cars looking for girls. At one time raggare automobiles interfered sufficiently with traffic flow in Stockholm that city officials invited leaders of the main groups, the Car Angels, the Car Comets, the Teddy Boys, and the Car Devils, to City Hall to discuss the problem. On New Year's Eve of 1957, a crowd of 3,000 persons, about two-thirds of them under 21, gathered in the center of Stockholm and bombarded police with empty tin cans and other objects. They forced several cars to stop and wrenched off their doors. One car was overturned and wrecked.[8] Gate-crashing has also been a problem in Sweden, as it has in the United States.[9] As a Swedish governmental report put it, "Groups of young people force their way uninvited into a party, or break into a private house or apartment, in the absence of the owners, and proceed to break china, mutilate furniture and deface walls."[10]

That the rise in Swedish delinquency is indirectly related to Swedish prosperity is not self-evident. But there does not seem to be any major social trend—except the increase in affluence—to blame for the delinquency problem. There are also some direct connections between delinquency and affluence. In Sweden, as in the United States, auto theft is predominantly a

TABLE 3–39.

NUMBER OF OFFENDERS RECORDED IN THE PENAL REGISTER OF SWEDEN PER 100,000 OF THE BASE POPULATION, 1946–55

	Age of Offenders and Their Crime Rates		
Year	15–17 Years	18–20 Years	21 Years and Older
1946	485	473	155
1947	469	506	148
1948	482	460	128
1949	485	535	144
1950	522	569	157
1951	637	697	188
1952	651	697	204
1953	634	718	202
1954	677	708	210
1955	671	743	235

SOURCE: "Post-War Juvenile Delinquency in Sweden," mimeographed (Stockholm: Department of Justice and the Swedish Institute, July, 1960), p. 6.

[8]"Post-War Juvenile Delinquency in Sweden," mimeographed (Stockholm: Department of Justice and the Swedish Institute, July, 1960), p. 19.

[9]Robert Wallace, "Where's the Party: Let's Crash It!" *Life* 55 (July 5, 1963): 62–67.

[10]"Post-War Juvenile Delinquency in Sweden," p. 20.

crime of adolescents, as Figure 3–2 shows.[11] Furthermore, while the rate of auto theft in Sweden rose from 29 per 100,000 population in 1950 to 126 per 100,000 population in 1957, the rate computed per 10,000 automobiles registered rose only from 90 per 10,000 registrations in 1950 to 116 per 10,000 registrations in 1957.[12] What does this mean? That the temptation to steal cars was proportional to the number of cars in use and the number of adolescents who felt dissatisfied with their share of them. Of course, older Swedish adolescents did not have to steal cars in order to drive them. Unlike the situation in Japan, teenage boys in Sweden who work in unskilled jobs may nevertheless earn enough to afford a secondhand car. The *raggare* gangs do not consist entirely of delinquents any more than the American hotrod clubs consist of delinquents. But some *raggare* boys and girls are not satisfied with their share in Sweden's high living standards. And they can be very delinquent indeed, as the following excerpts from an interview with a former member of the Road Devils show:[13]

Lappen was an unwanted child. He arrived just as the marriage of his parents was breaking up. Shortly after Lappen's birth, his father left his mother for another woman. Lappen's brother Bengt, 2 years older than he, was kept at home, and Lappen was temporarily sent to live with his maternal grandparents in Lapland; his mother could not take care of both children.[14] Lappen's mother earned 600 crowns a month [about $120] in a butcher shop. By Swedish standards this was a low income, and Lappen reported that he envied the clothes and spending money of some of his friends whose family earned 1,600 crowns a month [the man of the family earned a thousand and the woman 600]. When Lappen was 9 or 10 years old, he and three friends from relatively poor families began stealing candy and fruit from local stores so that they could have the same things as the other boys in the neighborhood. (Stig was one year older than Lappen, Borje one year older, and Jan one year younger.) The other neighborhood boys admired the courage of the thieves. "We took greater and greater chances because we had to show that we were just as good as those whose parents had a lot of money." The boys who did not need to steal stole anyway out of a sense of adventure. Lappen and his three friends became the leaders of a gang. Lappen's gang controlled 10 or 15 square blocks. Between the ages of 10 and 15, Lappen participated in many fights. As many as 200 boys were involved in some of the biggest fights. The fights were with gangs from outside the neighborhood and were usually over "honor and girls, if I may say so." Lappen differentiated between two types of boys from outside the neighborhood: Boys who came from essentially the same class and boys who were *sossar* [important]. Fights with boys from the same social level were relatively friendly. "We only fought to show who was best. After the fight, we were all friends." In addition to fighting, Lappen and his friends increased the scope of their stealing activities. They "borrowed" rowboats and bicycles. They also "borrowed" automobiles for joyrides.

When Lappen attended school he played hookey at least one day a week. He said it was because he "had it so easy. The next day I came back and knew what they had talked about." The teachers did not find out about his truancy because he would write notes to them and forge his mother's signature. His mother urged him to go to school. However, she didn't tell the teacher he played hookey when she had an interview with the teacher because ". . . she wanted it to be good for me in school. Mother wanted me to be something, to go to the university, but I wouldn't. My interest was motors. I wouldn't sit on a book." Lappen's relationship with his mother has never been very good. "She lives her life and I live mine. I like her but I do not love her."

At the age of 15, just about the time he quit school, Lappen had his first sex experience. His gang [the South End Club] had obtained a meeting room in a local youth club. Lappen had carefully

[11]In 1965 there were 486,600 auto thefts reported in the United States, 51 percent more than in 1960 and more than double the percentage increase in automobile registrations. Sixty-two percent of the persons arrested for auto theft were under 18; 88 percent of the persons arrested for auto theft were under 25. Federal Bureau of Investigation, *Uniform Crime Reports of the United States, 1965* (Washington, D.C.: Government Printing Office, 1936), pp. 17–18.

[12]"Post-War Juvenile Delinquency in Sweden," n. 8, p. 14.

[13]This interview was conducted in English in a reception center for young offenders near Uppsala, Sweden, in 1960. In addition to studying English in school, as all Swedes do, the prisoner had been a merchant seaman and had visited English-speaking countries. The opportunity to visit a reception center and interview inmates was graciously provided by Torsten Eriksson, Director-General, Swedish National Prisons Board.

[14]"Lappen" is a nickname meaning Laplander. At the age of 6, he spent 6 months in Lapland with his maternal grandparents when his mother was too sick to take care of him. When he returned to Stockholm, his friends noticed traces of a Lapland accent and dubbed him "Lappen." "I liked that name because not everyone knew my real name. If someone told it to the police, they might not catch me."

FIGURE 3–2.

ARRESTS FOR THE UNAUTHORIZED LOAN OR THE THEFT OF AUTOMOBILES IN FOURTEEN
MEDIUM-SIZED SWEDISH CITIES, 1950–1956, BY AGE OF OFFENDER

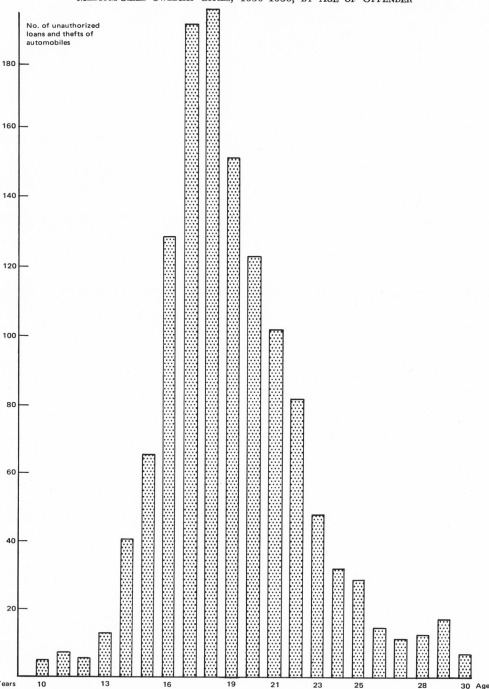

SOURCE: "Post-War Juvenile Delinquency in Sweden," mimeographed. (Stockholm: Department of Justice and the Swedish Institute, July, 1960), p. 16.

observed the caretaker's keys, and he had made a duplicate from memory. Consequently, he, Stig, and Borje had a key to the meeting room. One evening he took a girl friend into the room and locked the door. Stig and Borje were outside to see that members of the youth club did not try to come in. Other members of the gang were in the game rooms of the club to keep the caretaker busy enough so that he would not disturb Lappen. Since there was no bed or sofa in the room, his first experience with *knulla* [intercourse] occurred on a table. Subsequently, he engaged in *knulla* frequently, usually in the home of girls whose parents were working. Although he and his friends were *raggarbrud* [promiscuous], they resented it when girls were unfaithful. He told me of one member of the gang who was in love with a girl. When he discovered that he had been sharing her with numerous others, he was enraged. He told his friends. On some pretext the jealous lover and seven of his friends, including Lappen, rowed to a deserted island near Stockholm with the girl. They confronted her with her infidelity and, as punishment, forced her to remove her clothes, and then all except the injured boy friend had sexual relations with her in turn. They rowed back to the mainland leaving her to swim back as best she could.

When he left school, Lappen got a job as a car mechanic. On and off for the next three or four years, he worked in this occupation, earning 200–250 crowns a week [$40–$50]. Like many other Swedish boys of similar social background, he is fascinated by cars, especially big American cars. He eventually became a member of one of the four most important *raggare* clubs of Stockholm, the Road Devils. Lappen and his friends drank heavily, drove recklessly, and cruised around the city of Stockholm picking up girls who were "looking for a good time." They held noisy parties and dances. Some members stole accessories for their cars. Those who did not own a car "borrowed" cars for joyrides. Lappen was probably more delinquent than most of the *raggare*. He rolled homosexuals and drunks. He burglarized stores with one or two confederates—usually using *schmacha* [the smash and grab technique]. His last *schmacha* was a jewelry store window. He got enough jewelry and watches to sell to a fence for 2,000 crowns. With this money he bought his own car and gave up stealing.

As Lappen described his life as a *raggare* boy, it was a life of fun, of laughs. "I lived an expensive life and I done exactly what I want. If I wanted to go to Copenhagen, I gotta go to Copenhagen. When we would drive to a little town, the girls knew we came from Stockholm and looked up to us." There was dancing and singing in the streets. "When I want to dance, I dance." Every weekend there would be parties in the homes of various girls or boys that he knew. He would start out on a Saturday evening at one party and would move

on to others as the inclination moved him. He would usually bring vodka or Scotch or Spanish brandy as his contribution to the merriment. Ten to twenty young people would be present at a given party at one time, but there would be constant comings and goings. For example, Lappen would usually get to three or four parties by Sunday morning. "If I didn't have fun, I'd get home by 3 or 4 a.m. If I had fun, I'd get home by 6 or 7." Sometimes, however, the parties lasted all through Sunday.

In 1957 Lappen was convicted for breaking and entering and sent to Fagared, a youth prison near Gothenburg. When he was released, he did not return to Stockholm. Instead he took a room in Gothenburg and got a job as an auto mechanic. Somehow, while he was in the institution, he had fallen in love with a local girl. He distinguished his love for this 17-year-old girl from the many intimate relationships that he has had with girls in his neighborhood and in the *raggare*. (Girls are also members of the *raggare* clubs, but they rarely own cars.) "That year 1958 I shall never forget. It was the happiest year of my life. For the first time, I had a family. I played cards with her father and listened to the radio." The girl's father, an office worker, took a liking to Lappen. He discovered that the boy was living in a lonely furnished room and offered to rent a room to him in their house. Lappen eagerly accepted. During the period when he lived in his girl friend's house, he was, according to his account, a model young man. He didn't drink; he went to bed early; he worked steadily; and he spent his spare time with his girl friend. Unfortunately, she became pregnant. When they told her parents, he at first thought that they would allow him to marry her, which is what both of them wanted. But a few days later the father told him that he "was no longer welcome in the house." Without further discussion, Lappen left. The girl, being only 17, could not marry without her parent's consent. They insisted that she go to a hospital and have an abortion. Lappen returned to Stockholm. His letters to her were returned unopened. Soon he went back to his old life with the *raggare*. Twice he and another Road Devil broke into safes although Lappen was very nervous, and he let his partner handle the explosives.

"The boys in this place are like gamblers. If we win, we get money. If we lose, we are locked up. Because we are good losers, we can smile." He recognized that, when he got out of prison, he faced a choice between two very different ways of life. "I know that the right kind of life is to work and have a family, something to hope at. Maybe I had it too easy the last year now and it is difficult to get back to normal life. On the one side, I found a lot of fun and on the other side, the right side, there was only a hard life." I asked Lappen what the chances were of his not getting into trouble any more. "If I learn to trust people, I won't have any more trouble." I think what he meant was that he would not commit further crimes if he developed another relationship like the one he had with the girl from Gothenburg and her family.

Case studies like those of Lappen, Happy, and Toshiko illustrate the mechanism whereby affluence leads to crime: through arousing feelings of material deprivation that cannot be satisfied legitimately. It is unlikely that adolescents from such different cultures would react to affluence so similarly unless there were a common causal process at work. Bear in mind though that the Lappens, Happys, and Toshikos are in the minority in their countries. Feelings of deprivation do not inevitably lead to crime. On the contrary, they are rarely acted upon. Under what conditions does the impulse to steal lead to theft? If affluence not only arouses predatory motives but gives the potential predator some prospect for "getting away with it," it greatly increases the probability that the motives will find expression in action. As the next section of this report will show, urban industrial societies do precisely that for adolescents: They loosen social controls and thus provide the opportunity for delinquency.

AFFLUENCE AND PARENTAL CONTROL OVER CHILDREN

One of the effects of affluence is to increase the life expectancy of everybody in the society, including, of course, parents. This means that a child in a rich industrial society has a far better chance of having both his parents alive and well during his adolescence. Another effect of affluence is to increase the divorce and separation rate. Why? Because industrialization enables women to support themselves—and their children, if need be.[15] Hence marital unhappiness is more likely to result in divorce or separation in rich industrial societies than in poor under-developed societies. But the most important effect of affluence on the family is to strip it down to jet-age size (mother, father, and their dependent children) and to isolate it physically and emotionally from other relatives. This is not true of all families even in the United States. And some industrial societies—Japan is a good example—have gone less far in deemphasizing generational ties than has Sweden, Israel, and the United States. Still, families in industrial societies are characteristically small; they move from community to community as employment opportunities arise; they lack the bulwark of kinship and communal support that poorer societies had.

These effects of affluence on the family help to explain why delinquents come from broken or inadequate families in industrial societies. Broken and inadequate families cause delinquency in rich societies because these societies assign major responsibility to parents for the control of their children. In poorer rural societies, where in addition to their biological parents, neighbors, grandparents, uncles, aunts, and other assorted relatives supervise children, the death or divorce of parents does not lead to juvenile delinquency. In short, a truism of criminologists, that delinquents come from less stable families than nondelinquents, is a truism only for affluent industrial societies. And even for us it is not clear *why* it is true. Two quite different mechanisms have been suggested by experts to explain this relationship between parental inadequacy and juvenile delinquency:

Mechanism 1. Parental rejection and neglect damage the personality of the developing child. Lack of impulse control results from pathological socialization. The psychopathic or neurotic boy reacts with violence to trivial provocations, sets fires, and steals purposelessly.

Mechanism 2. Parental inadequacy and neglect, by reducing family control, thereby orient the boy toward his agemates in the neighborhood. The family and the peer group are in a sense competing for the allegiance of boys in high-delinquency neighborhoods. If the peer group is delinquent, a boy's desire for acceptance by his peers tempts him to participate in delinquent activities.

Some evidence supports both mechanisms; re-

[15]In 1890, women constituted 15.8 percent of the white civilian labor force; in 1957, they constituted 34.1 percent. In 1890, divorced, separated, and widowed women constituted 28.6 percent of working women; in 1957, these categories constituted 40.4 percent of working women. U.S. Bureau of the Census, *Historical Statistics of the United States, Colonial Times to 1957* (Washington, D.C.: Government Printing Office, 1960), p. 72.

search is needed to distinguish the more important one. Such clarification would be useful because if mechanism 1 predominates, juvenile delinquency will probably continue to rise in all urban industrial countries. It is unlikely that most family catastrophes can be prevented. Assuming that the emotional scars resulting from death, divorce, or the mental illness of a parent cause delinquency, then delinquency may be part of the price of living in a rich society. On the other hand, if mechanism 2 predominates, more effective programs of delinquency control can be designed than are available at present. Assuming that the main problem is a breakdown of family control over the child, thereby exposing him to the corrupting influences of the street corner gang, then supportive institutions can be developed to backstop parents.[16]

Supportive institutions may be needed anyway. After all, although "problem" families have less effective control over adolescents than "normal" families in affluent societies, under contemporary conditions all families have weak control over adolescents, especially over boys. This weakness of adult control is most obvious under pathological circumstances such as slum neighborhoods or broken homes. Its ultimate source, however, is not pathology but the increasing social fluidity resulting from the allocation of education, recreation, work, and family life to separate institutional contexts. These changes in social organization affect everyone in contemporary societies, but their impact is especially great on adolescents because adolescence is a period of transition. Youngsters must disengage themselves from the family into which they were born and raised and establish themselves in a new family unit. They must eventually withdraw from the system of formal education and assume an occupational role. While preparing to make these transitions and learning preparatory skills, many adolescents are socially adrift—except for such solidarities as

they form with youngsters in the same situation as they. This is one reason for the development of "teenage culture." It is not the whole explanation. The affluence of industrial societies creates the material basis for an adolescent market. That is to say, adults in the United States, Sweden, Great Britain, the Soviet Union, Israel, and other industrial societies give adolescents substantial discretionary purchasing power, which enables adolescents to demand (and obtain) distinctive clothing, motion pictures, phonograph records, recreational facilities, and eating and drinking places.[17]

Teenage culture helps to ease the transition between the family into which the child was born and the family the young adult will create by marriage. Peers give the adolescent an emotional anchorage, but they constitute an unpredictable influence. Unless adolescents are organized under adult sponsorship, as boy's clubs, Scouts, and church youth groups are, they may mutually encourage one another to engage in a wide variety of unconventional or rebellious behavior. Delinquent gangs represent an antisocial development of adolescent autonomy; they are of course less pleasing to adults than scouting or 4-H clubs. Gang formation is possible in contemporary societies because the institutional structure, in adjusting to the requirements of urban industrial life, has (unintentionally) undermined effective adult supervision of adolescents. Of course, some families maintain better control over adolescents than others; and adolescent girls are generally better supervised than adolescent boys. The very technology of industrial societies emphasizes the independence of the adolescent from parental observation. In the age of the automobile, an adolescent's home may be the place where he sleeps and little else. The car is not the only means of avoiding adult surveillance, but the car symbolizes the looseness of the ties between adults and adolescents because it is such an effective instrument for escaping the eyes of adults.

The increased freedom of adolescents from adult control cannot be revoked. Not only technology but ideology is on the side of youthful independence. Contemporary societies are or-

---

[16]In Sweden, unmarried mothers not only receive allowances for their children. They are visited regularly by social workers who attempt to give some of the guidance that a husband-father might provide. Nevertheless, children from broken families have a higher delinquency rate than children from intact families. The supportive institution is not fully successful.

[17]Mark Abrams, *The Teenage Consumer* (London: London Press Exchange, 1960).

ganized with the unit of participation the individual rather than the family. The child is not a representative of his family in the classroom or in the play group; as an adult he will participate in the economic and political systems as an individual also. This principle of individualism, implicitly embodied in social organization, is explicitly defined (outside of Iron Curtain countries) in the concept of "freedom." Adolescents are jealous of this prerogative. The freedom offered to adolescents is not always used wisely; the freedom to choose is the freedom to make mistakes. Delinquency is one mistake. On the other hand, many adolescents use their period of unsupervised freedom creatively: to establish commitments to educational and occupational goals, to learn how to relate to the opposite sex and, ultimately, to marry and have children. It would be throwing out the baby with the bath water to attempt to establish preindustrial control over adolescents to prevent some of them from using their freedom destructively.

AFFLUENCE AND EDUCATION: COUNTERVAILING FORCES ON DELINQUENCY

The new affluence has an important impact on the material aspirations of young people: on the desire for cars, transistor radios, cameras, and clothes. But affluence has also an impact on education. As Table 3–40 shows, substantial proportions of adolescents in industrial countries now remain in school instead of going to work, which was the usual pattern up to a generation ago. Even for the United States, the first country to embark on mass secondary education, the change is recent, as Table 3–41 shows.

Why does affluence have this effect on educational aspirations? One reason is the increased public support of education made possible by large national incomes. Another is the greater resources of individual families, making it possible for them to forego the financial contributions of working adolescents. Both of these factors make for an increased supply of educational opportunities. Education is a substantial investment, both for society and for the individual family; rich countries can make this investment

more easily. The demand for education—as opposed to the supply—depends on the motivation of young people themselves. This has been nega-

TABLE 3–40.

SCHOOL ATTENDANCE IN CONTEMPORARY NATIONS IN VARIOUS RECENT YEARS

Country	Base Year	*Percent of Age Group Enrolled in School*			
		5–14 Years	15–19 Years	20–24 Years	5–24 Years
United States ..	1958	89.9	66.2	12.0	69.9
Iceland	1957	73.2	57.9	6.8	56.7
Soviet Union ..	1958	71.5	48.6	8.2	49.1
Canada	1958	87.3	45.9	9.3	63.0
Norway	1957	77.3	35.7	9.5	55.2
Netherlands ...	1958	85.5	32.8	4.7	57.4
Sweden	1960	82.6	32.3	11.0	54.0
Belgium	1957	95.4	31.5	5.5	60.2
France	1958	90.1	30.8	3.8	58.6
Luxembourg ..	1957	76.3	25.2	5.4	44.0
Switzerland ...	1956	78.6	22.9	3.4	48.7
Ireland	1957	92.6	19.6	4.2	59.3
Denmark	1957	76.4	18.5	5.6	48.9
Germany, F.R...	1958	80.2	17.6	4.6	42.3
United Kingdom	1957	98.8	17.6	3.9	59.6
Yugoslavia	1956	66.3	16.9	4.1	37.8
Greece	1956–57	74.5	16.9	3.3	40.8
Italy	1957	78.8	15.7	3.9	42.5
Spain	1958–59	74.9	13.3	3.3	39.6
Austria	1957	84.8	13.1	3.7	46.5
Portugal	1957–58	56.2	8.8	3.1	32.6
Turkey	1959–60	44.7	3.3	1.1	25.1

SOURCE: Ingvar Svennilson (in association with Friedrich Edding and Lional Elvin), *Targets for Education in Europe in 1970* (Paris: Organization for Economic Cooperation and Development, January, 1962), pp. 107–08.

TABLE 3–41.

THE INCREASING NUMBER OF HIGH SCHOOL GRADUATES IN THE UNITED STATES, 1870–1956

School Year Ending	*High School Graduates*	
	Number	*Percent of Population 17 Years Old*
1870	16,000	2.0
1880	23,634	2.5
1890	43,731	3.5
1900	94,883	6.4
1910	156,429	8.8
1920	311,266	16.8
1930	666,904	29.0
1940	1,221,475	50.8
1950	1,199,700	59.0
1956	1,414,800	62.3

SOURCE: U.S. Bureau of the Census, *Historical Statistics of the United States, Colonial Times to 1957* (Washington, D.C.: Government Printing Office, 1960), p. 207.

tively demonstrated in recent crash programs in slum schools (e.g., the Higher Horizon program in New York) where substantial new resources did not make dramatic improvements in student accomplishments. Research is needed to clarify the conditions under which students are motivated to seek as much education as they can master. It is known that parental encouragement is important. And what if parents are not encouraging? Can teachers and other school personnel make up for this deficit? To some as yet unknown extent, they can.

The potentialities of fostering educational aspirations can perhaps be gauged by an unplanned experiment in the consequences of high aspirations. American children of Japanese, Chinese, and Jewish backgrounds do extraordinarily well in school and go to colleges and universities in disproportionate numbers. They also have extremely low delinquency rates.[18] What is the connection? These same ethnic groups are often considered drivingly ambitious. Do not their educational aspirations reflect this ambition? Japanese, Chinese, and Jewish parents want to insure their children a share in business and professional occupations; education is the means to this end. Being members of minority groups, they are perhaps more keenly aware of the necessity of education for socioeconomic success, but they are motivated in essentially the same way as white Anglo-Saxon Protestants. The connection between higher education and high-income employment is well understood and provides a principal motivation for college attendance.[19]

What about Negroes? Unlike the Japanese, Chinese, and Jews, American Negroes show massive educational disadvantage. But recent studies prove that Negro educational retardation does not reflect lack of interest in education. Negro school children, even though they may be performing poorly in the classroom, are as likely as white children to say that they want to go to college.[20] They are less likely to perceive education as feasible for them; hence they are less likely to plan on going and to put in the consistent studying that can make college attendance a reality. In the light of their underutilization of the educational escalator, it is no coincidence that Negro adolescents have a high delinquency rate. Whereas education is a legitimate opportunity for Japanese adolescents, delinquency constitutes for Negro adolescents a tempting alternative to poverty—what one sociologist has called an "illegitimate opportunity."[21] It would be oversimplifying to maintain (1) that all delinquents are envious and (2) that they would not be delinquent had they realized that education could get them a high standard of living. Some delinquents are not envious. Some envious adolescents are not delinquent. Some adolescents are not willing or able to wait for the economic payoff of education; they share the sentiments of a famous economist who said, "In the long run we are all dead."

Nevertheless, there is fragmentary but consistent evidence from various industrialized countries that the longer a youngster stays in school the smaller are the chances that he will commit crimes. For example, table 3–42 presents some Swedish data showing that the criminal conviction rate for boys born in Stockholm in

TABLE 3–42.

BOYS BORN IN STOCKHOLM IN 1940 WHO, BY THE AGE OF 21, ACQUIRED A RECORD IN THE CRIMINAL REGISTER, BY EDUCATIONAL ATTAINMENT

| *Highest Educational Attainment* | Boys with Criminal Records | | *All Boys* |
	Number	*Percent*	
Gymnasium	10	2.0	488
Realskola	34	9.9	445
Primary school	185	20.2	918
Unknown	7	14.3	49
Total	236	12.4	1900

SOURCE: Unpublished study of comparative adolescent delinquency being conducted by Jackson Toby, Carl-Gunnar Janson, and Shuichi Miyake.

[18]Jackson Toby, "Educational Maladjustment as a Predisposing Factor in Criminal Careers: A Comparative Study of Ethnic Groups" (Ph. D. Diss., Department of Social Relations, Harvard University, 1950).

[19]Jackson Toby, "The American College Student: A Candidate for Socialization," *American Association of University Professors Bulletin* 43 (June, 1957): 319–22.

[20]U.S. Office of Education, *Equality of Educational Opportunity* (Washington, D.C.: Government Printing Office, 1966).

[21]Richard A. Cloward, "Illegitimate Means, Anomie and Deviant Behavior," *American Sociological Review* 24 (April, 1959): 164–76.

1940 was 10 times as great if they completed primary school than if they completed *gymnasium*. The data in table 3–42 are unusually clean cut; few countries have as good criminal records as Sweden where it was possible to trace 94 percent of the cohort of Stockholm boys from birth until the age of 21.

Table 3–42 shows clearly that educational accomplishment prevents criminality, but it does not tell why. Therefore it does not immediately suggest policy recommendations. Would raising the age for compulsory school attendance reduce adolescent delinquency? Not unless mere custody of children in school is the reason for the correlation between educational attainment and nondelinquency. This is rather unlikely to be the case. The correlation almost certainly reflects the motivations of young people themselves. That is to say, the significance of graduation from *gymnasium* is that graduation from *gymnasium* fulfills the aspirations of Swedish young people. Most of them were interested in obtaining business and professional occupations. Some may have been interested in education for its own sake. But committing crimes would be incompatible with the fulfillment of either of these goals. Arrests label a boy to himself as well as to his classmates and teachers as belonging to a different world, a world the values of which are opposed to those of the school and incompatible with it.

Table 3–43 is a refinement of the data of table 3–42 taking into account the fact that the 1900 boys came from different socioeconomic circumstances. It is known that boys from working class families are less likely to seek higher education than boys from business, professional, and white-collar families. It is also known that boys from working class families are more likely to be arrested for delinquent behavior than boys from more elite occupational backgrounds. Table 3–43 examines the joint effect of socioeconomic background and educational attainment on criminality, thus providing an answer to the question: Which takes precedence? The answer is fairly clear. Those Stockholm boys who graduated from gymnasium had a low offense rate, and it did not make much difference whether their fathers were high status or low status. Three of the 71 working class boys who completed gymnasium

TABLE 3–43.

THE CRIME RATES OF BOYS BORN IN STOCKHOLM IN 1940, BY EDUCATIONAL ATTAINMENT AND THE SOCIOECONOMIC STATUS OF THEIR FAMILIES

	Boys with Criminal Records					
	In the Upper Class		In the Middle Class		In the Working Class	
Highest Educational Attainment	Number	Percent	Number	Percent	Number	Percent
Gymnasium ..	4	1.7	3	1.6	3	4.2
Realskola	4	5.3	15	8.6	15	8.0
Primary school	0	—	57	20.0	128	20.7
Unknown (49 cases)	—	—	—	—	—	—
Total	8	2.4	75	11.8	146	16.6

SOURCE: Unpublished study of comparative adolescent delinquency being conducted by Jackson Toby, Carl-Gunnar Janson, and Shuichi Miyake.

had a criminal record as compared with two of the 235 boys from upper class families. At the minimal educational level, on the other hand, parental status had an appreciable effect on criminality. Whereas 21 percent of the 618 working class boys with minimal education had a criminal record, none of the 25 upper class boys with minimal education had one. What are the implications of this finding? That a youngster who commits himself to education is unlikely to become delinquent regardless of his family background.

But why does educational commitment have this effect? Criminologists do not know for sure. One likely possibility is that youngsters who pursue successful careers at school are consciously doing so in order to enjoy the "good life" as adults. They desire to share in the material rewards of an affluent society, just as delinquents do, but they utilize a legitimate path to socioeconomic advancement. This is probably not the whole explanation. Whatever the initial motivation for desiring success at school—to please concerned parents, to obtain a well-paying job as an adult, to learn—involvement in the school program has consequences for the student's conception of the world. A relatively uneducated delinquent does not know as much about the pleasures an affluent society can offer as a university student. The university student may obtain pleasure out of reading a book, attending a concert or ballet, visiting a museum, appreciating natural beauty, fighting for social justice—as well as out of driving a powerful car, getting "high," and wearing fashionable clothes. Delinquents in affluent societies characteristically desire material pleasures intensely—so much so that they are willing to risk freedom for them—but they are aware only of a small part of the opportunities for gratification that their societies offer. Furthermore, opportunities they are unaware of are those that are awakened or cultivated by the educational system. These considerations suggest that another reason that education prevents crime is that education broadens the range of desires of young people and stimulates some desires that bear little relation to money income. This is, of course, speculation. Research is needed to establish the precise mechanism whereby educational achievement prevents crime.

CONCLUSION

Poverty is nothing new. It is affluence that is new. But the relationship between subjective dissatisfaction and objective deprivation is more complicated than was at first thought. Poverty cannot cause crime but resentment of poverty can, and, curiously enough, resentment of poverty is more likely to develop among the relatively deprived of a rich society than among the objectively deprived in a poor society. This is partly because affluent industrial societies are also secular societies; the distribution of goods and services here and now is a more important preoccupation than concern with eternal salvation. It is also because the mass media—to which television has been a recent but important addition—stimulate the desire for a luxurious style of life among all segments of the population. These considerations explain why the sting of socioeconomic deprivation can be greater for the poor in rich societies than for the poor in poor societies. They also throw light on the high crime rates of affluent societies and on the increase of adolescent delinquency rates with the increase in general prosperity. Relative to adults, adolescents feel like a poverty stricken

and powerless minority, and how they feel has consequences for how they behave.

The fact that adolescents mostly go to school and adults mostly go to work helps to explain the phenomenon of "teenage culture." It is not the whole explanation. The affluence of industrial societies creates the material basis for cultural differentiation. That is to say, industrial societies allocate to adolescents substantial discretionary purchasing power, and this enables adolescents to demand (and obtain) distinctive clothing, motion pictures, phonograph records, recreational facilities, and eating and drinking establishments. From the viewpoint of understanding delinquency, however, the extension of formal education is probably more important than the development of the adolescent market. The reason for this is that mass formal education has created serious problems of life goals for adolescents with educational disabilities. For academically successful adolescents, school is a bridge between the world of childhood and the world of adulthood. For children unwilling or unable to learn, school is a place where the battle against society is likely to begin.

Orientation to consumption seems to be an increasing characteristic of industrial societies. It permeates most strata, not merely adolescents, and it contributes to other phenomena besides delinquency, e.g., ostentatious expenditures for food, clothing, travel, housing. However, the impact of commercialism is greatest on working class adolescents because the impact on them of the educational system is less positive than for middle class youth. If they leave school as soon as they legally may, they have less opportunity to experience art, literature, serious music, science, religion, and meaningful work, than they have of being attracted to the gadgets and entertainments available in the marketplace. This isolation of school-leaving youths from what are generally conceded to be the accomplishments of industrial civilization may partially account for violent crimes. As Nelson Algren put it in his paraphrase of a literary idea of Richard Wright, ". . . when a crime is committed by a man who has been excluded from civilization, civilization is an accomplice of the crime."[22]

---

[22] Nelson Algren, "Remembering Richard Wright," *The Nation* 192 (January 28, 1961): 85.

Selective exposure to industrial society is not merely an internal problem. Anthropologists have called attention to the selective "diffusion" of culture traits to underdeveloped societies. Trinkets, tools, hard liquor, and Coca Cola are easier to export than arts and sciences or even religion.

H. G. Wells once remarked, "Human history becomes more and more a race between education and catastrophe." Is delinquency a catastrophe? Some might argue that delinquency is a small price to pay for life in a rich society where most people, including adolescents, have the freedom to choose the direction of their destiny. It is true that delinquency is rare in subsistence economies (where there is less to envy) and in totalitarian states (where social controls coerce would-be rebels). On the other hand, crime does cost a society something, not only the losses to victims but also the wasted years of delinquent youths. Most ex-delinquents regard the years spent in raising hell on the streets as well as those in prisons as irretrievable mistakes. Mass education can prevent some of

this waste. The appeal of education, like adolescent delinquency itself, is stimulated by affluence. But affluence needs reinforcement if youngsters from homes where parents do not value education are to believe that education is for them too. The primary benefit of education is of course intrinsic: the greater realization of the potentialities of young people. But a secondary consequence is to deflect adolescents from the destructive possibilities open to them in a free society. If the experience of American society with its Japanese, Chinese, and Jewish minorities is any precedent, the indirect consequence of educational upgrading will be the reduction of adolescent delinquency. True, these ethnic groups possessed special cultural values favorable to education, which were transmitted to children without planning. However, it seems likely that planned programs of educational upgrading, adequately financed and enthusiastically publicized, could duplicate the Japanese, Chinese, and Jewish unintended experiments in delinquency prevention. Is it worth a try?

28.

Walter E. Schafer and Kenneth Polk

WHAT THE SCHOOLS MUST DO TO HELP PREVENT DELINQUENCY

[Our] analysis should have made three things clear. First, juvenile delinquency in this country is partly heightened by conditions in American public education. Second, these conditions are deeply anchored into prevailing conceptions and organization of the educational system. Third, proposals for preventing, reducing and controlling delinquency cannot refer only to pro-

Source: Walter E. Schafer and Kenneth Polk, "Delinquency and the Schools," *1967 President's Commission on Law Enforcement and Administration of Justice: Task Force Report on Juvenile Delinquency and Youth Crime* (Washington, D.C.: Government Printing Office), pp. 258-60.

grams that relate directly to control problems in the schools, but must reach deeply to the underlying and core conditions that help produce educational failure, perceived irrelevancy, lack of commitment, and exclusion—and, therefore, delinquency. To stop short at proposing such stop-gap and surface proposals as more counselors, more social workers, more truant officers, special classes for troublemakers, and tighter enforcement of attendance laws would simply be a failure to recognize the broader dimensions of the problem. Their implementation would have only the slightest effect on prevention of delinquency. Unless basic, radical, and immediate educational changes are made, delinquency will continue to increase—and will be accompanied by the spread of other social ills that stem from the same roots. . . .

We have argued that in the past, our schools have been less than fully effective in preventing delinquency and, in fact, that they have inadvertently contributed to delinquency. If the educational system is to become more effective in the prevention of delinquency, the schools themselves and those who support them must face up to a dual challenge.

A. Schools must organize their programs and efforts in such a way that all youth get "bound into" legitimate and acceptable pathways through adolescence.

(1) In meeting this challenge, the schools must succeed in maximizing the chances of educational success by taking advantage of educational aptitudes and assets and by making up for any educational handicaps that may exist.

(2) Moreover, they must continue to hold the interest and allegiance of all youth throughout the educational career, even in the face of strong pressures toward delinquency.

(a) This will be done to the extent that the schools present a curriculum . . .

(i) that is relevant to present experiences and problems in the lives of pupils;

(ii) that is equally relevant to the future, especially at the secondary level, in the sense that current activities have a clear connection with future rewards;

(iii) that provides alternative avenues to productive and responsible adulthood, so that varying aptitudes, interests, and aspirations are taken into account.

(b) This will be done to the extent that the schools give youth a larger share in

(i) educational planning and decision-making;

(ii) the exercise of authority;

(iii) the instructional process.

B. Schools must organize their programs and efforts in such a way that students who fall behind or stray from the legitimate pathways through childhood and adolescence are "recaptured," "re-equipped," and re-committed.

(1) When students fall behind academically, the schools must make even more intense efforts to equip them to achieve at their highest possible levels.

(2) When students deviate from school or community rules of conduct, the schools must make even more intense efforts to "bind" them into the legitimate system, so they will become committed or recommitted to acceptable pathways toward adulthood. The schools must do this by:

(a) avoiding "system" and individual responses to students in trouble that serve to exclude, push away, or lock them out of conventional opportunities;

(b) making special efforts to channel such youth into existing opportunities for involvement in the educational process;

(c) creating additional opportunities for such youth.

C. If the educational system is to accomplish these ends, certain other conditions must be met as well.

(1) The schools must develop means for effectively involving parents in the educational process, so their general support of educational programs as well as understanding of and aid to their own children will be maximal.

(2) The schools must have a built-in capacity to assess their programs and outcomes and to make needed adaptations when conditions demand it.

(3) Innovations must be introduced into current operations in such a way that they will not be subverted or channeled into existing frameworks.

(4) Teacher training institutions must feed into the schools new staff who are adequately prepared to teach students who are high risks in terms of failure and delinquency.

29.

ERDMAN B. PALMORE AND PHILLIP E. HAMMOND

INTERACTING FACTORS IN JUVENILE DELINQUENCY

Cloward and Ohlin's theory of delinquent gangs implies that delinquency rates are proportional to the product, not the sum, of positions in legitimate and illegitimate opportunity structures. This implication is illustrated with data on 319 youths from Aid to Dependent Children welfare rolls.

Social scientists' understanding of delinquency is reasonably advanced in two respects. First, they have identified with fair accuracy the social structures that contain high rates of juvenile crime. And second, they have developed a number of theories regarding the social-psychological processes that lead youth to delinquency. The literature attests to the importance on the one hand of age, sex, race, social rank, and neighborhood, and, on the other hand, to alienation, guilt, frustration, and aspiration, as factors in explaining juvenile delinquency.[1]

One recent attempt to integrate both these aspects of knowledge about delinquency is Cloward and Ohlin, *Delinquency and Opportunity*.[2] The authors present a theoretical argument to explain the development and content of patterns of juvenile deviance or delinquent subcultures. Put briefly, their argument is that discontent or alienation *develops* from restricted access to legitimate avenues, while the *likelihood* and *direction* of actual criminal behavior depend on access to illegitimate avenues. Thus, an explanation of delinquency must take into account not only the impoverishment of legal paths of behavior but the "richness" and kind of illegal paths as well.

As Cloward and Ohlin note, a theory of delinquent subcultures need not explain every delinquent act; in their essay they restrict their attention to "those forms of delinquent activity which result from the performance of social roles specifically provided and supported by delinquent subcultures."[3] But much research into delinquency (including that reported here) is based on police and court records, and it is not always clear whether the delinquent acts result from subcultural forces or represent instead the extra-role behavior of individuals. Since "delinquency is normally an activity carried on in groups,"[4] however, the theory of delinquent subcultures may be relevant to the explanation of delinquency.[5] We shall assume its relevance in the following analysis of an implication of the Cloward-Ohlin theory regarding interacting factors in juvenile delinquency. Here we present an *ex post facto* illustration of this interaction. Although we make no effort to investigate delinquency as a subcultural phenomenon, our analysis is guided by the question: what results would be expected if the theory in *Delinquency and Opportunity* were adequate to

SOURCE: Erdman B. Palmore and Phillip E. Hammond, "Interacting Factors in Juvenile Delinquency," *American Sociological Review* 29, no. 6 (December, 1964): 848–54. Reprinted by Permission of the authors and the American Sociological Association.

The authors gratefully acknowledge the aid of the Ford Foundation, who supported the research reported here, and thank Hubert M. Blalock and Elton F. Jackson for their critical reading of the manuscript.

[1]For reviews of this literature, see any text on juvenile delinquency, e.g., Herbert A. Bloch and Frank T. Flynn, *Delinquency* (New York: Random House, Inc., 1956), pp. 60ff. For a succinct outline and appraisal of delinquency theory see Albert K. Cohen and James F. Short, Jr., "Juvenile Delinquency," in *Contemporary Social Problems*, ed. Robert K. Merton and Robert A. Nisbet (New York: Harcourt, Brace and World, Inc., 1961), pp. 89–112.

[2]Richard A. Cloward and Lloyd E. Ohlin, *Delinquency and Opportunity* (New York: The Free Press, 1960).

[3]Ibid, p. 9.

[4]Cohen and Short, op. cit., p. 103.

[5]This is especially true when the delinquents are persons of similar age living in a limited number of neighborhoods, and when many of the acts with which they are charged are acts typically engaged in by gangs. Both of these conditions apply to the data reported here.

the explanation of different rates of delinquent acts?

THE DATA

The study reported here investigated every youth in Greater New Haven born in 1942–44 whose surviving relative—most often the mother —was on the rolls of Aid to Dependent Children (ADC) in 1950.[6] The record of every youth was followed from his sixth birthday to his nineteenth, so that the age span would be the same for all subjects. Data was taken from the welfare office records and from school and police records in all cases. Socio-economic characteristics of the neighborhoods were derived from a 1950 study of New Haven,[7] and neighborhood delinquency rates were calculated from recent statistics of the New Haven Police Youth Bureau.

We concentrated on ADC cases for two reasons. First, social casework records were available for the years they were on ADC. Our information on family characteristics, for example, was obtained from these records. Second, this group is relatively homogeneous with respect to social class and home conditions. It is by definition in a deprived stratum, since neither the parents nor other relatives could support the children. Furthermore, the records show that virtually all these cases not only were economically deprived in 1950 but also came to ADC with a history of such deprivation. All but one of these ADC families were broken by death of a parent, divorce, separation, or desertion. This state of affairs tends to be chronic: 74 per cent of the sample were still on ADC rolls after five years, and 63 per cent were still receiving aid after 10 years.

At the outset, then, this population is at least grossly homogeneous in terms of social class, broken homes, and age span. Since lower-class youth from broken homes are known to have high delinquency rates, it is not remarkable

that by 1962, 34 per cent of the sample had become known to the police or juvenile court.[8] Interest thus shifts to *which* third of this deprived group became delinquent, and why.

THE FINDINGS

Three rather powerful factors associated with delinquency are race, sex, and school performance.[9] Table 3–44 summarizes the simultaneous effects of these factors. Each of the three factors has an independent effect, i.e., influences the delinquency rate when the other two factors are held constant. The range in these rates, from zero to 71 per cent, indicates that a considerable portion of the variation in delinquency in this population can be predicted, if not theoretically explained, by race, sex, and school performance.

TABLE 3–44.

THE EFFECTS OF RACE, SEX, AND SCHOOL PERFORMANCE ON DELINQUENCY

Percentage with One or More Arrests or Court Referrals
(Numbers in parentheses are base N's)

School Performance	Negro Males	White Males	Negro Females	White Females
Success	43(14)	38(37)	24(25)	0(75)
Failure	71(38)	61(61)	40(25)	23(44)

---

[8]In contrast, a "control" group (all youths of the same age as the welfare group, and included in the 1950 New Haven Study as Class 5, the lowest class) had a delinquency rate of 18 per cent. Though the two groups were similar with respect to age, sex, type of neighborhood lived in, and performance in school, they did differ radically on attributes associated with welfare cases. Compared with the control group, our sample contained twice as many persons living in public housing, twice the number who had moved three or more times during the 11-year period, three times the number of Negroes, and over ten times the number from broken homes. For further comparisons of these two groups see Erdman B. Palmore, "Factors Associated with School Dropouts and Juvenile Delinquency among Lower-Class Children," *Social Security Bulletin* 26 (October, 1963): 4–9. Of course, we recognize that reported delinquency is not necessarily equivalent to actual delinquency.

[9]School success is operationally defined as a grade average of A, B, or C; all others are defined as failure.

---

[6]A total of 353. Of this number 34 were eliminated because they died or moved from the area, or because insufficient data were available; therefore N = 319.

[7]See August B. Hollingshead and Frederick C. Redlich, *Social Class and Mental Illness* (New York: John Wiley & Sons, Inc., 1958).

The introduction of two more variables, however, not only increases the range in rates but also reveals a different pattern. Unlike race, sex, and school performance, whose effects generally are additive, "family deviance" and "neighborhood deviance" have non-additive or interaction effects; their influence on delinquency is differentially felt.[10]

One of the overwhelming impressions one gets from reading the case work records is the different *degree* to which these broken homes are "deviant." At one extreme are families that are relatively stable even though one parent is dead, deserted, or disabled. At the other extreme are units deviating grossly from societal norms: one or both parents are in prison or mental hospital, or the parent has had a series of marriages, separations, multiple illegitimacies, or "cut and run" affairs.[11] Negroes are more likely to live in one of these unstable or grossly deviant families (57 per cent, vs. 28 per cent of whites), and family deviance is somewhat related to delinquency (in the sample as a whole, 41 per cent from deviant families, vs. 31 per cent from non-deviant families were delinquent). The surprising observation is that family deviance influences the delinquency of Negroes but not that of whites, as Table 3–45 indicates.

TABLE 3–45.

THE EFFECT OF FAMILY DEVIANCE ON DELINQUENCY AMONG NEGROES AND WHITES

| *Family* | *Percentage with One or More Arrests or Court Referrals* | |
	Negroes	*White*
Deviant	55(58)	27(60)
Non-deviant	39(44)	29(157)
Difference	16	−2

<hr>

[10]An interaction effect occurs when the relation between two variables is not additive, that is, when the relationship differs under various conditions of a third variable. In much survey research, identifying interaction effects is thus analysis by "specification." See Paul F. Lazarsfeld and Morris Rosenberg, eds., *The Language of Social Research* (New York: The Free Press, 1955), pp. 115–26.

[11]Any person whose family displayed one or more of these gross deviations is characterized as being from a deviant family. Most of these deviant families had multiple illegitimate births and a series of illegitimate "affairs."

These data, which apply equally to males and females, lead one to infer that race and family deviance have an interactive effect on delinquency. A possible explanation, to be discussed presently, is suggested by the next table, where the impact of family deviance on Negro delinquency is concentrated among those failing in school.

Table 3–46 indicates that family deviance influences Negroes performing badly in school but has much less effect on those doing well. One could just as easily phrase the point this way: school failure has more effect on those from deviant families. Thus, school success seems to play a compensating role, protecting persons from the impact of a surrounding force that otherwise encourages delinquency.[12]

TABLE 3–46.

THE EFFECT OF FAMILY DEVIANCE ON DELINQUENCY AMONG NEGROES FAILING OR SUCCEEDING IN SCHOOL

| *Family* | *Percentage with One or More Arrests or Court Referrals* | |
	School Failure	*School Success*
Deviant	71(34)	33(24)
Non-deviant	45(29)	27(15)
Difference	26	6

Another relevant variable is deviance of the neighborhood environment. The great majority, of course, live in areas of great poverty. But some do not, and even the lower-class neighborhoods differ in the rates of crime and delinquency that occur year after year. Subjects were classified as living in a deviant neighborhood when their area was both of the lowest class and characterized by high delinquency rates.[13] Again, Negroes are more likely than whites to live in deviant neighborhoods (54 vs. 26 per cent), and neighborhood deviance is

<hr>

[12]This pattern does not emerge among the whites.

[13]The delinquency rate of the neighborhood is not completely independent of the percentage in our sample from that neighborhood who are delinquent, since the delinquents in our sample contribute to the over-all delinquency rate. This interdependence is insignificant, however, because our delinquents constituted only a small fraction of the total delinquents from any given neighborhood.

somewhat related to delinquency rates (42 vs. 30 per cent). But again, the impact of neighborhood deviance is restricted—this time to boys. (See Table 3–47.)

TABLE 3–47.

THE EFFECT OF NEIGHBORHOOD DEVIANCE ON DELINQUENCY AMONG BOYS AND GIRLS

Percentage with One or More Arrests or Court Referrals		
Neighborhood	Boys	Girls
Deviant	71(55)	14(56)
Non-deviant	47(95)	16(113)
Difference	24	–2

This pattern, which holds for both Negroes and whites, is another example of interacting factors: neighborhood deviance influences the delinquency of boys but not girls. And once more, this influence is further restricted almost entirely to boys failing in school; boys doing well in school appear to be little influenced by a deviant neighborhood. The protective or compensating role of adequate school performance is once again observed.[14]

INTERPRETATION

We have presented an uncomplicated notion several times—the notion that a factor has a "protective role" or differential effect, or that two factors have an interacting effect on a third. In summary: (1) A deviant family background increases Negro, but not white, delinquency. (2) A deviant neighborhood increases male, but not female, delinquency. (3) Either kind of deviant influence increases delinquency more among those failing in school than among those succeeding. Taken together, these findings illustrate an implication of Cloward and Ohlin's theoretical work in which illegitimate as well as legitimate opportunity structures are related to delinquency.

The youths in this research are lower-class, both in origin and by present circumstance. They also are or have been on welfare rolls. For those reasons alone, then, their life chances,

[14]This pattern emerges also among the girls.

their range of alternatives or "effective scope" is relatively narrow. Unable to avoid some contact with society's general value system, they too are confronted by a goal of success, self-esteem, or dignity.[15] Yet the probability that they will achieve this goal, whatever its particular form, is less than the probability for youths not from lower-class, welfare families.

We can specify this generalization, however, because the chances for "success" are not equally low throughout the lower class. For example, Negroes systematically have more difficulty than whites reaching comparable goals, and they know it. "The last hired and first fired," reflects in both belief and reality the different probabilities of getting and keeping a steady job. Correlatively, among lower-class youth the sexes differ in their chances of achieving "success." Girls typically can anticipate a future of marriage and motherhood, however imperfect, and regardless of hardships in performing the role, most will meet some acceptable criterion of success. For lower-class boys, on the other hand, aspirations of marriage and fatherhood are not enough. In the eyes of society a job and income are further criteria they must meet. And ironically, lower-class women can frequently find employment more readily than can men.

Reworded in Cloward and Ohlin's terms, our assertions are that lower strata generally, and Negroes and boys especially, face more barriers to legitimate goals. Their situation is more anomic. Similarly, school failure can be conceived of as another barrier to legitimate opportunity. Whether school failure stems from low intelligence or lack of motivation or deprived cultural background, it is clear that a youth failing or dropping out of school will find more

[15]Data that we do not have, on what values these persons in fact hold, would obviously improve this statement. As it stands it is an assumption, the same assumption central to the theoretical tradition being applied here. See Robert K. Merton, *Social Theory and Social Structure*, rev. ed. (New York: The Free Press, 1957), chaps. 4–5; Albert K. Cohen, *Delinquent Boys* (New York: The Free Press, 1955); and Cloward and Ohlin, op. cit. Herbert Hyman, in "The Value Systems of Different Classes," in *Class, Status and Power*, ed. Reinhard Bendix and Seymour M. Lipset (New York: The Free Press, 1953), pp. 426–42, has investigated this assumption and shown its potential importance to delinquency theory.

obstacles to the legitimate goals of our society than will other youths.

As different indicators of the variable "legitimate opportunity," therefore, these measures might be expected to have an *additive* effect on the degree of delinquency. That is, the more legitimate opportunities a person has, the less likely he is to engage in illegitimate behavior. Table 3–44 generally shows that this is the case —persons who have the least access to legitimate avenues (i.e., Negro boys failing school) are most likely to engage in illegitimate behavior (their delinquency rate is 71 per cent); persons who have most opportunity to learn and fulfill legitimate avenues (i.e., white girls succeeding in school) are least likely to engage in illegitimate behavior (their delinquency rate is 0 per cent). Other categories differ in delinquency rates depending on the extent of their legitimate opportunity.

Cloward and Ohlin make an important theoretical specification, however. Social structural conditions account not only for differential barriers to *legitimate* avenues but also, they argue, for differential opportunities to learn and execute *illegitimate* avenues.[16] If deviance, or illegitimate behavior, is to be explained, both kinds of opportunity should be incorporated in the analysis.

Stated in extreme terms, the theory says that irrespective of the degree to which legitimate avenues are unavailable, patterned deviance can occur only when deviant avenues (illegitimate means) are available.[17] We can infer, then, that the level of deviant behavior is predicted not by the *sum* of blocked legitimate opportunity plus illegitimate opportunity, but rather by the *multiplied* effect of the two variables. Thus, if one of the terms has a value of zero, deviance would not be increased by the other term.

We repeat, this is the *extreme* form of an inference from the Cloward-Ohlin theory. No research could claim to have adequate measures

ranging from zero to maximum opportunity. Nor are these two variables the only ones required for an adequate explanation of delinquency. Motivation, or the extent to which "societal" goals are indeed goals for given subjects, for example, is obviously important in understanding the vigor with which any avenue will be tried and thus the strength of reaction upon finding that avenue blocked. The theory nevertheless implies that, since "each individual occupies a position in both legitimate and illegitimate opportunity structures,"[18] the likelihood that he will pursue a deviant path is the product of his position in both structures. In short, illegitimate avenues will be *disproportionately* utilized by those whose legitimate opportunities are more restricted.[19]

Family deviance and neighborhood deviance can be conceived as measures of opportunity to learn and to execute illegitimate means. It seems reasonable to assume that children brought up in grossly deviant homes or in slum neighborhoods with high delinquency rates have more opportunity to observe and learn disregard for law, to learn how to reduce the visibility of illegal activities, and to find gang support and organized crime to facilitate delinquent behavior. If this is the case, then the simultaneous effect of family deviance and neighborhood deviance on delinquency might well be additive,[20] since both are measures of the same variable—illegitimate opportunity—but the simultaneous effect of one or more measures of *legitimate* opportunity, coupled with one or more measures of *illegitimate* opportunity, ought to be interactive.[21] And indeed Tables 3–45 through 3–48 reveal just that pattern: availabil-

---

[16]Cloward and Ohlin, op. cit., chap. 6.

[17]We say "in extreme terms" because, of course, social survey research is not in a position to measure, or hold constant, every avenue, legitimate and illegitimate. It is possible, though, to imagine true experiments on a variable such as school performance, where other factors are randomized.

[18]Cloward and Ohlin, op. cit., p. 150.

[19]And correlatively, a point for which we have no illustrative data: an increase in legitimate avenues will be disproportionately utilized by those with more restricted illegitimate opportunities.

[20]Though not shown in tabular form, the data clearly indicate that these two variables do have an additive effect on delinquency.

[21]Specifically it ought to be a particular form of interaction, a multiplicative effect. Were it possible to measure opportunity precisely, one could examine the implication in its strict form: illegitimate opportunity has no effect on persons whose legitimate avenues for success are adequate but has an increasing impact as legitimate avenues are less and less adequate.

TABLE 3–48.

THE EFFECT OF NEIGHBORHOOD DEVIANCE ON
DELINQUENCY AMONG BOYS FAILING OR
SUCCEEDING IN SCHOOL

Percentage with One or More Arrests or Court Referrals

Neighborhood	School Failure	School Success
Deviant	82(39)	44(16)
Non-deviant	53(60)	37(35)
Difference	29	7

ity of illegitimate opportunities (family deviance or neighborhood deviance) has greater impact on the deviance of those with fewer legitimate opportunities (Negroes, or boys, or school failures).

If two measures of each variable are used, the result is to sharpen the differential effect of illegitimate opportunity, as Table 3–49 shows. Table 3–49, of course, simply synthesizes data already shown, but it does show concisely that illegitimate opportunity has greater impact on persons with fewer legitimate avenues to legitimate goals (46 percentage points) than on those with many (11 percentage points). The number of cases is too small to permit refinements in Table 3–49, but the pattern of differences remains the same when, instead of race and school performance, any two of the three measures of legitimate opportunity are paired. A reasonable, if tentative, conclusion is that legiti-

mate and illegitimate opportunities have an interacting effect on juvenile delinquency.

SUMMARY

We have investigated the effect on delinquency of two basic variables: (1) legitimate opportunity as indicated by race, sex, and school success, and (2) illegitimate opportunity as indicated by family deviance and neighborhood deviance. We have used our data to illustrate an implication of Cloward and Ohlin's theory of delinquent gangs, that delinquency is proportional to barriers to legitimate opportunity *times* illegitimate opportunity.

Any measure of one of the opportunity variables, coupled with any measure of the other opportunity variable, should produce an interaction effect on delinquency. In the discussion above, four such effects were shown in tabular form. The probabilities[22] of finding the observed

[22]The test is Goodman's test of the difference between the differences in two proportions, Leo A. Goodman, "Modifications of the Dorn-Stouffer-Tibbetts Method for 'Testing the Significance of Comparisons in Sociological Data,'" *American Journal of Sociology* 66 (January, 1961): 355-59. Since many of the cells in the tables contain fewer than 100 cases, and since the subjects are not strictly a random sample but constitute a universe of local ADC cases of their ages for those years, the appropriateness of the test is debatable. Its use (two-tailed here) does provide a basis for contrasting patterns of results, however.

TABLE 3–49.

THE EFFECT OF ILLEGITIMATE OPPORTUNITY ON DELINQUENCY AMONG YOUTHS WITH
VARYING DEGREES OF LEGITIMATE OPPORTUNITY

Percentage with One or More Arrests or Court Referrals

	Degree of Legitimate Opportunity			
	Low		High	
	School Failure		School Success	
Degree of Illegitimate Opportunity	Negroes	Whites	Negroes	Whites
High: Both Family Deviance and Neighborhood Deviance	82(17)	63(8)	21(14)	0(4)
Medium: Either Family Deviance or Neighborhood Deviance	56(32)	39(46)	42(19)	15(46)
Low: Neither Family Deviance nor Neighborhood Deviance	36(14)	47(51)	17(6)	11(62)
Difference Attributed to Illegitimate Opportunity	46	16	4	–11

differences (between percentage differences) by chance are:

Family Deviance and Race	.13
Family Deviance and School Performance (for Negroes)	.30
Neighborhood Deviance and Sex	.01
Neighborhood Deviance and School Performance (for Boys)	.20

According to the theory, four other pairs of variables, which combine alternative measures of *either* legitimate *or* illegitimate opportunity, need not have differential impact on delinquency. Note that the following probabilities are higher:

Neighborhood Deviance and Family Deviance	.52
Sex and School Performance	.76
Sex and Race	.28
Race and School Performance	.68

These tests of significance are meant, of course, only as benchmarks. In addition to reservations about the test's applicability to these data, several other qualifications must be noted. First, these results should not be construed as a test of Cloward and Ohlin's theory. The latter is chiefly concerned with the nature or content of delinquent subcultures, rather than rates of delinquent acts; in addition, the relation between the measures used here and the *concepts* of legitimate and illegitimate opportunity is tenuous. School success, for example, reflects not only a legitimate means to respectability but probably indicates a higher level of aspiration as well. Sex, as another example, no doubt measures differential access to legitimate means, but in addition taps the differences between

male and female socialization in families; therefore, the finding that family deviance has more effect on female delinquency comes as no surprise though it is contrary to the theory discussed here.[23]

Put briefly, these data, taken entirely from records compiled for other purposes, cannot adequately confirm the theoretical implication regarding interaction effects. Further investigation will require sharper measures of avenues to opportunity structures, both legitimate and illegitimate. It would also benefit from measures of frustration, resentment, and so on, thus providing the social-psychological links between opportunity and delinquency that necessarily cannot be provided here.

To explain away unconfirmed predictions by claiming they have been tested with impure measures is to admit that the propositions that *were* upheld are open to question. Certainly no deception is warranted or intended, given these conditions. Our data, however, convincingly suggests that interaction effects of legitimate and illegitimate opportunity structures are worth looking for: either variable taken singly might leave out a significant portion of the story.

---

[23]This reversal of the general prediction is understandable on other theoretical grounds: girls are more influenced by their homes and more likely to pattern their behavior after adults in their families. See Jackson Toby, "The Differential Impact of Family Disorganization," *American Sociological Review* 22 (October, 1957): 502–12, and F. Ivan Nye, *Family Relationships and Delinquent Behavior* (New York: John Wiley & Sons, Inc., 1958).

The theory anticipates three more multiplicative effects, one of which we observed: neighborhood deviance has greater impact on the delinquency of school failures. The other two (family deviance and school performance; neighborhood deviance and race) do not conform to the theory.

30.

JON E. SIMPSON AND MAURICE D. VAN ARSDOL, JR.

RESIDENTIAL HISTORY AND EDUCATIONAL STATUS OF DELINQUENTS AND NONDELINQUENTS

The feasibility of the records matching approach is examined with data pertaining to the interrelations of residential mobility, educational status, and juvenile delinquency. Findings are reported by race and sex for comparisons of approximately 7,000 delinquent and 325,000 general population youth 14–17 years of age. Recent mobility was not systematically associated with delinquency; educational status was directly related to delinquency; and little interaction was observed between the mobility variables or between mobility and educational status.

Extended research based on official records has not resolved issues pertaining to the derivation and interpretation of juvenile delinquency rates. Much delinquency theory is barren of empirical content, and rate differential studies of delinquency etiology in urban areas have yielded limited results.[1] There are several reasons for these difficulties.

First, record systems of adjudicating agencies do not provide accurate social correlate data concerning "official" delinquents. Second, the range of sociological variables is limited to a small number since the official records are maintained for administrative purposes. Third, it is difficult to obtain base populations for computing delinquency rates and contrasting delinquent and nondelinquent populations.[2] Background data for delinquents collected from agencies, which comprise the rate numerators, may not be comparable to census or survey information about the general population which is usually the basis of the rate denominators. If numerators and denominators do not explicitly refer to the same phenomenon, delinquency rates will be in error.[3] Finally, official records have been un-

SOURCE: Jon E. Simpson and Maurice D. Van Arsdol, Jr., "Residential History and Educational Status of Delinquents and Nondelinquents," *Social Problems* 15, no. 1 (Summer, 1967): 25–40. Reprinted by Permission of the authors and The Society for the Study of Social Problems.

This investigation was supported in whole by Public Health Service Research Grant MH-06729 from the National Institute of Mental Health for the Southern California Records Matching Project. Agencies conducting the research are the University of Southern California, Department of Sociology and Anthropology, Population Research Laboratory and the Youth Studies Center. Patricia A. Nelson, Muriel Schad, and James Taggart assumed responsibility for the collection of data from the County of Los Angeles Probation Department files. Leo A. Schuerman offered important assistance in the analysis of the data, including the construction of special computer programs. John C. Beresford, Special Assistant, Demographic Fields, United States Bureau of the Census has ably coordinated activities of the Bureau of the Census necessary for this work. Georges Sabagh participated in the project design and assisted in the development of the tabulation program. Calvin Goldscheider and Clarence Schrag have made important contributions to the preparation of this paper.

[1] See, for example, the studies summarized by Terrance Morris, *The Criminal Area* (London: Kegan Paul, 1958); Bernard Lander, *Toward an Understanding of Juvenile Delinquency* (New York: Columbia University Press, 1954); Clifford R. Shaw et al., *Delinquency Areas* (Chicago: The University of Chicago Press, 1929); Clifford R. Shaw and Henry D. McKay, *Juvenile Delinquency and Urban*

Areas (Chicago: The University of Chicago Press, 1942); and Christen T. Jonassen, "A Re-Evaluation and Critique of the Logic and Some Methods of Shaw and McKay," *American Sociological Review* 14 (October, 1949): 608–14.

[2] Stanton Wheeler has correctly argued that conceptions of delinquency rate denominators should be broadened to include characteristics of police systems and the nature of victims and citizen populations, as well as the nature of crime-committing persons. Nevertheless, sociologists have yet to obtain the accurate information concerning crime-committing persons which is a prerequisite for Wheeler's broader objectives. See Stanton Wheeler, "Criminal Statistics: A Reformulation of the Problem," *1965 Social Statistics Section Proceedings of the American Statistical Association* (Washington, D.C.: American Statistical Association, 1965), pp. 28–35.

[3] To illustrate, a variable such as occupation may be defined in different ways and may differ over time—from a decennial census return to an earlier or later report in connection with an agency activity. Reliable rate computation requires a reconciliation of these differences.

favorably viewed as a result of repeated findings that: (1) youths known to the police or courts are not representative of juveniles committing delinquent acts, (2) some types of behaviors and offenders are more likely to be reported and adjudicated than others, and (3) placement of a juvenile on probation rather than in an institution may be a function of available space or family composition and other socio-economic biases.[4]

The difficulties encountered in obtaining data about delinquents through court records have led to alternative methods that have generated new methodological and conceptual problems. For example, community survey studies must obtain interviews within home or school contexts, determine how to identify delinquent and non-delinquent populations, and acquire large sam-

ples to permit detailed cross-tabulations. These requirements are increasingly difficult to accomplish. Ecological correlations relating indices of social, economic, and housing characteristics of urban subareas to delinquency rates;[5] analyses of specific types of delinquency, including gang studies;[6] provocative theoretical formulations advanced during the past decade;[7] and attempts to focus on the adjudicating process rather than delinquents[8] are other alternatives hindered by the paucity of comparative data.

Our premise is that records linkage merits intensive exploration as a new procedure to correct limitations of existing data collection techniques. This focus is a prerequisite to analyses of juvenile and adult offenders and their environments, reactions of citizen populations, or adjudicating processes. In our research, two disparate records systems—those of a metropolitan probation department and the U.S. Bureau of the Census—were merged to provide a better quality and broader range of data for delinquent populations than can be obtained from local data systems. The procedure involves physically matching, on an *individual case basis*, probation

[4]See Austin L. Porterfield, *Youth in Trouble* (Fort Worth, Tex.: Leo Potisham Foundation, 1946); James F. Short, Jr., and F. Ivan Nye, "Reported Behavior as a Criterion of Deviant Behavior," *Social Problems* 5 (Winter, 1957): 207–13; F. Ivan Nye and James F. Short, Jr., "Scaling Delinquent Behavior," *American Sociological Review* 22 (June, 1957): 326–31; F. Ivan Nye, *Family Relationships and Delinquent Behavior* (New York: John Wiley and Sons, Inc., 1958), Chap. 2–7; Thorsten Sellin and Marvin E. Wolfgang, *The Measurement of Delinquency* (New York: John Wiley and Sons, Inc., 1964); F. Ivan Nye, James F. Short, and Virgil J. Olson, "Socio-Economic Status and Delinquent Behavior," *American Journal of Sociology* 63 (January, 1958): 381–89; Albert J. Reiss and Albert L. Rhodes, "The Distribution of Juvenile Delinquency in the Social Class Structure," *American Sociological Review* 26 (October, 1961): 720–32; John P. Clark and Eugene P. Wenninger, "Socio-Economic Class and Area as Correlates of Illegal Behavior among Juveniles," *American Sociological Review* 27 (December, 1962): 826–34; Joseph W. Eaton and Kenneth Polk, *Measuring Delinquency: A Study of Probation Department Referrals* (Pittsburgh: University of Pittsburgh Press, 1961); Alex McEachern, "Characteristics of Probationers," in *Views of Authority: Probationers and Probation Officers*, ed. Alex McEachern, mimeographed (Los Angeles: Youth Studies Center, University of Southern California, 1961); Maynard L. Erickson and LaMar T. Empey, "Court Records, Undetected Delinquency, and Decision Making," *Journal of Criminal Law, Criminology, and Police Science* 54 (December, 1963): 456–69; Joseph Goldstein, "Police Discretion Not to Invoke the Criminal Process: Low Visibility Decisions in the Administration of Justice," *Yale Law Journal* (March, 1960), 543-94; and David Matza, *Delinquency and Drift* (New York: John Wiley and Sons, Inc., 1964), esp. Chaps. 4 and 5.

[5]For example, see Bernard Lander, op. cit., and William S. Robinson, "Ecological Correlations and the Behavior of Individuals," *American Sociological Review* 15 (June, 1950): 351–57.

[6]See James F. Short, Jr. and Fred L. Strodtbeck, *Gang Process and Gang Delinquency* (Chicago: The University of Chicago Press, 1965), for description of such research and citations to these studies.

[7]Among the best known are Albert K. Cohen, *Delinquent Boys* (New York: The Free Press, 1960); Walter B. Miller, "Lower Class Culture as A Generating Milieu of Gang Delinquency," *Journal of Social Issues* 14 (Summer, 1958): 5–19; and Richard A. Cloward and Lloyd E. Ohlin, *Delinquency and Opportunity* (New York: The Free Press, 1960).

[8]In addition to the sources cited in n. 4, see the research reports by Nathan Goldman, *The Differential Selection of Juvenile Offenders for Court Appearance* (New York: National Council on Crime and Delinquency, 1963); Yona Cohen, "Criteria for the Probation Officer's Recommendations to the Juvenile Court Judge," *Crime and Delinquency* 9 (July, 1963): 262–75; George E. Bodine, "Factors Related to Police Dispositions of Juvenile Offenders," unpublished paper, 1964 meetings of the American Sociological Association, Montreal, Canada; and Peter G. Garabedian, "The Control of Delinquent Behavior by Police and Probation Officers," unpublished paper, 1964 meetings of the Society for the Study of Social Problems, Montreal, Canada.

department records for juveniles with their 1960 census returns and those of their parents, siblings, and housing units. With this technique, data for the numerators and denominators of delinquency rates, as well as comparisons between delinquent and total populations, are based on the same phenomena—census variables.[9]

This paper has two purposes. The first objective is to outline records linking procedures for a metropolitan probation department and the U.S Bureau of the Census. The second objective is to illustrate how records linkage data can be used for rate and percentage comparisons of delinquents by social categories. With regard to the second aim, an investigation is made of the relationship of delinquency to: (1) residential histories, as measured by place of birth of youth, residence of head of household in 1955, and the year juvenile moved into present house; and (2) educational status, as indicated by school enrollment and relative grade level by age. Comparisons are limited to delinquent and total populations. Findings are discussed with reference to innovations and problems in records linkage which merit further consideration.

PROCEDURES

To obtain a universe of "delinquent" cases, summary information on case identification, name, age, sex, race, and offense was collected for the 23,543 juvenile referrals to the County of Los Angeles Probation Department from July 1, 1959 through December 31, 1960—an 18 month period centered on the April 1, 1960 U.S. decennial census date. The study population was limited to the 12,525 juveniles, age 10

to 17 inclusive, who were defined as official cases through the filing of formal juvenile court petitions as a result of alleged delinquent acts.[10]

Identification information derived from intake forms was submitted to the Bureau of the Census.[11] Key criteria used to establish match statuses were name, address, age, sex, and race of juvenile, and relationship of juvenile to head of household. Rules were developed to determine matching status when there were recording errors or when information was missing from Bureau of the Census or probation files. During the matching phase, a computer procedure was developed to replace the prior technique of visually matching agency information with enumeration schedules.[12]

Most of the detailed data in the 1960 Census were obtained on a 25 percent basis. The Census

---

[9]In addition to comparisons between subcategories of delinquent populations, records matching facilitates examination of delinquents and/or their households in terms of: (1) the general population delimited by the social categories which pertain to the delinquents; (2) nondelinquent siblings of delinquents; and (3) computer "matched" nondelinquent households within the same or other communities selected on the basis of the presence of youths with comparable characteristics. Finally, it is possible to analyze the type and prevalence of delinquency by neighborhood, i.e., enumeration district or census tract.

[10]A total of 9,407 cases were eliminated by the project staff as a consequence of the following criteria which were implemented in the order listed: under age 10 (primarily unofficial and/or dependency cases), unofficial (petition not filed, closed at intake or noncourt investigation), dependency (guardianship, parental neglect, transient, and court consents), and 18 years of age or older. The final universe of 12,525 cases reflects the additional loss of 1,611 cases because of duplication (280), residence outside of Los Angeles County at the time of census enumeration (756), Group Quarters residence (354) and under or over-age (175) based on Bureau of the Census records, and administrative errors (46). Individual offense categories accounted for 9 to 26 percent of the total cases with the following percentage distribution by offense type: auto theft (15), offenses against property (26), offenses against persons (9), sex delinquencies (10), major traffic offenses (14), narcotics (4), and delinquent tendencies (22). Neglect and other dependency referrals and minor traffic violations were previously eliminated from the universe.

[11]To achieve maximum efficiency in retrieving the required information from the detailed Probation Department case folders, only single page summary intake "face sheets" or "book sheets" were normally examined. These summary records were photocopied, coded as to match criteria, and then sent to the Bureau of the Census.

[12]For a description of these techniques see Jon E. Simpson and Maurice D. Van Arsdol, Jr., "The Matching of Census and Probation Department Records Systems," *1965 Social Statistics Section Proceedings of the American Statistical Association* (Washington, D.C.: American Statistical Association, 1965), pp. 116–21; and Jon E. Simpson, Maurice D. Van Arsdol, Jr., and Georges Sabagh, "Records Matching as a Technique for Social Research: An Illustrative Case," *Sociology and Social Research* 50 (October, 1965): 89–100.

listing books were therefore searched to establish sample status. The delinquents in the 25 percent sample were matched with the appropriate computer tape storage files. Both the delinquent juvenile and the presumed adult in the juvenile's household were matched to their comparable 1960 census records in 78.1 percent of the cases; the adult only was found in an additional 7.2 percent of the referrals; and neither the delinquent juvenile nor the adult was linked in the remaining 14.7 percent of the cases.[13]

A previous feasibility study for a sample of the probation department universe showed no substantial decrease in the matching rate as a result of using the full eighteen months rather than a shorter period of time.[14] Also, findings of the pilot study indicated that matched cases are representative of the universe with respect to sex, race, and offense classifications.[15]

As each case was located in the census storage file, all housing and population characteristics of the household and the delinquent were added to a project tape file. For comparisons of the delinquents and total population, a special tape file was constructed from the 25 percent

---

[13]Match failures for the delinquent population may represent, in part, high rates of underenumeration of official delinquents by the 1960 censuses, and the match rates may be lower than would be obtained with cases more "representative" of the total population. See Jack Silver, "Discussion," 1965 Social Statistics Section Proceedings of the American Statistical Association (Washington, D.C.: American Statistical Association, 1965), p. 140.

[14]The match rates obtained in this research compare favorably with other census records matching studies utilizing shorter periods of time adjacent to a census date, e.g., Lillian Guralnick and Charles B. Nam, "Census NOVS Study of Death Certificates Matched to Census Records," Milbank Memorial Fund Quarterly 37 (April, 1951): 144–53; Evelyn M. Kitagawa and Philip M. Hauser, "Methods Used in a Current Study of Social and Economic Differentials in Morality," in Emerging Techniques in Population Research (New York: Milbank Memorial Fund, 1963), pp. 250–66; and Earl S. Pollack, "Use of Census Matching for Study of Psychiatric Admission Rates," 1965 Social Statistics Section Proceedings of the American Statistical Association (Washington, D.C.: American Statistical Association, 1965), pp. 107–15.

[15]For the feasibility study results, Jon E. Simpson, Maurice D. Van Arsdol, Jr., and Georges Sabagh, op. cit., pp. 94–95. The analyses for the total study population are complete and substantiate the pilot study findings.

---

sample of the total population of Los Angeles County. The total population was comprised of all families with one or more children 10 through 17 years of age in the household. Tabulations for the delinquent and total populations reflect the sample weighting program used by the Bureau. This paper reports data for the weighted equivalent of 7,185 delinquent cases and 324,863 juveniles within the general population from 14–17 years of age.[16]

---

[16]The ratio weights were those used by the Bureau of the Census as adjustment factors to compensate for under and overenumeration in the 1960 Censuses. These ratio weights were applied to both the delinquent and the total samples. The weighting procedure probably underestimates delinquency rate levels as delinquents are expected to have a higher level of underenumeration in the 25 percent sample than are nondelinquents. A detailed explication of the weighting system used in this project may be found in Muriel Schuerman, Records Matching: An Investigation of the Procedures for Linkage of Local and Federal Records Systems (Master's thesis, Los Angeles: University of Southern California, forthcoming).

For the present discussion, a review by the Bureau of the Census of the 12,525 cases in the study population indicated that 2,676 were in the 25 percent sample enumeration, and 9,849 were non-sample cases. The 78.1 percent match rate for the sample enumeration cases resulted in the location of approximately 2,100 juveniles with their presumed adult(s) in the Census records. Application of the Census derived weight of 4.07—based on the population parameters of the study universe—provided a reconstructed total of 8,556 cases. The analyses in this paper are limited to the 7,185 delinquents 14–17 years of age. Data were also obtained for weighted equivalent of 1,371 delinquents 10–13 years of age. This latter segment was not included in this report due to the comparatively low rate of involvement with the court which confirms the assumption that most youth in this age range have not approached the threshold of official delinquency. Rates per 1000 population for all juveniles in the 10–13, 14–15, and 16–17 years of age categories were: 3, 16, and 22, respectively. For the males only, the rates were: 4, 24, and 36, respectively.

The sex ratio for the matched delinquents was 4 to 1 as compared to a 1 to 1 ratio in the general population. The correspondence on "ethnicity" was closer with the following percentages for the delinquent and total populations, respectively: Anglo American (68.3 and 81.7), Spanish surname (16.2 and 11.2), and Negro (15.4 and 7.1). Ethnicity was defined by Spanish surname, Negro, and Anglo, including white, not Spanish surname, Japanese, Indian and other. Similarities of delinquency rates for the Japanese, Indian and other ethnic categories justified inclusion with the Anglos. The total population was evenly distributed in the dichotomized age categories 14–15 and 16–17, but the delinquents

RESULTS

The relationship of official delinquency to mobility and educational status has often been examined, but earlier studies lead to inconsistent interpretations.[17] For example, it has been hypothesized that mobility leads to "anomie" and reduces the effectiveness of social control mechanisms supporting law-abiding behavior. On the other hand, a period of socialization into delinquent subcultures may be a prerequisite for delinquent behavior. Recent in-migrants in high delinquency areas may not immediately internalize prevailing "delinquent" value systems and may not become active participants or leaders within the existing gang structures.

For educational status, it has been argued that poor school performance is an important antecedent of delinquency. School attendance reflects progress toward socially approved goals. On the other hand, lack of school enrollment has been interpreted as leading to adjustment for those youths with poor school records. These arguments were reformulated in terms of the following assumptions:

1. Recent in-migration into metropolitan areas is not a precursor of juvenile delinquency. The time required to integrate new migrants into delinquent subcultures means that delin-

quency rates will generally increase with increased length of metropolitan residence.

2. School attendance and school performance are inversely related to official metropolitan delinquency.

3. School attendance and school performance are not related to past mobility. Youthful in-migrants to metropolitan areas and the juveniles involved in intrametropolitan residential mobility enter school systems which are essentially similar to those which they have previously experienced.

4. The relationships of school attendance and school performance to delinquency are not enhanced when past metropolitan in-migration and residential mobility are considered.

In summary, it was anticipated that recent mobility would not be associated with delinquency and that delinquency would be directly related to length of residence in the metropolis and school failure. It was further assumed that the interaction of these measures would not differentiate the delinquents from the total juvenile population.

Residential Mobility and Delinquency. As shown in Table 3–50,[18] data are available for

---

were overrepresented (56.9 percent) in the older category. Approximately 20 percent of the delinquents compared to 13 percent of the total population resided in non-intact households defined in terms of female head. Family status controls—intact versus non-intact families—were not included as the small number of cases in the latter category negated detailed cross-tabulations.

[17] For an overview of the significance of education and the school in the area of juvenile delinquency, John R. Eichorn, "Delinquency and the Educational System," in *Juvenile Delinquency: Research and Theory*, ed. Herbert C. Quay (Princeton, N.J.: D. Van Nostrand Company, Inc., 1965), pp. 298–322. General statements pertaining to the relationship of mobility and delinquency may be found in Robert G. Caldwell, *Criminology*, 2nd ed. (New York: The Ronald Press Company, 1965), Chap. 12; John M. Martin and Joseph P. Fitzpatrick, *Delinquent Behavior: A Redefinition of the Problem* (New York: Random House, Inc., 1964), Chap. 3; and Walter C. Reckless, *The Crime Problem*, 3rd ed. (New York: Appleton-Century-Crofts, 1961), Chap. 4. Also, see Leonard D. Savitz, *Delinquency and Migration* (Philadelphia: Commission on Human Relations, 1960).

[18] Numerators and denominators of the 25 percent sample were inflated to estimated population figures by Bureau of the Census ratio weights (see n. 16). Computed rates were then expressed to the base of 1000, weighted by the reciprocal of the matching rates for the appropriate population category, and adjusted from an 18 month to an annual basis. Rate numerators are by sex and ethnicity for juvenile offenders. Matching rate proportions used in the adjustment of rate numerators are as follows: male—.793, male-Anglo—.816, male-Spanish surname —.786, male-Negro—.713, and all females—.754.

Rate computation and adjustment procedures are illustrated for the total cases, male Anglo rate in Table 3–50. The constructed total population of 135,884 is inflated by a ratio weight factor of slightly more than 4 and represents a sample of approximately 33,500. Similarly the constructed delinquent population of 4,078 reflects a sample of approximately 1,000. The constructed delinquent population of 4,078 is divided by the constructed total population of 135,884 and multiplied by 1,000 to yield an initial rate of 30.01 per 1000. This initial rate is multiplied by .667 to adjust the rate from an 18 month to a 12 month base, and then divided by .816, the Anglo match rate proportion, which gives a rate of 25 per 1000. It is assumed that underenumeration is greater for Negroes than for the Spanish surname category and greater for the *(Footnote Continued)*

TABLE 3–50.

MOBILITY STATUS OF TOTAL AND DELINQUENT POPULATIONS 14–17 YEARS
OF AGE BY SEX ETHNICITY: PERCENTAGES* AND RATES[a] (PER THOUSAND)

		Males			Females
		Anglo[b]	Spanish Surname	Negro	
Total Cases	T.P.[c]	135,884	18,324	11,341	159,314
	Del.[d]	4,078	951	869	1,287
	Rate	25	44	72	77
Place of Birth of Youth					
Calif.	T.P.	55.8	64.8	38.0	55.7
	Del.	54.3	68.2	40.4	50.7
	Rate	24	47	77	6
South	T.P.	7.6	7.7	46.5	10.3
	Del.	7.6	10.0	48.7	15.9
	Rate	24	57	75	11
Other Regions	T.P.	33.1	15.0	15.2	29.6
	Del.	35.7	13.0	10.4	30.4
	Rate	26	39	49	7
Foreign	T.P.	3.5	12.5	0.4	4.5
	Del.	2.4	8.7	0.6	3.1
	Rate	17	31	—[e]	5
Residence of Household Head, 1955					
Same House	T.P.	49.5	47.1	42.9	48.1
	Del.	45.4	44.9	43.8	38.5
	Rate	22	42	74	6
L.A. County	T.P.	34.0	38.9	39.4	35.8
	Del.	38.8	42.0	40.2	45.7
	Rate	28	48	73	9
Calif.	T.P.	2.7	2.3	1.8	2.4
	Del.	2.4	2.3	0.6	1.2
	Rate	22	45	23	4
South	T.P.	1.8	2.0	7.7	2.3
	Del.	1.8	2.7	6.9	3.1
	Rate	24	60	64	10
Other Regions	T.P.	9.3	3.9	5.0	8.3
	Del.	9.6	2.3	5.9	7.5
	Rate	26	24	84	6
Foreign & Not Rep.	T.P.	2.8	5.8	3.2	3.0
	Del.	2.0	6.0	2.6	4.0
	Rate	17	46	60	9

Spanish surname category than for Anglos. Lack of Census data with which to estimate under-enumeration in the total population precluded adjustments for the rate denominators. All rate comparisons testing the assumptions concerning the influence of residential histories and educational status upon delinquency are made within, instead of between, the sex and ethnic categories. Inflation of rate denominators by reciprocals of the level of census enumeration by ethnicity would probably diminish slightly the rate differences between these categories.

An alternative rate construction procedure would

have involved not weighting the numerators for the ethnic categories by the reciprocal of the matching rates. This technique could have diminished the rate differences between males and females and among the male Anglo, male Spanish surname, and male Negro categories. It was assumed, however, that the differences in matching rates for these delinquent categories were greater than the differences in enumeration rates for the comparable categories in the total population, which are the bases of the denominators. If this assumption is correct, the inflated numerators would provide more accurate rates for comparisons of within sex and ethnic cat-

TABLE 3-50.—*Continued*

Year Youth Moved into Present House		Males			Females
		Anglo[b]	Spanish Surname	Negro	
1959–60	T.P.	21.0	25.0	27.0	23.2
	Del.	24.3	25.7	25.5	37.1
	Rate	28	45	68	11
1957–58	T.P.	18.4	18.5	21.0	18.3
	Del.	18.3	22.1	20.7	17.5
	Rate	24	53	71	7
1950–56	T.P.	40.5	38.0	39.2	39.9
	Del.	38.8	33.2	42.6	31.7
	Rate	24	39	78	6
1949 or Earlier	T.P.	20.0	18.4	12.8	18.6
	Del.	18.7	19.0	11.2	13.8
	Rate	23	46	63	5

*Percentages added vertically within total and delinquent populations each total 100.
[a]See n. 18 for explanation of rate computations.
[b]Anglo includes "white" and "all other" ethnic categories.
[c]T.P. = total population, based on inflated 25% sample.
[d]Del. = delinquent population, based on inflated 25% sample.
[e]Less than 200 cases in the general population and/or no delinquent cases.

three mobility indices: place of birth of juvenile, residence of head of household in 1955, and the year that juvenile moved into present residence.[19] Similar percentage distributions occur for the total male population and the male delinquents on each of the residential history variables with race controlled. Female delinquents manifest more recent mobility than the total female juvenile population. Similarities between delinquent and total populations are reinforced by comparable percentages in most of the mobility subcategories when evaluated by sex and ethnicity. While the South is the place of birth for approximately one-half of the Negro males, Anglo males and all females not born in

egories. See Earl S. Pollack, op. cit. The problem of rate adjustment for underenumeration of the general population recorded in a rate denominator is, of course, not peculiar to records matching studies. See, for example, George W. Barclay, *Techniques of Population Analysis* (New York: John Wiley and Sons, Inc., 1958), pp. 50–81. Unfortunately, additional data were not available with which to adjust the denominators.

[19]Results described in this report relating to the comparison of Bureau of the Census records with other records are based on work done by the Bureau of the Census and transmitted to the authors in a manner such that the identification of individuals was not possible and the confidentiality of reports to the Bureau of the Census was maintained.

California typically are from different regions than the South. Otherwise, the row percentages for Anglo, Spanish surname, and Negro males, and all females are quite stable.

Rate comparisons, with sex and race controlled, generally verify the assumption that recent in-migration into Los Angeles and/or intrametropolitan residential mobility are not precursors of official delinquency. To illustrate, the delinquency rate for all Anglo males of 25 per thousand may be contrasted with the highest and lowest rates of 28 and 17, respectively, for all subcategories of the three mobility measures. Variations are greater for Spanish and Negro males, but without a consistent trend. Thus, the rates are lower for Negro youths whose heads of households resided in the South instead of Los Angeles during 1955 and/or who moved into their present housing units within approximately one year prior to the 1960 Census in contrast with periods up to ten years. Finally, with few exceptions, the descending rank order of rates—Negro males, Spanish surname males, Anglo males, and all females—is maintained for all the residential mobility categories.

Education and Delinquency. The educational status index is derived from a combination of census questions pertaining to age, school enrollment, and grade level. Youths are classified as not enrolled in school; or as enrolled at below, within, or above the modal grade level for age through comparisons of grade level with the following modal values: 14 years of age, 8th or 9th grade; 15 years, 9th or 10th grade; 16 years, 10th or 11th grade; 17 years, 11th or 12th grade. Table 3–51 indicates that the Anglos have the most favorable educational experience—age-grade placement and school enrollment—followed by the Negro and Spanish surname populations. Results of the educational index show greater variation in the percentage distributions and the delinquency rates than for the residential history measures.

With sex and race controlled, the delinquents are over-represented in the school dropout category and under-represented within the modal grades. However, there are no large differences in percentages between delinquent and total population youth in above and below modal educational attainment. The percentage distributions for the delinquent and total populations and the comparative rates suggest that school enrollment, *per se*, regardless of relative

achievement, represents a deterrent to delinquency. The pattern for Negro males is less pronounced than for the other three population subcategories. As with mobility, there is a descending order of rates associated with each of the school achievement categories from Negro males, to Spanish surname males, Anglo males, and all females.

Interrelationship of Residential Mobility and Educational Status. Findings pertaining to the Anglo males for all possible two variable cross-tabulations of the three residential mobility variables and the educational measure are given in Table 3–52. The relationship of residence of head of the household in 1955 and educational status is not reported since the results duplicate the pattern found for place of birth of youth with school status and year juvenile moved into present house with school status. Additional analyses for Spanish surname males, Negro males, and all females provided similar patterns with allowance for rate variations.

The nominal percentage differences observed in comparisons between the delinquents and total population on each of the mobility variables are repeated in the cross-tabulations in-

TABLE 3–51.

EDUCATIONAL STATUS OF TOTAL AND DELINQUENT POPULATIONS 14–17 YEARS OF AGE BY SEX AND ETHNICITY: PERCENTAGES[*] AND RATES[a] (PER THOUSAND)

		Males			Females
		Anglo[b]	Spanish Surname	Negro	
Educational Status of Youth					
Above Mode	T.P.[c]	7.1	4.9	9.2	8.7
	Del.[d]	5.2	4.2	10.4	5.5
	Rate	18	38	81	4
Mode	T.P.	80.7	67.8	68.8	78.1
	Del.	73.1	57.9	64.7	68.1
	Rate	18	38	68	6
Below Mode	T.P.	5.6	13.7	10.0	5.0
	Del.	6.8	13.9	9.2	7.9
	Rate	30	45	66	11
Not Enrolled	T.P.	6.6	13.6	11.9	8.2
	Del.	14.9	24.0	15.8	18.4
	Rate	56	78	95	16

[*]Percentages added vertically within total and delinquent populations each total 100.0.
[a]See n. 18 for explanation of rate computations.
[b]Anglo includes "white" and "all other" ethnic categories.
[c]T.P. = total population, based on inflated 25% sample.
[d]Del. = delinquent population, based on inflated 25% sample.

volving pairs of mobility indices. The base rate for Anglo males is 25 per 1000 and only 4 of 56 rates with combinations of mobility variables were higher than 35 per 1000. When mobility is controlled, the previous finding that "out of school" status is the category most directly related to delinquency gains additional support. Data in Table 3–52 suggest that there is little interaction between the mobility variables or between mobility and educational status.

School Status and Selected Social Correlates. As a consequence of the above findings, a series of other variables were paired with educational status to determine: (1) if school enrollment would become more predictive of delinquency, and (2) if the effect of school enrollment would remain with other controls. Table 3–53 presents the outcomes for Anglo males in the comparisons of educational status by age of head, marital history of parents, education of head, and total family income. For purposes of the analysis, the polar categories of age of head were considered to contribute to delinquency through a discontinuity of attitudes between older parents and children or the younger parents' lack of experience with which to deal with youth problems. Family instability, as indicated by divorce or female head of household, was expected to be associated with delinquency. Education of head of household and total family income were expected to be inversely related to delinquency.[20]

The significance of school dropout status is again generally apparent. Consistent with previous data, the representation of delinquents and the total population youths in the below and above mode categories is substantially the same, with only a slightly more favorable pattern for the general population. Although the percentage differences between the delinquents and the total population on each of the sub-categories of the additional variables, as reported in the total column, are not as great as expected, the delinquents are characterized by greater family instability, lower educational at-

tainment of the head, and lower family income. Thus, for Anglo males, the basic relationship among the various categories of educational status is generally more distinctive, as measured by rates, with the interrelationships using education of head, family income, or marital history of parents rather than the mobility variables.

DISCUSSION

This paper has illustrated the feasibility and utility of the records matching procedure for delinquency research which focuses on characteristics of delinquent and nondelinquent populations. The "delinquent" cases in the County of Los Angeles Probation Department files can be traced and identified in the returns of the 1960 United States Census. This objective can be accomplished for a time span of 18 months bracketing the April 1, 1960 census date without major attrition of cases by month and without requiring elimination of subcategories of cases based on sex, race, or offense. The matching procedures can be effectively applied to other jurisdictions and adjudicating agencies. The tabulation plan, as illustrated by the selected findings on residential mobility and educational status, facilitates analyses previously impossible due to a lack of comparable data for the delinquent and total populations.

The data analyses can be summarized in a series of tentative generalizations concerning the interrelations of residential mobility, educational status, and juvenile delinquency.

1. Past residential mobility—as indicated by place of birth of youths 14 through 17 years of age in 1960, by place of residence of head of household in 1955, and number of years youth resided in present house—does not differ for delinquent and general population youths, and is not directly or systematically related to the 1960 based delinquency rates of the Los Angeles youth population. This finding holds for the male Anglos, Spanish surnames, and Negroes, and less definitively, for females aged 14 through 17 years.

2. Educational achievement, as described by enrollment status, is inversely related to delinquency for the Anglo, Spanish surname, and Negro males, and for the females. The relation-

---

[20]For a review of research and theory pertaining to these assumptions about the relationships of family characteristics and delinquency, see Donald R. Peterson and Wesley C. Becker, "Family Interaction and Delinquency," in Herbert C. Quay, *op. cit.*, Chap. 3.

TABLE 3–52.

INTERRELATIONSHIP OF MOBILITY VARIABLES AND EDUCATIONAL STATUS
OF TOTAL DELINQUENT ANGLO[e] MALES 14–17 YEARS OF AGE:
PERCENTAGES[a] AND RATES[b] (PER THOUSAND)

		Place of Birth				Year in House			
		Calif.	South	Other Regions	Foreign	1959–1960	1957–1958	1950–1956	1949–Earlier
Year Youth Moved into Present House									
1959–60	T.P.[c]	15.1	32.4	26.8	36.0				
	Del.[d]	18.3	35.1	30.8	27.3				
	Rate	29	26	30	13				
1957–58	T.P.	15.2	21.9	22.3	26.3				
	Del.	18.3	18.5	17.3	32.3				
	Rate	29	20	21	21				
1950–56	T.P.	41.2	36.2	41.0	34.2				
	Del.	36.8	38.6	42.0	36.4				
	Rate	21	26	27	18				
1949–Before	T.P.	28.4	9.4	9.9	3.5				
	Del.	26.6	7.8	9.9	4.0				
	Rate	22	20	26	—[e]				
Residence of Household Head, 1955									
House	T.P.	60.1	34.1	37.7	25.6	3.3	2.2	70.8	78.5
	Del.	53.9	40.6	35.3	17.2	2.8	1.7	67.5	97.5
	Rate	21	29	25	11	25	19	22	18
County	T.P.	34.5	37.0	32.4	33.5	57.2	67.4	22.9	14.8
	Del.	40.7	29.2	37.7	42.4	65.2	74.0	23.2	2.5
	Rate	28	19	31	22	32	27	24	2
State	T.P.	2.7	3.9	2.4	1.7	5.6	5.4	1.1	1.2
	Del.	2.5	4.2	2.1	0.0	5.2	5.2	0.6	0.0
	Rate	22	26	23	—	26	23	12	—
South	T.P.	0.5	14.9	1.1	0.7	5.0	2.7	0.6	0.8
	Del.	0.4	16.6	0.5	5.1	4.9	0.5	1.3	0.0
	Rate	19	27	14	—	28	48	52	—
Other Regions	T.P.	1.8	8.8	22.3	6.8	22.0	17.3	3.6	3.4
	Del.	2.0	9.4	21.6	4.0	18.3	16.1	5.8	0.0
	Rate	27	26	26	10	24	23	38	—
Foreign & Not Rep.	T.P.	0.5	1.2	4.1	31.7	6.9	5.0	1.0	1.2
	Del.	0.4	0.0	2.8	31.3	3.5	2.4	1.7	0.0
	Rate	18	—	18	17	14	12	38	—

ship between age-grade levels and delinquency is less clear and not consistent, particularly for Negro males.

3. A lack of school enrollment is more closely associated with delinquency than is school enrollment which is below the mode for age.

4. Interrelationships of the three mobility measures for the Anglo male youths of Los Angeles County are not related to delinquency and do not affect the influence of educational status.[21]

5. For Anglo males, educational status remains an important concomitant of delinquency when age of the head of household, marital history of parents, education of the head of

[21]This generalization also pertains to the data which has not been reported for Negro and Spanish surname males and all females.

TABLE 3–52.—*Continued*

	Place of Birth				Year in House			
	Calif.	*South*	*Other Regions*	*Foreign*	*1959– 1960*	*1957– 1958*	*1950– 1956*	*1949– Earlier*
Educational Status of Youth								
Above Mode ..........T.P.	7.6	5.4	6.7	5.5	5.4	6.5	7.2	9.1
Del.	6.2	1.3	4.9	0.0	4.3	8.2	3.7	6.4
Rate	19	6	19	—	23	31	12	16
Mode ...............T.P.	81.8	78.1	79.9	75.9	76.0	80.0	82.9	81.7
Del.	71.2	81.8	74.9	61.6	70.5	62.5	77.4	77.9
Rate	21	26	25	14	26	19	22	22
Below Mode ..........T.P.	5.1	7.2	5.6	10.5	8.2	6.7	4.7	3.7
Del.	8.3	4.2	4.5	14.1	8.6	7.4	5.6	6.3
Rate	39	14	21	23	30	27	28	39
Not Enrolled ..........T.P.	5.5	9.4	7.8	8.1	10.3	6.8	5.2	5.5
Del.	14.3	12.7	15.7	24.2	16.6	22.0	13.3	9.3
Rate	62	33	54	51	45	78	61	39

°Anglo includes "white" and "all other" ethnic categories.
ªPercentages added vertically within total and delinquent **populations** each total 100.0.
ᵇSee n. 18 for explanation of rate computations.
ᶜT.P. = total population, based on inflated 25% sample.
ᵈDel. = delinquent population, based on inflated 25% sample.
ᵉLess than 200 cases in the total population and/or no delinquent cases.

household, and family income are controlled.[22]

6. The relationships between educational status and delinquency for the Anglo male population are enhanced by the interaction of educational status with the same family variables noted in the prior generalization.

The finding that past residential mobility is not appreciably related to delinquency confirms the previous findings of Savitz[23] and contrasts with the "public" image of delinquency as a reflection of recent in-migration to the metropolis—particularly among Negroes. Also, our data suggest that school dropout behavior is not a satisfactory solution to youth problems at any social status level.[24] Educational status is inversely related to official delinquency as measured by Probation Department referrals. This

[22]The analyses for the delinquent youths other than Anglo males are not completed, but will be reported in another paper which will focus on educational status.
[23]Leonard D. Savitz, op. cit.
[24]Delbert S. Elliott has suggested that "dropout is a satisfactory solution for those from lower SES areas for the delinquency rate of such youth is lower after leaving school than it was while they were in school." See Delbert S. Elliott, "Delinquency, School Attendance, and Dropout," *Social Problems* 13 (Winter, 1966): 314.

pattern is found, with minor variations, for different categories of age of head of household, marital history of parents, education of head of household, and total family income. No matter what the in-school status of the Anglo males, delinquency rates are higher for those not in school. It might be argued that involvement in delinquency leads to dropping out of school. However, the number of delinquents not enrolled in school accounts for only a small portion of the total school dropouts, e.g., approximately 610 in a total of 8,900 Anglo males.

CONCLUSION

The records matching approach facilitates data analyses relevant to contemporary explanations of delinquency. Linkage of the records systems of local agencies and organizations at the federal level can be accomplished efficiently and will yield much information pertaining to the characteristics of "offender" populations. The success to date in linking records systems justifies the exploration of additional strategies in records merging.

Two possibilities may serve as illustrations.

TABLE 3–53.

EDUCATIONAL STATUS BY SELECTED VARIABLES FOR TOTAL AND DELINQUENT
ANGLO* MALES 14–17 YEARS OF AGE: PERCENTAGES[a] AND RATES[b]
(PER THOUSAND)

		Educational Status				
		Above Mode	Mode	Below Mode	Not Enrol.	Total
Age of Household Head						
Under 35 Years	T.P.[c]	4.8	72.3	10.5	12.4	4.5
	Del.[d]	4.1	66.0	13.4	16.5	4.7
	Rate	23	24	33	35	26
35 to 44 Years	T.P.	6.4	81.8	5.8	6.0	45.3
	Del.	4.1	75.0	6.3	14.7	46.4
	Rate	16	23	27	62	25
45 to 54 Years	T.P.	7.8	81.3	4.8	6.1	39.5
	Del.	6.7	71.6	5.7	15.9	36.2
	Rate	20	20	27	59	22
55 Years or Older	T.P.	8.3	76.9	6.0	8.8	10.7
	Del.	5.4	73.0	9.2	12.4	12.7
	Rate	18	27	43	40	29
Marital History of Parents						
Husband & Spouse Married Once	T.P.	7.6	82.0	5.0	5.5	65.8
	Del.	6.1	74.6	5.9	13.4	53.6
	Rate	16	18	24	49	20
Husband Once— Wife Two or More	T.P.	5.9	80.7	5.8	7.7	6.9
	Del.	5.1	74.6	4.9	15.4	10.7
	Rate	32	35	32	75	38
Husband Two or More— Wife Once	T.P.	5.8	80.7	6.3	7.3	5.4
	Del.	1.8	72.5	9.6	16.0	5.3
	Rate	8	22	37	54	24
Husband & Spouse— Two or More	T.P.	5.6	78.3	7.6	8.5	8.7
	Del.	3.7	78.8	4.6	13.0	10.8
	Rate	20	30	18	46	30
Female Head Married Once	T.P.	7.0	76.2	6.8	10.0	9.4
	Del.	6.3	62.3	13.5	17.9	13.0
	Rate	30	27	67	60	34
Female Head Married Two or More	T.P.	6.9	73.7	8.5	10.9	3.7
	Del.	1.4	71.0	4.7	22.8	6.7
	Rate	9	43	25	94	44

First, records linkage involving a number of jurisdictions would facilitate comparisons of diverse populations and different adjudicating systems. Secondly, the collection of survey data in connection with the census enumerations would add significant flexibility to delinquency research. The survey data could be matched with detailed offense data obtained at the local level, or with information pertaining to court actions as well as with census data. With con-

TABLE 3–53.—*Continued*

		Above Mode	Mode	Below Mode	Not Enrol.	Total
				Educational Status		
Education of Household Head						
7th Grade or Less .............T.P.		5.3	73.2	10.2	11.3	7.4
	Del.	3.4	64.1	9.1	23.4	9.4
	Rate	20	27	28	65	31
8th Grade ....................T.P.		5.6	76.5	7.4	10.5	10.8
	Del.	2.7	71.0	7.6	18.7	14.7
	Rate	16	30	33	58	34
High School 1 to 3 Years ........T.P.		6.1	78.8	6.8	8.3	21.6
	Del.	4.3	71.3	8.3	16.1	26.6
	Rate	21	28	37	60	30
High School 4 Years ...........T.P.		7.0	82.2	4.6	6.2	31.1
	Del.	3.8	75.4	6.4	14.4	27.7
	Rate	12	20	31	52	22
College 1 to 3 Years ...........T.P.		8.4	83.2	4.3	4.1	16.3
	Del.	10.8	77.1	4.8	7.2	13.3
	Rate	26	18	22	35	20
College 4 or More Years.........T.P.		9.6	84.5	3.6	2.3	12.9
	Del.	10.1	78.6	2.3	9.0	8.3
	Rate	17	15	10	63	16
Family Income						
Under $2,000 ..................T.P.		6.3	72.2	8.4	13.0	4.3
	Del.	4.3	65.2	9.5	21.0	5.0
	Rate	20	26	33	47	29
$2,000–3,999 ..................T.P.		6.4	74.8	8.3	10.5	6.2
	Del.	2.0	66.9	9.7	21.4	10.0
	Rate	12	35	46	80	40
$4,000–6,999 ..................T.P.		5.9	78.7	7.2	8.1	22.5
	Del.	4.4	68.4	9.2	18.0	27.1
	Rate	21	25	37	65	30
$7,000–9,999 ..................T.P.		6.4	82.2	5.6	5.8	28.8
	Del.	2.6	79.5	5.7	12.2	26.8
	Rate	9	22	23	48	23
$10,000–14,999 ................T.P.		7.9	82.4	4.3	5.4	25.0
	Del.	8.4	74.1	4.4	13.0	22.0
	Rate	23	20	22	52	22
$15,000 or More ...............T.P.		9.6	82.8	3.4	4.2	13.2
	Del.	11.0	76.6	3.9	8.4	9.1
	Rate	20	16	20	35	17

* Anglo includes "white" and "all other" ethnic categories.

a For Educational Status columns, percentages added *horizontally* within total and delinquent populations each total 100. For Total column, which provides distributions for each selected variable, percentages added *vertically* within total and delinquent populations each total 100.

b See n. 18 for explanation of rate computations.

c T.P. = total population, based on inflated 25% sample.

d Del. = delinquent population, based on inflated 25% sample.

stantly improving computer technologies and the wealth of existing data obtained by local, state, and federal agencies—e.g., school records, public assistance files, vital statistics, and census

returns supplemented by specially collected data —implementation of the records matching methodological design should serve to reduce the data vacuum in social problems research.

31.

KENNETH POLK

URBAN SOCIAL AREAS AND DELINQUENCY

Despite the dominant interest of sociology in class-based theories of delinquency, a number of empirical studies in recent years have failed to establish any meaningful relationship between the economic characteristics of urban areas and the ecological distribution of delinquency. When higher order correlation analyses were employed in such widely scattered cities as Baltimore,[1] Detroit,[2] Indianapolis,[3] and San Diego,[4] results

indicate little relationship between economic variables and delinquency as these are distributed ecologically in metropolitan areas. The present investigation is directed at an examination of the extent to which this negative evidence results jointly from, first, the application of inappropriate methods and, second, lack of theoreti-

tion of standardized regression coefficients and partial correlation coefficients shows that none of these three variables is consistently related to delinquency. In no instance do the higher order terms involving rent or income show any significant relationship to delinquency, while education bears some relationship in Detroit, but not in Baltimore or Indianapolis. (See his Tables 2 and 6, pp. 74 and 80.) The factor matrices are inconsistent, but somewhat more supportive of the conclusion. Nowhere in the eight variable matrices are the highest loadings for education and rent exhibited for the same factor where delinquency has its highest loading (income was not included in the eight variable analysis). In the ten variable case for Detroit, income, but not education or rent, emerged in the factor showing the highest loading for delinquency. In Indianapolis, on the other hand, all three (education, rent, and income) were found in the same factor with delinquency. The nineteen variable factor matrix for Indianapolis is not "clean," since a single factor with high loadings of education, rent, income, and delinquency is not found. There is a hint of convergence, however, since moderate to high loadings for all four variables (education, rent, income, and delinquency) are found in one or another of two factors (G1 and G4, Table 7, p. 81). Nonetheless, the overall inconsistency in the pattern between these central measures of economic status and delinquency suggests something other than economic position will have to be advanced to account for the ecological distribution of youthful misconduct.

SOURCE: Kenneth Polk, "Urban Social Areas and Delinquency," *Social Problems* 14, no. 3 (Winter, 1967): 320–25. Reprinted by Permission of the author and The Society for the Study of Social Problems.

[1] Bernard Lander, *Towards an Understanding of Juvenile Delinquency* (New York: Columbia University Press, 1954).

[2] David J. Bordua, "Juvenile Delinquency and 'Anomie': An Attempt at Replication," *Social Problems* 6 (Winter, 1958–59): 230–38. In the matrix of partial regression coefficients for Detroit, neither rent nor income showed any correlation with delinquency, although some correlation was found in the case of education.

[3] Roland J. Chilton, "Continuity in Delinquency Area Research: A Comparison of Studies for Baltimore, Detroit, and Indianapolis," *American Sociological Review* 29 (February, 1964): 71–83. Although the analyses of partial correlation and standard regression coefficients show little linking between economic variables and delinquency, Chilton concludes: "Our findings suggest that delinquency still appears to be related to transiency, poor housing, and economic indices; this supports the assumption of almost all sociological theories of delinquency, that delinquency in urban areas is predominantly a lower class phenomenon," ibid., pp. 82–83 (see Tables 2 and 6). This interpretation is derived principally from his factor analyses. Unfortunately it is not clear that the more "pure" measures of economic status, such as education, rent, and income, show any consistent relationship to delinquency. Inspec-

[4] Kenneth Polk, "Juvenile Delinquency and Social Areas," *Social Problems* 5 (Winter, 1957–58): 214–17.

cal precision in specifying how area economic characteristics relate to patterns of delinquency.

The failure to find a consistent and meaningful relationship between the economic status characteristics of areas and delinquency presents a curious and major disjunction of "facts" and "theory" in delinquency research. The most thoughtful and rigorous contemporary sociological theories of delinquency are virtually unanimous in their positing of social class as a (if not *the*) core factor producing delinquency.[5] Furthermore, in many such theories, the ecological dimension of class position is crucial. This is clear, for example, in the case of Miller, who argues that lower class culture creates an environment which generates delinquency.[6] The terms "culture" and "milieu" are concepts relating to aggregates of persons. For Cloward and Ohlin, likewise, access to opportunity structures is an aggregate characteristic with an ecological referent.[7] In such theories, the ecological setting of the class behavior exerts pressures which are seen as limiting and supportive of responses of youth. Miller, and Cloward and Ohlin, view the environment of the lower class community as one of the potent forces not only in shaping delinquency but in setting the particular kinds of delinquency that will be observed.

The fact that empirical studies of the ecology of delinquency are, at best, inconsistent in providing a factual base for these theories presents somewhat of a puzzle. If the theories reflect reality, differentials in the ecological distribution of delinquency should be linked to the patterning of social class residence of the urban complex. Data from the city of Portland, Oregon, shall be drawn to throw further light upon this problem. Male juveniles who were residents of this city and who were referred to juvenile court authorities for a delinquency offense during 1960 comprise the population of this study. The case records of these individuals were examined and data obtained regarding a number of variables, including an identification of the census tract area within which the youth resided. U.S. census tract data for the city in 1960 were used to obtain information on the social characteristics of the tracts, and to compute an age-specific delinquency rate for each tract.

THE INAPPROPRIATE METHOD PROBLEM

One problem may be that the approach used in these ecological studies of delinquency is inappropriate. The explanatory power of an ecological frame of reference is obscured by the use of a method of statistical analysis which does not permit examination of characteristics within various types of urban social areas. The "mosaic" nature of the organization of urban life is hopelessly blurred by product-moment correlations of census tract variables, and this blurring becomes especially confounded when higher order correlation terms such as partial correlation or standardized coefficients are employed.

More valid empirical and theoretical information will be obtained by looking at the nature of delinquency within specific kinds of urban social areas. This point probably can be made most directly by the use of an example. One way of executing such an analysis is to utilize the typology which results from the social area analysis scheme suggested by Shevky and Bell. Social area analysis allows examination of urban area types in terms of configurations of the economic, ethnic, and familism status scores. Each individual census tract, in other words, occupies a position in the three-dimensional social space defined by these variables. Using the method suggested by Shevky and Bell, a total of 32 different social area types are logically possible (when economic status and familism status each are cut at four levels and ethnic status is dichotomized).[8] In Portland, however, only 14

[5]Cf. Albert K. Cohen, *Delinquent Boys: The Culture of the Gang* (New York: The Free Press, 1955); Richard A. Cloward and Lloyd E. Ohlin, *Delinquency and Opportunity: A Theory of Delinquent Gangs* (New York: The Free Press, 1960); Walter B. Miller, "Lower Class Culture as a Generating Milieu of Gang Delinquency," *The Journal of Social Issues* 14, no. 3 (1958): 5–19.

[6]Miller, op. cit.

[7]Cloward and Ohlin, op. cit.

[8]Eshref Shevky and Wendell Bell, *Social Areas Analysis* (Stanford, California: Stanford University Press, 1955). The Shevky and Bell procedures were followed exactly in the case of the Index of Economic Status (derived from tract measures of occupation and education), and the Index of Familism (derived from tract measures of fertility,
(Footnote Continued)

types actually are found. There are only two types of high ethnic status areas (2BN and 3BN), and no tract is found at the lowest level of economic status. (See Figure 3–3.) In this diagram, for example, social area 4A is a high economic status, high family status, and low ethnic status area, while 2D is a low economic, low familism, and low ethnic status area.

When the delinquency characteristics of these social areas are examined, each of the three variables in the typology is found to contribute a unique effect to the distribution of delin-

women in the labor force, and single family dwelling units). In the case of the Index of Ethnic Status, since "other" subordinate ethnic groups in no case comprise a significant proportion of tract residents, the percentage of Negro dwellers is used as the measure of ethnic status. "High" ethnic status has been arbitrarily defined to mean tracts with 20 per cent or more Negro population. This was done to assure that tracts defined as "ethnic" had, in fact, ethnic characteristics. Since there are relatively few Negroes in Portland, using the midpoint of the distribution as suggested by Shevky and Bell would result, in this instance, in tracts with 5 per cent Negro population being called high ethnic status tracts.

quency. There is a general tendency for the highest levels of delinquency to be found at the lowest levels of economic status and familism and at the high levels of ethnic status, although in a moment it will be seen that this is a deceptive way of summarizing those relationships. The combined effort of economic and family status in low ethnic status tracts can be seen in the general increase in delinquency rates that accompanies the diagonal, downward progression to the low economic status, low familism status corner of the figure: 32.7 to 41.2; 13.1 to 28.5; 28.5 to 122.0; 20.6 to 72.3; and 26.8 to 67.8. Delinquency, in other words, tends to be lowest where there is a conjoining of high economic status and high familism (as in area 4A), and highest where low economic status and low familism occur together (as in area 2C).

One major exception to this generalization is the absence of delinquency in area 2D, the area with the lowest conjoined economic and family status score. In actuality, this is a peculiar kind of an exception. There is no juvenile delinquency here because there are virtually no

High A	1A	2A	44.8	3A	32.7	4A	13.1
B	1B	2BN 2B	(56.7)* 41.2	3BN 3B	(71.2)* 28.5	4B	20.6
C	1C	2C	122.0	3C	72.3	4C	26.8
D Low	1D	2D	0.0	3D	67.8	4D	74.0

Index of Familism

1   2   3   4

Low   High

Index of Economic Status

*Parentheses indicate delinquency rates in High Ethnic Status social areas (where the percentage of Negroes is 20 or greater).

FIGURE 3–3.

DELINQUENCY RATES BY SOCIAL AREAS, PORTLAND, 1960

young people. This is the "area of homeless men," the "skid-road" area of Portland, where the sex ratios approach 1,000 and fewer than five per cent of the residents are persons under 21 years of age. Despite the fact that this is unquestionably a lower class area, it certainly is not the lower or working class culture that receives attention in the sociological theories of delinquency.

But what of the general relationship between economic status and delinquency? The differential findings that result from a typological *vs.* a correlational assessment of the impact of economic conditions on delinquency when other variables are considered can be seen by examining the interplay of economic status, family status, and delinquency in the social space diagram. At the lowest levels of family status, i.e., in areas 2D, 3D, and 4D, delinquency *increases* as social class increases (0.0 to 67.8 to 74.0), in contrast to the *decrease* that accompanies increases in social class for other levels of familism, e.g., as in areas 2A, 3A, and 4A (44.8, 32.7, 13.1). This reversal in the direction of the relationship between class and delinquency will confound any single partial correlation coefficient, so that the single regression term cannot possibly express the relationship that exists between economic status and delinquency when familism is held "constant."

The traditional partial correlation coefficients or the standardized regression terms from multiple correlation analyses are estimates, and only estimates, of procedures which hold "constant" variables. These estimates which control for the linear effects of additional variables are extremely vulnerable to error when any deviation from a multivariate normal distribution occurs. In ecological studies, the curvilinear relationships between the independent variables and delinquency, even ignoring those *between* the independent variables, are of such variety that they defy description, as Chilton has noted.[9] As estimates, these higher order coefficients break down completely when the multidimensional space shows the differentials in the direction of relationship found in this Portland instance.

One reason, then, why ecological studies have

not been able to find any consistent relationship between the economic status of areas and delinquency is that the method employed is not sensitive to the types of economic status differentials that exist. Class is an important variable in the social space diagram, but the complexity of its impact cannot be summarized in one simple coefficient. There is no single statement that tells us the effect of economic status on the distribution of delinquency. It is only when we examine the specific types of areas that differential rates of delinquency between neighborhood economic status levels, or even differentials *at the same economic level,* can be understood and interpreted.

THE THEORETICAL PRECISION PROBLEM

A second difficulty in trying to relate ecological studies to sociological theories of delinquency has to do with the lack of clarity in specifying or translating the ecological components of these theories. The ecology of the modern city is more complex than most delinquency theories indicate. It is not sufficient to say that delinquency is higher in "lower class areas," because low economic status areas will differ considerably when family status and ethnic status vary. A lower class, white, "family" neighborhood is quite different from "Hobohemia" or a lower class Negro community, even though each occupies a similar position on an economic continuum. These differences are reflected in the diversity of delinquency rates in Portland at the lowest levels of economic status (2A, 44.8; 2B, 41.2; 2BN, 56.7; 2C, 122.0; and 2D, 0.0).[10]

One positive result of the typological approach to the study of the ecology of delinquency, then,

---

[9]Chilton, op. cit., p. 78.

[10]It is not necessarily implied that this particular typological framework solves the problem of theoretical precision. The intent here is to utilize social area analysis to demonstrate that typological analysis will yield different results than correlational analysis. If the argument were to be advanced that social area analysis is the appropriate way to execute such a study, a case would have to be made linking, theoretically, delinquency with both the social area indexes and the variables which make up these indexes (census tract measures of occupation, education, fertility, women in the labor force, single family dwelling units, and ethnicity). While this case might be made, space and data limitations preclude such in the present discussion.

is that of demonstrating the need for logical precision of theoretical constructs. If class-linked theories are to be expressed in such a way that their implications are to be seen in the ecological structure of the city, more than simple economic characteristics will have to be specified. There is no such thing as *a* lower class area, or *a* lower class culture. There are a number of such cultures, and it is the task of the theorist to specify which is being discussed.

An example of such specification can be found in the description of lower class culture provided by Miller. The work of Miller explicitly recognizes the family characteristics of the lower class neighborhood:

The one-sex peer group is a highly prevalent and significant structural form in the lower class community. There is a strong probability that the prevalence and stability of this type of a unit is directly related to the prevalence of a stabilized type of lower class child-rearing unit—the "female-based" household. This is a nuclear kin unit in which a male parent is either absent from the household, present only sporadically, or, when present, only minimally or inconsistently involved in the support and rearing of children. This unit usually consists of one or more females of child-bearing age and their offspring. The females are frequently related to one another by blood or marriage ties, and the unit often includes two or more generations of women, e.g., the mother and/or aunt of the principal child-bearing female.[11]

In Portland, the type of area described by Miller is virtually nonexistent except in lower class, Negro areas. Only in area 2BN are found the conditions which approximate Miller's "lower class culture." Delinquency rates are relatively high (56.7) in this area. With additional data,

---

[11]Miller, op. cit., pp. 13–14.

analysis of the family life backgrounds of individual delinquents in area 2BN reveals that 43 per cent of the delinquent youth come from homes where the father is absent, compared with 8 per cent in area 2A, 11 per cent in area 2B, 7 per cent in area 2C, and between 10 and 20 per cent in most other areas. Of all the lower class social areas of Portland, in other words, only in area 2BN do the economic, family, and delinquency characteristics approximate those described by Miller. Location of this area in the social space of Portland, therefore, requires that its *family and ethnic* characteristics be explicated in addition to the social class description. Any attempt to "test" Miller's hypothesis regarding class and delinquency in terms of a single, overall, summary correlation coefficient is doomed to failure. This hypothesis does not say that *overall* there is some type of inverse relationship between class and delinquency, but that a characteristic pattern of delinquency is to be expected within a very specific kind of urban area.

Given the use of inappropriate statistical techniques and the lack of conceptual precision of current sociological theories of juvenile delinquency, it is not surprising that ecological studies have given little support to contemporary delinquency theory. The ecological structure of the city does appear to function as one of the important determinants of the patterns of youthful misconduct. Hopefully, theories of delinquency will be developed which are complex enough to account for the differentials observable in the various social areas of the city. At the same time, to accompany such theories there would appear to be a need for a typological, rather than a correlational, analysis of the ecological distribution of delinquency.

32.

Charles V. Willie

THE RELATIVE CONTRIBUTION OF FAMILY STATUS AND ECONOMIC STATUS TO JUVENILE DELINQUENCY

A review of the literature indicates two basic conditions associated with juvenile delinquency that have been confirmed in several studies. They are (1) poverty and poor living conditions and (2) broken homes and inadequate family life.[1] It is sometimes assumed that poverty and family instability are so closely intertwined that one is but a reflection of the other. Probably the best summary on the association between family instability and economic insecurity is provided by Abram Kardiner and Lionel Ovesey. They state that "the broken home in the lower-class family is very commonly attributed to the precarious economic conditions under which these families live. This statement is not untrue; it is merely incomplete."[2]

The general hypothesis of this study is that economic status and family status make both joint and independent contributions to deviant behavior. Family instability is aggravated by economic insecurity but is not limited to poor

households. Also, inadequate family finances do not always result in broken marriages. It is of particular importance to study this hypothesis (1) since doubt has been cast upon the assumption that family instability and economic insecurity are but different reflections of the same phenomenon, and (2) because of the recent debate surrounding the Moynihan Report on *The Negro Family*,[3,4] which discusses the relationship between family instability, economic insecurity, and deviant behavior.

Daniel Patrick Moynihan concluded that federal government programs should be designed to enhance the stability and resources of the Negro family. What is unclear in this conclusion is the relationship between stability and resources. Belton Fleisher in a recent study of the economics of delinquency stated that "when family income increases . . . the number of women over 14 who are separated or divorced will decline. . . ."[5] It was suggested by Fleisher that family stability is a function of economic security. But Moynihan implied that upward mobility and economic security would continue to elude Negroes "unless the viability of the Negro family is restored."[6] Moynihan, of course, does not rule out increasing the economic resources of the Negro family as a way of contributing to its viability; but it is clear that his focus is upon the social integration of family members.

So a study is needed not only of the inde-

SOURCE: Charles V. Willie, "The Relative Contribution of Family Status and Economic Status to Juvenile Delinquency," *Social Problems* 14, no. 3 (Winter, 1967): 326–35. Reprinted by Permission of the author and The Society for the Study of Social Problems.

The author is Professor of Sociology at Syracuse University. Data for this study were gathered while the author was Research Director of Washington Action for Youth, a delinquency prevention project in the District of Columbia, sponsored by the President's Committee on Juvenile Delinquency and Youth Crime. Data on delinquency was secured from Dr. Hylan Lewis of Howard University. His assistance is acknowledged with appreciation, and so is the help of the research staff of Washington Action for Youth. This is a revised version of a paper presented at the Eastern Sociological Society Annual Meeting, New York, April 10, 1965.

[1] Leslie T. Wilkins, "Juvenile Delinquency: A Critical Review of Research and Theory," *Educational Research* 5 (February, 1963): 104–19.

[2] Abram Kardiner and Lionel Ovesey, *The Mark of Oppression* (Cleveland: The World Publishing Company, 1962), p. 344.

[3] United States Department of Labor, *The Negro Family—The Case for National Action* (Washington, D.C.: Government Printing Office, 1965).

[4] Lee Rainwater and William L. Yancy, "Black Families and the White House," *Transaction* 3 (July-August, 1966): 6–11, 48–53.

[5] Belton M. Fleisher, *The Economics of Delinquency* (Chicago: Quadrangle Books, Inc., 1966), p. 117.

[6] U. S. Department of Labor, op. cit., p. 30.

pendent contributions of family status and economic status to deviant behavior such as juvenile delinquency but also of their interaction effect. Which comes first—family stability or economic security? Does one give rise to the other? With reference to juvenile delinquency, this question might be asked: Is the rate higher among children of poor stable families than among children of affluent unstable families?

Because the findings to date about the correlation between delinquency rates and race are ambiguous, as pointed out by Roland Chilton in his study of Baltimore, Detroit, and Indianapolis,[7] a study of the relative contribution of economic and family status to juvenile delinquency should attempt to study whites and nonwhites separately to determine if the association (if there is any between race and delinquency) is similar or different in these two populations. Unequivocally, Fleisher has stated that "in areas of high tendency toward crime, a 10 per cent rise in income might well result in a 20 per cent decline in delinquency."[8] It should be determined, if possible, whether this phenomenon would be true both of white and nonwhite populations.

Chilton has wisely pointed out that "questions concerning the relationship of delinquency to the degree of organization of an area or to the degree of agreement on norms cannot be adequately answered with delinquency area data and procedures."[9] Social area data and ecological correlations are basic to the analysis in this study and therefore limit the kinds of inferences that may be drawn. No attempt is made to correlate delinquent behavior with certain sociological conditions such as anomie. This investigation has two goals which are quite modest: (1) to determine whether or not earlier findings regarding the association between economic status and juvenile delinquency and family status and juvenile delinquency hold when populations of whites and nonwhites are analyzed separately, and (2) to determine the joint effect, if any, of these two variables.

DATA AND METHOD

The study area was Washington, D.C. The basic unit of analysis was the census tract. Analysis of the association, if any, between juvenile delinquency and economic status and juvenile delinquency and family status was determined by computing Pearsonian correlation coefficients for 115 of the 125 census tracts in the city (the 10 tracts eliminated were sparsely settled or consisted of institutional populations).

There are, of course, dangers in using ecological correlations, which W. S. Robinson has discussed.[10] The dependent variable, juvenile delinquency, accounted for only three per cent of the youth population 10 to 17 years of age in the total city and varied from census tracts in which less than one per cent of the youth had been referred to court during the course of a year to a high-rate tract in which 11 per cent of the youth had been referred to court. The small proportion of the population in each census tract that was delinquent means that caution should be exercised in interpreting the findings. However, some of the problems of ecological correlations were guarded against by relating the dependent variable to independent variables such as socio-economic status (which was a composite value that characterized most of the people in a census tract) and the proportion of children in broken families (which varied from a small minority to a large majority of the families in many census tracts). Because the number of census tracts in the predominantly white area and in the predominantly nonwhite area of Washington was relatively small (41 predominantly white and 51 predominantly nonwhite tracts), this would further complicate a correlational analysis. And so patterns of variations within racial populations by socio-economic and family status were determined by using the methods of social area analysis.[11]

---

[7] Roland J. Chilton, "Continuity in Delinquency Area Research: A Comparison of Studies for Baltimore, Detroit and Indianapolis," *American Sociological Review* 29 (February, 1964): 75–78.

[8] Belton M. Fleisher, op. cit.

[9] Roland J. Chilton, op. cit., p. 83.

[10] W. S. Robinson, "Ecological Correlations and the Behavior of Individuals," *American Sociological Review* 15 (June, 1950): 351–57.

[11] Eshref Shevky and Marilyn Williams, *The Social Areas in Los Angeles* (Berkeley: University of California Press, 1949). Wendell Bell, "Economic Family and Ethnic Status: An Empirical Test," *American Sociological Review* 20 (February, 1955): 45–51. Eshref Shevky and Wendell Bell, *Social Areas Analysis* (Stanford, Calif.: Stanford University Press, 1955).

Data for the study are records of 6,269 youth referred to the District of Columbia Juvenile Court for reasons other than traffic offenses and dependency during a 33-month period from 1959 to 1962. Another study conducted by this author in Washington and using the data of a single fiscal year, 1963, revealed a high correlation between the rates for youth who came in contact with police only and youth who were referred to court; the Pearsonian correlation coefficient for 113 census tracts included in that study was .90. This means that a strong socio-economic bias, which could result in a much higher proportion of police contacts being referred to court in the poorer than in the more affluent neighborhoods, does not appear to contaminate these data. For the city as a whole, 37 per cent of the youth contacted by police were referred to court; the percentage in a more affluent socio-economic area was 32 and in a low-income area, 40. This was not a large difference in per cent of court referrals between populations of high and low socio-economic status. While the bias was not completely eliminated, it was controlled. This may be because Washington has a separate youth aid division in the police department staffed by officers who give full-time attention to youth and who must be consulted on all police contacts that are referred to court.

The 1960 census population 10 through 17 years of age was used as the base for computing rates. The base was limited to these particular age levels because less than five per cent of court-referred youth were under 10 years. Because these youth are not as vulnerable as those over 10 years, their inclusion in the population base would have distorted the actual incidence of delinquency by depressing the rate. Data for three years (33 months) were used to increase the reliability of rates since only a small proportion (about three per cent) were referred to court each year. The population base was multiplied by 2.75 to make it comparable to the 33-month study period so that annual rates could be computed for each census tract. The total city population in 1960 was approximately 764,000, about 45 per cent white and 55 per cent nonwhite.

The economic status and family status of the population, the former of which is more appropriately called socio-economic status in this study, was measured by a composite index score for each census tract and the per cent of broken homes. Five highly correlated variables were used in the index:[12] (1) percentage of the employed in the combined categories of operatives, service workers, and laborers; (2) median number of years of school completed by the population over 25 years of age; (3) estimated market value of owned homes; (4) the gross monthly rental for tenant-occupied dwellings; and (5) percentage of sound dwelling units. (The first factor was inverted so that it varied directly with the other four.) Distributions of each of the five variables were converted into standard scores with assigned means of 50 and assigned standard deviations of 10. The five standard scores for each census tract were simply averaged into a socio-economic status composite score. The per cent of children under 18 years of age not living with both parents was computed as an indicator of the family status of a census tract. Studies of indices of social status, such as one conducted by John Haer, indicate that a composite index of several variables is a better predictor of differentiation within a population than a single variable.[13] In delineating family status, a gross indicator like the number of children in one-parent families was believed to be sufficient. While one parent may be absent from the household due to death, divorce, or desertion, the functional consequence for the child—particularly if the absent parent is the father which is usually the case—is more or less the same. No one is present who has a primary responsibility, as Malinowski has described it, of orienting the child to the community at large.[14]

Census tracts were classified as white and

[12]Charles V. Willie, and Morton O. Wagenfeld, *Socio-Economic and Ethnic Areas, Syracuse and Onondaga County, New York, 1960* (Syracuse, N.Y.: Syracuse University, Youth Development Center, 1962).

[13]John L. Haer, "Predictive Utility of Five Indices of Social Stratification," *American Sociological Review* 22 (October, 1957): 541–46.

[14]Bronislaw Malinowski, "Parenthood: The Basis of Social Structure," in *Source Book in Marriage and the Family*, ed. Marvin B. Sussman (Cambridge, Mass.: Houghton Mifflin Company, 1955), p. 25.

nonwhite for the social area analysis; tracts in which two out of every three persons were white were classified as part of the white area. A similar procedure was followed in delineating the nonwhite area. In spite of the criterion used, 95 per cent of the total population in the white area was of Caucasian racial stock and 90 per cent of the total population in the nonwhite area was of that color category. Most of the census tracts in Washington are racially homogeneous; only about one-fifth of the population lives in racially mixed residential areas.

White census tracts were grouped into poor and affluent areas and into areas of few and many broken homes. Those census tracts above the city-wide socio-economic composite standard score of 50 (that is, those tracts in which the median family income was above $4,500) were included in the affluent area. The median family income for some census tracts in the affluent area were well above $10,000. Those census tracts below the city-wide average composite score (that is, those tracts with median family incomes below $4,500) were classified as part of the poor area. Several of the tracts in this area had medians that were below the $3,000 level of extreme poverty. The area of few broken homes consisted of those tracts in the affluent and poor areas in which the per cent of children not living with both parents was above the city-wide percentage. There were four area types into which census tracts with predominantly white populations were grouped: Area A, the affluent area characterized by few broken homes; Area B, the affluent area characterized by many broken homes; Area C, the poor area characterized by few broken homes; and Area D, the poor area characterized by many broken homes. The number of delinquents and the population 10 through 17 for all census tracts in an area were totaled. With these summations, delinquency rates per 1,000 youth were computed for each. Area A had 32 census tracts, Area B, 4 census tracts, Area C, 4 census tracts, and Area D, 1 census tract classified as white.

The same procedure was followed in delineating areas for the nonwhite population and in computing area delinquency rates. Area A had 6 census tracts, Area B, 2 tracts, Area C, 5 tracts, and Area D, 38 census tracts.

Classifying white and nonwhite populations into these four types of social areas made possible a comparative analysis controlled for variations in socio-economic and family status that tend to differentiate these two populations. The conditions of the populations in each of the areas were, of course, not identical because of the crude technique of dichotomizing the economic and family status variables above and below the city-wide average.

About 18 per cent of the total population of juvenile delinquents was eliminated from that part of the study which compared white and nonwhite areas. These were the youthful offenders who lived in racially mixed areas. The remaining population of 5,148 delinquents was divided this way: 737 or 14 per cent in the white areas and 4,411 or 86 per cent in the nonwhite areas. The large imbalance of delinquency within the different racial areas is further indication that any meaningful comparison of whites and nonwhites must control for socio-economic and family status. Although the number of census tracts was few in one or two of the four areas among white and nonwhite populations, no area had a base population of less than 300. Thus, the rates that were computed for comparative analysis were reasonably reliable.

FINDINGS

As reported in a previous study, the correlation coefficient for juvenile delinquency rates and socio-economic status scores was significantly different from zero and so was the correlation coefficient for delinquency rates and the per cent of children with one or both parents absent from home.[15] In this city-wide analysis, the correlation coefficient for juvenile delinquency and socio-economic status was −.65 and the correlation coefficient for juvenile delinquency and family instability was .64. This means that juvenile delinquency rates tended to increase as the socio-economic status level of census tracts decreased, and that juvenile delinquency rates tended to increase as the per cent of broken homes in the census tracts increased.

[15]Charles V. Willie, Anita Gershenovitz, Myrna Levine, Sulochana Glazer, and Roy J. Jones, "Race and Delinquency," *Phylon* 26 (Fall, 1965): 240–46.

These findings are in accord with those of other investigators mentioned at the beginning of the paper.

Although socio-economic and family status variables both correlated highly with juvenile delinquency rates (having coefficients of a similar magnitude), this did not mean that the two variables were identical. To determine the degree of association between these variables, socio-economic status scores were correlated with the per cent of children in broken homes; the correlation coefficient was −.65. This coefficient indicated that slightly more than 40 per cent of the variance in the ecological distribution of the family instability factor could be attributed to variation in levels of socio-economic status. While this was a high degree of association, the correlation coefficient also indicated that nearly 60 per cent of the variance must be attributed to factors other than socio-economic status. Clearly, the two variables did not duplicate each other. Although there was some overlap, they were not simply different ways of measuring the same phenomenon.

A multiple correlation coefficient was computed to determine the independent and joint contribution of economic and family status to the pattern of variation in juvenile delinquency on a city-wide basis. These two variables correlated with the dependent variable—juvenile-delinquency—at .71. The multiple correlation coefficient accounted for a larger proportion of the variance in the ecological distribution of juvenile delinquency than either family status or economic status separately correlated with the dependent variable.

Beta weights were obtained to continue the analysis of the independent and joint effects of these two factors upon the dependent variable. They indicate that about 16 per cent of the variance in the ecological distribution of juvenile delinquency rates could be attributed to variation in levels of socio-economic status; approximately 14 per cent could be attributed to variation in the distribution of the per cent of youth who lived in broken families; and about 20 per cent of the variance was due to the joint effect of these two factors. The finding that socio-economic and family status make a joint contribution to the pattern of variation

of juvenile delinquency within an urban community is important. It may help explain why the debate over whether economic status should be upgraded or family stability secured initially, as a way of dealing with deviant behavior, has not been resolved satisfactorily for advocates of either form of action.

This finding suggests that some juvenile delinquency is associated with unstable family life which is unstable because of impoverished economic circumstances; and some juvenile delinquency is associated with families which are economically impoverished and that these families are impoverished because they are unstable. Nevertheless, family status and economic status are independently associated with juvenile delinquency too. This fact should be remembered when assessing the joint effects of these variables. Obviously, the relationship between delinquency, family life, and economic circumstances is complex. A major error in many discussions about the relative importance of different independent variables in preventing deviant behavior has been the tendency to oversimplify.

The contribution of socio-economic and family status to variations in the pattern of juvenile delinquency in separate white and nonwhite populations is presented now. Fourfold tables were constructed for this analysis.

The data in Tables 3–54 and 3–55 indicated both similar and different ecological patterns of distribution for juvenile delinquency in white and nonwhite populations. The white and nonwhite areas are similar in that circumstances contributing to the lowest and highest delinquency rates were the same for both races. The area of affluent socio-economic status in which there were few broken homes (as seen in cell A of Tables 3–54 and 3–55) tended to have the lowest delinquency rate in the city, while the highest rate was found in that area characterized by low socio-economic status and many broken homes (as seen in cell D of Tables 3–54 and 3–55) for white and nonwhite populations. These areas provided the least favorable and most favorable circumstances for the development of delinquent behavior. Apparently, these circumstances affect whites and nonwhites in similar ways.

TABLE 3–54.

JUVENILE DELINQUENCY RATE PER 1,000 YOUTH 10 THROUGH 17 YEARS OF AGE IN NONWHITE AREA, BY FAMILY STATUS AND SOCIO-ECONOMIC STATUS, WASHINGTON, D.C. JULY, 1959–MARCH, 1962

Juvenile Delinquency Rate among Nonwhites		
	Area of Few Broken Homes	*Area of Many Broken Homes*
Affluent Area	a 19.7	b 20.9
Poor Area	c 26.5	d 42.4

TABLE 3–55.

JUVENILE DELINQUENCY RATE PER 1,000 YOUTH 10 THROUGH 17 YEARS OF AGE IN WHITE AREA, BY FAMILY STATUS AND SOCIO-ECONOMIC STATUS, WASHINGTON, D.C. JULY, 1959–MARCH, 1962

Juvenile Delinquency Rate among Whites		
	Area of Few Broken Homes	*Area of Many Broken Homes*
Affluent Area	a 10.6	b 30.4
Poor Area	c 19.6	d 44.3

White and nonwhite populations differed in the way in which delinquency rates were distributed between affluent areas characterized by many broken households and poor areas consisting of many stable or intact families. Data for this analysis are found in cells B and C of Tables 3–54 and 3–55. Among the affluent, the absence of one or both parents from the home tended to be associated with a higher delinquency rate for whites than nonwhites. And among the poor, the presence of both parents in the household tended to be associated with a lower delinquency rate among whites than nonwhites. It would appear that family status had a greater affect upon the white than nonwhite population in contributing to a lower delinquency rate.

Differences between rates for comparable white and nonwhite areas are not great, never exceeding 11 points. This means that one should exercise caution in drawing inferences from these data. A persistent pattern, however, does merit attention. Further analysis of the data is pursued to confirm or cast doubt on tentative conclusions based on analysis of patterns discussed above. (See Table 3–56.)

The goal of this analysis was to examine further the differential contribution of family and economic status to delinquency among white and nonwhite populations alluded to, especially the possibility that family status may be more specifically and immediately associated with delinquency among whites than nonwhites. Since the most favorable circumstance for the development of juvenile delinquency was similar for both racial categories—that is, a low-income area characterized by many broken families—cell D in Tables 3–54 and 3–55 was identified as the high-rate area, having a similar juvenile delinquency rate for both races, i.e., 44 and 42 for whites and nonwhites respectively.

The analysis was designed to determine which area type exhibited the greatest difference in delinquency rate between it and the high-rate area. Rates for Areas A, B, and C, therefore, were subtracted from the rate in Area D for both white and nonwhite populations. For the white population, the greatest difference was between Areas D and A; this was also the case for the nonwhite population. The delinquency rate in this low-rate area was 76 per cent lower in the white population and 54 per cent lower in the non-white population than the delinquency rate in the high-rate area. In this respect, the two racial populations were similar as mentioned above. They differed, however, in the kinds of areas that resulted in the second and third greatest difference. For the white population, Areas D and C exhibited a 56 per cent difference in rates while Areas D and B revealed a 51 per cent difference in rates among nonwhites. The second greatest difference for whites occurred in an area characterized by high family stability and low economic status, while among nonwhites the second greatest difference occurred in an area characterized by high economic status and low family stability.

TABLE 3–56.

A COMPARISON OF THE JUVENILE DELINQUENCY RATE IN THE HIGH-RATE
AREA WITH THE RATES IN THREE OTHER SOCIAL AREAS, FOR WHITE AND
NONWHITE POPULATIONS, WASHINGTON, D.C. 1959–62

| | Per Cent of Change in Delinquency Rate for Three Social Areas Compared with the High-Rate Area[*] | | | |
| | White Areas | | Nonwhite Areas | |
	Per Cent of Change from High-Rate Area	Rank	Per Cent of Change from High-Rate Area	Rank
High family stability and high economic status[a]	76	1	54	1
High family stability and low economic status[b]	56	2	36	3
High economic status and low family stability[c]	31	3	51	2

[*]The high-rate area is Cell D in Tables 3-54 and 3-55.
[a]Cell A in Tables 3-54 and 3-55.
[b]Cell C in Tables 3-54 and 3-55.
[c]Cell B in Tables 3-54 and 3-55.

Although the economic circumstances were relatively favorable, the white population had a delinquency rate that was only 31 per cent lower than the high-rate area, when there was a considerable amount of family instability in the area. But nonwhite households that lived under similar affluent economic circumstances tended to exhibit a 51 per cent difference in delinquency rate below that of the high-rate area even though the area consisted of many unstable households. The area among nonwhites which registered the smallest difference in delinquency rate between it and the high-rate area was the one characterized by high family stability and low economic status.

Thus, it would appear that the extremes—those circumstances that were the most and least favorable for the development of delinquent behavior—had similar consequences for white and nonwhite populations. But in between these most and least favorable circumstances, whites were more affected by family composition while nonwhites were more affected by economic circumstances. Because of the kinds of data and methods used in this analysis, these differential effects cannot be stated with certainty. But the findings do suggest that different approaches may be needed for white and nonwhite populations in the United States to solve some problems of deviancy, like juvenile delinquency.

There are, of course, no innate differences between these two races that would cause one to be more affected by economic or family circumstances than the other. One possible explanation of the differential affects of family and economic status in white and nonwhite populations is their different positions in the opportunity system as described by Cloward and Ohlin.[16] In Washington, D. C., 80 per cent of the white population lives in economically affluent areas while 67 per cent of the nonwhite population lives in neighborhoods of poverty or marginal economic condition. Since poverty was no longer an overwhelming problem for most white people, family instability was a major remaining and outstanding problem contributing to the incidence of juvenile delinquency.

Although the per cent of nonwhite children growing up in one-parent families was greater than the per cent of white children who had this kind of experience, the impoverished economic circumstances of nonwhites was overwhelming. In the light of the data and analysis

---

[16]Richard A. Cloward and Lloyd E. Ohlin, *Delinquency and Opportunity* (New York: The Free Press, 1960).

of this study, it is hypothesized that nonwhites may be able to deal with the family instability factor which is associated with juvenile delinquency only after notable improvements have been experienced in their economic circumstances. The hypothesis is advanced on the basis of the findings in this study, particularly the findings pertaining to the white population which is largely beyond the pale of poverty.

Out of this analysis, then, has come the sociological principle that the solutions of some social problems occur in a serial pattern, that the solution of one problem makes possible the solution of another. There is an ordering of social events into a sequential pattern. Obviously, white and nonwhite populations are in different stages of the series. Most whites have passed beyond the stage of economic insecurity.

This means that efforts to strengthen family ties and increase family stability in the nonwhite population probably will not be very successful until opportunities for economic upgrading are provided. This society may have the possibility of helping a population achieve greater family stability to prevent delinquency only after it has assisted a population to achieve greater economic security. The longitudinal unfolding of life in the social system needs to be studied in a much more refined way. This study has suggested the significance of this kind of investigation and called attention to the inadequacy of explanation that does not take into consideration a serial or developmental view of social conditions.

CONCLUSIONS

A general conclusion emerging from this study is that juvenile delinquency will not be greatly reduced in Washington, or in cities like Washington with a large nonwhite population, until there is a substantial increase in the nonwhite population's economic status. The low rate of delinquency among white youth who are members of a population that has achieved economic affluence is further evidence supporting this conclusion. Other conclusions of the study are these:

Socio-economic and family status are phenomena that have overlapping but different ecological patterns of distribution in an urban community.

Socio-economic and family status make independent as well as joint contributions to variations in the ecology of juvenile delinquency.

The preventive potential of two-parent households against juvenile delinquency tends to be impaired by circumstances of poverty.

The preventive potential of affluent economic status against juvenile delinquency tends to be impaired by family instability.

Delinquency rates are similar for members of white and nonwhite populations who live in the most disadvantaged environment characterized by many broken homes and low income.

Community programs designed to prevent juvenile delinquency associated both with family instability and economic insecurity will probably have greater success if they focus first upon increasing the economic status of a population.

The full answer, however, to the question of whether community programs should attempt first to create more economic security or develop greater family stability depends upon the target population and the stage through which it is passing. More than four out of every five youth referred to juvenile court in Washington, D.C. are Negro. If a community is really interested in reducing delinquency in this kind of a city, it would appear, according to the findings of this study, that much assistance must be rendered to the nonwhite population, in the form of increased economic opportunities.

CHAPTER IV

Perceptions and Self-Perceptions of Delinquents and Their Peers

EDITOR'S INTRODUCTION

WHILE THE LITERATURE pertaining to the self-perceptions of delinquent youth has been relatively sparse, even sparser is literature pertaining to the perceptions of delinquents. The first four papers in this section all deal with the role of self-concept as a factor in delinquency. Utilizing relevant findings by the Gluecks, Gough, and others, Walter Reckless and his associates at Ohio State University developed one of the earlier research projects designed to assess the role of self-concept in the etiology of delinquency. The first paper, by Reckless, Dinitz, and Murray, presents the results of a study of 125 "good" boys from high delinquency, virtually all-white areas of Columbus. Data was obtained by employing self-administered questionnaires to the boys. The authors hypothesize on the basis of their pilot study that "positive" self-concept helps to deter the acquisition of delinquent values, even in delinquent settings. The next paper, by Michael Schwartz and Sandra Tangri, employs a different measure of self-concept, viz., a ten-scale Semantic Differential form. As in the study by Reckless and his associates, Schwartz and Tangri also employ a study group of sixth graders, but whereas the former utilized an all-white study group, the latter employed an all-black study group. A further point of difference between the two studies is that Schwartz and Tangri attempted to distinguish between a boy's self-concept and his perceptions of the way others see him.

The third paper in this section, by Reckless and Dinitz, represents a recent backward look by the authors upon research on the relationship between self-concept and delinquency. The authors suggest lines along which subsequent work might fruitfully develop.

Leon Fannin and Marshall Clinard's paper is the fourth and last paper in this section which deals with self-concept and delinquency. The authors depart somewhat from the earlier research papers in this section by focusing on samples of lower and middle class white delinquents committed to a training school. Fannin and Clinard employed depth interviewing in probing the boys' self-concept. Finding some differences between lower and middle class boys with respect to self-concept, the authors then consider the implications of this finding for further research into deviant and nondeviant behavior.

The next paper, by Teele and his associates, moves to the consideration of sociometric ratings, choice reciprocity and teacher perceptions for antisocial and normal boys in primary and secondary schools. Findings in this study are viewed in connection with Renato Taiguiri's work on social preferences and social perception.

The last paper in this section, by Short, Rivera, and Tennyson, represents a study of perceptions of legitimate and illegitimate opportunities among comparable groups of gang-nongang, Negro-white, and lower class-middle class boys. This paper, then, also relates to the work of Cloward and Ohlin, but on the level of perceived opportunities rather than objective opportunities as dealt with earlier by Palmore and Hammond.

33.

Walter C. Reckless, Simon Dinitz and Ellen Murray

SELF CONCEPT AS AN INSULATOR AGAINST DELINQUENCY

This study is concerned with sixth-grade boys[1] in the highest delinquency areas in Columbus, Ohio, who have not become delinquent and who are not expected to become delinquent. What insulates an early teen-age boy against delinquency? Is it possible to identify certain components that enable young adolescent boys to develop or maintain non-delinquent habits and patterns of behavior in the growing up process?

METHODOLOGY

In order to study the non-delinquent boy, all 30 sixth-grade teachers in schools located in the highest white delinquency areas in Columbus were asked to nominate those white boys in their school rooms who would not, in their opinion, ever experience police or juvenile court contact. Treating each nominee separately, the teachers were then requested to indicate their reasons for the selection of a particular boy. Of the eligible students, 192, or just over half, were selected and evaluated by their teachers as being "insulated" against delinquency. A check of police and juvenile court records revealed that 16 (8.3 per cent) of those nominated had some type of law enforcement record, and these boys were eliminated from further consideration. Repeated neighborhood visits failed to locate 51 others. In the remaining cases both the boy and his mother were interviewed.

The 125 "good" boys comprising the final sample were given a series of four self-administered scales to complete. These included, in somewhat modified form, (1) the delinquency proneness and (2) social responsibility scales of the Gough[2] California Personality Inventory, (3) an occupational preference instrument,[3] (4) and one measuring the boy's conception of self, his family and other interpersonal relations.[4] At the same time, though not in the presence of the nominee, the mother or mother-surrogate was interviewed with an open-ended schedule to determine the boy's developmental history, his patterns of association, and the family situation. (Now nearing completion is a comparable study of sixth-grade boys in the same classrooms who were nominated by the same teachers as being likely to come into contact with the police and juvenile court.)

Source: Walter C. Reckless, Simon Dinitz, and Ellen Murray, "Self Concept as an Insulator against Delinquency," *American Sociological Review* 21 (1956): 744–46. Reprinted by Permission of the authors and the American Sociological Association.

Paper read at the annual meeting of the American Sociological Society, September, 1956. This research was supported by a grant from The Ohio State University Development Fund.

[1]Sixth-grade students were selected for study because they represent the threshold age group for entry into legal and social delinquency. In Columbus, Ohio, the delinquency rate doubles between the ages of 11 and 12. For details on age and census tract rates see John S. Ely, "An Ecological Study of Juvenile Delinquency in Franklin County" (Master's thesis, Ohio State University, 1952).

[2]For a detailed description of the delinquency proneness scale see Harrison G. Gough, "Systematic Validation of a Test for Delinquency," reprint of a paper delivered at the annual meeting of the American Psychological Association, September, 1954; Harrison G. Gough and Donald Peterson, "The Identification and Measurement of Predispositional Factors in Crime and Delinquency," *Journal of Consulting Psychology* 16 (1952): 207–12; and Harrison G. Gough, "A Sociological Theory of Psychopathy," *American Journal of Sociology* 53 (1948): 359–66. In correspondence with us, Gough suggested the inclusion of the social responsibility scale as a "partial index of the 'social control' factor in personality . . . [and] an index of delinquency proneness based upon both scales would be a better measure for your study." Both scales were used with Gough's expressed permission and consent.

[3]This instrument was developed in a study of juvenile vulnerability to delinquency. See James E. Morlock, *Predicting Delinquency in a Homogeneous Group of Pre-Adolescent Boys* (Doctoral diss., Ohio State University, 1947).

[4]This measure was based in part on the Glueck findings concerning family variables and delinquency. See Sheldon and Eleanor Glueck, *Unraveling Juvenile Delinquency* (New York: The Commonwealth Fund, 1950).

FINDINGS

An analysis of the scores made by these 125 nominees on the delinquency vulnerability (De) and social responsibility (Re) scales seemed to justify their selection as "good" boys. Out of a possible total De score of 54, scores ranged from a low of 4 to a high of 34 with a mean of 14.57 and a standard deviation of 6.4. This mean score was significantly lower than that of school behavior problem boys, young delinquents or reformatory inmates investigated in other studies. In fact, the average De score of the sample subjects was below that obtained in all but one previous study using the same scale.[5]

For a twelve year old group, the nominees scored remarkably high on the social responsibility scale. The mean Re score for the group was 28.86 with a standard deviation of 3.60 and a range of 12 to 40 out of a possible 42 points. This mean score was appreciably higher than that achieved by school disciplinary cases, delinquents, and prisoners tested in other studies. The correlation between the two sets of scores was −.605, indicating a significant and negative relationship between delinquency vulnerability and social responsibility as measured by these instruments.

In response to self-evaluation items, the 125 boys portrayed themselves as law-abiding and obedient. Specifically, the vast majority defined themselves as being stricter about right and wrong than most people, indicated that they attempted to keep out of trouble at all costs and further indicated that they tried to conform to the expectations of their parents, teachers and others.[6] The nominees did not conceive of themselves as prospects for juvenile court action or detention,[7] and they stated that their partici-

pation in such activities as stealing had been minimal and that their friends were either entirely or almost completely free of police and juvenile court contact.[8] As part of their conformity pattern, the respondents rarely played "hookey" from school and almost without exception indicated a liking for school. Finally, the "good" boys visualized themselves as being about average in ability, activity level, and aggressiveness. When asked "What do you think keeps boys out of trouble?" the respondents listed parental direction (a good home), non-deviant companions, and work, as well as other conventional answers. It would therefore appear that the internalization of these non-deviant attitudes played a significant role in the "insulation" of these boys.

Nominee perceptions of family interaction also appeared to be highly favorable. As noted in a previous paper, the 125 families were stable maritally, residentially, and economically.[9] There appeared to be close parental supervision of the boys' activities and associates, an intense parental interest in the welfare of the children, and a desire to indoctrinate them with non-deviant attitudes and patterns. This parental supervision and interest seemed to be the outstanding characteristic of the family profiles. It extended over the entire range of their sons' activities—from friendship patterns, leisure activities, and after school employment to movie attendance and the performance of well-defined duties at home. Thus, as regards companions for example, the mothers almost without exception stated that they knew the boys' friends, that these friends were "good" boys and that, in fact, the boys couldn't have chosen better companions. The mothers also knew the where-

---

[5]Based on data furnished by Gough.

[6]Nearly 60 per cent of the boys thought they were stricter about right and wrong than most people; 85 per cent tried to escape trouble at all costs; 81 per cent stressed their obedience to their parents' wishes, and 81 per cent were concerned with the reaction of friends and others to their behavior. These and other data were based on responses to items in one or more of the four instruments used.

[7]For example, 70 per cent of the boys in answering the questions on the Morlock scale seemed certain that they would never be brought before the

juvenile court; only one respondent believed he would have future contact with the court. Two-thirds indicated certainly about never being taken to jail. Some 57 per cent did not rule out the possibility of becoming policemen.

[8]In only 12 per cent of the cases had any of the friends of these boys experienced police or juvenile court contact.

[9]For a complete discussion of the family backgrounds of the nominees see Walter C. Reckless, Simon Dinitz, and Ellen Murray, "The 'Good' Boy in a High Delinquency Area," *Journal of Criminal Law, Criminology, and Police Science,* vol. 48, no. 1, pp. 18–25.

abouts of their sons at almost all times and many insisted on this knowledge.

Despite this intensive supervision, the boys did not feel themselves to be unduly restricted. In general, the nominees appeared satisfied with the amount of parental affection and attention and with the quality of discipline and punishment given them. They viewed their home life as pleasant and their parents as understanding.

Low and high scorers on the delinquency proneness scale and their respective mothers did not differ significantly in their evaluations of these various aspects of family interaction. Of the 22 home background variables tested—ranging from the percentage of boys from broken homes to parental favoritism—none was found to be significantly related to the delinquency proneness scores. This finding was hardly surprising in view of the non-representative character of the sample group and the relatively small amount of variation in the family settings. It may also well be that in defining his interpersonal and family relationships favorably, the "good" boy, regardless of the degree of his "goodness" as measured by various scales, is in fact expressing the positive attitudes and perceptions that are important components in his "goodness."

While there was no appreciable variation in aspects of family interaction between the low and high scorers, the boys as a group and their mothers as a group did differ significantly in some of their evaluations. These differences were largely centered around the activity level of the boys, the definitions of the fairness and severity of parental punishment, and the amount of bickering in the home. Mothers thought their sons to be more active, punishment to be less frequent and severe, and parental tranquility to be more pervasive than did the nominees. Most significantly, perhaps, the mothers expressed less satisfaction with the role played by the boys' fathers than did the boys. Briefly, the mothers pictured their husbands as being relatively aloof and rigid in their affectional relationships with their sons. The nominees, however, could not differentiate between their parents in this regard.

These divergences in perceptions may largely reflect age, sex, and role differences in expectations of what constitutes satisfactory family relationships. Consequently, predictive tables based on the parents' conceptions of the boy and his relationships would necessarily be different in many particulars from those based on the boys' conceptions.

CONCLUSION

"Insulation" against delinquency on the part of these boys may be viewed as an ongoing process reflecting an internalization of non-delinquent values and conformity to the expectations of significant others. Whether the subjects, now largely unreceptive to delinquent norms of conduct, will continue to remain "good" in the future remains problematic. The answer to this question, it is felt, will depend on their ability to maintain their present self-images in the face of mounting situational pressures.[10]

While this pilot study points to the presence of a socially acceptable concept of self as the insulator against delinquency, the research does not indicate how the boy in the high delinquency area acquired his self image. It may have been acquired by social definition of role from significant figures in his milieu, such as a mother, a relative, a priest, a settlement house worker, a teacher, etc. It might have been a by-product of effective socialization of the child, which had the good fortune of not misfiring. On the other hand, it may have been an outgrowth of discovery in social experience that playing the part of the "good" boy and remaining a "good" boy bring maximum satisfactions (of acceptance) to the boy himself. Finally, there is a strong suspicion that a well-developed concept of self as a "good" boy is the component which keeps middle- and upper-class boys, who live in the better neighborhoods, out of delinquency. The point is that this component seems to be strong enough to "insulate" the adolescent against delinquency in the unfavorable neighborhoods.

---

[10]See Daniel Glaser, "Criminality Theories and Behavioral Images," *American Journal of Sociology* 61 (March, 1956): 433–44.

34.

MICHAEL SCHWARTZ AND SANDRA S. TANGRI

A NOTE ON SELF-CONCEPT AS AN INSULATOR AGAINST DELINQUENCY

Much theory and research on juvenile delinquency is focused on self-concept or self-esteem. Cohen, for example, has argued that the delinquent gang permits working-class boys to recoup self-esteem lost through defeat in middle-class institutions.[1] Reckless and his associates have been major contributors to this line of research and appear to have demonstrated that the quality of self-concept may be an excellent predictor of delinquency. Reckless' research seems to lend some credence to Cohen's formulation, since it indicates that poor self-concepts leave boys vulnerable to delinquency. Of course, this work does not indicate whether or not a poor self-concept is the product of defeat in school or other middle-class institutions.

The work of Reckless is interesting from several other points of view. It attacks the question of delinquency from a social-psychological as opposed to either a psychoanalytic or social structural perspective. That is, Reckless views a delinquent or "pre-delinquent" as trying to resolve his problems in terms of his own "personal equation." Individual behavior is viewed as a function of the articulation of society and self, and the question of delinquency becomes a research problem in socialization processes. This approach also appears to explain both delinquency and *non*-delinquency with a single set of variables. That is, self-concept or self-evaluation potentially accounts for the non-delinquent boy in a high delinquency area as well as for the delinquent boy in the same area.

The research of Reckless and his associates

has been reprinted in a number of books of readings, and it is our impression that school administrators, probation officers and others in direct contact with youth are aware of it and try to act in terms of it. Nevertheless, the work seems to have some problems, examination of which will open some important research doors.

Essentially, the Reckless studies have four parts. The first is a study of 125 white boys in the sixth grade in schools in the highest delinquency area of Columbus, Ohio.[2] These are "good" boys, having been nominated by their teachers as unlikely ever to experience police or juvenile court contacts. Each was administered the delinquency proneness (De) scale and the social responsibility scale (Re) from Gough's California Personality Inventory (CPI), and a questionnaire on occupational preference (the data from which do not appear among the results). Each was asked about his concept of himself, his family, and his interpersonal relations. The boys' mothers were interviewed also.

The results obtained for the "good" boys were: (1) low scores on the De scale and high scores on the Re scale; (2) "self-evaluations which were law-abiding and obedient"; and (3) very favorable perceptions of family interaction and lack of resentment of close family (maternal) supervision. (4) Their families were maritally, residentially and economically stable. The authors concluded that "insulation against delinquency is an ongoing process reflecting internalization of non-delinquent values and conformity to the expectations of significant others."

This study alone is difficult to assess because it lacked a control or comparison group. But a follow-up study of these "good" boys four years

SOURCE: Michael Schwartz and Sandra S. Tangri, "A Note on Self-Concept as an Insulator against Delinquency," *American Sociological Review* 30, no. 6 (December, 1965): 922–26. Reprinted by Permission of the authors, and the American Sociological Association.
[1]Albert K. Cohen, *Delinquent Boys: The Culture of the Gang* (New York: The Free Press, 1956).

[2]Walter C. Reckless, Simon Dinitz, and Ellen Murray, "Self Concept as an Insulator against Delinquency," *American Sociological Review* 21 (1956): 744–46.

later provides an interesting comparison.[3] Of the original group of 125 "good" boys, now age 16, 103 were located, and 99 were still in school. Teachers nominated 95 of the 99 boys as "good" boys again. The boys and their mothers were again interviewed and the boys again completed the De and Re scales. The boys' responses on the tests were consistent with their earlier performance; again they reported favorable family interaction patterns; and only four of the renominated "good" boys had had any police contact. Apparently these boys were insulated against delinquency over a four year period.

A similar longitudinal study was conducted with a group of 101 "bad" boys, that is, boys who were nominated by their teachers as likely to have police and juvenile court contacts. Of these 101 "bad" 12-year-old boys, 24 were already on record for previous offenses. Again, the boys and their mothers were interviewed, and the boys were administered the De and Re scales. The results were as follows. The "bad" boy scores

were significantly higher on the De and lower on the Re scales than those made by the "good" boys of the first study. Indeed, this mean delinquency vulnerability score was higher than that achieved by any of the non-delinquents and non-disciplinary sample subjects treated in other studies. Similarly, the mean social responsibility score was lower than those recorded in other studies for all but prisoners, delinquents and school disciplinary cases. These scores seem to validate the judgments of the teachers in selecting these boys as ones who would get into future difficulties with the law.

Not only do these scales appear to differentiate between the potentially delinquent and non-delinquent, but even more importantly they were found to discriminate within the sample of nominated delinquents between those boys who had and those who had not experienced previous court contact.[4]

The follow-up study of the "bad" boys succeeded in locating 70 boys, now 16 years of age.[5] Twenty-seven (39 per cent) had had serious and frequent police and court contacts. The "bad" boys' mean scores on the De and Re scales had not changed and were still worse than the "good" boys' scores. The "bad" boys, then, seem to be more vulnerable to delinquency, and on the basis of the scale scores and the interview data, Reckless and his associates conclude that the discriminating factor is quality of "self-concept." The "bad" boys see themselves as likely to get into trouble in the future; their mothers and teachers agree. The "good" boys see themselves as unlikely to get into trouble; their mothers and teachers agree.

Our research is not a replication of this work, although it was stimulated by several important problems in the Reckless studies. First, Reckless assumes that mothers and teachers are significant others and that the boys incorporate mothers' and teachers' evaluations into their own self-concepts. Now, a delinquent may know at the cognitive level that others such as mother and teacher evaluate him negatively. But does he incorporate those perceived evaluations into his own concept of self? A "bad" boy who sees himself as likely to get into trouble may do so less as a consequence of poor self-concept than as an accurate prediction of future events based on prior experience. Reckless does not distinguish between an individual's knowledge of others' expectations as matters of fact and those that become part of his self-evaluation. His treatment of self-concept is most unclear.

The primary problem raised by Reckless' treatment of self has to do with the kinds of conclusions one can draw about the self from any collection of questionnaire or interview responses. Since almost anything a person says may have some bearing on the self, one must extract from the statement *that aspect* or implication relevant to self. Otherwise, everything is "self," and the value of the term is lost. An indiscriminate collation of items from the CPI and questions asked of mothers, sons, and teachers, all treated as self-concept, does not produce a meaningful definition of the term.

[3] Frank R. Scarpitti, Ellen Murray, Simon Dinitz, and Walter C. Reckless, "The 'Good' Boys in a High Delinquency Area: Four Years Later," *American Sociological Review* 25 (1960): 555–58.

[4] Simon Dinitz, Walter C. Reckless, and Barbara Kay, "A Self Gradient among Potential Delinquents," *Journal of Criminal Law, Criminology and Police Science* 49 (1958): 231.

[5] Simon Dinitz, Frank R. Scarpitti, and Walter C. Reckless, "Delinquency Vulnerability: A Cross Group and Longitudinal Analysis," *American Sociological Review* 27 (1962): 515–17.

Finally, this research is missing a theoretical link. *Why* should poor self-concept leave the individual vulnerable to delinquency? One could argue, for example, that a poor self-concept ought to produce behavior conforming to the demands of significant others like mother or teacher. Or does a poor self-concept lead to a rejection of the rejectors and the attribution of significance to others who prove more rewarding (say, delinquent peers)? Does poor self-concept leave one vulnerable to delinquency only where delinquent alternatives to conformity are available? If so, does this mean that an upper middle-class boy with a poor self-concept and restricted opportunity for delinquency is apt to be a conflicted neurotic? Reckless has forced these and other significant questions upon us, and therein lies his greatest contribution.

THE PRESENT STUDY

These comments on previous work in no way demonstrate that self-concept does *not* differentiate nominated "good" boys from nominated "bad" boys. Our concern here was to devise measurement procedures suitable for determining the extent to which such a distinction does obtain between the two groups. Furthermore, we wished to investigate the extent to which varying self-concepts are a function of the consistency of self-definitions given to the boys by significant others, as those definitions are perceived by the boys themselves, and to determine, as far as possible, who the significant others really are. Another objective was to distinguish between a boy's judgments of the way others see him as a fact apart from his judgments in terms of self-evaluation. In other words, does a boy say that "My mother doesn't think I'm very nice, but it doesn't really matter what she thinks anyway" (his perception of the facts of the matter), or does he say, "My mother doesn't think I'm very nice, so I guess I'm not" (thus incorporating an evaluation perceived as given by a significant other).

In short, we began by asking whether a group of nominated "good" boys and a group of nominated "bad" boys can be distinguished in terms of quality of self-concept. Second, we asked about the relation between the self-concepts of

"good" and "bad" boys and the perceived evaluations that others make of the boys. And finally, we asked which "others" seem to be perceived in terms of evaluation and which are less significant.

DATA

In the spring of 1964, sixth-grade teachers, and the principal and assistant principal in a single inner-city, all-Negro school in the highest delinquency area of Detroit were asked to nominate "good" and "bad" sixth-grade boys, i.e., to designate which boys they felt would never have police or court contacts and which boys they felt sure would have such contacts.

All 101 sixth graders were given a ten-scale Semantic Differential form to fill out. The polarities were: good-bad, useful-useless, superior-inferior, smart-stupid, square-cool, tough-soft, selfish-unselfish, friendly-unfriendly, kind-cruel, and important-unimportant. Seven of these pairs have high factor loadings on the evaluation factor Osgood found in his work;[6] the smart-stupid and tough-soft pairs are similar to ones Osgood used; and "cool-square" comes from the local argot. The phrases to be rated on these polarities were, "I Am," "My Friends Think I Am," "My Mother Thinks I Am," and "My Teachers Think I Am." Instructions were given orally by the authors, and they put several examples on the classroom blackboard with the concepts "Apple" and "My Shirt." Interestingly, these Negro students seemed to have vastly less difficulty with the instrument than middle-class white adolescents and adults have. Practically no subject failed to complete the instrument in its entirety, while in the senior author's experience college students have much more difficulty. Perhaps this is because sixth graders are cognitively less complex than college students.

The Semantic Differential forms of the boys nominated as "good" and "bad" (N's are 27 and 24, respectively) were separated and scored. (Since every boy was nominated as either "good" or "bad," the total of 51 includes all of the sixth-grade boys. The girls' data were not

---

[6]Charles E. Osgood, George J. Suci, and Percy Tannenbaum, *The Measurement of Meaning* (Urbana: University of Illinois Press, 1957).

included in this analysis.) The scoring procedure took two forms. The self-concept score was taken from the ratings of the "I am" page. A score of one is given to a check mark on the space nearest the positive pole, such as

good:$\sqrt{}$: : : : : :bad,

and a score of seven is given to a check mark nearest the negative pole, such as

good: : : : : :$\sqrt{}$:bad.

The scales are thus scored from one to seven and the range of possible scores over ten scales is ten to 70.

The second scoring procedure was the computation of Di^2 scores. We wished to know not only whether the "good" boys have better self-concepts, but also the extent to which good self-concept goes with consistency of perceived feedback. To determine the consistency of perceived feedback the individual receives from significant others, we matched the scores for "My Friends Think I Am" and "My Mother Thinks I Am," for example, on a scale-by-scale basis. If a boy thinks his friends would give him a 2 on the good-bad scale, and his mother would give him a 5, then his $Di^2 = (2-5)^2$ or 9. Summing the Di^2 scores over all ten scales yields a discrepancy score, and this score was obtained for each combination of significant others.

RESULTS AND DISCUSSION

The mean self-concept score for the "good" boys was 23.48 while the mean self-concept score for the "bad" boys was 27.29 (the smaller the score, the more positive the self-concept). These data support the Reckless, et al., notion that two such nominated groups do have different qualities of self-concept, although our data are based on a measure of self less ambiguous than the measures used by Reckless.

Differences between what "My Friends Think I Am" and what "My Mother Thinks I Am" were smaller for the "good" boys than for the "bad" boys: the mean ΣDi^2 score for the "good" boys was 34.51, while the mean ΣDi^2 score for the "bad" boys was 62.38. Similarly, comparing what "My Friends Think I Am" with what "My Teachers Think I Am" produced a mean ΣDi^2 score of 22.19 for "good" and 49.79 for "bad" boys. These data are summarized in Table 4–1, and may be considered support for a dissonance hypothesis of poor self-concept. The greater perceived inconsistency among reference groups manifested by the "bad" boys may also be taken as a measure of the quality of socialization, thus tending to support the Reckless studies' De-scale data, assuming that the De scale does represent quality of socialization.

The next question is whether mother's, friends' and teachers' evaluations of the boys, as the boys perceive them, are related to the boys' own evaluations of themselves. Correlations among the total scores for "I Am," "My Mother Thinks I Am," "My Friends Think I Am," and "My Teachers Think I Am" are shown in Table 4–2.

These intercorrelations vary greatly, and they

TABLE 4–1.

SELF-CONCEPT AND DISCREPANCY SCORES FOR 27 "GOOD" AND 24 "BAD" BOYS

	Range		Mean		Standard Deviation			
	Good	Bad	Good	Bad	Good	Bad	*t*	*P*
I Am	12–37	16–42	23.48	27.29	6.14	6.45	2.12	<.05
My Friends Think I Am	16–45	10–58	26.44	32.83	10.21	11.87	2.03	<.05
My Mother Thinks I Am	10–40	10–60	23.44	30.04	8.33	10.75	2.42	<.05
My Teachers Think I Am	10–45	16–64	26.85	36.16	7.46	10.95	3.50	<.001
Σd_i^2 Friends vs. Mother	1–105	11–360	34.51	62.38	28.33	68.18	2.02	<.05
Σd_i^2 Friends vs. Teachers	3–124	5–164	22.19	49.79	7.69	12.79	3.02	<.01

TABLE 4–2.

CORRELATIONS BETWEEN SELF-CONCEPT AND PERCEIVED MOTHER'S, FRIENDS'
AND TEACHERS' CONCEPTS

	"Good" Boys			"Bad" Boys		
	I Am	Friends Think I Am	Mother Thinks I Am	I Am	Friends Think I Am	Mother Thinks I Am
Friends	.27	..	..	.28	..	..
Mother	.18	.60*	..	.67[a]	.54*	..
Teachers	.42*	.68*	.32	.22	.61*	.41*

*Significant at .05 level.
[a]Significant at .001 level.

are not easy to interpret. For example, the correlations between "I Am" and "My Friends Think I Am" for both "good" and "bad" boys are not significantly different from zero. Yet the relevant literature on this age group indicates an enormous dependency on peers for approval and self-definition. Perhaps what we observe in adolescent gangs or cliques is not dependency in an identification sense, but rather role-playing behavior, and the reflected images are accepted as fact and not as evaluations to be incorporated into the self-concept. Forced to re-examine our assumption that peers are truly *significant* others, we infer that peer dependency develops at a later age. Our boys were only 12 years old, and might not yet have developed a high level of dependency.

The differences between groups in the correlations between "I Am" and "My Mother Thinks I Am" proved very interesting. Although no significant correlation exists for the "good" boys, a very strong one does exist for the "bad" boys, accounting for about 45 per cent of the variance. This result was not anticipated. A plausible, though *post facto* explanation is that a close relation between self-concept and perception of mother's concept implies that mother remains very significant over a protracted time period, especially during the time when more masculine identifications are "normally" formed. Failure to give up mother obviously restricts the possibility that others might become significant in the boy's environment, which in turn restricts the possibility that others can control the boy's behavior by reflecting either negative or positive self-images. Note that the correlation between

self-image and perceived teachers' image for "bad" boys is not different from zero, whereas for "good" boys, it is the largest and only significant correlation, much larger than the minor correlation with the mother's image. Perhaps, then, defining self as "good" or "bad" is largely a function of the individual's own attribution of significance to others in varying situations. Among the directions indicated for further research, testing hypotheses concerning mother's control of independence training is an example.

An alternative interpretation is as follows. If it is true that peer evaluations are not, at this age, incorporated into a self-image, and therefore render little or no psychological support, and if a boy's teachers reject him (as is clearly the case when a teacher nominates the boy as "bad"), then where can a "bad" boy turn for support? At this age, it seems to be toward mother. Perhaps defeat in the broader environment, i.e., the school, forces the boy back to the family group. It is not that his mother fails to "let go," but rather that the son seeks to retain a relationship that a clinician would insist he ought to have given up. Even though mother seems to define him (as he perceives it) less favorably than the "good" boy thinks his mother defines him, she represents the primary source of self-definition, and her limited knowledge of his behavior on the streets leaves the "bad" boy relatively more free, in the psychological sense, to engage in delinquent behavior.

Whether the primary factor is the mother's failure to encourage her son's independence or the teacher's rejection, which forces the boy to rely on his mother, the results are similar, and the senior author's observations (as research director for a government-sponsored delinquency control project) support our interpretation of these data. A certain amount of latent homosexuality was evident among some of the older "bad" boys; sex, sex talk, and heterosexual encounters in general often seemed characterized by aggression more than by affection. Others have discussed the Negro matriarchy in terms of its potential for encouraging homosexuality among young men, but these data indicate an additional factor—that a Negro boy risks being driven back into a relationship to which he has no alternatives, if he is to find support for his conception of self.

The Reckless et al. studies have not tapped these complex aspects of self. Here, we have made the distinction between fact and evaluation (or cognitive vs. cathectic modes) somewhat clearer. The high correlations between what these boys perceive as their friends' opinions of them and what they perceive as their mothers' and teachers' opinions, together with the lower correlations with their own conceptions (Table 4–2), suggest that a boy attributes to these others elements of his "self" definition that he finds irrelevant for his own evaluation

of himself. Some aspects of what others say about one are relevant to one's own self-definition and other aspects are not. Reckless, however, treats all such perceptions as self. Moreover, some of the "others" whom the investigator may deem "significant" for the individual are clearly not significant at all—at least not enough to make the reflected self-definitions acceptable.

Our data have several implications, which we shall simply list in conclusion. First, self-concept, while still a vague and inadequately developed notion, is a much more complex phenomenon than the usual rhetoric of symbolic interaction would indicate. Second, the so-called "self-component" in vulnerability to delinquency may yet prove to be an extremely important road to follow for prediction and control. Finally, any solutions to the sociological problems of delinquency must, inevitably, incorporate social-psychological concepts. The cognitive structure that intervenes between delinquency and opportunity is a function of unique socialization experiences wherein lie an individual's reasons for choosing a deviant response to blocked opportunities. For those who wish to understand these reasons, self-concept research seems to provide fruitful directions.

35.

WALTER C. RECKLESS AND SIMON DINITZ

PIONEERING WITH SELF-CONCEPT AS A VULNERABILITY FACTOR IN DELINQUENCY

This paper presents a retrospective assessment of a pioneering line of research on the self-concept as an insulator against delinquency. The

SOURCE: Walter C. Reckless and Simon Dinitz, "Pioneering with Self-Concept as a Vulnerability Factor in Delinquency," *Journal of Criminal Law, Criminology and Police Science* 58, no. 4 (1967): 515–23. Reprinted by Special Permission of the Journal of Criminal Law, Criminology and Police Science (Northwestern University School of Law), Copyright © 1967, Volume 58, Number 4.

authors were in search of a clue—a possible self-factor—which might shed light on what it is that steers youths in high delinquency areas of a large city away from involvement in delinquency. Certainly, criminologists and sociologists are well aware of the simple fact that a large percentage of adolescents in high delinquency areas manage to keep out of official trouble with the law, walk around the street-corner gang and avoid its so-called "subculture," stay in school rather than drop out, identify with the norms and values of the dominant society, and turn their backs on the availability of illegitimate means to ends in their neighborhood environment. What, then, are the components which enable adolescents to develop and maintain non-delinquent patterns of conduct despite the adversities of family, class position, and neighborhood?

It was decided that the best subjects for an initial inquiry would be the sixth-grade boys in high delinquency areas. Attention was focused on white sixth-grade boys, so as not to complicate the research design with race and sex variables. One might well ask: why sixth-grade boys? The answer is that they are approximately 12 years of age and are at the threshold of adolescence as well as the threshold of officially complained-upon delinquency. Complaints on boys for delinquency begin to increase at this age and keep on increasing through the succeeding years of adolescence. In addition, it begins to be feasible to interview a child, at the age of 12, about himself and his world as he sees it. Attempts to obtain, by verbal interviews or pencil and paper inventories, subjective data from young children about themselves run into difficulty. This does not mean, however, that one cannot procure objective data from pre-adolescent children.

As a start, the authors in 1955 gained permission to ask sixth-grade teachers in predominantly white elementary schools in high delinquency areas of Columbus, Ohio—teachers who interact with their pupils the entire school day for an entire school year—to indicate from among the white boys in their classes those who would never get into trouble with the law. Despite the fact that most of the teachers were middle-class females, the authors maintain—and we think very rightly so—that they have a sense of the direction in which their pupils are going. Kvaraceus' work in developing a delinquency proneness measure certainly bears out our contention that teachers' behavior ratings, evaluations, or prognostications are quite accurate.[1]

A CLOSE LOOK AT SAMPLING AND PROCEDURE

Thirty sixth-grade teachers nominated 192 white boys in their classes who in their opinion would not experience police or juvenile court contact. The range was from 15 to 100 percent of the white boys in the 30 classes and the average per class was 6.4 boys.

The teachers at the time of making their nominations of the so-called "good boys" were asked to give their reasons for each nomination. They mentioned 1,033 reasons or 5.4 reasons per boy; 45 percent represented favorable personal characteristics, attitudes, and interests; 27 percent, one or more aspects of favorable home situations; 20 percent, participation in character-building youth organizations, religious activities, conforming in-school behavior, after-school employment; 7 percent, negative evaluations such as being excessively timid, naive, or overprotected so as to preclude involvement in delinquent behavior.

Sixteen of the 192 "good boys," constituting 8.3 percent of the teachers' nominees, turned out to have had, after clearance was made, previous contact with the police or the juvenile court. In 13 of the 16 cases, one or more members of the family had also had contact with the courts. Members of 42 additional families also had court contact, although the boys were not involved.

The authors eliminated these 16 boys, who already had contact with the law, from their "good boy" sample. In addition, when interviewers tried to locate the remaining 176 boys (out of the original 192), they could not find 51 boys, probably due in small part to wrong address, but in most part to removal of the family from the community in the interim of the several months between the teachers' nominations and the field follow-up. The project was left with a sample of 125 (192 minus 16 minus 51).[2]

A schedule was developed to be administered on an individual basis to each of the 125 "good

---

[1]William C. Kvaraceus, *Anxious Youth: Dynamics of Delinquency* (Columbus, Ohio: C. E. Merrill Books, 1966), pp. 102–108.

[2]Walter C. Reckless, Simon Dinitz, and Ellen Murray, "Teacher Nominations and Evaluations of 'Good' Boys in High-Delinquency Areas," *Elementary School Journal* 57 (1957): 221.

boys" in their own homes. Among other formal scales and inventories included in the schedule were 50 items which attempted to assess the boy's perception of himself in relation to his family, friends, school, and possible involvement with the law. We called these items self-concept items, because the responses represented the boy's perception of himself in reference to the significant others in his immediate world.

Two research interviewers contacted the mother at home and obtained permission to interview her and her son. The one interviewer administered the schedule to the boy in one room; the other interviewer administered a specially prepared schedule to the mother in another room simultaneously.

The following school year, namely 1956, the authors returned to the same 30 sixth-grade classrooms and asked the teachers, most of whom were the same ones they interviewed in 1955, to nominate the white boys in their rooms, who would, in their opinion, almost certainly experience police or juvenile-court contact in the future.

The teachers named 108 white boys, constituting about 25 percent of the eligible boys. Twenty-four of the 108 nominated "bad boys" (23 percent) had already had contact with the police and juvenile court (as against 8.3 percent of the "good boy" nominees). In view of a much shorter time span between teacher nomination and home interview, we lost only 7 boys in the "bad boy" sample, reducing it to 101 cases. The interview schedules for the boy and the mother were the same in the 1956 101 "bad boy" sample as in the 125 "good boy" sample of the previous year.

The scores on the two directionally-oriented scales of the California Psychological Inventory (*De* scale and *Re* scale), which were included in the schedule administered to each boy, were different in the expected directions: significantly more favorable for the "good boys" than for the "bad boys" or more unfavorable for the "bad boys" than the "good boys." Because the *De* scale of the CPI (now called the Socialization scale, measuring directionality toward and away from delinquency) and the *Re* scale of the CPI (measuring directionality toward social re-

sponsibility) are standardized scales, with national and even some international norms, the authors felt that the convincingly and significantly more favorable showing of the "good," and the more unfavorable showing of the "bad-boy" sample, tended to validate the teacher's nominations. Likewise, these scale scores provided corroboration for the more favorable answers on the self-concept items received from the "good" than from the "bad boys." In addition to these associations, the answers of the mothers to questions about their sons, paralleling virtually all of the questions used in the self-concept inventory for the boys, also added an additional dimension of validation. Thus, the teachers, the mothers, the *De* and *Re* Scales, and the boys' responses to the self-concept questions were highly consistent.

FOLLOW-UP FOUR YEARS LATER

Four years after initial contact (1959 for the "good" and 1960 for the "bad boys"), the authors set about determining how many of the boys were known to the juvenile court. Out of the total of 125 in the 1955 sample of "good boys," they were able to locate and assess 103; out of the 101 in the 1956 sample of "bad boys," 70. Incidentally, attrition was not related to scale scores or self-concept responses in either cohort. Those who remained in the community had scored neither better nor worse on the *De* and *Re* scales or on the self-concept responses than those who left.

Twenty-seven of the 70 "bad boys" (39 percent) had contact with the juvenile court for delinquency in the four year follow-up period —not including the court contacts in the instance of 24 out of the original 101 sample, prior to our study. Each of the 27 out of the traceable 70 "bad boys" averaged over 3 contacts with the juvenile court throughout the four-year period or from the time the boys were approximately 12 to the time they were 16 years of age.

In contrast, just four out of the 101 "good boys" who were followed had a one-time record in the juvenile court in the ensuing four-year period of follow-up—and only for very minor offenses. Ninety-nine of the 103 "good boys" were still in school, although half of them had passed legal age for drop-out. Of the 99 still in school, all but four impressed their teachers as unlikely to get into future difficulty. Their responses to the re-administered self-concept items were quite favorable, just as favorable as they were four years previously and the mothers' evaluations were just as favorable as four years earlier.

There was a remarkable four-year cohort stability on all of the directional indicators in both the "good" and "bad boy" samples: self-concept projections, teachers' prognostications, mothers' evaluations, scores on the *De* and *Re* scales of the CPI.

Furthermore, the authors were able to compare the traceable 103 "good," and the 70 "bad boys," on the Nye-Short self-reporting delinquency check list (using 7 of the original Nye-Short items) and they found that the latter scored more unfavorably than the former. (This self-reporting check list was not available to us in 1955 and 1956.) Hence, "professed" involvement corroborated reported involvement in delinquency as well as the direction of the self-concept responses, and the teachers' expectations.

At this point it is important to duplicate the theoretical underpinning of our quest to discover what insulates a boy in the high delinquency areas against involvement in delinquency.

In our quest to discover what insulates a boy against delinquency in a high delinquency area, we believe we have some tangible evidence that a good self-concept, undoubtedly a product of favorable socialization, veers slum boys away from delinquency, while a poor self-concept, a product of unfavorable socialization, gives the slum boy no resistance to deviancy, delinquent companions, or delinquent subculture. We feel that components of the self strength, such as a favorable concept of self, act as an inner buffer or inner containment against deviancy, distraction, lure, and pressures. Our operational assumptions are that a good self-concept is indicative of a residual favorable socialization and a strong inner self, which in turn steers the person away from bad companions and street corner society, toward middle class values, and to awareness of possibility of upward move-

ment in the opportunity structure. Conversely, the poor concept of self is indicative of a residual unfavorable socialization (by 12 years of age probably not the result of participation in delinquency subculture) and indicative of weak inner direction (self or ego), which in turn does not deflect the boy from bad companions and street corner society, does not enable him to embrace middle class values, and gives him an awareness of being cut off from upward movement in the legitimate opportunity system.

We feel that the selective operation of the self element is not specified in the response to the models of behavior presented to the person by his associates in differential association theory (Sutherland) and is even less specified in delinquency subculture theory (Cohen), as well as "opportunity structure" theory (Cloward and Ohlin).[3]

CROSS-SECTIONAL STUDIES

In 1957, the authors administered 717 schedules to sixth-grade children in 24 classes in eleven elementary schools of Columbus, Ohio, chosen according to census tract indexes of socioeconomic status as well as high and low delinquency. Eight of the schools (with 17 sixth-grade classes) served disadvantaged areas with high delinquency rates, while 3 served middle-class areas where delinquency rates were low. All the sixth-grade pupils present in class on the appointed day were administered a schedule. The schedule consisted of 46 items from the *De* scale, 38 items from the *Re* scale (both from the California Psychological Inventory which is a factor-analyzed version of the Minnesota Multiphasic Inventory), 56 self-concept items, plus certain social background items. During the administration of the inventories, the sixth-grade room teacher was interviewed elsewhere by a research assistant. With her cumulative record cards before her, the teacher rated each child in her class as either headed for trouble with the law, not sure, or not headed for trouble with the law.

[3]Simon Dinitz, Frank R. Scarpitti, and Walter C. Reckless, "Delinquency Vulnerability: A Cross Group and Longitudinal Analysis," *American Sociological Review* 27 (1962): 517.

Since the schedule was administered in school, a standard introductory statement requesting cooperation and allaying fears was used. On the front page of the schedule the following statement appeared in bold type: *Remember this is not a test. We simply want to know how you feel about things. There are no right or wrong answers. The right answer for you is how you feel about things.* Dr. Dinitz read aloud each question, reminding the pupils of the response pattern: true or false; yes or no.

Dr. Ernest Donald analyzed 354 boys' schedules from among the total of 717. Because the teachers nominated too few girls as headed for trouble with the law to warrant comparisons, the Donald analysis applied only to white and colored sixth-grade boys in both the high and low delinquency areas of Columbus, Ohio in 1957.[4] The various subgroups in the 1957 sample of 354 sixth-grade boys consisted of the subgroups shown in Table 4–3.

TABLE 4–3.
The Sample of Sixth-Grade Boys by Subgroups, Columbus, Ohio, 1957

Subgroup	Number
Teacher's nomination:	
Not headed for trouble (good)	222
Headed for trouble* (bad)	132
Race:	
White	234
Negro	120
Area:	
Low delinquency (good)	125
High delinquency (bad)	229
Nomination by race:	
Good white	155
Good Negro	67
Bad white	79
Bad Negro	53
Nomination by race by area:	
Good white (good)	86
Good white (poor)	69
Good Negro (poor)	67
Bad white (good)	39
Bad white (bad)	40
Bad Negro (bad)	53

*Including the teacher's evaluation of "not sure." The teacher rated each boy in terms of whether she thought he was headed for trouble with the law, not sure, or not headed for trouble with the law.[5]

[4]Ernest P. Donald and Simon Dinitz, "Self-Concept and Delinquency Proneness," *Interdisciplinary Problems of Criminology,* Papers of the American Society of Criminology, ed. Walter C. Reckless and Charles L. Newman (1965), pp. 49–59.

[5]Ibid., p. 50.

It was possible to relate the favorable and unfavorable responses on each of the 56 self-concept items with the dichotomous nominations of the sixth-grade teachers (headed for trouble with the law, including not sure, versus not headed for trouble with the law). Table 4–4 lists 16 of the 56 self-concept items, used in the 1957 schedule, which were found to be differentiated by teacher nomination at the .05 level of confidence and beyond (9 items at the .001; 3, at the .01; 1, at the .02; and 3, at the .05 level of confidence). Note that the items through number 39 were answered by *yes* or *no*; items 42 and 46 were answered by a response format of *often, sometimes, never*; item 50, as will be seen on inspection, was answered by checking one out of three possibilities.

TABLE 4–4.
Significant Self-concept Items According to Teacher Nomination, Associated with High and Low Scores on the *DE* Scale of the California Psychological Inventory

Original Schedule No.	Self-Concept Items
1....	Will you probably be taken to juvenile court sometime?
2....	Will you probably have to go to jail sometime?
6....	If you found that a friend was leading you into trouble, would you continue to run around with him or her?
11....	Do you plan to finish high school?
12....	Do you think you'll stay out of trouble in the future?
17....	Are grown-ups usually against you?
21....	If you could get permission to work at 14 would you quit school?
23....	Are you a big shot with your pals?
24....	Do you think your teacher thinks you will ever get into trouble with the law?
25....	Do you think your mother thinks you will ever get into trouble with the law?
26....	Do you think if you were to get into trouble with the law, it would be bad for you in the future?
27....	Have you ever been told that you were headed for trouble with the law?
39....	Have most of your friends been in trouble with the law?
42....	Do you confide in your father?
46....	Do your parents punish you?
50....	Do you think you are quiet _____ average _____ active _____.[6]

[6]Ibid., p. 51.

When the favorable and unfavorable responses on these 16 self-concept items were related to high and low scores on the *De* scale of the California Psychological Inventory (which also measures direction toward or away from delinquency), all but one item (number 25) reached the minimum .05 level of statistical significance. Certainly, there is corroboration here; teacher nomination, response to self-concept items, and scores on the *De* scale are going in the same direction.

Five of the 16 significant self-concept items according to teachers' nomination, as presented in Table 4–4, were discriminated by the race of the sixth-grade (1957) Columbus boys (items 2, 12, 23, 39, 52); seven, by high and low delinquency area (items 1, 2, 12, 25, 26, 27, and 39); 6, by I.Q. level, 94 and above, 93 and below (items 2, 17, 23, 27, 30, and 42); 1, by reading achievement (item 17); and 7 by arithmetic achievement (1, 2, 11, 12, 24, 26, and 29).

After having spotted the 16 significant self-concept items, it was possible to obtain a total self-concept score on the 16. High total scores were in the unfavorable (delinquency) direction. When the mean (total) scores on the 16 self-concept items were computed for various subgroups of the sixth-grade boy sample (1957), the difference in the means for white and colored boys was (a) slight (although significant statistically); (b) somewhat larger for boys by type of area (again statistically significant); (c) not significant for white boys in high and in low delinquency areas; (d) significant for white boys in good areas and colored boys in bad areas; and (e) not significant for white boys and Negro boys (both) in areas of high delinquency.

By way of comparison, the mean self-concept score for boys with high *De* scores and that for boys with low *De* scores differed most of all and at a significance level of .00001.[7] In commenting on these findings relative to self-concept scores by various subgroups of the sixth-grade Columbus boys, Donald had this to say:

One is almost ready to hazard the guess that race and type of neighborhood, whatever they may

signify in the accumulated socialization of 12-year-old boys, are relatively unimportant in determining self-concepts. On the other hand, a large mean score difference on the self-concept items is found when the sixth-grade boys are divided by favorable and unfavorable direction of socialization as measured by the scores on the *De* scale. Evidently the big thing which determines the boy's self-concept orientation is something other than race and neighborhood. Might we say that it is the quality of family interaction and impact, apart from class and race, plus the impact of other supplementary relationships found within the child's world?[8]

Further details on the entire 717 (1957) "big run," giving the mean scores for girls as well as boys on the *De* and *Re* scales, I.Q., Reading Achievement, and Arithmetic Achievement, by sex, race, type of area, and teacher nomination were presented in a special article, published in 1958.[9] In addition, an analysis of 400 of the 717 (1957) sixth-grade children, girls as well as boys, all from high delinquency areas, was published in 1960.[10]

SOUNDINGS IN BROOKLYN AND AKRON

Prior to Donald's 1963 item analysis of the authors' self-concept items, using 354 schedules of sixth-grade boys in the 1957 Columbus, Ohio sample, and establishing 16 discriminating items which could be summated into a total score, the authors received permission in 1959 to administer a schedule to 697 sixth-grade children in six elementary schools of Brooklyn, serving high, medium, and low delinquency areas. The object here was to determine whether the trends noted in Columbus applied to the more complex, heterogeneous, urban environment of New York.

The Brooklyn schedule consisted of 46 items of the *De* scale; 34 self-concept items, including 9 which deal with a general view that the child has of himself, 7 with his view of his home and parents, and 8 with his view of how his father deals with him (a sort of father rejection assess-

---

[7]Ibid., pp. 52–53.

[8]Ibid., p. 54.

[9]Simon Dinitz, Barbara A. Kay, and Walter C. Reckless, "Group Gradients in Delinquency Potential and Achievement Scores of Sixth Graders," *American Journal of Orthopsychiatry* 33 (1958): 598.

[10]Jon E. Simpson, Simon Dinitz, Barbara A. Kay, and Walter C. Reckless, "Delinquency Potential in Pre-Adolescents in High Delinquency Areas," *British Journal of Delinquency* 10 (1960): 211.

ment), and 10 with his projection about getting into trouble with the law; and 7 items taken from the Nye-Short inventory of self-reported delinquency involvement. However, it was not possible to obtain the sixth-grade teachers' prognostications of delinquency vulnerability in the Brooklyn project.

The findings on the Brooklyn study were never published. It was expected, however, that the sixth-grade males would test more unfavorably than the sixth-grade females, Negro more than white, high-delinquency area more than low-delinquency area pupils, Puerto Rican sixth-graders about the same as Negro sixth-graders, on all or most of the measures in the schedule. The greatest over-all differences between the various subgroups among the 1959 Brooklyn sixth-grade pupils occurred in mean scores on the *De* scale, which measures direction toward and away from delinquency. The 10 self-concept items dealing with projected involvement with the law made less sharp distinctions than the *De* scale between the various subgroups, although practically all differences between the means scores were significant. The mean subgroup scores on the self-concept items which focused on the father's rejection of the child were not significant, while most of the mean scores on the child's view of his home and parents did not distinguish the various subgroups in Brooklyn. The mean scores on the Nye-Short self-reported involvement in delinquency, likewise, for the most part did not differentiate the various subgroups. The authors wished that they could have gone into Brooklyn with a self-concept scale based on the 16 discriminating items which Donald analyzed and with more sophisticated measures of self-reported involvement.

The authors received considerable encouragement from the results of a 1959 Akron, Ohio, study made by Dr. Edwin L. Lively.[11] Lively administered the authors' Brooklyn schedule to 1171 pupils, boys and girls, in Akron: 192 in sixth-grade, 324 in seventh-grade, 325 in eighth-grade, and 300 in ninth-grade rooms, divided among schools serving lower and middle class

neighborhoods as well as high and low delinquency areas. It was possible in this study to tell whether the mean scores by various subgroups (sex, race, high-low delinquency area, and teacher prognostication) had stability with increasing age in adolescence (roughly 12 through 15).

The mean scores on the *De* scale (now called the Socialization scale) of the CPI, the 10 self-concept items projecting involvement with the law, and the 7 items dealing with the child's view of his home, were quite stable throughout the four age samples (sixth, seventh, eighth, and ninth graders). The scores on the 8 items dealing with the child's view of his relations with his father (mostly rejection items) were not stable for the subgroups of the four age levels. The mean scores on the 7 self-reported involvements in delinquency increased with age (which trend seems logical).

Very interesting, as far as directional corroboration is concerned, is the fact that scores on the five instruments analyzed in the Akron study (*De* scale—now called Socialization scale, home items, law involvement items, father rejection items and self-reported delinquency) intercorrelated very well indeed ranging from +.27 to +.65, and at about the same levels of intercorrelation for each age sample: sixth, seventh, eighth and ninth grade.[12] (One should remind himself that if the coefficients of correlation had been in the high seventies, eighties, or nineties, he should suspect that any two measures which highly correlated would be assessing the same component of self.) This directional corroboration plus the corroboration of stability with age gave re-assurance to the authors that a self factor seems to be involved in vulnerability toward or insulation against delinquency.

A disconcerting note, however, needs to be inserted at this point. The authors attempted to administer the Brooklyn schedule in representative sixth, seventh, eighth, and ninth grades of two large metropolitan school systems after the excellent results in Akron. But they were turned down in both instances, due to the politi-

[11]Edwin L. Lively, Simon Dinitz, and Walter C. Reckless, "Self-Concept as a Predictor of Juvenile Delinquency," *American Journal of Orthopsychiatry* 32 (1962): 1.

[12]Edwin L. Lively, "A Study of Teen-Age Socialization and Delinquency Insulation by Grade Levels" (Ph.D diss., Ohio State University, 1959), pp. 70–71.

cal dynamite which could be caused by administering schedules to children. And just recently a new National Institute of Mental Health regulation requires that the principal investigators of research projects obtain parental permission before administering scales and inventories to school children.

APPLICATION TO PREVENTION

In 1959, the authors were asked by the Columbus, Ohio, school system, to attempt some practical application of their findings. A demonstration on a very limited scale was undertaken to determine the feasibility of presenting appropriate models of behavior to sixth-grade boys, selected by teachers as headed for trouble. (Parental permission was obtained and the program occupied the last school period plus a half hour over school-closing time each day.) The main thrust of this demonstration was directed toward helping the vulnerable sixth-grade boy internalize effective models of behavior, thus building up or strengthening his self-concept. The worker in charge of the model-building sessions was also trained to be a most significant other (adult) in the lives of the participants.

Three years of such limited demonstration projects led to the formulation of a large demonstration-research project, supported by grants from the National Institute of Mental Health, to discover whether appropriate presentation of realistic models of behavior in the classroom could "beef up" a vulnerable boy's self. The design followed the theory and procedures of our original work on the self-concept as the insulating agent against trends toward delinquency.

The authors selected eight junior high schools of the inner city of Columbus, Ohio, which served disadvantaged and high delinquency neighborhoods. These 8 junior high schools were fed pupils by 44 elementary schools. In May of 1963, the authors, after having received the go-ahead signal from the granting agency, asked the sixth-grade teachers of the 44 elementary schools to nominate the boys in their classes who, in their opinion were likely to get into trouble with the law and likely to drop out of school as well as the boys who were likely not

to get into trouble with the law and likely to stay in school. In each school, the principal reviewed and confirmed the sixth-grade teacher's rating.

The over-all average was about 75 percent "good;" 25 percent "bad boys." The following September when the boys reached the eight junior high schools, the nominated vulnerable ("bad") boys were randomly divided into two groups: an experimental, and a control group. The project also called for a continuing follow-up of a sample of 15 percent of the so-called "good boys."

Preliminary data on the validity of these teacher-nominations of their students as vulnerable, doubtfully vulnerable or not vulnerable to later involvement with the law have been obtained. These data tend to support the contention that teacher-nominations are reasonably valid indicators of case outcomes of the 176 boys nominated as "good" (not vulnerable) in May, 1963; 154 or 87.5% had no contact with the police as of August, 1966. Of the unsure nominees, 69.4% avoided police contact in the comparable 3-year period, while just 53.7% of the nominated "bad" (vulnerable) boys were free of contact in the same three and one-fourth year time period.

The Columbus junior high schools at the time of the intervention demonstration operated "self-contained classes," which ran for three consecutive school periods (of forty minutes each) with the same teacher. In these self-contained classes, world geography, Ohio history, and English were taught in mixed groups, boys as well as girls. The project called for placing the experimental group (randomly split half of the vulnerable boys) into an all-boy self-contained class of approximately 25 boys. It called also for retaining the other half of the vulnerable boys as well as the nonvulnerable boys in the regular mixed self-contained classes.

Permission was obtained from parents to gather the experimental group into a special all-boy section. When the boys and parents asked why, our reply was that Mr. Jones, the teacher, wanted Joe in his class and wanted an all-boy section.

Four male seventh-grade project teachers were selected by the authors (the principal investigators). They were specially trained to present "model" materials, as a youth development supplement to the regular diet of world geography, Ohio history, and English. They were trained also to play the role of the most significant adult in the lives of these boys in the experimental classes. They were involved in a summer tooling-up program, met with the project's research director each day after school, and with the project's consulting child psychiatrist each Saturday morning as a group.

Each of the four project teachers had two experimental self-contained classes: one in the morning at one junior high school and one in the afternoon at another junior high school. Thus, there was one experimental all-boy self-contained class in each of the 8 junior high schools serving children from disadvantaged, high-delinquency areas. The four project teachers worked with the research director in developing appropriate "lesson plans" to get on target of presenting models of behavior in an effective way. In addition, the project teachers, as a result of their Saturday morning discussions with the project's consulting psychiatrist, developed a class-room climate or atmosphere conducive to internalization of the regular class fare and the project's supplementation. The experimental group was found, on an average, to be reading at the fourth-grade level. Consequently, the project used seventh-grade materials written at a fourth-grade comprehension level and it availed itself of various reading-therapy procedures.

The youth-development supplementation (presentation of models of behavior) was fed into the experimental all-boy classes at the same time, in all eight groups—feeding in the same lesson plans—such as finding out something about the man on your city block who has the reputation of being the best worker so as to put on the board (on such and such day). During the first year of operation (1963–1964), the project teachers worked valiantly to develop lesson plans which had possibility of model take-over. These plans were standardized and used in the same way, to supplement the regular school fare, in two successive years, namely 1964–1965 and 1965–1966. During the last two years of the project, it was possible for the project teachers to use their after-school overtime for making home visits.

The demonstration-research design consisted of an experimental group and two control groups, in three cohorts, 1963–1964, 1964–1965, and 1965–1966. Standard information was accumulated on each boy. Certain inventories were administered to the three groups in September and again in May of each year, at the close of the school year. Available school information on reading and arithmetic achievement, absences, conduct, school performance, is being collected for the file. Yearly clearance (every year until 1970) of all three sub-groups (the experimental group and the two control groups) is made through school records and through the files of the juvenile bureau of the police department in the summer of each follow-up year, to record truancy, non-attendance, and complaints for delinquency. Each yearly cohort will have four yearly clearances and by the time of the fourth clearance each boy will have passed his sixteenth birthday and will have had the legal opportunity to quit school and go to work.

Is the youth development supplement, in terms of presentation of appropriate models of behavior, strong enough preventive medicine? Does it reach the adolescent boy and presumably his self? Will the teacher-nominated vulnerable boys, who received Dr. Reckless and Dinitz's vitamins do better over a four-year period than their untreated first-cousins (also vulnerable boys) and even the teacher-nominated "good boys?" This is the question. The authors will have some answers in the fall of 1970.

CONCLUSION

It is no longer sufficient for sociologists who study criminal and delinquent behavior to call attention to the possible impact of disorganized and disadvantaged neighborhoods, family tensions and insufficiencies, bad companions and street-corner gangs, and the availability of illegitimate means to ends. Who responds to carriers of patterns of delinquency and crime? Who resists and goes the other way? We live in a society of alternates, where the self has more and more opportunities for acceptance or rejection of available confrontations. Consequently, sociologists as criminologists must join the search for the self-factors which determine direction of behavior or choice among alternates and in this endeavor they must work with their colleagues in psychology and psychiatry in an effort to discover what self-factors actually determine the direction of behavior and how they can be controlled.

The proposal herein has been to explore the self-concept as one important self-factor which controls the direction of the person. There is certainly some preliminary evidence in the authors' work to date, to indicate that the self-concept might be one of the important self-factors in determining the "drift" toward or away from delinquency and crime. The authors do not presume that such a self-factor would operate in instances of deep character and emotional disturbances. But for the large majority of unofficial and official offenders as well as effective conformers to the dominant norms of a democratic, industrial, urban, mobile society, it is certainly feasible to operate on the hypothesis that self-factors determine direction of behavior toward or away from delinquency and deviance in general.

The authors feel they uncovered some corroborating evidence, namely that the self-concept of early adolescent might be one of the self-factors which controls directionality. Certainly, teachers' prognostications of sixth-grade boys—even the mothers' evaluations—plus the *De* scale (now called Socialization scale) indicate that directionality, toward or away from delinquent behavior, can be sensed and assessed. If, in the future, effective assessment of self-reported delinquency can be made, sociologists as well as behavioral-science researchers will have another effective instrument to gauge directionality of the youth.

It seems to the authors that these indicators of directionality toward or away from deviance point to the strong possibility of a favorable-to-unfavorable self-concept in the young person, which is acting as the controlling agent. Our large cross-sectional study in 1957 certainly indicated that self-concept factors, the teachers' prognostication of direction of the youth, the *De* scale's assessment of direction were interrelated. And the authors, if they might be spared glib-

ness, do not think it is the subtle "rub-off" of the teacher's sense of the individual youth's direction which causes an internalization of a favorable image of himself (although this might happen in rare instances). And in the 1955 and 1956 samples, when the mother's projections of direction in which the son was travelling were obtained, the authors did not feel that in the overwhelming majority of instances the mother's faith or lack of faith in the directional outcome of her boy was the "looking glass" which gave the boy his image (although this might happen in more instances than in the impact of the sixth-grade teacher's sense of direction on the boy). The authors believe that a youth in American society obtains his self-concepts from many experiential sources, inside and outside the home and school.

The findings from the Akron study point to stability of direction as assessed by teacher's nomination and other instruments of assessment. Here again, the authors' interpretation is that directional stability in comparable samples of the sixth, seventh, eighth and ninth grades reflects the operation of a self-factor. However, this is not as convincing evidence as if the same sample of children could be tested during four successive years of adolescence. Nevertheless, the authors felt they received indications of longitudinal stability in the operation of a self-factor in the four-year follow-up of the 1955 "good boy" sample and the 1956 "bad boy" sample.

Undoubtedly, there is a need for the development of an effective self-concept measure which can assess the direction toward or away from delinquency or deviant behavior generally. There is need also to develop measures of other self-factors which control directionality. When such factors are uncovered and when they are effectively measured, then it should be possible to chart workable programs to prevent delinquency and to re-enforce the components of self which enable the youth to be an effective conformer.

Certainly, the authors' experience in Brooklyn indicates that it is necessary to use much more discriminating instruments than the ones they used and it could very well be that much more sensitive instruments are needed to record differences in self-development among sixth-graders in high, medium, and low delinquency areas as well as white, colored, and Puerto Rican sixth-graders than among sixth-grade white and colored adolescents in different areas of Columbus and Akron, Ohio.

In the meantime, more faith can be placed in the sixth-grade teacher's evaluations or her assessments of the directionality of her male pupils. Sophisticated studies could be made of the predictive efficacy of her ratings. More use could be made of her ratings, say in May of each year after 35 weeks of daily contact, for designing preventive programs or attempting individualized corrective therapy. More sophisticated

effort should also be expended on attempting to develop improved measures of self-reported delinquency.

One of the most difficult tasks would be to follow a large stratified sample of children who were evaluated at the first-grade level by the Gluecks' family-factor prediction instrument, to obtain teacher's prognostication, a self-reported delinquency measure, and an assessment of self-concept at the sixth-grade level, and to make an official delinquency clearance on each youth in the sample at 18 years of age, no matter how many times he may have changed residence.

36.

LEON F. FANNIN AND MARSHALL B. CLINARD

DIFFERENCES IN THE CONCEPTION OF SELF AS A MALE AMONG LOWER AND MIDDLE CLASS DELINQUENTS

This study investigated differences between lower and lower-middle class white delinquents in conception of self as a male, and behavioral correlates of such differences.

Despite the theoretical importance of self-conception from the symbolic interactionist viewpoint, attempts by sociologists to exploit it in empirical research have been comparatively limited.[1] Probable reasons for this include the theoretical complexity of the concept and the consequent difficulty in formulating operational procedures.[2] Thus, conception of self is difficult to

SOURCE: Leon F. Fannin and Marshall B. Clinard, "Differences in the Conception of Self as a Male Among Lower and Middle Class Delinquents," *Social Problems* 13, no. 2 (Fall, 1965): 205–14. Reprinted by Permission of the authors and The Society for the Study of Social Problems.

The authors would like to acknowledge their thanks to the Ford Foundation for a Small Research Grant which made this study possible.

[1]Some of the studies that have focused upon the self include Marsh Ray, "The Cycle of Abstinence and Relapse among Heroin Addicts," *Social Problems* 9 (1961): 132–40; Frank R. Scarpitti, Ellen Murray, Simon Dinitz, and Walter C. Reckless, "The 'Good' Boy in a High Delinquency Area: Four Years Later," *American Sociological Review* 25 (1960): 555–58; John W. Kinch, "Self-Conceptions of Types of Delinquents," *Sociological In-*

quiry 32 (Spring, 1962): 228–34. Much of the theoretical and empirical work dealing with self-conception during the last 15 years has been in the area of clinical psychology, with a strong emphasis usually upon the discrepancy between self and ideal self as an index of adjustment. See, for example, Victor C. Raimy, "Self Reference in Counseling Interviews," *Journal of Consulting Psychology* 12 (1948): 153–63; Rosalind F. Dymond, "Adjustment Changes over Therapy from Self-Sorts," in *Psychotherapy and Personality Change,* ed. Carl R. Rogers and Rosalind F. Dymond (Chicago: University of Chicago Press, 1954), pp. 76–84; Renate G. Armstrong, William O. Hambacher, and James F. Overley, "Self Concepts of Psychiatric and Normal Subjects as Revealed by the Way Test," *Journal of Clinical Psychology* 18 (1962): 271–76.

[2]Thus, the "social self" is considered by various writers to include not only self-conceptions, but a number of "elementary selves," conscious and unconscious evaluation of behavior through role taking, consequent feelings of gratification or mortification, stabilized and unstabilized internalized "others" as standards, and a built-in component of indeterminacy, the "I." In addition, all these are in a state
(Footnote Continued)

utilize partly because an individual has many self-conceptions, not simply one, which undergo modifications through time. A person conceives of himself, for example, as a male, with certain descriptive traits attached to this conception, but also as a son, an engineer, attractive, criminal, likable, and so on.

Some self-conceptions may have greater importance than others because they are more generalized and thus function in a wider variety of social actions. Self-conceptions related to many occupational roles, such as those ascribed to the military elite, high level business executives, or confidence men, would appear to be of this nature.[3]

Another such generalized self-conception, and the subject of this study, is that attached to sex status. Indeed, of all self-conceptions this may be one of the most decisive, as there are relatively few actions in which the participants conceive of themselves as sexless, or are so conceived by others. A "proper" sex self-conception may thus sharply limit approved behavioral alternatives.

The present study focused upon possible differences in the degree to which certain "masculine" traits were held by delinquents from the lower and middle classes. That male self-conceptions may vary by social strata, and be related to behavioral differences, is suggested by a number of studies, particularly those of Miller, Cohen, and Wolfgang, despite some contradic-

tory results.[4] It seemed reasonable to hypothesize that: (1) lower class males would conceive of themselves as tougher, harder, more powerful, and dangerous, and place greater value upon physical prowess and aggression than middle class males; consequently, (2) they probably would be involved more often in physically violent offenses, and define and act with less verbal sophistication and dexterity, but more physical aggression, in dating and sexual behavior.

RESEARCH PROCEDURES

Characteristics of the Samples. Data to test these hypotheses were collected from random samples of lower and lower-middle class white delinquents committed to a training school in a mid-western state. All boys present at the school during the summer of 1962 who were 16 or 17 years old, and who had resided in urban areas of at least 300,000 population, were given a class rank on the basis of their fathers' or guardians' levels of occupation and education. The distribution of these ranks was then differentiated into lower, working, and lower-middle class levels.

Delinquents from the working class were eliminated to obtain class levels as disparate as possible. Class levels higher than the lower-

of flux, as the self is a process, not a static entity. See George H. Mead in *Mind, Self, and Society,* ed. C. W. Morris (Chicago: University of Chicago Press, 1934), pp. 47, 68–69, 136–38, 142–44, 154, 178; Anselm L. Strauss, *Mirrors and Masks* (New York: The Free Press, 1959), pp. 49ff.; Tamotsu Shibutani, *Society and Personality* (Englewood Cliffs, N.J.: Prentice-Hall, Inc., 1961), pp. 214–36; and S. Frank Miyamota and Sanford M. Dornbusch, "A Test of Interactionist Hypotheses of Self-Conception," *American Journal of Sociology* 61 (1956); 399–403.

[3] See Morris Janowitz, *The Professional Soldier* (New York: The Free Press, 1960), pp. 228–29; Charles H. Coates and Roland J. Pellegrin, "Executives and Supervisors: Contrasting Self-Conceptions and Conceptions of Each Other," *American Sociological Review* 22 (1957): 217–20; Peter F. Merenda and Walter V. Clarke, "Influence of College Experience on the Self-Concepts of Young Male Job Applicants," *Journal of Psychological Studies* 12 (1961): 49–60.

[4] See Walter B. Miller, "Lower Class Culture as a Generating Milieu of Gang Delinquency," *Journal of Social Issues* 14 (1958): 5–19; Albert K. Cohen, *Delinquent Boys* (New York: The Free Press, 1955), pp. 24–32; Albert K. Cohen and James F. Short, Jr., "Juvenile Delinquency," in *Contemporary Social Problems,* ed. Robert K. Merton and Robert A. Nisbet (New York: Harcourt, Brace, & World, Inc., 1961), pp. 77–126; Marvin E. Wolfgang, *Patterns in Criminal Homicide* (Philadelphia: University of Pennsylvania Press, 1958), pp. 188–89; also see Leon F. Fannin, "A Study of the Social Class Affiliation and Societal Reaction to Convicted Sex and Non-Sex Offenders" (Ph.D. diss., University of Wisconsin, 1962), pp. 169–71, 178–79. For a broader perspective concerning the possible relationship between self-conception and stratification, see G. Morris Carstairs, *The Twice-Born: A Study of a Community of High-Caste Hindus* (London: The Hogarth Press, 1961); Hugh H. Smythe, "The Eta: A Marginal Japanese Caste," *American Journal of Sociology* 58 (1952): 194–96. On the basis of such data, it might by hypothesized that the more discontinuous a stratification system, the more each stratum will generate disparate self-conceptions over a wide range of traits.

middle[5] were desired but only one boy represented a higher level. The lower and middle classes were treated as separate statistical populations, and 25 cases were randomly selected from each; the sampling fractions were 23.4% and 75.8%, respectively. The limitations in using institutionalized cases and small samples were fully recognized.

Data Collection. Depth interviewing and self-conception scales elicited the most crucial information, with official records used to determine class affiliation and reported delinquent histories. The interviews were structured, although the respondents were unaware of it, and it was believed a high degree of rapport was attained with most of the boys.

Operationally, self-conception as a male was defined by the relative intensity of specific traits which the delinquents felt characterized them when they were placed, verbally, in varying situations that made them explicitly aware of their sex status. Their responses to these situations were then elicited through intensive probing by open-ended questions and by forced-choice scales.

These scales were constructed on the basis of a technique developed by Bennett,[6] whereby the respondent selects traits, three at a time from a list of 15 until none remain, which are ranked "most" or "least" descriptive of himself, or of others, or of situations, and so on. The trait lists provided by Bennett were not used as such because they would not have elicited enough of the type of information desired; rather, four new lists were developed (see Tables 4–5 and 4–6 below). Lists I and II contained a majority of traits believed to be positively evaluated by American males while Lists III and IV contained a majority of traits negatively evaluated.

Each list of 15 traits was administered three times, with the situation under which the respondents selected traits varied each time. They were asked to rank the traits contained in each list according to: (1) how they felt the traits

actually described them as males (actual, or perceived, self); (2) how they *would like* to be as males (ideal self); and (3) how they felt *other people in general* believed them to be as males (generalized looking-glass self). These selections were scored from zero to four points for each trait, so that those which the boys felt described them most closely had the highest values.

SELF-CONCEPTIONS AND SOCIAL CLASS

The findings indicate that while the male self-conception is very similar across class lines, there are a few crucial differences which apparently are related to a diverse range of behavior patterns.

A partial test of the first hypothesis, stating in the null form that *there is no significant difference in the conception of self as a male held by lower and middle class delinquents,* is provided by analysis of the delinquents' responses to the Trait Lists (see Tables 4–5 and 4–6). Almost one-third (32.2%) of the means calculated from Lists I and II and over one-fifth (22.2%) of the means from Lists III and IV are significantly different by class ($p < .05$), and since these differences are largely in the expected direction, the null hypothesis is tentatively rejected.

Tough Guys and Loyal Comrades. Lower class boys felt themselves to be (actual self) tougher, more powerful, fierce, fearless, and dangerous than middle class boys. It was unexpected, however, that they did not feel themselves to be significantly more violent, hard, and pugilistic. Middle class delinquents, on the other hand, conceived of themselves as being more loyal, clever, smart, smooth, and bad. This greater stress upon loyalty by the middle class is surprising,[7] even though the lower class also ranked it very high.

When responses depicting the ideal self and the generalized looking-glass self are studied, essentially the same traits separate the class levels, with some interesting exceptions. The lower class would like to be (ideal self) tougher, harder, and more violent than the middle class, while the latter would like to be more loyal,

[5]To avoid repetition, lower-middle class will be referred to hereafter as middle class.

[6]Edward Bennett, *Personality Assessment and Diagnosis* (New York: The Ronald Press Company, 1961), pp. v, 69–80, 173–87, 253–70.

[7]Miller, op. cit.

TABLE 4-5.

Social Class Comparison of Item Means from Trait Lists I and II for Actual, Ideal, and Generalized Looking-Glass Selves

Trait Lists	Actual Self		Ideal Self		Generalized Looking-Glass Self	
	Lower Class	Middle Class	Lower Class	Middle Class	Lower Class	Middle Class
List I						
Fearless	1.89*	1.52*	1.37	1.81	1.74	2.00
Loyal	3.05*	3.71*	2.63*	3.71*	2.21*	3.16*
Brave	2.58	2.49	2.79	2.76	3.00	3.00
Strong	2.26	2.33	2.47	2.62	2.37	2.21
Active	2.79	3.29	2.64	2.71	2.16	2.89
Tough	1.88*	1.45*	1.63*	.91*	1.74	1.79
Athletic	2.47	2.52	3.05	2.90	2.18	2.42
Hard	1.42	1.29	1.47*	1.05*	1.88*	1.42*
Reckless	1.11	1.00	.84	.71	1.00	1.05
Courageous	2.59	2.90	3.05	3.19	2.89	3.05
Loud	1.40	1.24	1.16	1.00	1.68*	.89*
Powerful	2.04*	1.50*	1.90	1.91	2.42*	1.63*
Rough	1.68	1.14	1.05	1.24	1.21	1.60
Smart	1.89*	2.86*	3.00	3.19	2.20	2.42
Violent	.95	.76	.95*	.29*	1.32*	.47*
List II						
Clever	1.95*	2.95*	3.00	2.38	2.53	2.89
Cruel	1.21	.95	.89	1.05	1.42*	.63*
Lucky	2.32	2.05	2.89*	3.62*	2.47	2.63
Fierce	2.58*	1.05*	1.95	1.67	1.47	1.42
Bad	1.14*	1.57*	.84	1.05	1.32*	1.74*
Wild	1.05	1.19	1.16	.81	1.53	1.21
Proud	3.11	3.71	3.47*	3.06*	2.74*	3.21*
Dangerous	1.11*	.57*	.95	.67	.54*	1.00*
Bold	2.21	2.24	2.21	2.14	2.37*	1.74*
Firm	2.16	2.52	2.79*	3.14*	2.42	2.78
Shrewd	2.11	2.05	1.42	1.76	1.88*	1.69*
Cunning	2.79	2.14	1.95	1.90	2.00	1.74
Stern	2.32	2.81	2.74	2.71	2.68	2.26
Smooth	2.26*	2.72*	2.53	2.71	2.79*	2.63*
Fighter	1.68	1.48	1.21	1.33	1.84*	2.53*

*Differences between means for lower and middle classes are significant at the .05 level (Student's test). The range for any mean is 0 to 4.

TABLE 4-6.

Social Class Comparison of Item Means from Trait Lists III and IV for Actual, Ideal, and Generalized Looking-Glass Selves

Trait Lists	Actual Self		Ideal Self		Generalized Looking-Glass Self	
	Lower Class	Middle Class	Lower Class	Middle Class	Lower Class	Middle Class
List III						
Proper	1.63	1.33	1.69	1.48	1.42	1.32
Loving	2.26	2.43	2.74	3.00	1.75*	2.63*
Graceful	1.58	1.24	2.00	1.95	1.92	1.42
Modest	1.58	1.57	1.89*	.95*	1.69	1.47
Respectable	2.63	2.43	3.00*	3.62*	2.63	2.37
Shy	1.74	2.10	.53	.19	1.42	1.16
Sympathetic	1.53*	2.57*	1.32	1.81	1.79	2.21
Gentle	1.95	1.86	2.68*	2.02*	2.11	2.26
Courteous	2.26	2.10	2.05	2.33	2.42	2.32
Peaceful	2.68	2.43	2.58	2.51	2.37	2.58
Friendly	2.84*	3.52*	3.05	3.10	3.16	3.68
Soft	.96	.86	1.05	.67	1.21	.74
Neat	2.78*	2.14*	2.57*	3.05*	2.68	2.89
Affectionate	2.05	2.14	1.53*	2.05*	1.69	1.95
Tender	1.53	1.28	1.32	1.27	1.74*	1.00*
List IV						
False	.95	.71	.79	.71	1.32*	.68*
Kind	2.89*	3.33*	3.21	3.29	3.32	3.37
Sweet	1.79	1.88	2.53	2.68	2.32	2.78
Upright	2.32	2.71	2.78	2.95	2.21	2.37
Sensitive	2.74	2.62	2.37*	2.52	2.11*	2.78*
Feeble	.63	.62	.37*	.85*	1.11*	.47*
Delicate	1.84	1.52	1.84	1.95	1.85	1.53
Helpless	1.17	1.14	.89	.76	1.44*	.89*
Safe	2.89	2.81	2.68	3.05	2.68	3.07
Timid	1.89	1.95	1.79	1.62	1.89	1.58
Afraid	1.37	1.71	1.11	1.14	.95	1.32
Fearful	1.84	1.62	2.11*	1.23*	2.32	2.21
Quiet	3.68	3.10	3.21	2.97	3.11	2.84
Loved	2.58*	3.33*	3.74	3.66	2.32*	3.11*
Weak	1.42*	.95*	.58	.62	1.05	1.00

*Differences between means for lower and middle classes are significant at the .05 level (Student's test). The range for any mean is 0 to 4.

lucky, and firm. When their interpretations of how other people in general view them are analyzed (generalized looking-glass self), approximately the same findings hold, except that the middle class felt others believed them to be more dangerous, bad, and pugilistic. It would seem to be quite clear that the norms from which these delinquents believed others evaluated them were sharply different, because the lower class had been actually involved in more assaults, robberies, fights, and other delinquencies (see below) than the middle class and yet the latter felt others believed them to be more "dangerous" and "bad."

The more negatively connoted traits used in Lists III and IV were far less discriminatory except for a sharp difference in responses to "love" and related traits. Middle class boys felt they were loved to a significantly greater degree and felt others also believed them to be more loving. In addition, they conceived of themselves as being more friendly, sympathetic, and kind.

These differences were strongly supported and supplemented by the results gained from informal interviewing. While discussing the type of "reputation" desired among their closest male friends, and among females and police, lower class boys stressed their ability and willingness to fight, their physical power over others, and their fear of nothing. These traits appear to be similar to those ascribed by Sykes to prison inmates who attempt to prove their masculinity to others and to themselves, in a one-sexed community, by over-emphasizing such "masculine" traits.[8] Middle class boys, on the other hand, stressed loyalty to friends above all, their desire to be clever and smooth, and also to be daring.

An additional trait which appeared to more adequately characterize the lower class boys was a greater degree of callousness in their relations with others, particularly in regard to "enemies" (which may reflect a relative lack of propathic role taking). This trait was perhaps clearer in their relations with homosexuals and adolescent females.

While exciting exploits and incredulous adventures were highly evaluated by members of both class levels, it appeared that middle class boys conceived of themselves as more daring. They liked to take risks and regale others with their fascinating tales. Some of the adventures they told during the interviews were injected with much the same drama they had probably seen in movies and on television, particularly when they viewed themselves as "desperate heroes."

From an over-all perspective, then, it would appear these classes differ chiefly in that significantly more lower class delinquents feel themselves to be "tough guys," while more middle class delinquents feel themselves to be "loyal and daring comrades."

These class differences cannot be explained by differential membership in gangs, where a stress upon toughness would be expected, as an almost identical proportion participated in gangs, namely 84% of the lower and 80% of the middle class ($p > .70$).

The degree to which these boys conceived of themselves as tough guys, however, varied within the class levels. Briefly, the range of such conceptions appeared to run typologically from the "bruising marauder" to the "fearful warrior." The former is a boy who is constantly proving his toughness by fighting unrelentingly at the slightest provocation, or who initiates brawls because he "likes to fight." His perception of ridicule, or the merest hint of disbelief about his masculinity, is extremely acute and he will settle the matter immediately by force. He is looked upon with respectful apprehension by his peers as a "nut," "crazy bastard," "a real goner," and as "dangerous" because he is always stirring up trouble; he is, in short, a disliked deviant.

The fearful or reluctant warrior is a "brittle tough guy" who does not like fighting or physical violence but considers himself at least minimally "tough." This self-conception is to a large extent defensive[9] and could probably be changed comparatively easily if he were placed in social situations other than the tough world in which he lives.

---

[8]Gresham M. Sykes. *The Society of Captives* (Princeton, N.J.: Princeton University Press, 1958).

[9]The functions of the "tough guy" self-conception need thorough study if only because there are probably others in addition to status acquisition-retention and defense.

SELF-CONCEPTIONS RELATED
TO BEHAVIOR

It had been hypothesized that if these differences in self-conceptions by class had meaning, this would probably be reflected in behavioral differences, such as frequency of physical violence, occupational aspiration, and attitudes toward sexuality. To a large extent these expectations were fulfilled. Six statistical tests were made and five allowed rejection of the null hypothesis.

Physical Violence. One of the more important of the tests was a comparison of the frequency with which reported and unreported robberies and assaults were committed by members of the two class levels. The vast majority of all lower class delinquents, 84%, had committed at least one such offense compared to 28% of the middle class (p < .01); 28% of the lower and 8% of the middle class had committed 10 or more violent offenses.

Class level was also related to the frequency of fighting with other boys. Lower class delinquents fought singly and in groups significantly more often (p < .05) than middle class delinquents, with 20% of them averaging five or more fights per month compared to 4.0%. The possibly greater lack of propathic role taking characteristic of lower class boys also appeared in their techniques of fighting. More of them used weapons, and more advocated "stomping" (kicking a fallen opponent, particularly in the face). As one very "tough guy" answered when questioned about the frequency and circumstances under which stomping should be used: "Always! You're a sucker if you don't because the other guy would sure as hell do it to you. I always try to kick the guy's teeth out myself, but anywhere's good."

Lower class boys also regularly carried weapons on their persons significantly more often than middle class boys (p < .02); 80% usually carried a knife, gun, or "knuckles," compared to 48% of the middle class. The most frequent reason given for having a weapon close at hand was self protection.

One factor which ran counter to expectations was the similarity in the frequency of forcible rape committed by boys of both classes (p >

.05); the proportions having done this were 12% in the lower and 16% in the middle classes, but differences in class definitions of "rape" may have been an important obscuring variable.

Occupational Aspirations. While occupational aspirations are influenced by a wide variety of factors, it was anticipated that one which might help to explain the different aspirations of the lower class would be their orientation toward certain categories of work as related to their male self-conceptions.

Eighty per cent of the lower class boys wanted a type of adult occupation in which they could work with their hands, while only 36% of the middle class desired this (p < .01). Some of the reasons given for these lower aspirations were that it was a "real man's" type of work while a desk job was somewhat effeminate; it was "better" for a man to work with his hands; you had to "have something on the ball" to work with machines while anyone could work at a desk job; and white collar work was in some sense "cheating" because it was *not really work.* Finally, an occupational role of greater attraction for lower class boys was that of the combat infantryman, or even better, the "fighting marine."

Sexuality. Masculinity was also expressed differently by members of the two class levels in their orientation and behavior toward adolescent females.[10] Toughness, callousness, and physical prowess appeared to be dominant for the lower class, while sophistication, dexterity, and verbal manipulation seemed prominent for the middle class.

Dating was viewed by the lower class, for example, primarily as the *means* to an end (sexual intercourse) while the middle class stressed dating as an *end* in itself (the fun element in going out). Sixty-eight per cent of the lower

---

[10]See Clark E. Vincent, "Ego Involvement in Sexual Relations: Implications for Research on Illegitimacy," *American Journal of Sociology* 65 (November, 1959): 287–95. It has also been suggested that attitudes of females toward premarital sex relations are related to class: see Eugene J. Kamin and David H. Howard, "Postmarital Consequences of Premarital Sex Adjustment," *American Sociological Review* 23 (October, 1958): 556–62, and J. C. Ball and N. Logan, "Early Sexual Behavior of Lower-Class Delinquent Girls," *Journal of Criminal Law, Criminology and Police Science* 51 (1960): 209–15.

class boys believed intercourse was the normal goal in dating a girl, while 40% of the middle class felt this way ($p < .05$).

For the lower class boy, sexual intercourse was to be achieved by the raw force of his masculinity; he would not "seduce" his date so much as he would "conquer" her. The aura of his maleness should be enough for the girl, without stopping to demean himself by clever, witty, and manipulative verbal "propaganda." The female should surrender herself to this image of the "all man" rather than be converted to willingness by gentle and smoothly coined phrases. The latter approach to the lower class is sissified. In short, when attempting to gain sexual intercourse, the lower class boy more often viewed himself as a "rough and manly conqueror" while the middle class boy thought of himself more often as a "slick seducer."

Similarly, the "teaser" as a female type was evaluated differently by members of the two class levels.[11] To lower class boys, she more often represented unmitigated and unforgivable viciousness and deserved "anything her date would do to her," including a beating. To middle class boys she was scorned and considered indecent for "leading a guy on like that" but should not be "slapped around." At most she probably should be "dumped out of the car and made to walk home."

DISCUSSION

A number of implications emerged from this study's findings, although the small size of the samples and the relative primitiveness of the procedures used to elicit self-conception data must be kept in mind. The data suggest that a significant proportion of offenses involving physical violence may be committed by delinquents who stress certain "masculine" traits in their self-conceptions as males, which help channel and legitimize such violence. Self-conception

may act as a closure factor,[12] restricting the possibilities of behavior to a narrowed universe. In terms of rehabilitating violent offenders, consequently, it would seem feasible that a highly selective program directed toward the limited ends of changing this aspect of the self-conception might prove more helpful than a global effort at pervasive personality change, or other current techniques. It cannot be inferred, obviously, that all deviant aggression by males can be explained by this type of self-conception,[13] as the latter may result from behavior, but it may help to explain a portion of it.

Another implication of the findings is that this tough guy self-conception may be related to a wide range of other types of behavior, deviant and nondeviant, including drinking patterns, leisure habits, divorce and desertion, illegitimacy, and so on. This needs intensive investigation, as do other types of self-conceptions.

Finally, empirically oriented analyses of the components of social interaction may help to better understand deviant and nondeviant behavior; this refers not only to further studies of the types and interrelation of self-conceptions, but also to analyses of the various aspects of role taking, the relationship between role taking and role playing, the internalization of significant and generalized others and their specific influence upon behavior, and the complex interrelationships of these factors within the "social self."

SUMMARY

The conception of self as a male held by lower and lower-middle class delinquents was probed by informal depth interviewing and by forced-choice scales. While self-conceptions were found to be quite similar, lower class boys did conceive of themselves as being tougher, more fearless,

---

[11]Other types of female roles which these delinquents recognized, however, were much the same across class lines, and similar to those described by: William Foote Whyte, "A Slum Sex Code," *American Journal of Sociology* 49 (July, 1943): 24–31.

[12]Edwin M. Lemert, "An Isolation and Closure Theory of Naive Check Forgery," *Journal of Criminal Law, Criminology and Police Science* 44 (1953): 296–307.

[13]Richard R. Korn and Lloyd W. McCorkle, *Criminology and Penology* (New York: Holt, Rinehart & Winston, Inc., 1959), pp. 336–39; John Paul Scott, *Aggression* (Chicago: University of Chicago Press, 1958), pp. viii, 5–6; Arnold H. Buss, *The Psychology of Aggression* (New York: John Wiley and Sons, Inc., 1961), p. 28.

powerful, fierce, and dangerous, while middle class boys felt they were more clever, smart, smooth, bad, and loyal. Descriptively, these were labeled as "tough guy" and "loyal and daring comrade" self-conceptions.

These self-conceptions were then found to be related to specific types of behavior. The "tough guys" significantly more often committed violent offenses, fought more often and with harsher means, carried weapons, had lower occupational aspirations, and stressed toughness and related traits in the reputation they desired and in sexual behavior.

Rehabilitative and preventive efforts to decrease violent offenses might be more profitable if focused upon this aspect of the offender's social self. The possible relation of the tough guy self-conception, and other types of self-conceptions, to varying types of behavior was also pointed out.

37.

JAMES E. TEELE, MAXWELL J. SCHLEIFER, LOUISE CORMAN
AND KARIN LARSON

TEACHER RATINGS, SOCIOMETRIC STATUS, AND CHOICE-RECIPROCITY OF ANTI-SOCIAL AND NORMAL BOYS

Although the literature reflects great interest in the sociometric study of school children, studies documenting the relationship of sociometrically-determined status to teacher rankings of students, with the latter based on perceived peer popularity, are scarce.[1] Of studies subsequent to the pioneering work of Moreno relating peer and teacher ratings, those of Gronlund and of Bonney are outstanding.[2] Moreno found that the accuracy of teachers' judgments was highest in the kindergarten and declined as grade level increased.[3] Bonney and Gronlund both concluded from their findings that teachers overrate the students who exhibit adult-desired personality traits and underrate those who, although possessors of interpersonal skills, are not responsive in class and, indeed, may even appear to be anti-social. The stability of these findings, however, is questionable, since Moreno's study group was limited to the first eight grades, Bonney's to high school grades, and Gronlund's principal study to sixth grade classes.

The present paper reports on a partial replication of the studies by Moreno and Bonney. At least two features apparently unique to the

SOURCE: James E. Teele et al, "Teacher Ratings, Sociometric Status, and Choice-Reciprocity of Anti-Social and Normal Boys."

From *Group Psychotherapy* Vol. XIX, 1966, No. 3–4, J. L. Moreno, M.D. Editor, Beacon House Inc. Publisher. Permission granted by publisher and authors.

The research on which this study is based is sponsored by the Judge Baker Guidance Center, in cooperation with the Newton Public Schools, and is supported by the National Institute of Mental Health, Grant 5-R11-MH 00811-04. We are grateful to C. N. Alexander and E. F. Borgatta for their valuable comments on an earlier version of this paper.

[1] Jacob L. Moreno, of course, presented data on this relationship. See *Who Shall Survive* (Washington, D.C.: Nervous and Mental Disease Publishing Co., 1934).

[2] See Norman E. Gronlund, *The Accuracy of Teachers' Judgments Concerning the Sociometric Status of Sixth Grade Pupils*, Sociometry Monograph No. 25 (New York: Beacon House, 1951); and Merl E. Bonney, "Sociometric Study of Agreement between Teacher Judgments and Student Choices," *Sociometry* 10 (May, 1947): 133–46.

[3] Moreno, op. cit., p. 134.

study reported on here are: (1) grades 2 through 11 are covered and (2) some known anti-social boys are included in the study group. This last feature is of considerable importance, since teachers are being increasingly employed in screening procedures aimed at the early identification of problem children.[4] To our knowledge this is the only published sociometric study which has taken place in classrooms containing boys who have been previously identified by psychiatric personnel as anti-social. Thus, this study permits such operations as the following: (1) a comparison of the teacher assessments of the anti-social and of the normal boys; (2) a comparison of the sociometric peer assessment of anti-social boys and of boys not so identified; (3) an analysis of teacher-peer agreement on assessments of anti-social and normal boys; (4) a comparison of choice reciprocity in anti-social and normal boys.

METHOD

The screening on which this study is based took place in Newton, Massachusetts, in 1963. Among the participating schools, all boys 9 to 16 years of age and showing anti-social problems in school were named by teachers. A total of 450 boys were identified by the teachers who completed questionnaires on these boys. Based on a careful examination of the questionnaires as well as the boy's school records, the psychiatrists on our project rated the boys according to whether or not their behavior approximated the description of the diagnostic category: anti-social character disorder. In this paper, those whom the psychiatrists felt most closely fit this category are referred to simply as "strongly anti-social," and those not fitting this category are referred to as "moderately anti-social." We have done so since the records of these boys show them to have committed many anti-social acts, with the "strongly anti-social" having more records.[5]

A total of 103 boys were judged to be "strongly anti-social." The classroom (grade schools) or home room (junior and senior high schools) of each of the 103 "strongly anti-social" boys was identified in January, 1964, and in each of the 70 rooms involved the sociometric questionnaire was distributed by teachers and completed by all students present.[6] Altogether, 1,944 sociometric questionnaires were completed. Of the "strongly anti-social" boys, 84 completed the sociometric test. The 19 "strongly anti-social" boys who did not take this test break down as follows: eight boys had transferred to schools outside of the study area, six had dropped out of school, three were in detention, one had moved out of town, and one refused to complete the form. Within the original teacher-identified group of 450 boys, this left 347 boys who were rated as being only "moderately anti-social"; of these, 139 were located within the classrooms in which the "strongly anti-social" boys were located. Thus, 223 of the 1,088 boys who took this test were rated as either "strongly" or "moderately anti-social;" the rest of the boys in these classrooms had not been referred as having anti-social problems, and will be treated here as our group of normal boys.

In addition, teachers were asked to complete a questionnaire designed to obtain their perception of peer popularity ratings. Only the extremes (popular and unpopular choices) were utilized in some of the analyses to be presented. The majority of the classes had only one "strongly anti-social" boy present and no class contained more than two of such boys.

There are a couple of qualifications which

---

[4]For example, see B. B. Khleif, "Teachers as Predictors of Juvenile Delinquency and Psychiatric Disturbance," *Social Problems* 11 (Winter, 1964): 270–82.

[5]For a description of the screening procedures used in the identification process, see James E. Teele and David Ricks, "Newton-Baker Project:

The Selection Phase of a Clinically-Oriented Field Experiment," (paper presented at the 1964 meetings of the American Orthopsychiatric Association, Chicago).

[6]Among other requests, grade school children were asked to list the five boys in class (or girls, depending on the respondent's sex) whom they would "prefer to be sitting close to," while secondary school children were asked to list their five closest friends in the classroom (sex specific). Teachers were asked to name three boys and three girls who were popular, as well as the three boys and three girls who were unpopular.

We are indebted to Mr. John Cullinane, formerly employed at the Division of Pupil Personnel Services and Special Education, Newton Public Schools, for his valuable assistance in the administration of the sociometric questionnaires in 1964.

should be kept in mind when contemplating the findings: (1) the teachers' questions were double-barreled, i.e., they were asked to name students who were either "popular and helpful" or "unpopular and disruptive."[7] (2) the teachers' perceptions of peer popularity are necessarily limited by what they can observe in the classroom and this undoubtedly limits their ability to assess peer popularity.

FINDINGS

The first task undertaken was an assessment of the relationship between teachers' and peers' ratings on popularity. As suggested, this analysis partially replicates the work of Moreno and Bonney. Results shown in Tables 4–7 and 4–8 apparently resemble those of Moreno for those grades included in both studies (Grades 2 through 8). That is, the higher the grade, the lower the magnitude of the relationship. However, with the exception of grade 5, there is an increase in the number of children involved as grades elevate—the result being that each of the coefficients shown in Table 4–7 for grades compared with Moreno is significant beyond the .01 level, two-tailed tests. Since Moreno did not indicate the number of children within each of his grade breaks, his results are not comparable with the present results in terms of levels of significance. On the basis of the present results, then, no firm differences by grade level with regard to agreement between teachers and peer ratings exist, with the exception of the agreement involving eleventh grade boys.

Results of cross-tabular analyses (Table 4–8) permit comparison with Bonney's work. Bonney found that teachers were most accurate with respect to students who were most popular on peer ratings. The present data not only are consistent with Bonney's findings but tend to confirm and extend his findings to the elementary school grades. Besides the amazing overall consistency for boys and girls on teacher agreements, these proportions support Bonney's finding that teachers were more accurate for those students in the high and middle groups on popularity (45%) than for those low on popularity (28%) although it should be kept in mind that Bonney's study group was restricted to high school students.[8] Still, when the analysis of the present study data was restricted to our three senior grades, it was found that teachers were more accurate for the most popular students. Perhaps one reason the present proportions are lower than Bonney's is that teachers were asked, as we indicated earlier, to name both students who were "popular and helpful" and those who were "unpopular and disruptive."

TABLE 4–7

AGREEMENT BETWEEN TEACHERS' AND PEER POPULARITY RATINGS BY GRADES (N = 1017)[a]

Grades	N	r
Grades 2 & 3		
Boys	27	+ .54*
Girls	29	+ .54*
Grade 4		
Boys	38	+ .45*
Girls	31	+ .58*
Grade 5		
Boys	32	+ .66*
Girls	35	+ .52*
Grade 6		
Boys	59	+ .53*
Girls	54	+ .39*
Grades 7 & 8		
Boys	149	+ .25*
Girls	167	+ .24*
Grades 9 & 10		
Boys	183	+ .30*
Girls	147	+ .21*
Grade 11		
Boys	37	+ .24
Girls	29	+ .59*

*$P < 01$, two-tailed test.

[a] Sociometric choices were summed and the three boys and three girls receiving the highest numbers of choices were rated as *most* popular and the three boys and three girls receiving the least numbers of choices were rated as *least* popular. Tied ranks were included. The residual children, that is those who were neither least nor most chosen comprised the *middle* group but were not employed in the present table nor in Table 4-8 although they were included in the analysis presented for Table 4-10. For purposes of the presentation, teacher ratings were restricted to those made for *peer least and most popular* with the teacher ratings grouped into "unpopular," "popular," and "no mention" categories.

---

[7] We did this because of the presence of antisocial boys in these classes, although the phrasing was ambiguous. In subsequent years (1965 and 1966), we altered these procedures slightly, and kept the two dimensions of popularity and helpfulness separate. These data are being analyzed at present, and findings spanning the three years will be presented later.

[8] Bonney, op. cit.

TABLE 4–8.

AGREEMENT BETWEEN TEACHERS' JUDGMENTS (IN PROPORTIONS) AND PEER SOCIOMETRIC CHOICES BY GRADE
(N = 1017)

Grade	Proportion of Least Popular Rated Unpopular by Teachers				Proportion of Most Popular Rated as Popular by Teachers			
	Boys	100% =	Girls	100% =	Boys	100% =	Girls	100% =
2+3	43%	14	47%	15	54%	13	50%	14
4	47%	19	46%	13	42%	19	33%	18
5	29%	17	31%	16	60%	15	37%	19
6	31%	32	32%	25	52%	27	42%	29
7+8	23%	77	18%	89	29%	72	37%	78
9+10	11%	100	7%	69	23%	83	26%	78
11	37%	19	31%	13	39%	18	44%	16
				Total Agreement				
All Grades	24%	278	21%	240	34%	247	35%	252

At this point we undertook the analysis of the relationship between the prior school behavior (clinicians' ratings) and subsequent teacher ratings. Results of this analysis show that there is a firm relationship between the boys' prior behavior and the current teacher assessments (Table 4–9). The magnitude of this relationship is remarkably similar for both elementary school (r = .30) and junior and senior high school boys (r = .27) though the percentages reveal a sharper relationship for the grade school boys. Thus, 61 per cent of the grade school boys previously identified as strongly anti-social were reported to be unpopular with peers and disruptive in class by subsequent teachers as against 45 per cent for their high school counterparts. The most striking thing about these data is that of the total number of 84 boys—grade and high school combined—only one was reported as being "popular and helpful." What makes this finding interesting is that the teachers involved in the sociometric study had not been informed as to the identities of the boys previously identified as "strongly anti-social."[9]

However, on the basis of the data shown in Table 4–9, the present procedures leave much to be desired with respect to teacher identification—a matter compounded perhaps of differing perceptions and evaluations, uneven knowledge, and differing classroom situations. Thus, for example, in the elementary schools, 10 of the 26 boys previously identified as strongly anti-social were not mentioned by current teachers. However, our records show that these boys still are functioning poorly and involved to a not inconsiderable degree in anti-social behavior. This suggests that the current teachers, in the cases of these 10 boys, had insufficient evidence regarding the extent of anti-social behavior outside the classroom.

Still another cause for concern might be the 35 grade school boys previously not mentioned as anti-social who were tagged by current teachers as unpopular and disruptive. This should be of less concern since the total number of "unpopular and disruptive" boys was artificially enlarged by the stipulation that each teacher name three such boys. However, the more pressing question is raised in the preceding paragraph where the issue is: Who gets identified for the second time?[10] Although the relationship is significant, it is not really very satisfactory when the goal is prediction.

[9]Although we do not omit the possibility that the teachers shared their impressions of some of the boys with each other, it is unlikely that our findings result from such sharing, since extensive precautions were taken by the project to keep the names of study group boys secret.

[10]We are following the school and community careers of all of the "strongly anti-social" boys and of a large number of the boys in the other two categories, and will attempt at a later date to more fully assess the identification power of the teacher ratings. Police contact data is being systematically collected, and will be useful in establishing the value of the screening procedures employed and of the sociometric data. Both the school data and teacher-peer assessments may prove to be valuable in the prediction of later police contacts.

TABLE 4–9.

PRIOR SCHOOL BEHAVIOR AND TEACHER RATINGS

	Grade School Boys (N = 322)						
	Teacher Ratings						
Prior School Behavior	Unpopular & Disruptive		Not Mentioned		Popular & Helpful		100% =
	N	%	N	%	N	%	
Strongly Anti-social	16	61.5	10	38.5	0	—	26
Moderately Anti-social	12	36.0	15	46.0	6	18.0	33
Not mentioned as Anti-social	35	13.0	169	64.0	60	23.0	263

r = 30, P < 001, two-tailed test

	Junior and Senior High School Boys (N = 766)						
Strongly Anti-social	26	44.8	31	53.5	1	1.7	58
Moderately Anti-social	20	18.9	79	74.5	7	6.6	106
Not mentioned as Anti-social	62	10.3	425	70.6	115	19.1	602

r = 27, P < 001, two-tailed test

Another vital question focused on in the present study was: what is the relationship between the prior rating on the anti-social measure and subsequent sociometric ranking? For peer choices, as for teacher ratings, the relationship is stronger for the elementary school boys (r = .21) than for the junior and senior high school boys (r = .14). Moreover, none of the grade schoolers previously identified as strongly anti-social were among the most chosen boys while eight (14%) of the 58 identified as strongly anti-social were among the most popular boys in the high schools.[11] Conversely, 72% and 50% of strongly anti-social grade schoolers and high school boys, respectively, were least chosen by their peers. Among the elementary school boys, although the magnitude of the correlation is higher for the relationship between teacher rating and prior behavior (Table 4–9) than for the one between peer choices and prior behavior (Table 4–10), the latter analysis reveals a more satisfying "fit" for the "strongly anti-social" group. Among the junior and senior high

school boys, the higher of the two correlations again involves the teachers. In this case, there is little to choose from between the peer and teacher ratings with respect to the characterization of the boys as unpopular, although the teachers appear to underestimate the popularity of the anti-social secondary school boys. This appears to be reasonable since adults were involved in both referral and identification in addition to the sociometric study while school peers were involved in only the latter step. That is, recalling Bonney's finding that teachers underrate students whose habits seem anti-social, adults identified the "strongly anti-social boys" to begin with, so in any re-identification effort it should be expected that adults would show higher agreement with the original screening results than would students.[12] The fact that the difference between teachers and peers in the re-identification effort is greater for secondary school boys suggests that the differences in attitudes held by students and teachers toward anti-social behavior widen as children move upward in age.[13] Other writers, of course, have addressed themselves to both the fact of the adolescent-adult estrangement and to the fact

---

[11] The fact that few of the "strongly anti-social" boys were popular with their peers is highly consistent with findings recently presented by James S. Coleman. Coleman emphasized that adolescents as a whole are not anti-social and, moreover, that the adolescent culture does not reward delinquency. See *The Adolescent Society* (New York: The Free Press, 1961).

[12] Bonney, op. cit.

[13] An alternative explanation for this slight difference in absolute magnitudes may be that the secondary school teachers have less time with particular students than do elementary school teachers.

TABLE 4–10.

PRIOR SCHOOL BEHAVIOR AND PEER RATINGS

	Grade Schools (N = 322)						
	Peer Ratings						
Prior School Behavior	*Least Chosen*		*Middle Group*		*Most Chosen*		*100%=*
	N	%	N	%	N	%	
Strongly Anti-social	19	72.0	7	28.0	—	—	26
Moderately Anti-social	12	36.4	12	36.4	9	27.3	33
Not mentioned as Anti-social	52	19.7	147	55.7	65	24.6	263

r = 21, P < 001, two-tailed test

Junior and Senior High School Boys   (N = 766)

Strongly Anti-social	29	50.0	21	36.2	8	13.8	58
Moderately Anti-social	34	32.1	55	51.9	17	16.0	106
Not mentioned as Anti-social	136	22.6	317	52.6	149	24.8	602

r = 14, P < 001, two-tailed test

that the estrangement seems greater today than in past times.[14]

In the present study, this adolescent-adult estrangement is graphically attested to by the data shown in Table 4–11. The data there show the results of an analysis of the *pattern of agreement* between teachers and peers for each of the three categories of prior behavior: strongly antisocial, moderate anti-social, and not mentioned as anti-social. In every case, the area of disagreement is greater within the secondary schools than in the elementary schools. Moreover, the extent of the disagreement is largest with respect to the anti-social boys (strongly and moderately) in the secondary schools.

It is also observable in Table 4–11 that grade school peer boys and teachers "confirmed" that 44.4 per cent of the "strongly anti-social" boys were among the least chosen and were rated by teachers as unpopular with peers *and* disruptive in class. However, peers and teachers also "agreed" that 23.5 per cent of the "moderately anti-social" grade school boys were having serious problems of relationship, a finding indicating that the clinicians might have had insufficient information for judging the extent to which these boys were anti-social. And, indeed, the clinicians involved stated that it *was* often difficult to tell whether a latency-age boy's

aggressive and conflictful behavior was transitory or was a stable pattern of behavior calling for intervention. This difficulty, according to clinicians, did not exist to the same extent for adolescent boys, and the data for the secondary school boys tend to substantiate this claim. While a smaller proportion of secondary school boys (25 per cent) than grade school boys (44.4 per cent) of those originally classified as "strongly anti-social" were "confirmed" as peer and school problems, it is also true that substantially fewer (6.5 per cent) of the secondary school boys rated by clinicians as "moderately anti-social" were later rated as "least chosen and unpopular," respectively, by peers and teachers. Likewise, the "moderately anti-social" boys in grade schools were likelier to be later rated as "most chosen and popular" than was the case in secondary schools. In brief, then, the data presented in Table 4–11 indicates that although the overall disagreement between peer and teacher ratings is greater in the secondary schools, with converse agreement in the elementary schools, the notion that elementary schools present a superior opportunity for screening potential delinquents does not automatically follow. Given the attendant diagnostic difficulties—psychiatric caution with respect to younger boys seems justified.

Davids and Parenti, in their study of social

[14]For example, see Coleman, op. cit.

TABLE 4–11.

AGREEMENT OF PEER AND TEACHER RATINGS AND PRIOR BEHAVIOR

Agreement of Peers and Teachers	Grade School Boys (N = 322)						
	Strongly Anti-social		Moderately Anti-social		Not Mentioned as Anti-social		Total
	N	%	N	%	N	%	
Most Chosen and rated Popular/helpful	0	0.0	6	17.7	32	12.3	38
Ignored by tchrs. and middle range on peer choices	4	14.8	7	20.6	117	44.8	128
Least chosen and un-popular/disruptive	12	44.4	8	23.5	10	3.8	30
Disagreement between peers and teachers	11	40.8	13	38.2	102	39.1	126
Total	27	100.0	34	100.0	261	100.0	322

	Junior High and High School Boys (N = 766)						
Most chosen and rated popular/helpful	0	0.0	0	0.0	47	7.9	47
Ignored by tchrs. and middle range on peer choices	14	23.3	35	32.7	270	45.0	319
Least chosen and un-popular/disruptive	15	25.0	7	6.5	14	2.4	36
Disagreement between peers and teachers	31	51.7	65	60.8	268	44.7	364
Total	60	100.0	107	100.0	599	100.0	766

choices in children and which included an investigation of group structure in groups of normal and disturbed children, found that both the degree of popularity and the reciprocation of friendships were significantly associated with good emotional adjustment.[15] We were, of course, interested in finding out if our findings would "parallel" those of Davids and Parenti, i.e., would the more aggressive or anti-social boys be less likely to have their friendship choices reciprocated than the normal boys? As seen earlier, (Table 4–10) both the strongly and moderately anti-social boys were likelier to be unpopular with their peers than were those not referred. Consistent with this earlier finding, the strongly anti-social boys were substantially less likely than the moderately anti-social boys to have their choices reciprocated, and both of these groups were less likely than the "normal"

boys to have their choices reciprocated (Table 4–12). Thus, the findings of Davids and Parenti appear to be paralleled by the present findings although it should be kept in mind that there are apparent differences between the two studies.

The finding that anti-social boys (both "moderately" and "strongly") have far fewer reciprocal choices than the "normal" boys becomes quite meaningful when viewed within the framework of Tagiuri's discussion of sentiments and perceptions. Tagiuri pays special attention to several aspects of peer ratings and the perception of peer ratings which have relevancy for the present study, for example, accuracy and reciprocation. He states that the bulk of the writings in this field—since the earlier work by Moreno and by Bonney—"have focused almost exclusively on accuracy of various kinds and its correlates."[16] Tagiuri agrees with Cronbach

[15] Anthony Davids and Anita Negrin Parenti, "Personality, Social Choice, and Adults' Perception of These Factors in Groups of Disturbed and Normal Children," *Sociometry* 21 (September, 1958): 212–24.

[16] See Renato Tagiuri and Luigi Petrullo, eds. *Person Perception and Interpersonal Behavior* (Stanford, California: Stanford University Press, 1958). See esp. chap. 21, by Tagiuri: "Social Preference and Its Perception."

TABLE 4–12.

PRIOR BEHAVIOR AND MEAN NUMBER OF RECIPROCAL CHOICES INVOLVING BOYS

	Elementary School Boys		
	Strongly Anti-Social	Moderately Anti-Social	Not Mentioned as Anti-Social
Mean Number of Reciprocal Choices	1.24	2.09	2.30

t between 1 and 2 = 2.83, significant at .01 level (two-tailed test)
t between 1 and 3 = 4.82, significant at .001 level (two-tailed test)
t between 2 and 3 = .88, not significant

	Junior High and High School Boys		
	Strongly Anti-Social	Moderately Anti-Social	Not Mentioned as Anti-Social
Mean Number of Reciprocal Choices	1.40	1.84	2.15

t between 1 and 2 = 2.59, significant at .01 level (two-tailed test)
t between 1 and 3 = 5.36, significant at .001 level (two-tailed test)
t between 2 and 3 = 3.10, significant at .01 level (two-tailed test)

that the difficulties involved in such studies make the interpretation of findings problematic.[17] Obviously, the limitations of which Tagiuri writes (diverse criteria of judgments and diversity of tasks, skills, and situations) apply to that part of the present study which deals with "agreements." These limitations do not exist, however, when we deal with peer ratings (Table 4–10) or with choice reciprocity (Table 4–12). Even though the extent of reciprocation is undoubtedly affected by the correct perception of others' feelings about oneself, the conditions affecting reciprocity among peers would seem more equitable than is the case when teachers are asked to assess popularity of students. Moreover, the comparison of "normal" and "anti-social" boys on extent of reciprocity gets us away, in part, from the problem of contamination of measures since the "purity" or "contamination" of the measure of reciprocity should operate for both the "normal" and the "anti-social" boys. Similarly, when we deal with the relationship between prior school behavior and peer ratings we are not confronted with a distinct possibility which

exists when we deal with the accuracy of teacher perceptions: the easy availability of school records. This, of course, is not to say that the data dealing with teacher perceptions are not of great interest; rather we only wish to point out the cautions which should accompany the interpretation of these data.

In considering the findings on reciprocation, it is obvious that the anti-social boys chose boys who did not choose them in return. The finding probably does not mean that the anti-social boys intended not to choose those who chose them, though it is possible that this is the case; rather it is believed here that the *perceptions* of the anti-social boys are faulty, and that they overrate their popularity with their peers in general and with selected peers in particular.[18] Clinicians as well as social psy-

[17]See Lee J. Cronbach, "Processes Affecting Scores on 'Understanding of Others' and 'Assumed Similarity,'" *Psychological Bulletin* 52 (1955): 177–93. Also see Lee J. Cronbach, "Proposals Leading to Analytic Treatment of Social-Preception Scores" in Tagiuri and Petrullo, op. cit.

[18]Indeed, in a relevant and stimulating study, David Goslin found that normal children who perceived themselves differently from the way they were perceived by other members of the group tended to be isolated from the group. Appropriately, Goslin viewed his findings as support for the Meadian approach to social interaction, i.e., "rejected individuals had not developed complete social selves and were unable to take the roles of others successfully in evaluating their own positions in the social system"; see "Accuracy of Self Perception and Social Acceptance," *Sociometry* 25 (September, 1962): 283–96; 296.

chologists who are interested in the dynamics of delinquency might be well-advised to consider more seriously the roles of empathy and social perception, although they should not lose sight of the conceptual problems discussed by Borgatta and others.[19]

It is possible, of course, that the comparative isolation of the anti-social boys is due to their behavior rather than to any perceptual weakness. Here one could fruitfully employ an assessment of what Tagiuri calls self-referent accuracy with respect to guessing reciprocated choices of self and others. If such an operation showed the anti-social boys to accurately perceive their low status vis-a-vis reciprocity, one would be confronted with a quite different problem than were one to find that the boys did not correctly guess their low status. In the former case, one would probably be concerned with the possibility of negative self-image *or* of societal—or peer-alienation (which would suggest that such boys are "hard" and apparently do not care, even about their peers—here the isolation is due strictly to behavior and not to faulty perception), while in the latter case one would obviously be more concerned with the perceptual ability of the boys (such boys might change their behavior when confronted with the fact of their unpopularity).

There are undoubtedly a variety of interpretations which could be placed on the findings of this study. We singled out the findings pertaining to reciprocity since we were impressed by the difference between "strongly anti-social" and "normal boys" with respect to this matter. Based on the Davids-Parenti study and the present one, along with the study reported on by Richardson and his associates,[20] it would seem that a tentative generalization can be presented, namely, that *children tend to reject those children whose behavior may be defined as being deviant, regardless of whether the deviance is of a physical, a psychiatric, or a social character.* Such a generalization, if true, has substantial implications with respect to both the theories and techniques of treatment or control employed by corrective agents.

SUMMARY

The investigation presented here focused on the following analyses: (1) a partial replication of earlier studies by Moreno and Bonney which focused on the relationship between peer popularity and teachers' estimates of peer popularity; (2) the relationship of these peer and teacher ratings, separately and in combination, to a measure of anti-social behavior based on prior teacher and clinical assessments; (3) the extent of sociometric reciprocation among boys rated as "strongly anti-social," "moderately anti-social," and "normal."

The findings may be summarized as follows:

(1) Moreno's findings that the accuracy of teachers' judgments declined as grade level increased is not confirmed in the present study. We find that with the exception of eleventh grade boys, there is a correlation between peer ratings and teacher perceptions at all grade levels. However, further research, covering all grades, is necessary before confidence can be placed in these findings.

(2) Bonney's finding that teachers were more accurate for those more popular with peers appears to be strongly confirmed by the results of the present study.

(3) The strongly anti-social boys were least popular with their peers and were perceived as such by the teachers. This finding pertains to both elementary and secondary school boys.

(4) The strongly anti-social boys were also less likely than either of the two comparison aggregates to have their sociometric choices reciprocated.

[19]For a penetrating review of research issues around the concepts of empathy and perception, see Edgar F. Borgatta, "Analysis of Social Interaction and Sociometric Perception," in *The Sociometry Reader*, ed. J. L. Moreno with others (New York: The Free Press, 1960). For earlier discussions of empathy and associated concepts, see: Leonard S. Cottrell Jr., "The Analysis of Situational Fields in Social Psychology," *American Sociological Review* 7 (1942): 370–82; Rosalind Dymond, "A Scale for the Measurement of Empathic Ability," *Journal of Consulting Psychology* 13 (1949): 127–33; and George H. Mead, *Mind, Self, and Society* (Chicago: University of Chicago Press, 1934).

[20]For a study of the reaction of children to the physical disabilities of other children, see Stephen A. Richardson, Norman Goodman, Albert H. Hastorf, and Sanford M. Dornbusch, "Cultural Uniformity in Reaction to Physical Disabilities," *American Sociological Review* 26 (April, 1961): 241–47.

The findings were discussed with respect to other studies—especially those of Davids and Parenti and of Tagiuri. Special consideration was given to the finding on reciprocation and implications for theory were discussed.

Perhaps the most salient implication of our generalization that children tend to reject "deviant" peers is to increase the support for those who oppose facile incarceration or confinement of anti-social children. Such a confinement, it would seem, would only induce *a feeling of rejection* and especially for those whose perceptual faculties are weak and who were unaware of their low status.

More concretely, it seems to us that this heavy censure by school peers of anti-social behavior could be used instead as an instrument of social control if the agents of control would make use of it. In order to do this, of course, a greater understanding of the peer mechanisms of social control is necessary—a matter recently emphasized in the literature.[21]

---

[21]Coleman, op. cit.

38.

James F. Short, Jr., Ramon Rivera and Ray A. Tennyson

PERCEIVED OPPORTUNITIES, GANG MEMBERSHIP, AND DELINQUENCY

Certain aspects of the opportunity structure paradigm were operationalized in a study of delinquent gangs in Chicago. Negro and white lower-class gang boys were compared with lower-class nongang boys from the same neighborhoods, and with middle-class boys, of the same race. The ranking of the six race-by-class-by-gang-status groups on official delinquency rates corresponded more closely to ranking on perceptions of legitimate opportunities than to ranking on perceptions of illegitimate opportunities, which is consistent with the assumption that illegitimate opportunities intervene after legitimate opportunities have been appraised and found wanting. Gang members perceived legitimate opportunities as available less often than nongang boys, lower-class boys, less often than middle-class, and Negro boys, less often than white. Differences in perceptions of illegitimate opportunities were in the reverse direction, as expected.

Not since the advent of psychoanalysis has a theory had such impact on institutionalized delinquency control as the theory, explicit or implied, in *Delinquency and Opportunity*.[1] Given the impetus of major foundation and federal support, the theory has been extensively adopted as a rationale for action programs in many areas of the country. There is some danger that, like psychoanalysis, "opportunity structure theory" may be rationalized and elaborated so rapidly and extensively as to discourage, if not

---

SOURCE: James F. Short, Jr., Ramon Rivera, and Ray A. Tennyson, "Perceived Opportunities, Gang Membership, and Delinquency," *American Sociological Review* 30, no. 1 (February, 1965): 56–67. Reprinted by Permission of the authors and the American Sociological Association.

This research is supported by grants from the Behavior Science Study Section of the National Institute of Mental Health (M-3301 and MH-07158); the Office of Juvenile Delinquency and Youth Development, Welfare Administration, U. S. Department of Health, Education, and Welfare in cooperation with the President's Committee on Juvenile Delinquency and Youth Crime (#62220); the Ford Foundation; and the Research Committee of Washington State University. We are grateful for this support and for the support and encouragement of staff members at the University of Chicago, Washington State University, and the Program for Detached Workers of the YMCA of Metropolitan Chicago, whose wholehearted cooperation makes the entire enterprise such an exciting "opportunity." An earlier version of this paper was read at the annual meetings of the Pacific Sociological Association, 1963.

[1]Richard A. Cloward and Lloyd E. Ohlin, *Delinquency and Opportunity: A Theory of Delinquent Gangs* (New York: The Free Press, 1960).

render impossible, empirical testing, pragmatic validation, or demonstration of worth by any other criterion of "good theory." *Delinquency and Opportunity* has been widely praised for its theoretical integration, e.g., as "a logically sound deductive system that is rich in its implications for delinquency causation and control," but the same critic also notes that "examined in terms of its logical, operational, and empirical adequacy, the theory poses a number of questions concerning the accuracy of some of its postulates and theorems."[2] Our paper will bring data to bear on certain aspects of the opportunity structure paradigm as we operationalized it in a study of delinquent gangs in Chicago.

Figure 4–1 reproduces in paradigm form the principal elements of "opportunity structure theory" concerning *criminal* and *conflict* subcultures. It subdivides the "Innovation" category

[2]Clarence Schrag, "Delinquency and Opportunity: Analysis of a Theory," *Sociology and Social Research*, 46 (January, 1962): 167–75.

FIGURE 4–1.

SOCIAL CONTEXT AND MODES OF DELINQUENT BEHAVIOR: A PARADIGM

Structural Features	*Type of Subculture*	
	Criminal	*Conflict*
I. Independent Variables A. Culturally prescribed success goals	(Integrated Areas) Internalized	(Unintegrated Areas) Internalized
B. Availability of legitimate means to success goals	Limited; hence intense pressures toward deviant behavior	Limited; hence intense pressures toward deviant behavior
II. Intervening Variables		
A. Institutional norms	Incomplete internalization	Incomplete internalization
B. Availability of illegal means to success goals	Available	Unavailable
1. Relations between adult carriers of conventional and criminal values	Accommodative; each participates in value system of other	Conflicted; neither group well organized; value systems implicit, and opposed to one another
2. Criminal learning structure	Available; offenders at different age levels integrated	Unavailable; attenuated relations between offenders at different age levels
3. Criminal opportunity structure	Stable sets of criminal roles graded for different ages and levels of competence; continuous income; protection from detection and prosecution	Unarticulated opportunity structure; individual rather than organized crime; sporadic income; little protection from detection and prosecution
4. Social control	Strong controls originate in *both* legitimate and illegal structures	Diminished social control; "weak" relations between adults and adolescents
III. Dependent Variable		
A. Expected type of collective response among delinquents	Pressures toward deviance originate in limited accessibility to success goals by legitimate means, but are ameliorated by opportunities for access by illegal means. Hence, delinquent behavior is rational, disciplined, and crime-oriented	Pressures toward deviance originate in blocked opportunity by *any* institutionalized system of means. Hence, delinquent behavior displays expressive conflict patterns

of Merton's deviance paradigm, referring to acceptance (internalization) of culturally prescribed success goals and rejection (incomplete internalization) of institutional norms or culturally prescribed means, by those for whom legitimate means to success goals are restricted.[3] To this the paradigm adds Cloward's four sets of defining conditions for the relative availability of illegitimate means to success goals,[4] and the two hypothesized types of "collective response among delinquents" produced by the preceding conditions.[5]

In our research in Chicago we have attempted to measure variables specified in this paradigm and to investigate their interrelations. For this purpose we have studied lower-class "delinquent gangs" involved in a "detached worker" program of the YMCA of Metropolitan Chicago, control groups of lower-class nongang boys from the same neighborhoods as the gang boys, and middle-class nongang boys.[6] Elements of the paradigm were operationalized in terms of the *perceptions* reported by the boys studied.[7] In

this paper we direct attention to perceptions of legitimate and illegitimate opportunities by Negro and white lower-class gang and nongang boys and middle-class boys of both races, and to the relations among these perceptions. Detailed discussion of the relation of perceived opportunities and patterns of behavior derived from self-reports and, for gang boys only, from detached-worker ratings, is deferred for later presentation.[8]

Data reported elsewhere establish different levels of aspiration among the boys studied, but they show that regardless of race, class, or gang membership, mean levels of both occupational and educational aspirations considerably exceed fathers' achieved levels of occupation and education.[9] In this sense the independent variable—internalization of culturally prescribed success goals—may be said to have a positive value among all the boys studied. For the first intervening variable in the paradigm, however—internalization of institutional norms—our gang members are less positive than the other boys studied. With "values" data from semantic differential scales, we established the fact that all groups assign equally high value and degree of legitimacy to such "middle-class" im-

[3]Robert K. Merton, *Social Theory and Social Structure* (New York: The Free Press, 1958), chap. 4.

[4]Richard A. Cloward, "Illegitimate Means, Anomie, and Deviant Behavior," *American Sociological Review* 24 (April, 1959): 164–76.

[5]Cloward and Ohlin use a different theoretical rationale to explain "retreatist" subcultures, but our data are not relevant specifically to this aspect of the theory. See Cloward and Ohlin, op. cit., pp. 25–27, 178ff.

[6]Selection and description of study populations and other characteristics of the research program are described in previous publications and in greatest detail in a forthcoming book. See, for example, James F. Short, Jr., Fred L. Strodtbeck, and Desmond Cartwright, "A Strategy for Utilizing Research Dilemmas: A Case from the Study of Parenthood in a Street Corner Gang," *Sociological Inquiry* 32 (Spring, 1962): 185–202; James F. Short, Jr., "Street Corner Groups and Patterns of Delinquency: A Progress Report," *American Catholic Sociological Review* 24 (Spring, 1963): 13–32; and James F. Short, Jr., and Fred L. Strodtbeck, *Group Process and Gang Delinquency* (Chicago: University of Chicago Press, 1965), esp. chap. 1.

[7]Cloward and Ohlin refer to "common perceptions" of opportunities, and Schrag explains that one of the basic postulates of the theory is that "perceived disadvantage, regardless of the accuracy of the perception, is for lower-class youth the functional equivalent of objectively verified disadvantage in that it has the same effect on overt behavior." (Schrag, op. cit., p. 168.) This is not to deny the importance of *objective* opportunities, legitimate and illegitimate. The former can be dem-

onstrated to be greater for whites than Negroes, and for middle- than for lower-class persons. It is more difficult to demonstrate gang-nongang differences except in terms of the cumulative *effects*— school performance, relations with the police, etc. —which favor nongang boys. Differences in objective illegitimate opportunities are similarly difficult to demonstrate, though the illegal enterprises are more likely to be present in a lower-class than in a middle-class environment.

[8]Behavior factors based on detached-worker ratings of gang boys are reported in James F. Short, Jr., Ray A. Tennyson, and Kenneth I. Howard, "Behavior Dimensions of Gang Delinquency," *American Sociological Review* 28 (June, 1963): 411–28. Self-reported behavior factors are presented in Short and Strodtbeck, op. cit., chap. 7.

[9]See James F. Short, Jr., "Gang Delinquency and Anomie," in *Deviant Behavior and Anomie*, ed. Marshall B. Clinard (New York: The Free Press 1964); see also Jonathan Freedman and Ramon Rivera, "Education, Social Class, and Patterns of Delinquency" (paper read at the annual meetings of the American Sociological Association, 1962). Elliott's study of "200 delinquent and nondelinquent boys attending two adjoining high schools in a large West Coast city" supports these findings. See Delbert S. Elliott, "Delinquency and Perceived Opportunity," *Sociological Inquiry* 32 (Spring, 1962): 216–27.

ages as "Someone who works for good grades at school" and "Someone who likes to read good books"—again indicating that certain values are common to all groups—but gang boys of both races hold more positive attitudes toward *deviant* images than do the other boys.[10] These deviant images represented hypothesized "delinquent subcultures"; e.g., conflict ("Someone who is a good fighter with a tough reputation"), criminal ("Someone who knows where to sell what he steals" and "Someone who has good connections to avoid trouble with the law"), and retreatist ("Someone who makes easy money by pimping and other illegal hustles" and "Someone who gets his kicks by using drugs"). Middle-class boys generally attribute to these deviant images a lower value and less legitimacy, as we expected.

This paper is concerned with other elements in the paradigm, based on data from one part of an extensive interview schedule administered by specially trained interviewers to more than 500 boys in the six categories (race by class status and gang membership) under study. Respondents were instructed to indicate whether each of a series of statements was true of the "area where your group hangs out." In this way we hoped to measure perceptions of relatively specific legitimate and illegal opportunities. Perceptions of legitimate means to success goals, for example, were sampled by a series of statements concerning the *educational* and *occupational* orientations, abilities, and prospects for "guys in our area." We hoped by the impersonal referent to avoid the personalized ambitions and expectations which were the subject of inquiry in another part of the interview and thus to obtain measures referring to the boys' perceptions of general opportunities for legitimate and illegal achievement in their respective areas.

Aspects of the availability of illegal means to success goals to which attention was directed concerned the relative integration of the carriers of criminal and noncriminal values (in terms of the respectability of persons making

money illegally and the orientation of local police toward law violation); adult "connections" and opportunities for learning and abetting criminal activities; the availability of criminal role models; and the probability of successful criminal enterprise in the area. Finally, because Cloward and Ohlin stress the importance of these matters for social control, perceptions of appropriate adult role models and their interest and sincerity concerning the problems of adolescents were also covered. The list of statements is in Table 4–13, together with the percentage of boys in each group answering "true."[11]

In most cases responses to the statements concerning open legitimate opportunities and adult helpfulness form a gradient: gang boys are least likely to answer "true," followed by nongang and then by middle-class boys of each race. For negatively stated legitimate opportunity questions, and for the two negative adult power ("clout") statements, this gradient is reversed.[12] White gang boys generally are more sanguine than Negro gang boys about occupational opportunities and adult "clout," while Negroes tend to be slightly more optimistic concerning education and adult helpfulness. For all these areas, white middle-class boys have the most *open* view of "opportunities."

Conversely, gang boys are more likely to perceive illegitimate opportunities as open than are other boys, and these perceptions are held by more Negro than white boys in each stratum. The latter finding is somewhat surprising, in view of the acknowledged white domination of organized crime in Chicago. Informal observation suggests that vice organized on a large scale does flourish in Negro communities, and that "independent entrepreneurship" in such forms as small (and large) policy wheels, marijuana peddling, street-walking prostitutes, pool sharks, professional burglars and robbers, and the like, is more common in lower-class Negro

---

[10]The data are reported in Robert A. Gordon, James F. Short, Jr., Desmond S. Cartwright, and Fred L. Strodtbeck, "Values and Gang Delinquency: A Study of Street Corner Groups," *American Journal of Sociology* 69 (September, 1963): 109–28.

[11]In the interview schedule the statements were not labeled according to which "opportunity structures" were being studied, and they were arranged in different order.

[12]Elliott, op. cit., finds that delinquents consistently perceive lower opportunities for educational and occupational "success" than do nondelinquents. For evidence of other gradients among boys in the present study, see Gordon, et al., op. cit., and Short and Strodtbeck, op. cit.

TABLE 4–13.

PERCENTAGE OF BOYS ANSWERING "TRUE" TO OPPORTUNITY STRUCTURE
QUESTIONS, BY RACE, CLASS, AND GANG STATUS

Interviewer: "Once again I want you to think about the area where your group hangs out. I'm going to read a few statements to you, and all you have to do is say 'True' or 'False' after each statement. If you think the statement is true about the area, say 'True'; if you don't think it's true, say 'False.'"	Per Cent Answering "True"					
	Negro			White		
	Lower Class Gang $N=206$	Lower Class Nongang $N=89$	Middle Class $N=26$	Lower Class Gang $N=90$	Lower Class Nongang $N=79$	Middle Class $N=53$
Legitimate Educational Opportunities						
1. In our area it's hard for a young guy to stay in school. (−)*	48.5	28.1	7.7	52.2	21.5	0.0
2. Most kids in our area like school. (+)	43.2	49.4	80.8	32.2	60.8	94.3
3. Most of the guys in our area will graduate from high school. (+)	30.6	44.9	96.2	32.2	65.8	100.0
4. In our area, there are a lot of guys who want to go to college. (+)	37.4	47.2	84.6	16.7	44.3	98.1
5. College is too expensive for most of the guys in the area. (−)	75.7	76.4	53.8	80.0	65.8	7.5
6. As far as grades are concerned, most of the guys in our area could get through college without too much trouble. (+)	46.6	43.8	50.0	43.3	40.5	73.6
Legitimate Occupational Opportunities						
7. It's hard for a young guy in our area to get a good paying honest job. (−)	77.2	62.9	46.2	56.7	31.6	9.4
8. Most of the guys in the area will probably get good paying honest jobs when they grow up. (+)	51.9	59.6	61.5	65.6	79.7	92.5
9. For guys in this area honest jobs don't pay very well. (−)	56.3	47.2	26.9	40.0	22.8	3.8
10. Guys in this area have to have connections to get good paying jobs. (−)	53.9	51.7	30.8	56.7	44.3	22.6
11. In this area it's hard to make much money without doing something illegal. (−)	54.9	38.2	23.1	37.8	13.9	0.0
Integration of the Carriers of Criminal and Non-Criminal Values						
12. Some of the most respectable people in our area make their money illegally. (+)	44.2	19.1	15.4	24.4	10.1	3.8
13. The police in this area get paid off for letting things happen that are against the law. (+)	51.5	37.1	30.8	42.2	36.7	20.8
Criminal Learning Structures						
14. There are connections in this area for a guy who wants to make good money illegally. (+)	57.8	49.4	38.5	47.8	35.4	5.7
15. Young guys can learn a lot about crime from older people in the area. (+)	75.2	66.3	34.6	52.2	35.4	11.3
16. There are adults in this area who help young guys make money illegally. (+)	59.2	49.4	30.8	42.2	26.6	15.1

*Signs in parenthesis indicate the "valence" of a "True" answer relative to the opportunity structure area indicated.

TABLE 4–13.—*Continued*

Interviewer: "Once again I want you to think about the area where your group hangs out. I'm going to read a few statements to you, and all you have to do is say 'True' or 'False' after each statement. If you think the statement is true about the area, say 'True'; if you don't think it's true, say 'False.'"	Per Cent Answering *"True"*					
	Negro			*White*		
	Lower Class Gang N = 206	*Lower Class Nongang* N = 89	*Middle Class* N = 26	*Lower Class Gang* N = 90	*Lower Class Nongang* N = 79	*Middle Class* N = 53
Visibility of Criminal Careers						
17. In this area there are some people who make their living by doing things that are against the law. (+)	83.0	73.0	69.2	70.0	60.8	30.2
18. Some of the young guys in our area will be making a living someday by doing things that are against the law. (+)	83.0	79.8	73.1	75.6	59.5	39.6
Elite Criminal Opportunities						
17. (A) A lot of these guys who make money illegally do not operate alone. They have to answer to people above them who are calling the shots. (−)	62.6	62.9	65.4	45.6	40.5	18.9
18. (A) A lot of these guys won't be operating alone either. They'll have to answer to people above them who'll be calling the shots. (−)	70.4	70.8	65.4	62.2	53.2	30.2
19. A guy from this area has a chance of really making it big in the rackets. (+)	45.1	30.3	34.6	35.6	24.1	3.8
20. None of the people who make big money in the rackets live in this area. (−)	54.4	66.3	38.5	56.7	75.9	60.4
Adult "Clout"						
21. Not many really successful people live in this area. (−)	63.6	59.6	19.2	42.2	26.6	0.0
22. Adults in this area haven't much clout (pull). (−)	55.3	42.7	23.1	48.9	48.1	13.2
Adult Helpfulness						
23. There are adults in this area who help young guys get jobs. (+)	82.5	93.3	92.3	78.9	89.9	94.3
24. Adults in the area do a lot to help young guys keep out of trouble. (+)	67.0	91.0	61.5	50.0	73.4	88.7

than in lower-class white communities.[13] In any case, illegitimate opportunities appeared to be open to more Negro than white boys.

To reduce these data further, we assigned an opportunity structure score to each item. Except for items 17(A) and 18(A) answers were scored 2, 1, or 0, with 2 assigned to *open* opportunity perceptions, whether legitimate or illegiti-

mate. Thus, for questions in Table 4–13 followed by (−), a "true" answer received a 0, "Don't know," a 1, and "False," a 2. The reverse procedure was applied to questions followed by (+).

Statements 17(A) and 18(A) are difficult to score. At first we assumed that a positive response to these questions indicated that illegitimate opportunities were perceived as closed. Boys were asked these questions only if they

[13]See Short and Strodtbeck, op. cit., esp. chap. 5, "Racial Differentials in Gang Behavior."

had already responded positively to questions 17 and 18. Thus, a "true" response to the statement that "A lot of these guys who make money illegally do not operate alone. They have to answer to people above them who are calling the shots," was taken to mean that the "really big" hoodlums were not available as role models; hence, to this extent illegitimate opportunities for "making it big" were perceived as closed. On the other hand, a boy might answer *false* to this statement on the grounds that those who were making money illegally were involved in such petty pursuits as not to warrant concern or control by the syndicate, or, particularly in the case of middle-class white boys, illegal pursuits might be in the nature of white-collar crime and so not subject to syndicate control. In the latter case, a "false" answer still would be consistent with an *open* perception of opportunity, while in the former it would not. Answers to "elite criminal opportunities" questions are the only exceptions to the observed gradient for perceptions of illegitimate opportunities, suggesting that boys within each class of respondents may have interpreted these questions less uniformly than they did the others.

Before answers to these questions are dismissed as invalid, however, they should be examined more carefully. Note that responses to questions 17(A) and 18(A) follow a pattern: more Negro than white boys say that people in their areas who make money illegally have to "answer to people above them." Unfortunately the question did not specify where these "higher ups" lived or whether they were visible to the boys. We may infer, however, that a higher proportion of persons making money illegitimately in the white areas were among the "higher ups" in organized crime than was the case in Negro neighborhoods.

The middle-class boys' answers to the entire set of four "elite" questions are especially interesting. Negro middle-class boys are far more likely to indicate that local area people have "a chance of really making it big in the rackets" and far less likely to say that locals do not "make big money in the rackets." Drake and Cayton[14] and Frazier[15] have described important

criminal and otherwise "shady" elements in the Negro middle class. Frazier, in particular, indicates that influential segments of the "black bourgeoisie" are "recruited from the successful underworld Negroes, who have gained their money from gambling, prostitution, bootlegging, and the 'numbers.' "[16] Frazier attributes the flashy consumption patterns of the new Negro middle class to the influence of these elements and contrasts this way of life with that of the old upper and middle classes who "erected an impenetrable barrier between themselves and Negroes who represented the 'sporting' and criminal world."[17] The white middle-class boys, who were chosen precisely because they were the "cream" of YMCA Hi-Y clubs, are very unlikely to be exposed to this sort of community influence. Such differences as these, if they are real, should find expression in other data from these subjects.[18]

These ambiguities in interpretation led us to score "elite" criminal opportunities in two ways —with and without questions 17(A) and 18(A). When they were included, we followed our original assumptions, adjusting the scoring so that if either question was not asked, implying closed opportunities, the boy was scored zero for the question; if the question was asked and a "true" answer recorded, a score of 1 was given; "undecided" was scored 2, and "false," 3.

---

[14]St. Clair Drake and Horace R. Cayton, *Black Metropolis: A Study of Negro Life in a Northern City*, vol. 2 (New York: Harper & Row, 1962).

[15]E. Franklin Frazier, *Black Bourgeoisie* (New York: Crowell Collier & Macmillan, Inc., 1962).

[16]Ibid., p. 109.

[17]Ibid., pp. 109–10.

[18]We were first alerted to differences between our Negro and white middle-class boys when they came to our offices for testing, and later by analysis of semantic differential data. See Gordon et al., op. cit. It should be emphasized that primary data for this paper represent perceptions rather than objective measures of opportunities or of the communities in which these boys live. Other investigators have emphasized the extent to which middle-class Negroes are like their white counterparts in terms of the character and stability of their institutions and their community leadership, and in interracial situations. Life styles, interaction patterns with whites, and leadership among middle-class Negroes vary greatly, however. See, for example, the discussion in Robin M. Williams, Jr. et al., *Strangers Next Door; Ethnic Relations in American Communities* (New York: Prentice-Hall, Inc., 1964), esp. chaps. 7–10; also James Q. Wilson, *Negro Politics: The Search for Leadership* (New York: The Free Press, 1960).

Table 4–14 presents mean opportunity structure scores, by race, class, and gang status of respondents. The trends apparent in Table 4–13 appear here, also.

In addition, it is clear that for *legitimate* opportunities, gang-nongang and middle-class differences *within* racial categories are greater than the Negro-white differences for each of the three gang and class strata. For *illegitimate* opportunities, differences between races are greater than within-race differences.

PERCEIVED OPPORTUNITIES AND AN OFFICIAL DELINQUENCY RATE

In Table 4–15, ranking on each of the summary opportunity scores is compared with the official delinquency rates of the six race-by-class-by-gang-status groups.[19] As far as the *ordering* of

[19]These rates refer to the mean number of offenses known to the police, per boy, in each group. Data are based on John M. Wise, "A Comparison of Sources of Data as Indexes of Delinquent Behavior" (Master's thesis, University of Chicago, 1962).

the six groups is concerned, perception of *legitimate* opportunities is more strongly associated with delinquency rates than is perception of illegitimate opportunities. This is consistent with the assumption that perceived legitimate opportunities are independent variables, while perceived illegitimate opportunities intervene, after legitimate opportunities have been appraised and found wanting. Legitimate achievement tends to be the universal standard in our culture, highly valued even by very deviant individuals.[20] Note, however, that *within* racial categories, perception of illegitimate opportunities does order the groups according to official delinquency rates.

Official delinquency rates measure the hypothesized dependent variables only in a very gross sense. The gang-nongang distinction probably measures participation in delinquent subcultural activity, and adding the middle-class—lower-class division permits a test of the theory in terms somewhat broader than it was originally set forth. Here the theory holds up well: gang

[20]See Gordon et al., op. cit.

TABLE 4–14.

MEAN OPPORTUNITY STRUCTURE SCORES, BY RACE, CLASS, AND GANG STATUS

Aspect of Opportunity Structure*	Negro			White		
	Lower Class Gang N = 206[a]	Lower Class Nongang N = 89	Middle Class N = 26	Lower Class Gang N = 89	Lower Class Nongang N = 75	Middle Class N = 53
Legitimate Educational (0–12)	4.8	5.7	9.0	3.8	6.4	11.2
Legitimate Occupational (0–10)	4.2	5.2	6.6	5.4	7.3	9.1
Integration of Carriers of Criminal and Noncriminal Values (0–4)	2.1	1.4	1.2	1.5	1.0	0.5
Criminal Learning Structures (0–6)	4.0	3.6	2.3	3.0	2.2	0.7
Visibility of Criminal Careers (0–4)	3.4	3.2	3.0	3.0	2.5	1.4
Criminal Opportunities (0–10)	4.7	4.0	4.6	4.7	4.3	4.6
Adult "Clout" (0–4)	1.5	1.9	3.0	2.0	2.4	3.7
Adult Helpfulness (0–4)	3.0	3.7	3.2	2.6	3.2	3.7
Criminal Opportunities (0–4)	1.8	1.2	1.8	1.5	1.0	0.9
Summary Scores Legitimate Educational and Occupational Opportunities (0–22)	9.0	11.0	15.6	9.3	13.7	20.2
Illegitimate Opportunities (0–24)	14.3	12.3	11.0	12.1	10.0	7.2
Illegitimate Opportunities Less Inclusive (0–18)	11.4	9.5	8.2	9.0	6.7	3.5
Adult Power and Helpfulness (0–8)	4.5	5.6	6.2	4.7	5.6	7.4

*Figures in parentheses indicate the possible range for each score.
[a]Ns vary slightly for some scores, due to nonresponse. Scores are based in each case on the number of boys who actually gave meaningful responses.

TABLE 4–15.

MEAN OPPORTUNITY STRUCTURE SCORES KNOWN TO THE POLICE,
BY RACE, CLASS, AND GANG STATUS*

Legitimate Educational and Occupational Opportunities (0 to 22)	Perception of Illegitimate Opportunities (Less Inclusive) (0 to 18)	Perception of Adult Power and Helpfulness (0 to 8)	Total Opportunities Score[a] (−18 to 30)	Mean Number of Offenses Known to Police, per Boy
NG (9.0)	NG (11.4)	NG (4.5)	NG (2.1)	NG (3.14)
WG (9.3)	NLC (9.5)	WG (4.7)	WG (5.0)	WG (2.73)
NLC (11.0)	WG (9.0)	NLC (5.6)	NLC (7.1)	NLC (0.47)
WLC (13.7)	NMC (8.2)	WLC (5.6)	WLC (12.6)	WLC (0.31)
NMC (15.6)	WLC (6.7)	NMC (6.2)	NMC (13.6)	NMC (0.06)
WMC (20.2)	WMC (3.5)	WMC (7.4)	WMC (24.1)	WMC (0.02)

*NG stands for Negro gang members, NLC Negro lower-class boys, and so on.

[a]Total Opportunities Score is designed to reflect both legitimate and illegitimate pressures toward delinquency. It is obtained by adding together legitimate educational and occupational opportunities and adult power and helpfulness scores, and from this sum subtracting illegitimate opportunity scores. Hence it should be negatively correlated with delinquency.

boys of both races perceive greater restrictions on legitimate opportunities than do nongang boys in the same neighborhoods or middle-class boys. Thus, the *negative* pressure toward deviance is greater for gang boys. Within each racial group, gang boys perceive better illegitimate opportunities; hence the greater "pull" toward deviance. While perceived adult power and helpfulness, combined, rank the groups very much as do official delinquency rates, adult power alone turns out, as predicted, to be negatively related to delinquency, while helpfulness, which may be exercised by carriers of criminal as well as noncriminal values, is related inconsistently to delinquency among Negro boys.

Adult power and helpfulness are both hypothesized by Cloward and Ohlin to be negatively related to the emergence and maintenance of conflict subcultures. "The term that the bopper uses most frequently to characterize his relationships with adults is 'weak.' . . . He views himself as isolated and the adult world is indifferent. The commitments of adults are to their own interests and not to his. Their explanations of why he should behave differently are 'weak,' as are their efforts to help him."[21] This description holds up well with respect to "clout." Gang boys score lower than the others and Negro gang boys—by far our most conflict

oriented[22]—score lowest of all. But helpfulness scores are comparatively high for all groups, and they are lowest for the less conflict-oriented white gang boys.[23]

Differences between nongang and gang boys on both scores are sufficient to suggest that these factors are important in selection for gang membership, though their relation to a particular type of delinquent subculture—conflict—is inconsistent with the theory. The previously noted higher illegitimate opportunity scores registered by the Negro boys are also inconsistent, but the greater visibility and availability of petty criminal activities in lower-class Negro communities

[21]Cloward and Ohlin, op. cit., pp. 24–25.

[22]For documentation, see Short, Tennyson, and Howard, op. cit., and Short and Strodtbeck, op. cit., esp. chaps. 1, 5, and 9. It was in large part because they were involved in gang fighting that most of the Negro gangs received the attention of newspapers, police, and the Program for Detached Workers with which this research program was associated. Close observation of the gangs over periods ranging from several months to more than three years suggests that nearly all the Negro gangs had at one time been more involved in "conflict subcultures" than had any of the white gangs. Finally, detailed analysis of behavior ratings by detached workers indicates greater conflict involvement by Negro than white gangs.

[23]These findings are consistent with boys' ratings of a series of adult roles in the same interview. See James F. Short, Jr., Ramon Rivera, and Harvey Marshall, "Adult-Adolescent Relations and Gang Delinquency: An Empirical Report," *Pacific Sociological Review*, Fall, 1964.

may account for this. Similarly, the comparatively low Negro middle-class scores on "clout" and helpfulness are consistent with Frazier's descriptions of the superficial show put on by Negro middle-class "society," which he regards as a somewhat futile attempt to compensate for status insecurities relative to whites.[24]

The hypothesis that perceived adult power is inversely related to gang conflict is essentially a social control argument. But helpfulness, when exercised by illegitimate adults, may be conducive to involvement in a criminal subculture. To investigate this possibility, we examined the relation *between* perceptions of various types of opportunities.

THE RELATION BETWEEN LEGITIMATE AND ILLEGITIMATE OPPORTUNITIES

The product-moment correlations between opportunity scores, for all boys and for gang boys only, by race, are in Table 4–16. Legitimate opportunity scores tend to be positively correlated with one another, as are illegitimate opportunity scores, and between legitimate and illegitimate scores correlations are negative. There are exceptions to this general pattern, however; for example, perceptions of legitimate educational and occupational opportunities are significantly correlated for all groups except white gang boys. The low correlation in the latter group suggests that perceptions of legitimate educational and occupational opportunities often are not mutually reinforcing.

The relation between adult power and perceived illegitimate opportunities suggests greater "integration" of the carriers of criminal and conventional values in white neighborhoods: the correlations are low but *positive* among white boys, and *negative* among Negroes. For both races, adult helpfulness is negatively correlated with illegitimate opportunities.

Correlations between perceived illegitimate opportunities are higher for white boys, particularly those involving the criminal *elite* measures. Thus, while white boys perceive illegitimate opportunities as less available than do Negro boys, "integration" as we have opera-

tionalized it is actually more characteristic of white than Negro gang areas. Negro gang boys perceive illegitimate opportunities as relatively open, but they tend to perceive illegitimate adults as neither powerful nor helpful. White gang boys, however, tend to perceive illegitimate adults as powerful but not very helpful. A similar pattern occurs in data from another section of the interview, in which boys were asked to indicate four characteristics of several adult roles in their local areas. Among Negro gang boys, 38 per cent, compared with 53 per cent of white gang boys, felt that adults making money illegally have "a lot of clout," while only about one boy in five in both racial groups felt that such adults are "interested in the problem of teen-agers." Lower-class nongang boys consistently rated legitimate adult roles higher than gang boys did on scales reflecting their interest in and degree of contact with teen-agers, their "clout," and the extent to which they are considered "right guys."[25]

In the present analysis, the relations between various opportunity scores reveal no significant or consistent differences that explain behavioral differences between gang and nongang lower-class boys. The most striking differences are between middle-class Negro boys and all other groups in the correlation between adult helpfulness and perceived elite criminal opportunities. This correlation is positive for both elite scores (.34 for the more inclusive measure, .20 for the less inclusive measure) among Negro middle-class boys, but both correlations are negative in all other groups. Adult "clout" was also correlated positively with the two elite criminal opportunity scores among Negro middle-class boys (.22 and .30), and among white gang members, but negatively in the other groups. Again, reference to Frazier's perceptive analysis is pertinent.[26]

SUMMARY

Legitimate occupational opportunities are perceived as available less often by gang than by nongang boys, and most often by middle-class

[24]Frazier, op. cit.

[25]A more detailed report of these data is in Short, Rivera, and Marshall, op. cit.
[26]Frazier, op. cit.

TABLE 4-16.
CORRELATIONS AMONG OPPORTUNITY STRUCTURE SCORES, BY RACE[b]

	Legitimate Educational		Legitimate Occupational		Adult Clout		Adult Helpfulness		Criminal, Noncriminal Integration		Criminal Learning Opportunities		Visibility of Criminal Careers		Criminal Opportunities Elite (Less Inclusive)		Criminal Opportunities Elite (Inclusive)	
	W*	N[a]	W	N	W	N	W	N	W	N	W	N	W	N	W	N	W	N
Legitimate Educational	**1.00**		.48	.38	.45	.34	.35	.27	—.36	—.17	—.49	—.22	—.42	—.23	—.27	—.13	—.06	—.03
Legitimate Occupational	.13	.34	**1.00**		.42	.35	.28	.29	—.26	—.32	—.31	—.37	—.26	—.30	—.25	—.23	—.10	—.08
Adult "Clout"	.10	.22	.28	.37	**1.00**		.29	.32	—.14	—.25	—.13	—.23	—.19	—.23	.04	—.01	.10	.05
Adult Helpfulness	.23	.32	.23	.35	.19	.32	**1.00**		—.23	—.26	—.19	—.15	—.26	—.14	—.27	—.21	—.19	—.13
Criminal, Noncriminal Integration	—.26	—.19	—.18	—.33	.05	—.23	—.27	—.29	**1.00**		.49	.51	.37	.32	.46	.32	.20	.14
Criminal Learning Opportunities	—.26	—.20	—.15	—.31	.16	—.22	—.20	—.19	.59	.52	**1.00**		.54	.43	.52	.27	.19	—.02
Visibility of Criminal Careers	—.28	—.27	—.17	—.39	.10	—.22	—.34	—.16	.37	.34	.46	.37	**1.00**		.38	.21	.00	—.14
Criminal Opportunities Elite (Less Inclusive)	—.21	—.18	—.24	—.25	.24	—.04	—.32	—.24	.60	.31	.64	.29	.49	.23	**1.00**		.73	.70
Criminal Opportunities Elite (Inclusive)	—.03	—.05	—.15	—.07	.19	.01	—.23	—.15	.32	.08	.41	—.03	.16	—.10	.74	.66	**1.00**	

*White: p < .05 = .13 (all boys) and .21 (gang boys); p < .01 = .18 (all boys) and .27 (gang boys)

[a] Negro: p < .05 = .11 (all boys) and .14 (gang boys); p < .01 = .14 (all boys) and .18 (gang boys)

[b] Italicized coefficients below the diagonal represent gang boys only; coefficients above the diagonal represent all boys, including gang members.

boys. White boys are more likely than Negro boys to perceive such opportunities as available, in each of the strata examined. With respect to legitimate educational opportunities, the same pattern occurs, except that the racial difference does not occur among gang boys. Race and class-by-gang-status gradients are both present concerning adult "clout," but not perceived adult helpfulness, among lower-class boys. These data are consistent with the apparently greater *protest* orientation of white as compared with Negro gang boys.[27] Gradients within racial groups are consistent with inferences from the Cloward and Ohlin theory.

Differences in perceptions of illegitimate opportunities reverse most of those found for legitimate opportunities, as expected. These differences are inconsistent with the greater conflict orientation of Negro gang boys, but when adult "clout" is correlated with criminal opportunity scores, and other data are introduced, "integration" of criminal opportunities and between criminal and legitimate opportunities is greater for white than for Negro boys. Even for white gang boys, however, the negative correlations between adult helpfulness and criminal opportunity scores, and their small positive correlations with adult "clout" suggest a low degree of "integration" between the carriers of criminal and conventional values.[28]

The logic of the theory clearly presumes that perceptions of opportunities *precede* involvement in delinquency, while our data reflect perceptions "after the fact." We cannot fully resolve this problem. Evidence concerning the relation of *individual* gang boys' perceptions of opportunities to their behavior as individuals, is relevant, however, and its mention permits brief discussion of the somewhat different causal model that has emerged from the larger study of which this paper is a partial report. Correlations between opportunity scores and theoretically relevant behavior scores for individual gang boys are low. For example, *conflict factor scores*,

consisting of a combination of individual and gang fighting (with and without weapons), assault, and carrying concealed weapons, are not systematically related to perceptions of either legitimate or illegitimate opportunity scores. That is, boys with high scores do not have lower opportunity scores.[29] It seems unlikely, therefore, that data reported in this paper reflect the boys' efforts to rationalize delinquent behavior by "blaming" the lack of opportunity. Although this does not solve the problem of temporal order, it is presumptive evidence against an alternative interpretation based on the assumption of "after-the-fact" (of delinquency or gang membership) influences on perception.

Our argument is not that the latter are unimportant. Other data from our study suggest that social structure influences the development of ethnic, class, life-cycle, and perhaps "delinquent" subcultures with relatively distinctive content. Social structural theories are therefore appropriately applied to the social distribution of many phenomena—to delinquency "rates" rather than to individual episodes or degrees of involvement in delinquency. It is to the question of "rates" or the social distribution of delinquent subcultures, that the Cloward and Ohlin theory is addressed—appropriately. To account for selection into subcultures—into gang membership, for example—from the youngsters available, and for individual behavior within the context of a subculture, requires reference to "levels" of explanation other than social structure.[30] We have found it necessary to invoke personality level

---

[27] See Short, Tennyson, and Howard, op. cit., and Short and Strodtbeck, op. cit., chap. 5.

[28] This, perhaps, explains why we had such difficulty locating criminal gangs. See Short and Strodtbeck, op. cit., chaps. 1 and 9.

[29] Derivation of the scores is detailed in Short, Tennyson and Howard, op. cit. Full presentation of the data concerning individual opportunity perception and behavior is beyond the scope of this paper.

[30] See David Bordua's critique of social structural theories in this regard. David Bordua, "Delinquent Subcultures: Sociological Interpretations of Gang Delinquency," *Annals of the American Academy of Political and Social Science*, 338 (November, 1961), and his "Sociological Theories and Their Implications for Juvenile Delinquency," Children's Bureau, *Juvenile Delinquency: Facts and Facets*, No. 2 (Washington, D.C.: Government Printing Office, 1960). See, also, Short and Strodtbeck, op. cit., and James F. Short, Jr., "Social Structure and Group Process in Explanations of Gang Delinquency" (paper read at the Fifth Social Psychology Symposium, University of Oklahoma, 1964, to be published in the Symposium volume).

variables, as Inkeles suggested,[31] and *group process* considerations, to explain delinquent behavior *within* our gangs.[32] The give and take of

interaction among gang boys, and between gang boys and others; a variety of role relations within the gang and status considerations related to these roles and to opportunities present in situations of the moment—these are prime determinants of what happens in the gang, of who becomes involved in what type of behavior, and with whom.[33] This *level* of explanation "washes out" variations in perceptions of opportunities related to social structure as a major determinant of individuals' behavior in the gang context.

[31] Alex Inkeles, "Personality and Social Structure," chap. 11 in *Sociology Today,* ed. Robert K. Merton, Leonard Broom, and Leonard S. Cottrell, Jr. (New York: Basic Books, Inc., 1959). From the present study, see Robert A. Gordon and James F. Short, Jr., "Social Level, Social Disability, and Gang Interaction," chap. 10 in Short and Stodtbeck, op. cit.

[32] See, esp., Short, "Gang Delinquency and Anomie," op. cit.; Short and Strodtbeck, op. cit., and by the same authors, "The Response of Gang Leaders to Status Threats: An Observation on Group Process and Delinquent Behavior," *American Journal of Sociology* 68 (March, 1963): 571–79, and "Why Gangs Fight," *Trans-Action* 1 (September-October, 1964): 25–29; and Strodtbeck and Short, "Aleatory Risks v. Short-Run Hedonism in Explanation of Gang Action," *Social Problems,* Fall, 1964.

[33] The point is made in more general theoretical terms in Albert K. Cohen, "The Sociology of the Deviant Act: Anomie Theory and Beyond," *American Sociological Review,* vol. 30, no. 1 (February, 1965).

CHAPTER V

On the Assessment of the Prevention and Treatment of Delinquency

EDITOR'S INTRODUCTION

THE PAPERS in this section deal variously with the problems of intervention, of prevention, of prediction, and of treatment. The first paper, by Malcolm Klein, is the only one of the papers whose explicit focus is the problem of intervention with juvenile gangs. Earlier, in Chapter III, section A, some of the theories concerning the etiology of subcultural delinquency were presented. In introducing that section, the editor noted that there seemed to be less research on the etiology of gang delinquency than there was on the etiology of individual delinquency. A similar situation seems to prevail with respect to research on intervention. While Klein's paper is not based on research, he does suggest some research questions and problems pertaining to the use of detached workers in programs of intervention with street gangs. Klein's paper is valuable in that it focuses on areas not often mentioned by those theorizing about subcultural delinquency, namely, the interagency conflicts (e.g., between the public and detached worker programs) concerning how best to deal with delinquent gangs. It would seem that students of gang delinquency would do well to consider these interagency conflicts on intervention in the light of theories about the etiology of gang delinquency. Perhaps this will foster appreciation of the large gap between etiological theories and various intervention practices, especially with respect to subcultural delinquency.

The next paper, by Joan and William McCord, focuses on the Cambridge-Somerville Youth Study, an extensive, long-term experiment in the prevention of individual delinquency. While the authors state that the results of this experiment were negative (in that as many boys in the treated as in the control group became delinquents) they also note the value of the experiment in producing a fund of information for future researchers. Indeed, the paper by Robert Stanfield, presented earlier in Chapter III, section B, involved a further analysis of data produced in the Cambridge-Somerville Youth Study.

Following the paper by the McCords is a piece drawn from the book by Ashley Weeks: *Youthful Offenders at Highfields.* This is a report by Weeks of the results of a short-term treatment experiment carried out by the State of New Jersey and involving boys sent to correctional facilities either at Highfields or at Annandale. Boys at Highfields in no case remained longer than four months, while the large majority of boys at Annandale remained at least twelve months. The primary analysis was on the extent of recidivism among boys released from the two facilities. Other analyses by Weeks focused on changes in expressed attitudes toward the boys' families, the law, and their own outlook on life.

Eleanor Glueck, in her paper, "Efforts to Identify Delinquents," reviews various attempts, both in the United States and abroad, to utilize the well-known Social Prediction Table developed by Sheldon and Eleanor Glueck, in their extensive research on delinquency prediction. While much of this work has involved retrospective studies, the author also discusses various attempts to employ the Prediction Table prospectively. Although reserving final judgment as to the efficiency of the Social Prediction Table, she indicates that the instrument has been effectively used in studies in various countries.

Don Gottfredson, in the next paper, also focuses on the prediction problem. He also considers the use of clinical assessment as an aid to prediction in this paper, taken from the Task Force Report of the President's Committee on Juvenile Delinquency. Gottfredson considers the various problems associated with attempts to develop predictive instruments for individual delinquents and criminals. These include the need to establish: valid and reliable predictors, valid and reliable performance criterion classifications (i.e., the behavior to be predicted), and measures of predictive efficiency. Other items discussed by Gottfredson in connection with predicting include the base rate (i.e., the proportion of individuals in a population who fall into a category which is to be predicted), the selection ratio, the sampling procedure, and the use of prediction instruments (such as in parole prediction).

While social scientists generally agree that the efficient prediction of delinquency does not imply the causation of delinquency, it is useful for students of delinquency to bear in mind that causation, correlation, and prediction are not, therefore, *unrelated*. Travis Hirschi and Hanan Selvin, in their paper "False Criteria of Causality in Delinquency Research," take a critical look at a number of the assertions of noncausality in the literature on delinquency. It is revealing to compare, for example, some of the variables used in prediction instruments with the factors considered by Hirschi and Selvin in their examination of statements about causal relations in the literature on delinquency.

The paper by Edward Rolde and his associates describes the philosophy and practices of a maximum security institution for juveniles in an eastern state. This paper, written especially for this volume and heretofore unpublished, discusses the wide gap between the stated goals of the institution and its actual practices with respect to the rehabilitation of delinquents. It was published because the literature on delinquency is nearly bereft of such descriptions, except for the occasional sensational accounts by journalists. Indeed, Rolde and his associates provide a service in reminding social scientists of the value of long-term observation from a position within the structure of such an institution.

The last paper in this section describes some of the issues considered by the Supreme Court of the United States in the historic case resulting in the Gault Decision. This paper, by Howard Brown, describes some of the dissatisfaction with the manner in which the juvenile courts were functioning in this country, dissatisfaction which resulted in the Gault Decision. The juvenile courts, created originally from a desire to treat children rather than to punish them had deteriorated, for a variety of reasons (many of these reasons lying beyond the courts' control) to where they were not only unable to provide effective treatment facilities, but to a point where their informal practices disregarded the constitutional rights of children. Brown elaborates on this situation and then discusses the possible effect of the Gault case.

39.

Malcolm W. Klein

JUVENILE GANGS, POLICE, AND DETACHED WORKERS: CONTROVERSIES ABOUT INTERVENTION

A detached worker (gang worker, street worker, street-club worker) is an individual, usually with social work orientation, who is assigned to one or more urban street gangs. His *modus operandi* differs from that of the usual agency worker in that his primary task is to attach himself to the delinquent gang where and as it exists—on the street corner, on the playground, in a garage, at a hamburger stand, or in any other spot where the boys seem to congregate. The general idea is that if gang members will not respond to ordinary social agency programs, then the programs must move out to the streets in order to achieve change in gang behavior.

Almost every major urban center in the United States now has some type of "detached-worker" program for work with delinquent youth. Often more than one exists within a given city. Among the most notable of these have been the Chicago area project, the detached-worker program of the Chicago YMCA, the Chicago Youth Development Project, the New York City Youth Board, Youth for Service in San Francisco, and the Group Guidance program of the Los Angeles County Probation Department.

As a by-product, these programs have tended to focalize and often to polarize the value differences between law-enforcement agencies and social agencies. In at least two cases this polarization has become highly visible to the public and has led to open controversy between the agencies involved. In New York, conflict between the Police Department and the Youth Board led to development of some new and different action guidelines for the Youth Board.[1] In Los Angeles the controversy led to a one-month suspension of the Group Guidance program while the police and probation departments worked out an agreement specifying the nature of the activities and program that the Group Guidance Section of the Probation Department would undertake. It was only after the agreement was reached that the program was reinstituted.[2]

These two instances have not been marked by any total resolution of value differences—nor should one expect such a total resolution. Indeed, they may in time become nothing more than models of conflict between enforcement and detached-worker agencies. It is the intent of this paper not to take a position about these conflicts but rather to specify some of the major differences in assumptions underlying the two positions in these conflicts and to suggest that for most of the assumptions there are data presently available or obtainable that can be used to test them. When two agencies can look at one set of data and draw diametrically opposite findings, then obviously the argument is less over the nature of reality than over philosophies of gang intervention. In fact, the nature of the inter-agency conflicts suggests that both sides to these controversies may be working more from myth than from fact.[3]

[1] *Dealing with the Conflict Gang in New York City*, Interim Report No. 14 (New York: Juvenile Delinquency Evaluation Project of the City of New York, 1960), pp. 27–28.

[2] See "Second Annual Progress Report: Study of Delinquent Gangs, July 1, 1962–June 30, 1963" (Los Angeles: Youth Studies Center, University of Southern California, and Los Angeles County Probation Department, 1963).

[3] A particularly lucid and forthright discussion of interagency conflict and the underlying values involved can be found in Walter B. Miller, "Inter-institutional Conflict as a Major Impediment to De-

Source: Malcolm W. Klein, "Juvenile Gangs, Police, and Detached Workers: Controversies about Intervention," *Social Service Review* 39, no. 2 (June, 1965): 183–90. Reprinted from *The Social Service Review*, Vol. XXXIX, No. 2, June, 1965. Copyright 1965 by the University of Chicago. Permission granted by Publisher and author.

Anyone who attempts to step into the conflict between representatives both of police and of detached-worker agencies is likely to be shouted down by each group for being antagonistic to a particular point of view. This paper is an attempt to take a neutral position without interruption, something more easily done on paper than in person.

Listed below are some, but by no means all, of the questions about which arguments between enforcement and detached-work agencies seem to revolve. In each case there are underlying assumptions that could be tested with data at hand or data that are not difficult to collect. Perhaps a brief specification of these underlying assumptions and some suggestions about sources of data will motivate one or more research workers to determine their validity.

1. *Do "sponsored" gangs create more trouble than "unsponsored" gangs?* A "sponsored" gang —and this is evidently not a very useful term— is one to which a detached worker has been assigned. The statement is often made by police officials that the effect of worker supervision is in the long run an increase in the number of gang fights, gang incidents, and individual delinquencies associated with the gang. In Los Angeles the police reported figures suggesting that supervised gangs accounted for three and one-half to four times as many gang incidents as unsupervised gangs. The Group Guidance Section retorted that this should be true because workers are assigned to the most troublesome gangs just as more firemen are assigned to the worst fires and fire areas. Moreover, the fact that a worker is assigned to a gang means that more is known about it and naturally its activities are more likely to come to light than those of gangs that are not clearly identified or followed.

Obviously there are many questions about this set of arguments. For instance, what was the pattern of gang incidents before supervision was begun? What has it been since the advent of supervision, and for what period of time?

(Detached workers will often say that it takes them one to three years to have a significant effect on some gangs.) In order to evaluate changes in gang incidents, one must consider the age of the youngsters. In American cities, delinquency generally reaches its peak at around the age of 16 or 17. One expects it to rise before this age is reached and then to decrease. This fact must be separated from any analysis which attempts to pinpoint the effectiveness of a detached worker.

Which boys are the target of supervision? Does the detached worker concentrate his time on the hard-core delinquents or on the fringe members in an attempt to move them away from gang membership? How intensive is supervision? Does the worker spend five days a week with the boys or only one or two? Does he have a significant effect on arrest records, or also on the number of court appearances and the disposition of cases? One must also distinguish between minor and major delinquent activities. There are a number of ways of doing this: one can use the distinction between Part One and Part Two crimes as employed in the *Uniform Crime Reports* by the Federal Bureau of Investigation, or one could use one of several indexes of seriousness developed by Robin[4] and Sellin and Wolfgang[5] in Philadelphia and by McEachern[6] in Los Angeles.

For example, an interesting attempt to compare gangs is being made by the Division of Research of the Los Angeles County Probation Department. A large area gang in East Los Angles seems to be separated into two segments. One of these received services from a detached worker and the other did not. Both groups initially were quite similar in costs to the community. It will be interesting to see whether the costs of the gang patterns of the groups differ

---

linquency Prevention," *Human Organization* 17 (Fall, 1958): 20–23. See also Mary E. Blake, "Youth Workers and the Police," *Children* 8 (September-October, 1961): 170–74, and William Dienstein, "Conflicts of Beliefs about Causes of Delinquency," *Crime and Delinquency* 6 (July, 1960): 287–93.

[4]Gerald D. Robin, "Gang Member Delinquency in Philadelphia," in *Juvenile Gangs in Context: Theory, Research, and Action*, ed. Malcolm W. Klein and Barbara G. Myerhoff (Los Angeles: Youth Studies Center, University of Southern California, 1964), pp. 107–16.

[5]Thorsten Sellin and Marvin Wolfgang, *The Measurement of Delinquency* (New York: John Wiley & Sons, Inc., 1954).

[6]A. W. McEachern and Riva Bauzer, "Factors Related to Disposition in Juvenile Police Contacts," in Klein and Myerhoff, op. cit., pp. 192–210.

after a period of service to only one of them. In another research project in Los Angeles an attempt is being made to determine empirically whether gang incidents and individual gang delinquencies decrease among four major clusters of gangs after three years of detached-worker service. Similar research ventures are under way in Chicago. The point here is simply that the question of an increase or decrease of delinquent activity in the presence of detached workers is one that can be answered with data. It need not be merely a subject of speculation or untested assumptions.

2. *Does supervision of gangs lead to increased status?* This question has become particularly important in Los Angeles because the detached workers in that city are probation officers. It is the position of the police that this fact alone tends to give official sanction and status to gang membership. Elsewhere, too, it is often believed that the assignment of a worker to a gang gives public recognition to that gang's "toughness." It has been reported by gang workers and researchers across the country, for instance, that neighboring gangs not being served often tend to increase their activity with the explicit purpose of obtaining a worker; that is, they seem to be saying, "Man, we're so tough that they have to assign a worker to us." This matter of status increase associated with the assignment of a worker can be more than a mere assumption. It is a hypothesis that can be tested through the use of data.

For instance, one could, in a carefully constructed interview, attempt to ascertain from the boys themselves whether the assignment of a worker has increased their feelings of status within the general community and within the delinquent subculture. One could question community adults in the same manner. Since the assignment of the worker, have adults been more aware of the existence of the gang? If so, has this awareness come about merely because of the worker's prominence or because gang activities have increased or become more visible? If awareness of status increases after assignment of a worker, which gang members and which kinds of people in the community become more aware of the gang?

Even more important is the underlying assumption that an increase in status—for the gang or for individuals—leads to an increase in delinquency. Do the boys who feel an increase in status also seem to be getting into more difficulty? Are they being arrested more? Are they being arrested for more serious acts than before? How do they view this increase in status if and when it takes place? Is it a positive or a negative sort of status? Does it have to do with them as individuals or as members of the given group? Is it status as club members, or is it status as gang members, or is it status as delinquents?

One of the subunits of a gang cluster being studied in Los Angeles, a group of approximately 25 boys 14 to 16 years of age, seems to separate "club" status and gang status; rather than just belonging to a gang the boys see themselves as belonging both to a gang and to a club, as supervised by a detached worker. Do they really make a genuine distinction between these two kinds of status? Which one is more important to them? Is the worker successful in getting them to attach more importance to their club status than to their gang status? Each of the above is a question which can be answered by careful research and need not be left to speculation only.

3. *Does supervision lead to greater cohesion within the gang?* It is generally believed, by both enforcement agencies and detached workers and their administrative directors, that a more cohesive gang is likely to be a more delinquent gang. In addition, it is suspected that the more cohesive group tends to be the more conflict-oriented group—that is, one in which violent crimes and assaultive acts are predominant. Cohesiveness of any group can be measured by means of various techniques, including direct interview and observation. The author has attempted a cohesiveness analysis of four gang clusters. At this point data from detached workers alone—even without going to the boys for information—can be collected which clearly distinguish between more cohesive and less cohesive gangs. It then remains to follow the pattern of cohesiveness over a period of two or three years and to follow the pattern of delinquency during this same period.

Cohesiveness, of course, refers to several

factors. One is the over-all cohesiveness of all boys who consider themselves affiliated with the gang. Another is the existence of clique structures or subgroups within the total gang. Findings suggest that gangs with distinct clique structure are also higher in over-all cohesiveness. Furthermore, it appears that the cliques that emerge from such analyses are almost completely made up of the "core" or "hardcore" members of the gang. If so, breaking up of the clique structure of the inner core may also lead to a breaking up of general gang cohesiveness.[7] This is a position diametrically opposed to that of Yablonsky,[8] who suggests that the proper mode of approach to these gangs is to peel off the fringe members of the gang much as one would peel off the leaves of an artichoke, and then to deal severely with the hard-core members. (The analogy to splitting logs is perhaps more pertinent than that of peeling artichokes. When you are splitting a log with a very hard knot in it, is it best to go around the knot? Or is it best to attack the knot directly, and in so doing split the entire piece in half with one solid blow, or several if necessary?)

In dealing with cohesiveness, it is also important to make a distinction between the early and later stages of assignment by gang workers. It is possible that cohesiveness is initially increased by the presence of the detached worker. He offers activities, and perhaps status, but certainly a focal point around which organization can take place. Under such circumstances an increase in cohesiveness can be expected. But as the group's cohesiveness increases, can the worker at the same time begin to weaken cohesion before a troublesome increase in gang delinquency occurs? Here is the focal point of the argument. Data collected over a period of two or three years with supervised gangs can provide the answer to such a question. The preliminary impression from the author's current research is that cohesion does indeed increase in the beginning, but that later it tends to

decrease. It may be that decrease can be achieved faster by removal of the worker from the gang even before he feels that the gang is ready for termination of service.

4. *Is gang leadership psychopathic?* Yablonsky and many enforcement officials have indicated that gang leaders are by and large psychopathic, sociopathic, or, in some other sense, clearly sick individuals. No doubt some boys in gangs are genuinely sick and do have the potential to influence certain other members of the gangs in a destructive direction. But to what extent do they possess general leadership of their groups? To find out, one could undertake an analysis of the kinds of activities influenced by the "psychopathic" members as opposed to those influenced by relatively "healthy" gang leaders, persons who also very clearly exist in gang structures.

One of the first tasks for any gang worker is to attempt to replace negative leadership with so-called positive leadership. To what extent this can actually be done is still problematic, but it is the stated goal of gang work insofar as leadership is concerned. Both observational and sociometric analysis of gang leadership can provide many answers to this question of whether the gang, *ipso facto*, is psychopathically led.

5. *Are truce meetings between rival gangs helpful or harmful?* A number of detached-worker programs hold truce meetings between gangs or get-togethers between gang leaders when "rumbles"[9] are under way or threatened. Obviously, bringing together the leaders of two rival gangs in which feelings are strong is a delicate matter. The truce meeting may lead to some resolution of the differences, but it may also lead to a heightening of hostilities. A number of police officials maintain that the net effect of truce meetings is to let the members of each rival gang know exactly whom to pounce on next time. One means of looking at this—granted, it would be hard to get an agency to agree to such an approach—would be to hold truce meetings in half of those instances in which they seem to be indicated and to avoid

---

[7] Malcolm W. Klein, "Internal Structures and Age Distributions in Four Delinquent Negro Gangs" (paper presented at the 1964 annual meeting of the California State Psychological Association, held in Los Angeles).

[8] Lewis Yablonsky, *The Violent Gang* (New York: Crowell Collier & Macmillan Co., 1962).

[9] "Rumble" is the generally accepted term for a gang fight or extended period of gang conflict. Other terms with similar meaning are "humbug," "beef," and "hassle."

such meetings in the other half of such cases. After a sufficient period of time perhaps a large enough number of cases could be logged to attempt some answer to the question of the effectiveness of truce meetings.

Other data are also needed. For instance, suppose that a truce meeting is followed by certain acts of a delinquent nature. Are these acts in any way related to the matters brought up during the truce meeting? For instance, if a truce meeting deals with intergang hostilities and if after the truce meeting several of the boys go out and commit statutory rape, is it then legitimate to consider their act a result of the truce meeting? Second, if delinquent acts do take place following a truce meeting, who participated in them? Were the participants gang leaders or fringe members of the gangs? Were they members of one gang acting against its rival, or were the acts committed against persons or property unrelated to the rival gang? To what extent did the boys at the truce meeting manage to pass the word along to other gang members to "cool it"? One must ask and answer questions such as these before achieving any genuine evaluation of the effectiveness of truce meetings.

6. *Do gang workers increase anti-police feelings among gang members?* The police, perhaps because they are aware of the value differences between the detached workers and themselves, believe that gang members increase their hostility to police when they receive supervision by detached workers. Detached workers, of course, maintain that this is not their intent, and they add that they counsel gang members about the nature of the legitimate and necessary role of the police officer. On the other hand, there have been instances in which activities or statements by detached workers have been used by boys to justify their own hostile feelings toward the police.

This is a matter to be investigated through careful research. Attitudes can be measured. More specifically, attitudes toward the police can be measured both before and after the assignment of a worker to an area. Because gang members are a highly heterogeneous lot of youngsters, it could well be assumed that feelings toward police will be more a function of

the boy himself than of the nature of the detached worker. That is, no matter what he says about the police, the detached worker may have a positive effect on the attitudes of some boys and a negative effect on the attitudes of others. Research could delve into this problem and attempt to distinguish between these differences and also attempt to determine what types of statements by detached workers lead to attitude changes. How do the boys differentially view the statements made by detached workers (or by anyone else, for that matter)?

Each of the above instances is an example of questions which can be studied empirically. Although this list could be extended, these questions are adequate to establish the point of this paper, that many of the assumptions underlying the controversies between police and detached workers are nothing more than that—assumptions, beliefs, convictions—and that data can be collected to validate or invalidate the assumptions in whole or in part.

There are of course other problems in such controversies. For instance, there is some disagreement on the importance of the collaboration between the police and detached workers. All agencies officially say that co-operation and collaboration are highly important. In fact, they often say that no detached-worker program can be effective unless it has the co-operation of local enforcement agencies. However, a number of detached workers (not agencies) believe that they can work independently of the police, and some police officers prefer to work with juveniles without contact with detached workers to whom these juveniles are known.

Another source of controversy revolves around "finking," that is, providing police with information about the boys. The detached-worker position, stated in its extreme, is that, if the worker does "fink," the boys will inevitably know it, and the worker will have lost his chance to establish rapport. Once the boys have any substantial reason to accuse the worker of being a fink, the worker can no longer have any effect on the boys. On the other hand, the police position, stated very clearly, is that withholding information about serious delinquent acts is tantamount to defying law and order; every citizen has a duty to make illegal infractions known to the duly constituted authorities. Furthermore, refusal to provide such information suggests to the police that the worker is on the side of the boys, rather than on the side of society. The most crucial case concerns firearms. While most detached-work programs state as official policy that firearms are to be turned over to the police, the fact remains that many individual workers ignore the policy, either because their rapport with the boys is tenuous, or because they fear losing rapport.

Rosters pose another critical example. Very often gang workers develop rosters of gang members. Very often the police request these rosters, since their intelligence role requires them to gather as much information as possible on actual or potential criminals and delinquents. When refused access to rosters, as they often are, police understandably come to feel that the worker is working against them, rather than with them. On at least one occasion in Los Angeles gang members themselves were so concerned about "finking" that they refused to give the worker their names for fear that they would

then be open to increased "harassment" by the police.

In summary, now is the time for police and detached-worker agencies to stop arguing about what delinquents are like, about what is or what is not appropriate intervention policy, about whose right it is to intervene. Both police and detached workers know what the respective positions are, and those who have been involved with both of them also know these positions. It is time for a disinterested, scientific look at data pertinent to the controversies. Responsible enforcement and social work administrators must come together and consider dispassionately what sorts of data are helpful in understanding the nature of the differences and in resolving the problems. Once requests for data have been made, there can be great strides in the development of empirically based programs for the handling of juvenile gangs. The problem of delinquent gangs is not decreasing, and the time for argument and controversy is rapidly drawing to a close.

40.

Joan McCord and William McCord

A FOLLOW-UP REPORT ON THE CAMBRIDGE-SOMERVILLE YOUTH STUDY

ABSTRACT

The Cambridge-Somerville Youth Study was founded in 1935 with the double purpose of preventing delinquency and providing research in the area of delinquency prevention. 325 boys were selected to receive preventive treatment, and a carefully matched group of 325 boys was provided as a control group. The treatment program utilized many of the practices prevalent in welfare work: family guidance, medical and academic assistance, co-ordination of community agencies, and supplementary entertainment for the boys. This article traces into adulthood the lives of 253 of the "treatment" boys and their 253 matched mates in the control group. Although the boys were counseled for an average of five years, whatever benefits they may have received were not reflected in their criminal rates: As many treated boys as control boys had been convicted of crimes; they had committed approximately equal numbers of crimes and did not differ significantly in the ages when such crimes were committed. Nevertheless, evidence gleaned from this program suggests that early treatment and intensive contact with the boy may be an effective means toward crime prevention.

One of the most extensive attempts to prevent delinquency and crime was the famous Cambridge-Somerville Youth Study. Founded in 1935 by Richard Clark Cabot, a physician and social philosopher on the faculty of Harvard University, the project aimed at decreasing delinquency in two densely populated, factory dominated cities, Cambridge and Somerville, Massachusetts.

With the aid of a $500,000 grant, Dr. Cabot established a center for the project. After careful interviews, the staff selected subjects from among hundreds of boys referred by schools, welfare agencies, police, and churches as difficult children or as ones who were average in behavior and personality. Each boy was given medical and psychological examinations. Social workers consulted the families and reported on their homes. On the basis of this information, each boy was matched to another as closely similar in background and in personality as was possible. One in each pair was then selected, by toss of a coin, to receive the services of the Youth Study. Thus 325 boys were to be given friendly, regular attention from counselors, as well as whatever medical and educational service seemed needed. A matched set of 325 boys, a control group, was to be left to the usual services of the community.[1]

Beginning in 1939, for an average of five years, the "treatment boys" were given assistance ranging from academic tutoring to psychological counseling. The intensity and calibre of treatment varied from counselor to counselor and boy to boy. In some cases, as Dr. Cabot had hoped, treatment involved an intimate friendship between boy and counselor. In most cases, however, the treatment relationship was less close. Treatment had many aspects: talks between the boys and counselors, trips and other recreation for the children, and medical aid whenever it was required. In addition, many counselors, focusing on school problems, tutored their boys in reading and arithmetic. Others acted primarily as co-ordinators for welfare and family agencies, the YMCA, and summer camps. Large numbers of boys were encouraged to participate in shop classes or informal games at the project's center. Religion formed an important part of the treatment: Boys and their

Source: Joan McCord and William McCord, "A Follow-up Report on the Cambridge-Somerville Youth Study," *The Annals of the American Academy of Political and Social Science* 332 (March, 1959): 89–96. Permission granted by publisher and author.

[1] See Edwin Powers and Helen Witmer, *An Experiment in the Prevention of Delinquency* (New York: Columbia University Press, 1950) for a detailed discussion of the original selection and the treatment of the subjects.

families were encouraged to attend church, and ministers and priests were alerted to their problems. Police departments, particularly the juvenile bureaus, kept in close touch with the project. Counselors often visited the boys' families to offer advice and general support.

The Cambridge-Somerville Youth Study differed from most social agencies in three ways: Its subjects were selected by the staff and were therefore, in a sense, "drafted" into the project. It tried to maintain contact with the boys and their families until the boys were about seventeen instead of "closing" cases after shorter treatment. Most importantly, it incorporated a control group of boys who could later be examined in an objective assessment of the effectiveness of the treatment program.

The first attempt to measure effectiveness was carried out while the program was in progress. Psychological tests, checks on school adjustment, and a review of court records failed to uncover significant differences between the treatment and the control groups.

In 1948, almost three years after the project had ended treatment, a second assessment was made by Edwin Powers, the project's Director, and Helen Witmer, a social scientist. At that time it was found that, according to juvenile court and criminal records, the treatment group had committed as many and approximately as serious offenses as had the control group. Dr. Witmer's ratings of the terminal adjustment of the boys also indicated few differences between the treatment and control groups. Since the conclusions of Powers and Witmer are fully presented in *An Experiment in the Prevention of Delinquency*,[2] we will not attempt to duplicate their report.

In 1956 the authors of this article received a grant from the Cabot Foundation to trace the lives of these boys now that they had reached manhood. We dropped from our study those who had died or who had received very little treatment; also, of course, we dropped their matched mates from the control group. We then secured criminal records for the remaining boys who had passed through Massachusetts or Federal courts. By 1948, 90 per cent

of a random sample of 200 boys from the study were still living in the Boston area.

We had decided that the presence or absence of criminal behavior would be our criterion of success in treatment and that criminality would be determined through official court convictions. Objections can be made both to the criterion of success and to the method by which we measured it. We might, for example, have attempted to gauge the general mental health, adjustment, or character of the men. Yet since the major avowed aim of the project was the prevention of crime—and since other standards of success seemed relatively difficult to define or measure—we concluded that criminality should be the yardstick of success.

We recognize, of course, the many defects of official criminal records as a standard of criminality. An earlier study made by the Cambridge-Somerville staff revealed that many delinquent acts known to the counselors had gone undetected by the police. Admittedly, official records are incomplete and, in some cases, may reflect a variety of community biases. Nevertheless, no satisfactory substitute has yet been developed. Moreover, we believe that a confirmed criminal is unlikely to pass through the first thirty years of his life without being apprehended at least once. Furthermore, most of our subjects emerged from deteriorated neighborhoods; therefore the usual middle-class biases in court convictions would be equally applicable to all the boys. Thus, for a variety of reasons, court convictions appeared to be the most practical, objective standard of crime.[3]

---

[2]Ibid.

[3]Social scientists have attempted to measure criminality through self-reports. Sheldon and Eleanor Glueck, in *500 Criminal Careers* (New York: Alfred A. Knopf, Inc., 1930), reported interviews with criminals whom they had questioned on undetected crimes they had committed. A number of the subjects admitted additional crimes. Yet, using this method, one is unable to dissociate bragging or dishonesty from the truth. Ivan Nye, more recently, in *Family Relationships and Delinquency* (New York: John Wiley & Sons, Inc., 1958), used a questionnaire administered to a group of high school students as a measure of crime. Yet Nye validated the "reported behavior" questionnaire by showing that it differentiated between incarcerated delinquents and non-institutionalized high school students —the standard which he attempted to eschew. (Incidentally, the questionnaire failed to tab as delinquent 14 per cent of the incarcerated subjects.)

The final group used for this assessment of treatment was made up of 506 men predominantly from lower-class and lower-middle-class backgrounds. Approximately half of these men, divided equally between the treatment and the control group, had been considered pre-delinquent. Their median I.Q. in childhood was 98; their median age, when treatment began, was 11.

COMPARISON OF TREATMENT GROUP AND CONTROL GROUP

When we compared the court records of the boys who had received treatment with those of the control group, we found that a slightly greater number of treatment boys had been convicted for at least one crime,[4] although their number of convictions was slightly lower. Neither of these differences, however, is statistically significant.

	Number of Boys Convicted	Number of Convictions
Treatment group	107	315
Control group	95	344

Both Professor Gordon Allport, in his foreword, and Edwin Powers had expressed the hope that the treatment boys would evidence better adjustment as they matured.[5] To check this possibility, we grouped the boys according to the age at which they committed crimes. We found that a slightly larger number of treatment boys had criminal records in each of three groups: those convicted only as juveniles, those convicted only after "maturation," and those convicted as both juvenile and as adult criminals. These differences, too, were not statistically significant.

Age of Criminality	Number of Boys Convicted	
	Treatment Group	Control Group
Under 18 only	34	29
18 or older only	35	32
Under and over 18	35	34

[4]Twenty-seven treatment boys and 35 control boys had records only for traffic offenses. We did not consider these boys as criminal.

[5]Powers and Witmer, op. cit.

Nor was there a significant difference in the number of crimes committed during either the juvenile or the adult period.

Age of Boy	Number of Convictions	
	Treatment Group	Control Group
Under 18	152	157
18 and over	163	186

Thus again we had failed to uncover evidence that the treatment had successfully deterred criminality.[6] We looked in another direction for such evidence. Although the treatment and control groups had been carefully matched before treatment began, we knew that much had been discovered since the 1930's about the causes of crime.[7] To control against erroneous matching, we held constant the affectional attitudes of the parents, their techniques of discipline, and the neighborhoods in which the subjects had been reared.[8] Nevertheless, we found no statistically significant differences in favor of the treatment group. Nor did we find differences in favor of the treatment group when we held constant the intelligence and the personalities of the boys.

As a result of these various analyses, we were forced to conclude that the treatment program, considered in its totality, had been ineffectual as a preventative of crime.

[6]Another criterion of the effect of treatment could be commitment to reform schools, jails, and prisons. A number of biases affect whether a delinquent will go to an institution (judges sometimes consider the home situation or appearance in court). Consequently, we believe that incarceration is less satisfactory than conviction as a standard of criminality. However, the reader may be interested in this aspect of the analysis: Equal proportions of boys from the treatment and control groups were sent to reform schools and equally high proportions, upon release, were convicted for further crimes. Yet only half as many men from the treatment as from the control group were committed to jails and prisons (X^2 5.7; $P < .02$). A number of possible interpretations of this finding are discussed in *Origins of Crime* (New York: Columbia University Press, 1959).

[7]See, for example, Sheldon and Eleanor T. Glueck, *Unraveling Juvenile Delinquency* (Cambridge, Mass.: Harvard University Press, 1950).

[8]See William and Joan McCord, in collaboration with Irving Kenneth Zola, *Origins of Crime* (New York: Columbia University Press, 1959) for a complete description of this analysis.

COMPARISON OF VARIATIONS IN TREATMENT

A comparison of treatment and control groups failed to indicate that the treatment, in general, had been beneficial. One possibility suggested itself as perhaps being responsible for the failure: During World War II, many counselors had joined the armed forces, and the turnover in counselors had been marked. We thought these changes might account for the over-all failure of treatment. Yet when we compared criminal rates—per cent convicted of crimes—we found that they did not significantly reflect this factor.

Number of Counselors		Per Cent Convicted of Crimes
One	(N:72)	43
Two	(N:88)	30
Three	(N:47)	53
More than three	(N:46)	48

Despite changes in counselors, the first counselor could be expected to have a degree of influence unmatched by his successors. One of the results of the turnover in counselors was that few boys maintained their relationships with their first counselors for an extended period of time. We anticipated that the duration of treatment by the first counselor would influence criminal rates. Again, we found no confirmation for this view.

Length of Treatment by First Counselor		Per Cent Convicted of Crimes
Less than two years	(N: 38)	47
2-3 years	(N:134)	39
More than 3 years	(N: 81)	42

Since neither the number of counselors nor the length of treatment by the first counselor seemed to be responsible for the apparent failure of treatment in preventing criminality, we next considered the total duration of treatment. One could argue that programs utilizing the tactics of the Cambridge-Somerville Youth Study must operate over extended periods of time. Length of treatment, to a considerable extent, reflected the staff's estimate of the seriousness of a case. Yet we found no support for the belief that lengthy treatment decreased criminality.

Total Length of Treatment		Per Cent Convicted of Crimes
Less than 4 years	(N: 82)	35
4-6 years	(N: 65)	29
More than 6 years	(N:106)	53

In addition to variations in the duration of treatment, there was, of course, wide variation in the intensity of treatment. In almost every case, counselors devoted close attention to family problems. Nevertheless, there were considerable differences in the amount of interaction they had with the boys themselves. Using six months as the minimum time span, we divided the boys according to the greatest intensity of contact they had with any counselor.

Greatest Intensity of Contact		Per Cent Convicted of Crimes
Once a week	(N:32)	25
Once in two weeks	(N:84)	51
Once a month	(N:47)	43
Less than once a month	(N:82)	33

If we assume that cases considered most serious were seen at least once in two weeks, then the comparison between the group seen every two weeks and those seen every week (for a minimum of six months) gives a measure of the efficacy of intensive treatment. When the criminal rates for these two groups are compared, we find that those seen every week had a significantly smaller incidence of criminality (X^2 6.4; $P < .02$). This finding suggests that frequent contact between a boy and an adult counselor may deter criminality and that sporadic contact has little effect.

Besides reflecting the intensity of treatment, the effectiveness of treatment was found to be related to the age of the boys when they first became participants in the program (X^2 18.9; d.f. 4; $P < .001$).

Age on Nearest Birthday		Per Cent Convicted of Crimes
5-8	(N:39)	26
9	(N:35)	29
10	(N:47)	66
11	(N:56)	45
12-13	(N:76)	37

Clearly, early treatment appeared to have been most beneficial; possibly, the drop in crime rate for older boys—over 10 years old—was due to the fact that a higher proportion continued to have guidance through the difficult adolescent period.

We hypothesized that the sex of the counselors, too, might make a difference in the effectiveness of treatment. One might assume, on the one hand, that female counselors would best satisfy a rejected child's desire for maternal care —or, on the other hand, that male counselors would be most effective for they would furnish a masculine model for the boy. To check the relationship between the sex of the first counselor and treatment, we held the boy's age constant.

	Sex of First Counselor			
	Female		Male	
Age of Boy	Per Cent Convicted		Per Cent Convicted	
5-9	(N:42)	29	(N:32)	25
10	(N: 6)	67	(N:41)	66
11-13	(N:48)	29	(N:84)	46

The group of boys in the 11- to 13-year age group who had female counselors had a significantly lower crime rate than did those guided by male first counselors (X^2 3.9; $P < .05$). This may be a reflection of independent variables which we were unable to measure, but it appears that female guidance may be more valuable than male guidance for adolescent boys. On the other hand, the very young boy seems to respond equally to male and female counseling. These findings would seem to recommend a reversal in programs which leave adolescent guidance to men and frequently discourage the treatment of very young children by males.

In summary, these comparisons point again to the general ineffectiveness of those forms of counseling which consisted in family assistance plus infrequent interaction with the boy. The analyses suggest, however, that frequent contact with the child—particularly if begun when the child is under 10 or by a female after the boy has reached adolescence—may effectively prevent criminality.

A CONTROLLED TEST OF INTENSIVE TREATMENT

One of the greatest difficulties in testing the effects of treatment is the large number of independent factors which may be responsible for variations in results. Having discovered that intensive contact seemed beneficial while the more common "general guidance" approach seemed useless in crime prevention, we sought a controlled test of "the best" treatment offered by the Cambridge-Somerville Youth Study.

Selecting cases which had received the most "intensive" therapy proved to be a rather tangled problem for standards of "good treatment" vary widely. Since the experiment had been initiated by Dr. Cabot, we decided to use his criteria as a basis for the assessment.

In almost every case, as we have noted, counselors worked with the families of their boys. Similarly, there was widespread attention paid to educational and medical handicaps of the boys. Naturally, "good treatment" involved the counselor's alertness to the needs of the family and acceptance by them.

In addition, we established four criteria for judging which boys had undergone the most intensive therapy—standards with which, we believe, Dr. Cabot would have agreed.

First, a counselor had to maintain a relationship with the child for an absolute minimum of two years.

Second, the counselor had to visit the child an average of once a week throughout the two year period.

Third, the counselor had to have a close relationship with the child. Only if the boy volunteered statements which seemed to indicate his regard and respect for the counselor did we judge their bond as an intimate one.

Fourth, the discussions between the boy and his counselor had, at some point, to touch on the child's basic personality problems: his relation with his parents; his sexual feelings; his attitudes toward authority and his peers; or his feelings of guilt, anxiety, aggression.

After combing the case records, we found, unfortunately, that only twelve cases satisfied these requirements. These boys were some of the most potentially delinquent cases in the project; they had been subjected to a variety of influences which research has shown to be productive of crime. In order to test the effects of treatment on this group, we needed to hold constant those factors which might have some influence on crime but were not directly related to treatment. Therefore each of the twelve boys who received intensive treatment was matched individually to another boy from the treatment group. We matched treated boy to treated boy because information on this group was so much more complete than on the control boys.

Each pair was equated on eight factors: the mother's attitude toward her son, the father's attitude toward his son, the child's personality, method of parental discipline, general home atmosphere, neighborhood, intelligence, and the delinquency prognosis score which had been assigned at the beginning of the experiment.

We were able to find boys who, on these factors, closely resembled the twelve boys who had received the Cambridge-Somerville project's most intensive care.[9] The mothers and the fathers of every pair resembled each other in their attitudes toward their sons. Each pair of boys was of the same general personality type. Except for one set, the pairs matched in terms of the parental discipline which they had received. Eleven of the twelve pairs had similar home atmosphere. Only one set differed by more than a single rating point in neighborhood. Using the Stanford-Binet intelligence scores, we were able to match the boys (within five points) in eight of the twelve pairs. Eight of the twelve

_____
[9]When difficulties occurred in the matching, we used a "preference" table which gave greater importance to those factors which research had shown to be the most important in delinquency causation. Naturally the matching was done without knowledge of the court records of any of the boys.

pairs had been given a delinquency prognosis within one point on an eleven-point scale.

When we had finished this matching, two groups of remarkably similar boys could be compared with each other. One set of boys had received, for at least two years, the very best attention which the project offered; the other set received the less intensive, and, as we have seen, largely inadequate services of the program.

The results of the comparison are suggestive: While six of the boys who received the most intensive treatment committed at least one crime, eleven of their matched comrades became criminal (X^2 3.9; P < .05).

Unfortunately, only a handful of boys underwent the intensive treatment. The small number of cases makes generalization difficult. Nevertheless, the results seem to indicate that intimate, long-term, "supportive" counseling may help to prevent criminality.

SUMMARY

Three forms of analyses were used to check the efficacy of the Cambridge-Somerville Youth Study in preventing crime. In the first form, we compared 253 boys who had received treatment with 253 boys, carefully matched in personality and family background, who had received no special treatment. In this comparison, we found that the general program—consisting of guidance for the family, medical and academic assistance for the boys, co-ordination of community agencies, and supplementary entertainment of the boys—had been no more effective in crime prevention than other community services: Approximately equal numbers of treated boys and control boys had committed approximately equal numbers of crimes in childhood and adulthood.

In the second form of analysis, we concentrated upon variations within the treatment group. Negatively, we found that neither the change in counselors nor the length of treatment —which, for many boys, was shorter than had been planned—could be held responsible for the failure. On the other hand, we found evidence that the program might have been more successful had a greater number of boys been seen at least once a week by their counselors and had treatment been started during the first decade of the boys' lives. In addition, we found that male counselors were apparently as effective as female counselors with very young boys, although they were less effective with adolescents.

As a final method for assessing the project, we focused upon twelve boys who had received intensive treatment. We matched each of these twelve boys to another who had similar parents, personality, discipline, home atmosphere, and intelligence, yet had received no intensive treatment. We concluded from this closely controlled comparison that intimate, long-term, "supportive" counseling may prevent crime.

Thus, using the standard of "official" criminal behavior, we must conclude that the Cambridge-Somerville Youth Study was largely a failure. Some individuals undoubtedly benefited from the program; but the group, as a whole, did not. Yet even in its failure, the program must be regarded as a magnificent experiment, for its provision of a control group and its careful attention to research have produced a fund of information invaluable to future studies of the causation and prevention of crime.

41.

H. Ashley Weeks

THE HIGHFIELDS PROJECT

STUDY DESIGN

The Highfields Project for the Short-Term Treatment of Youthful Offenders inaugurated in New Jersey has been in operation since July 5, 1950. This report is an attempt to measure and evaluate various aspects of the Highfields Project for the first several years of its life.

The Short-Term Treatment of Youthful Offenders Program evolved from the need felt by many New Jersey judges for a new law to permit them to make definite sentences of not more than three months to the existing New Jersey facilities such as the reformatories and training schools. These judges believed that such a law would act as a deterrent to many boys—it would demonstrate to delinquent boys that commitment and incarceration for a much longer period would be their lot if they did not mend their ways. The judges felt that many delinquent boys were not yet serious enough offenders to warrant

their being sent to The New Jersey State Home for Boys at Jamesburg or to one of the state's reformatories for an indeterminate period of confinement. Such boys had demonstrated that their misbehavior was serious enough to raise doubts in the minds of the judges as to whether they could be placed or continued on probation with safety to the community and protection to themselves. Juvenile court judges are frequently loath to commit a boy to an institution which he is not likely to leave short of a year. They feel, with justification, that a boy often becomes worse when he is kept too long in an institution.[1]

The director of Correction and Parole of the Department of Institutions and Agencies of New Jersey, Dr. F. Lovell Bixby, was in sympathy with the ideas of the judges. He knew that judges frequently face a grave dilemma: should they commit a delinquent or place him on probation? He believed, however, that it was not enough just to remove a boy from his community, that a program or plan of treatment had

Source: H. Ashley Weeks, "The Highfields Project," *Youthful Offenders at Highfields* (Ann Arbor: The University of Michigan Press, 1958), pp. 1–10, 20–24, 118–28. Permission granted by publisher and author.

[1] There is much evidence to show that the longer the stay in a correctional institution the more likely a person is to fail on parole when he is released.

to be a part of the boy's short-term stay. During World War II, Dr. Bixby had had a chance to observe at first hand the program of rehabilitation which was being tried among army prisoners at the Fifth Service Command, Rehabilitation Center, Fort Knox. So impressed was he with the possibilities of the group psychotherapy idea for the rehabilitation of civilian offenders that he asked Dr. Lloyd W. McCorkle, one of the chief therapists at Fort Knox, to come to New Jersey after the war. As a result, programs involving group psychotherapy were set up and tried at many of the state correctional institutions.

When the judges made their proposal for a short-term facility for delinquents, Dr. Bixby suggested that a treatment program embodying group psychotherapeutic techniques be added to the short-term idea. The plan which was drawn up incorporated many new and imaginative features.

Dr. Bixby has written that he "began to believe that guided group interaction (the name given to group therapy programs in New Jersey) would be an even more effective instrument of reform if it were applied in a setting more consistent with its basic principles." He found support for his belief in an article entitled "Psychiatry as Seen in the Advanced Mobile Base Hospitals,"[2] by Lieutenant Howard R. Rome, a psychiatrist in the United States Naval Reserve. Dr. Bixby quotes the following passage from Rome's article: "Group therapy is an educational procedure. All aspects of it must be educational. By controlled graduated activity in all spheres insight is acquired. . . . Group psychotherapy must be lived in constantly, not merely exposed to intermittently. This is done by carefully scheduled twenty-four-hour-a-day routine. With subtle management the machinery of the organization can be hidden. Work, play, classroom study, meals, recreation, and rest are organized on a group plan."

THE PROPOSED PROGRAM

The New Jersey program for the short-term

treatment of youthful offenders originally included these points:

Boys, while still officially on probation, would live, work, and play together in a unit which would house only a few boys at any one time.

Small groups of boys—not more than ten in any one group—would meet each day with the director, a trained guided group interactionist, in sessions designed to uncover their problems and help them begin to solve them.

The boys would live as nearly normal lives as possible. There would be no outward symbols of incarceration, force, or even control. There would be no officers or guards. The personnel would consist only of the director, who would be responsible for establishing and maintaining a therapeutic climate, a man and his wife to supervise housekeeping and to assume the role of houseparents, and a handyman or jack-of-all-trades to assist the boys in developing their hobbies and in making themselves useful around the place.

There would be no formal educational program, but boys would listen to the radio and read newspapers and magazines and other material. This material would be thoroughly discussed and would give the residents a chance to evaluate and interpret together the information and opinions with which these mass media continually bombard us all.

The boys would work on some constructive project, not for vocational training but to gain work experience, and they would be paid a small wage for this work.

There would be hobby and craft projects in which all would participate. Each boy would be expected to select and finish one such project during his residency, whether it be "writing a short story, building a radio cabinet, overhauling a gasoline engine, or almost anything else that the individual feels he would like to do."

The boys would be allowed to go to local villages, accompanied by an adult, to shop, attend the movies, have a soda, or indulge in other approved activities of interest to them. On Sundays, religious activities and experiences would be available in the nearby community churches. There would be many opportunities to maintain community contacts. Periodically,

---

[2]Cf. F. Lovell Bixby, "Short Term Treatment of Youthful Offenders," *Focus* 30 (March, 1951): 33–36. Lieutenant Rome's article can be found in *American Journal of Psychiatry* (July, 1943).

during their short stay, they would be granted furloughs home. These would be in the nature of test situations and would also furnish experiences that could be discussed in the group sessions.[3]

As actually established, the project embodies some changes in the original plan as proposed by Dr. Bixby. The guided group interaction sessions are not held every night, but only five nights during each week. Usually, there are no sessions Thursday and Saturday nights. So far as is known, there is no specific discussion session in which the boys evaluate and interpret the information they have received from the mass media. Of course, certain attitudes and expressions received from their reading or listening are often brought forward in the sessions and aired and analyzed there, but this as observed by the writer is more by happenstance than design. Nor is there any hobby or craft program in which all participate. Boys can and do carry on projects, but again it is because of an individual interest and not by design. With these exceptions the program is very similar to the one Dr. Bixby originally conceived.

Certain criteria for the kind of residents were set up. In the first place, it was decided to limit the project to delinquent boys 16 and 17 years of age. Boys under this age would have to have school facilities provided for them in accordance with the state law, and those over 17 are beyond the age when they may be handled as juveniles by the courts of the state. It was also decided to limit the project to first commitment boys, that is, boys who had not formerly been committed to a state industrial school or other place of confinement. It was reasoned that boys who had had former institutional experience might be so conditioned in their behavioral reactions that it would be difficult for them to participate wholeheartedly and freely in the guided group interaction sessions.[4] The kind of resident to be sent to Highfields was further limited by the exclusion of known sexual perverts and feeble-minded and/or psychotic boys.

Before Highfields began to accept boys, discussions were held with the judges of the four

large northeastern counties which have separate juvenile courts. It was explained to them that Highfields was not necessarily a substitute for either probation or incarceration, but a third choice. Whenever a judge had a boy before him who was 16 or 17 years of age and met the other criteria, the judge could consider whether the short-term treatment afforded at Highfields might be preferable to commitment or regular probation. A specialized facility such as Highfields would be helpful when he was in doubt. He could still place a boy on probation provided the boy would agree to spend a relatively short term (up to four months) under the treatment program.[5] If he decided a boy was suitable for Highfields, he could ascertain whether a bed was available there, and if it was he could see whether a boy would volunteer to go to Highfields. If a bed was not available, the former choice was still possible—incarceration or probation.

Because the short-term treatment program was an experimental one, it was assumed that the state would not immediately be willing to finance it. Fortunately, The New York Foundation was looking for a worthy experimental project they could help finance. When the foundation learned about the plans for the short-term treatment of youthful offenders it agreed to help finance the project for the first two years of its operation.

THE NEED FOR RESEARCH

Many times in the past, treatment and preventive programs have been started and continued with no evaluation or attempt to find out whether they were accomplishing their aims. In June, 1954, the conferees attending a meeting of the Special Juvenile Delinquency Project carried on by the Children's Bureau noted the contrast between the amount of money spent on programs to combat delinquency and the lack of expenditure for collecting data as to the achieve-

---

[3]Cf. *Focus*, pp. 35–36.

[4]From time to time these criteria have been disregarded in the interest of a particular boy.

[5]Judges are loath to institutionalize a delinquent if they can possibly avoid it. This can be seen from the fact that boys often have long histories of delinquency and court appearances without commitment. They frequently are placed on probation again and again, or continued on probation. The ordinary delinquent has three or more official prior delinquencies before he is committed to a penal institution. This is true not only in New Jersey but elsewhere.

ments of the programs. They called this contrast "shocking."[6] The initiators of the New Jersey program wanted to know what was being accomplished. From the outset Dr. Bixby and Dr. McCorkle emphasized the desirability of having an outside independent agency study and evaluate the results of the program. They were instrumental in securing financial support for such a research undertaking from the Vincent Astor Foundation.

The Vincent Astor Foundation, through the auspices of one of its trustees, Mr. Barklie Henry, asked Professor Ernest W. Burgess to select a group of persons to serve as a Scientific Advisory Committee to advise the Foundation as to the merits of research which might be undertaken in connection with the project. The Department of Sociology, Graduate Schools of Arts and Science, New York University, was asked to draw up a design and submit it to the Committee.[7]

The Scientific Advisory Committee accepted the design and recommended to the Board of Trustees of the Vincent Astor Foundation that it make a grant to New York University for the purpose of carrying on an evaluation of the short-term treatment program over a five-year period. The grant was made.

ORIGINAL RESEARCH DESIGN

In order to secure the information needed to evaluate the program proposed by Dr. Bixby, it appeared that there were three basic questions which should be answered:

1. Do delinquents participating in the short-term treatment program show a higher, the same, or a lower recidivist rate than boys participating in other kinds of treatment programs?

2. Do delinquents participating in the short-term treatment program change their expressed attitudes, values, and opinions toward their families, law and order, and their own outlook on life?

3. Do delinquents participating in the short-term treatment program change their basic personality structures or at least the overt manifestations of their personalities?

These questions were based on certain theoretical considerations. It is generally assumed that correctional training, whether punitive or therapeutically oriented, changes and improves the overt behavior of the person undergoing the training. The lay public as well as the professionals at work in the field hope that the experiences persons have in correctional facilities will be reflected in an improvement in the behavior they exhibit after they are released. As Dr. Bixby has written: "The objective of all correctional procedures is the permanent protection of society through the rehabilitation of the greatest possible number of convicted offenders."[8] Recidivist rates, then, should be a general measure of the effectiveness of a correctional program.

But recidivism is not the sole measure of effectiveness. Persons who have experienced correctional training may be favorably affected by the treatment only to have the good effects discounted by the fact that they are returned to the same family, the same neighborhood, and the same detrimental social groupings and influences which contributed to their anti-social behavior in the first place. But whether or not they subsequently get into further trouble with the law, the treatment they receive, if effective, should alter their attitudes, values, and opinions, and this alteration should be observable at the time they leave the treatment facility. We felt that the short-term treatment program should especially bring about changes in values, attitudes, and opinions. Guided group interaction sessions, we believed, should encourage the participants to recognize their problems in terms of their behavior, attitudes, and values and allow them to explore alternative solutions to their problems.

Fundamentally, attitudes and values serve to motivate certain kinds of behavior and inhibit other kinds. A person who despises the police, feels that laws are totally unfair or apply only to the other fellow, and is antagonistic toward or has no respect for his family or other authority, must be motivated differently from one

[6]*Summary of Conference Finding,* Special Juvenile Delinquency Project, Children's Bureau, Department of Health, Education and Welfare, June 30, 1954, p. 20.

[7]Mr. Barklie Henry, Mr. C. F. Bomer, and later Mr. Hoyt Ammidon of the Vincent Astor Foundation invariably attended the meetings of the committee, as did Mr. Albert Elias when he became Director of Highfields.

[8]"A Plan for the Short-Term Treatment of Youthful Offenders," mimeographed, p. 1.

who has opposite attitudes and values. Of course, some specific values may be held which are similar for the lawbreaker and the law-abider; but when this is the case, the object toward which the values are directed is probably narrower and more restricted for the lawbreaker than it is for the law-abider. In other words, the lawbreaker may have a feeling of loyalty, may uphold the norms of the group, but the object of this loyalty is restricted, for example, to his gang or individual members of it and not to society as a whole. The true gang delinquent growing up in high delinquency areas is motivated certainly by many of the same values as are prevalent in the larger society, but these values are restricted and operate only in reference to his own in-group and fail to operate in reference to what he considers the out-group —the group, as he sees it, which is against him and repressive in its actions toward him.

In the third place, there are persons who, because of adverse conditions in their life histories, become psychologically maladjusted. These persons frequently engage in delinquent behavior because of their deep-seated anxieties and perplexities. Many delinquents have distorted conceptions of reality. For example, although this is not always verbalized, boys—and girls too —often feel that all adults are against them, that they are alone in a hostile world, and that they must battle to retain their personal significance. Treatment, to be effective, must change these basic personality manifestations in order to give a more realistic picture of society.[9]

In order to insure meaningful answers to the questions we were asking, an experimental design was called for. Therefore, we advocated securing pre- and post-information on each boy sent to the short-term treatment project and like information on boys who were handled in other ways. These other ways might include release with no further action by the court, probation, committal to a training school or reformatory,

or even to a jail or other local place of incarceration. Theoretically, at least, samples of boys similar in every way to those sent to the short-term treatment facility could be drawn from those handled in each of these other ways, and comparisons made between them and the boys experiencing the short-term treatment program.

New Jersey has an excellent Diagnostic Center at Menlo Park, and it was suggested that all boys be screened at the Center and complete diagnostic workups on each boy be obtained when he first came to the attention of the court and again when he was discharged from whatever treatment he had been undergoing. Comparisons could then be made in terms of the changes revealed between the two workups and the particular treatment accorded the various groups of boys.[10]

As the research plan was discussed with the judges of the four separate juvenile courts, it appeared that the great majority of boys would probably be committed to Annandale Farms, the New Jersey State Reformatory for Males, if there were no room for them at Highfields. It could be assumed that if Highfields did not exist almost all of the more serious delinquents as old as 16 or 17 would be sent to the reformatory at Annandale. Thus, it was decided for research purposes to use as a control group boys of the same ages as those eligible for Highfields who were committed to this reformatory. The control group would, of course, be selected according to the other criteria established for Highfields eligibility: it would be composed of boys who had not previously been in a state correctional institution, who did not appear to be feebleminded or psychotic and who were not known sexual perverts.

Originally, it was also planned to select boys similar to the Highfields group who were placed on probation for the first time or continued on probation. Some reasons why this was not done will be discussed later.

HIGHFIELDS

. . . During the spring of 1951 the following policy, initiated with the co-operation of the juvenile courts and parole offices, became the

---

[9]We think of these two types as (1) the social deviant or gang delinquent and (2) the psychologically maladjusted. They are essentially the same types that Dr. Richard L. Jenkins calls the adaptive and the maladaptive delinquent. See Richard Jenkins and Sylvia Glickman, "Patterns of Personality Organization Among Delinquents," *The Nervous Child*, vol. 6, no. 3 (1947), pp. 329–39.

[10]See copy of the original design, Appendix A.

standard operating procedure carried on for the remainder of the study. Each time a judge decided to send a boy to either Highfields or Annandale, his office notified the research division at New York University and one of the staff traveled to the probation office or parental school of the respective court, where the tests were administered. Each time a boy was released from Highfields the director notified the research office and a member of the staff went to the respective probation office and administered the same tests as were given before. When a boy in the control group was released from Annandale the institution parole officer notified the district parole officer that the boy was in the control sample. This officer in turn notified the research office and arrangements were made to meet with the parolee and administer the tests. In this way almost all of the boys were tested just before they went to their respective facilities and just after they were released.[11] A few boys from counties which do not have a full-time juvenile court, such as Burlington, Monmouth and Mercer, were first tested after they arrived at Highfields and shortly before they were released from there.[12] No procedure was established whereby the research office was notified when boys were sent to one or the other facility from these counties. Occasionally, through some unusual contingency, the research office was not notified when boys were sent to Highfields or to Annandale by the four larger counties. With Highfields boys this did not appreciably delay the testing because we were informed that the boy had arrived and the tests had not been given, but in the case of Annandale the information was not

so readily forthcoming. For this reason, about every two or three months during the course of the study we checked the records at Annandale and tested any boy who had not hitherto been tested. In this way, we secured as complete a sample as possible of all boys who met our criteria.

Because it was believed there might be a fictitious inflationary "halo" reflected in the results of the tests taken so soon after release from either facility, each boy who was still available (that is, still on probation or parole or had not joined the armed services) was called in to his probation or parole office and was given all the tests a third time, after he had been back in his community six months or more.[13]

The administration of these tests and the filling in of the interview schedule took, on the average, somewhat over two hours on the first contact. The post-test could be administered in much less time because it was not necessary to interview again; and then, too, the boys knew the staff and there was no problem of establishing rapport. However, it should be mentioned that often the boys were somewhat more resistant to filling in the post-test, especially when, as originally was the case, we asked them to do so before they had had a chance to get home and see their families and friends. When this was discovered, we arranged the post-test a day or so after the boy had been home.

In addition to the testing, we have, through co-operation of the probation and parole offices, kept in touch with each boy over the length of the study. Periodically, we received reports from the respective offices on each boy's adjustment. If he got into further trouble and was returned to the court and recommitted to any correctional facility we were immediately notified.

[11]Without the co-operation, interest, and awareness on the part of the judges of the juvenile court or the probation and parole officers, and the superintendent of the reformatory of the necessity for this procedure the research staff would have had much more difficulty than it encountered. We recognize that the procedure added to their already heavy burdens and we are exceedingly grateful.

[12]By far the greatest number of boys were sent to Highfields from the four counties with full-time juvenile courts; only relatively few were sent from all other counties of the state. Boys at Annandale from other than the juvenile court counties were selected for the control sample in about the same proportion as they were found in the Highfields population.

[13]This was not carried on after the first year or so, for several reasons. First, almost all of the boys tested were those making favorable adjustments, as many of those who failed on probation or parole had done so before the end of a six-month period and were recommitted. Second, by examining the various test scores it could not be seen that the boys changed much from the first post-test to the second. And finally, it added another burden to the probation and parole staffs to call these boys in. Often it was difficult to find a time when they could be tested. No boy was post-post-tested after November, 1952.

For the purposes of this study the following definition of a recidivist, or failure, was adopted. A recidivist is one who, for any reason, was returned to court and/or violated probation or parole and as a result was committed to an institution. When we speak of failures or recidivists, we mean only boys who, subsequent to their first stay in either Highfields or Annandale, have been committed a second time. This commitment may be in Annandale, as is the case with most of the boys in our sample who have failed, or in a jail for a period of 30 days or longer, or penal institution in another state. Boys who have been called in to the probation or parole office or even brought before the court and admonished or warned but were not recommitted but continued on probation or parole are not failures by this definition.

Beginning November 1, 1951, and continuing until January, 1953, another phase of the research was designed and carried out.[14] This was an attempt to ascertain whether persons who know a boy intimately see any changes in him after he has been out of his respective facility for six weeks or more.

The procedure for this phase of the research was as follows:

1. At the time the boy was first interviewed —before he entered Highfields or Annandale—he was asked if he had any objections to our talking about him with (1) one of his parents or his guardian or another relative, (2) a boy or girl friend, (3) the proprietor of the place where he "hung out," (4) a policeman or other representative of the law, and (5) his probation officer. If he had no objections (very few objected) we asked for names and addresses.

2. Each of the persons suggested was interviewed in order to find out about the boy's behavior and the interviewee's attitudes toward it at the time he got into his present trouble.

3. After the boy had been out of either facility for two months, each of **these persons** was interviewed again and was asked the same type of questions concerning the boy's behavior as at the first interview. A comparison of the pre- and post-interview shows whether they think the boy's behavior has changed or whether opinions and attitudes toward the boy have altered. It was felt that these interviews would also indicate whether there were any unusual community situations which would make it especially difficult for the boy to adjust.

No boys committed to Annandale were pre-tested after February, 1954, and no boys sent to Highfields after April of this same year. It was necessary to cut off the Annandale cases earlier than the Highfields ones because of the longer commitment period of the reformatory boys. Few boys, unless recalled by the committing judge, are released from Annandale earlier than 12 months. Therefore, boys committed through February, 1954 would not leave Annandale before the end of January, 1955; and because we wished to allow at least a six-month period after release to ascertain whether or not a boy made good, none could be included who would not be out of the institution for at least six months by the end of August, 1955. The same reasoning was applied to the Highfields cases. Boys at Highfields stay as long as four months. All of the boys admitted to Highfields through April, 1954, therefore, would normally be released by the last of August and would have been on probation in their communities for at least six months by the end of February, 1955. The main reason for the earlier six-month cutoff date for the Highfields boys was that many more Highfields than Annandale boys had to be processed. It was also felt that numerically enough boys were in the Highfields sample and nothing would be gained by extending the time. Both groups of boys were finally followed up until October, 1955.

From February, 1951, when the first boys were tested, to the last of April, 1954, 233 boys were sent to Highfields by the courts, an average of about 61 boys a year.

From this beginning date to the end of January, 1954, the same courts committed 122 boys to Annandale. Nearly three-quarters of the boys sent to Highfields came almost equally from two of the most populous counties. One of these counties committed very few boys to Annandale—only three—whereas the second county committed almost two-thirds of the Annandale sample. This discrepancy in commit-

---

[14]This addition to the study was made possible by a grant-in-aid from the Rockefeller Foundation, to whom we are exceedingly grateful.

ment rates was an indication that the High-fields and Annandale samples might not be exactly comparable. We shall compare the two samples in order to convey just how they differ.[15]

◦ ◦ ◦

SUMMARY AND CONCLUSIONS

What answers can be given to the three questions which were proposed to guide this research?

1. Do delinquents participating in the short-term treatment program show a higher, the same, or a lower recidivist treatment rate than boys participating in other kinds of treatment programs?
2. Do delinquents participating in the short-term treatment program change their expressed attitudes, values, and opinions toward their families, law, and order, and their own outlook on life?
3. Do delinquents participating in the short-term treatment program change their basic personality structures or at least the overt manifestation of their personalities?

Answer to the First Question. There is no doubt that the Highfields Program for the Short-Term Treatment of Youthful Offenders is effective with a large proportion of the boys sent to the project. The data show that over the length of this study, when all boys sent to the project by the counties of New Jersey are included, 63 in every 100 Highfields boys, in contrast to 47 in every 100 Annandale boys, complete their treatment and do not get into further difficulty serious enough to require that they be reinstitutionalized.

This better over-all record of the total 229 boys sent to Highfields appears to be due in the main to the large difference between the relative number of Negro boys from the two facilities with successful outcomes. There is very little difference in the relative number of white boys from the two facilities with successful outcomes, but 59 in every 100 Highfield Negroes as compared with only 23 in every 100 Annandale

Negroes complete their stay and do not get into further difficulty.

There is no reason to believe from the data available that this large discrepancy is accounted for by differences in the backgrounds of Negro boys sent to the two facilities. When the number of background variables related to outcome are held constant, Highfields still has relatively more Negro boys with low and high scores who are successful than does Annandale. Nor is the difference accounted for by the disproportionate number of white and Negro boys sent to either facility by each county. A comparison of the counties has shown that the county which sends the most Negroes to Annandale also sends the most Negroes to Highfields. In this county the proportion of boys with successful outcomes is basically the same as it is for all the counties which send boys to Highfields: about three in every five white and Negro boys complete their treatment period at Highfields and get into no further difficulty after release, whereas about the same ratio of Annandale white boys but only three in every ten Annandale Negro boys complete their stay and get into no further difficulty after release.

It must be remembered that boys are sent to Highfields while they are officially on probation to the court from which they are sent.[16] Because this is the case, boys can be sent back to the

---

[15] When we began the Highfields research, 15 boys had already been there and were released at the end of their treatment or sent back to the court as unsuitable for residence at Highfields. These boys are not, of course, included in our analysis. It should be pointed out, however, that the results would not be altered in any significant way if they were.

---

[16] The fact that boys sent to Highfields are officially on probation should not be construed to mean that they are less serious delinquents than boys sent to Annandale. Probation is an integral part of the Highfields program. There is little doubt that almost all of the boys in the Highfields sample would have been sent to Annandale or a similar facility, rather than placed on probation, if Highfields were not in existence.

The original research design included the drawing of a second control group from boys placed on probation. This plan was abandoned because of the impossibility of securing a sample of boys on probation which would be reasonably similar to the Highfields sample. It was not possible to find enough boys 16 to 17 years of age on probation with the same frequency of prior delinquencies and serious kinds of delinquencies as those of the Highfields boys to say nothing of the similarity of many other background variables. There is every reason to believe that boys sent to Highfields are more like boys of the same age sent to Annandale than they are to boys placed on probation. All available information points to the fact that the great majority of Highfields boys are serious delinquents and have long histories of delinquency.

court if, in the opinion of the director, they are failing to adjust. About one-fifth of the boys, during the length of this study, have been declared unsuitable for residence. These include boys who ran away from Highfields (some within a few days or even a few hours after they first arrived), boys who found that the group and the program offered too great a threat to them, and boys who were so disruptive that they threatened the stability of other boys and the group as a whole. The majority of these boys were returned to the court within the first few weeks they were at the project. They cannot be considered to have really experienced the Highfields program.

The elimination of the boys who have been returned to the court results in an even more striking contrast between the success rates for Highfields and Annandale boys. More than three-quarters (77 per cent) of the Highfields boys who completed treatment have been successful. In other words, for every 100 boys who complete residence in the respective facility, the Highfields program rehabilitates 28 more than does the traditional program of caring for such boys.

Furthermore, a separate comparison of the success rates for white and Negro boys from the two facilities shows that Highfields has a higher success rate than Annandale for each group. Eight in every ten Highfields white boys are successful, whereas only six in every ten Annandale white boys are successful. Highfields Negroes succeed at more than double the rate of Annandale Negroes: seven out of ten Negroes are successful after their Highfields treatment, but only slightly over three in ten Negroes are successful after their Annandale stay.

When the differential in length of time after release is held constant the rates for Highfields boys are even more favorable than they are when time is not considered. Eight Highfields boys in every ten are successful a year after being released (there is no difference between whites and Negroes), whereas only five Annandale boys in every ten are likewise successful at the end of the same period of time. Seventeen more Highfields white boys in every 100 and almost 50 more Negro boys in every 100 are rehabili-

tated 12 months after release than Annandale white and Negro boys.

There is no reason to believe that these differences in success rates are due to the fact that Highfields may get a "better type" of boy. The expectancy tables constructed on the basis of background variables found to be related to outcome for white and Negro boys have shown that the differences in the relative number of adverse background variables for Highfields and Annandale boys do not account for the differences in outcome.

The simple fact is that all boys who complete their stay at Highfields have a better chance of being successful than do boys who complete their stay at Annandale, and this is especially the case for Highfields Negro boys.

A word of caution is in order here. The fact that Negroes at Highfields appear to profit so much more than they do at Annandale does not necessarily indicate that Highfields-type facilities should be established solely for Negroes or that a higher proportion of Negroes should be sent to the present Highfields project. From the data collected, it cannot be concluded that Negroes would profit to the same extent if a facility were established for them alone or if a higher proportion of them were sent to the present facility. It appears that the success of the Negoes sent to Highfields may be related to the ratio of Negroes to whites there. At present, it is rare that there are, at any one time, more than four or five Negroes at the project in a total of 18 to 20 boys. If the number were increased to eight or nine the whole acceptance and integration of the Negroes into the group might be different. This integration and acceptance is a fundamental aspect of the program at Highfields. A facility solely for Negroes would not allow the give-and-take between the white and Negro boys both in the guided group interaction sessions and in all their daily living experiences. In our opinion, the fact that white and Negro boys can discuss their common problems together is an important factor in the relatively low failure rate of the Negro boys who have been at Highfields.

Not only are higher proportions of Highfields than Annandale boys successful, but as time has passed since Highfields first opened in 1950 the proportion of boys who are successful has tended to increase. Also as time has gone by, relatively fewer boys have been returned to the court as unsuitable for residence. Of the 85 boys who entered Highfields during the last year of the study—from April, 1953 to April, 1954—only eight were sent back to the court as unsuitable for residence; and of those who completed their treatment nine out of ten had not got into further difficulty requiring institutional care, although every boy had been released and back in his community for more than a year. Sixteen of the 77 boys who completed treatment during this period were Negroes, and every one of them had a successful outcome. In fact, all but two Negro boys have had successful outcomes after Highfields treatment since April, 1952. Of course, a few more failures can be expected as the boys are out longer, but the data indicate that the great majority, over three-quarters, of the boys who fail do so within the first year after release. It appears certain that as the Highfields program has become stabilized and traditions have crystallized, it has become even more effective than it was at first.

Answer to the Second Question. There is very little evidence that Highfields boys, over the length of their treatment, change their attitudes toward family and toward law and order, and their outlook toward life, so far as the eight scales used to measure these attitudes show.

Highfields white boys showed no appreciable change on six of the eight scales. They became more favorable on the scale measuring attitude toward obeying the law, and less favorable on the scale measuring attitude toward law enforcement.

Annandale white boys also did not show many changes from pre- to post-test. On five of the eight scales there were no appreciable changes. They became more favorable on the scale measuring attitude toward general authority and less favorable on the scale measuring attitude toward law enforcement. Annandale white boys were more inclined to mark the neutral category on the post-test than they were on the pre-test on the scale measuring attitude toward the family.

On five of the eight scales Highfields Negro boys showed no appreciable difference from pre- to post-test. On three of the scales—attitude toward parental authority, attitude toward law enforcement and attitude toward behavior norms —Highfields Negro boys became more unfavorable on the post-test than they were on the pre-test.

The Annandale Negro boys showed the greatest tendency to change. On only three of the eight scales did these boys show relatively no difference between pre- and post-test responses. These scales were: attitude toward law enforcement, attitude toward general authority, and attitude indicating acceptance of others. On five of the scales the Annandale Negro boys moved in a favorable direction and on one, attitude toward parental authority, they moved unfavorably.

Although there does not appear to be much evidence that Highfields or Annandale white or Negro boys change their responses on the eight scales, there is evidence that the attitude responses of the boys are related to outcome. Actually, the pre-test responses of all white boys sent to either Highfields or Annandale on five of the scales significantly differentiate the boys who are likely to be successful from those who are likely to be unsuccessful. These scales are: attitude toward family, attitude toward parental authority, attitude toward obeying the law, attitude toward acceptance of others, and attitude toward behavior norms. On each of these scales boys with more favorable attitudes are more likely to have successful outcomes than boys with less favorable attitudes. An expectancy table constructed on the basis of the cumulative effect of these attitude variables, makes clear that white boys in both Highfields and Annandale who have low scores (zero or one) are much more likely than those with high scores to have successful outcomes; but *there is no appreciable difference between the success rates of Highfields and Annandale white boys who fall in the same score group, whether low or high.*

Only two of these scales show a relationship with outcome for Highfields and Annandale white boys who have completed their stay at either of the facilities: attitude toward obeying the law and attitude toward behavior norms. An expectancy table constructed on the basis of these two scales shows that Highfields white boys with no adverse attitude variables are more likely to be successful than those with one or more variables. This table does not discriminate for Annandale white boys who have completed treatment.

The attitude responses of all Negroes sent to either Highfields or Annandale show a significant relationship with outcome on three of the scales. These same scales also discriminate for only the Negro boys who complete their stay in either of two facilities. The scales which differentiate are: attitude toward family, attitude toward acceptance of others, and attitude toward behavior norms.

On the attitude toward family scale, Negro boys with less favorable attitudes are more likely than those with more favorable attitudes to have successful outcomes; this is especially pronounced for the Highfields Negroes. On the other two scales Negroes with more favorable attitudes are more likely than those with less favorable attitudes to have successful outcomes, as is the case with white boys. The expectancy table constructed on the cumulative effect of these three scales shows very little discrimination for all Negroes sent to Highfields, but discriminates significantly for all Negroes sent to Annandale. The expectancy table based on these same scales discriminates for both Highfields and Annandale Negroes who have completed treatment. Negro boys with low scores who have completed treatment in either facility are more likely to be successful than those with high scores, but *Annandale Negroes with either low or high scores have lower success rates than do Highfields Negroes.*

Actually, there is much more discrimination on these scales than the above discussion of the expectancy tables would indicate. We have discussed only the pre-test responses on the attitude scales which discriminate in the same direction for boys in both facilities. In addition, some of the other scales show a relationship between the pre-test and/or post-test responses of the boys and outcome. A given scale may discriminate for Highfields boys but not for Annandale

boys, or vice versa, or discriminate in opposite ways for boys in the two facilities.

It is interesting that on six of the eight scales the highest success rate is found for the Annandale Negro boys whose post-test responses fall in the most favorable categories. An expectancy table based on Annandale Negroes' post-test responses shows that boys with low scores have much higher success rates than boys with high scores. Only for Annandale Negroes is there this consistency. In all other groups the highest success rate is likely to be found in any of the three categories. This may indicate that few Annandale Negroes can succeed unless they have favorable attitudes, but that Highfields Negroes can hold favorable or unfavorable attitudes and still succeed because they have learned to live with their attitudes without undue disturbance.

Answer to the Third Question. There is no evidence that Highfields white or Negro boys change much from pre- to post-test, judging from the over-all responses they made to the ten scales adapted from the Army's Psychoneurotic Screening Adjunct to measure the boys' personality structure.

Highfields white boys show an over-all difference in response of as much as ten percentage points between pre- and post-tests on only one scale; and Highfields Negro boys show this much difference on but two. The white boys shift in the direction of better adjustment, whereas the Negroes shift toward poorer adjustment on one of the scales and toward better adjustment on the other.

Annandale white and Negro boys shift at least ten percentage points between pre- and post-tests on more scales than do Highfields white and Negro boys. Annandale white boys show an over-all difference in response of as much as ten percentage points between pre- and post-tests on five of the ten scales; Annandale Negro boys show this much over-all difference in response on three scales. Two of these scales are the same as those on which the Annandale white boys shift, but none is the same as those on which the Highfields Negroes shift. On one of the scales the Annandale Negroes shift in the direction of poorer adjustment, but on the other two scales the shift is toward better adjustment. On all five scales the Annandale white boys shift in the direction of better adjustment.

There is no consistent relationship between the boys' responses to either the pre- or post-test and outcome. The scales on which there is the most change from pre- to post-test are not necessarily the scales which show the greatest relationship between the boys' responses and outcome. A number of the scales which showed a relationship between boys' pre-test responses and outcome do not show the same relationship between the boys' post-test responses and outcome.

According to the analysis of the Miale-Holsopple Sentence Completions given to a sample of Highfields and Annandale boys, Highfields boys tend to change from pre- to post-test more than Annandale boys, and in a different way. But, as Dr. Holsopple writes: "There is no reason to suppose that the primary goals or basic drives of either group were substantially changed. With the Annandale group on the one hand, the goals remained distorted to unclear, the drives unrecognized or unaccepted. In contrast, among the Highfields group, there was movement toward a clearer view of primary goals and substantially increased acceptance of primary drives."

These changes, however, do not appear to be related to outcome. Just about as many Highfields as Annandale boys whose tests were analyzed have unsuccessful outcomes. It would be worth knowing whether the boys who change the most and in a favorable direction on these tests are the ones who are most likely to be successful. This cannot be ascertained from this analysis because it was done for the group of boys in each sample rather than for the individual boys making up the respective samples.

CONCLUSION

This research points out the fact that a higher proportion of Highfields than Annandale boys succeed and that this is true even when the background variables which are related to their success or failure are held constant. It has shown that it is possible by using background and attitudinal variables, to differentiate boys who are likely to have high and low success rates even before they enter the respective facility. It has not shown that the boys' attitudes as measured by the tests change appreciably during their residence and treatment. It may well be that the instruments used in this research do not get at the kinds of changes which the Highfields white and Negro boys undergo during their period of treatment. When almost three more Highfields than Annandale white boys in every ten and five more Highfields than Annandale Negroes in every ten who complete their treatment succeed, there must be some explanation for it.

Highfields rehabilitates this high proportion of boys in a four-month period, whereas most other facilities keep boys at least three times as long. Not only is this fact important in itself, but it is important because Highfields is relatively much less expensive per boy treated than is the conventional facility. The "yearly per capita cost" of the residential aspects of the Highfields and Annandale programs, as figured by the state, is about the same, but this is misleading because it does not take into consideration the total number of boys who have experienced the Highfields program during the course of a year.[17] On a strict per capita basis the Highfields program costs one-third as much as the traditional program for each boy treated. Because of the differential in the outcome rates, this cost differential would be much greater if it took into consideration the number of boys each facility rehabilitated.

It is hoped that research will continue at Highfields so that the many facets of the program can be explored and better understood. It would be very worth while to know which boys at Highfields change, how this change takes place, and what form it takes.

---

[17]The yearly per capita cost on current maintenance while in the institutions was $1,413.95 for Highfields and $1,479.75 for Annandale during 1953 (see: *Mental Deficiency in New Jersey*, 1953). These per capita costs are figures on the basis of the number in the facility at the end of the fiscal year and not the total number treated during a year.

42.

ELEANOR TOUROFF GLUECK

EFFORTS TO IDENTIFY DELINQUENTS

In *Federal Probation* (September, 1956) appeared an article by the writer entitled, "Spotting Potential Delinquents: Can It Be Done?" In this article a description was given of what is now called the *Glueck Social Prediction Table for Identifying Potential Delinquents,* and the findings of several retrospective applications of this Table were briefly summarized. As the device approaches validation, interest in it is becoming greater and although experimentation must continue, this seems an appropriate time to summarize the efforts to check it, especially as the chapter in *Predicting Delinquency and Crime*[1] entitled "Checkings of Table Identifying Potential Delinquents" was prepared at an earlier stage and does not, therefore, incorporate the most recent attempts to check the Table.

The purpose of the predictive instrument is to distinguish at school entrance those children who are and those *who are not* in danger of developing into persistent offenders. (It is equally important to identify the latter, especially in high-delinquency areas). Its purpose is also to distinguish delinquents from pseudo-delinquents and nondelinquents among those manifesting difficulties.

The Table, first published in *Unraveling Juvenile Delinquency*[2] derives from a comparison of 500 persistent delinquents and 500 nondelinquents matched by age, intelligence, ethnic origin and residence in depressed areas of Boston.

The Social Prediction Table, which is one of four predictive instruments based on the findings of *Unraveling Juvenile Delinquency*[3] comprises five factors in the family background (Affection of Mother for Boy, Affection of Father for Boy, Discipline of Boy by Father, Supervision of Boy by Mother, Family Cohesiveness), found in *Unraveling Juvenile Delinquency* markedly to differentiate delinquents from nondelinquents. As it was learned in *Unraveling Juvenile Delinquency* that half the delinquents had shown their first overt signs of antisocial behavior before age 8, and 90 percent at 10 or younger, it was necessary to limit the selection of differentiative factors to those clearly operative in a child's life prior to the time he might evidence the earliest signs of maladaptive behavior. (The interested reader is asked to refer to *Unraveling Juvenile Delinquency*, chapter twenty, pps. 259, 260, and to *Predicting Delinquency and Crime*, chapter two, pps. 23–31, for a description of the method of constructing the Table.)

A predictive table, is, strictly speaking, only an "experience" table until it has been successfully applied to other samples of cases. For this reason, checkings on many and varied samples need to be made. During the period of the earliest efforts to check the device, attention was largely focused on determining the extent to which it would have been possible by retrospective application of the Table to already adjudicated delinquents and also to nondelinquents, to have correctly identified them at age five or six as the persistent offenders or the nonoffenders they actually turned out to be.

SOURCE: Eleanor Touroff Glueck, "Efforts to Identify Delinquents," *Federal Probation,* June, 1960, pp. 49–56. Permission granted by publisher and author.

[1]Sheldon and Eleanor Glueck, *Predicting Delinquency and Crime,* with an "Introduction" by the Chief Justice of the United States, the Honorable Earl Warren (Cambridge, Mass.: Harvard University Press, 1959), chap. 10, pp. 127 ff.

[2]Sheldon and Eleanor Glueck (New York: The Commonwealth Fund, Cambridge, Mass.: Harvard University Press, 1950), chap. 20, pp. 258 ff.

[3]A second predictive device grew out of differences in the character structure of delinquents and nondelinquents (ibid., pp. 263, 264); a third from the temperamental differences between them (ibid., pp. 264, 265), and a fourth from differences in their response to certain intelligence tests (only recently published in *Predicting Delinquency and Crime,* p. 239).

The wisdom of ascertaining to what extent the predictive cluster (derived from the comparison of 500 persistent offenders in Boston and 500 matched nondelinquents) is present in many and varied samples of cases should be self-evident. The search for "causes" of delinquency (by which is here meant *persisting* antisocial behavior) may be narrowed, should the predictive cluster of factors be found present in great measure in other samples of already persistent offenders and in nonoffenders differing from the original sample in age, ethnic origin, intelligence level (and so on). Their far greater presence in delinquents and their far lesser presence in nondelinquents should lend confidence to their significance for a clearer understanding of certain aspects of the causation of delinquency.

RETROSPECTIVE STUDIES PREVIOUSLY REPORTED IN FEDERAL PROBATION QUARTERLY

The first retrospective study was undertaken in 1952 by Black and Glick of the Jewish Board of Guardians on 100 delinquent boys at the Hawthorne-Cedar Knolls School.[4] The second, also in 1952, was made by Richard E. Thompson,[5] candidate for Honors at Harvard University, Department of Social Relations, on 100 boys originally encompassed in the well-known Cambridge-Somerville Youth Study.[6]

The third checkup on cases other than the ones on which the Table was based, was made in 1953 by the New Jersey State Department of Institutions and Agencies, on 51 parolees;[7] the fourth, in 1956, by clinicians of the Douglas A. Thom Clinic for Children in Boston on 57

"antisocial" young children.[8] A fifth check by Thompson, also made in 1957, comprised 50 boys who had appeared in the Boston Juvenile Court in 1950 and 50 girls committed by the Boston Juvenile Court to the care of the Massachusetts Youth Service Board during 1954–55.[9]

In addition to these already published studies, two as yet unpublished "retrospective" efforts, one in 1957 by Selma J. Glick and Catherine Donnell applied the Table to 150 unmarried mothers,[10] and another in 1957 by Glick, to 81 boys from upper-income families ($7,500 a year and over).[11]

This completes the roster of *retrospective* applications of the five-factor Social Prediction Table as reported in the article "Spotting Potential Delinquents: Can It Be Done?"

In most of these inquiries, it was found that in nine out of ten instances the offenders involved would have been correctly identified at age six as potentially persistent offenders; and in the few remaining investigations a slightly lesser result was derived. It is of particular significance that in the first of the two studies by Thompson (see n. 5 for reference), it was ascertained that true *nondelinquents,* even though evidencing behavioral difficulties in school (thought by teachers and clinicians to be prodromal of delinquency), were correctly identified by the Table in 91.3 percent of instances. (This is in contrast with 58.7 percent, 53.5 percent, and 56.9 percent of correct predictions by three clinicians charged with selecting boys for the Cambridge-Somerville Youth Study.) It is to be noted also that in the study of unmarried mothers (the first application of the Table to girls) evidence began to suggest that the

[4]Bertram J. Black and Selma J. Glick, "Predicted vs. Actual Outcome for Delinquent Boys," New York, Jewish Board of Guardians, 1952.

[5]Richard E. Thompson, "A Validation of the Glueck Social Prediction Scale for Proneness to Delinquency," *Journal of Criminal Law, Criminology and Police Science,* November-December, 1952.

[6]Edwin Powers and Helen Witmer, *An Experiment in the Prediction of Delinquency* (New York: Columbia University Press, 1951).

[7]"Predicting Juvenile Delinquency," *Research Bulletin* No. 124, April 1955, State Department of Institutions and Agencies, Trenton, N. J.

[8]Eveoleen N. Rexford, Maxwell Schleifer, and Suzanne T. Van Amerongen, "A Follow-up of a Psychiatric Study of 57 Antisocial Young Children," *Mental Hygiene,* April, 1956, pp. 196–214.

[9]Richard E. Thompson, "Further Validation of Glueck Social Prediction Table for Identifying Potential Delinquents," *Journal of Criminal Law, Criminology, and Police Science,* vol. 48, no. 2 (July-August, 1957).

[10]Selma J. Glick and Catherine Donnell, "Background Factors in 150 Cases of Jewish Unmarried Mothers," presented in part in the *Jewish Social Service Quarterly,* vol. 30, no. 2 (Winter, 1958). The Section on Prediction was omitted from the printed paper.

[11]Letter, May 31, 1956.

predictive instrument might be applicable to girls as well as boys.

PROSPECTIVE STUDIES REPORTED IN FEDERAL PROBATION QUARTERLY

In addition to a resumé of retrospective studies, the writer made brief mention of two ongoing projects of a different nature, in which the identification of true delinquents and true non-delinquents was being attempted before clear evidence of their status was apparent—one, an investigation set up in 1953 by the New York City Youth Board in two public schools in very high delinquency areas where the Table was being applied to all first-grade boys shortly after school entrance, that is, roughly at age six; the other called the Maximum Benefits Project initiated in 1954 under the auspices of the Commissioners' Youth Council of the District of Columbia in two elementary schools in very high delinquency areas and including girls as well as boys (179 children) already manifesting severe behavioral difficulties in school.

In the New York City Youth Board inquiry the objective is to determine whether and to what extent the Social Prediction Table, if applied even before clear signs of antisocial behavior, will serve to distinguish on the basis of *subsequent* evidence, the true delinquents in a high delinquency area from the nondelinquents; while in the Maximum Benefits Project the purpose (among others) is to determine whether the Social Prediction Table, if applied to children reported by teachers as already showing evidences of severe behavioral difficulties, will correctly differentiate, as determined by subsequent followup, the potential delinquents from the pseudodelinquents. Both inquiries are still in process and will, it is hoped, continue until the subjects are 17. A brief resumé of the findings to date follows.

FURTHER RETROSPECTIVE STUDIES IN THE UNITED STATES

Subsequent to the appearance of "Spotting Potential Delinquents: Can It Be Done?" several other retrospective checkings of the Social Pre-

diction Table have been made—one at the Thom Clinic in Boston where Dr. Virginia Clower applied the Table in 1956 to 100 boys "chosen at random for a wide variety of behavior and emotional difficulties" who had been referred to the Clinic during 1953 and 1954. The results showed that of 31 boys in this group who had been diagnosed by the clinicians as "antisocial characters," all "without exception" were placed by the Prediction Table in the group having a high likelihood of persistent delinquency. And in 1957, the Clinic, continuing its experimental application of the Social Prediction Table, again reported a consistently high degree of correlation between the clinical diagnoses and the rating by the Social Prediction Table:

> Our impression is that the Scale almost invariably gives high scores to the child with aggressive, destructive behavior problems, whether these problems are seen in an individual with an antisocial character formation, neurosis or psychosis. The work we have done so far suggests a positive correlation between the ability of the child to manage aggression and his score on the Glueck scales. That is, the less tendency to act out aggressive impulses, the lower the score.[12]

In 1957, Selma J. Glick applied the Prediction Table to a small group of boys who were independently diagnosed by the clinical staff of the Jewish Board of Guardians as true delinquents on intake into the Clinic and she found that the Table itself, "without psychiatric and psychological studies of the children would have properly identified the same cases."[13]

Still another retrospective study completed since the publication of "Spotting Potential Delinquents" encompasses 28 inmates of Sing Sing Prison who had been juvenile offenders. In this were involved a team of researchers at the Post-Graduate Center for Psychiatric Research headed by Bernard Glueck, Jr., M.D.,[14] and the findings presented at the Third International Congress of Criminology in London (1955) by Mrs. Isa Brandon. The prisoners included rapists, men committing sexual assaults, heterosex-

---

[12]Letter from Dr. Eveoleen N. Rexford, Director, Douglas A. Thom Clinic for Child Guidance, dated May 16, 1957.
[13]Letter, May 17, 1957.
[14]Now professor of psychiatry in the Medical School of the University of Minnesota.

ual pedophiles, homosexual pedophiles, and non-sexual offenders. Coauthored by Bernard Glueck, Jr., M.D., and Mrs. Brandon, the report stated that regardless of offense, 71 percent of the men would have been correctly identified by the Social Prediction Table in their early years as headed for criminal careers; and that 90 percent of the "nonsexual" offenders would have been correctly identified.[15]

Also during 1957, the South Shore Courts Clinic of Quincy, Massachusetts, which was set up by the Massachusetts State Department of Mental Health and charged with the study and diagnosis of children referred by the local Juvenile Court, applied the Table to 50 young offenders in an effort to determine its usefulness to clinicians. The results of the pilot study were sufficiently encouraging to the project director, B. R. Hutcheson, M.D., and to the research director, J. I. Hurwitz, Ph.D., to suggest the possibility that the Table may be of aid in differentiating between true delinquents and accidental offenders.

The above constitutes a brief resumé of American retrospective studies applying the Social Prediction Table that have come directly to the writer's attention.

In addition to the actual applications of the Table, diverse inquiries about it reflecting widespread interest have come, for example, from police departments (notably the Juvenile Aid Bureau of the New York City Police Department); from school systems in different parts of the United States, including Rochester, Denver, Los Angeles, and Tacoma; from school counselors; from family service societies; from youth authorities, notably the Southern Reception Center for Children of the State of California; from institutions for young children, including schools for retarded children; from child guidance clinics; from mental hospitals; from Community Chests and Councils; from Governor's Committees on Children and Youth; from child psychiatrists, psychologists, pediatricians, ministers; and more recently, from a nursery school training center.

RETROSPECTIVE STUDIES IN FOREIGN COUNTRIES

Some checkings of the Social Prediction Table have been attempted also in foreign countries, notably in Japan and France. A third is in the planning stage in Belgium.

In addition have come expressions of earnest interest in a means for early differentiation between potential delinquents and true nondelinquents from England, Holland, Germany, Sweden, India, Israel, Australia, New Zealand, Uruguay and other South American countries. And worldwide interest is reflected in a resolution presented and passed at the Third International Congress of Criminology held in London in September, 1955:

Because of the close relationship between recidivism and early delinquency, it is advisable to encourage the development and use of prognostic devices, including predictive tables in the prediction of early delinquency. . . . That an indispensable aspect of any improved prognostic technique is the validation of the predictive methods on samples of cases other than those on which they were developed in order to transform them as far as possible into effective instruments for prognosis.[16]

It is noted in the Program of the Third International Penal and Penitentiary Congress of the Spanish American countries, which is to be held in Lisbon in the summer of 1960, that the Fifth Section is to be devoted to "Pronostics Criminologiques:"

Le choix de ce sujet dérive de la décision adoptée par le II Congrès pénal pénitentiaire de Sao-Paulo qui recommandait comme sujet de travail du prochain Congrès l'étude de l'examen médico-psychiatrique, psychologique et social des délinquants, spécialement en ce qui concerne les délinquants par habitude.[17]

(a) *Japan.* Japanese interest in a means for the early identification of potential delinquents is especially keen, and is manifested not only by

---

[15]Unpublished paper presented at the Third International Congress of Criminology, London, September, 1955.

[16]See *Summary of Proceedings,* Third International Congress of Criminology, Bedford College, London, September 12–18, 1955, 251 pp., published by the British Organizing Committee on behalf of the International Society for Criminology, 1957. The resolution was adopted by a vote of 260 to 10 (see pp. 222–23. Conclusion of Section 4).

[17]For Program, see *Revue de Science Criminelle et de Droit Pénal Comparé,* Paris, Octobre-Décembre 1959, nouvelle Série, numéro 4, p. 915.

the recent organization of a Criminology Study Society within the Ministry of Justice, a major effort of which is devoted to prediction studies, but also by the publication of a two-hundred page book in Japanese by a public prosecutor and a psychiatrist, entitled *Introduction to the Glueck Prediction Method.*[18]

The first of the Japanese attempts to apply the Social Prediction Table was made by Tokuhiro Tatezawa, probation officer of the Yokohama Family Court, on 30 delinquents appearing before a juvenile court in Morioka, Japan, and a control group of 30 nondelinquent boys from a public school in the same neighborhood.[19]

The application of the Table appears to have been successful because 87 percent of the delinquents and 92 percent of the nondelinquents were correctly identified by the Social Prediction Table. This first retrospective Japanese checking assumes particular significance in the light of the marked cultural differences between Japanese and American delinquents and nondelinquents:

This prediction study revealed that the factors used in the Gluecks' prediction table show rather high predictive power when applied to the Japanese juvenile cases which have their own cultural and social background.[20]

Subsequently, other inquiries were made in Japan, and some are still under way:

Our Criminology Study Society has been successfully carrying out a series of studies for the validation of Glueck Social Prediction Scales. A Progress Report on one of these studies revealed that the Social Prediction Scale would have successfully detected 92 percent of 70 persistently delinquent juveniles, had it been applied to these cases as early as when they were nine years of age.[21]

(b) *France.* An ongoing study in Strasbourg, France, was initiated in 1958 by Professor

Jacques Léauté of the Institut de Science Criminelle of the Faculty of Law of the University of Strasbourg, and is being carried on in cooperation with M. Didier Ansieu (Professor of Psychology and Head of the Institut Psycho-Pédagogie of the University of Strasbourg), Dr. René Oberlé (psychologist at the Centre d'Observation of the Juvenile Court in Strasbourg), and Dr. Berge (Head of the Institut Psycho-Pédagogie of the Lycée Claude Bernard, Paris). They made a pilot study in 1958, applying the Social Prediction Table to 46 delinquents at the Centre d'Observation de Délinquants Juvénile in Strasbourg and found that 91.4 percent of these boys would have been correctly identified as potential delinquents had the prediction table been applied to them at the age of six. It is of special interest that the psychologist, M. Oberlé, who was charged with the details of the study, was initially skeptical of the ability of the Prediction Table to identify the delinquents and is now convinced of its usefulness.

Encouraged by the result of the pilot project, Professor Léauté and his coworkers applied the Table early in 1959 to two additional groups of offenders totalling 203 boys, one group being already adjudicated delinquents and the other, though never arrested, was brought before the juvenile court by their parents on complaint of incorrigibility. Of the 140 delinquents in the first group, 89.9 percent would have been correctly predicted as potential delinquents at age six; while of the 63 boys in the second group, almost all were identified as potential delinquents.

A comparison of the findings regarding the incidence of the five predictive factors among the French delinquents and predelinquents, as compared with the 500 delinquents of *Unraveling Juvenile Delinquency* (on the basis of which cases the Social Prediction Table was constructed), is of interest:

In *Unraveling Juvenile Delinquency,* 27.9 percent of the mothers of the delinquents were found to be indifferent or hostile to the boys as compared with 46.4 percent of the French delinquents and 49.2 percent of the French predelinquents; as regards "Affection of Father," 59.8 percent of the fathers of our delinquents of *Unraveling* were found to be indifferent or

[18]Haruo Abe and Kokichi Higuchi, Tokyo, Ichiryusha Publishing Company, 1959.
[19]Tokuhiro Tatezawa, "A Study of Prediction of Juvenile Delinquency," mimeographed by Ministry of Justice, Japan, 1956, and distributed by the Criminology Study Society.
[20]Ibid., p. 30.
[21]Letter from Haruo Abe, Public Prosecutor, Ministry of Justice, November 21, 1958. Additional studies have been reported (all confirmatory) since the completion of this article.

hostile to them, as compared with 75 percent of the fathers of the French delinquents and 69.8 percent of the fathers of the French predelinquents; as regards "Supervision by Mother," it was unsuitable in 93 percent of the cases of 500 delinquents of *Unraveling*, as compared with 95.7 percent of the French delinquents and 93.7 percent of the French predelinquents; in regard to "Discipline by Father," it was other than firm and kindly in 94.3 percent of the 500 delinquents of *Unraveling* as compared with 100 percent of the French delinquents and 98.4 percent of the French predelinquents; finally, as regards "Family Cohesiveness," the family was not completely cohesive in 84 percent of instances among the 500 delinquents of *Unraveling Juvenile Delinquency* as compared with 95.7 percent of the French delinquents and 98.4 percent of the French predelinquents.[22]

(c) *Interest in Other Foreign Countries.* A study to test the usefulness of the Table is now being formulated in Brussels by Professor Aimée Racine of the University of Brussels, director of the Centre d'Étude de la Délinquance Juvénile[23] with a subsidy from the Belgian Ministry of Justice. This study has the support of the Secretary-General of the Ministry, M. Paul Cornil, and of M. DeCant, Public Prosecutor, as well as of the Ministry of Public Health (especially of its Conseil Supérieur de la Famille, the Chairman of which was, until recently, Professor Fernand Collin of the Law Faculty of Louvain University, and who is largely responsible for initiating interest in a prediction validation project in Belgium).

It is our intention to prepare a motion to be sub-

mitted to the Conseil Supérieur, in which we request the Government to give first priority to the study of the detection of possible delinquency among Belgian youth.[24]

There are other significant evidences of interest in foreign countries in the early identification of potential delinquents which might be mentioned. For example, in Holland, Professor Willem Nagel of the Criminological Institute of the University of Leiden has been charged with, and has recently completed, the preparation of a report to the Dutch Ministry of Justice on the possible uses of prediction tables in Holland. This is a complete survey of predictive theories and devices, including a description of the Glueck Prediction Tables. The Dutch Ministry of Justice is now engaged in determining next steps in the application of such devices.

In Germany, Judge Wolf Middendorff of Freiburg/Breisgau has prepared a Report for the German Ministry of Justice on American and European Prediction Studies, in which considerable space is given to the Social Prediction Table. This is now in process of publication. In India, Mr. D. V. Kulkarni, Chief Inspector of the Certified Schools in Bombay, and Mr. Chinnea Doraiswami, Deputy Inspector General of Prisons and Correctional Schools of India, have each expressed the hope that they might develop some experimental applications of the Social Prediction Table. From New Zealand, Mr. Henry Field, professor of educational psychology of Canterbury University College in Christchurch, wrote in February, 1957:

I am satisfied that this work of prediction is of fundamental importance and that it points the way to successful measures of prophylaxis and prevention.

In July, 1956, a report on juvenile delinquency in Australia, prepared by the Advisory Committee to the Honorable Chief Secretary of Victoria[25] indicates that "research in this field should be undertaken in Victoria with the objective of ascertaining the extent to which, and

---

[22]Findings reported to Professor and Mrs. Sheldon Glueck in July, 1958 in Strasbourg, and in June, 1959 in Paris by Professor Léauté and some of his coworkers and supplemented by a letter from Professor Léauté, February 25, 1960. As regards the incorrigible boys, in accordance with Article 375 of the French Code Civil (September 1, 1945), a parent or guardian may, if a child is unmanageable, request the judge of the juvenile court to examine into the situation. Article 376 requests that the judge make an investigation and that he may for this purpose order that a child be held in an observation center; (already adjudicated delinquents may also be held in such a center). The incorrigibles are regarded as predelinquents and the results of the application of the Social Prediction Table have indeed proved them to be such.

[23]49, rue du Châtelain, Bruxelles 5, Belgique.

[24]Letter, January 28, 1958.

[25]Report of Juvenile Delinquency Advisory Committee to The Honorable A. G. Rylah, M.L.A., Chief Secretary of Victoria, The Honorable Mr. Justice John V. Barry of the Supreme Court of Victoria (Chairman); Printed at Melbourne, July 17, 1956, 96 pp. See p. 32ff., "Prediction Studies."

the manner in which, these methods may be properly used here."

These are a few illustrations of the far-flung interest in a means for identifying delinquents and for experimenting with the Social Prediction Table.

PROJECTS DIRECTED TOWARD THE IDENTIFICATION OF POTENTIAL DELINQUENTS

I return now to two ongoing experiments in which the Social Prediction Table has been applied:

(1) by the New York City Youth Board to 224 boys in the first grade of two schools in high delinquency areas of New York City, in advance of, or without knowledge of, any overt signs of antisocial behavior, in order to determine the extent of ultimate agreement between predicted and actual delinquency or nondelinquency.

(2) by the Maximum Benefits Project, to 179 boys and girls in all grades of two elementary schools in high-delinquency areas in the District of Columbia referred to the Project staff by teachers as manifesting severe behavioral difficulties. Among the questions raised in this inquiry is the extent to which the behavioral symptoms are indeed prodromal of future delinquency according to the Prediction Table when checked against the later behavior of the children.

Both inquiries are still in progress and it is hoped will continue until the youngsters are 17. Meanwhile, the New York City Youth Board[26] has briefly reported in January 1960 that "follow-up" data covering a seven-year period is available on 223 of the initial sample of 224 boys who are now 12½ to 13 years old and scattered in 89 different schools: Of 186 boys predicted at school entrance as *nondelinquents,* 176, or 94.6 percent are still *nondelinquent;* of 37 boys predicted as delinquents, 13 are already adjudicated delinquents and 4 more are "unofficial" offenders, a total of 46 percent; of 191 boys who are still nondelinquents, regardless of how predicted, 176, or 89.7 percent, had

been correctly predicted as nondelinquents; of 27 boys already delinquents, 17, or 63 percent, had been correctly predicted as delinquents.

In considering these interim results, it should be kept in mind that the boys are only now approaching the peak years of delinquency and arrest. It is essential that the followup continue until they are 17, since it was found in *Unraveling Juvenile Delinquency*[27] that about half of the 500 Boston delinquents did not make their first court appearance until they were between 13 and 16 years old.

As regards the Maximum Benefits Project, a preliminary report issued in 1958 states that "The Glueck criteria . . . have proven in our opinion to be a very effective predictive device."[28]

In a later interim report it is stated that of 58 children already having police or court records four years after the beginning of the study, 57 had been previously identified by the Social Prediction Table as potential delinquents.

And a more recent summary of the Project made in preparation for the 1960 White House Conference on Children and Youth now stresses that "The Glueck Scores, in conjunction with the teacher referrals, appear to be effective tools in the identification of potential delinquents:"

Since the average child still has 5.9 years to go before reaching 18, and since the incidence of juvenile court appearances increases in the teenage group, we are inclined to think the percentage will draw near expected levels.[29]

GENERAL TREND OF FINDINGS

The accumulated evidence thus far gathered from "retrospective" and "prospective" studies both in the United States and in foreign countries all seems to be tending in the same direc-

---

[26]79 Madison Avenue, New York City.

[27]*Unraveling Juvenile Delinquency*, Appendix A, p. 294.

[28]Emory F. Hodges, C. Downing Tait, Jr., and Nina B. Trevvett, "Preliminary Report of the Maximum Benefits Project," made to the Eugene and Agnes E. Meyer Foundation; Commissioners' Youth Council, 1145 19th Street N.W., Washington, D.C., September, 1958 (mimeographed), p. 18.

[29]Emory F. Hodges, C. Downing Tait, Jr., and Nina B. Trevvett, "Four Years of Work with Problem Children in Elementary Schools," Maximum Benefits Project (mimeographed, 1959). Address as above.

tion. A total of 18 inquiries in which the Social Prediction Table has been applied, are all suggestive of its usefulness. The studies include four samples of nondelinquents (the latter incorporated into the first of the two investigations by Thompson in 1954, in the New York City Youth Board study, in the Maximum Benefits Project, and in the first of the Japanese inquiries); three studies include girls (the second Thompson study, the study by Glick and Donnell of 150 unmarried mothers, and the Maximum Benefits Project).

The results thus far indicate that regardless of ethnic origin, color, religion, intelligence level, residence in urban or rural areas, economic level, or even sex, the predictive cluster is equally potent, not only on American but on Japanese and French samplings.

The Table has to date been applied to some 1,600 young children and adolescents—preponderantly males—in three American States (Massachusetts, New Jersey, and New York) and the District of Columbia, and in two foreign countries (Japan and France), each time with highly encouraging results. This does not mean that Professor Sheldon Glueck and I, who are responsible for the construction of this device based on 500 delinquents and 500 matched nondelinquents of *Unraveling Juvenile Delinquency,* are satisfied that it is beyond the stage of testing. We urge that checkings continue and that careful record be kept of the work done.

The instrument appears to hold promise not only for the identification of emotionally healthy potential delinquents, but also for the identification of neurotic, psychotic, or psychopathic children who are likely to give overt expression to their conflicts in aggressive behavior. Some gleanings of the capacity of the Table to identify this latter group of potential delinquents come from the experiments with it in the Thom Clinic by Rexford, Van Amerongen and Schleifer;[30] by Glick at the Jewish Board of Guardians; and in the study of 28 cases at Sing Sing Prison.

The Table also holds promise of distinguishing among children already manifesting behavior difficulties, those who are and who are not likely to develop into persistent offenders.

RESOLUTION OF DIFFICULTIES IN APPLYING TABLES

A pioneer venture must to some extent proceed by trial and error, and the one of checking even a carefully constructed predictive device is no exception. Difficulties have emerged in the course of the experimental use of the Social Prediction Table that could not have been fully anticipated, and this has provided an invaluable opportunity to find ways of coping with them.

A device of this kind, the use of which is in part at least based on observational skills and the capacity to make judgments on data gathered from home interviews as well as from already recorded data in the files of social agencies, police, probation departments and other repositories of information about children and their families, is naturally subject to pitfalls. It has become abundantly clear that the difficulties stem from variations in the training and experience of those applying the Tables (psychiatrists, social workers, psychologists and others) as well as from occasional inadequacies in data. Questions have arisen, for example, as to the particular subcategory of one or another of the five factors into which to place a case. Likewise, there have at times emerged disagreements among different investigators in the same inquiry about the rating of some factors, especially affection of parents for a child which psychoanalytically oriented observers interpret in accordance with Freudian depth psychology and others on the basis of *surface* manifestations of parental affection. In addition to the difficulties encountered in the rating of parental affection, is the rating of "Discipline by Father" (as well as "Affection of Father") in instances in which the father or a father-substitute had never been a part of the family group, or left the home before the child was three years of age. Still another difficulty relates to the assessment of "Family Cohesiveness" in instances in which children were reared solely by the mother or mother-substitute.

These and similar considerations led us to

---

[30]See Eveoleen M. Rexford, "Antisocial Young Children and Their Families," *Dynamic Psychopathology in Childhood,* ed. Lucie Jessner and Eleanor Pavenstedt (New York: Grune and Stratton, Inc., 1959), pp. 186–220. See esp. pp. 197–200.

investigate the possibility that the rating of one or another of the five factors could be dispensed with in instances in which the data appeared insufficient for purposes of making an accurate judgment, or was altogether lacking. This was accomplished with the aid of the Research Bureau of the Harvard Business School (which had on punch cards for each of the thousand cases of *Unraveling Juvenile Delinquency* the five factors comprising the original Table). Correlations were systematically pursued between the total scores for the Five Factors ("Affection of Mother for Boy," "Affection of Father for Boy," "Supervision by Mother," "Discipline by Father," and "Family Cohesiveness") and every possible combination of 4, 3, and 2 factors, eliminating those combinations in which the Coefficient of Correlation was less than .90. Actually, the coefficients were found to range from .932 in a Table made up of two factors to .987 in a Table made up of four factors. (The interested reader is invited to examine *Predicting Delinquency and Crime*, Appendix B, Tables IX-1 to IX-1e, pp. 233 to 235, for all possible combinations of four and fewer factors that nevertheless retain a very high predictive potential. These shortened prediction tables were completed just in time to be added to the galley proof of *Predicting Delinquency and Crime*.)

In instances in which the Five-Factor Table cannot be used, one or another of the shorter Tables should meet any problem reflected in the course of the validation efforts, except those arising from lack of sufficient training in gathering and interpreting the needed data. Some illustrations of how the shortened prediction Table would meet the problems that have been revealed in the course of attempts to check the Social Prediction Table against various samples of cases might be helpful. For example, the inconsistency of ratings of "Affection of Mother" or "Affection of Father" by workers of differing "persuasions" has been eliminated by confining the scoring in certain instances to the three remaining factors ("Supervision by Mother," "Discipline by Father," and "Family Cohesiveness"). The Coefficient of Correlation between the Three-Factor Total Scores and the Total Scores for the Five Factors is .961). To those who may conclude that the elimination of these

factors implies that they are not potent in the etiology of delinquency, the writer wishes to emphasize that this is not the case; for these two factors were found in *Unraveling Juvenile Delinquency* markedly to differentiate delinquents from nondelinquents; it is rather to be stressed that the remaining three factors reflect parental affection and it is for this reason that the fewer number of factors have been found in the original sample to be as potent as the greater number in differentiating between persistent delinquents and true nondelinquents.

The problem of rating "Discipline by Father" in a situation in which he has not been part of the family group since a child was three years old is met in turn by the use of a Two-Factor Table ("Supervision by Mother," "Family Cohesiveness"), the coefficient of correlation between the Total Scores for the Two Factors being .932 in the cases included in *Unraveling Juvenile Delinquency*. And the rating of "Family Cohesiveness" in instances in which one of the parents, usually the father or a father-substitute has not been an integral part of the family group since the child in question was three years of age, is now met by considering the relationship between mother and children as "cohesive" if the ties between them are close and warm, rather than rating such a situation as having only some elements of cohesiveness by reason of a father's absence. Our attention was particularly directed to this clarification because in both the Youth Board and the Maximum Benefits Projects this kind of family pattern, rarely present in the cases of *Unraveling Juvenile Delinquency*, emerged in a particular ethnic group that had not been there included.

By reducing the burden of data-gathering and increasing the accuracy of the rating of cases, the Social Prediction Table becomes more usable and more efficient. Certainly, nonpsychiatric workers should not encounter difficulties in the rating of "Supervision by Mother," "Discipline by Father," and "Family Cohesiveness."[31]

The New York City Youth Board has already corrected errors of rating resulting from the first two difficulties, but must yet give consideration to the third; and the Maximum Benefits

---

[31]Definitions of terms appear in Appendix B, pp. 245ff. of *Predicting Delinquency and Crime*.

Project is now in process of rerating cases to take account of all three of the above-mentioned difficulties.

It is clear that the accuracy of the predictive device is being sharpened and it is to be hoped that experimentation by the Youth Board and the Maximum Benefits Project will continue to the advantage of those who may ultimately wish to apply the Social Prediction Table. There is still much to learn, however, and many difficulties to be resolved in connection with any large-scale use of this or any other device for the identification of potential delinquents.

There are additional problems that would follow the general acceptance of this device as a means for differentiating soon after school entrance among those children who are not and those who are likely to develop into persistent offenders unless suitable measures of intervention are applied. Among them might be mentioned the wisdom of using such devices at all. In this connection, the interested reader is asked to consult *Predicting Delinquency and Crime*, chapter twelve, "Some Objections to Predictive Devices," as a means of orientation in the pros and cons.

Still another basic issue has to do with meeting the challenge of "doing something" following the identification of potential delinquents. The way points to the early treatment of families and children by the constituted agencies of society when the interpersonal relations between the parents and a particular child make him vulnerable to delinquency. The rationale for such intervention is embraced in the already accepted philosophy of "reaching out" casework and poses only the problem of the *stage at which* this "reaching out" is to be initiated, i.e., *after* signs of antisocial behavior have become clearly evident or *in advance* of them.

Beyond this is the need for a new profession of "family educators" drawn from among psychiatrists, social workers, psychologists, ministers, pediatricians, public health nurses, teachers and others whose first task it would be to explore *methods* of reeducating the families of children found to be vulnerable to delinquency. Despite the many forms that delinquency may take and the many "types" of delinquents, the common denominator is aggressive antisocial behavior and it is to the prevention and control of this that family educators must direct themselves.

43.

Don M. Gottfredson

ASSESSMENT AND PREDICTION METHODS IN CRIME AND DELINQUENCY

Prediction, a traditional aim of science, is a requisite to any effective crime and delinquency prevention or control program. If we seek to control delinquent and criminal behavior, then first we will need to be able to predict it.

William James warned that we cannot hope

Source: Don M. Gottfredson, "Assessment and Prediction Methods in Crime and Delinquency;" *1967 President's Commission on Law Enforcement and Administration of Justice: Task Force Report on Juvenile Delinquency and Youth Crime* (Washington, D.C.: Government Printing Office), pp. 71–87.

to write biographies in advance. He asserted also, however, that we *can* establish general expectations. "We live forwards, but we understand backwards," he said, pointing out that any prediction method provides merely a way of summarizing previous experience in the hope of finding a useful guide to future decisions (87).

The problems of prediction in delinquency and related areas have interested many people. This has led to an extensive literature and a variety of techniques for developing and evaluating predictions. The resulting prediction methods have brought about arguments concerning the research methods used and inferences drawn, suggestions for practical uses, and complaints concerning misuses. This work has suggested avenues for further research and possibilities for more effective practice in the entire field of crime and delinquency, including delinquency prevention; and where prevention fails, each step in the process of the administration of criminal justice, from arrest to final discharge.

The nature of the prediction problem in this field is the same in many others.[1] A large body of literature is available concerning attempts to predict behavior in many sectors of social life. Examples are found in the prediction of social adjustment (79), of academic achievement (24, 59, 99), of vocational interest and performance (2, 133, 134, 136), and of the outcomes of marriage (16, 17).

Along with prediction studies in various social problem areas, the literature addressing theoretical and technical issues in prediction has grown. It includes studies of the logic of prediction (116), of the role of prediction in the study of personality (62, 80, 84, 96, 100, 101, 103, 104, 123), of psychometric problems (5, 6, 21, 26, 27, 55, 66, 83), and of the role of prediction methods in evaluating studies of different treatments (50, 57, 67, 98, 152).

The objective in this paper will be to summarize some of this extensive work in order to identify the major general problems, limitations, and potentials of methods for prediction of delinquency or crime. The general nature of the prediction problem will be reviewed. The steps followed in prediction research, some simplifying assumptions that commonly are made, and some requirements of useful prediction methods will be identified. Some basic concepts underlying prediction efforts and a number of general problems commonly found will be discussed. Some factors which influence the utility of prediction methods will be identified. This will help

in evaluation of the "state of the art." Finally, various applications, in both research and practice, will be reviewed. This will suggest further research needs and point up some implications concerning appropriate roles for prediction methods in crime and delinquency treatment and control programs.

The scope of this paper will be limited to some problems of prediction for individuals. More global prediction problems (e.g., estimations of population trends, or predictions of the number of offenses or offenders to be expected in a given place at a given time) may be very useful in correctional planning, or in testing hypotheses derived from social theories (94, 151), but they will be excluded. A vast literature concerning personality assessment generally, and evaluation of offenders specifically, is relevant to the prediction problem. No attempt will be made to review comprehensively, or even to list, the many delinquency prediction devices which have been proposed, discussed, and argued about. A number of bibliographies are available (9, 57, 62, 98, 124). No attempt will be made to discuss the methods and problems of the standardization of tests, or the preparation of norms, or to review even generally the large number of methods available and in widespread use in the clinical assessment of personality (26).

Some statistical problems will be discussed briefly; but no attempt will be made to present a full discussion of assumptions underlying the use of various techniques. The basic concepts of probability and statistical inference will not be discussed, even though they are basic to any prediction.

THE NATURE OF THE PREDICTION PROBLEM

The common goal of the assessment methods to be discussed is the prediction of an individual's performance, that is, an assessment of his *expected* behavior, at some future time. The criterion of performance, of course, must be defined in terms of attributes or characteristics other than those used in whatever operations are performed in arriving at the prediction. The prediction problem, viewed in this way, involves

[1]This review of prediction problems has been adapted largely from the excellent summary given by Bechtoldt (7), and it has been aided considerably by the summary of much of the pertinent literature provided by Gough (62).

two independent assessments of persons; the two assessments are separated in time. On the basis of one assessment, "predictor categories" are established (by various means). These are items of information believed to be helpful in prediction; they are the "predictors." The second assessment establishes "criterion categories"; these are the classifications of performance to be predicted. The predictions represent estimates of the expected values for the criterion categories, and these estimates are determined from earlier empirical investigations of the relations between the two sets of categories. On the basis of previously observed relationships between the predictor and criterion categories, an attempt is made to determine, for each category of persons, the most probable outcomes in terms of the criterion.

Predictions are sometimes qualified by making them conditional upon the occurrence of some later specific event, and then they are said to be conditional predictions (79). The determination of specific conditional factors which are relevant to the criterion classifications is a crucial problem, not only for prediction; it is a critical problem also in the evaluation of the effectiveness of treatment and control programs. The goals of delinquency prevention and correctional programs may be defined in terms of changing the probabilities of delinquent and criminal behavior.

A predictor category may represent any attribute or measure describing the individual. It may be defined by his own report, or by observations or judgments of others; it may be defined by what he can do or by how he perceives the world. It may be a measure of what he has done, and in this case it may include any of his past achievements or difficulties. It might be defined by exposure to specific treatment programs.

The criterion classification is based upon performance. In the area of crime and delinquency, the measurement of the performance criterion has special features which are critical but often overlooked.

THE CRITERION PROBLEM

Requirements of reliability and validity must be met for the criterion classifications, as for the predictors. These requirements usually are discussed with reference to predictor variables; measures of differences among individuals which are believed to be predictive must meet certain basic requirements if we are to have confidence in them. Often it is forgotten that these same requirements apply equally to the things we wish to predict. A criterion of delinquency, of criminal behavior, or of probation or parole violation, is itself a measure of individual differences. It may be accurate, explicit, and clear in meaning, or inaccurate, vague, and ambiguous. A number of factors reduce the reliability and validity of the performance criteria commonly used in this field. To the extent that this occurs the validity of prediction will be reduced.

The need for improvement of reliability and validity of measures of criminal and delinquent behavior is a much neglected field, and it is only beginning to receive careful attention as a measurement problem (128). Criteria of delinquency, criminal behavior, and of parole or probation violations are ordinarily quite crude. For example, a common criterion of delinquency is a definition in terms of confinement. If among the confined population some are wrongly convicted, while the nonconfined group contains any individuals who are in fact engaged in delinquent behavior, the validity of the criterion is reduced to that extent. Criteria may not depend solely on the behavior of the person about whom the prediction is made, but they also may depend upon the behavior of others. In the above example, the classification may depend upon the behavior of the police and the courts as well as the accused. Commonly used parole violation criteria, when a designation as a "parole violator" is made on the basis not only of the parolee's behavior, but also on the response of the parole agent or the paroling authority provide another example. In this situation, an increase in "parole violations" may reflect increased offending behavior by parolees, increased surveillance by parole agents, or changes in policy of the paroling authority. The argument may be carried a step further, since the behavior of a victim might be an important component in determining the "delinquency" or "parole violation." The reliability and validity of criterion categories often are related closely to the efficiency of law enforcement and the administration of criminal justice. They may be affected by policy changes in the relevant social agencies and by changes in the categories of behavior which, in a changing social context, become defined as socially acceptable or unacceptable. The need for development of more adequate assessments of delinquent and criminal behavior, in order to provide criterion measures which are not artificially tied to social agency responses to that behavior, is apparent.

An acceptable criterion of delinquency is critical to any prediction effort since it provides the standard for identification of relevant predictor variables. It constitutes the basis for determining the validity of the prediction method, and it thereby determines whether or not the prediction method will be useful for any specific practical applications.

The reliability and discrimination of criterion measures must be evaluated in terms of consistencies over periods of time and over samples of situations. If this is not done, we can have little confidence that the prediction method will "work" when later applied to new samples. A ruler made of rubber, stretching variably each time a wooden table is measured, cannot be depended upon to provide a reliable measure; similarly, a wooden ruler will be inadequate if the table continuously expands and contracts.

No procedure can predict consistently a criterion which has no reliability; but while high reliability in the criterion is desirable, it does not follow that it is completely necessary. Low reliability introduces random variation which decreases the strength of relations between the predictors and the criterion; but it does not introduce systematic irrelevant variables (137). One consequence of this is that useful prediction methods may be developed despite relatively crude criteria; another is that improvement of the criterion measures may provide one avenue to improved prediction.

THE STEPS FOLLOWED IN PREDICTION STUDIES

Five steps must be followed in any prediction study; the list below is modified from the steps identified by Horst (80), by Sarbin (123), and by Bechtoldt (7).

First, the criterion categories of "favorable" performance or of "delinquency" must be established. This involves the definitions of the behavior to be predicted and the development of procedures for classification of persons on the basis of their performance.

Second, the attributes or characteristics on which the predictions are to be based must be selected and defined. These predictor candidates are those that are expected to have significant relationships with the criterion classifications. Critics of prediction methods sometimes argue that the procedures ignore individual differences among persons. Actually, individual differences, often assumed to be a source of error in other problems, provide the basis for any prediction effort. If the persons studied are alike with respect to the predictor candidates, no differential prediction can be made. If they are alike with respect to the criterion categories, there is no prediction problem.

Third, the relationships between the criterion categories and the predictor candidates must be determined, in a sample representative of the population for which inferences are to be drawn.

Fourth, the relationship determined on the basis of the original sample must be verified by application of the prediction procedures to a new sample (or new samples) of the population. This verification, commonly called cross-validation, is a crucial step; but it is often omitted. Without it, there can be little confidence in the utility of a prediction method for any practical application; nevertheless applications are often suggested. Those who argue for applications of prediction methods while ignoring this critical step properly should be excluded from the argument until they learn what the first question is. There may be good reasons for not using demonstrably valid prediction methods in any specific application, but there can be no justification for confident use of these methods in the absence of cross-validation studies.

Fifth, the prediction methods may be applied in situations for which they were developed, provided that the stability of predictions has been supported in the cross-validation step and appropriate samples have been used.

SIMPLIFYING ASSUMPTIONS

In prediction studies certain assumptions commonly are made in order to simplify operational procedures. As a result, statistical procedures which are not justified on the basis of logical implications of assumptions underlying measurement in science nevertheless are followed. For example, numerals are used to represent differences in attributes, since this serves a practical purpose. Qualitative dichotomous attributes may be assigned numbers such as zero and one, with various statistics then computed. Qualitative variables with multiple categories may be scaled in various ways with numerical scores assigned. These practices, of ignoring a number of measurement problems pertinent to the use of various statistical procedures (130), undoubtedly will continue since the results are useful. It would not seem wise to ignore these problems, however, since the improved measurement of individual differences with hypothesized relationships to later delinquency behavior offers another means for the eventual improvement of prediction.

A second example of a simplifying assumption, common in prediction studies, is that the criterion magnitudes are linear functions of the predictor variables. A number of authors have pointed out that increased accuracy of prediction may require the use of non-linear relations (80, 67, 98, 143, 149). In response it may be argued that a linear equation may provide a useful first approximation (7) or turn out to be entirely adequate (26). It may be argued also that nonlinearity of relationships may not be critical, since linearity might be secured by modifying the measuring devices or by a transformation of scales or scores. Furthermore, as pointed out by Bechtoldt, "empirical evidence indicates that sampling fluctuations of regression parameters are of such magnitude that very large representative samples would be required to provide accurate estimates of non-linearity (7, 35)."

An additional example of a simplifying assumption, usually implicit in the procedures for developing prediction methods, is that the relations among predictor candidates, and between predictor candidates and the criterion, hold for subgroups of a heterogeneous population. The prediction methods are ordinarily based upon a study of a total sample of offenders, or of combined delinquent and nondelinquent populations, with no attempt to establish any relatively homogeneous subgroupings within the larger population (53, 55). This suggests a third approach toward improvement of prediction; predictive efficiency might be improved through separate study of various subgroups of persons.

REQUIREMENTS OF PREDICTOR CLASSIFICATIONS

Two requirements for any predictor candidate, aside from the relationship with the criterion, are *discrimination* and *reliability*. *Discrimination* is reflected in the number of categories to which significant proportions of persons are assigned. A classification which assigns all individuals to one class does not discriminate. An index of discrimination has been developed (33), and it may be shown that the best procedure is one which provides a rectangular distribution of categorizations for the sample. For a dichotomous item, the most discriminating item is one that has fifty percent of the cases in each of the two categories (1). However, when two or more items are used the maximum number of discriminations made by the total prediction instrument may or may not be obtained with items at this fifty percent level; the intercorrelations of items and their reliabilities must be considered (13, 19, 34, 69, 120).

One consequence of the requirement of discrimination is that the predictor items found useful in one jurisdiction may not be helpful in another. For example, in parole prediction studies in California, where 15 to 20 percent of the parolee population has a history of opiate drug use, this item has been found useful in parole prediction studies (56). However, in the State of Washington, where fewer than one percent of adult parolees have histories of drug use, the item would not be expected to be a helpful predictor.[2] The requirement of discrimination points to the need for cross-validation studies in various jurisdictions and points up one hazard in untested acceptance of prediction measures developed from study elsewhere in a single jurisdiction. (Considerations of sampling and of the concept of validity, discussed below, result in the same conclusion.) A classification procedure may discriminate but not be valid for a given criterion, and there seems to be no reason that the extent of discrimination would provide an effective weighting of the item in arriving at a prediction device.

Reliability refers to the consistency or stability of repeated observations, scores, or other classifications. If a procedure is reliable, then repetitions of the procedure lead to similar classifications. The topic of reliability of measurement is a large one indeed, and it has been discussed by many writers (25, 73, 74, 82).

Valid prediction is not possible with completely unreliable measures, but all measurement is relatively unreliable. This means that some variation is always expected. It also means that if valid prediction is demonstrated, then the predictor attributes may not be completely unreliable. The main interest in a prediction method is how well the method works; so more importance is attached to the question of validity than of reliability. This does not mean the issue of reliability is unimportant; the improvement of reliability of predictor variables provides another means for the possible improvement of prediction and therefore deserves much study. Unfortunately, analyses of the reliability of individual predictor items (or of a total prediction instrument) frequently are not reported in delinquency prediction studies.

PROBABILITY AND VALIDITY

No estimate of future behavior, arrived at by any means, can be made with certainty; a statement of degree of probability is a more appropriate prediction. Individual prediction, with which this paper is concerned, is actually a misnomer. Predictions properly are applied not to individuals but to groups of persons, similar

with respect to some set of characteristics (123). In any prediction problem individuals are assigned to classes, and then statements are made about the expected performance of members of the classes. The expected performance outcomes, for specific classifications of persons, ought to be those which provide the most probable values for the population as a whole (12, 72).

The validity of a prediction method refers to the degree to which earlier assessments are related to later criterion classifications. The question of validity asks how well the prediction method "works." Any prediction instrument or method, however, may be thought of as having and lacking not one but many validities of varying degrees. For example, an intelligence test might provide a valid prediction of high school grades. It might provide a much less valid, but still useful, measure of expected social adjustment, and it might have no validity for prediction of delinquency. The validity of prediction refers to the relationship between a specific criterion measure and some earlier assessment, and it is dependent upon the particular criterion used. A prediction method has as many validities as there are criterion measures to be predicted.

Evidence of validity with respect to the specific criterion of interest obviously is necessary before any practical application of the method. Nevertheless, "prediction" studies in the field of crime and delinquency frequently are reported in which the verification, or "cross-validation" step has been omitted.

The concept of validity of prediction is "the tie that binds" all prediction efforts together (101). This is the case whether they are considered clinical or statistical, and regardless of the specific procedures used in developing the method. The "proof of the pudding" in any prediction study is the degree to which the method is valid with respect to specific criterion classifications.

PREDICTORS

The predictor items, on which expectations are based, may be obtained from the self-report of the subjects concerned, reports of observers or judges, records of past performance, or by

---

[2] J. Thompson, Washington State Probation and Parole Board, personal communication.

direct observation by the individual making the prediction. Thus, predictor items may include psychological test scores, measures of attitudes or interests, biographical items, ratings, or indeed any information about the subject.

The objective in most prediction studies has been the formulation of empirical rules based upon observed relationships between individual attributes and the criteria of interest. Those engaged in these studies have tended to consider their problems in these strict empirical terms. The focus of interest has been in the empirical relationships between the predictors and the criterion. If the resulting prediction procedures work, they are accepted as useful.

Some writers have asked whether a theoretically blind prediction technique can provide the basis for effective interventions in the crime and delinquency field (140); this suggests that criminological theory can be helpful in development of more useful prediction instruments. It may be suggested also that the development of prediction methods provides opportunities for the hypothesis testing necessary for development of theory. Prediction methods do not require that hypotheses be derived from a single, consistent theoretical framework; any hypotheses (and conflicting ones) may provide a source of predictor candidates. They do require that these hypotheses be tested as the prediction methods are developed. The strictly empirical, atheoretical approach of many prediction studies has, as Toby points out, led to neglected opportunities for improvement of both prediction and criminological theory.

THE EVALUATION OF PREDICTION

A number of measures have been developed for the assessment of predictive efficiency. Traditionally, for a qualitative criterion such as "Delinquent vs. Non-Delinquent," the efficiency of prediction has been expressed in terms of the proportion of individuals correctly assigned to these criterion categories (72). For quantitative predictions, efficiency is usually expressed as some function of the correlation between the predictor and criterion measures. Some measures provide interpretations of a validity coefficient with special reference to the accuracy of prediction of individual scores. They include the coefficient of alienation (75) and the index of forecasting efficiency (80). Efficiency of prediction may be assessed also by the relative number of correct predictions in terms of exceeding some critical value of the criterion (81). Sometimes the correlation coefficient is regarded as a direct index to the efficiency of prediction (13); the square of the correlation coefficient, called the coefficient of determination, measures the proportion of variance in the criterion classifications which is "accounted for" by the items included in the prediction method. Another means of evaluating the efficiency of prediction is in terms of the increase in accuracy of prediction when the prediction method is used, as compared with selecting cases at random (88).

Ohlin and Duncan proposed an index of predictive efficiency defined by the percentage change in errors of prediction by the prediction method rather than the "base rate," i.e., the proportion of persons in the criterion category to be predicted (108). Their later method (31) was modified by Duncan and Duncan and called the "mean cost rating" (32), a procedure which reflects the degree to which a classification method accurately assigns persons to a dichotomous criterion classification.

Evaluations of predictive efficiency by means of these and other available measures can provide useful comparisons of the predictive accuracy of various prediction approaches, and they provide general statements concerning the efficiency of prediction. Such comparisons of efficiency of predictions, when the expectancies are arrived at by various methods, are needed but are quite rare in the crime and delinquency field.

It should be noted that (depending upon the purpose to which the prediction method is to be put) prediction methods with even quite low validity may be useful (27). On the other hand, prediction methods with high validity in one sample may be of little use in an application which concerns a sample from another population, or the degree of validity required may depend upon other components of the problem. A number of factors influence the utility of prediction methods and bear upon issues of practical applications.

FACTORS INFLUENCING THE UTILITY OF PREDICTION

Predictive efficiency and the utility of prediction methods both are affected by various factors other than the relationship between the predictor items and the criterion. Besides the reliability of predictor candidates, these factors may include the "selection ratio," the "base rate," the method of combining predictor variables, the representativeness of the sample on which the prediction method has been based, and the number of predictor variables. Each of these should be discussed briefly as a basis for consideration of existing prediction methods.

THE SELECTION RATIO

In any selection problem, such as placement on probation or parole, some individuals are chosen and some are rejected. The ratio of the number who are chosen to the total number available is called the selection ratio (7). The usefulness of a selection procedure depends not only upon the validity of the prediction method but depends also upon this ratio. If the selection ratio is low, as for example when only a few individuals are to be accepted for parole, fairly low validity coefficients in a prediction device may prove useful. If only a few individuals are to be rejected, then a much higher validity would be required for the same degree of effectiveness as an aid in selection.

THE BASE RATE

The "base rate" refers to the proportion of individuals in some population who fall into a category which is to be predicted. Fortunately for society, but unfortunately for those who aspire to predict delinquency, delinquency is a rather uncommon state of affairs (76). Even more fortunate for society at large is that shocking crimes against persons are relatively infrequent in proportion to the population as a whole; but at the same time that we wish most to predict these relatively rare occurrences, the predictive task is made more difficult by the base rate. The base rate affects both our ability to discover predictors which differentiate criterion categories and the accuracy of prediction when methods are applied to new samples.

This means that for relatively rare occurrences we may expect greater difficulty in finding predictive information. At the same time, a prediction method (in order to be useful) must be a more efficient one if the event to be predicted is relatively rare.

The first problem is that if there are relatively few "failures" or "delinquents" in a population we'll be hard put to find items which discriminate between the successes and the failures.[3] It will be more difficult to find useful predictors, because the variation in the criterion is reduced, and it is this variation which must be analyzed in the search for predictors.

The effect of base rates on the accuracy of prediction has been discussed by Meehl and Rosen (105), by Cureton (28), and with illustrations in the field of delinquency by Gough (62), Hanley (76), Grygier (67), and Walters (145).

In order for a prediction method to be useful, it must provide more information than that given by the base rate alone. For example, if 90 percent of the children in the population can be expected to be nondelinquent in any event, then there is little value in a method unless the proportion of non-delinquent individuals among those expected to be non-delinquent can be significantly increased over the 90 percent value (141). Frequently, however, a prediction method is devised on the basis of study of a sample containing equal (or about equal) numbers of delinquents and non-delinquents. Then it is applied to the general population where the proportion who actually become delinquent is considerably lower. This procedure can be expected to result in a serious overestimation of the practical effectiveness of the prediction device. In order to evaluate the utility of the prediction method, it is necessary to know not only how well it discriminates between the future delinquents and non-delinquents, but how common is delinquency in the general population.

It is important to know also the relative costs and utilities of forestalling delinquency in a

---

[3]It can be shown also that as a sample proportion of failures (or of successes) becomes smaller, larger samples are needed in order to reduce error in estimating the numbers of successes and failures in the total population.

predicted delinquent in relation to the possible costs of misclassifying an individual who will not become delinquent (27). Similarly, in probation or parole selection applications it is important to know not only the probable outcomes of probation or parole and the associated costs but the expected outcomes and costs of denial of these alternatives to confinement.

METHODS OF COMBINING PREDICTORS

If a number of predictor items are to be used in establishing a single prediction, then the items may be combined in various ways. Either the predictors all may be used without weighting them, or some procedure for weighting the various predictor items may be used, or some type of "configural" method may be employed.

The most widely used method of combining predictors has been the assignment of unit weights; many predictive characteristics are used without a weighting system. Each item found to be related to the criterion is assigned one point regardless of the strength of its association; and the sum of the points thus assigned provides a measure of the probability of delinquency, parole violation, or some other criterion classification. This has been a popular procedure (15, 36, 63, 109, 110, 117, 118, 119, 138, 139, 147, 126). As pointed out by Grygier, it is democratic as well as popular, considering all predictors equally; however, it may be inefficient (67). This procedure ignores intercorrelations among the predictors, but if a large number of items is used there is nevertheless a good argument for it. It may be assumed that as the number of positively correlated variables increases, the correlation between any two sets of weighted scores approaches one and the effect of differential weighting of the various items tends to disappear. If the number of measures to be added together is not large, however, the dispersions and intercorrelations of the measures may influence significantly the weights expected on theoretical grounds to increase predictive efficiency.

The second method (really a set of methods) employs a smaller number of predictive characteristics and some weighting system. Items with the highest correlations with the criterion are generally selected and various methods of weighting are applied.

The best known of these is found in the series of prediction studies by the Gluecks (38, 39, 40, 41, 42, 43, 44, 45, 46, 47, 48). Contingency coefficients are found, in order to measure the association of the initial assessments with the criterion classification, and to select significant predictors. Each item is weighted in scoring by assigning it the percent figure for the criterion among persons characterized by the predictor attribute. As in the case of assignment of unit weights, correlations among predictors are ignored, and there is no reason to suppose that an "optimal" weighting procedure would result. The weighting is based upon discrimination in the criterion classification and ignores overlapping of items. In two studies, the method was not found superior to assignment of unit weights (106, 144).

Two theoretically better models are provided by multiple linear regression and by linear discriminant function. These methods take account of the intercorrelations of the predictor variables as well as the correlations with the criterion. In multiple regression, the linear equation is found such that weights are assigned in order to minimize the squared deviations of observed and expected criterion values. If Fisher's discriminant function is used, the weights in the linear equation are found such that the criterion classification groups are maximally separated (in terms of the mean values for the prediction scores, in relation to their pooled standard deviations).

These methods have been used in a number of studies. Multiple regression was used by Mannheim and Wilkins (98), in their English Borstal prediction study, and they reported that more efficient prediction was thereby achieved than that found with assignment of unit weights. The method was employed in parole prediction by Kirby (90), and it has been the method used in a number of California Parole Prediction Studies (51, 52, 56). The discriminant function has been employed for prediction in various areas, including problems in classification of students (3), of farmers (11), of air force radio operators (146), of aviation cadets (93), and military delinquents (70).

A series of studies conducted for the United States Naval Retraining Command represents one of the most careful and sophisticated studies in delinquency prediction but is perhaps less well known than others (5, 70, 66, 85, 71). Discriminant functions were developed, from study of an initial sample of 20,000 naval recruits, and from study of the proportion defined as offenders from various follow-up sources (1,339 persons). Among other results, the study demonstrated clearly that a pencil and paper Delinquency Potential Scale (developed in the same study) made a unique contribution to the separation of the offender and non-offender groups.

Regression analyses have many advantages. One is the theoretically optimal weighting of predictors (in terms of the linear assumption). Another is the special utility of the method for selection of predictors, since they may be selected after determining the proportionate reduction of unaccounted-for variance in the criterion by inclusion of each item; that is, the gain in prediction by adding the item may be determined readily as an increase in the coefficient of determination.

The method has some shortcomings. One may be the assumption of linearity already discussed. Another is that the weights are derived from the correlation matrix (for all predictor candidates and the criterion) for the total sample of subjects. It is therefore assumed implicitly that these correlations are adequate estimates of comparable coefficients for subsamples, that is, for subgroups of persons, within the larger sample. This assumption may be demonstrably false (53).

Configural prediction methods also have been used in delinquency prediction, again with variations of method. In other areas, they generally have not been found to provide increases in predictive efficiency over linear models (26). One method, described by MacNaughton-Smith (95) has been called "predictive attribute analysis." This approach also has been used in parole predictions by Wilkins (153), by Grygier (67), and by Ballard (6). A closely related procedure is the "configural analysis" method of Glaser (37), also used in parole prediction studies by Mannering and Babst in Wisconsin (97). When both linear regression and the configural analysis methods were applied to the same set of Wisconsin data, results of these methods gave similar predictive efficiency (54). A shortcoming of the general approach is that the successive partitioning of the sample into subgroups may involve a capitalization on sampling error (55).

The basis for the method proposed by MacNaughton-Smith is a successive partitioning of a sample into subgroups on the basis of the single item found in each subgroup to have the closest association with the criterion. That is, first the single most predictive item is found and the total sample is divided on this attribute. Each of the two resulting subsamples is studied further, in order to identify, within each, the single best predictor. Then the two subsamples are further subdivided and the process repeated until no further items significantly associated with the criterion are found.

Another configural approach is given by the method called association analysis. The method, developed by Williams and Lambert for studies in plant ecology (154), has been employed in delinquency prediction by Wilkins and MacNaughton-Smith (153), and by Gottfredson, Ballard and Lane (53). The method provides an empirical means for subdividing a heterogeneous population into subgroups which are relatively homogeneous with respect to the attributes studied. It is more properly called a classification method; unlike other prediction methods, the criterion classifications are ignored in establishing the subgrouping. The establishment of the classifications is not dependent upon the relationships of predictor candidates to the criterion; the classification may provide, nevertheless, a valid prediction method.

A combination of association analysis and regression methods has been suggested. Association analysis would be used in order to define relatively homogeneous subgroups of persons. Then regression methods would provide the means for development of prediction devices for each subgroup so identified. This or similar procedures providing for separate prediction studies for meaningful subgroups of offenders may provide an avenue to improved prediction.

Despite the variety of methods which have

been used for combining predictors, empirical comparisons of resulting predictive efficiency are rare; and they are needed (62).

SAMPLING

A shortcoming of many delinquency prediction studies is the use of samples, studied for development of the prediction method, which are not representative of the populations to which generalizations are to be made. If systematic biases are introduced by the sampling procedure, then the validity in new samples will be decreased. General application of prediction methods based upon study of non-representative samples, as in a study completed in a high delinquency area, is very questionable; the same is true of application of probation or parole prediction procedures in jurisdictions other than those studied in developing the measures. In any such intended application, further cross-validation is necessary, attention to the base rate problem is imperative, and continued assessment of the stability of predictive validity over time is essential.

NUMBER OF PREDICTOR VARIABLES

When multiple regression is used as the method of combining predictor variables, the stability of predictions for new samples tends to decrease with an increase in the number of items included in the equation. Adding items to the original set of predictors will not reduce the accuracy of prediction in the original sample, however (80, 115). If only the original sample is studied, the investigator risks being misled by an accumulation of errors; his only safeguard is found in study of new samples. This emphasizes again the need for cross-validation studies.

For stable predictive validity a small number of items which are not only predictive but relatively independent of one another is sought. In this situation, each item makes an unique contribution to the prediction.

PREDICTIVE INFORMATION

In the Glueck studies, already mentioned, attempts have been made to identify potential delinquents at a very early age. Various prediction tables have been developed. One of these, called "Social Factors" has been evaluated intensively over a long term. The tables rest on the determination of predictive items in a study comparing 500 delinquents and 500 non-delinquents.

In a ten year validation study, with retention of a three factor scale including "supervision of the boy by his father," "supervision of the boy by his mother," and "family cohesiveness," as well as a two factor scale including "supervision of the boy by his mother" and "family cohesiveness," the investigators concluded:

The Glueck Social Prediction Table, after nine years of study and experimentation, is showing evidence of being a good differentiator between potential delinquents (serious and persisting) and non-delinquents.

They asserted also that:

The Three-Factor Table yielded approximately a 70 percent accuracy in predicting delinquents and an 85 percent accuracy in predicting non-delinquents (22, 23).

The procedures used by the Gluecks in developing their methods and the conclusions reached on the basis of their study have been strongly supported and severely criticized. A 1951 symposium of reviews in the *Journal of Criminal Law and Criminology* was generally highly favorable. The most incisive criticisms have been addressed to the sampling methods used and the base rate problem. It has been argued that a non-representative sample was studied, the research having been carried out in a high delinquency area in New York City (121, 92). The criticisms of Rubin and of Shaplin and Tiedman (129) discuss the sampling problem and the point that delinquents were not studied in their youth (extrapolations having been made from data obtained after the boys had been institutionalized in adolescence).

Similar strong objections by Reiss (119), by Gough (62), by Grygier (67), and by Hanley (76) emphasize the implications of the base rate problem and demonstrate its importance for applications in delinquency prediction. The reported accuracy of the Glueck Tables is based on the situation with equal numbers of delinquents and controls. When the base rate is set at a more realistic figure in terms of the incidence of delinquency generally, the tables turn out to be far less discriminating than claimed. The criticism is also made by Walters (145), who demonstrates that a base rate of between two and four percent makes prediction from the tables quite inaccurate. It is clear that if the base rate problem is ignored, the practical effectiveness of the Glueck Tables will be greatly overestimated.

A sequential procedure for identifying potential delinquents has been offered by Stott (132). Based upon the incidence of symptoms of non-delinquent behavior disturbances among probationers and controls, the *Bristol Social Adjustment Guide* was developed. A preliminary screening is completed by teachers on the basis of six yes-no items concerning behavior disturbances found to be associated with delinquency. If a boy is rated adversely on one or more items, then the full *Guide* is used in assessment. Evidence from a Glasgow survey suggests these procedures as promising, but they have not been validated in the United States.

Of various prediction measures developed by Kvaraceus, the non-verbal KD Proneness Scale has undergone the most extensive validation (91). Sixty-two circles each include four pictures based on concepts concerning reported differences between delinquents and non-delinquents. The subject indicates the item he likes most and the one he likes least. Validation data are available from a careful three year follow-up study of 1,594 junior high school students (and for a small sample of retarded children in special classes). While some evidence of validity was reported, inconsistencies in the results of the validation study led the author to urge caution in the employment of this tool for prediction on a routine or perfunctory basis. Reported as the most significant result was that teacher nominations (based on pupil behavior) were found equally effective and sometimes more effective as predictors of future delinquency.

A procedure reported by Bower as a method for identification of children most vulnerable to or handicapped by emotional disorders also makes use of teacher ratings in a sequential

screening process (10). The usefulness of the screening process has been extensively studied. Results indicate that it is a practical approach for identification of emotionally disturbed children not otherwise recognized in the school situation; further validation studies again are needed.

A number of additional prediction methods, aimed at the identification of future delinquents, give evidence of promise; all need further validation, and all require validation in specific jurisdictions before application (131, 112, 148, 114).

The Minnesota Multiphasic Personality Inventory is a widely used empirically derived set of personality scales which may be used in group administration (77). The validity of this instrument in delinquency prediction has been investigated in a sample of 4,048 ninth grade boys and girls in Minneapolis (78). Two years after administration of the test, county and city records were checked and it was found that 591 (about 22 percent of the boys and 8 percent of the girls) had been brought before the courts or the police. The criterion of delinquency employed was a broad one, including three levels of seriousness of offenses.

Two subscales of the test, namely the "Psychopathic Deviancy" subscale and the "Hypomanic" subscale were found predictive of delinquency. Considerable attention was given to the contribution of profiles of the *MMPI* as an aid to understanding the dynamics of delinquent behavior. Also, 33 *MMPI* items discriminating pre-delinquent from normal boys later were identified (79); further validation of these items as a separate scale is needed.

The *MMPI* was originally prepared for adult use, and it has been noted that it contains a large number of emotionally charged items to which parents and teachers frequently raise objections (92). The predictive utility of the *MMPI* in the prediction of delinquency among prisoners (in terms of misbehavior during confinement) has been investigated by Paton (111), and by Jacobson and Wirt (86).

There are many other psychological assessment procedures which may help in development of improved prediction methods. As recently as 1950, a review of the literature concerning comparisons of delinquents and non-delinquents on personality measures led to the conclusion that no consistent significant differences between these two groups were to be found (127). More recent studies, using more recently available instruments, demonstrate that a number of these do discriminate between delinquents and non-delinquents. Already mentioned is the Psychopathic Deviate scale of the *MMPI* which has been found in a number of studies consistently to differentiate delinquents and non-delinquents (107, 78). Another discriminator is the Socialization scale of the *California Personality Inventory* (58, 61); another is the already mentioned *Delinquency Potential Scale*. These studies themselves demonstrate that there are measurable personality differences between delinquents and non-delinquents.

In a 1961 review, Argyle points to a large number of reported differences between delinquents and non-delinquents on personality measures (4). These are enumerated under categories of tests of cheating, and of moral values; measures of extra-punitiveness; of attitude toward parents, toward authority, and toward peer groups; measures of level of aspiration, of motor control, time span, compulsiveness, and emotional maturity; measures of cruelty and aggressiveness, and of skill and social perception; and measures of neuroticism.

Still other personality measures have identified variables discriminating delinquent and non-delinquent subjects. Differences in ability between delinquent and non-delinquent boys were described by Zakilski (156). Another study demonstrated that institutionalized delinquent boys obtained lower scores than controls on a "perceptual-completion" measure (89). Differences in measured levels of aspiration were described in yet another study (20), and differences in Porteus Maze Test performance have been identified in still another (30). Differences were reported in Rorschach responses by delinquent and normal adolescents in the Glueck study; the same study reports a high degree of discrimination between delinquent and normal Rorschach records when these are made by skilled clinical workers (126).

There are promising results, though they do not hold forth much hope of immediate applicability. Often, the data describe differences between delinquent and control samples which may not be assumed to be representative of the general population, and the problem of the base rate is ignored. This does not mean they are unimportant in pointing the way to improvement of predictive efficiency. The utility of discriminators such as these in a prediction study which includes adequate investigation of the validity problem, and investigates the consequences of application of realistic base rates, can only be settled by the empirical study which is needed.

In a lengthy history of parole prediction studies, a number of consistently reported differentiators of parole performance criteria have been found. The most useful guides to prediction of parole violation behavior are indices of past criminal behavior. This result, discouraging in terms of treatment concerns, finds support in most parole prediction studies (56, 38, 138, 15, 18, 37, 126, 142, 109, 98).

Offenders against persons have been found at least since 1923 to be generally better risks, so far as parole violations are concerned, than are offenders against property (147). Glaser includes an excellent review of evidence, from a variety of jurisdictions, that leaves little room for doubt as to the predictive nature of offense classifications (37).

In general, the probability of parole violation decreases with age (45, 41, 18, 122, 155). The contention that offenders who are older at release are less likely to return to crime is supported by parolee data from the States of Wisconsin, New York, California, and the United States Federal System. Similar results have been found, as Glaser notes, for many decades, and in numerous jurisdictions, both in the United States and abroad.

Histories of opiate drug use or of alcoholic difficulties are unfavorable prognostic signs for parole performance; this has been found for both male and female parolees (49, 52, 56). Burgess and Tibbetts found a "drunkard" classification to yield an unfavorable sign, as did Ohlin. Similarly, Schiedt considered alcohol use important. The social types from earlier work were redefined by Glaser into seven general categories, "toward which the subjects seemed to be developing prior to their offenses," taking account of alcoholic difficulties.[4]

The use of aliases has been found, in California studies, to be predictive of unfavorable parole performance among both male and female adult prisoners. When the offender's history reflects a criminal record for others in the person's immediate family, this too is an unfavorable prognostic sign.

Recent studies indicate that a combination of life history information, which provides the main basis for prediction in most studies, when combined with data from personality testing may result in a superior prediction of parole violations (64, 57). Measures of "social maturity," have been found helpful in prediction in a number of studies. "Social Maturity" has been defined variously, but in each case has had its roots particularly in studies by Gough (60), by Gough and Peterson (63), and by Grant (65).

CLINICAL ASSESSMENT AS AN AVENUE TO IMPROVEMENT OF PREDICTION

Comparisons of empirically derived and "subjective experience" derived behavior predictions, along with the extensive literature dealing with this topic, have been well reviewed by Meehl (100) and by Gough (62). When statistical prediction devices are pitted against clinical judgment and the accuracy of prediction compared, statistical prediction has generally fared better. A less competitive, more collaborative, attack on prediction problems is needed.

As indicated twenty-five years ago by Horst, "The statistician and the case study investigator can make mutual gains if they'll quit quarreling with each other and begin borrowing from each other (80)." In the same vein, DeGroot has argued there is more to be gained through efforts to improve statistical prediction by way of clinical prediction than through continuation of arguments or comparisons of the predictive accuracy of the two approaches (29). This suggests that the clinician be given the best available statistical prediction device, and that he

[4]A review of literature concerning the predictive utility of age, offense, prior record, race, intelligence, and body build is given by Glaser (37).

then attempt to improve, by any means, upon the accuracy of predictions which may be made through its use. When it can be demonstrated that he can do so, then the attempt should be made to define adequately the information used in establishing the expectancy. If this can be done, then a reliable measure can be developed; and ultimately it can be included in the statistical prediction device.

Prediction devices, developed by any method, can do no more than summarize experience. They can do this quite objectively and efficiently; and therefore they can provide an adequate means of summarizing that which is known about the prediction of delinquency or crime. Possible predictors which are as yet only vaguely felt or ill-defined may be refined into more adequate hypotheses which then may be tested for possible inclusion in the prediction device. In this way, a means is provided not only for the summarization of knowledge but for its extension.

CLINICAL ASSESSMENT AND DELINQUENCY PREDICTION

Personality assessment techniques of a different variety are in widespread use in schools, in private clinical practice, in evaluations prepared for courts, and diagnostic studies in detention. They are used in making decisions about individuals, often on the basis of assumptions concerning predictive validity with respect to future delinquency, criminal behavior, or probation or parole violation. A whole literature of clinical psychology, psychiatry, and social work is relevant to the problem of predictions based upon interviews, projective tests, or other samples of the person's behavior. How can the utility of this vast array of assessment methods be considered briefly?

Cronbach and Gleser have suggested an important, useful distinction between two general types of assessment methods (27, 26). Their discussion is based upon a model from information theory in which two aspects of any communication system are distinguished: bandwidth and fidelity.

Some procedures, like the interview, the psychologist's report from projective testing, written evaluations prepared by clinical or custodial institution staff, or a social history report, provide a wide variety of information. Each of the "wide band" procedures is characteristically found to be unsatisfactory, by any usual standards of reliability and validity, for prediction of specific behavior. This does not mean they are useless; it means that the wider coverage is purchased at the price of low dependability (fidelity). What purposes, then, do these procedures fulfill?

Evidence that interviews, for example, are useful in prediction, is preponderantly negative; repeatedly, comparisons have shown statistical prediction devices to be more valid. But, as Cronbach and Gleser point out, even the most forceful advocates of statistical prediction insist on an interview when *they* must make a decision. Since interviewer judgments disagree notoriously with one another and have little relationship to outcomes, we must ask why we persist in interviewing.

The interviewer can address any aspect of the other person's personality, character and life situation. His delinquency history, employment record, relations with his family, group identifications, feelings about authority, his disappointments and expectations are some frequent topics. The interview may reveal something of his abilities and interests, his sexual attitudes, his major conflicts, defenses against anxiety, his values and his plans. It is a sequential process which can turn in any direction to follow leads, unexpected but judged important during the interview, that any structured objective test or prediction procedure cannot. This flexibility and potential scope is its virtue, because by covering a broad range of information it may shed light on *many different decisions*. It is clear that the interview may not bear only on a single problem or relate to a single criterion classification we wish to predict. It may suggest a further treatment plan, particular areas of weakness to be guarded against, and special potentials for favorable adjustment in certain situations.

The "wide band" methods are exhaustive but undependable; that is, they cover more of the ground we wish to know about—but any one prediction from this wide range of information cannot be depended upon to be valid. The narrow range procedures may give more accurate information with respect to *one* decision outcome when adequate validation data is available; but they give no guidance at all with respect to *other* decision outcomes.

What about "narrow band" procedures? These include any objective psychological test with established validity for prediction of a single behavioral criterion, parole or probation violation prediction devices, some delinquency prediction scales, certain college aptitude tests, and the like. Their virtue is dependability (high fidelity)—compared with the interview and other broad scope methods. Their limitation is that they cover relatively little ground; that is, they bear only on that part of the decision which is concerned with the specific question they help answer.

The narrow scope (and therefore both the potential power and limited utility) of such a prediction device is apparent. Though it gives a more dependable prediction of outcome than generally obtained by broad band methods, it is relevant only to the *specific* criterion defined for the purpose of study. Unless it has been shown valid also for predicting other specific outcomes of interest to the decision maker, it provides no guidance for decisions based on expected behavior in other areas. It may tell nothing about appropriate treatment placement.

In general, a narrow range procedure such as an objective test, delinquency scale, or parole prediction device is more reliable (that is, different people will tend to agree on the scores for various others). It is more valid (that is, it predicts better). But it covers only a limited sector of all behavior in which there is interest. In short, it has limited range but high fidelity; if the narrow scope is unrecognized, the procedure may provide a good answer to the wrong question.

How can these two types of information be profitably used together? We wish to utilize the best features of each, recognizing the limitations of both, in order to make optimal decisions on the basis of available knowledge.

The optimal use of both, however, will depend upon the nature of the decision problem. It will depend upon the resources available, the alternative courses of action, and the goals of crime and delinquency programs. This suggests that optimal procedures for one agency might not be the best for others with differing resources, alternatives, or goals. Recently developed methods in applied statistical decision theory are pertinent to this problem; and development of applications of these methods to delinquency and crime prevention, treatment, and control problems offers one of the most promising available routes to increased effectiveness of the social agencies concerned.

APPLICATIONS OF PREDICTION METHODS

Despite the painstaking studies, item analyses, and validation studies implied by the preceding pages, all currently available prediction methods still have only relatively low predictive power. In most instances the problem of any application is confounded by the base rate problem and by inadequate cross-validation in samples from populations in which practical applications might be proposed.

The routine use of any available instruments in programs for early identification and treatment of delinquency has been regarded by many as somewhat dangerous on one or more of three grounds. First, the available validity data is questionable. Second, there is the base rate problem; and finally, there is apprehension concerning the "self-fulfilling prophecy." The latter concern is with the possible negative effects of a classification procedure itself upon the persons classified, through labeling them undesirably. Toby asks:

How can early identification and intensive treatment programs avoid "self-fulfilling prophecies?"

If the treatment program concentrates its efforts on youngsters who are especially vulnerable to delinquency, how can it justify its discriminatory policy except by stigmatizing pre-delinquents? And may not the delinquency-producing effects of the stigmatizing equal or exceed the delinquency-preventing benefits of the treatment? (140).

In any proposed application, the question of validity of prediction is only one component of the decision problem. The objective of the decision should be to minimize errors and to make them less costly.

In the absence of a perfection which is not expected, any prediction (made by any procedure) is uncertain; the result will be errors of two kinds. Some persons will be expected to be delinquents who will not be identified later as delinquent. Some will be expected to be nondelinquent but later will be found to be delinquent. The concept of the "self-fulfilling prophesy" calls attention to the probability that the two types of error may not have equal consequences. It suggests that it may be much more damaging to treat as delinquents those persons misclassified as expected delinquents than to treat pre-delinquents as if they were not expected to be delinquent.

The application of statistical decision theory methods as a means of minimizing errors in placement or selection decisions will require the assignment of values to the outcomes, i.e., to the consequences, of the decision alternatives; the positive and negative values of outcomes of both correct and incorrect decisions must be considered. This points again to the need for attention to problems of measurement of the consequences of decisions, that is, to the criterion problem. It will require careful and explicit statement of the objectives of any given decision, but this may be a healthy exercise for the decision makers concerned.

Programs of early identification and prevention of delinquency have been recently reviewed by Kvaraceus (92). Pointing to the low predictive power of available instruments, he indicates that "as yet, no simple, practical, and valid tests for delinquency prediction can be found on the test market." He notes also a growing conviction that separate techniques or tests must be developed for middle-class youngsters and for lower-class children and that it may be easier to predict certain types of delinquents compared with others.

Related suggestions are made by Toby. Along with demonstrating that in both the Cambridge-Somerville Youth Study (113) and the New York City Youth Board Prediction Study (135) attention to the social context can improve the accuracy of predictions, he discusses the needs for integration of prediction efforts within a consistent theoretical framework.

The entire July, 1962 issue of the journal of *Crime and Delinquency* was given to discussion of parole prediction devices. Most of this discussion relates to the applicability of parole prediction methods to individual selection for parole. Before discussing this role, however, it should be noted that parole prediction methods have demonstrated utility (in one practical situation) in broad screening programs and for parole supervision caseload assignments (50).

In the first application, as an aid to a program intended to reduce confinement costs, a large prison population was screened, first by the parole prediction device, then by further clinical criteria. The result was a small group of men referred for parole consideration at a date earlier than originally scheduled, with substantial monetary savings and no increase in parole violations, as a result. In the second application, the parole prediction measure aided the establishment of minimal supervision caseloads for both male and female parolees. Persons classed as having a high probability of successful parole completion received minimal supervision (experience having demonstrated that these cases may be given less supervision with no increase in the parole violation rate) with the result that parole workers might be assigned to spend their effort in areas where help is more needed. Again, a substantial saving of money was reported.

When applications to parole selection are considered, in the light of the "band width-fidelity" concept discussed above, it appears that the best use of prediction methods will depend upon not only the established validity of the prediction method but also upon the goals of a particular decision in a specific social agency. Ultimately, the contribution of any prediction method to a particular decision process should be assessed in reference to available decision alternatives and in terms of costs and utilities (27).

The most useful role, and at any rate the most immediately feasible application, for pre-diction methods may be found not in selection or placement applications but in treatment evaluation research (98, 51, 52, 50, 57). Studies of effectiveness of any treatment or control program may be conducted according to experimental or statistical designs. Experimental designs provide the most rigorous approach. In the field of crime and delinquency, however, this approach often is beset with problems or is simply not feasible. When this is the case, statistical means of control must be substituted for the lacking experimental controls. The prediction method can provide a measure of the expected performance for any group of subjects. Then the expected and actual outcomes, for a specific criterion classification, may be compared. One such approach may be described as follows:

Prediction devices, to estimate the likelihood of agency program outcomes, first must be developed and tested. These represent experience with various groups of people, summarized by appropriate statistical methods; they provide a way of quantifying expectations based upon past experience. They are needed for application to each person *before* assignment to treatment. When persons are assigned to specific kinds of treatments, then we may ask whether the actual outcome is more or less favorable than *expected* (from past experience with other, similar groups). Since we wish to find treatments that improve the chances of success, we will be pleased if the prediction device is made invalid by helpful treatment.

If the outcome following treatment can be predicted not only before treatment but *regardless* of treatment, then it is very hard to argue that this treatment makes any difference with respect to the specific outcome studied. However, persons assigned to a given treatment may "succeed" (or "fail") significantly more often than expected from their risk classifications. If the validity of the prediction device has been established on other groups, then the observed differences in outcomes must be due to treatment, or to factors associated with treatment, or to both.

Further research, using experimental designs, might then be developed in order to test hypotheses about the source of the difference. Meanwhile, decision makers at least can be made aware of the relationship—positive, negative, or none—between the program and the outcomes. The most useful role for prediction methods, therefore, will be found when their development and validation is studied continuously as one component of an agency-wide information system for assessment of the effectiveness of programs.

IMPLICATIONS

In each social agency responsible for crime and delinquency treatment and control programs, a systematic study of "natural variation" is needed. Improvement of predictive efficiency and evaluations of differing treatment alternatives are closely related problems; in a concerted effort they can be attacked together. The main requirements are:

1. Systematic collection of reliable data for "predictor candidates" at critical decision points within the total system.
2. Repeated studies of the relations between predictor categories and criterion categories defined in terms of agency goals.
3. Repeated validation of any prediction methods devised.
4. Periodic determination, on the basis of prediction methods, of expected outcomes of various programs within the agency.
5. Comparisons of criterion outcomes expected (by the prediction method) and observed (in actual practice).
6. Development of experimental programs to identify the sources of discrepancies between expected and observed results, when such differences are found.
7. Periodic provision, to decision makers of the agency, of information concerning the probable criterion outcomes of program decision alternatives.

In any agency, a continuous cycle of development of prediction methods, repeated validation, comparisons of program outcomes, modification of practice, research, and practice is needed. This requires systematic collection of information over the total system and repeated study of relationships to correctional goals. Prediction methods should occupy a prominent place in this cycle, primarily because they are needed as tools for the assessment of programs.

The next need will be for collaborative studies by agencies in various jurisdictions and by agencies whose responsibilities focus at different points in the continuum of correctional services from arrest to discharge. Examples of areas in which careful development of prediction methods, and extensive validation studies, are needed may be found throughout this continuum. Applications may be envisioned, but not yet proposed, as aids in selection or placement and the research applications of prediction methods can be immediately helpful.

Potential applications may be found at each stage of the process of the administration of justice. Problems of early identification of delinquency have been reviewed briefly. Immediately upon arrest of an alleged offender, other prediction problems arise. The general problem of "release on recognizance," includes at least the prediction question of appearance for trial. This problem demands (in fairness to the courts and to the accused) much more empirical study than ever has been attempted. Prediction of probation outcomes has received little study, despite the needs for assessment of variations in criterion outcomes associated with probation supervision alternatives. Prediction methods, with adequate validation, are needed for evaluation studies of a variety of community treatment programs. They are needed equally as tools for assessment of the wide variety of programs conducted in confinement, in detention, in jails, or in prisons. They are needed as aids in determining probable outcomes of alternative programs after institutional release.

This review shows that work is needed particularly in a number of areas:

1. Improvement of measures of the criteria of delinquency or crime to be predicted is required. This includes the development of more reliable measures, more specifically related to the behavior of offenders, and the assessment of reliability over time. There is a broader question, however, of explicit identification of the goals of social agencies concerned with delinquency and its correction. This general problem has led Wilkins to remark that one of the most important problems is not *how* to predict but *what* to predict (150).
2. Cross-validation studies of available measures in

order to test their applicability in various jurisdictions is needed, and repeated assessment of validity along with social change will be in order.

3. Development of prediction measures for specific subgroups, rather than for samples of total populations of children or of offenders is apparently a promising route to improved prediction.

4. Empirical comparisons of various methods in use for combining predictors are needed.

5. Leads from studies demonstrating a variety of discriminators of delinquent and non-delinquent samples should be followed up systematically to improve current prediction methods.

6. Attempts to improve statistical prediction methods by testing hypotheses from clinical practice represent another avenue to improved prediction.

7. Studies of specific decision functions, utilizing recently developed tools in applied decision theory, are needed at various points in the correctional process, wherever decisions are made about offenders. These will require assessment of the social and monetary costs and values associated with errors and successes along the correctional continuum.

8. Prediction methods should be built into the information system of each social agency responsible for custody, treatment, or release of offenders. This can permit necessary, repeated validation studies, or necessary modifications, of available prediction tools. It can permit programs for systematic feedback to decision makers concerning the predictive relevance of information used in arriving at individual decisions. It can provide helpful tools for evaluations of programs, thereby enabling administrators to assess the probable consequences of program decisions.

There is much to be learned about the prediction of delinquency and crime, and with presently available instruments caution is ordinarily required when applications are proposed. Yet much has been learned; methods are available for improvement of these instruments, and we should use them. The resulting prediction methods can summarize that which is known. More important, they can provide very useful tools for discovery of that which is not yet known concerning effective interventions to prevent delinquency and crime.

REFERENCES

1. ADKINS, B. C., *Construction and Analysis of Achievement Tests,* Washington, D.C.: Superintendent of Documents, 1947.

2. ADKINS, B. C., "Selecting Public Employees," *Pub. Personnel Rev.,* 1956, 17: 259–267.

3. AHMAN, J. S., "An Application of Fisher's Discriminant Function in the Classification of Students," *J. Educ. Psychol.,* 1955, 46: 184–188.

4. ARGYLE, M., "A New Approach to the Classification of Delinquents with Implications for Treatment," in *Enquiries Concerning Kinds of Treatment for Kinds of Delinquents, Monograph No. 2,* Sacramento, California: Board of Corrections, July, 1961, 15–26.

5. BALLARD, K. B., JR., BOBINSKI, C. A., GRANT, J. D., *A Pilot Study of Factors in Retraining Which Change Delinquency Attitudes,* Third Technical Report, Rehabilitation Research, U.S. Naval Retraining Command, Camp Elliott, San Diego, California, January, 1956.

6. BALLARD, K. B., JR., AND GOTTFREDSON, D. M., *Predictive Attribute Analysis and Prediction of Parole Performance,* Vacaville, California: Institute for the Study of Crime and Delinquency, December, 1963.

7. BECHTOLD, H. P., "Selection," in Stevens, S.S., *Handbook of Experimental Psychology,* New York: John Wiley & Sons, Inc., 1951, 1237–1266.

8. BLACK, B. J., AND GLICK, S. J., *Recidivism at the Hawthorne Cedar Knolls School: Predicted vs. Actual Outcome for Delinquent Boys,* Hawthorne-Cedars, Research Monograph No. 2, New York: Jewish Board of Guardians, 1952.

9. BLUM, R. N., "Predicting Criminal Behavior: An Annotated Bibliography," *J. of Corr. Psychol.,* Monograph No. 1, 1957.

10. BOWER, *The Education of Emotionally Handicapped Children,* a report to the California Legislature prepared pursuant to Sec. 1, of Chap. 2385, Statutes of 1957, Sacramento, California: State Dept. of Education, March, 1961.

11. BRANDON, G. E., AND POTTER, A. K., "An Application of the Linear Discriminant Function," *Rural Sociol.,* 1953, 18: 321–326.

12. BRIDGEMAN, P. W., *The Logic of Modern Physics,* New York: Crowell Collier & Macmillan, Inc., 1932.

13. BROGDEN, H. E., "On the Interpretation of the Correlation Coefficient as a Measure of Predictive Efficiency," *J. of Educ. Psychol.,* 1946, 37: 65–76.

14. BROGDEN, H. E., "Variation in Test Validity with Variation in the Distribution of Item Difficulties, Number of Items, and Degree of their Intercorrelation," *Psychometrika,* 1946, 11: 197–214.

15. BURGESS, E. W., in Bruce, Burgess and Harno, *The Working of the Indeterminate Sentence Law and the Parole System in Illinois.* Springfield: Illinois State Board of Parole, 1928, 205–249.

16. BURGESS, E. W., AND COTTRELL, L. S., JR.,

Predicting Success or Failure in Marriage, New York: Prentice-Hall, Inc., 1939.

17. BURGESS, E. W., AND WALLIN, T., *Engagement and Marriage,* Philadelphia: J. B. Lippincott Co., 1953.

18. CALDWELL, N. G., "Preview of a New Type of Probation Study Made in Alabama," *Federal Probation,* June, 1951.

19. CARROLL, J. B., "The Effect of Difficulty and Chance Success on Correlations between Items or between Tests," *Psychometrika,* 1945, 10: 1–19.

20. CASSELL, R. N., AND VAN VORST, R., "Level of Aspiration as a Means for Discerning between 'In Prison' and 'Out of Prison' Groups of Individuals," *J. Soc. Psychol.,* 1954, 40: 121–135.

21. CATTELL, R. B., "Measurement vs. Intuition in Applied Psychology," *Charact. and Personal.,* 1937, 6: 114–131.

22. CRAIG, M. M., AND GLICK, S. J., "Ten Years Experience with the Glueck Social Prediction Table," *Crime and Delinquency,* July, 1963, 249–261.

23. CRAIG, M. M., AND GLICK, S. J., *A Manual of Procedures for the Application of the Glueck Prediction Table,* New York: New York City Youth Board, Office of the Mayor, 1964.

24. CRAWFORD, A. B., AND BURNHAM, B. S., *Forecasting College Achievement,* New Haven: Yale University Press, 1946.

25. CRONBACH, L. J., "Test Reliability: Its Meaning and Determination," *Psychometrika,* 1947, 12: 1–16.

26. CRONBACH, L. J., *Essentials of Psychological Testing,* 2nd ed., New York: Harper & Row, Publishers, 1960.

27. CRONBACH, L. J., AND GLESER, G. C., *Psychological Tests and Personnel Decisions,* Urbana: University of Illinois Press, 1957.

28. CURETON, E. E., "Recipe for a Cookbook," *Psychol. Bull.,* 1957, 54: 494–497.

29. DE GROOT, A. D., *Via Clinical Statistical Prediction,* invited address, Western Psychological Association, San Jose, April, 1960.

30. DOCTOR, R. S., AND WINDER, C. L., "Delinquent vs. Non-Delinquent Performance on the Porteus Qualitative Maze Test," *J. Consult. Psychol.,* 1954, 18: 71–73.

31. DUNCAN, O. D., OHLIN, L. E., REISS, A. J., AND STANTON, H. R., "Formal Devices for Making Selection Decisions," *Amer. J. Sociol.,* 1953, 48: 573–584.

32. DUNCAN, O. D., AND DUNCAN, B., "A Methodological Analysis of Segregation Indexes," *Amer. Sociol. Rev.,* 1955, 20: 210–217.

33. FERGUSON, G. A., "On the Theory of Test Discrimination," *Psychometrika,* 1949, 14: 61–68.

34. FLANAGAN, J. C., "General Considerations in the Selections of Test Items and a Short Method of Estimating the Product Moment Coefficient from the Data at the Tails of the Distribution," *J. Educ. Psychol.,* 1939, 30: 674–680.

35. FLANAGAN, J. C., "The Aviation Psychology Program in the Army Air Forces," *Army Aviation Psychology Research Program Report 1,* Washington, D.C.: Government Printing Office, 1948.

36. GILLIN, J. L., "Predicting Outcome of Adult Probationers in Wisconsin," *Amer. Sociol. Rev.,* 1950, 15: 550–553.

37. GLASER, D., *The Effectiveness of a Prison and Parole System,* New York: The Bobbs-Merrill Co., Inc., 1964, chap. 3.

38. GLUECK, S., AND GLUECK, E. T., *500 Criminal Careers,* New York: Alfred A. Knopf, Inc., 1930.

39. GLUECK, S., AND GLUECK, E. T., *Five Hundred Delinquent Women,* New York: Alfred A. Knopf, Inc., 1934.

40. GLUECK, S., AND GLUECK, E. T., *One Thousand Juvenile Delinquents,* Cambridge: Harvard University Press, 1934.

41. GLUECK, S., AND GLUECK, E. T., *Juvenile Delinquents Grown Up,* New York: Commonwealth Fund, 1940.

42. GLUECK, S., AND GLUECK, E. T., *Criminal Careers in Retrospect,* New York: The Commonwealth Fund, 1943.

43. GLUECK, S., AND GLUECK, E. T., *Unravelling Juvenile Delinquency,* New York: The Commonwealth Fund, 1950.

44. GLUECK, S., "Pre-Sentence Examination of Offenders to Aid in Choosing a Method of Treatment," *J. Crim. Law Criminol.,* 1951, 41: 717–731.

45. GLUECK, S., AND GLUECK, E. T., *Later Criminal Careers,* New York: The Commonwealth Fund, 1957.

46. GLUECK, S., AND GLUECK, E. T., *Predicting Delinquency and Crime,* Cambridge: Harvard University Press, 1959.

47. GLUECK, E. T., "Efforts to Identify Delinquents," *Federal Probation,* June, 1960, 24: 49–56.

48. GLUECK, E. T., "Toward Improving the Identification of Delinquents," *J. Crim. Law Criminol.,* 1962, 53: 164–170.

49. GOTTFREDSON, D. M., *A Shorthand Formula for Base Expectancies,* Sacramento, California: California Department of Corrections, December, 1962.

50. GOTTFREDSON, D. M., "The Practical Application of Research," *Canadian J. Corr.,* October 4, 1963, 5: 212–228.

51. GOTTFREDSON, D. M., AND BONDS, J. A., *A Manual for Intake Base Expectancy Scoring (Form CDC BE61A),* Sacramento, California:

California Department of Corrections, April, 1961.

52. GOTTFREDSON, D. M., BALLARD, K. B., JR., AND BONDS, J. A., *Base Expectancy: California Institute for Women*, Sacramento, California: Institute for the Study of Crime and Delinquency and California Department of Corrections, September, 1962.

53. GOTTFREDSON, D. M., BALLARD, K. B., JR., AND LANE, L., *Association Analysis in a Prison Sample and Prediction of Parole Performance*, Vacaville, California: Institute for the Study of Crime and Delinquency, November, 1963.

54. GOTTFREDSON, D. M., BALLARD, K. B., JR., MANNERING, J. W., AND BABST, D. V. *Wisconsin Base Expectancies for Reformatories and Prisons*, Vacaville, California: Institute for the Study of Crime and Delinquency, June, 1965.

55. GOTTFREDSON, D. M., AND BALLARD, K. B., JR., *Association Analysis, Predictive Attribute Analysis, and Parole Behavior*, paper presented at the Western Psychological Association meetings, Portland, Oregon, April, 1964.

56. GOTTFREDSON, D. M., AND BALLARD, K. B., JR., *The Validity of Two Parole Prediction Scales: An 8 Year Follow Up Study*, Institute for the Study of Crime and Delinquency, Vacaville, California, 1965.

57. GOTTFREDSON, D. M., AND BALLARD, K. B., JR., *Testing Prison and Parole Decisions*, unpublished manuscript, July, 1966.

58. GOUGH, H. G., "A Sociological Theory of Psychopathy," *Amer. Sociol. Rev.*, 1948, 53: 359–366.

59. GOUGH, H. G., "What Determines the Academic Achievement of High School Students?," *J. Educ. Res.*, 1953, 321–331.

60. GOUGH, H. G., *Systematic Validation of a Test for Delinquency*, paper presented at the American Psychological Association meeting, New York, September, 1954.

61. GOUGH, H. G., "Theory and Measurement of Socialization," *J. Consult. Psychol.*, 1960, 24: 23–30.

62. GOUGH, H. G., "Clinical vs. Statistical Prediction in Psychology," chap. 9, in Postman, L., ed., *Psychology in the Making*, New York: Alfred A. Knopf, Inc., 1962, 526–584.

63. GOUGH, H. G., AND PETERSON, D. R., "The Identification and Measurement of Predispositional Factors in Crime and Delinquency," *J. of Consult. Psychol.* 1952, 26: 207–212.

64. GOUGH, H. G., WENK, E. A., AND ROSYNKO, V. V., "Parole Outcome as Predicted from the CPI, the MMPI, and a Base Expectancy Table," *J. Abnorm. Psych.*, December, 1965, 70: 6.

65. GRANT, J. D., *The Navy's Attack on the Problems of Delinquency*, mimeographed, Rehabilitation Research, U.S. Naval Retraining Command, Camp Elliott, San Diego, California, April 6, 1955.

66. GRANT, J. D., BOBINSKI, C. A., AND BALLARD, K. B., JR., *Factors in Retraining Which Affect Delinquency Proneness*, Fifth Technical Report, Rehabilitation Research, U.S. Naval Retraining Command, Camp Elliott, San Diego, California, January, 1956.

67. GRYGIER, T., *Treatment Variables in Nonlinear Prediction*, paper presented to the Joint Annual Meeting of the American Society of Criminology and the American Association for the Advancement of Science, Montreal, December, 1964.

68. GUILFORD, J. P., *Personality*, New York: McGraw-Hill Book Company, 1959.

69. GULLIKSEN, H., "The Relation of Item Difficulty and Inter-Item Correlation to Test Variance and Reliability," *Psychometrika*, 1945, 10: 79-91.

70. GUNDERSON, E. K., GRANT, J. D., AND BALLARD, K. B., JR., *The Prediction of Military Delinquency*, mimeographed, San Diego, California: U.S. Naval Retraining Command, 1956.

71. GUNDERSON, E. K., AND BALLARD, K. B., JR., *Discriminant Analysis of Variables Related to Nonconformity in Naval Recruits*, mimeographed, Eleventh Technical Report, Rehabilitation Research, U.S. Naval Retraining Command, Camp Elliott, San Diego, California, August, 1959.

72. GUTTMAN, LOUIS, "Mathematical and Tabulation Techniques. Supplemental Study B," in Horst, P., *The Prediction of Personal Adjustment*, New York: Social Science Research Council, 1941, 253–364.

73. GUTTMAN, L., "A Basis for Analyzing Test-Retest Reliability," *Psychometrika*, 1945, 10: 255–282.

74. GUTTMAN, L., "Test-Retest Reliability of Qualitative Data," *Psychometrika*, 1946, 9: 81–95.

75. HALL, C. L., *Aptitude Testing*, New York: The World Publishing Company, 1928.

76. HANLEY, C., "The Gauging of Criminal Predispositions," in Toch, H., *Legal and Criminal Psychology*, New York: Holt, Rinehart & Winston, Inc., 1961, 213–242.

77. HATHAWAY, S. R., AND McKINLEY, J. C., *The Minnesota Multiphasic Personality Inventory Manual*, Rev. New York: The Psychological Corp., 1951.

78. HATHAWAY, S. R., AND MONACHESI, E. D., *Analyzing and Predicting Juvenile Delinquency with the MMPI*, New York: The Psychological Corp., 1954.

79. HATHAWAY, S. R., AND MONACHESI, E. D., "The Personalities of Pre-Delinquent Boys," *J. Crim. Law Criminol.*, 1957, 48: 149–163.

80. HORST, P., *The Prediction of Personal Ad-*

justment, New York: Social Science Research Council Bulletin No. 48, 1941.

81. HORST, P., "Mathematical Contributions. Supplemental Study E," *The Prediction of Personal Adjustment*, Social Science Research Council, New York: 1941, 407–47.

82. HORST, P., "A Generalized Expression for the Reliability of Measures," *Psychometrika*, 1949, 14: 21–32.

83. HUNT, H. F., "Clinical Methods: Psychodiagnostics," in Stone, C. B., and Taylor, V. W., eds., *Annual Review of Psychology*, Stanford: Annual Reviews, Inc., 1950, 1: 207–220.

84. HUNT, W. A., "An Actuarial Approach to Clinical Judgment," in Bass, B. N., and Berg, I. A., *Objective Approaches to Personality Study*, Princeton, N.J.: Van Nostrand Co., Inc., 1959, 169–191.

85. IVES, V., GRANT, M. Q., AND BALLARD, K. B., JR., *Interpersonal Variables Related to Recidivism in Military Delinquency*, mimeographed, Eighth Technical Report, Rehabilitation Research, U.S. Naval Retraining Command, Camp Elliott, San Diego, California, December, 1957.

86. JACOBSON, J. L., AND WIRT, R. D., *Studies in Psychological and Sociological Variables in State Prison Inmates, Section No. 1, 18 Variable Profile*, Minneapolis: University of Minnesota, December, 1961.

87. JAMES, W., "Pragmatism. A New Name for Some Old Ways of Thinking," 1907, reprinted as "Pragmatism's Conception of Truth," in *Essays in Pragmatism*, New York, Hafner Publishing Co., Inc., 1955.

88. JARRETT, R. F., "Percent Increase in Output of Selected Personnel As an Index to Test Efficiency," *J. Appl. Psychol.*, 1948, 32: 135–145.

89. JONES, D. S., LIVSON, N. H., AND SARBIN, T., "Perceptual Completion Behavior in Juvenile Delinquents," *Percept. Mot. Skills*, 1955, 5: 141–146.

90. KIRBY, B. C., "Parole Prediction Using Multiple Correlation," *Amer. J. Sociol.*, 1953–4, 59: 539–550.

91. KVARACEUS, W. C., "Forecasting Juvenile Delinquency: A Three Year Experiment," *Exceptional Children*, April, 1961, 18: 429–435.

92. KVARACEUS, W. C., "Programs of Early Identification and Prevention of Delinquency," *Social Deviancy among Youth*, 65th Yearbook of the National Society for the Study of Education, Chicago: National Society for the Study of Education, 1966, 189–220.

93. LACKMAN, R., *The Predictive Use of the Linear Discriminant Function in Naval Aviation Cadet Selection*, U.S. Naval Sch. Aviat. Med. Res. Rep. 1953, Rep. 11 N.M. 001057.16.02–11p.

94. LUNDEN, W. A., "Forecast for 1955: Predicting Prison Population," *The Presidio*, 1952, 19, no. 2.

95. MACNAUGHTON-SMITH, P., "The Classification of Individuals by the Possession of Attributes Associated with a Criterion," *Biometrics*, June, 1963.

96. MCARTHUR, C.,"Analyzing the Clinical Process," *J. Counsel. Psychol.*, 1954, 1: 203–207.

97. MANNERING, J. W., AND BABST, D. V., *Wisconsin Base Expectancies for Adult Male Parolees*, Progress Report No. 4, Wisconsin State Department of Public Welfare, Bureau of Research and Division of Corrections, April, 1963.

98. MANNHEIM, H., AND WILKINS, L. T., *Prediction Methods in Relation to Borstal Training*, London: Her Majesty's Stationery Office, 1955.

99. MAY, M. A., "Predicting Academic Success," *J. Educ. Psychol.*, 1923, 14: 429–440.

100. MEEHL, P. E., *Clinical vs. Statistical Prediction*, Minneapolis: University of Minnesota Press, 1954.

101. MEEHL, P. E., "Clinical vs. Actuarial Prediction," in *Proceedings, 1955 Invitational Conference on Testing Problems*, Princeton, N.J.: Educational Testing Service, 1956, 136–141.

102. MEEHL, P. E., "The Tie That Binds," *J. Counsel. Psychol.*, 1956, 3: 163–164, 171, 173.

103. MEEHL, P. E., "When Should We Use Our Heads Instead of the Formula?" *J. Counsel. Psychol.*, 1957, 4: 268–273.

104. MEEHL, P. E., "A Comparison of Conditions with Five Statistical Methods of Identifying MMPI Profiles," *J. Counsel. Psychol.*, 1959, 6: 102–109.

105. MEEHL, P. E., AND ROSEN, A., "Antecedent Probability and the Efficiency of Psychometric Signs, Patterns, or Cutting Scores," *Psychol. Bull.*, 1955, 52: 194–215.

106. MONACHESI, E. D., *Prediction Factors in Probation*, Hanover, N.H.: The Sociological Press, 1932.

107. MONACHESI, E. D., "Personality Characteristics and Socio-Economic Status of Delinquents and Non-Delinquents," *J. Crim. Law Criminol.*, 1950, 40: 570–583.

108. OHLIN, L. E., AND DUNCAN, O. D., "The Efficiency of Prediction in Criminology," *Amer. J. Sociol.*, 1949, 54: 441–451.

109. OHLIN, L. E., *Selection for Parole: A Manual of Parole Prediction*, New York: Russell Sage Foundation, 1951.

110. OHLIN, L. E., *Some Parole Prediction Problems in the United States*, paper presented at the Third International Congress of Criminology, London, September, 1955.

111. PATON, J. H., "Predicting Prison Adjustment with the Minnesota Multiphasic Personality Inventory," *J. Clin. Psychol.*, 1958, 14: 308–313.

112. PORTEUS, S. D., *Qualitative Performance in the Maze Test*, Vineland, N.J.: The Smith Publishing House, 1942.

113. POWERS, E., AND WITMER, H., *An Experiment in the Prevention of Delinquency*, The Cambridge-Somerville Youth Study, New York: Columbia University Press, 1951.

114. QUAY, H., AND PETERSON, D. R., "A Brief Scale for Juvenile Delinquency," *J. Clin. Psychol.*, April, 1958, 14: 139–142.

115. REED, R. R., "An Empirical Study in the Reduction of the Number of Variables Used in Prediction: Supplementary Study C" in Horst, P., *The Prediction of Social Adjustment*, New York: Social Science Research Council, 1941.

116. REICHENBACH, M., *Experience and Prediction*, Chicago: University of Chicago Press, 1938.

117. REISS, A. J., JR., "The Accuracy, Efficiency, and Validity of a Prediction Instrument," Ph. D. diss., Dept. of Sociology, University of Chicago, 1949.

118. REISS, A. J., JR., "Delinquency as a Failure of Personal and Social Control," *Amer. Sociol. Rev.*, 1951, 16: 196–207.

119. REISS, A. J., JR., "Unravelling Juvenile Delinquency: II. An Appraisal of the Research Methods," *Amer. J. Sociol.*, 1951, 57: 115–21.

120. RICHARDSON, M. W., "The Combination of Measures: Supplemental Study D," in Horst, P., *The Prediction of Personal Adjustment*, New York: Social Science Research Council, 1941, 379–401.

121. RUBIN, S., "Unravelling Juvenile Delinquency: I. Illusions in a Research Project Using Matched Pairs," *Amer. J. Sociol.*, 1951, 57: 107–114.

122. SALINE, T., "Recidivism and Maturation," *National Probation and Parole Association Journal*, July 3, 1958, 4: 211–230.

123. SARBIN, T. R., "The Logic of Prediction in Psychology," *Psychol. Rev.*, 1944, 51: 210–228.

124. SAVITZ, L. D., "Prediction Studies in Criminology," *International Bibliography on Crime and Delinquency*, New York: National Council on Crime and Delinquency, 1965.

125. SCHACTEL, E. G., "Notes on the Use of the Rorschach Test," in Glueck, S., and Glueck, E. T., *Unravelling Juvenile Delinquency*, New York: Commonwealth Fund, 1950.

126. SCHIEDT, R., *Ein Beitrag Zum Problem der Ruckfallsprognose*, Munchen, 1936.

127. SCHUESSLER, K. F., AND CRESSEY, D. R., "Personality Characteristics of Criminals," *Amer. J. Sociol.*, 1950, 55: 483–484.

128. SELLIN, T., AND WOLFGANG, M. E., *The Measurement of Delinquency*, New York: John Wiley & Sons, Inc., 1964.

129. SHAPLIN, J. T., AND TIEDMAN, D. V., "Comment on the Juvenile Prediction Tables in the Glueck's *Unravelling Juvenile Delinquency*," *Amer. Sociol. Rev.*, 1951, 16: 544–548.

130. STEVENS, S. S., "Mathematics, Measurement, and Psychophysics," in Stevens, S. S., *Handbook of Experimental Psychology*, New York: John Wiley & Sons, Inc., 1957, 1–49.

131. STOGILL, M., *Behavior Cards: A Test-Interview for Delinquent Children*, The Psychological Corp.

132. STOTT, D. H., "A New Delinquency Prediction Instrument Using Behavioral Indications," *International Journal of Social Psychiatry*, 1960, 6: 195–205.

133. STRONG, E. K., JR., *Vocational Interests of Men and Women*. Stanford, Calif., Stanford University Press, 1943.

134. STRONG, E. K., JR., *Vocational Interests Eighteen Years After College*, Minneapolis: University of Minnesota Press, 1955.

135. TAYLOR, D. W., "An Analysis of Delinquency Based on Case Studies," *J. Abnorm. Soc. Psychol.*, January, 1947, vol. 42.

136. THORNDIKE, E. L., et al., *Prediction of Vocational Success*, New York: Commonwealth, Fund, 1934.

137. THORNDIKE, E. L., *Personnel Selection*, New York: John Wiley & Sons, Inc., 1949.

138. TIBBITTS, C., "Success and Failure on Parole Can Be Predicted," *J. Crim. Law Criminol.*, 1931, 22: 11–50.

139. TIBBITTS, C., "The Reliability of Factors Used in Predicting Success or Failure on Parole," *J. Crim. Law Criminol.*, 1932, 22: 844–853.

140. TOBY, J., "An Evaluation of Early Identification and Intensive Treatment Programs for Pre-Delinquents," *Social Problems*, 1965, 13: 2.

141. TOOPS, H. A., "Philosophy and Practice of Personnel Selection," *Educ. Psychol. Measmt.*, 1945, 5: 95–124.

142. TRUNK, H., *Sociale Prognosen Strafgefangenen*, 28 Monatsschrift fur Kriminolobiologie und Strafrechtsreform, 1937.

143. VERNONE, P. E., "The Assessment of Children: Recent Studies in Mental Measurement and Statistical Analysis," *Studies in Education No. 7*, London: University of London Institute of Education and Evans Bros. Ltd., 1955, 189–215.

144. VOLD, G. B., "Prediction Methods Applied to Problems of Classification within Institutions," *J. Crim. Law and Criminol.*, 1936, 26: 202–209.

145. WALTERS, A. A., "A Note on Statistical Methods of Predicting Delinquency," *Brit. J. Delinquency*, 1956, 6: 297–302.

146. WARD, J. H., JR., *An Application of Linear and Curvilinear Joint Functional Regression in Psychological Prediction*, U.S.A.F. Pers. Train. Res. Cent., Res. Bul., 1954, No. AFPTRC TR54 86, W29p.

147. WARNER, S. B., "Factors Determining Parole from the Massachusetts Reformatory," *J. Crim. Law Criminol.*, 1923, 14: 172–207.
148. WASHBURNE, J. W., *The Washburne Social Adjustment Inventory*, Harcourt, Brace & World, Inc.
149. WILKINS, L. T., *Classification and Contamination*, a memorandum from the Research Unit, Home Office, London, December, 1955.
150. WILKINS, L. T., "Who Does What with What and to Whom?" Sacramento, California, Department of Corrections, *The Research Newsletter*, March 1, 1959.
151. WILKINS, L. T., *Delinquent Generations: A Home Office Research Unit Report*, London: Her Majesty's Stationery Office, 1960.
152. WILKINS, L. T., "What is Prediction and Is It Necessary in Evaluating Treatment?" in *Research and Potential Application of Research in Probation, Parole, and Delinquency Prediction*, New York: Citizens Committee for Children of New York, Research Center, New York School of Social Work, Columbia University, July, 1961.
153. WILKINS, L. T., AND MACNAUGHTON-SMITH, P., "New Prediction and Classification Methods in Criminology," *The Journal of Research in Crime and Delinquency*, 1954, 1: 19–32.
154. WILLIAMS, W. T., AND LAMBERT, J. M., "Multivariate Methods in Plant Ecology: Part I, II, and III," *J. Ecol.*, 1959, 47: 83–101; 1960, 48: 680–710; 1961, 49: 717–729.
155. WOOTON, B., *Social Science and Social Pathology*, New York: Crowell Collier & Macmillan, Inc., 1959, chap. 5.
156. ZAKILSKI, F. C., "Studies in Delinquency: II. Personality Structure of Delinquent Boys," *J. Genet. Psychol.*, 1949, 74: 109–117.

44.

TRAVIS HIRSCHI AND HANAN C. SELVIN

FALSE CRITERIA OF CAUSALITY IN DELINQUENCY RESEARCH

Smoking per se is not a cause of lung cancer. Evidence for this statement comes from the thousands of people who smoke and yet live normal, healthy lives. Lung cancer is simply unknown to the vast majority of smokers, even among those who smoke two or more packs a day. Whether smoking is a cause of lung cancer, then, depends upon the reaction of the lung tissues to the smoke inhaled. The important thing is not whether a person smokes, but how his lungs react to the smoke inhaled. These facts point to the danger of imputing causal significance to superficial variables. In essence, it is not smoking as such, but the carcinogenic elements in tobacco smoke that are real causes of lung cancer.[1]

The task of determining whether such variables as broken homes, gang membership, or anomie are "causes" of delinquency benefits from a comparison with the more familiar problem of deciding whether cigarette smoking "causes" cancer. In both fields many statistical studies have shown strong relations between these presumed causes and the observed effects, but the critics of these studies often attack them as "merely statistical." This phrase has two meanings. To some critics it stands for the belief that only with experimental manipulation of the independent variables is a satisfactory causal inference possible. To others it is a brief way

SOURCE: Travis Hirschi and Hanan C. Selvin, "False Criteria of Causality in Delinquency Research," *Social Problems* 13, no. 3 (Winter, 1966): 254–68. Reprinted by Permission of the authors and The Society for the Study of Social Problems.

This is publication A-56 of the Survey Research Center, University of California, Berkeley. We are grateful to the Ford Foundation for financial support of the larger study from which this paper is drawn. An early account of this study, which does not include the present paper, is *The Methodological Adequacy of Delinquency Research* (Berkeley: Survey Research Center, 1962). Ian Currie, John Lofland, Alan B. Wilson, and Herbert L. Costner made useful criticism of previous versions of this paper.

[1]This is a manufactured "quotation"; its source will become obvious shortly.

of saying that observing a statistical association between two phenomena is only the first step in plausibly inferring causality. Since no one proposes trying to give people cancer or to make them delinquent, the fruitful way toward better causal analyses in these two fields is to concentrate on improving the statistical approach.

In setting this task for ourselves we can begin with one area of agreement: all statistical analyses of causal relations in delinquency rest on observed associations between the independent and dependent variables. Beyond this there is less agreement. Following Hyman's reasoning,[2] we believe that these two additional criteria are the minimum requirements for an adequate causal analysis: 1) the independent variable is causally prior to the dependent variable (we shall refer to this as the criterion of "causal order"), and 2) the original association does not disappear when the influences of other variables causally prior to both of the original variables are removed ("lack of spuriousness").[3]

The investigator who tries to meet these criteria does not have an easy time of it.[4] Our examination of statistical research on the causes of delinquency shows, however, that many investigators do not try to meet these criteria but instead invent one or another new criterion of causality—or, more often, of noncausality, perhaps because noncausality is easier to demonstrate. To establish causality one must forge a chain of three links (association, causal order, and lack of spuriousness), and the possibility that an antecedent variable not yet considered may account for the observed relation makes the third link inherently weak. To establish noncausality, one has only to break any one of these links.[5]

Despite the greater ease with which noncausality may be demonstrated, many assertions of noncausality in the delinquency literature turn out to be invalid. Some are invalid because the authors misuse statistical tools or misinterpret their findings. But many more are invalid because the authors invoke one or another false criterion of noncausality. Perhaps because assertions of noncausality are so easy to demonstrate, these invalid assertions have received a great deal of attention.

A clear assertion that certain variables long considered causes of delinquency are not really causes comes from a 1960 *Report to The Congress:*

Many factors frequently cited as causes of delinquency are really only concomitants. They are not causes in the sense that if they were removed delinquency would decline. Among these factors are:

Broken homes
Poverty
Poor housing
Lack of recreational facilities
Poor physical health
Race
Working mothers.[6]

According to this report, all of these variables are statistically associated with delinquency, i.e., they are all "concomitants." To prove that they are not causes of delinquency it is necessary either to show that their relations with delin-

---

[2]Herbert H. Hyman, *Survey Design and Analysis* (New York: The Free Press, 1955), chaps. 5–7.

[3]Hyman appears to advocate another criterion as well: that a chain of intervening variables must link the independent and dependent variables of the original relation. We regard this as psychologically or theoretically desirable but not as part of the minimum methodological requirements for demonstrating causality in nonexperimental research.

[4]Hirschi and Selvin, op. cit.

[5]Popper calls this the asymmetry of verifiability and falsifiability. Karl R. Popper, *The Logic of Scientific Discovery* (New York: Basic Books, Inc., 1959, esp. pp. 27–48. For a fresh view of the verifica-

tion-falsification controversy, see Thomas S. Kuhn, *The Structure of Scientific Revolutions* (Chicago: University of Chicago Press, 1962). Kuhn discusses Popper's views on pp. 145–146. Actually, it is harder to establish non-causality than our statement suggests, because of the possibility of "spurious independence." This problem is discussed in Hirschi and Selvin, op. cit., pp. 38–45, as "elaboration of a zero relation."

[6]U.S. Department of Health, Education, and Welfare, *Report to The Congress on Juvenile Delinquency* (Washington, D.C.: Government Printing Office, 1960), p. 21. The conclusion that "poor housing" is not a cause of delinquency is based on Mildred Hartsough, *The Relation Between Housing and Delinquency*, Federal Emergency Administration of Public Works, Housing Division, 1936. The conclusion that "poor physical health" is not a cause is based on Edward Piper's "unpublished Children's Bureau manuscript summarizing the findings of numerous investigators on this subject." Since we have not examined these two works, the following conclusions do not apply to them.

quency are spurious or that they are effects of delinquency rather than causes. Since all of these presumptive causes appear to precede delinquency, the only legitimate way to prove non-causality is to find an antecedent variable that accounts for the observed relations. None of the studies cited in the *Report* does this.[7] Instead, the assertion that broken homes, poverty, lack of recreational facilities, race, and working mothers are not causes of delinquency appears to be based on one or more of the following false "criteria":[8]

1. Insofar as a relation between two variables is not *perfect*, the relation is not causal.
   a. Insofar as a factor is not a *necessary condition* for delinquency, it is not a cause of delinquency.
   b. Insofar as a factor is not a *sufficient condition* for delinquency, it is not a cause of delinquency.
2. Insofar as a factor is not *"characteristic"* of delinquents, it is not a cause of delinquency.
3. If a relation between an independent variable and delinquency is found for *a single value of a situational or contextual factor,* then the situational or contextual factor cannot be a cause of delinquency.[9]

4. If a relation is observed between an independent variable and delinquency and if a psychological variable is suggested as *intervening* between these two variables, then the original relation is not causal.
5. *Measurable* variables are not causes.
6. If a relation between an independent variable and delinquency is *conditional* upon the value of other variables, the independent variable is not a cause of delinquency.

In our opinion, all of these criteria of non-causality are illegitimate. If they were systematically applied to any field of research, no relation would survive the test. Some of them, however, have a superficial plausibility, both as stated or implied in the original works and as reformulated here. It will therefore be useful to consider in some detail just why these criteria are illegitimate and to see how they appear in delinquency research.

FALSE CRITERION 1

Insofar as a relation between two variables is not perfect, the relation is not causal.

Despite the preponderance of Negro delinquency, one must beware of imputing any causal significance to race per se. There is no *necessary* concomitance between the presence of Negroes and delinquency. In Census Tracts 9-1 and 20-2, with populations of 124 and 75 Negro juveniles, there were no recorded cases of delinquency during the study period. The rates of Negro delinquency also vary as widely as do the white rates indicating large differences in behavior patterns that are not a function or effect of race per se. It is also of interest to note that in at least 10% of the districts with substantial Negro juvenile populations, the Negro delinquency rate is lower than the corresponding white rate.[10]

There are three facts here: (1) not all Negroes are delinquents; (2) the rates of Negro de-

---

[7] The works cited are: broken homes, Negly K. Teeters and John Otto Reinemann, *The Challenge of Delinquency* (New York: Prentice-Hall, Inc., 1950), pp. 149–54; poverty, Bernard Lander, *Toward an Understanding of Juvenile Delinquency* (New York: Columbia University Press, 1954); recreational facilities, Ethel Shanas and Catherine E. Dunning, *Recreation and Delinquency* (Chicago: Chicago Recreation Commission, 1942); race, Lander, op. cit.; working mothers, Eleanor E. Maccoby, "Children and Working Mothers," *Children* 5 (May-June, 1958): 83–89.

[8] It is not clear in every case that the researcher himself reached the conclusion of noncausality or, if he did, that this conclusion was based on the false criteria discussed below. Maccoby's article, for example, contains a "conjectural explanation" of the relation between mother's employment and delinquency (i.e., without presenting any statistical evidence she suggests that the original relation came about through some antecedent variable), but it appears that the conclusion of noncausality in the *Report* is based on other statements in her work.

[9] All of the foregoing criteria are related to the "perfect relation" criterion in that they all require variation in delinquency that is unexplained by the "non-causal" variable. A more general statement of criterion 3 would be: "if variable X is related to delinquency when there is no variation in variable T, then variable T is not a cause of delinquency." In order for this criterion to be applicable, there

must be some residual variation in delinquency after T has had its effect.

Although both forms of this criterion fairly represent the reasoning involved in some claims of non-causality, and although both are false, the less explicit version in the text is superficially more plausible. This inverse relation between explicitness and plausibility is one reason for the kind of methodological explication presented here.

[10] Bernard Lander, *Towards an Understanding of Juvenile Delinquency* (New York: Columbia University Press, 1954), p. 32. Italics in original. An alternative interpretation of the assumptions implicit in this quotation is presented in the discussion of criterion 6, below.

linquency vary from place to place; (3) in some circumstances, Negroes are less likely than whites to be delinquent. These facts lead Lander to conclude that race has no causal significance in delinquency.

In each case the reasoning is the same: each fact is another way of saying that the statistical relation between race and delinquency is not perfect, and this apparently is enough to disqualify race as a cause. To see why this reasoning is invalid one has only to ask for the conditions under which race *could be* a cause of delinquency if this criterion were accepted. Suppose that the contrary of the first fact above were true, that *all* Negroes are delinquent. It would then follow necessarily that Negro delinquency rates would not vary from place to place (fact 2) and that the white rate would never be greater than the Negro rate (fact 3). Thus in order for race to have "any" causal significance, all Negroes must be delinquents (or all whites non-delinquents). In short, race must be perfectly related to delinquency.[11]

Now if an independent variable and a dependent variable are perfectly associated,[12] no other independent variable is needed: that is, perfect association implies single causation, and less-than-perfect association implies multiple causation. Rejecting as causes of delinquency those variables whose association with delinquency is less than perfect thus implies rejecting the principle of multiple causation. Although there is nothing sacred about this principle, at least at the level of empirical research it is more viable than the principle of single causation. All studies show that more than one independent variable is needed to account for delinquency. In this field, as in others, perfect relations are virtually unknown. The researcher who finds a less-than-perfect relation between variable X and delinquency should not conclude that X is not a cause of delinquency, but merely that it is not the *only* cause.[13]

For example, suppose that tables like the following have been found for variables A, B, C, and D as well as for X:

TABLE 5-1.

DELINQUENCY BY X, WHERE X IS NEITHER A NECESSARY NOR A SUFFICIENT CONDITION FOR DELINQUENCY, BUT MAY BE ONE OF SEVERAL CAUSES

	X	Not X
Delinquent	40	20
Nondelinquent	60	80

The researcher using the perfect relation criterion would have to conclude that none of the causes of delinquency has yet been discovered. Indeed, this criterion would force him to conclude that there are *no causes* of delinquency except *the* cause. The far-from-perfect relation between variable X and delinquency in the table above leads him to reject variable X as a cause of delinquency. Since variables A, B, C, and D are also far from perfectly related to delinquency, he must likewise reject them. Since it is unlikely that *the* cause of delinquency will ever be discovered by quantitative research, the researcher who accepts the perfect relation criterion should come to believe

[11] Strictly speaking, in this quotation Lander does not demand that race be perfectly related to delinquency, but only that all Negroes be delinquents (the sufficient conditions of criterion 1-b). Precedent for the "perfect relation" criterion of causality appears in a generally excellent critique of crime and delinquency research by Jerome Michael and Mortimer J. Adler published in 1933. "There is still another way of saying that none of the statistical findings derived from the quantitative data yields answers to etiological questions. The findings themselves show that every factor which can be seen to be in some way associated with criminality is also associated with non-criminality, and also that criminality is found in the absence of every factor with which it is also seen to be associated. In other words, what has been found is merely additional evidence of what we either knew or could have suspected, namely, that there is a plurality of related factors in this field." *Crime, Law and Social Science* (New York: Harcourt Brace & World, Inc.), p. 53.

[12] "Perfect association" here means that all of the cases fall into the main diagonal of the table, that (in the 2 × 2 table) the independent variable is both a necessary and a sufficient cause of the dependent variable. Less stringent definitions of perfect association are considered in the following paragraphs. Since Lander deals with ecological correlations, he could reject race as a cause of delinquency even if it were perfectly related to delinquency at the census tract level, since the ecological and the individual correlations are not identical.

[13] We are assuming that the causal order and lack of spuriousness criteria are satisfied.

that such research is useless: all it can show is that there are *no* causes of delinquency.

FALSE CRITERION 1-a

Insofar as a factor is not a necessary condition for delinquency, it is not a cause of delinquency.

The "not necessary" (and of course the "not sufficient") argument against causation is a variant of the "perfect relation" criterion. A factor is a necessary condition for delinquency if it must be present for delinquency to occur— e.g., knowledge of the operation of an automobile is a necessary condition for auto theft (although all individuals charged with auto theft need not know how to drive a car). In the following table the independent variable X is a necessary (but not sufficient[14]) condition for delinquency.

TABLE 5-2.

DELINQUENCY BY X, WHERE X IS A NECESSARY BUT NOT SUFFICIENT CONDITION FOR DELINQUENCY

	X	Not X
Delinquent	67	0
Nondelinquent	33	100

The strongest statement we can find in the work cited by the Children's Bureau in support of the contention that the broken home is not a cause of delinquency is the following:

We can leave this phase of the subject by stating that the phenomenon of the physically broken home is a cause of delinquent behavior is, in itself, not so important as was once believed. In essence, it is not that the home is broken, but rather that the home is inadequate, that really matters.[15]

This statement suggests that the broken home

is not a necessary condition for delinquency (delinquents may come from intact but "inadequate" homes). The variable with which the broken home is compared, inadequacy, has all the attributes of a necessary condition for delinquency: a home that is "adequate" with respect to the prevention of delinquency will obviously produce no delinquent children. If, as appears to be the case, the relation between inadequacy and delinquency is a matter of definition, the comparison of this relation with the relation between the broken home and delinquency is simply an application of the illegitimate "necessary conditions" criterion. Compared to a necessary condition, the broken home is "not so important." Compared to some (or some *other*) *measure* of inadequacy, however, the broken home may be very important. For that matter, once "inadequacy" is empirically defined, the broken home may turn out to be one of its important causes. Thus the fact that the broken home is not a necessary condition for delinquency does not justify the statement that the broken home is "not [a cause of delinquency] in the sense that if [it] were removed delinquency would decline."[16]

FALSE CRITERION 1-b

Insofar as a factor is not a sufficient condition for delinquency, it is not a cause of delinquency.

A factor is a sufficient condition for delinquency if its presence is invariably followed by delinquency. Examples of sufficient conditions are hard to find in empirical research.[17] The nearest one comes to such conditions in delinquency research is in the use of predictive devices in which several factors taken together

---

[14]To say that X is a necessary condition for delinquency means that all delinquents are X (i.e., that the cell in the upper right of this table is zero); to say that X is a sufficient condition for delinquency implies that all X's are delinquent (i.e., that the cell in the lower left is zero); to say that X is a necessary and sufficient condition for delinquency means that all X's and no other persons are delinquent (i.e., that both cells in the minor diagonal of this table are zero).

[15]Teeters and Reinemann, op. cit., p. 154.

[16]*Report to The Congress*, p. 21. Two additional illegitimate criteria of causality listed above are implicit in the quotation from Teeters and Reinemann. "Inadequacy of the home" could be treated as an intervening variable which interprets the relation between the broken home and delinquency (criterion 4) or as a theoretical variable of which the broken home is an indicator (criterion 5). These criteria are discussed below.

[17]In his *Theory of Collective Behavior* (New York: The Free Press, 1963) Neil J. Smelser suggests sets of necessary conditions for riots, panics, and other forms of collective behavior; in this theory the entire set of necessary conditions for any one form of behavior is a sufficient condition for that form to occur.

are virtually sufficient for delinquency.[18] (The fact that several variables are required even to approach sufficiency is of course one of the strongest arguments in favor of multiple causation.) Since sufficient conditions are rare, this unrealistic standard can be used against almost any imputation of causality.

First, however, let us make our position clear on the question. Poverty per se is not a cause of delinquency or criminal behavior; this statement is evidenced by the courage, fortitude, honesty, and moral stamina of thousands of parents who would rather starve than steal and who inculcate this attitude in their children. Even in the blighted neighborhoods of poverty and wretched housing conditions, crime and delinquency are simply nonexistent among most residents.[19]

Many mothers, and some fathers who have lost their mates through separation, divorce or death, are doing a splendid job of rearing their children.[20]

Our point of view is that the structure of the family *itself* does not cause delinquency. For example the fact that a home is broken does not cause delinquency, but it is more difficult for a single parent to provide material needs, direct controls, and other important elements of family life.[21]

The error here lies in equating "not sufficient" with "not *a* cause." Even if every delinquent child were from an impoverished (or broken) home—that is, even if this factor were a necessary condition for delinquency—it would still be possible to show that poverty is not a sufficient condition for delinquency.

In order for the researcher to conclude that poverty is a cause of delinquency, it is not necessary that all or most of those who are poor

become delinquent.[22] If it were, causal variables would be virtually impossible to find. From the standpoint of social action, this criterion can be particularly unfortunate. Suppose that poverty were a necessary but not sufficient condition for delinquency, as in Table 5–2. Advocates of the "not sufficient" criterion would be forced to conclude that, if poverty were removed, delinquency would not decline. As the table clearly shows, however, removal of poverty under these hypothetical conditions would *eliminate* delinquency!

To take another example, Wootton reports Carr-Saunders as finding that 28% of his delinquents and 16% of his controls came from broken homes and that this difference held in both London and the provinces. She quotes Carr-Saunders' "cautious" conclusion:

We can only point out that the broken home may have some influence on delinquency, though since we get control cases coming from broken homes, we cannot assert that there is a direct link between this factor and delinquency.[23]

Carr-Saunders' caution apparently stems from the "not sufficient" criterion, for unless the broken home is a sufficient condition for delinquency, there must be control cases (nondelinquents) from broken homes.

In each of these examples the attack on causality rests on the numbers in a single table. Since all of these tables show a non-zero relation, it seems to us that these researchers have misinterpreted the platiture "correlation is not causation." To us, this platitude means that one must go beyond the observed fact of association in order to demonstrate causality. To those who employ one or another variant of the perfect relation criterion, it appears to mean that there is something suspect in any numerical demonstration of association. Instead of being the first evidence for causality, an observed association becomes evidence against causality.

[18]In the Gluecks' prediction table, those with scores of 400 or more have a 98.1% chance of delinquency. However, as Reiss has pointed out, the Gluecks *start* with a sample that is 50% delinquent. Had they started with a sample in which only 10% were delinquent, it would obviously have been more difficult to approach sufficiency. Sheldon Glueck and Eleanor Glueck, *Unraveling Juvenile Delinquency* (Cambridge: Harvard University Press, 1950), pp. 260–62; Albert J. Reiss, Jr., "Unraveling Juvenile Delinquency. II. An Appraisal of the Research Methods," *American Journal of Sociology*, 57, no. 2 (1951): 115–20.

[19]Teeters and Reinemann, op. cit., p. 127.

[20]Ibid., p. 154.

[21]F. Ivan Nye, *Family Relationships and Delinquent Behavior* (New York: John Wiley & Sons, Inc., 1958), p. 34. Italics in original.

[22]We are of course assuming throughout this discussion that the variables in question meet what we consider to be legitimate criteria of causality.

[23]Barbara Wootton, *Social Science and Social Pathology* (New York: Crowell Collier & Macmillan, Inc., 1959), p. 118.

FALSE CRITERION 2

Insofar as a factor is not "characteristic" of delinquents, it is not a cause of delinquency.

Many correlation studies in delinquency may conquer all these hurdles and still fail to satisfy the vigorous demands of scientific causation. Frequently a group of delinquents is found to differ in a statistically significant way from a nondelinquent control group with which it is compared. Nevertheless, the differentiating trait may not be at all characteristic of the delinquent group. Suppose, for example, that a researcher compares 100 delinquent girls with 100 nondelinquent girls with respect to broken homes. He finds, let us say, that 10% of the nondelinquents come from broken homes, whereas this is true of 30% of the delinquent girls. Although the difference between the two groups is significant, the researcher has not demonstrated that the broken home is characteristic of delinquents. The fact is that 70% of them come from unbroken homes. Again, ecological studies showing a high correlation between residence in interstitial areas and delinquency, as compared with lower rates of delinquency in other areas, overlook the fact that even in the most marked interstitial area nine tenths of the children do not become delinquent.[24]

This argument is superficially plausible. If a factor is not characteristic, then it is apparently not important. But does "characteristic" mean "important"? No. Importance refers to the variation accounted for, to the size of the association, while "being characteristic" refers to only one of the conditional distributions (rows or columns) in the table (in Table 5–2, X is characteristic of delinquents because more than half of the delinquents are X). This is not enough to infer association, any more than the statement that 95% of the Negroes in some sample are illiterate can be taken to say anything about the association between race and illiteracy in that sample without a corresponding statement about the whites. In Table 5–3, although Negroes are predominantly ("characteristically") illiterate, race has no effect on literacy, for the whites are equally likely to be illiterate.

More generally, even if a trait characterizes a large proportion of delinquents and also char-

TABLE 5–3.

LITERACY OF NEGROES AND WHITE

| | Race | |
	Negro	White
Literate	5	5
Illiterate	95	95

acterizes a large proportion of nondelinquents, it may be less important as a cause of delinquency than a trait that characterizes a much smaller proportion of delinquents. The strength of the relation is what matters—that is, the *difference* between delinquents and nondelinquents in the proportion having the trait (in other words, the difference between the conditional distributions of the dependent variable). In the quotation from Barron at the beginning of this section, would it make any difference for the imputation of causality if the proportions coming from broken homes had been 40% for the nondelinquents and 60% for the delinquents, instead of 10 and 30%? Although broken homes would now be "characteristic" of delinquents, the percentage difference is the same as before. And the percentage difference would still be the same if the figures were 60 and 80%, but now broken homes would be characteristic of *both* nondelinquents and delinquents!

The "characteristic" criterion is thus statistically irrelevant to the task of assessing causality. It also appears to be inconsistent with the principle of multiple causation, to which Barron elsewhere subscribes.[25] If delinquency is really traceable to a plurality of causes, then some of these causes may well "characterize" a minority of delinquents. Furthermore, this "inconsistency" is empirical as well as logical: in survey data taken from ordinary populations it is rare to find that any group defined by more than three traits includes a majority of the cases.[26]

---

[24]Milton L. Barron, *The Juvenile in Delinquent Society* (New York: Alfred A. Knopf, Inc., 1954) pp. 86–87.

[25]Ibid., pp. 81–83.
[26]There are two reasons for this: the less-than-perfect association between individual traits and the fact that few traits are simple dichotomies. Of course, it is always possible to take the logical complement of a set of traits describing a minority and thus arrive at a set of traits that does "characterize" a group, but such artificial combinations have too

FALSE CRITERION 3

If a relation between an independent variable and delinquency is found for a single value of a situational or contextual factor, that situational or contextual factor cannot be a cause of delinquency.

No investigation can establish the causal importance of variables that do not vary. This obvious fact should be even more obvious when the design of the study restricts it to single values of certain variables. Thus the researcher who restricts his sample to white Mormon boys cannot use his data to determine the importance of race, religious affiliation, or sex as causes of delinquency. Nevertheless, students of delinquency who discover either from research or logical analysis that an independent variable is related to delinquency in certain situations or contexts often conclude that these situational or contextual variables are not important causes of delinquency. Since personality or perceptual variables are related to delinquency in most kinds of social situations, social variables have suffered most from the application of this criterion:

Let the reader assume that a boy is returning home from school and sees an unexpected group of people at his doorstep, including a policeman, several neighbors, and some strangers. He may suppose that they have gathered to welcome him and congratulate him as the winner of a nationwide contest he entered several months ago. On the other hand, his supposition may be that they have discovered that he was one of several boys who broke some windows in the neighborhood on Halloween. If his interpretation is that they are a welcoming group he will respond one way; but if he feels that they have come to "get" him, his response is likely to be quite different. In either case he may be entirely wrong in his interpretation. *The important point, however, is that the external situation is relatively unimportant.* Rather, what the boy himself thinks of them [it]

and how he interprets them [it] is the crucial factor in his response.[27]

There are at least three independent "variables" in this illustration: (1) the external situation—the group at the doorstep; (2) the boy's past behavior—entering a contest, breaking windows, etc.; (3) the boy's interpretation of the group's purpose. As Barron notes, variable (3) is obviously important in determining the boy's response. It does not follow from this, however, that variables (1) and (2) are unimportant. As a matter of fact, it is easy to see how variable (2), the boy's past behavior, could influence his interpretation of the group's purpose and thus affect his response. If he had not broken any windows in the neighborhood, for example, it is less likely that he would think that the group had come to "get" him, and it is therefore less likely that his response would be one of fear. Since Barron does not examine the relation between this situational variable and the response, he cannot make a legitimate statement about its causal importance.

Within the context of this illustration it is impossible to relate variable (1), the group at the doorstep, to the response. The reason for this is simple: this "variable" does not vary—it is fixed, given, constant. In order to assess the influence of a group at the doorstep (the external situation) on the response, it would be necessary to compare the effects of groups varying in size or composition. Suppose that there was no group at the doorstep. Presumably, if this were the case, the boy would feel neither fear nor joy. Barron restricts his examination of the relation between interpretation and response to a single situation, and on this basis concludes that what appears to be a necessary condition for the response is *relatively unimportant!*

In our opinion, it is sometimes better to say nothing about the effects of a variable whose range is restricted than to attempt to reach some idea of its importance with inadequate data. The first paragraph of the following statement suggests that its authors are completely aware of this problem. Nevertheless, the concluding paragraphs are misleading:

much internal heterogeneity to be meaningful. What, for example, can one say of the delinquents who share the following set of traits: not Catholic, not middle class, not of average intelligence?

The problem of "characteristic" traits arises only when the dependent variable is inherently categorical (Democratic; member of a gang, an athletic club, or neither) or is treated as one (performs none, a few, or many delinquent acts). In other words, this criterion arises only in tabular analysis, not where some summary measure is used to describe the association between variables.

[27]Barron, op. cit., pp. 87–88. Italics added.

We recognized that the Cambridge-Somerville area represented a fairly restricted socio-economic region. Although the bitter wave of the depression had passed, it had left in its wake large numbers of unemployed. Ten years after its onset, Cambridge and Somerville still showed the effects of the depression. Even the best neighborhoods in this study were lower middle class. Consequently, our results represent only a section of the class structure.

In our sample, however [*therefore*], there is not a *highly* significant relation between "delinquency areas," or subcultures, and crime. If we had predicted that every child who lived in the poorer Cambridge-Somerville areas would have committed a crime, we would have been more often wrong than right. Thus, current sociological theory, by itself, cannot explain why the majority of children, even those from the "worst" areas, never become delinquent.

Social factors, in our sample, were not strongly related to criminality. The fact that a child's neighborhood did not, by itself, exert an independently important influence may [*should not*] surprise social scientists. Undeniably, a slum neighborhood can mold a child's personality–but apparently only if other factors in his background make him susceptible to the sub-culture that surrounds him.[28]

False Criterion 4

If a relation is observed between an independent variable and delinquency and if a psychological variable is suggested as intervening between these two variables, then the original relation is not causal.

There appear to be two elements in this causal reasoning. One is the procedure of *conjectural interpretation*.[29] The other is the con-

[28]William McCord and Joan McCord, *Origins of Crime* (New York: Columbia University Press, 1959), pp. 71 and 167.

In a study restricted to "known *offenders*" in which the dependent variable is the *seriousness* of the *first offense* Richard S. Sterne concludes: "Delinquency cannot be fruitfully controlled through broad programs to prevent divorce or other breaks in family life. The prevention of these would certainly decrease unhappiness, but it would not help to relieve the problem of delinquency." Since the range of the dependent variable, delinquency, is seriously reduced in a study restricted to *offenders*, such conclusions cannot follow from the data. *Delinquent Conduct and Broken Homes* (New Haven: College and University Press, 1964), p. 96.

[29]Like conjectural explanation, this is an argument, unsupported by statistical data, that the relation between two variables would vanish if the effects of a third variable were removed; here, however, the third variable "intervenes" causally between the original independent and dependent variables.

fusion between *explanation,* in which an antecedent variable "explains away" an observed relation, and *interpretation,* in which an intervening variable links more tightly the two variables of the original relation. In short, the vanishing of the partial relations is assumed, not demonstrated, and this assumed statistical configuration is misconstrued.

This criterion is often encountered in a subtle form suggestive of social psychological theory:

The appropriate inference from the available data, on the basis of our present understanding of the nature of cause, is that whether poverty, broken homes, or working mothers are factors which cause delinquency depends upon the meaning the situation has for the child.[30]

It now appears that neither of these factors [the broken home and parental discipline] is so important in itself as is the child's reaction to them.[31]

A factor, whether personal or situational, does not become a cause unless and until it first becomes a motive.[32]

The appropriate inference about whether some factor is a cause of delinquency depends on the relation between that factor and delinquency (and possibly on other factors causally prior to both of these). All that can be determined about meanings, motives, or reactions that *follow from* the factor and *precede* delinquency can only strengthen the conclusion that the factor is a cause of delinquency, not weaken it.

A different example may make our argument clearer. *Given* the bombing of Pearl Harbor, the crucial factor in America's response to this situation was its interpretation of the meaning of this event. Is one to conclude, therefore, that the bombing of Pearl Harbor was relatively unimportant as a cause of America's entry into World War II? Intervening variables of this type

[30]Sophia Robison, *Juvenile Delinquency* (New York: Holt, Rinehart and Winston, Inc., 1961), p. 116.

[31]Paul W. Tappan, *Juvenile Delinquency* (New York: McGraw-Hill Book Company, 1949), p. 135.

[32]Sheldon and Eleanor Glueck, *Family Environment and Delinquency* (Boston: Houghton-Mifflin Company, 1962), p. 153. This statement is attributed to Bernard Glueck. No specific reference is provided.

are no less important than variables further removed from the dependent variable, but to limit analysis to them, to deny the importance of objective conditions, is to distort reality as much as do those who ignore intervening subjective states.[33]

This kind of mistaken causal inference can occur long after the original analysis of the data. A case in point is the inference in the *Report to The Congress*[34] that irregular employment of the mother does not cause delinquency. This inference appears to come from misreading Maccoby's reanalysis of the Gluecks' results.

Maccoby begins by noting that "the association between irregular employment and delinquency suggests at the outset that it may not be the mother's absence from home per se which creates adjustment problems for the children. Rather, the cause may be found in the conditions of the mother's employment or the family characteristics leading a mother to undertake outside employment."[35] She then lists several characteristics of the sporadically working mothers that might account for the greater likelihood of their children becoming delinquent. For example, many had a history of delinquency themselves. In our opinion, such conjectural "explanations" are legitimate guides to further study but, as Maccoby says, they leave the causal problem unsettled:

It is a moot question, therefore, whether it is the mother's sporadic employment as such which conduced to delinquency in the sons; equally tenable is the interpretation that the emotionally disturbed and antisocial characteristics of the parents produced both a sporadic work pattern on the part

of the mother and delinquent tendencies in the son.[36]

Maccoby's final step, and the one of greatest interest here, is to examine simultaneously the effects of mother's employment and mother's supervision on delinquency. From this examination she concludes:

It can be seen that, whether the mother is working or not, the quality of the supervision her child receives is paramount. If the mother remains at home but does not keep track of where her child is and what he is doing, he is far more likely to become a delinquent (within this highly selected sample), than if he is closely watched. Furthermore, if a mother who works does arrange adequate care for the child in her absence, he is no more likely to be delinquent . . . than the adequately supervised child of a mother who does not work. But there is one more lesson to be learned from the data: among the working mothers, a majority did not in fact arrange adequate supervision for their children in their absence.[37]

It is clear, then, that regardless of the mother's employment status, supervision is related to delinquency. According to criterion 3, employment status is therefore not a cause of delinquency. It is also clear that when supervision is held relatively constant, the relation between employment status and delinquency disappears. According to criterion 4, employment status is therefore *not* a cause of delinquency. This appears to be the reasoning by which the authors of the *Report to The Congress* reject mother's employment as a cause of delinquency. But criterion 3 ignores the association between employment status and delinquency and is thus irrelevant. And criterion 4 treats what is probably best seen as an intervening variable as an antecedent variable and is thus a misconstruction of a legitimate criterion. Actually, the evidence that allows the user of criterion 4 to reach a conclusion of noncausality is, at least psychologically, evidence of *causality*. The disappearance of the relation between mother's employment and delinquency when supervision is held relatively constant makes the "How?" of the original relation clear: working mothers are less likely to provide adequate supervision

[33]"Write your own life history, showing the factors *really* operative in you coming to college, contrasted with the external social and cultural factors of your situation," Barron, op. cit., p. 89.

[34]Op. cit., p. 21.

[35]Eleanor E. Maccoby, "Effects upon Children of Their Mothers' Outside Employment," in *A Modern Introduction to The Family*, ed. Norman W. Bell and Ezra F. Vogel (New York: The Free Press, 1960), p. 523. In fairness to the Children's Bureau report, it should be mentioned that Maccoby's argument against the causality of the relation between mother's employment and delinquency has a stronger tone in the article cited there (see n. 7) than in the version we have used as a source of quotations.

[36]Ibid.

[37]Ibid., p. 524.

for their children, and inadequately supervised children are more likely to become delinquent.

FALSE CRITERION 5

Measurable variables are not causes.

In tract 11-1, and to a lesser extent in tract 11-2, the actual rate [of delinquency] is lower than the predicted rate. We suggest that these deviations [of the actual delinquency rate from the rate predicted from home ownership] point up the danger of imputing a causal significance to an index, per se, despite its statistical significance in a prediction formula. It is fallacious to impute causal significance to home ownership as such. In the present study, the author hypothesizes that the extent of home-ownership is probably highly correlated with, and hence constitutes a measure of community anomie.[38]

As a preventive, "keeping youth busy," whether through compulsory education, drafting for service in the armed forces, providing fun through recreation, or early employment, can, at best, only temporarily postpone behavior that is symptomatic of more deep-seated or culturally oriented factors. . . . Merely "keeping idle hands occupied" touches only surface symptoms and overlooks underlying factors known to generate norm-violating behavior patterns.[39]

The criterion of causation that, in effect, denies causal status to measurable variables occurs frequently in delinquency research. In the passages above, home ownership, compulsory education, military service, recreation, and early employment are all called into question as causes of delinquency. In their stead one finds as causes anomie and "deepseated or culturally oriented factors." The appeal to abstract as opposed to more directly measurable variables appears to be especially persuasive. Broad general concepts embrace such a variety of directly measurable variables that their causal efficacy becomes almost self evident. The broken home, for example, is no match for the "inadequate" home:

[T]he physically broken home as a cause of delinquent behavior is, in itself, not so important as was once believed. In essence, it is not that the home

is broken, but rather that the home is inadequate, that really matters.[40]

The persuasiveness of these arguments against the causal efficacy of measurable variables has two additional sources: (1) their logical form resembles that of the legitimate criterion "lack of spuriousness"; (2) they are based on the seemingly obvious fact that "operational indices" (measures) do not *cause* the variations in other operational indices. Both of the following arguments can thus be brought against the assertion that, for example, home ownership causes delinquency.

Anomie causes delinquency. Home ownership is a measure of anomie. Anomie is thus the "source of variation" in both home ownership and delinquency. If the effects of anomie were removed, the observed relation between home ownership and delinquency would disappear. This observed relation is thus causally spurious.

Home ownership is used as an indicator of anomie, just as responses to questionnaire items are used as indicators of such things as "authoritarianism," "achievement motivation," and "religiosity." No one will argue that the responses to items on a questionnaire *cause* race hatred, long years of self-denial, or attendance at religious services. For the same reason, it is erroneous to think that home ownership "causes" delinquency.

Both of these arguments beg the question. As mentioned earlier, conjectural explanations, although legitimate guides to further study, leave the causal problem unsettled. The proposed "antecedent variable" may or *may not* actually account for the observed relation.

Our argument assumes that the proposed antecedent variable is directly measurable. In the cases cited here it is not. If the antecedent variable logic is accepted as appropriate in these cases, all relations between measurable variables and delinquency may be said to be causally spurious. If anomie can "explain away" the relation between *one* of its indicators and delinquency, it can explain away the relations between *all* of its indicators and delinquency.[41]

---

[38]Lander, op. cit., p. 71.

[39]William C. Kvaraceus and Walter B. Miller, *Delinquent Behavior: Culture and the Individual* (National Education Association, 1959), p. 39.

[40]Teeters and Reinemann, op. cit., p. 154.

[41]As would be expected, Lander succeeds in disposing of all the variables in his study as causes

No matter how closely a given indicator measures anomie, the indicator is not anomie, and thus not a cause of delinquency. The difficulty with these conjectural explanations is thus not that they may be false, but that they are *non-falsifiable*.[42]

The second argument against the causality of measurable variables overlooks the following point: it is one thing to use a measurable variable as an indicator of another, not directly measurable, variable; it is something else again to assume that the measurable variable is *only* an indicator. Not owning one's home may indeed be a useful indicator of anomie; it may, at the same time, be a potent cause of delinquency in its own right.

The user of the "measurable variables are not causes" criterion treats measurable variables as epiphenomena. He strips these variables of all their causal efficacy (and of all their meaning) by treating them merely as indexes, and by using such words as *per se, as such,* and *in itself*.[43] In so doing, he begs rather than answers the important question: Are these measurable variables causes of delinquency?

FALSE CRITERION 6

If the relation between an independent variable and delinquency is conditional upon the value of other variables, the independent variable is not a cause of delinquency.

The rates of Negro delinquency also vary as widely as do the white rates indicating large differences in behavior patterns that are not a function or effect of race per se. It is also of interest to note that in at least 10 percent of the districts with substantial Negro juvenile populations, the Negro delinquency rate is lower than the corresponding white rate.[44]

The appropriate inference from the available data, on the basis of our present understanding of the nature of cause, is that whether poverty, broken homes, or working mothers are factors which cause delinquency depends upon the meaning the situation has for the child.[45]

Both of these quotations make the same point: the association between an independent variable and delinquency depends on the value of a third variable. The original two-variable relation thus becomes a three-variable conditional relation. In the first quotation, the relation between race and delinquency is shown to depend on some (unspecified) property of census tracts. In the second quotation, each of three variables is said to "interact" with "the meaning of the situation" to cause delinquency.

One consequence of showing that certain variables are only conditionally related to delinquency is to invalidate what Albert K. Cohen has aptly named "the assumption of intrinsic pathogenic qualities"—the assumption that the causal efficacy of a variable is, or can be, independent of the value of other causal variables.[46] Invalidating this assumption, which Cohen shows to be widespread in the literature on delinquency, is a step in the right direction. As many of the quotations in this paper suggest, however, the discovery that a variable has no *intrinsic* pathogenic qualities has often led to the conclusion that it has no pathogenic qualities at all. The consequences of accepting this conclusion can be shown for delinquency research and theory.

Cloward and Ohlin's theory that delinquency is the product of lack of access to legitimate means *and* the availability of illegitimate means assumes, as Palmore and Hammond have shown,[47] that each of these states is a necessary

---

of delinquency—even those he says at some points are *"fundamentally* related to delinquency."

[42]While Lander throws out his measurable independent variables in favor of anomie, Kvaraceus and Miller throw out their measurable dependent variable in favor of "something else." "Series of norm-violating behaviors, which run counter to legal codes and which are engaged in by youngsters [delinquency], are [is] only symptomatic of something else in the personal make-up of the individual, in his home and family, or in his cultural milieu." Op. cit., p. 34. The result is the same, as the quotations suggest.

[43]The appearance of these terms in the literature on delinquency almost invariably signals a logical difficulty.

[44]Lander, op. cit., p. 32. This statement is quoted more fully above (see n. 10).

[45]See n. 30.

[46]"Multiple Factor Approaches," in *The Sociology of Crime and Delinquency,* ed. Marvin E. Wolfgang et al. (New York: John Wiley & Sons, Inc., 1962), pp. 78–79.

[47]Erdman B. Palmore and Phillip E. Hammond, "Interacting Factors in Juvenile Delinquency," *American Sociological Review* 29 (December, 1964): 848–54.

condition for the other—i.e., that lack of access to legitimate and access to illegitimate means "interact" to produce delinquency. Now, if "conditional relations" are non-causal, neither lack of access to legitimate nor the availability of illegitimate means is a cause of delinquency, and one could manipulate either without affecting the delinquency rate.

Similarly absurd conclusions could be drawn from the results of empirical research in delinquency, since all relations between independent variables and delinquency are at least conceivably conditional (the paucity of empirical generalizations produced by delinquency research as a whole shows that most of these relations have already actually been found to be conditional).[48]

Although conditional relations may be conceptually or statistically complicated and therefore psychologically unsatisfying, their discovery does not justify the conclusion that the variables involved are not causes of delinquency. In fact, the researcher who would grant causal status only to unconditional relations will end by granting it to none.

Any one of the criteria of causality discussed in this paper makes it possible to question the causality of most of the relations that have been or could be revealed by quantitative research. Some of these criteria stem from perfectionistic

interpretations of legitimate criteria, others from misapplication of these legitimate criteria. Still others, especially the argument that a cause must be "characteristic" of delinquents, appear to result from practical considerations. (It would indeed be valuable to the practitioner if he could point to some easily identifiable trait as the "hallmark" of the delinquent.) Finally, one of these criteria is based on a mistaken notion of the relation between abstract concepts and measurable variables—a notion that only the former can be the causes of anything.

The implications of these standards of causality for practical efforts to reduce delinquency are devastating. Since nothing that can be pointed to in the practical world is a cause of delinquency (e.g., poverty, broken homes, lack of recreational facilities, working mothers), the practitioner is left with the task of combatting a nebulous "anomie" or an unmeasured "inadequacy of the home"; or else he must change the adolescent's interpretation of the "meaning" of events without at the same time changing the events themselves or the context in which they occur.

Mills has suggested that accepting the principle of multiple causation implies denying the possibility of radical change in the social structure.[49] Our analysis suggests that rejecting the principle of multiple causation implies denying the possibility of *any* change in the social structure—since, in this view, nothing causes anything.

[48]After reviewing the findings of 21 studies as they bear on the relations between 12 commonly used independent variables and delinquency, Barbara Wootton concludes: "All in all, therefore, this collection of studies, although chosen for its comparative methodological merit, produces only the most meager, and dubiously supported generalizations." Op. cit., p. 134.

[49]C. Wright Mills, "The Professional Ideology of Social Pathologists," *American Journal of Sociology,* 44 (September, 1942): 165–80, esp. 171–72.

45.

Edward Rolde, John Mack, Donald Scherl and Lee Macht

THE MAXIMUM SECURITY INSTITUTION AS A TREATMENT FACILITY FOR JUVENILES

I. INTRODUCTION AND PURPOSE

The purpose of this paper is to describe the philosophy and practice of a maximum security institution for juveniles in one of the eastern states. The description covers the period from 1962 through 1968. The official goals of the institution are treatment and rehabilitation. In reality, the day to day life of the institution centers around punishment. Of equal importance to what is happening within the institution, is the fact that the public, relevant government agencies, and the academic community are aware of what has been happening, and have been unable or unwilling to effect changes.

The literature on institutions for juveniles tends to concentrate on those institutions that are most progressive and treatment oriented. Knowledge of punitive programs, such as the one described in this paper, is also of central importance to those trying to improve delinquency programs. Such knowledge is central in monitoring, on a national basis, the progress of delinquency rehabilitation efforts, and in understanding the background of the current disenchantment with experience in the field over the past 50 years. The realities of the punishment institution provide the background for the position taken in the Gault decision, that the juvenile is receiving the worst of two worlds, being neither treated nor protected.[1] Despite the enlightenment and successes of many delinquency programs, the authors' personal experience and the experience of many others suggest that the program described in this paper is typical of a large number of institutions for juveniles.

Source: This article was written for this volume.
[1]In re Gault (Supreme Court, May 15, 1967).

II. THE INSTITUTION

The institution that the authors are describing is the maximum security institution for juveniles in one state. We will refer to the institution in this article as State. The state referred to is part of a region of the United States which contains numerous children's facilities and academic establishments of world renown. Several institutions for juveniles within the state have served as the locations of some of the classic studies of the literature on delinquency.

The Youth Authority of the state was established in its present form in the late 1940's. The legislative mandate to the authority has been used as an example of progressive policy. The goals set forth by the state legislature are treatment and rehabilitation for return to society. These goals are constantly referred to and kept prominent by the Youth Authority itself. Consistent with these goals, the Authority has the mandate of prevention of delinquency, research, and aftercare, as well as responsibility for institutions for juveniles within the state.

The Youth Authority operates several institutions. The explicit purpose of State is to provide the maximum possible security for those young men that the Youth Authority feels should be placed in this environment. There are two major mechanisms through which boys are assigned to State. First, it is the place to which boys are sent who have committed "serious" crimes. The category of crime that is considered "serious" varies somewhat from time to time. Murder and sexual molestation of minors have been constantly placed in this category; in recent years, some examples of drug abuse have been added. The second group of youngsters commonly sent to State consists of boys who cannot be contained or tolerated in other institutions. The boys in this group tend to have long arrest records, most often for related minor crimes. They tend also to have long institutional records, including numerous escapes and incidents of trouble-making. The final common denominator of a boy's being sent to State is the Youth Authority's view that nothing less than the maximum security available is enough to insure that he does not escape back to society.

In recent years, the population of State has ranged between 75 and 90. The age of the inmates is in most instances between 13 and 18; occasionally there have been boys a little younger or a little older. The majority of youngsters carry the psychological-psychiatric diagnosis of "psychopath," or "severe antisocial personality disturbance." Most come from the lower socio-economic levels. However, the entire range of psychiatric diagnosis and socio-economic background is represented. The most common period of confinement within the institution is eight months. This period of time is predetermined by a general policy of a release to home after eight months, irrespective of the boys' personal or family history or his institutional course. Boys institutionalized for murder are kept for slightly longer periods of time. The recidivism rate is very high, and many boys return for a number of successive terms.

State occupies a building which was first used by the Youth Authority in the early 1950's. It was built in the early part of the century and was used for many years as an adult women's prison. The building is located in a relatively isolated area, some distance from the nearest town and about one hour's drive from the nearest urban center. The physical appearance of the building would be familiar to anyone knowledgeable of the history of American prisons. The building is surrounded by a high thick wall, solid and stark. The boys live in individual cells, barred and screened, with peep holes serving as the only openings through otherwise solid doors.

According to commonly accepted criteria for the definition of bureaucracy,[2] the administration of State can be best described as pre-

bureaucratic, i.e., relationships among the staff tend to be on a personal basis rather than related to role function. There are approximately 50 full time staff members. The superintendent manages the institution with a minimum of codified rules. In essence, almost all staff members report to him directly. There is little systematic communication between other staff members, and even little informal communication between staff members with differing functions, such as between school teachers and Masters.

The Youth Activities division is one of the major sources of non-civil service positions within the State. There is, therefore, relatively little protection against the hiring of grossly unqualified persons. At the same time, positions do conform to the state tenure laws, and it is virtually impossible for an individual to be removed from his position once he has achieved tenure.

Our association with the institution began in 1962 and has continued over the past six years to the present time (1968). Our original contact was made in connection with the case of a boy who received a psychiatric referral after having been institutionalized for matricide. Since that time, the authors, depending on their availability, have succeeded each other as psychiatric consultants to the institution on a weekly basis. Our role at the institution evolved from individual psychotherapy with a single boy, to general consultation with a variety of staff members about problems of the institution and society. The development of our consultation, its successes and failures, will be described elsewhere.[3] Our aim here is to describe the institution and its programs.

Our relatively long term presence at the institution implies that we have been of value there; that we feel able to work with both the boys and with the institution staff and its administration. Our long term work at the institution would not have been possible if the boys and the staff and administration had not wanted our services. However, our presence has not implied and did not necessitate that we have been in agreement with the administration in its overall

---

[2]Robert K. Merton, "Bureaucratic Structure and Personality" in *Social Theory and Social Structure* (New York: The Free Press, 1957).

[3]Edward Rolde, Donald Scherl, John Mack, and Lee Macht, "The Process of Change in a Maximum Security Institution for Juveniles," in preparation.

philosophy and actions, nor that the administration has felt in agreement with our general philosophy and approach.

III. THE INSTITUTION PROGRAM

It is clear that the institution conveys to the boys neither an attitude of concern nor a willingness to offer help and rehabilitation. To the inmates, the institution is a place to pass their sentence. As expressed by Eldridge Cleaver,[4] the institution represents the establishment, the enemy of those confined within it, a hostile force with which the inmates are engaged in a constant battle. A number of characteristics have impressed us as indicating custodial and even more important, punitive goals. These characteristics are dealt with in the following paragraphs.

A. PHYSICAL FACILITIES

There are a number of long-standing deficiencies in the physical plant of the institution that cause a great deal of discomfort to the boys. The inadequacy of the heating system is a prime example. The heating system of the building is inadequate to the extent that during the winter months approximately 50 percent of the boys' rooms receive essentially no heat. The temperature in the rooms has often been almost as low as the outside temperature. On the colder days of winter, water freezes in the rooms; a pitcher of water will have ice forming in it, a wet towel will stand frozen. On severely cold days, some of the boys are moved to a central recreation hall to sleep, but boys regularly spend long periods of time in their rooms even under very cold conditions. During the winter months, many of the boys are extremely uncomfortable, and the cold and lack of administrative action to deal with it are a constant preoccupation of the inmate population.

The heating of the building has been inadequate since its takeover by the Youth Authority. At a recent court hearing on another topic, a young man who had been an inmate of the institution, described the discomfort and concern of the boys a decade previously. There has

been little indication that anyone in authority felt strongly enough to have made a realistic effort to remedy the situation.

Although the lack of heat probably causes the most discomfort, there are other long-standing deficiencies. For example, there is often large scale seepage of water into the building. At times there have been several inches of water in the arts and crafts room, and the boys and their instructor could be seen working in a water level reaching above their shoes. The common denominator of these deficiencies is that they are accepted. They have existed for a long time; there are no real plans for change. The discomfort that they cause is rationalized under a tacit assumption, that if the boys had behaved themselves, they wouldn't be in the institution. The physical facilities express the philosophy that the worst is excusable with such a population.

B. PUNISHMENT

Punishment is the basic mechanism of the day by day, hour by hour management of the boys, even though it is not one of the explicit mandates of the institution or of the Youth Authority. It can be stated by the institution that corporal punishment is not allowed. At the same time, it is apparent that boys are frequently handled roughly by the custodial staff. Physical punishment is not an organized and supervised part of the system, but tends to be informally employed, inconsistently and often arbitrarily and capriciously. The informality and the unofficial sanctioning of force was represented in a nickname that the boys had for the superintendent. He was often referred to as the "Big Bopper," an allusion to both his use of physical force and to his position as a father analogue at the institution.

Solitary confinement is one of the major means of punishment at the institution. It is frequently used for a wide variety of infractions, large and small. The area in the building used for solitary confinement is referred to as the "hole" by both staff and inmates, and is located in an isolated part of the building. Boys are placed in small cells wearing their shorts, and with no other possessions. The cells are bare except for a mat-

[4]Eldridge Cleaver, *Soul on Ice* (New York: McGraw-Hill Book Company, 1968).

tress, and a single suspended light bulb. Generally there is no reading matter provided, nor any other form of sensory stimulation. There is no guard stationed in the area. The only human contact takes place when food is placed in the room, or when the boys are brought to a nearby lavatory for bodily functions. Boys are placed in these cells for unspecified periods of time; 30 days is a frequent period of confinement, but longer terms are not unusual.

There are no codified rules of procedures. Individual guards have the authority to impose the confinement, although the superintendent reviews the decision. Solitary is often used without real investigation of the instigating situation. After fights between two boys, both boys have often been confined, without staff knowledge of which was the instigator. The effects of the prolonged isolation have frequently been severe. There have been numerous occasions when solitary confinement was used when the psychological state of the boy argued against such a measure—in boys in panic states, or with newly admitted boys suffering from drug-induced psychosis. There has been no medical or psychiatric consultation sought in relation to this aspect of State's program.

All aspects of institution life are influenced by the use of punishment as the major modality of management. Almost all reinforcement is negative: boys lose privileges by transgression, rarely do they have much to gain by socially acceptable behavior. Fear and resentment are much more common sentiments than feelings of accomplishment. Many incidents that start out as little more than youthful exuberance are expanded out of proportion by instant, arbitrary, harsh measures, and soon become protracted struggles with the establishment. Many situations that would appear amenable to a few minutes of conversation never receive such attention. Since any contact by a boy with a staff member has a high chance of bringing a negative reaction, it becomes essentially impractical for a boy to bring up any legitimate grievance. The major skill is how to keep out of the way of the staff. The social skills that are taught by example are most often the use of force and manipulation. Few staff members feel that the boys have much to gain from their stay in State.

C. TREATMENT AND REHABILITATION

The boys spend a major portion of their time sitting in the "recreation hall," with no organized programs or facilities. Little schooling is provided. Approximately one hour a day of schooling is scheduled for each boy. There is no system of accreditation for studies. The trade program centers around bookbinding and upholstery; however most of the time scheduled in these trades is actually spent in idleness. More important, these trades have little relevance for the boys. There are no trades that the boys feel would have meaning for them, trades such as mechanics and electrical work. In short, there is no significant positive program for either time passed in the institution or for the learning of skills to be used on the outside.

Institution policy prohibits staffs from taking an active role in dealing with the community or with people who play a part in the boys' lives outside the institution. There are neither programs of graduated release nor a work program outside of the institution. Counseling and consultant staff are prohibited from having family meetings, or from having significant relationships with the probation staff or other agencies who would have responsibility for service to the boy when he leaves the institution. The rationale of not dealing with the community is to avoid potential sources of trouble for the institution. The avoidance of difficulty is the goal, therefore positive programs have little to offer and there is little reason to have them.

D. STAFFING

The staffing pattern of the institution is consistent with its punitive orientation. There is very little professional contact with State. There is, in addition, an attempt to isolate and to minimize the roles of those professionals who do become involved. The weekly visit of a member of our group is the only contact the institution has with professionally trained psychologists, psychiatrists, sociologists, or social workers. Our contact with State began on our own initiative. At the time of our original contact, there had been no psychiatric consultation for a number of years. Lack of funds is often given as the official reason for lack of professional personnel, but there are many indications that the administration feels that the professions do not have any significant contribution to make to the management of boys within the institution.

The nonprofessional personnel of the institution affect its policy more than the absence of professional personnel. The past ten years have been a period of widespread interest in non-professional programs in the domain of juvenile delinquency and related areas. Numerous individuals of varying educational backgrounds have demonstrated vision and experience in reaching youngsters. This category of individuals has not been welcome at State. A number of staff members at State are concerned with positive approaches, but these individuals must work as individuals, and the potential that they have is constantly dissipated and at odds with the dominant organization and power structure of the institution.

The morale and sense of mission of the entire staff is repeatedly undermined by political appointments. The Youth Authority of the State is under frequent political pressure to provide jobs, and the Youth Authority institutions have a reputation within the state as a fertile source of political "patronage." Frequently an individual having obviously little qualification for a position will be directly appointed to an institution by the central office of the Authority. For example, the year before the writing of this article, one of the nurse's positions was filled by a woman trained as a beautician. The woman arrived, on the job and payroll, without the prior knowledge of the superintendent. As long as basic security is maintained, many types of incompetency can be tolerated.

IV. PUBLIC AND PROFESSIONAL ACCEPTANCE OF THE PUNISHMENT MILIEU

State exists and has prospered as a punishment oriented institution. This is a fact of the institution and of the lives of the boys within it, but it is also a statement about the society of which State is a part. The society uses State to deal with youngsters that it labels as antisocial. Since they are aware of this use, the continued existence of State serves as an example of the public support and the professional tolerance of the punishment orientation.

A. REPORTS ON THE PROGRAM AT STATE

In response to criticism and questioning, three investigations of the Youth Authority and its institutions and programs were carried out during the early and mid 1960's. The first was by a State legislator, the second was by a State committee appointed by the Governor and composed of prominent citizens and professionals, and the third was by a team from the United States Department of Health, Education and Welfare.

These reports agreed with each other, and stated clearly that State was not living up to its therapeutic and rehabilitative mandate. Quotations from the description of State in one of the reports give a representative picture of the language and sentiment of those documents. "The institute's long-range objective, 'to provide an intensive therapeutic program necessary in the treatment and rehabilitation of deep-seated aggressive, behavior problems,' is impossible with the limited staff and program. . . . the physical plant of the institute is inadequate and represents a major obstacle to program development. . . . Security Masters Staff see themselves solely as security and custody staff. . . . Approximately 25 percent of the boys participate in the academic program."

There is clear documentation that the findings of these reports were made available to the public, in addition to the government and professional community. The headlines of an article appearing in a major newspaper in the state reported, "Scathing U.S. Report Blasts State Youth Board." The Public was informed that the United States Government Commission clearly described the Youth Authority in negative terms. The newspaper article quoted the report's findings as follows: "poor staffing, inadequate financing and . . . overcrowding, poorly designed institutions, lack of coordinated planning, evidence of political interference and considerable unnecessary detention of children." The public was informed in the same newspaper article that the United States Government report had made charges against the Youth Authority, charges such as "improperly structured and managed; children held in cold storage with no attempt to diagnose them . . . top administrative roles confusing and overlapping . . . trained personnel lacking and no orderly system of issuance of policies, rules and regulations." The informed public was well aware that the Youth Authority was not fulfilling its mandate of treatment and rehabilitation.

The most striking feature of these years was that no significant changes were made in response to these investigations and the reporting of them to the public. The leadership, organization and general budget for the Youth Authority remained stationary. There was no discernible change at State.

The lack of change did not result from public apathy. There is strong, organized and active support for the status quo. The groups supporting the status quo tend to be those most in favor of a punishment orientation. The support of the continued existence of a punishment orientation is often explicit and direct. For example, a prominent clergyman who is a staunch defender of State has spoken publicly in support of the institution with the argument that "punishment cleanses."

B. Attitude of the Academic Community toward State

Interested members of the academic community are also aware of the general orientation of State. They receive personal reports from visitors to the institution, and have had access to the investigation reports. State is widely viewed as a punitively oriented institution with little therapeutic or rehabilitative value. The universal condemnation of the institution among the academic community is illustrated by the fact that the authors know of no psychiatrists, psychologists or sociologists who are among the defenders of the system. This is a remarkable fact considering the diversity of opinion usually found within these groups.

While they express disapproval of State, many members of the professional community have mixed feelings about the usefulness of a punitively oriented group. It is common for boys to arrive from other institutions with a picture of State as a "hell on earth." This impression is most often gained from the professional staff at the other institutions, where it is common for staff to threaten a boy with being sent to State if he misbehaves. Paradoxically, therefore, many who are most critical of State actually use its existence in their dealings with boys.

In many instances members of the professional community take the position that punishment has a very definite place in the rehabilitation program of some boys. Recently the Youth Authority dealt with the case of a 13 year old boy adjudged delinquent after the murder of a younger boy. Several professionals who had seen the boy felt that it was important for his psychological development that he experience a sense of punishment, as a necessary step in his own acceptance of his return to society. There were, therefore, many recommendations that the boy be sent to State, even though those making the recommendations felt that he would receive no treatment there. We do not intend to discuss the question of the usefulness of punishment; the question is a complex one. We do intend to make the point that boys are often sent to State in order to receive punishment as opposed to treatment.

V. DISCUSSION: THE SIGNIFICANCE OF STATE

The institution being described here is adjacent to one of the relatively wealthy urban areas of the United States, and near some of the nation's leading academic centers. State is in a position to be an example of what the modern United States society has to offer juveniles. However, the program centers around punishment, despite a clear mandate to treat and rehabilitate, and conditions remain unchanged despite public, governmental and professional awareness of them. The conditions at State can be taken as a comment on the society of which it is a part. These conditions are congruent with a society that is greatly concerned with the problem of "law and order" and much less concerned with the rehabilitation of young men that it labels as antisocial.

The authors' personal experience suggests that conditions similar to State are common in the United States. Reports of those with wide experience with institutions in the United States tend to confirm this impression. Menninger describes a widespread punishment orientation.[5] Janowitz states "there is no adequate body of data on the types of quality of programs to be found in correctional institutions throughout the nation. Yet on the basis of a variety of sources, especially measures of staff/inmate ratios, we estimate that at least half of public institutions are basically custodial (obedience/conformity format) and have only limited features of the re-education/development format."[6] The sociologic literature concentrates on describing and evaluating the more progressive treatment and rehabilitative programs. The public and the academic community know most about institutions in the United States from reports of Highfields,[7] Provo[8] and Fricot Ranch.[9]

Coverage of negative aspects of institutionalization is most often reserved for the "exposé" where the bias of the description is often difficult to evaluate. The sensationalism of the exposé gives the impression that what is being reported is aberrant or unusual, and that except for the corruption of the few, treatment and rehabilitation would be the rule. The punishment orientation of State cannot be dismissed as aberrant or as a malfunction. The punishment orientation is all-pervasive and long-standing.

Descriptions of institutions such as State are important in understanding how society deals with those that it labels deviant, and what it is like for most youngsters so labeled. The progress of institutions such as State is an important descriptive element in the evaluation of the success of the treatment mandate of the juvenile court system.

More information on the realities of institutions such as State will also be useful in studying institutionalization itself as a modality in dealing with juvenile delinquency. Several studies of innovative programs compare their results with what they term "the usual State School." The Provo experiment included a control group of boys who were sent to the Colorado State Reformatory; the Highfields experiment included a control group from the New Jersey state school at Allendale. The relevant state schools are not adequately described. Without more detailed descriptions of the programs at these institutions, it is difficult to interpret differential findings pertaining to control and treatment groups.

The literature on the sociology of prisons suggests that institutions as such cannot be rehabilitative, and that the formation and influence of an inmate society is a major reason for inevitably negative results.[10,11] Studies by Wheeler and by Wheeler and Baum have been productive in demonstrating the process by which the inmate relates to, and is influenced by the inmate society.[12,13] Comparative studies of institutions suggest that the reaction of the inmates may vary in characteristic ways according to variations in institutional organizations and programs.[14] More detailed studies of punishment orientation such as the one at State will be helpful in examining the important distinction between the effects of punishment and the effects of control.

SUMMARY

We have described a state institution for juveniles as it has existed up to 1969. The institution presents a punitive orientation, even though its official mandate describes therapeutic and rehabilitative goals. The punitive orientation has been actively supported over a number of years.

[5]Karl Menninger, *The Crime of Punishment* (New York: The Viking Press, Inc., 1966).

[6]Morris Janowitz, "Introduction," in *Organization for Treatment*, by D. Street, R. Vinter and C. Perrow (New York: The Free Press, 1966).

[7]H. Ashley Weeks, *Youthful Offenders at Highfields* (Ann Arbor: University of Michigan Press, 1958).

[8]Lamar T. Empey and Jerome Rabow, "The Provo Experiment in Delinquency Rehabilitation," *American Sociological Review* 26 (October, 1961): 679-95.

[9]C. F. Jesness, "The Fricot Ranch School Study: An Analysis of a Training School Experience," Fricot Progress Report No. 3 (August, 1962) California Youth Authority, Division of Research.

[10]Donald Clemmer, *The Prison Community* (New York: Holt, Rinehart & Winston, Inc., 1960).

[11]Gresham Sykes, *The Society of Captives* (Princeton, N.J.: Princeton University Press, 1958).

[12]Stanton Wheeler, "Socialization in Correctional Communities," *American Sociological Review* 26, no. 5 (October, 1961): 699, 700.

[13]Martha Baum and Stanton Wheeler, "Becoming an Inmate" in *Controlling Delinquents*, ed. S. Wheeler (New York: John Wiley and Sons, Inc., 1968).

[14]Street et al., op. cit.

Descriptions of institutions such as State are important in addition to descriptions of more progressive therapeutic and rehabilitative programs. The existence of the punitive orientation of State is a characteristic of present day United States society, an important fact of life for many adolescents, and the basic factor in the effects of the institution on the boys within it.

46.

Howard G. Brown

JUVENILE COURTS AND THE GAULT DECISION: I. BACKGROUND AND PROMISE

At the turn of the century, new ideas for dealing with juvenile delinquents arose in this country and quickly spread throughout the Western World. There was widespread dissatisfaction with administration of justice as it affected children, especially with the practice of giving children long criminal sentences and mixing them in jails with hardened criminals. The leaders of the movement were convinced that society's duty to erring children was not discharged by the simple administration of the routine, impersonal criminal procedures then operating. They proposed that the States accept responsibility for making a diagnostic study of the child and his milieu and for prescribing a course of treatment that would help rehabilitate and perhaps completely reform him. They proposed quarantine rather than punishment for children needing physical control.

Underlying these proposed changes was the assumption that the causes of juvenile delinquency and the means of preventing further misconduct were known. Such knowledge was to be brought to bear upon children, much in the same way that scientific advances were being used to heal injury or cure disease. Children were to be "cured" of delinquency and restored to the community as useful citizens. Broad, summary powers were to be given to juvenile court judges to accomplish this purpose.

The judge, with his hand on the shoulder of the child, was to act as a wise and loving parent. He would induce or compel the child, with or without the parents' consent, to undergo care and treatment, often custodial, for his and the community's best interest. His concern was to be not with what the child had done but with what he is and which of the many community resources and what part of the wide knowledge at the court's disposal should be brought to bear on him and his family to make them more socially acceptable and law-abiding.

The first juvenile court embodying these ideas was established in Illinois in 1899. Within a short time such courts were established in all of the States and in most other Western countries.

Innovations that start with great fanfare and high ideals and spread like wildfire often give rise to excesses, and this is what occurred in the juvenile court movement. Great departures from time-tested procedures took place in the name of salvage, rehabilitation, and correction, the beneficent end being held to justify almost any means. Law was supplemented and even supplanted by other social sciences in efforts to deal with a child's unacceptable behavior. While the compulsory nature of the courts and the legal system was retained, the safeguards of public hearing, counsel, due process of law,

Source: Howard G. Brown, "Juvenile Courts and the Gault Decision: I. Background and Promise," *Children* 15, no. 3 (May-June, 1968): 86–89. Reprinted by Permission of the author and CHILDREN, U.S. Department of Health, Education, and Welfare, Social and Rehabilitation Service, Children's Bureau.

and formal procedure were discarded in view of the high intent and purpose of the courts and their supposed power and ability to help rehabilitate the child.

These juvenile court practices gained general acceptance. The summary procedures and lack of formality that became characteristic of them were approved by most appellate courts when questions about them were raised. Because juvenile proceedings were regarded as civil rather than criminal proceedings, the constitutional rights of the child were disregarded with impunity.

UNEXPECTED PROBLEMS

But unforeseen problems developed. Trained, skilled, and kindly judges were not always available to discharge the awesome responsibility of being a wise parent to all children in the community who were in trouble with society. Treatment resources, facilities, and staff with the necessary knowledge to diagnose and deal with the problems of a delinquent child were not adequately provided. The volume of delinquency cases became so unmanageable that enough time, staff, and resources were not available to enable the courts to give each case the intensive consideration, attention, and care needed.

Moreover, delinquency did not decline. Many children who went through the juvenile courts were not changed. Even under the most favorable circumstances, children were not always rehabilitated as the theory had promised.

People began to realize that while social science and medicine had made great strides in understanding human behavior, great areas were still unexplored. To make a diagnosis and a prognosis of a person's behavior, at least that of a troubled adolescent, turned out to be a complex matter about which much less was known than had been assumed. Courts and their staff members were not always able to find and use means of effecting the desired change in children. What a wise parent should be and do about a bewilderingly complex child and the problems he presented the community was often a mystery.

Dissatisfaction with juvenile court justice also began to arise from the summary fashion in which juvenile proceedings were often carried out. Cases were processed without the child or his parents being given notice of the charges or apprised of the right to counsel. In fact, the right to counsel was often not recognized. Incompetent and untrained staff members were often used to make social investigations and administer social treatment. The judge often acted not only in his judicial capacity but also as prosecutor and defense counsel. It took superhuman ability to discharge these three functions with dignity, impartiality, and justice, and it often proved impossible to convince the parties that such functions had been so discharged. In many communities the courts had no treatment facilities to rely on—the institutions for juveniles were no more than junior jails.

Criticism of the juvenile courts mounted during the past decade. Articles appeared in law reviews criticizing the absence of due process and the deprivation of children's constitutional rights and privileges. Appellate courts began to recognize abuses that were taking place. Professional organizations began to take cognizance of the limitations and the difficulties involved. The National Council of Juvenile Court Judges, in 1961, began training programs for judges and conducted an institute on the role of attorneys in juvenile court. The University of Chicago held an institute on "Justice for the Child" in 1962. The National Council on Crime and Delinquency published a handbook on "Procedure and Evidence in the Juvenile Court" in 1962.

In 1966, the Supreme Court of the United States handed down its first decision involving the rights of children under a juvenile code in the case of *Kent* v. *United States*.[1] The Court pointed out that cases in juvenile courts were legal proceedings and that basic to the theory of any legal disposition was some concept of due process. The President's Commission on Law Enforcement and Administration of Justice in its report issued early in 1967[2] pointed out

---

[1] *Kent* v. *United States*, 383 U.S. 541 (1966).

[2] President's Commission on Law Enforcement and Administration of Justice, Task Force on Juvenile Delinquency, "The Challenge of Crime in a Free Society," Washington, D.C., 1967.

the limitations of the juvenile courts and the crises that were occurring in them.

IN RE GAULT

With so many expressions of dissatisfaction being made with the way juvenile courts were functioning, the decision of the Supreme Court in the Gault case,[3] handed down May 15, 1967, was hardly a surprise.

In the Gault case, a boy of 15 had been found delinquent by a juvenile court in Arizona and committed to a State institution for six years for a minor offense that would have been a misdemeanor had he been an adult. At the "trial" or informal hearing, he had not been represented by counsel, no prior notice of the charge had been given to him or his parents, no sworn testimony had been introduced, and he had been required to incriminate himself without warning of any privilege against self-incrimination.

The very fact that the Gault case, disclosing such a bad state of affairs, could get all the way to the Supreme Court, after having gone through a trial court and a review on habeas corpus at the trial level and on appeal to the State supreme court, was substantial evidence that something was drastically wrong with both the theory and practice in juvenile delinquency proceedings.

Basically, the decision recognizes and extends the principle set forth in the Kent case: that due process of law applies to juveniles in an adjudicatory hearing as well as to adults. The Court was unwilling to establish a new or specialized class of due process for children. It found that the traditional constitutional safeguards are necessary protections and must be applied in that part of juvenile proceedings concerned with determining whether or not the State has a right to intervene in the lives of children and their families.

Specifically, the Court holds that in cases that may involve custody, transfer, and institutional placement of a delinquent child, the following constitutional rights must be observed:

[3]In re *Application of Gault* 387 U.S. 1, 87 S. Ct. 1428 (1967).

1. Adequate and specific notice in writing of the charge of alleged misconduct, set forth with particularity, must be given to the child or his parents in advance of the court hearing so that a reasonable opportunity to prepare a defense will be afforded.

2. At an adjudication hearing that may result in curtailment of the freedom of a child, the child and parents must be notified of the child's rights to be represented by counsel unless knowingly and intelligently waived. If they are unable to afford counsel, they must be advised that counsel will be appointed at public expense.

3. The privilege against self-incrimination is as applicable in the case of juveniles as it is with respect to adults, unless intelligently waived.

4. In the absence of a valid confession or admission, a determination of delinquency must rest upon sworn testimony in open court from witnesses whom the accused has had opportunity to confront and cross-examine.

The majority opinion expressly excepts from the effect of this decision anything that happens in the court prior to the hearing on adjudication and any proceedings held in regard to the disposition of a case. It does not guarantee, however, that questions of constitutional rights may not hereafter be raised with reference to what happens before or after the adjudication hearing. In effect, it challenges the various States to find ways and means to operate these pre- and post-adjudicatory proceedings that will not infringe on children's interests under the Bill of Rights and that will retain the unique merits or the original vision of juvenile courts.

THE POSSIBLE EFFECT

Contrary to some expressed opinion, the Gault case does not sound the death knell of the juvenile court in the United States. The fundamental concept of treatment and rehabilitation is not disturbed. But the court's right to deprive a child of freedom in providing treatment is limited to delinquency cases in which it has been established, by a trial in which due process is observed, that the State has a right to intervene.

Adherence to the precepts of due process in the trial will increase the demands on the juvenile courts in terms of time, expense, and procedural regularity. It may cause some courts to withdraw from precourt study and examination and from such treatment programs as informal probation and to limit their post-trial proceedings to referrals for study and treatment.

However, children are more likely to have a fair and impartial hearing and to depart from the hearing with the impression that justice has been done. This may render them more amenable to change.

The juvenile court movement has not been set backward by this decision. Rather, it has been given new direction and guidelines for operating when legal process is brought to bear on the activities of young people.

FACING REALITIES

The juvenile court, as a social institution, has had many salutary effects on other institutions. Its philosophy has provided an example for improving methods of social control of deviant behavior in adults. The widespread use of probation, the increasing practice of releasing persons without bail, the provision of treatment and rehabilitation, the reliance on the skill of the social and physical sciences, and the beginnings of scientific research into social prob-lems—all of these developments have been fostered, developed, encouraged, and, in part, made real by ideas generated and illustrated by work done in juvenile cases.

But the limitations of professional skill in dealing with the problems of maladjusted adolescents must be recognized, as must the widespread failure to bring what knowledge and skill are available to bear upon these problems. Such recognition may ultimately lead to some substantial rethinking of some of the methods of operating social controls.

Progress means change, and change means holding conclusions as tentative and not as absolute truths. The hypothesis of yesterday must give way to the realities of today to give hope to tomorrow.

The founders of the juvenile court movement were idealistic, dedicated, hard-working people. From their vision and devotion we must gain new dedication to give new leadership to the movement's new direction. The National Council of Juvenile Court Judges, the National Council on Crime and Delinquency, the Children's Bureau, the American Bar Association, the National Association of Social Workers, foundations, universities, and other groups must take up the challenge to make the dreams of the future more effective. Perhaps then we can come closer to the ultimate goal of scientific diagnosis and treatment of human behavior problems.

Index of Names

Index of Subjects

BOOK MANUFACTURE

Juvenile Delinquency: A Reader was typeset at Kopecky Typesetting, Inc. Printing by offset and binding was by Kingsport Press, Inc. John Goetz designed the internal material. Charles Kling & Associates designed the cover. The paper is Perkins & Squier's Gladfelter Old Forge. The type is Caledonia with Baskerville and Caledonia display.